Critical Concepts of
Canadian Business Law

Fifth Edition

Jan D. Weir, B.A., J.D.

Learning Solutions

New York Boston San Francisco
London Toronto Sydney Tokyo Singapore Madrid
Mexico City Munich Paris Cape Town Hong Kong Montreal

Previously published as:

Critical Concepts of Canadian Business Law, Third Edition
By Jan D. Weir and Shane A. Ellis
Copyright 2004, 2001, 1997 by Pearson Education Canada
Published by Addison Wesley
Toronto, Canada

Pearson Learning Solutions, 501 Boylston Street, Suite 900, Boston, MA 02116
A Pearson Education Company
www.pearsoned.com

Printed in Canada

7 8 9 10 V0ZN 15 14 13 12

000200010270586667

BK/LF

ISBN 10: 0-558-74638-1
ISBN 13: 978-0-558-74638-4

Contents

Part 4—Forms of Business Organizations

Foreword

I am pleased to contribute a foreword to *Critical Concepts of Canadian Business Law* written by my former partner Jan Weir.

The work is designed to enable students pursuing a business-related education to acquire general knowledge of business law. The importance of this objective for future business readers cannot be overstated. The book contains the most comprehensive survey of the law relating to business, accompanied by a number of hypothetical fact situations that serve as teaching aids. In my opinion, it will make a substantial contribution to the knowledge of business law among students at the college and university level.

I congratulate the author for the efforts exerted in bringing this fine work to publication.

The late Honourable Justice John Sopinka of the Supreme Court of Canada

Preface

Why This Book

The seed motivation for writing this book started with the writer's first meetings with clients and the realization that a new lawyer could argue the latest issues in the Supreme Court of Canada, but could not answer the simple questions the clients brought.

The writer kept track of these problems and resolved to one day write a book that was not a précis of law school courses, which are topics intriguing to the legal academic mind, but of the issues that most frequently impacted on business clients, mundane though they may be. The guide to content became not only personal experience, but the items that recurred on continuing education programs, as these were selected by practicing lawyers for other lawyers.

Writers of self help series books innovated a very different approach based on a way that people were beginning to more efficiently absorb information. The paragraph text was no longer the most effective way. In fact, it was boring to most students who had adapted to the more modular structured presentation that was reflected in the popular 'Dummy' series books.

The approach of using small "bits" of information has proved the most appealing to students and increased in appeal perhaps because of its use on the Internet. It is a process of information absorption very different from that most instructors are used to. However, if the instructors will take the time to use a chapter of this book with the students and get a comparative feedback with similar topics in other texts, they may find the students prefer, and benefit from, this model of instruction over the traditional text book.

The story approach, emphasized in this book, underlies all topics. Each legal topic is presented with several illustrations formulated to reveal its inherent drama. For when the graduates are at their office desks they will not likely remember avoiding the limitations of privity principles but they will remember the story of the misplaced comma that cost a business a million dollars—and the necessity for a lawyer's careful drafting advice for a contract involving significant amounts of money; the patrons of a game park who were attached by Bengal tigers—and the risk of running an inherently dangerous business; or the little girl who went down her backyard pool slide becoming an instant paraplegic on her second use—and the responsibility of a business for warning of possible dangerous use of products.

Only The Essentials

The word "critical" was chosen to reflect the objective of selecting from among the many issues most frequently confronted by businesses, only the most crucial, without all the mind-dulling details. Space is therefore devoted to teaching that one topic through several illustrations in different forms. Every major topic is expressed in at least four and sometimes more formats. For example, the topic of misrepresentation in Chapter 7: Defects in Contracts and Remedies:

a) There is a short narrative introduction of the topic.
b) The Critical Concepts summarize the essential points of a misrepresentation in bulleted format.
c) The Critical Concepts are followed by the brief of an actual case illustrating the principle.
d) Then follows a question or two, "Business Law Applied", which questions are simple illustrations in question format. The answers are in the Critical Concepts and designed to help the student understand these concepts.
e) At the end of the chapter, "In Summation" the topic is again restated in bulleted format. While similar to the Critical Concepts it is restated in different terminology and it may give students a different insight.
f) There are more complicated questions at the end of the chapter—"Closing Questions".
g) On the Website there are review exercises again done effectively in the bulleted format but this time not only restating the issue but leaving the critical term blank.

Interactive Approach

Instructors are often told that student attention span is somewhere between ten and twenty minutes. Some change must be introduced at about that time so that the students can hold their attention. The above structure permits the instructors to do this.

The modules are short enough so that the instructor can use this text in the classroom. There is, in effect, a suggested lesson plan for every major topic. Although each instructor has their preferred method of presenting a topic, they can give a short introduction of the topic in under ten minutes and then ask the students to read a part of the text, for example the reported case brief or the "Business Law Applied" questions. These are short enough and simple enough in language so that the average student can easily comprehend them in the class situation without prior preparation. The modules permit the opportunity for the instructor to use any of them in the classroom, thus varying his/her presentation and permitting a more interactive method of teaching.

Narrative And Case Method

The presentation of an issue is a balance of both narrative and case study methods. The premise is that it not important for students to learn to analyze cases or even to extract legal principles from several pages of text explanation. It is more important for them to be able to clearly see the principle of law so the briefs and critical concepts are made as simple as possible. However, when taken over a number of topics the concepts are challenging for most students.

Risk management has always been a topic that pervades all sections of the book. Sometimes it is identified by the "Business Alert" feature, but more often it is included simply as a question: What could have been done to prevent the result in the situation presented?

Law As Students Will Confront It

One particular concern about teaching contract law is the fact that standard terms in business contracts often modify or completely reverse the common law principles. Business people will see actual contracts frequently in dealings. Therefore, at the end of the contract chapters actual examples of contracts are given. Some of the questions refer to these contracts so that the students will not only have a general idea of how the legal issues actually apply to these contracts; but will understand that it is important for them to seek legal advice before signing major contracts as they may be giving away important rights. Most business people understand how to negotiate for price but they do not understand the consequences of many of the other terms.

Standard form contracts are good outlines of the issues that will most frequently arise in business deals and also a review of contract law principles.

The Danger of a Little Knowledge

By the end of the first year of practice all lawyers realize that they have completely wasted all law school tuition fees. Every client knows the law without going to law school. Clients do not ask for an opinion, they tell you the law. There is always a danger that in teaching students a little knowledge of the law, they will believe they can be their own lawyer. It is hoped that through the examples shown and the emphasis on the unforeseeable and often unexpected happenings in business deals, combined with the knowledge that terms in contracts can completely reverse common law statements of the law, students will learn caution and use their knowledge only to identify legal issues and seek advice where there is any significant consequence involved.

Student Centred

The use of the book so far has suggested that students will read it independently, they will enjoy the examples, and find them informative and of practical value to improve their job skills.

ESL Sensitive

From experience in developing curriculum and teaching ESL, the language used in the text has been selected to make the concepts more comprehensible to those students who have learned English as their second language.

Jan Weir

Taking Advantage of the Unique Features

1. **Critical Concepts** attempt to answer the perennial favourite question of students: "What do I really need to know?" Often the lists are summaries of preceding material, but sometimes they include succinct new points that require no further explanation.

■ **Critical Concepts of** Assault and Battery

- Assault is threatening another with violence, with the ability to carry out the threat causing fear in the victim.
- Battery is the least touching of another without consent and with the intention to cause harm.
- Self-defence is a complete defence to assault and battery.

---

2. **Business Alert!** points out common and/or especially damaging legal pitfalls that may be encountered in business. The items illustrate the consequences of failing to apply certain legal concepts to business dealings, or discuss how to avoid those consequences.

Business Alert!   Deposits   Be careful in giving any deposits. The business receiving them may not be able to refund them. It is a common complaint by purchasers of franchises that they have given large deposits in the order of $100,000 for initiation payments, but the franchise company has gone bankrupt. If giving a large deposit, have a credit check done on the company. Credit bureaus such as Dunn & Bradstreet will do credit checks for members of the public. Also, make certain the deposit is acknowledged to be held "in trust" for your purpose so it can't be used in the business generally. If the deposit is held in trust and the business goes bankrupt, it cannot be used to pay off other creditors and will be returned in full. Try to get a personal guarantee of the return of the deposit from the owner of the company. If that individual won't give a personal guarantee, be cautious!

---

3. Though this text attempts to use plain language whenever possible, sometimes the use of specialized terminology is unavoidable. When that occurs, **Legalese** provides an explanation of the term to help students understand it in context.

Consideration   **Consideration** derives from the same word as the term *consider*, which means to mentally weigh the merits of an issue, or in other words to take it seriously. The paying of something of value indicates that you have considered the matter and are agreeing to be bound.   **Legalese**

---

4. It is always useful to illustrate a point through a real incident that had to be resolved in the judicial arena. **Case summaries** cut through the legalese and highlight the main point. Cases were selected both to highlight the business context and to illustrate particular legal concepts.

Khosla v. Korea Exchange Bank of Canada, [2008] CanLII 56011 (ON S.C.)

Satwant Khosla was a solicitor who acted for clients who purchased a house. The house was sold using a fraudulent power of attorney. The fraudster was a tenant in the house.

The purchasers borrowed the purchase price of $492,000.00 and had it paid into Khosla's bank account in trust for themselves. Khosla drew a cheque in the name of the true owner of the house. Hence the true owner was the payee named on the cheque.

One month before closing the fraudster, using authentic identification taken from the owner, opened a bank account in the owner's name at the Korea Exchange Bank of Canada ("Korea Bank"). The fraudster deposited the cheque from the payment of the purchase price of the house in that bank account and shortly thereafter withdrew the funds and disappeared.

Khosla's insurer, a title insurance company, paid the purchasers their money, then using its right under the insurance policy [subrogation right] sued the Korea Bank using Khosla's name, for conversion of the cheque.

The Court's Decision

The Court held that there was well settled law that conversion was a strict liability defence. That meant that neither innocence on the bank's part, nor negligence by Khosla was a defence if the elements for conversion were established.

Conversion is wrongful interference with the property of another in a manner inconsistent with the owner's right to possession. The damage amount regarding cheques is the face amount of the cheque. Khosla, as drawer of the cheque, had the right to possession.

A bank commits conversion by collecting, i.e. obtaining the money from the drawer's [Khosla's] bank and then paying it to a person who is not the payee named on the cheque. Here the bank did not pay the funds to the true owner of the property, who was the payee on the cheque, but to a fraudster.

The bank was liable to pay Khosla the full amount of the face amount of the cheque plus interest.

5. **Business Law—Applied** questions follow each subject unit and are designed to discover whether the students "get it" before moving on. The questions are not meant to provide detailed review or analysis; often, they are effectively simple illustrations in question format.

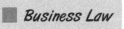

Business Law Applied

㉖ **You run a** small wholesaling outlet. Alf DeVry is your customer-service representative and has been a good employee for several years. One day, Alf is very angry with a particularly troublesome customer, and loses his "cool." Alf punches him, breaking his nose. The customer claims you, as his employer, are liable for this injury. Are you?

6. Where we have felt that quoting actual legislation would help students' understanding, **excerpts from legislation** have been included. Often, however, relevant statutes have been summarized in plain language.

The Charter of Rights and Freedoms Prevails

"Section 52(1). The Constitution of Canada is the supreme law of Canada, and any law that is inconsistent with the provisions of the constitution is, to the extent of the inconsistency, of no force and effect" (*The Constitution Act, 1982*).

The complete *Charter of Rights and Freedoms* is reproduced at the end of this chapter.

7. In Summation provides an executive summary of all major principles. Law schools are currently using the overview approach with apparent success, relying on bulleted summaries of areas of law. This method is employed at the end of each chapter.

In Summation

Defects in a Contract

■ A contract is based on the assumption that each party has freely given consent to perform the promises contained in it. If this is not the case, there are five main areas of concern the courts will consider in deciding whether to allow a claim by one party that consent was not freely given.

Misrepresentation

■ This is a statement, made by one party at the time of contracting, which is designed to persuade the other party to enter into the agreement, but which does not appear in the final contract. The

8. Closing Questions provide an in-depth review and analysis of the chapter. They vary in degree of difficulty but generally provide a good self-test to determine whether students truly understand and can apply the chapter content.

Closing Questions

2. Dewey, Cheatem and Howe is an accounting firm which is considering using an application service provider (ASP) to do its on-line billings and to store its back-up data from all computers.
   a) What business risks is the firm facing if it uses the services of the ASP as contemplated?
   b) What terms in the ASP's service contract would likely cover that risk and with what result?
   c) How could the firm protect itself with the legal or business solutions respecting this contract? Which is likely to be the more effective, the legal or the business solutions?

3. In the case of *Trigg v. MI Movers International Transportation* the exemption clause in the contract was not enforceable against Mr. Trigg because he had not read the clause. In the case of *Fraser Jewelers (1982) Ltd. v. Dominion Electric Protection Co.*, the president of Fraser Jewelers also claimed he had not read the exemption clause, but it was enforced against him. Are these cases reconcilable. If so, how?

9. The list of suggested **websites** at the end of each chapter points the student to readable explanations of legal concepts and expanded discussions of the practical implications of certain points.

Websites

www.rcmp-grc.gc.ca/scams/ecbweb.htm—The Economic Crime Prevention site. RCMP website includes the latest scams, business frauds, etc.

www.scambusters.com—Internet ScamBusters. Avoiding scams via Internet commerce.

strategis.ic.gc.ca/sc_consu/engdoc/homepage.html?categories=e_con—Industry Canada, Consumer Information. Includes tips to avoid consumer scams.

www.phonebusters.com—Information on the latest fraud schemes.

10. Appendices at the back of certain chapters include sample **contracts** that the students can refer to and analyze, which will help them put the legal issues raised into a real-world context.

Appendix 6

Used Car Bill of Sale

| | DAY | MONTH | YEAR |

PURCHASER'S INFORMATION

PURCHASER'S NAME: FIRST   MIDDLE INITIAL   LAST

PURCHASER'S ADDRESS

CITY/TOWN   PROVINCE   POSTAL CODE

HOME TELEPHONE NO.   BUSINESS TELEPHONE NO.

DRIVER'S LICENCE NO.   EXPIRY DATE

CAR INFORMATION

YEAR   MAKE   MODEL   COLOUR   STOCK#

SERIAL OR V.I.N. #

DISTANCE TRAVELLED   ☐ KMS   PURCHASER'S   IF MANUFACTURER'S WARRANTY
☐ MILES   INITIALS   APPLICABLE; TIME IS MEASURED FROM:

THIS CAR WILL BE DELIVERED WITH
A SAFETY STANDARDS CERTIFICATE ☐ YES _____   ☐ NO
CERTIFICATE NUMBER

TERMS OF SETTLEMENT

SELLING PRICE	
ADMINISTRATION FEE	
TRADE-IN ALLOWANCE (IF ANY)	
NET DIFFERENCE (ADD LINES 1 AND 2 AND DEDUCT LINE 3)	
P.S.T. ON NET DIFFERENCE	
LICENCE FEE	
GASOLINE	
PAYOUT LIEN ON TRADE-IN	
G.S.T. PAYABLE ON TRADE-IN	
BALANCE DUE	
DEPOSIT: ☐ CHEQUE ☐ CASH ☐ CREDIT CARD	
PAYABLE ON DELIVERY (CERTIFIED FUNDS ONLY)	
INSURANCE: ☐ LIFE ☐ ACCIDENT ☐ LOSS OF INC.	
P.S.T. ON INSURANCE	
LIEN REGISTRATION FEE	
BALANCE FINANCED SUBJECT TO APPROVAL	
NET AMOUNT TO BE FINANCED	
COST OF BORROWING %	
TOTAL BALANCE DUE $	

DEALER GUARANTEE

IS THERE A DEALER GUARANTEE ON THIS CAR? ☐ YES ☐ NO
IF YES, COMPLETE THIS SECTION.

_____ DAYS OR _____ KM
(WHICHEVER COMES FIRST)

DESCRIPTION _____

TERMS OF THE CONTRACT

1. **PURCHASER'S OFFER:** By signing this form I have made an offer to purchase the car described above ("the car"). I understand that this offer becomes a binding contract between the dealer and me when it is accepted by the signature of an authorized official of the dealer.

2. **CAR SOLD "AS IS":** I agree that if the appropriate space below is initialed by me, the car is sold "As Is" and is not represented as being in a road worthy condition, mechanically sound or maintained at any guaranteed level of quality. The car may not be fit for use as a means of transport and may require substantial repairs at my expense.

_____   If this space is not initialled by me, this clause
Purchaser's Initials   does not form part of this agreement.

3. **ACKNOWLEDGEMENT OF TERMS:** I acknowledge having read all terms of the contract, including those on the reverse. I understand that they form part of this agreement. I also agree that no verbal promises have been made to me by the dealer or its employees. The dealer and I agree that the written terms contained in this contract make up the entire agreement between us.

SIGNATURES:
Purchaser's: _____

Co-Signer (if any): _____

TERMS ON BACK FORM PART OF THIS CONTRACT

VENDOR'S ACCEPTANCE

DATE REGISTRATION No.   NAME OF OFFICIAL (PLEASE PRINT)

ACCEPTOR'S REGISTRATION No.   TITLE

DATE   SIGNATURE

The text is modularized to provide maximum in-class interaction with the material. Any of the features outlined above can be used in a variety of ways to stimulate in-class discussion. For example, "Business Law—What's Your Opinion?" could be used for in-class review, while "Closing Questions" could form the basis for mock trials.

Any response from instructors is welcome and it is hoped that this edition will spur debate on and reform of the approach and content of business law courses. Our business law courses need constant pruning and revising to keep pace with the fast-changing pace of business practice and business law.

Supplements

Instructor's Manual: This manual contains additional teaching ideas—including background information, case summaries, news articles that illustrate how legal concepts work in the real world, and photocopy masters of cases, charts, and assignments—as well as suggested answers for "Business Law—What's Your Opinion?" and "Closing Questions."

Test Item File: This testbank includes multiple-choice, true/false, and short-essay questions for each chapter. It is available in printed and electronic formats.

Pearson Education Canada TestGen: This computerized version of the Test Item File allows instructors to edit existing questions, add new questions, and generate custom tests.

Companion Web Site: The Companion Web Site for *Critical Concepts of Canadian Business Law*, Third Edition, offers student resources such as practice questions, key terms, weblinks to related sites, answers to Business Law: Applied questions, and streaming CBC videos with cases. Visit the site at www.pearsoned.ca/weir.

CBC/Pearson Education Canada Video Library for Business Law: The CBC and Pearson Canada have combined their expertise in educational publishing and global reporting to create special video support for the text. The library consists of four video segments from the CBC program *Venture*. Each segment is complemented by a Case Study in the Instructor's Manual.

How This Book Is Different

The genius underlying the effectiveness of the common law is that it is based on real situations. Judges have a concrete case in front of them and devise an abstract principle from that situation. That principle may be adjusted or modified, but again only based on actual cases, and usually in very small increments. The approach used in this book is similar and based on the assumption that students will be able to understand what is at issue better if they have concrete situations presented at the earliest occasion. This is in contrast to the usual approach of giving a series of explanations of the abstract principles of law and related corollary rules.

In this text, while a short explanation of the abstract issue is first presented, students are quickly given example after example of the application of the issue.

That time honored teaching belief in the effectiveness of repetition captured in the phrase "the 3 tellems"—tell them what you are going to tell them, tell them, and tell them what you told them—is amply applied. A single issue is repeated under a different face a number of times.

The basic principles of business law that a business-person needs to know do not change significantly. The students do not need leading edge cases on esoteric principles. However, there are new cases that better illustrate a principle or that will catch and hold a student's interest. These have been selected for this new edition. It is hoped with these cases that reflect the drama of the law, students will catch some of the passion for this discipline that has attracted the instructors.

Acknowledgments

Probably no book is a result of a single effort and this one is no exception. The ideas contributed by many people have influenced the revisions small and large. The author and publisher would also like to thank the reviewers whose feedback on the previous edition and the new manuscript provided some valuable suggestions for the new edition:

To those who have not undertaken the excruciating task of writing a textbook, the important contributions to the refinement of the finished product by the publisher's professional staff would be unrecognized. So special recognition has to be given to Gilaine Waterbury, acquisition editor for taking the time to discover the unique approach of the book, to Bradley Keist, Theresa Festa, Seamas Culligan, Jennifer Roach, and Leah Feinberg, who creatively found better ways to make the form better reveal the distinct functions of the features of the text.

While a number of instructors have taken the time to make helpful suggestions, professors Susan Lieberman, Murray Horowitz and Tapas Payne stand out among the contributors to the improvement of this edition.

Many practicing lawyers have also made suggestions of tips and topics that they frequently encounter but which are usually not covered in texts. My colleagues at the Law Chambers, Toronto, have been especially generous in donating their time to review sections for practical advice. Joel Shuster, P. Adm., C.A., has assisted with frequent issues the small businessperson raises with advisers.

Photograph of Osgoode Hall by Binnie Chee reproduced with permission of Pinto Wray James LLP.

Table of Cases

Table of Statutes

Fundamental Rights

Why Study Business Law?

By studying business law you will learn the legal rules that govern businesses, but you will also learn valuable business practices. For in studying business law you will learn the unexpected. Many of the situations that you will read about are not easily foreseeable and often took at least one business by surprise. As you would when studying history, you will learn the mistakes that others have made so that hopefully you will not repeat them.

The study of law is the study of business in crisis. The reported cases are a result of a fight between at least two businesses which could not agree or reach a compromise solution, and which had to spend a great amount of time and expense fighting over legal and factual issues. A judge had to decide between the two conflicting positions. There was only one winner.

Using this text you will study primarily by the case method, the method used in law schools; however, there will also be narrative explanations of the principles. There are summaries of actually reported cases for each major topic. The questions, which follow the cases and which are at the end of the chapters, are most often based on practical situations from the authors' files or from reported cases. Thus, although some situations may seem bizarre, they actually did happen.

This course is practical and meant to help you to improve your business skill. The topics that have been selected are those that most frequently occur in modern business situations. What you will be reading actually happened to a business. Large businesses know the importance of considering legal consequences, and not only have in-house legal departments but additionally retain large law firms to advise them regularly. Small businesses often do not realize the importance of legal risk or don't have the financial resources to have lawyers on staff. This book is written from the perspective of the small-business entrepreneur who does not have easy access to lawyers (and who may regard a lawyer's services as the ultimate grudge purchase). This person typically knows, for example, how to negotiate a contract regarding price but is often unaware of how other terms in most contracts, especially standard form contracts, shift risks. This is particularly true of the ever-present disclaimer clause. You will learn to understand these terms in real agreements and the need to have them reviewed by a lawyer if there is a significant transaction involved.

Businesses are becoming increasingly sophisticated in using law suits to harm competitors. Thus, it is important for you to know how to protect your business from attacks by other businesses, such as stealing key employees or trade secrets. There are an increasing number of laws that give consumers rights. At various times in establishing a new business, you will be signing contracts, bank guarantees, and partnership agreements, incorporating companies, and carrying out other such activities. By studying business law you will understand the legal responsibilities and the pitfalls respecting these various situations.

You are at this point a consumer protected by a large number of consumer-protection laws that ensure fairness in most transactions. However, when you leave your present institution and enter into transactions as a businessperson, you will have few of these protections. The law of business is designed to promote competition, that is, the survival of the fittest.

Bill Gates is a good example of someone who used business law effectively to establish his Microsoft Empire. He knew that he should negotiate a term in a contract with IBM so that Microsoft kept the rights to the DOS system, which was the first foundation of the Microsoft Empire. He successfully fought a patent battle with Apple Computer to get the rights to use the mouse-graphic interface, which became the basis for Windows. Some criticize business law as being cutthroat, and however extreme that description and however undesirable, that is likely the best way to understand it. If you do not have a general knowledge of business law, you may find yourself in the same situation as some of the people in the cases that you are going to read.

Thus, one answer to the question, "Why should we bother to study business law?," may be: business self-defence.

Analyzing Court Decisions

Law is developed by decisions on actual cases. Lawyers must analyze cases such as the above to abstract more-general principles to attempt to predict how the law will apply to new situations where there is no similar decided case. In some questions, you will be shown this process of analysis at its most simplified level. This may assist you in understanding that many times a lawyer does not have a precise precedent and has to give an opinion based on his or her best estimate of how the principles developed to that point in time will be applied to your case.

In reading a reported case in this text it may be helpful to make a **brief**, which is a summary of a case (for use at trial) including evidence and law, or a summary of a court decision such as those used in this text. Use the following outline:

brief

a summary of a case (for use at trial) including evidence and law, or a summary of a court decision such as those used in this text

- the facts
- the legal principle to be applied, stated in one sentence
- the arguments for both sides
- the application of the legal principle (the result)

The Constitution of Canada

The Formation of Confederation

Prior to the formation of the country of Canada, the collection of British colonies, that would eventually form this country (including Quebec now under British control), faced a number of problems including: deterioration in relations with the United States and the possibility of loss of land to that foreign power and the increasing unwillingness of Britain to come to the defence of its colonies along with other factors. The solution, aided by the building of the railways and the possibility of a trans-continental railway, was unification on an east-west direction by way of confederation.

The Division of Powers Under the Constitution

In 1867, the four colonies of British North America—Upper Canada (now Ontario), Lower Canada (now Quebec), Nova Scotia, and New Brunswick—decided to form a new country, to be called Canada. The colonies had to decide which powers they would keep for themselves and which should be handed over to the new central, or federal, government. The *British North America (BNA) Act*, passed by the British Parliament in 1867, outlined the division of powers. Matters of common interest across Canada, such as the Post Office, were given to the federal government. One matter of particular interest to business is the regulation of trade and commerce, which includes advertising. Matters of a local provincial nature, such as city hospitals, were given to the provinces.

For the most part, sections 91 and 92 of the *BNA Act* divide legislative powers between the federal and provincial governments, and list specific areas of power. The federal government also has the power to make laws for the peace, order, and good government of Canada (this is colloquially known as the POGG clause of the constitution) in relation to all matters except those given exclusively to the provincial governments by section 92. This phrasing is intended to give the federal government authority over matters not specifically mentioned in section 92 as being of national concern.

Matters specifically set out in section 91 include:

- unemployment insurance (section 91(2A))
- postal service (section 91(5))
- regulation of trade and commerce (section 91(2))
- incorporation of banks and issuing of paper money (section 91(15))
- criminal law (section 91(27))

Section 92(16) gives the provinces exclusive jurisdiction over "all matters of a merely local or private nature in the province." This is a very wide clause, capable of embracing a large range of topics.

The *BNA Act* was drafted in 1867, and was intended to cover all areas of government. But who, at that time, when milk was delivered to the door in horse-drawn carts, could have anticipated computers and the Internet, or the importance of environmental pollution issues? The constitution today must be interpreted, and responsibility for such issues assigned to either provincial or federal government.

One guiding principle in deciding who is in charge is, obviously, whether the matter is of national concern, crossing provincial boundaries, or if it is purely local. In pollution control, for example, it is the federal government that regulates pollution caused by shipping, since that activity seldom takes place only within one province. The provinces, however, also have water pollution legislation to protect local lakes and rivers.

Critical Concepts of The Scheme for Division of Powers in the Constitution

- Specific matters to federal government
- Specific matters to provincial governments
- Matters not listed in either of above to the federal government under POGG, or to provincial governments under s. 92(16)

UltraVires   When a matter is outside a government's designated power, that matter is said to be ***ultra vires***. The term is derived from the Latin *ultra*, meaning beyond, and *vires*, meaning power.

Legalese

Bringing the Constitution Home

During the 1960s and 1970s, the provincial and federal governments were anxious to make several changes to the *British North America Act*. Specifically they wished to change the act:

- to allow amendment to it without having to go before the British Parliament
- to agree to a new division of the law-making powers among the federal and provincial governments
- to add a guaranteed set of rights and freedoms

Accordingly, in 1982, the *BNA Act*—the Constitution—was patriated, or brought home to Canada. The power to make changes to it now rests with the governments of Canada. The *Charter of Rights and Freedoms* was incorporated into the Constitution at that time. However, no agreement was reached on a new division of powers among federal and provincial governments—the issue of division of powers continues to be a perplexing political concern.

The name of the *British North America Act* was officially changed to the *Constitution Act*, and the new Canadian Constitution was called the *Constitution Act, 1982*.

Legalese

Civil Rights   Section 92.13 of the Constitution mentions **civil rights**. Because of more recent civil rights movements, there is now some confusion about the use of this term. *Civil rights* is a very general term that is derived from the same Latin root as the word *citizen* (*civitas*). It refers to the rights of citizens and includes areas of law such as contracts, *torts*, and so on. In order to distinguish between the more modern, but narrow, use of the term, Canadian legal writers refer to laws that deal with *discrimination* as human rights, or civil liberties, legislation.

Business Law Applied

(**Note to students:** In answering the "Business Law—Applied" questions, you should justify every answer by referring to a principle of law. You will find that these are often contained in the critical concepts or in sections of statutes.

Other principles may be contained in the text or in the reported cases. In any event, your answer should refer specifically to the principle of law and indicate also where it is found in the textbook. In other words, you must give the authority for your answer.)

❶ **You are a** policy advisor in the Attorney General's department. You are asked to give your opinion as to which level of government, federal or provincial, has the power to make laws relating to the following topics. Examine sections 91 and 92 of the Constitution provided by your instructor, and identify the specific section and item number that enables you to provide your opinion.

a) bankruptcy
b) the solemnization of marriage in the province
c) murder
d) a railway that runs only between two cities within one province
e) the protection of inventions

Businesses Use Division of Powers

Governments, both federal and provincial, often pass laws to regulate business activities. Because of the division of powers in the Constitution, business can challenge a law as being *ultra vires* that level of government.

Example: A provincial government passed a law creating its own currency and issues dollar bills. This would be *ultra vires* because of several sections of the Constitution—91, 14; 15 and 18.

Irwin Toy (case discussed later under a Charter point) challenged a law regarding advertising directed at children which was passed by the Quebec legislature as being *ultra vires* provincial jurisdiction claiming it was aimed at controlling broadcasting, a federal matter. The Court found that the essence of the legislation was to protect children within the province and was a valid execution of provincial power. It was significant that the act was not aimed at broadcasters but businesses.

In the following case a business tried to challenge a criminal conviction under Federal legislation claiming that the subject matter was completely within the jurisdiction of a province.

The "R" in the next case stands for Regina which is Latin for the Queen. Many criminal cases begin with that name.

Legalese

R. v. Crown Zellerbach Canada Ltd., [1988] CanLII 63 (S.C.C.)

The Federal government charges against *Crown Zellerbach* for dumping wood waste in the waters of Beaver Cove, an area within the province of B.C. but on the coast in that the water flowed into Johnson Strait which is connected to the Pacific Ocean. A map is available on the internet.

The relevant act, the *Ocean Dumping Control Act*, prohibited dumping any substance into seawater without a permit. *Crown Zellerbach* did not have a permit.

Crown Zellerbach defended on the basis that the Cove was entirely within the province of British Columbia and hence the matter was governed exclusively by provincial jurisdiction under the Constitution. The government defended its legislation under the Peace, Order and Good Government clause ("POGG").

The Court's Decision

The court upheld the legislation on the basis of the international concerned doctrine. This doctrine was developed to apply to new matters that did not exist at the time of confederation.

Here the matter of ocean pollution was a matter of concern to the nation as a whole. The pollution of marine water is clearly distinguishable from pollution of fresh water. This distinction also ensures that the legislation will meet the test that it would have minimal impact on provincial jurisdiction.

The legislation was upheld and *Crown Zellerbach* was convicted.

The Canadian Charter of Rights and Freedoms

The Supremacy Clause

The *Canadian Charter of Rights and Freedoms* is a piece of legislation that sets out the fundamental rights of all Canadians. When the Constitution was patriated, the *Canadian Charter of Rights and Freedoms* was enacted. It was made an integral part of the Constitution, so that the Charter would be difficult to change. An act such as the *Bill of Rights*, or the *Canadian Human Rights Act*, can be amended by a majority of the Canadian Parliament. However, the Constitution can only be altered according to a complex formula that involves agreement among the federal and provincial governments. Two attempts to amend the Constitution—the Meech Lake Accord and the Charlottetown Accord—failed, demonstrating how difficult it is to amend a provision of the Constitution.

The *Charter of Rights and Freedoms* changed the concept of the supremacy of Parliament. Before, the government in power could make any laws that it wanted, the only qualification being that the division-of-powers section of the Constitution entitled Parliament to pass that particular legislation.

When the Charter came into being, a new qualification was put on laws—they must also be in accordance with the principles of the Charter. Those principles take precedence over any of the laws enacted by the federal or provincial governments. Hence, the Charter, with some limitations, is superior to the acts of Parliament and the provincial legislatures.

Companies have successfully used the Charter to attack the legislation that affects their businesses. In one of the first successful Charter cases, Southam Publishing Inc.,[1] which owned many of the newspapers and magazines across Canada, challenged a section of the *Combines Investigation Act* (now the *Competition Act*) which permitted search warrants to be issued without the usual protections that apply to the issuance of police search warrants. That section was struck, or declared invalid, and so also was a search warrant that had been issued against Southam.

The tobacco companies had federal legislation that banned all commercial advertising of tobacco products successfully struck on the basis that the act was an unjustified infringement of freedom of expression.[2]

The Charter of Rights and Freedoms Prevails

"Section 52(1). The Constitution of Canada is the supreme law of Canada, and any law that is inconsistent with the provisions of the constitution is, to the extent of the inconsistency, of no force and effect" (*The Constitution Act, 1982*).

The complete *Charter of Rights and Freedoms* is reproduced at the end of this chapter.

■ *Critical Concepts of* The Constitution and the Charter of Rights and Freedoms

- The Constitution outlines which government (federal or provincial) can make which law
- The Charter determines whether the law conforms to certain protected rights
- The Charter, as part of the Constitution, prevails over all other laws

The Charter Does Not Always Apply

The Charter applies primarily to laws, but not to all situations where an individual's rights are violated. In some circumstances, human rights acts may apply, since they regulate actions such as discrimination by individuals, corporations, or governments. Examine section 32 of the Charter and decide to which of the following situations the Charter applies.

---

1. *Hunter v. Southam*, [1984] 2 S.C.R. 145.

2. *R.J.R. MacDonald v. Canada (Attorney General)*, [1995] 3 S.C.R. 199.

Charter of Rights and Freedoms Flow Chart

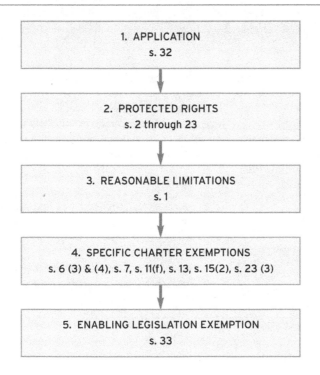

```
┌─────────────────────────────────────┐
│         1. APPLICATION              │
│              s. 32                  │
└─────────────────────────────────────┘
                  │
                  ▼
┌─────────────────────────────────────┐
│        2. PROTECTED RIGHTS          │
│           s. 2 through 23           │
└─────────────────────────────────────┘
                  │
                  ▼
┌─────────────────────────────────────┐
│       3. REASONABLE LIMITATIONS     │
│                s. 1                 │
└─────────────────────────────────────┘
                  │
                  ▼
┌─────────────────────────────────────────────────┐
│         4. SPECIFIC CHARTER EXEMPTIONS           │
│  s. 6 (3) & (4), s. 7, s. 11(f), s. 13, s. 15(2), s. 23 (3) │
└─────────────────────────────────────────────────┘
                  │
                  ▼
┌─────────────────────────────────────┐
│    5. ENABLING LEGISLATION EXEMPTION │
│                s. 33                │
└─────────────────────────────────────┘
```

◼ *Business Law*   Applied

❷ **You are a** policy analyst in the Attorney General's office in Ottawa. The following matters have been referred to you for your comments as to whether the Charter applies.

  a) A section of the criminal code which makes abortion illegal
  b) The firing of an employee by the Bay
  c) The refusal by the British Columbia Pulp and Paper Company Limited to hire a Sikh because he wears a turban
  d) A provision of the *Nova Scotia Liquor Control Act* that prohibits lap dancing in licensed taverns

Only Certain Rights Are Protected

After deciding that the Charter applies, the next step is to decide if the matter involved violates a right protected by the Charter. The charter guarantees many rights. "Fundamental freedoms" are one type of such rights and are found in section 2. Other rights are listed in sections 3 to 23. The complete Charter has been put in the appendix to this chapter so that you can read the relevant section with each topic.

In the early cases, the courts merely struck down legislation if it offended a right guaranteed by the Charter. More recently, the courts have moved toward requiring a government to pass legislation that is in conformity with the Charter.

RBC v. Welton, [2008] 89 O.R. (3d) 532

The RBC believed it had been defrauded by lending money based on mortgages on property whose value was falsely inflated. The lawyer, Molson, acted on both sides of the transactions—for both the lender bank, RBC, and the borrowers.

An RBC bank investigator got copies of relevant documents regarding Molson's trust account from the TD Bank and determined that a large series of fraud had been committed against the RBC. Although Molson's trust account information was confidential and protected by the *Personal Information Protection and Electronic Documents Act* ("PIPEDA"), one section of that Act, Section 8, permitted a business to disclose information to investigative authorities as defined under that Act, one of which was a bank investigator.

Molson and several clients challenged the disclosure of the trust account information claiming that Section 7 of PIPEDA violated Section 8 of the Charter which provides "everyone has the right to be secure against unreasonable search and seizure". The Applicant's claim that RBC was acting similar to a government investigator regarding a fraud charge and that Section 7 of PIPEDA should provide for a judicial supervisor over disclosure of this type of information such as a justice of the peace does in issuing a search warrant in a criminal investigation.

The Court

The Court rejected the argument that RBC was acting in a government function investigating criminal fraud. It was acting to protect itself from civil fraud. Therefore the Charter did not apply in these circumstances.

However, even if the Charter did apply, the exception in Section 7 of PIPEDA was reasonable, indeed necessary, for banks to prevent fraud.

Business Law Applied

❸ **Again, in** your position as policy analyst for the federal Attorney General, decide if any of the following situations relate to a right protected by the Charter. Make reference to a specific section of the Charter in your answer.

a) A provincial legislature passes a law stating:

"No person shall bear arms of any type for any purpose within the limits of any city in this province."

b) The federal government passes this law:

"No person on being arrested need be informed that he/she has a right to consult a lawyer."

c) A city passes this by-law:

"Smoking shall be prohibited in any restaurant in this city."

d) The federal government, in a time of peace, passes this law:

"The present government shall continue in power for 10 more years."

Confidentiality of Business Documents

There is a saying that one person's garbage is another's treasure. Businesses regularly dispose of paper documents and copies of documents and information stored electronically on hard drives at desktop computers, laptops, blackberries and other similar devices. It is said that a garbage bag may be accurately described as a bag of information whose contents, viewed in its entirety, paint a fairly accurate and complete picture of a business's activities.

It is known that competitors sometimes hire private investigators to search the garbage of other businesses. In the case *Meditrust Health Care Inc. v. Shopper's Drug Mart* 2002 CanLII 4710 (ON C.A.) a private investigator from Meditrust allegedly found evidence that a vice president of Shopper's Drug Mart had sent out false letters disparaging Meditrust products. See the CBC video, case no. 2 "Trash Talk" on the video library for this text.

Can police do the same if they are investigating possible criminal charges against a business? Can the target business raise the defence under Section 8 of the Charter that the search and seizure is unreasonable because the business has an expectation of privacy in garbage. The following case was decided in a criminal context but it may have applications for businesses.

R. v Patrick
[2009] SCC 17

Police suspected Patrick was manufacturing ecstacy. They took bags of garbage from garbage cans placed on a stand (without lids) just inside Patrick's property line.

Patrick moved to have the search declared illegal on the basis that it was unreasonable and in violation of Section 8 of the Charter in that he had an expectation of privacy in the information that the contents revealed to the police.

The Court's Decision

The court found that the search was not unreasonable and hence not in violation of Section 8 of the Charter because the householder had sufficiently abandoned his interest and control to eliminate any objectively reasonable privacy interest when he placed his garbage bags for collection in the open container at the back of his property adjacent to the lot line.

The court rejected the submission that Section 8 protects an individual's privacy in garbage until the last unpaid bill rots in the dust. Patrick's motion to strike the search was denied.

Businesses frequently dispose of not only paper documents but electronic versions of documents.

Given the court's ruling that the information and garbage is not subject to an expectation of privacy, businesses are well advised to consider not only policies regarding the shredding of paper documents but the complete elimination of data on copies of any electronic storage devices that they are disposing of. It is now well understood that deleting is not erasing. Data recovery specialists can often reconstruct much of the data from any type of hard drive or other storage device. The hard drives have to be erased by special software or removed and destroyed.

Business Alert!

Lawsuits for Protected Rights Used to Change Laws

The combination of the rights protected by the Charter and section 52 of the Constitution, which gives these rights priority over government-made laws, has resulted in the changing of many laws. For example, the once-mandatory sentence of a minimum of seven years for importing narcotics has been struck down.

One of the most controversial acts by the Supreme Court of Canada has been its pronouncements that it has the power to add protected rights to the Charter by analogy to those already listed in it. Since one of the protected rights is sex, the Supreme Court had said that by analogy to those grounds, sexual orientation is also a protected right.

Gay activists applaud this step by the court, saying governments move too slowly in affording them such protection. Critics say that judges are violating democratic principles by making laws in place of elected legislators. They are not accountable to voters for the enactment of those laws.

Limitations Over Protected Rights

Even if a protected right is violated, the court can uphold the law if it feels that the violation or limitation is reasonable in a free and democratic society. The *Irwin Toy* case below deals with the issue of what is a reasonable limitation on the protected right. Commercial advertising is a method of expression that is protected under the Charter. But are there situations where that freedom should be restrained? The power of the court to impose a reasonable limitation is set out in section 1 of the Charter.

The Charter and Advertising

Organizations have used the Charter to challenge limits on advertising both successfully and unsuccessfully. The Canadian Federation of Students successfully had a Bus Transit Authority policy restricting political advertising on the outside of its buses struck. The policy restricted political advertising and "advertising liable to cause offence to any person or group". The students wanted to place advertising, which among other statements, said "Tuition Fees—ROCK THE VOTE.COM". The bus line refused to run the ad, but the Supreme Court of Canada said that it had to do so and struck the Transit Authoritie's policy. (*Canadian Federation of Students v. Greater Vancouver Transit Authority*, 2006 BCCA 529 (CanLII))

However, a strip club was not so successful. The City of Montreal passed a noise by-law restricting any noise produced by sound equipment inside a building that could be heard outside the building. The club placed a loudspeaker outside its entrance. The announcer and music regarding the dance performers could be heard outside on the street.

The City fined the Club. The club challenged the by-law claiming Section 2(b) Charter Protection. The Court found that the announcer's statements had expressive content that was protected by Section 2(b) of the Charter; however, the noise by-law was justified by Section 1 by the City's need to restrict noise pollution and that the by-law minimally impacted on the right of freedom of expression (*Montreal (City) v. 2957-1366 Quebec Inc.*, 2005 SCC 62 (CanLII)).

Irwin Toy Ltd. v. Quebec (Attorney General), [1989] 1 S.C.R. 927

Irwin Toy sought a declaration from the court that certain provisions of the Quebec *Consumer Protection Act* were contrary to the *Charter of Rights and Freedoms*. The legislation in question prohibited commercial advertising directed at persons under 13 years of age. Irwin Toy alleged that this infringed upon its freedom of expression (section 2(b) of the Charter) and that such an infringement could not be justified in a free and democratic society (as set out in section 1 of the Charter).

The Court's Decision

The court held that the Quebec legislation did infringe on the rights protected in section 2(b) of the Charter. The government's purpose was to prohibit a certain kind of expression—commercial expression aimed at children.

However, the infringement could be justified under section 1 of the Charter. The evidence showed that children under age 13 are vulnerable to commercial manipulation, and that society has a pressing and substantial concern in preventing such manipulation. The means chosen by the government to address this concern was proportional to the objective, since children's products could still be advertised in other ways, and non-commercial advertising directed at children was also allowed.

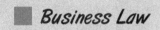 **Applied**

④ **Smith was caught** at the border bringing hashish into Canada. He was convicted of importing under section 5(2) of the *Narcotics Control Act*. That section prescribes a minimum term of seven years in jail. Smith wants to challenge this conviction on a Charter argument.

 a) Does the Charter apply?
 b) Does this section of the *Narcotics Control Act* violate any protected rights under the Charter?
 c) Even if it does violate a protected right, is it reasonable to permit this violation?
 d) Would it matter if Smith had one ounce of hashish or 30 pounds?

Specific Charter Exemptions

There are exceptions to every rule. The protected rights in the Charter are subject to certain exemptions set out in the various sections. Discrimination, for example, is permitted if it helps a disadvantaged group. Affirmative action programs are one of the specific exemptions under section 15(2). Other specific exemptions are set out in the Charter flow chart, above.

Business Law   **Applied**

⑤ **The federal government** has passed an employment-equity law that requires the federal civil service to hire new recruits in proportions that will result in the service being composed of the same proportion of visible minority groups as are in the general Canadian population.

 a) Does this law violate any protected Charter rights? Refer to a specific section of the Charter.
 b) Is there an exception that would save this law from being struck down? Refer to a specific section of the Charter.

The Notwithstanding Clause

A clause in the Charter permits governments to enact laws that can violate rights and freedoms under sections 2 or 7–15 of the Charter, so long as they expressly state that the law is being passed under section 33. This section is called the notwithstanding, or override, clause. It is from the clause's use of the term *notwithstanding* that the shorthand reference is derived. A law passed under section 33 expires automatically after five years. This allows for review of legislation that encroaches on Charter rights.

When the charter was being approved, it was felt that the Quebec government would not agree unless the notwithstanding clause was incorporated. Then-Prime Minister Trudeau stated that he agreed to the incorporation of section 33 "with dread." While most governments have been reluctant to make use of the notwithstanding clause, the Quebec government has done so in a series of laws to restrict the use of the English language in the province of Quebec.

Human Rights Legislation

Not every action which discriminates, or infringes on, what we view as our basic rights is a matter for the *Charter of Rights and Freedoms*. The Charter applies to the actions of governments in making or administering laws.

The actions of individuals, corporations, and governments (when acting like a private person, as opposed to making or administering laws) are governed by human rights legislation. Human rights legislation is aimed at acts of discrimination in three main areas:

- employment
- housing
- provision of goods and services

Say, for example, a business refuses to hire a person because that individual is a member of a minority group. Human rights legislation would apply because the situation:

- is an act of discrimination
- involves a business (viewed as an individual by the law, whether a corporation or not)
- is in the area of employment

■ *Critical Concepts of* Application of Fundamental Rights Legislation

- Constitution—states which government (federal or provincial) can make which laws.
- *Charter of Rights and Freedoms*—tells whether the laws passed by all governments, federal and provincial, comply with certain specified principles.
- *Human Rights Acts*—deal with discrimination by persons in employment, housing, and provision of goods and services.

The Canadian Human Rights Act

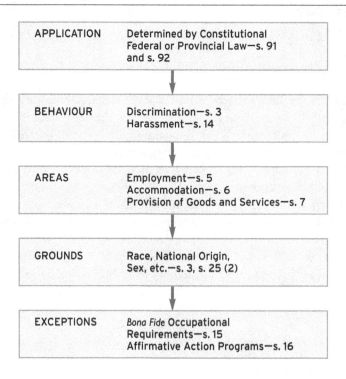

Knowing Which Legislation Applies

The federal and provincial governments, as well as those of the Northwest Territories and Yukon, have all enacted human rights legislation. Most of these statutes have very similar names—the *Human Rights Act* of the province. The practical way to find out whether the federal act or the act of your province applies to a particular situation is to call any of the human rights commission offices listed in the telephone directory. They will be able to advise you, as they are set up to deal with the public without the intervention of lawyers.

The technical answer to deciding the appropriate legislation is found in the division of powers in the Constitution. The *Canadian Human Rights Act* applies strictly to matters in section 91 of the Constitution, which covers the specifically named areas as well as government agencies and private businesses whose activities cross provincial borders. The Canadian National Railway and Air Canada, for example, must comply with the federal legislation. Zellers, on the other hand, has branches throughout Canada, but it is not part of the firm's business to cross provincial boundaries, and therefore it is subject to the human rights act of the province where each branch is located.

Discrimination

In law, **discrimination** is the act of treating someone differently on grounds that are prohibited by human rights legislation. A person can discriminate in ways that are not prohibited under the act. For example, a landlord could refuse a tenant because of the tenant's inability to pay. An employer can refuse to hire someone because of poor references.

discrimination
the act of treating someone differently on grounds that are prohibited by human rights legislation.

Employers are prohibited from discriminating not only in hiring, but also in advertising for job applicants, as well as in the job-interviewing process.

Discrimination includes actions such as harassment, as well as what has been called systemic discrimination, constructive discrimination, or adverse-effect discrimination. These are all different names for the same thing.

Prohibited Grounds for Discrimination

Section 3 of the *Canadian Human Rights Act* sets out the grounds for discrimination. Sex is specifically stated to include pregnancy. Section 25 extends the meaning of disability to include drug and alcohol dependency.

The grounds for charging discrimination vary among the federal and provincial acts for the different areas, such as for employment, accommodation, and provision of goods and services. In addition, the courts, by interpreting the statute, have declared that, as well as with the Charter, they can add certain grounds by analogy—for example, sexual orientation does not appear in section 3, but according to a decision of the courts, that ground should be considered part of it. Some provincial acts have been amended to include sexual orientation. In other provinces, the provincial human rights commissions consider that sexual orientation is included.

Section 3, Canadian Human Rights Act

---

3 (1) For all purposes of this Act the prohibited grounds are: race, national or ethnic origin, colour, religion, age, sex, sexual orientation, marital status, family status, disability and conviction for which a pardon has been granted.

3 (2) Where the ground of discrimination is pregnancy or childbirth, the discrimination shall be deemed to be on the ground of sex.

■ *Critical Concepts of* Prohibited Grounds

- The federal *Human Rights Act* lists the usual prohibited grounds for discrimination, such as sex, religion, country of origin, and so on. The act defines sex to include pregnancy or childbirth, and defines disability to include drug and alcohol addiction.
- Because of a court ruling, sexual orientation was added by amendment.
- The Canadian Human Rights Commission has stated that it interprets disability to include AIDS.

Zurich Insurance Company v. Ontario (Human Rights Commission), [1992] 2 S.C.R. 321

Michael Bates challenged Zurich Insurance Company's policy of charging higher rates for males under 25 than for females and married men. The insurance company conceded that the classification system for its premiums discriminated on the basis of sex, age, and martial status, but that the discrimination was reasonable and *bona fide* within the meaning of section 21 of the *Ontario Human Right Code*, which stated that the right to contract without discrimination is not infringed:

> ...where a contract of automobile...insurance...differentiates or makes a distinction, exclusion or preference on reasonable and *bona fide* grounds because of age, sex or marital status...

The court found that the insurance company operated its system in good faith, which met the test of *bona fide*. The issue of reasonableness was difficult in a human rights business context. The underlying philosophy of human rights legislation is that an individual has a right to be dealt with on his or her own merits and not on the basis of group categorization. This right must be balanced with the needs of a business to operate the business safely, efficiently, and economically.

A practice is reasonable if it is based on sound insurance practice and there is no practical alternative. The higher premium for under-25 male drivers was based on statistical evidence compiled in Ontario since 1920 which showed that this group had the highest number of claims, the highest loss per vehicle, and the highest average claim cost of all categories.

This was a reasonable basis for its discrimination and the under-25 male-driver premium policy was upheld.

Business Alert! Job Interviewing   The Law Society of Upper Canada circulated the following as examples of questions that, in light of human rights legislation, are inappropriate to ask in an interview.

- How old are you?
- How will your seniority negatively affect the office operations?
- Are you what is referred to as a "mature student"?
- What is your religion? Are you devout?
- Are you married? Do you have a girlfriend?
- Would your wife be happy living in Ottawa? Are you a "family man"?
- Do you plan to have children?
- Do you plan to get pregnant, and if so, when?
- Are you using birth control?
- How many children do you have? What are your daycare arrangements? How will you cope?
- Where were you born? What is your ancestry? How many years have you been resident in Canada?
- What clubs do you belong to?

Once the applicant has been given a job, questions necessary for employment records, such as age and marital status, can be asked.

Some questions that are related to a *bona fide occupational requirement* (discussed in the material which follows) can be asked at the interview stage.

Business Law   Applied

⑥ **Jan Nada has** been a cocktail waitress at the Hot House for two years. The Hot House is a very trendy downtown bar, designed to appeal to sophisticates. The waitresses are obviously chosen because of their looks, and the uniforms are very close fitting. Nada becomes pregnant and, at four months, this is obvious. Her boss fires her.

a) Does Nada have any grounds for a complaint under the *Human Rights Act*? Assume that the applicable provincial legislation is the same as the federal *Human Rights Act*. For now, ignore any defences of the employer.

⑦ **You work in** the human resources department and your company has devised a new job-application form. Some of the questions on it are:

- What is your age?
- What is your marital status?
- Where is your country of origin?
- Do you have a criminal record?
- Do you ever use non-prescription, recreational drugs?
- What is your previous work experience?

a) Write a memo to your boss advising on whether human rights legislation allows the company to ask these questions. Refer to the relevant section(s) in your memo.

Systemic Discrimination

The act recognizes that a seemingly neutral policy may in fact result in discrimination. For example, a policy by a police force requiring a certain minimum height and weight for police officers could exclude minority groups whose racial characteristics include a lighter weight and a smaller frame. The same issue has been raised in relation to women and fire departments. The police and fire departments have argued that height and weight are *bona fide* requirements for the job. The question of systemic discrimination is one of intention. Can an individual be said to have discriminated if that person did not intend to do so? The courts have answered this question in the affirmative in interpreting both the *Canadian Human Rights Act* and the provincial legislation. **Systemic discrimination** is discrimination that is the consequence of a policy, whether the effect of discrimination was intended or not; for example, a policy that a police officer be 6-feet tall would discriminate on gender and race.

systemic discrimination
discrimination that is the consequence of a policy, whether the effect of discrimination was intended or not

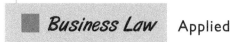

Business Law Applied

⑧ Action travail des femmes (ATF) is a public-interest pressure group originally funded by the federal government, but now incorporated and financed independently. The group alleged that the Canadian National Railway Company (CN) refused to hire women in certain unskilled, blue-collar positions, and was therefore guilty of discriminatory hiring and promotion practices contrary to the *Canadian Human Rights Act*. This was not a complaint by, or on behalf of, any one individual, but was on behalf of women workers in general in the local area.

The lobby group claimed that the percentage of women in the CN workforce was far below the percentage of women available in the general workforce in the area. Therefore, CN's policy of hiring had an adverse effect on working women. Here are the statistics for 1981:

	Percent of Total Labour Force	Percent of CN Workforce
Women workers	40.7	6.11

a) Could the ATF complaint be successful based on the statistical evidence alone?
b) Would the lobby group have to show actual incidents of discrimination by CN against particular women?
c) What is this type of discrimination called?
d) What are the advantages and disadvantages of the use of this type of discrimination in being able to prove discrimination?

Harassment

Harassment on any of the prohibited grounds is also forbidden, and is considered a type of discrimination. Sexual harassment in particular has become a focal point of human rights legislation in recent years. Harassment is any unwanted physical or verbal conduct that offends or humiliates the individual at whom it is directed. It can take many forms, such as:

- threats, intimidation, or verbal abuse
- unwelcome remarks or jokes about subjects such as race, religion, disability, or age
- displaying sexist, racist, or other offensive pictures or posters
- sexually suggestive remarks or gestures
- unnecessary physical contact, such as touching, patting, pinching, or punching
- physical assault, including sexual assault

Harassment can consist of a single incident or several incidents over a period of time, and will be considered to have taken place if a reasonable person ought to have known that the behaviour was unwelcome. Threatening, intimidating, or discriminating against someone who has either filed a complaint, or who is providing evidence or assistance in complaint proceedings, is a summary conviction offence under the federal *Human Rights Act*.

Flirtation/Harassment

Sexual harassment is a major concern in the workplace. The restrictions on sexual harassment are relatively new, and the law is still developing. Normal social behaviour—flirtation—and harassment may well overlap. The difficulty is deciding when the behaviour is part of what is socially acceptable and when it passes beyond.

Human rights legislation recognizes that flirtation is not abnormal, and that it should not be prohibited for people of equal status in their employment situations. However, if a person has supervisory authority over the other person, there is zero tolerance of sexual approach. The employee may feel that his or her job is at risk if there is a refusal.

Evidence of sexual harassment may be difficult to prove because the incident often takes place in private. The case becomes the word of the complainant against the word of the person allegedly harassing. Harassment is also a difficult question because people ordinarily speak of sex in euphemistic or suggestive terms rather than in direct language. The harassment may not be explicit, but suggestive. Even one incident is sufficient to be considered harassment.

Employer's Responsibilities   Employers are jointly responsible with the offending employee for any harassment that occurs in the workplace. Under all human rights acts, it is the employer's duty to be proactive in preventing harassment. Employers must:

Business Alert!

- make it clear that harassment will not be tolerated
- establish a no-harassment policy
- make sure every employee understands the policy and procedures for dealing with harassment
- inform supervisors and managers of their responsibility to provide a harassment-free work environment
- investigate and correct harassment problems as soon as they come to light, even if a formal complaint has not been received

The employer should be prepared to take appropriate disciplinary action against an employee found to have harassed someone.

The employer has a defence of due diligence. Due diligence can be thought of as being proactive. If the employer can establish that it did the above-noted in an effort to prevent harassment or discrimination, it may be acquitted, even though the employee is found guilty. **Due diligence** is a defence to certain charges, by doing everything reasonable to prevent the problem leading to legal liability.

due diligence
a defence to certain charges, by doing everything reasonable to prevent the problem leading to legal liability

Harassment is a possible ground for dismissal. In one court action, the court found that an employer was justified in firing a male employee who had sexually harassed a female co-worker under his supervision.

Disability—An Employer's Responsibility to Accommodate

Since an employer must not discriminate because of disability, there is a duty on employers to take a positive step to avoid discrimination. For example, a religious employee should not be forced to work on a religious holiday if other employees can do so. An employer must provide a business environment in which a person with a disability can function.

Creating a workplace that is, for example, fully wheelchair accessible can involve some expense, and businesses sometimes raise the concern of the cost per employee. If the business can prove undue hardship, it will be exempt from this requirement.

In general, the duty to provide an environment that avoids discrimination because of disability involves a combination of factors, including:

- accessible premises (entrances, washrooms, elevators)
- adaptive technology (Braille printers, or speech synthesizers)
- support services (a person to read to a visually impaired employee)
- job restructuring to shift responsibilities around where necessary
- modified work hours, to adapt to the schedules of those requiring medical treatment such as dialysis

Exemptions

Bona Fide *Occupational Requirement*

There are several exceptions set out in the *Human Rights Act* that permit discrimination under very restricted circumstances. The one most frequently applied in the business situation is known as a ***bona fide* occupational requirement (BFOR)**, which is a genuine requirement for a job, such as, for example, the need to wear a hard hat when working on a construction site. A BFOR is a defence that excuses discrimination on a prohibited ground when it is done in good faith and for a legitimate business reason.

bona fide occupational requirement (BFOR)

a genuine requirement for a job, such as, for example, the need to wear a hard hat when working on a construction site; a BFOR is a defence that excuses discrimination on a prohibited ground when it is done in good faith and for a legitimate business reason

Rejected BFORs   A BFOR commonly raised by employers as defences to human rights complaints is customer preference. This has almost universally been rejected as a BFOR. For example, it was ruled that a male applicant could not be refused a job as a drapery installer on the basis that a male did not have the requisite care, taste, and delicacy to install drapes. Physical capability has also been rejected. In one case, it was ruled that a woman could not be refused a job on the basis that she was not able to lift heavy truck equipment, and that it was dangerous for a woman to be left alone in an office at night.

In a highly controversial case a Sikh RCMP officer sought to wear a turban as part of his Mountie uniform claiming his right to freedom of religion. The RCMP agreed and decided that Human Rights legislation required it to permit this exception to the normal requirement because wearing the traditional Mountie hat could not be justified as a *bona fide* occupational requirement. A group of retired RCMP officers unsuccessfully challenged this ruling in court.

Efficiency and Safety   An employer may claim that a *bona fide* occupational requirement is necessary because of business profitability or safety to the public. When public safety is involved, a court is more likely to find that a BFOR exemption exists. Many cases heard before various provincial tribunals have dealt with the fact that firefighters must retire at the age of 60, because of public safety. The courts have upheld this mandatory retirement policy for firefighters, but have stated that in other circumstances individual testing should be used if at all possible to determine whether a person is fit for the job.

Is Drug Testing a BFOR?   Previous or existing dependence on alcohol or drugs is specifically defined as a disability by section 25 of the *Canadian Human Rights Act*. Is employment-related drug testing then a violation of this section? Can drug testing be justified as a *bona fide* occupational requirement if it is a violation?

A Health and Welfare Canada survey reported that 85 percent of Canada's labour force drank, and 10 percent considered themselves heavy drinkers. Illicit drug use was reported by 8 percent. Such substances affect the user's motor functions, decision-making capacity, and planning skills, both during use and in the hangover or withdrawal stages.

Studies have shown that alcohol is frequently a contributing factor in accidents in the workplace. Alcohol and drugs also contribute to absenteeism, higher turnover rates, increased sick benefits, more workers' compensation and insurance claims, lower productivity, lower-quality services, theft, and trafficking.

Employers are particularly concerned about substance abuse because of possible accidents:

- on the job, especially those involving other employees
- caused by intoxicated employees—ranging from those involving company-owned motor vehicles, to major disasters such as tankers running aground and spilling oil

Companies are discussing the use of drug testing to try to eliminate some of these problems.

There is some disagreement over the necessity for drug testing, since these tests may also reveal other conditions, such as AIDS or diabetes. Employees are concerned that their privacy is being invaded, or that they might be fired because they have AIDS.

The Toronto-Dominion Bank established a policy of administering drug and alcohol tests randomly to employees who have access to cash and to the confidential financial information of customers. The program was found to be too wide ranging, and the TD Bank and human rights groups are conferring on establishing a policy that meets the needs of the bank without unnecessary violations of employee rights. It is anticipated that there will be many challenges to such testing programs; the development of guidelines for when such programs are in violation of human rights legislation will be one of the tasks facing human rights tribunals in the future.

Bhinder v. Canadian National Railway Company, [1985] 2 S.C.R. 561

Bhinder became an employee of CN in April, 1974. He worked for more than four years as a maintenance electrician in the Toronto coach yard, servicing the turbo train between the hours of 11:00 p.m. and 7:30 a.m. The company announced on November 30, 1978, that, with effect from December 1, 1978, all employees at the Toronto coach yard would be required to wear a hard hat while at work. Bhinder, a Sikh, forbidden by his religion to wear anything on his head except a turban, refused to wear a hard hat.

He was informed in a letter from the general foreman, dated December 5, 1978, that there could be no exceptions to the hard hat rule, that he would be required to comply and wear a hard hat commencing December 6, 1978, and that he would not be permitted to work if did not do so. Bhinder was not prepared to work in any capacity other than that of an electrician, and there were no positions open for electricians in which the wearing of the hard hat was not required.

His employment with CN ceased on December 5, 1978. He successfully complained to the Human Rights Commission, which charged CN with discrimination on the grounds of religion. The matter was appealed to the Supreme Court of Canada.

The Court's Decision

The court concluded that the requirement to wear a hard hat was discrimination against Bhinder on the prohibited grounds of freedom of religion. The question then was whether it could be justified as a *bona fide* occupational requirement. The court established two principles about this defence:

- it was up to the employer to prove that its policy was a *bona fide* occupational requirement
- the section in the *Canadian Human Rights Act* that permits BFORs should be narrowly interpreted.

In applying these principles, the court found that the CN had established a *bona fide* occupational requirement because the wearing of hard hats was a reasonable policy, justified for the safety of the workers. Bhinder's complaint was dismissed.

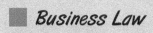 **Business Law** Applied

9 Star Caterers Inc. has obtained a new contract to supply food to a college cafeteria. The company wants to have all employees undergo a test for AIDS. Morris Brown, an employee, knows he is HIV-positive, and does not want Star to discover this.

a) Does Brown have any grounds under human rights legislation for challenging the mandatory AIDS testing?
b) Does Star Caterers Inc. have any defence?

Affirmative Action and Other Special Programs

Like the Charter, human rights legislation makes exceptions for affirmative action and other special programs. This is done in an effort to relieve the effect of discrimination on minority groups.

It is felt that many people will not complain because of the fear of pressure and consequences. The cost of processing individual complaints is high, and delays before tribunals, and courts, if there is an appeal, are lengthy. Prevention is felt to be a far more effective and efficient remedy. It also has the advantage of not singling out individuals as complainants.

Remedies

The federal and provincial human rights acts all have similar provisions allowing for several remedies upon finding of a violation. The main remedies allow the tribunal to order a person found at fault:

- to stop a discriminating practice
- to adopt a special program and plan to cure the problem
- to pay a money award as compensation to the complainant
- to reinstate a complainant into employment

The term *person* includes a business or corporation. The question in the *Action Travail v. CN* case above was whether a tribunal had the power to make the company adopt an employment equity program. The tribunal ordered CN to hire one woman in four as new employees until the level of female workers reached 13 percent of the company's total workforce—the national average for women working in equivalent jobs.

Private Settlement

Many complaints today are settled before they ever reach a board of enquiry. In these circumstances, a business should obtain a written **release** (a written or oral statement freeing another party from an existing duty) from the employee, guaranteeing that the individual will not make a claim under human rights legislation or bring a civil court action. A **claim** is a written statement or basic summary of a plaintiff's allegations against a defendant in a lawsuit. Releases are important because as well as defending a complaint made to a human rights commission, employers might also face a civil court action if the employee regards the harassment as constructive termination (see p. 451) and sues for wrongful dismissal.

Confidentiality   Many businesses want to avoid publicity, or setting a precedent in the amount of awards, and insist that a release contains a confidentiality clause—a gag clause—in which the complainant agrees not to reveal details of the settlement. (**Confidentiality** is the obligation not to disclose any information without consent.) These clauses are effective against the individual employees, but may not bind the respective human rights commission.

release
a written or oral statement freeing another party from an existing duty

claim
a written statement or basic summary of a plaintiff's allegations against a defendant in a lawsuit

confidentiality
the obligation not to disclose any information without consent

Business Alert!

In Summation

The essential concepts you see here are the basics of this chapter. They are the thread only—you must add the beads to form the necklace. Try using this list as a test. If there's a particular point that you don't recall, review that section of the chapter.

The Constitution

- The ability to make laws is divided between the federal and provincial governments according to specific matters. Residual powers are given to the federal government for matters not specifically listed.

- *The Constitution Act, 1982*, incorporated the *British North America Act* and the *Charter of Rights and Freedoms*, and qualifies the laws that the federal or provincial governments may enact. An amending formula requiring extraordinary measures to change any element of the constitution was also included.

Charter of Rights and Freedoms

▨ One aspect of the Charter focuses on controlling the government's power to make law. Here neither the federal nor any provincial government can make a law that violates the rights that are listed in the Charter. There are five concepts discussed in the text relating to the Charter:

a) Application. The Charter applies to governments when making laws, while human rights legislation applies to acts of government and individuals respecting certain prohibited behaviour, particularly discrimination and harassment.

b) Protected Rights. Only some rights are protected. For example, the right to freedom of the press is specifically mentioned, but the right to bear arms, which is part of the United States Constitution, is not set out as a Charter right.

c) Reasonable Limitations. Even if the right is protected, a law can be passed in violation of this protected right if it is reasonable to limit the right. A law limiting advertising is a violation of the freedom of expression of a business, but in the case of advertising directed at children under age 13, it may be reasonable to limit the right of freedom of expression because of the societal interest in protecting children from manipulation through advertising.

d) Specific Charter Exemptions. There are specific exemptions listed in the Charter for areas where laws can be passed even though they are in violation of protected rights. The most common example is affirmative action programs. These programs discriminate in favour of minority groups. While discrimination is generally prohibited, it is permitted in a law that benefits a disadvantaged group.

e) Legislative Exemptions. The controversial "notwithstanding clause" permits a government to pass a law which states that the law is valid in spite of the Charter.

Human Rights Legislation

▨ Human rights legislation ensures individuals are not discriminated against by the actions of other individuals, corporations, and governments.

▨ The federal and provincial governments have passed laws dealing with human rights. The law applicable, federal or provincial, to any given situation, basically reflects the division set up in sections 91 and 92 of the Constitution.

▨ The *Canadian Human Rights Act* lists a number of grounds on which discrimination is not permitted, such as religion, country of origin, and disability. Harassment stemming from any of these grounds will also be considered a type of discrimination. The act also recognizes that systemic discrimination may occur through the enforcement of policies by various organizations.

▨ There are very few exemptions from the prohibited grounds for discrimination, and only when there are very real occupational reasons behind the action or decision.

▨ Human rights commissions or councils have been established at the provincial and federal levels with definite procedures for handling investigations, decision making, and the determination of remedies for human rights violations.

Closing Questions

1. A provincial government proposes to pass an act called the *Provincial Postal Rate Act*. This legislation states: "All local mail within the province shall be sent for the rate of 10 cents."

a) Advise the Attorney General of Canada whether a provincial government has the power to pass legislation concerning the post office. Give a specific reference in the Constitution to justify your position.

2. A city council considers designating areas that permit prostitution. Its argument is that the city has control over uses of city areas through zoning by-laws. For example, an area can be zoned as residential-only, or the city can permit uses such as slaughterhouses or garbage dumps.

a) Do you think a city zoning by-law to regulate prostitution is within the provincial power?

3. A provincial government enacted a statute entitled the *Wages Act*. This act provides that if a business goes bankrupt, then the workers' claim for unpaid wages for the six months prior to bankruptcy will take precedence over all other claims against the company. The right to sue for wages is a matter of contract law, and hence is considered within the category of civil rights.
   a) Is the above legislation within the powers of the provincial government?
   b) What are possible categories in federal and provincial jurisdictions?
   c) Is this a matter that affects employment contract, or priority in bankruptcy?

4. Analyze the Big M Drug Mart decision according to the outline given after that case brief in the chapter.
   a) Can you think of arguments other than the ones given in the case brief?
   b) Write a decision that applies the same legal principles, but that comes to an opposite conclusion.
   c) Does logic necessarily govern the outcome of a decision? If not, what do you think does?

5. Corporal John Kanzawa of the Canadian Army has been charged with dereliction of duty, and is to appear before a military tribunal composed of army officers for court-martial proceedings. Corporal Kanzawa does not want to be tried by army officers, preferring a trial by jury.
   a) Is the right to a trial by jury a right protected by the Charter?
   b) Is there an exemption to this right?

6. In your position as policy analyst for the federal Attorney General's office, determine whether the *Charter of Rights and Freedoms*, the *Canadian Human Rights Act*, or provincial human rights legislation applies to each of the following situations.
   a) A provincial *Elections Act* denies the right to vote to any person serving a sentence for a criminal offence. A prisoner wishes to challenge this law.
   b) An employee of the post office believes that she was fired because of race.
   c) An employee of the Bay in Vancouver feels that he is being discriminated against because of age.
   d) An employee of Bell Canada in Halifax feels that she is being sexually harassed.

7. A federal government agency employed electricians in groups of ten on a short-term contract basis. There were seven such groups working on a particular project. In each, only one electrician was black; the others were members of other minority groups or were white.

   The project was entering a new phase, and the project manager ordered the foreman of each group not to renew the contract of one person per group. In each case, the individual let go was the member of the group who was black.

   The black electricians complained to the human rights commission. They said that while they were employed there was no incidence of racism, but claimed that the mass layoff was discrimination against them because of race.
   a) Could the black electricians prove their case without evidence of discriminatory acts by their employer?

8. KidTalk Inc. manufactures a line of cellphones for the pre-teen market. They are the hit toy of the year largely because of the very effective advertising campaign directed at the pre-teen market. Parents are upset. The Manitoba government passes a law that prohibits KidTalk from advertising on daytime television, in order to restrict the company's campaign aimed at children. KidTalk wants to challenge the legislation:
   a) What grounds could it use to attack the legislation?
   b) Based on the cases that you have studied so far, would one of them support either of the parties' position?
   c) Because of the effectiveness of the legislation, KidTalk has to downsize. Employees who are fired claim they are primarily from one minority group. Do they have any remedy against KidTalk?

9. a) Find a website which contains a copy of the *Canadian Charter of Rights and Freedoms* and report the website address to your class.
   b) Find a website that has the *R. v. Big M Drug Mart Ltd.* case. What is the difference between the brief or summary of the case in the text and the full case on the website?

Websites

www.nlc-bnc.ca—This is the site of the National Library of Canada, which provides links to all federal and provincial statute law and other information regarding the federal and provincial governments and the National Library.

www.duhaime.org—Online law dictionary by B.C. lawyer, Lloyd Duhaime.

www.human-rights-coalition.bc.ca—Links to most human rights legislation and commissions in Canada.

www.acjnet.org—Access to Justice Network. Links to most significant Canadian legal sites, including case law and statutes.

www.adrr.com—*ADR* and Mediation Resources. General information on the use of alternative dispute resolution.

www.ccla.org—Canadian Civil Liberties Association.

www.legalline.c—Free legal information on 870 topics. Primarily for Ontario.

Most governments and courts have websites which post provincial statutes and recent case decisions. To find one for your province simply do a search for your province name and the word *statute* or *courts*.

The Constitution Act, 1867, Sections 91 and 92

VI. Distribution of Legislative Powers

Powers of the Parliament
Legislative Authority of Parliament of Canada

91. It shall be lawful for the Queen, by and with the Advice and Consent of the Senate and House of Commons, to make Laws for the Peace, Order, and good Government of Canada, in relation to all Matters not coming within the Classes of Subjects by this Act assigned exclusively to the Legislatures of the Provinces; and for greater Certainty, but not so as to restrict the Generality of the foregoing Terms of this Section, it is hereby declared that (notwithstanding anything in this Act)the exclusive Legislative Authority of the Parliament of Canada extends to all Matters coming within the Classes of Subjects next hereinafter enumerated; that is to say,

1. Repealed. (44)
1A. The Public Debt and Property. (45)

2. The Regulation of Trade and Commerce.
2A. Unemployment insurance. (46)

3. The raising of Money by any Mode or System of Taxation.

4. The borrowing of Money on the Public Credit.

5. Postal Service.

6. The Census and Statistics.

7. Militia, Military and Naval Service, and Defence.

8. The fixing of and providing for the Salaries and Allowances of Civil and other Officers of the Government of Canada.

9. Beacons, Buoys, Lighthouses, and Sable Island.

10. Navigation and Shipping.

11. Quarantine and the Establishment and Maintenance of Marine Hospitals.

12. Sea Coast and Inland Fisheries.

13. Ferries between a Province and any British or Foreign Country or between Two Provinces.

14. Currency and Coinage.

15. Banking, Incorporation of Banks, and the Issue of Paper Money.

16. Savings Bank.

17. Weights and Measures.

18. Bills of Exchange and Promissory Notes.

19. Interest.

20. Legal Tender.

21. Bankruptcy and Insolvency.

22. Patents of Invention and Discovery.

23. Copyrights.

24. Indians, and Lands reserved for the Indians.

25. Naturalization and Aliens.

26. Marriage and Divorce.

27. The Criminal Law, except the Constitution of Courts of Criminal Jurisdiction, but including the Procedure in Criminal Matters.

28. The Establishment, Maintenance, and Management of Penitentiaries.

29. Such Classes of Subjects as are expressly excepted in the Enumeration of the Classes of Subjects by this Act assigned exclusively to the Legislatures of the Provinces.

And any Matter coming within any of the Classes of Subjects enumerated in this Section shall not be deemed to come within the Class of Matters of a local or private Nature comprised in the Enumeration of the Classes of Subjects by this Act assigned exclusively to the Legislatures of the Provinces. (47)

Exclusive Powers of Provincial Legislatures
Subjects of Exclusive Provincial Legislation

92. In each Province the Legislature may exclusively make Laws in relation to Matters coming within the Classes of Subjects next hereinafter enumerated; that is to say,

1. Repealed (48).

2. Direct Taxation within the Province in order to the raising of a Revenue for Provincial Purposes.

3. The borrowing of Money on the sole Credit of the Province.

4. The Establishment and Tenure of Provincial Offices and the Appointment and Payment of Provincial Officers.

5. The Management and Sale of the Public Lands belonging to the Province and of the Timber and Wood thereon.

6. The Establishment, Maintenance, and Management of Public and Reformatory Prisons in and for the Province.

7. The Establishment, Maintenance, and Management of Hospitals, Asylums, Charities, and Eleemosynary Institutions in and for the Province, other than Marine Hospitals.

8. Municipal Institutions in the Province.

9. Shop, Saloon, Tavern, Auctioneer, and other Licences in order to the raising of a Revenue for Provincial, Local, or Municipal Purposes.

10. Local Works and Undertakings other than such as are of the following Classes:
    (a) Lines of Steam or other Ships, Railways, Canals, Telegraphs, and other Works and Undertakings connecting the Province with any other or others of the Provinces, or extending beyond the Limits of the Province:
    (b) Lines of Steam Ships between the Province and any British or Foreign Country:
    (c) Such Works as, although wholly situate within the Province, are before or after their Execution declared by the Parliament of Canada to be for the general Advantage of Canada or for the Advantage of Two or more of the Provinces.

11. The Incorporation of Companies with Provincial Objects.

12. The Solemnization of Marriage in the Province.

13. Property and Civil Rights in the Province

14. The Administration of Justice in the Province, including the Constitution, Maintenance, and Organization of Provincial Courts, both of Civil and of Criminal Jurisdiction, and including Procedure in Civil Matters in those Courts.

15. The Imposition of Punishment by Fine, Penalty, or Imprisonment for enforcing any Law of the Province made in relation to any Matter coming within any of the Classes of Subjects enumerated in this Section.

16. Generally all Matters of a merely local or private Nature in the Province.

Canadian Charter of Rights and Freedoms

Schedule B, Constitution Act, 1982 (79)

Whereas Canada is founded upon principles that recognize the supremacy of God and the rule of law:

Rights and freedoms in Canada

1. The *Canadian Charter of Rights and Freedoms* guarantees the rights and freedoms set out in it subject only to such reasonable limits prescribed by law as can be demonstrably justified in a free and democratic society.

Fundamental freedoms

2. Everyone has the following fundamental freedoms:
   a) freedom of conscience and religion;
   b) freedom of thought, belief, opinion and expression, including freedom of the press and other media of communication;
   c) freedom of peaceful assembly; and
   d) freedom of association.

Democratic rights of citizens

3. Every citizen of Canada has the right to vote in an election of members of the House of Commons or of a legislative assembly and to be qualified for membership therein.

Maximum duration of legislative bodies

4. (1) No House of Commons and no legislative assembly shall continue for longer than five years from the date fixed for the return of the writs of a general election of its members.

Continuation in special circumstances

   (2) In time of real or apprehended war, invasion or insurrection, a House of Commons may be continued by Parliament and a legislative assembly may be continued by the legislature beyond five years if such continuation is not opposed by the votes of more than one-third of the members of the House of Commons or the legislative assembly, as the case may be.

Annual sitting of legislative bodies

5. There shall be a sitting of Parliament and of each legislature at least once every twelve months.

Mobility of citizens

6. (1) Every citizen of Canada has the right to enter, remain in and leave Canada.

Rights to move and gain livelihood

   (2) Every citizen of Canada and every person who has the status of a permanent resident of Canada has the right
   a) to move to and take up residence in any province; and
   b) to pursue the gaining of a livelihood in any province.

   (3) The rights specified in subsection (2) are subject to

Limitation

   a) any laws or practices of general application in force in a province other than those that discriminate among persons primarily on the basis of province of present or previous residence; and
   b) any laws providing for reasonable residency requirements as a qualification for the receipt of publicly provided social services.

Affirmative action programs

   (4) Subsections (2) and (3) do not preclude any law, program or activity that has as its object the amelioration in a province of conditions of individuals in that province who are socially or economically disadvantaged if the rate of employment in that province is below the rate of employment in Canada.

7. Everyone has the right to life, liberty and security of the person and the right not to be deprived thereof except in accordance with the principles of fundamental justice.

Life, liberty and security of person

8. Everyone has the right to be secure against unreasonable search or seizure.

Search or seizure

9. Everyone has the right not to be arbitrarily detained or imprisoned.

Detention or imprisonment

10. Everyone has the right on arrest or detention
    a) to be informed promptly of the reasons therefor;
    b) to retain and instruct counsel without delay and to be informed of that right; and
    c) to have the validity of the detention determined by way of *habeas corpus* and to be released if the detention is not lawful.

Arrest or detention

11. Any person charged with an offence has the right
    a) to be informed without unreasonable delay of the specific offence;
    b) to be tried within a reasonable time;
    c) not to be compelled to be a witness in proceedings against that person in respect of the offence;
    d) to be presumed innocent until proven guilty according to law in a fair and public hearing by an independent and impartial tribunal;
    e) not to be denied reasonable bail without just cause;
    f) except in the case of an offence under military law tried before a military tribunal, to the benefit of trial by jury where the maximum punishment for the offence is imprisonment for five years or a more severe punishment;
    g) not to be found guilty on account of any act or omission unless, at the time of the act or omission, it constituted an offence under Canadian or international law or was criminal according to the general principles of law recognized by the community of nations;
    h) if finally acquitted of the offence, not to be tried for it again and, if finally found guilty and punished for the offence, not to be tried or punished for it again; and
    i) if found guilty of the offence and if the punishment for the offence has been varied between the time of commission and the time of sentencing, to the benefit of the lesser punishment.

Proceedings in criminal and penal matters

12. Everyone has the right not to be subjected to any cruel and unusual treatment or punishment.

Treatment or punishment

13. A witness who testifies in any proceedings has the right not to have any incriminating evidence so given used to incriminate that witness in any other proceedings, except in a prosecution for perjury or for the giving of contradictory evidence.

Self-crimination

14. A party or witness in any proceedings who does not understand or speak the language in which the proceedings are conducted or who is deaf has the right to the assistance of an interpreter.

Interpreter

15. (1) Every individual is equal before and under the law and has the right to the equal protection and equal benefit of the law without discrimination and, in particular, without discrimination based on race, national or ethnic origin, colour, religion, sex, age or mental or physical disability.

Equality before and under law and equal protection and benefit of law

(2) Subsection (1) does not preclude any law, program or activity that has as its object the amelioration of conditions of disadvantaged individuals or groups including those that are disadvantaged because of race, national or ethnic origin, colour, religion, sex, age or mental or physical disability.

Affirmative action programs

16. (1) English and French are the official languages of Canada and have equality of status and equal rights and privileges as to their use in all institutions of the Parliament and government of Canada.

Official languages of Canada

(2) English and French are the official languages of New Brunswick and have equality of status and equal rights and privileges as to their use in all institutions of the legislature and government of New Brunswick.

Official languages of New Brunswick

(3) Nothing in this Charter limits the authority of Parliament or a legislature to advance the equality of status or use of English and French.

Advancement of status and use

English and French linguistic communities in New Brunswick	**16.1.**(1) The English linguistic community and the French linguistic community in New Brunswick have equality of status and equal rights and privileges, including the right to distinct educational institutions and such distinct cultural institutions as are necessary for the preservation and promotion of those communities.
Role of the legislature and government of New Brunswick	(2) The role of the legislature and government of New Brunswick to preserve and promote the status, rights and privileges referred to in subsection (1) is affirmed.
Proceedings of Parliament	**17.** (1) Everyone has the right to use English or French in any debates and other proceedings of Parliament.
Proceedings of New Brunswick legislature	(2) Everyone has the right to use English or French in any debates and other proceedings of the legislature of New Brunswick.
Parliamentary statutes and records	**18.** (1) The statutes, records and journals of Parliament shall be printed and published in English and French and both language versions are equally authoritative.
New Brunswick statutes and records	(2) The statutes, records and journals of the legislature of New Brunswick shall be printed and published in English and French and both language versions are equally authoritative.
Proceedings in courts established by Parliament	**19.** (1) Either English or French may be used by any person in, or in any pleading in or process issuing from, any court established by Parliament.
Proceedings in New Brunswick courts	(2) Either English or French may be used by any person in, or in any pleading in or process issuing from, any court of New Brunswick.
Communications by public with federal institutions	**20.** (1) Any member of the public in Canada has the right to communicate with, and to receive available services from, any head or central office of an institution of the Parliament or government of Canada in English or French, and has the same right with respect to any other office of any such institution where
	a) there is a significant demand for communications with and services from that office in such language; or
	b) due to the nature of the office, it is reasonable that communications with and services from that office be available in both English and French.
Communications by public with New Brunswick institutions	(2) Any member of the public in New Brunswick has the right to communicate with, and to receive available services from, any office of an institution of the legislature or government of New Brunswick in English or French.
Continuation of existing constitutional provisions	**21.** Nothing in sections 16 to 20 abrogates or derogates from any right, privilege or obligation with respect to the English and French languages, or either of them, that exists or is continued by virtue of any other provision of the Constitution of Canada.
Rights and privileges preserved	**22.** Nothing in sections 16 to 20 abrogates or derogates from any legal or customary right or privilege acquired or enjoyed either before or after the coming into force of this Charter with respect to any language that is not English or French.
Language of instruction	**23.** (1) Citizens of Canada
	a) whose first language learned and still understood is that of the English or French linguistic minority population of the province in which they reside, or
	b) who have received their primary school instruction in Canada in English or French and reside in a province where the language in which they received that instruction is the language of the English or French linguistic minority population of the province, have the right to have their children receive primary and secondary school instruction in that language in that province.
Continuity of language instruction	(2) Citizens of Canada of whom any child has received or is receiving primary or secondary school instruction in English or French in Canada, have the right to have all their children receive primary and secondary school instruction in the same language.

(3) The right of citizens of Canada under subsections (1) and (2) to have their children receive primary and secondary school instruction in the language of the English or French linguistic minority population of a province

Application where numbers warrant

    a) applies wherever in the province the number of children of citizens who have such a right is sufficient to warrant the provision to them out of public funds of minority language instruction; and

    b) includes, where the number of those children so warrants, the right to have them receive that instruction in minority language educational facilities provided out of public funds.

24. (1) Anyone whose rights or freedoms, as guaranteed by this Charter, have been infringed or denied may apply to a court of competent jurisdiction to obtain such remedy as the court considers appropriate and just in the circumstances.

Enforcement of guaranteed rights and freedoms

    (2) Where, in proceedings under subsection (1), a court concludes that evidence was obtained in a manner that infringed or denied any rights or freedoms guaranteed by this Charter, the evidence shall be excluded if it is established that, having regard to all the circumstances, the admission of it in the proceedings would bring the administration of justice into disrepute.

Exclusion of evidence bringing administration of justice into disrepute

25. The guarantee in this Charter of certain rights and freedoms shall not be construed so as to abrogate or derogate from any aboriginal, treaty or other rights or freedoms that pertain to the aboriginal peoples of Canada including

Aboriginal rights and freedoms not affected by Charter

    a) any rights or freedoms that have been recognized by the Royal Proclamation of October 7, 1763; and

    b) any rights or freedoms that now exist by way of land claims agreements or may be so acquired.

26. The guarantee in this Charter of certain rights and freedoms shall not be construed as denying the existence of any other rights or freedoms that exist in Canada.

Other rights and freedoms not affected by Charter

27. This Charter shall be interpreted in a manner consistent with the preservation and enhancement of the multicultural heritage of Canadians.

Multicultural heritage

28. Notwithstanding anything in this Charter, the rights and freedoms referred to in it are guaranteed equally to male and female persons.

Rights guaranteed equally to both sexes

29. Nothing in this Charter abrogates or derogates from any rights or privileges guaranteed by or under the Constitution of Canada in respect of denominational, separate or dissentient schools.(93)

Rights respecting certain schools preserved

30. A reference in this Charter to a Province or to the legislative assembly or legislature of a province shall be deemed to include a reference to the Yukon Territory and the Northwest Territories, or to the appropriate legislative authority thereof, as the case may be.

Application to territories and territorial authorities

31. Nothing in this Charter extends the legislative powers of any body or authority.

Legislative powers not extended

32. (1) This Charter applies

Application of Charter

    a) to the Parliament and government of Canada in respect of all matters within the authority of Parliament including all matters relating to the Yukon Territory and Northwest Territories; and

    b) to the legislature and government of each province in respect of all matters within the authority of the legislature of each province.

    (2) Notwithstanding subsection (1), section 15 shall not have effect until three years after this section comes into force.

Exception

Exception where express declaration

33. (1) Parliament or the legislature of a province may expressly declare in an Act of Parliament or of the legislature, as the case may be, that the Act or a provision thereof shall operate notwithstanding a provision included in section 2 or sections 7 to 15 of this Charter.

Operation of exception

(2) An Act or a provision of an Act in respect of which a declaration made under this section is in effect shall have such operation as it would have but for the provision of this Charter referred to in the declaration.

Five year limitation

Five year limitation

(3) A declaration made under subsection (1) shall cease to have effect five years after it comes into force or on such earlier date as may be specified in the declaration.

Re-enactment

(4) Parliament or the legislature of a province may re-enact a declaration made under subsection (1).

Five year limitation

(5) Subsection (3) applies in respect of a re-enactment made under subsection (4).

Citation

34. This Part may be cited as the *Canadian Charter of Rights and Freedoms.*

Legal Research

A website that contains all Canadian federal and provincial statutes and many court decisions is: http://www.canlii.org. CanLII is a non-profit organization managed by the Federation of Law Societies of Canada.

The citations for many of the case briefs in the text are given with CanLII citations. However, most other cases referred to in the text can also be found by searching the case name on this website.

Here is what the first Search page looks like. You can fill in the case name or statute in Box no. 2. However, one tip: the search program often does not recognize the "v." in case names. So it is more efficient to put in one or both of the parties names, not the complete citation. For example to find the decision of: *RBC v. Welton* (2008), 89 O.R. (3d) 532; enter the names "RBC Welton".

Statute names can be entered here or you can click on the federal or provincial name on the left hand menu and be brought to a section dedicated to that jurisdiction.

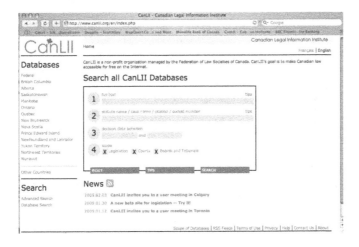

The Canadian Court System

Law and the Legal System

We all encounter laws and the legal system at some time or other in our lives—whether we are buying or selling a house, looking after the estate of a deceased loved one, or getting stopped for speeding on the way to work. When you enter the world of business, encounters with laws and the legal system are likely to be even more frequent. How much time off must you give your employees? Should you incorporate? Can you sue your supplier for delivering goods which were not of the quality you expected? Do you have to pay for injuries suffered by a customer who fell in your store?

There are many ways to define "law." However, laws can be broadly viewed as rules of conduct that are enforced by government-sanctioned agencies (such as the courts or the police). The laws that are set out for individuals and business to follow—or, if not, to face the legal consequences—may be categorized in a variety of ways:

- private or civil law—a set of laws that attempt to resolve disputes between individuals (or businesses). For example, if someone trips over a ladder you left across the entrance to your store and injures himself, you and that person would have a dispute governed by private or civil law.
- criminal or regulatory law—a set of laws that attempt to resolve disputes between society generally and certain individuals (or businesses). The results of running afoul of these rules are charges or the issuance of tickets. For example, if you published some misleading advertising in the local newspaper, you may be charged under the *Competition Act*. It sets out rules for advertising that society feels are in its own best interests. If you parked your delivery truck in a No Parking zone, you would be charged under the local traffic by-law and be issued a ticket. The municipality has regulated parking in the interests of the community as a whole.

Constitutional or administrative law—a set of laws that attempt to resolve disputes between individuals and governments, or between governments and governments, when governments are acting in their capacities as lawmakers. For example, if you are charged under a piece of legislation requiring all bike riders under age 25 to wear helmets, you may try to have the legislation overruled, by claiming that the government that enacted it did not follow the rules of the Constitution (perhaps by discriminating against you on the basis of age).

It is important to note that the goals of each of these types of law are different. Civil law attempts to obtain compensation for the wronged party; criminal or regulatory law attempts to extract punishment (for example, a fine or jail time) from the offending party; and Constitutional or administrative law nullifies certain actions of government if certain rules are not followed. The terminology used is also different—civil law speaks of suing and liability, and the parties involved are called the plaintiff and defendant; criminal or regulatory law speaks of charges or offences, and of guilty or not guilty, and the parties involved are the prosecutor and the accused. Finally, the processes are different. Civil matters are heard in one court, criminal in another, and Constitutional matters are often heard as a separate part of civil or criminal trials.

Note that one incident could lead to an encounter with both the criminal law process and the civil law process. For instance, if you are speeding to make a delivery and run over someone who is crossing the street, that injured person may sue you *and* you may well face charges under the *Highway Traffic Act* of your province. You may have to pay damages to the injured party as well as pay a fine.

Why is all this important? You need to realize that certain actions that you take in the business world may have a variety of consequences. It's important to weigh the possible consequences of your conduct in the business world. You may need to get a lawyer's advice before you take certain action. You may face a civil suit from someone you have allegedly wronged, and you may face criminal charges relating to the same incident. As well, you should know that the actions of government and its agents are not beyond legal challenge if certain rules have not been followed; however, sometimes the legal rules won't help you achieve your goals. Sometimes the only way to challenge government action is at the ballot box, or by way of protest. In short, some understanding of the legal rules that pertain to businesses, and of the legal system (with the aid of this book), will help you run your business with minimal legal cost in both time and money.

The Common Law System

Judge-Made Law

Judges frequently met and discussed similar cases, and tried to discover those principles that extended generally to all of England and were common to all the people. It is from this that the term common law arose. One such principle was that the eldest son was to be the sole heir to his ancestors. Another was that a transfer of land had to be in writing under seal, or it was ineffective.

It has been said that the unique feature of English culture is not the development of the parliamentary system, for that may be found in many parts of the world, but the survival of a common law system. Many countries today, most of which are former members of the British Empire, including the United States and Canada (except Quebec), use the common law system.

Courts of Equity

This concentration on the strict application of laws—known as the black-letter-law approach—became rigid and was viewed as unfair. So the monarch started his own court to apply fairness, or equity. Now two systems were in place, each with its own court—the common law and equity.

For example, if Joseph Levitt defaulted on his mortgage payment to Susan Scott, in common law court, Susan Scott could take Joseph Levitt's house immediately and sell it. But in a court of equity, Joseph Levitt was given an automatic extension of six months to pay the mortgage.

The courts of equity devised remedies to soften the harsh results of some of the common-law principles. The two courts were merged in 1873, so Canadian courts can apply both common law and equitable law. Where there is a conflict between the two, the laws of equity prevail.

However, it is important to understand that in the Court of Equity, the Judges did not apply their own view of fairness; rather the Courts developed laws that were intended to incorporate principles of fairness. It is a mistake, that even young lawyers make, to believe that a party can go to court and simply say to the judge in spite of the law do what is fair. Judges must apply the law whether the source is equity or common law, and not their own believe of what is fair in a situation.

Binding Precedent

Precedent is the principle in the common law system which requires judges to follow a decision made in a higher court in the same jurisdiction. Once a common principle is declared, it is to be applied in similar circumstances by all judges of equal or lower rank. This principle is called *stare decisis*.

The decisions of individual judges are written down. Certain of these decisions are selected and collected in volumes resembling large sets of encyclopedias. Cases are referred to by a special citation, which tells in which book the case is located. For example, the landmark case in tort law cited as *Donoghue v. Stevenson [1932], A.C. 532* means that the case can be found on page 532 of the 1932 edition of the report on all appeal cases. It is from these law reports that lawyers and judges learn what the law is on a given point. Today many written decisions are available on-line. The on-line databases contain search features. You can see an example at www.lexum.ca: if you want to find a case on punitive damages, you search for that term.

The intent of the common law was to eliminate as far as possible the discretion of the individual judge—the law, not a judge's personal belief of what is fair and good, should govern. The outcome of a case should not depend on which judge hears it.

Stare decisis   *Stare decisis*: when a court has once laid down a principle of law as applicable to a certain set of facts, it will adhere to that principle, and apply it to all future cases where facts are substantially the same. *Decisis* comes from the same Latin root, *decisio*, as our modern word *decided*, meaning *settled* or *unquestionable*.

precedent
the principle in the common law system which requires judges to follow a decision made in a higher court in the same jurisdiction

Legalese

Legal Analysis

When courts decide a case, it is on specific facts; however, a general principle can be abstracted from the concrete that is then applied by analogy to other similar situations. In the decision of *Donahue v. Stevenson*, a manufacturer of beverages was found liable to a person who drank (but had not purchased) the beverage because the bottle contained a partially decomposed snail which made the consumer ill. From this concrete situation a general principle can be derived that any manufacturer who puts a defective product on the market which injures anyone will be held responsible for the injury. An even wider principle can be deduced: where any person (not only manufacturers) can foresee that his or her failure to exercise due care can harm another, that person has a duty to take reasonable care not to harm another.

Thus, from an individual case a very wide principle of law is developed. This case, decided in 1933, was considered a radical innovation to respond to the newly expanding market of consumer products provided by suppliers who didn't deal directly with the end user. It is the foundation for the law of product liability that is so important to product safety today. Also, that case expanded the concept that every person has a legal duty to others in society.

Government-Made Law

statutes

summarized or codified
short-code formats of
common law, comprising acts
or legislation passed by
Parliament

Common law was created by judges. But as the principles became settled, they were sometimes gathered together as **statutes**, summarized or codified short-code formats of common law, comprising acts or legislation passed by Parliament. The *Partnership Act* is an example of a set of principles developed by judges, then put into a statute form that has remained mostly unchanged since.

In some cases, the principle of *stare decisis* meant judges could not alter laws to reflect changing social conditions. Thus, new laws, or modifications to existing laws, had to be introduced by government. Sometimes government has set up special groups to study and advise on new statutes. The *Competition Act* is an example of such a statute—it contains laws concerning abusive monopolistic power and unfair trade practices, such as misleading advertising. These are modern problems, and their solution requires input from many sources, such as economists and businesses. A judge sitting alone on a case would not have access to such resources, and so could not develop principles of law that took into account the complexities of the modern business environment.

Even in government-made laws there is room for judicial interpretation of the legislation. For example, the *Sale of Goods Act* (discussed in Chapter 8) covers only "goods." Sometimes a judge will have to decide whether the thing purchased should be categorized as a good or a service. If you buy a meal in a restaurant, are you buying goods (food) or services (someone preparing the food and serving it to you)? In a case called *Gee v. Whitespot* (1993), 32 D.L.R. (4th) 238, the judge decided that purchasing a meal was buying goods, and therefore the *Sale of Goods Act* applied to the complaint.

The introduction of the *Charter of Rights and Freedoms* has recently given the courts a wider role in modifying the laws (see Chapter 1).

The Civil Law (Quebec) System

The legal system in Quebec is different from that in the rest of Canada, and follows a civil-code system rather than a common law approach. Under the civil code, derived from the Greco-Roman approach and later the Napoleonic code, the law is established by government in a written code. The Canadian Criminal Code is another example of a code system that is not made by judges, but is passed by Parliament. A judge cannot create a new criminal offence—only governments can.

If you are doing business in the province of Quebec, be aware that the laws may be quite different from those in the rest of Canada.

Rule of Law

The Rule of Law if stated in modern speech would be: "Law rules!" which means that law is supreme. No one—president, king or prime minister—is above the law. Even a President of the United States, Richard Nixon, was forced to resign in 1974 to avoid impeachment proceedings because he knew that members of his political party were spying on the headquarters of the opposition party.

In early recognition of the importance of the supremacy of law Plato (350 BCE) wrote:

> "Where the law is subject to (below) some other authority and has none of its own, the collapse of the state, in my view, is not far off; but if law is the master of the government and the government is its slave, then the situation is full of promise and men enjoy all the blessings that the gods shower on a state."

The foundation for ensuring the Rule of Law is a country's constitution. In Canada, by our constitution at the time of confederation, the two levels of government were restricted to only passing laws within their own jurisdiction.

An essential component to ensure the effectiveness of the Constitution is a separation of powers between the government and the courts with an independent judiciary. The court can declare whether laws passed by the government are in accordance with the Constitution. However, this may only decide, (as was the case as our constitution was drafted at Confederation), whether they are within the power granted to the level of government, not whether they are fair.

An early example of the implementation of the Rule of Law was the revolt of the Barons of England against King John (made famous as an oppressor in the tale of Robin Hood) who was made to sign the Magna Carta that forced the king to accept that his will was subject to the law and guaranteed a number of rights. One of the most discussed ones is that no one could be arrested and held in prison unless they were given precise notice of any law they had broken. Citizens had the right to be brought before a judge who would review whether the charges had merit.

One of the early remedies to protect this right was called the Writ of *Habeas Corpus* which translates literally "bring the body". If a person were arrested and placed in jail, he had a right to petition a judge. The judge would send a Writ of *Habeas Corpus* to the jailer and the jailer had to bring the prisoner before the judge and justify his confinement.

That protection has been implemented in Canadian criminal procedure. A justice of the peace reviews any information laid by the police before a warrant for search or arrest is issued. An Information is a document seeking approval by the police to arrest someone who is suspected as having committed a criminal offence. Anyone arrested must be brought before a justice of the peace within twenty-four hours for a bail hearing. If an accused is kept in custody pending a bail hearing the accused is brought before a justice of the peace or a judge every seven days so the judge can review the accused's situation to make certain he is being treated properly.

While the principle of the Rule of Law ensures everyone, even leaders, must obey the law, there is little check on the justice of the law in this concept. Apart from the control that voters may have in a democracy over the fairness of laws, the Charter of Rights and Freedoms was enacted to guarantee that laws could not be passed that violated the principles set out in it. To safeguard this protection the Charter was made part of the Constitution and made supreme.

The role of the courts has been traditionally considered as also subject to the Rule of Law in that their function is limited to deciding whether laws are valid under the Constitution: either under the division of powers sections or the Charter. However, courts cannot force the government to make laws. Only if the government makes a law can the court rule on it.

This limitation was in issue in the case of Omar Khadr, a Canadian citizen of Egyptian heritage, who at the age of fourteen was brought by his mother to Afganistan to train with Al Qaeda. At age sixteen the boy allegedly threw a grenade that killed a U.S. medic during a firefight. The U.S. government charged him with war crimes and held him prisoner at Guantanamo Bay military prison awaiting trial. The military subjected the boy to interrogation procedures that violated the Canadian Charter's protection for questioning. Canadian government representatives questioned the boy during the time these objectionable procedures were employed and made the transcripts available to the U. S. military. Thus even though Khadir was in the U.S. and charged with violating U.S. laws, the Supreme Court of Canada held it had jurisdiction to rule on the situation and apply Canadian laws.

While the court stated it could find that Khadr's Charter rights of fundamental justice had been violated, it could not do more than make this declaration; it could not direct the government to take any action such as seek repatriation (Canada (Prime Minister) v. Khadr, 2010 SCC 3).

The Canadian Court System

The court system in Canada today has its roots in the history of England, developing over centuries and altering radically with each age. It is currently in a state of change as citizens wonder whether it is the best system for a society entering the 21st century. Litigants are experimenting with other private procedures, such as mediation or arbitration, to resolve disputes, replacing or supplementing the traditional court process. Such procedures are known as **ADR (alternative dispute resolution).**

ADR (alternative dispute resolution)

private procedures, such as mediation or arbitration, to resolve disputes, replacing or supplementing the traditional court process

The trial process began with a method of resolving disputes that was used in the Middle Ages. In trial by combat, the two opposing parties either fought themselves or hired a professional fighter—a champion—to fight on their behalf. The fight took place in an enclosed area, called a court.

King Henry II (1133-1189) started an alternative system for settling disputes. He appointed judges, who travelled from London to various districts to make the decisions. These judges, who were the first to be allowed to hear cases without the personal presence of the king, were to learn the local customs of the people and apply these to the whole district.

The Court Structure

There are basically two types of courts in Canada—trial and appeal. Only appeal-court decisions are binding in the sense of creating *stare decisis*. Each province has its own court of appeal, and the final court of appeal is the Supreme Court of Canada, in Ottawa. There are many different names for the various courts in all the provinces, but basically they divide into the two functions. Some higher trial-division courts function as appeal courts for lower trial-division courts.

The trial-level court is the one with which most of us are familiar from television and movies. There, a judge presides, either with or without a jury, and hears witnesses, who are examined and cross-examined by lawyers.

The appeal court normally hears appeals based on the transcripts of the trial. Because it does not actually see the witnesses, and cannot therefore judge their credibility, appeal courts are reluctant to change findings of fact made by a trial judge or jury. Appeals are usually based on matters of law.

A common basis for an appeal on law is that no appeal-court decision on that point exists in the province, or that there are conflicting decisions. Since Canada is a confederation—a union of separate states—each province is still a separate jurisdiction; therefore a decision of, say, the Ontario Court of Appeal is not binding on any level of court in, for example, the Manitoba court system. Only a Supreme Court of Canada decision is binding throughout Canada.

If the same type of case, involving a new point of law, is heard on the same day by a trial judge in Ontario and one in Manitoba, it is possible that each court will give a different decision. That decision might be appealed to the court of appeal in each province—which also may result in conflicting decisions. The matter would go on to the Supreme Court of Canada, and there the principle that will apply in all of Canada is decided.

The Role of the Lawyer

The form of combat changed from physical to verbal, but the use of the champion who fought for another's cause continued. The champion became the *barrister*, or trial lawyer.

The first barristers were members of the ruling class who were independently wealthy. Some attended the courts and spoke on behalf of the illiterate peasants who could not properly present their own case. These lawyers believed they had a responsibility to the lower classes as part of the *noblesse oblige*, or obligation of the nobility. They did not charge a fee for their work.

The gowns that barristers wear today in the higher courts are similar to the academic gowns worn in the 17th century. Students at some schools even wore gowns to class at that time.

As economic conditions changed, the wealth began to shift to the middle class. Barristers could no longer afford to work for nothing, and added a purse to their gowns. But, because of their pride and the tradition of not taking a fee, the purse was thrown over their shoulder—thus, a client who had enough money to pay would slip up behind the barrister and place a coin in the barrister's purse without the barrister's knowing it. The client could pay, and the barrister's pride remained intact. Today, the barrister's gown still has a stylized purse—not often recognized for what it is—thrown over the shoulder in recollection of this tradition.

Lawyers in Canada are technically called barristers and solicitors. **Solicitors** are lawyers who deal with commercial and other legal matters that do not involve going to court. **Barristers** are lawyers who represent clients in court. In England, where the profession developed, these were two separate functions, and remain so today. In pioneer times in early Canada, there were not enough professionals to allow for specialization, and so each lawyer was qualified both as a barrister and a solicitor.

Lawyers **Lawyer:** Yer denotes occupation, and is used after words ending with a *w*. *Law/yer*—one who uses the law.

Barrister: *Bar/ister*—a combination of *bar*, the railing that separates the court officials from the public, and *ster*, a suffix that indicates status (as used in the word *minister*).

Solicitor: This derives from the Latin *sollus*, meaning entire, and *citus*, to set in motion. The word *solicit*—to request or make appeals—comes from the same root.

Attorney: This term is used commonly to signify a lawyer in the United States. It means one who acts for another, or who has been assigned the rights of another to act in the other's place. It derives from the old French word *atorné*, to assign, which means, in this context, to give someone authority to act on your behalf. *Attorney* in Canada has a more restricted meaning, as in the term *power of attorney*. The person named in the power of attorney is called an attorney, and has the power to act for the person who signed the document for the matters specifically set out in it. The head of the government legal department is often called an Attorney General.

Juries

There is a difference between civil and criminal juries. The right to a jury in most serious criminal offences applies everywhere in Canada, but civil juries have been abolished in about half of the provinces. Where a civil jury is available, it is usually composed of six people, not twelve as is a criminal jury.

Juries decide issues of fact, not law. The judge instructs the jury in the law they must apply to the facts that the jury determines. For example, a homeowner is sued by a pedestrian for not clearing the snow from the sidewalk in front of the house. The evidence is that the snowfall occurred overnight, and ended by 7:00 a.m. The pedestrian slipped at 4:00 p.m. the same day. The judge would instruct the jury that, by law, they must decide how soon after such a snow-fall a reasonable homeowner would have cleared the sidewalk.

American jury awards have become notorious. They are so much larger than those in other countries that many European nations, as well as Australia, have passed specific laws, informally called blocking statutes, to prevent the enforcement of U.S. jury awards in their countries. Canadian juries typically do not give large awards. In fact, in many cases, it is the defending insurance-company lawyer who chooses the jury because of the Canadian jury's reluctance to find liability or make large awards. Also, Canadian courts of appeal will set aside lower jury awards which they consider unjustified—U.S. courts of appeal will not generally do this.

The large awards given by juries in the United States have made an impact on how Canadians view the civil court system. The population in general does not realize the vast difference between Canadian and U.S. jury awards, and decries what is seen as outrageous amounts of money being awarded for minor suffering. One of the most controversial cases in the early 1990s was that of a woman who spilled coffee on herself and was awarded US $3.5 million against McDonald's. This award was reduced on appeal to $800,000. Such cases are not representative of Canadian jury findings of liability or awards, and make the task of Canadian lawyers in advising clients regarding potential court claims more difficult. Some people, influenced by the American jury decisions, feel that if they are injured, someone automatically has to pay, and pay a large amount, no matter how trivial the injury.

solicitors
lawyers who deal with commercial and other legal matters that do not involve going to court

barristers
lawyers who represent clients in court

Legalese

attorney
a lawyer in the United States

The Stages in a Lawsuit (Higher-Level Courts)

Pleadings

A lawsuit involves several different stages. It is commenced by a document issued under the seal of the court. In some provinces this document is called a writ of summons, and in others it is called a statement of claim. There is a charge for issuing one of these with the courts, which can be substantial (it varies by province, but is in the range of $150 to $250). After the initial document is issued by the courts, it has to be served on the party who will be the defendant in the lawsuit. Then the other party will file a document called the statement of defence, giving his answer to the allegations set out in the statement of claim. The statement of defence is filed with the courts, and then served on the plaintiff (the person who started the lawsuit). The statements of claim and defence are referred to as the pleadings—they are very brief outlines of each party's case.

Legalese   Plaintiff   The word **plaintiff** derives from an old French word, *plaint*, which means accuse or charge. *Complaint* derives from the same word. The plaintiff is the person who starts the lawsuit.

The court will also award an amount for legal costs—an amount that helps to defer the actual expenses involved in conducting the legal action. These include the fee, normally between $75 and $100, paid for issuing a claim, as well as an amount for lawyers' fees, rarely exceeding $500.

Discovery of Documents

While the pleadings set out the basic claim and defence, particularly in business litigation, documentary evidence can be key to assessing the case. The next stage of a lawsuit is an exchange of documents by both sides of the case. Each side provides a list of the relevant documents it has, usually sworn in the form of an affidavit. Each side can then examine the documents in possession of the other side—unless one side is using special legal rules to claim that the opposing side is not entitled to look at a particular document. If there are a lot of documents in the case, they are scanned and entered into a computer database for easy review and management.

E-mail and files on a computer are considered documents and must be revealed in each party's affidavit of documents.

Legalese   Affidavit   An **affidavit** is a document sworn under oath, used as evidence in a judicial proceeding. Instead of physically getting up in a court and swearing to tell the truth, a person swears to tell the truth in the written document. Affidavit derives from *affiance* (Old French) which means to promise or swear. The words *fiancée* and *fiancé* derive from the same term, as does *affirm*.

Examination for Discovery

After receiving the opposite party's documents, the next step is usually the examination for discovery. This is a process in which each side gets to ask the other any relevant questions pertaining to the case. Though the proceeding does not take place in a courtroom, the person giving the testimony is sworn in, and there is a court reporter present, taking down the evidence word for word. A transcript is produced from the court reporter's work, so that the lawyers can review and use it in the proceedings.

Examinations for discovery are a very useful part of the court process. Sometimes a lawyer can get the other side to make an admission useful to his or her case. As well, the person testifying is committed to certain answers on paper, and cannot change the story at trial without his or her credibility coming into question. Discovery can also be used to encourage settlement. Once the whole story comes out, the sides are better able to assess their chances for success. Settlement before a trial may well be the desirable course of action.

Pretrial Conference

If no settlement is forthcoming, there may be an opportunity for an assessment by an independent third party—usually in the form of a pretrial conference or a case conference. In this process, the parties meet with a judge or senior trial **counsel** (a lawyer, usually a barrister), who hears the case and gives an opinion on who has the stronger one. Cases often settle at this stage, after both sides hear the view of one of these experienced legal professionals. The success of these meetings has caused some provinces to move them up earlier in the conduct of the lawsuit.

counsel
a lawyer, usually a barrister

The Trial Process

After all this, if the parties still cannot agree on a settlement, a trial will be conducted. It should be noted that a very small fraction of all lawsuits actually end up in a trial. Surveys suggest that almost 80 percent of actions do not reach trial for several reasons—including the time and expense that a trial would entail, as well as the uncertainty of the outcome.

The trial itself is based on a combat model, and is purely adversarial. That means each party's lawyer tries to win and there is no compromise. At the end, there is a winner and a loser. An ancient Arab felt the full force of this process, for there is an old Arab curse that says: "May you be involved in a lawsuit in which you know you are right!"

The trial process can be viewed as containing two sections: first—fact finding; and then, application of law to those facts. What the parties claim in their pleadings are considered allegations. They are not facts until a judge so decides based on the evidence that the parties present to establish those facts.

The fact finding process is governed by the law of evidence. From experience gained over centuries of hearing disputes, judges developed rules to assist in dealing with the fact finding process. The laws of evidence perform a critical sort function. They exclude some evidence judges have found to be so unreliable and hence potentially misleading, that it should not even be admitted into the fact finding stage of the trial.

One of the most well known of these rules is the Hearsay Exclusion rule. Witnesses can only testify to what they know from direct personal knowledge not from what others have told them. For simplification hearsay can be thought of as a repetition by a witness of what someone else said (or wrote). The person who originally said the statement is not in the courtroom. If you have ever palyed the game of "Broken Telephone" in which a person at the beginning of a line repeats a phrase to the next person in line and so on down the line, you will have seen why the courts do not trust testimony that is a repetition of what some one else has said.

Example: Hearsay: during a pedestrian knockdown traffic accident trial, the defendant driver, who is accused of running a red light, says: "I have proof the light was green. My friend John was standing on the corner and he told me he saw for certain the light was green." But John is not called as a witness. The repetition of what John has allegedly said is hearsay.

Hearsay is not rejected because it is untrue. In the example above John may very well have said that. It is rejected because of its form. The courts have heard so many people claim to repeat what others say, but when that person is called as a witness, that person often has quite a different version of the statement.

So the judges decided that they could not rely on hearsay statements, but decided to exclude them and require that the person who made the statement be called. Again referring to the example above, if John were called he might not confirm that he was even on the street corner, or that he recalls the light. Under cross-examination it might be disclosed that he actually needs to wear glasses and wasn't wearing them at the time, his view was blocked because a large truck was in the intersection as well and many other possibilities. Humorous examples of cross-examining an eye-witness to destroy their testimony were used in the popular movie *My Cousin Vinnie*. They demonstrate why judges require first hand and not hearsay evidence.

Exclusion Based on Form. The concept of exclusion based on form is a bit unusual. An example from the audit process may assist. When an auditor wants to verify the amount of a business loan, it does not ask the business owner to get a statement from the bank. Rather the auditor writes directly to the bank and requires that the bank respond directly to the auditor. By the form of this process, it has a greater degree of reliability. While even this is not 100% certain, the probability of tampering with the evidence is much less than if the business person was allowed to bring the letter from the bank to the auditor.

Exceptions to Hearsay

Having pronounced the hearsay rule, the judges then quickly developed a large number of exceptions to it because some hearsay is reliable or not controversial. For instance, if you are asked 'what is your age', that is hearsay. You probably don't remember your birth and even if you could, you could not read a calendar at that time. You rely on what your mother told you.

In most cases you age is not questioned. If it was, however, there is an exception that allows government records such as birth, marriage, death and such to be admitted without calling the string of people who contributed to the making of the records such as doctors, nurses, hospital administration, government ministry clerks, etc. The Courts accept there is a guarantee of reliability, or truth, in the process in that none of those persons would have motive to distort the evidence and the records are made in the usual course of business.

Business Records

Proof of fact by business records is commonly necessary in business litigation. These records are often hearsay and would require that the employees who made them would have to be called. This could be a serious problem because the employees may be out of the country, sick or even dead. Perhaps a large number of employees would be involved and given the modern use of the internet, many may be living in a large number of countries. So a business records exception to the Hearsay Rule was developed.

Example: Business Record Exception. A business that manufactures cell phones has to prove loss of profits as part of its claim. It has records on its computers of all of its sales for the past five years. These records are made by any number of the twenty staff in its accounting department some of whom are in Toronto, Canada and some of whom are in New Delhi, India, some have left the employment. All input was by data entry from invoices. The litigation started 2 years ago.

Under business records exception to the hearsay rule, if the business can prove that the records were made in its ordinary course of business, and that seems probable in the above example, then the records are admissible without having to call each of the staff who actually made the entry.

That business has to give notice in advance of the trial and permit the opposite party to inspect the records if demanded.

What is the guarantee of truth of business records? Businesses will usually keep accurate records for their own purposes. In the above example the records go back five years three of which were before the litigation became known. In addition, the ability of the opposite party to inspect is a further guarantee of the truth.

The Standard of Proof

Who wins? If the plaintiff can meet the civil "standard of proof," he or she will win. Standard of proof refers to how strong a case the plaintiff must have to win. In a civil case, it is a "balance of probabilities"—in other words, "more likely than not," or a 51 percent probability. In a criminal trial the standard of proof (usually on the Crown) is considerably higher—beyond a reasonable doubt—and so the Crown has to have a very strong case to convict someone under the criminal law.

Evidence and Fact Finding

There is often a difference between testimony given by a witnesses and eventual findings of fact at the end of a trial. The human memory is changeable; it does not operate like a photograph. For example, you may recall driving to the house of someone that you have not visited for some time. You are absolutely certain, no doubt about it, that the house is on the north side of the street. You are looking with full concentration on the north side to locate the house, when suddenly you see it on the south side of the street. You say, "I could have sworn that house was on the north side."

Your memory changed. It sometimes happens that by the time a matter gets to trial, often two to five years after the event, memories are not accurate. Sometimes, just in the re-telling, like in the "broken telephone" exercise, the story changes and so does the memory. Some cross-examination techniques are aimed specifically at identifying and exposing problems with perception and changed memory.

Judgment

At the end of the trial, the judge pronounces a conclusion in the form of a judgment. Sometimes he or she does this immediately after the end of the trial, sometimes months afterward (depending on the complexity of the case). If a party is unhappy with the outcome, there is a possibility of appeal to a higher court, and ultimately perhaps to the Supreme Court of Canada.

Stages of a Law Suit

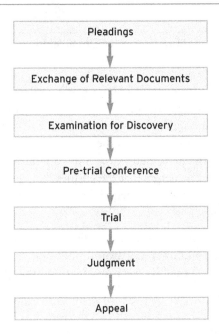

The Impact of Electronic Documents on Litigation

Computers have affected the use of evidence in litigation. Relevant e-mail and other electronic data stored on computer hard drives are documents which must be disclosed. Sometimes lawyers obtain a court order to have the opposite party's hard drive inspected by a computer technician to see if all documents have been produced and to recover any deleted documents and earlier drafts.

Documents that are "deleted" are not completely erased from a hard drive. Usually only the first letter of the file is turned to a symbol such as an asterisk so that when the original file name is entered, there is no match and the file will not be found. However, the file remains until all "bits," which are randomly scattered over the hard drive, have been overwritten. A data-recovery expert can often recover much of the content of deleted files.

Even technically sophisticated people get caught by this. Bill Gates was confronted with recovered deleted e-mail comments that were damaging to his company's case in an antitrust suit brought by the U.S. government against Microsoft.

There has been some suggestion that judges may tend to give more weight to e-mail messages over their paper counterparts on the belief that e-mail reflects the true thoughts of the author. Written letters are often edited by other parties but that rarely happens to e-mails.

shenanigans

"Throw down your E-mail address!"

Business Alert!   Destruction of Business Documents   The near universal use of computers and the ease of printing on paper and of copying and storing documents electronically has caused new concerns in business litigation. Often the news media reports cases of business documents surfacing in high profile inquiries and litigation to the embarrassment of the author.

It is now crucial for a business to determine a document retention/destruction policy in advance of any litigation to avoid charges that the business has destroyed the documents to eliminate harmful evidence. In general, three principles are recommended to determine a document retention policy:

(i)   records should be destroyed as a class rather than selectively,

(ii) records pertaining to known litigation should not be destroyed, and

(iii) confidential records should be destroyed in a way that preserves their confidentiality.

Business Alert!   During a trial it may come out that one or both of the parties have been involved in tax fraud to either avoid income tax or payment of GST or PST. Judges have noted this in their decisions and instructed the Registrar of the court to send the decision to the relevant government departments.

Social Networking Sites

Another relatively new development in litigation is the use of information posted on social networking sites. Pages from those sites, if they contain relevant information must be disclosed.

For example, if a plaintiff is involved in a motor vehicle accident and claims disability and loss of enjoyment of life, pictures on his Facebook page showing him drinking and dancing at a party would be relevant. Note that the entire Facebook contents may have to be produced as it would be reasonable to conclude that there would likely be relevant photographs. The fact that a site is private does not alter the disclosure obligation.

Employers, who have been sued for wrongful dismissal, have successfully used employees' postings on Facebook and similar sites against former employees in lawsuits.

The Small Claims Court

The procedure of a small claims court is very similar to that of a higher court (described above), but it is more streamlined. The small claims court is basically a do-it-yourself court, designed to be used without the need for a lawyer. Small claims court clerks are trained to help people conduct their own litigation.

The small claims court offices are usually listed under the provincial ministry of the Attorney General, and they supply free pamphlets on how they function. It is easy to sue in the small claims court, and therefore they are of great use to a business in collecting unpaid accounts, bad cheques, and the like.

If you feel uncomfortable conducting an action by yourself, you can retain a lawyer, a law student, or a paralegal to assist you.

Which Small Claims Court?

There are many small claims courts within a province, and even within any particular city. You must file your claim in the office closest to:

- where the problem occurred—for example, where the contract was made, or
- where the defendant lives, or carries on business

It is often advisable to choose the court closest to where the defendant lives or carries on business, for any judgment obtained will have to be enforced through that court. If you file your claim in a different court, then you will be required to take the extra step of registering the judgment in the court closest to the defendant anyway.

Monetary Limits

Small claims court can deal, literally, only with small claims. The monetary limit varies with each province, and changes from time to time. Because of the rising costs of litigation, provincial governments are raising the monetary limits of claims. You can easily check on the current monetary limit by calling your closest small claims court. If your claim exceeds that limit, you can waive the excess and still proceed in that court. This is often done, because the expense of lawyers' fees and delays in higher courts mean the net recovery will be less than it would be in a small claims court.

How to Start a Small Claims Court Action

An action is started by having the court issue a claim. Formal documents in a court action are called pleadings. The main ones are a statement of claim and a statement of defence.

You can obtain a form for a claim free from any small claims court office. It merely asks you to fill in background data, such as your own name and address, and the defendant's name and address, and to give a very short statement of the reasons for your claim.

You should attach any documents, such as an NSF cheque, purchase orders, or invoices, to support your claim.

Interest and Costs

You can claim interest on the sum owed if interest is part of the contract. For example, if someone purchased goods from a business whose purchase order said that interest at

2 percent per month (26.82 percent per annum) would be charged on the unpaid balance after 30 days, then interest at that stated amount could be included in the claim. Even if interest is not agreed upon, the courts will allow interest at a rate established by the Rules of Court. This rate is roughly equivalent to the current prime rate.

Fast Judgments

Many small claims court actions are not defended. If that is the case, the clerk of the small claims court may sign a judgment for you in the office. If the claim is of some complexity, the clerk may refer the matter to an uncontested hearing before a judge. In any event, the time taken to obtain such a judgment is much faster than if the matter is defended.

The Defendant's Options

There are several possible responses to a claim. The defendant:

- may feel that none, or only a part, of the money is owing, and must then file a defence;
- may have a claim—a counterclaim—against the plaintiff;
- may be responsible to the plaintiff, but may in turn have a claim against another party for some or all of the amount owed to the plaintiff. This is called a third-party claim.

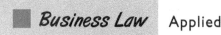

Business Law Applied

① **Ukani Enterprises Inc.** wants to sue Moez Amyn because he has not paid for supplies delivered to him. Amyn owes $8,000, and the limit of the small claims court in Ukani's province is $6,000. After Ukani consults a lawyer and is quoted a fee of $3,000, the firm realizes that it would be better to proceed in small claims court. Ukani Enterprises drafts a claim for $8,000, but the clerk at the court refuses to accept it, saying it is over the limit.

a) Is there any way Ukani could proceed in the small claims court? If so, how?

Trial

If the claim is defended, it will have to go to trial. Small claims court judges are used to dealing with people prosecuting their own claims, and they will assist. All you have to do is tell your story as briefly and concisely as possible, and show the judge all documents related to the claim. Make certain the defendant has copies of all documents well in advance of the trial.

Getting the Money

Obtaining a judgment does not mean that you will get paid. There is no magic in a judgment. If the debtor does not have any assets, the individual cannot be made to pay. Also, the courts do not automatically enforce a judgment: the successful party must do so. There are several ways to enforce a judgment. If:

- you do not know whether the debtor has assets, or where they might be located, you can ask to have the individual brought in front of the court to reveal assets by a process known as an examination of a debtor, or a judgment debtor examination
- someone else owes money to the debtor, such as an employer or a bank, you can ask the court to seize this money from the third party directly by a process known as garnishment

- the debtor owns personal property, such as a car or boat, you can ask the court to seize this property and have it sold by auction
- the debtor owns real estate, the court will seize and sell this property

While debtor's prison has been abolished, if a debtor is served with an appointment by the court to attend on an examination, but refuses to do so, that is contempt of court. For repeated violations, the small claims court may issue a warrant for arrest, and have the debtor detained in jail. Usually, the debtor is released after one night. However, it is a very effective remedy.

Business Law   Applied

❷ **Natasha Pushkov has** a judgment against Al's Carpentry Shop for $2,000 because of poor-quality work. Al refuses to pay. Pushkov believes Al is doing current work, and probably has money in a bank account. She has no idea at which bank that account is located.

a) How can Pushkov find out where Al's bank account is?
b) If Al fails to appear, what can be done to him?

Collecting Accounts   In collecting accounts, the race is to the swift. A business must have a system in place for identifying overdue accounts, and taking immediate action.

Business Alert!

- Have customers agree in their purchase orders to pay all accounts within 30 days, or to pay interest on any overdue amount. The interest must be stated at an annual rate, e.g., 2 percent per month (26.82 percent per annum).
- Set up a collection procedure—preferably a phone call—that operates routinely whenever accounts are not promptly paid.
- Follow up with a demand letter insisting that if the account is not paid by a certain date, then collection proceedings will be started.
- If these actions are unsuccessful, consider going to small claims court, or hiring a collection agency or lawyer, to sue on the outstanding debt.

The Class Action Law Suit

The difficulty of an ordinary citizen's bringing a court action against a huge multinational corporation was dramatized in the public eye by the thalidomide cases in the 1970s. An ordinary family with a baby severely deformed by a prescription drug not only faced the emotional trauma of the situation, but they would also have to meet significant additional medically related expenses. Then they would face bringing a lawsuit against a large drug company that could hire the best team of lawyers and medical experts, and that could afford to spend millions of dollars in defence of the case. The plaintiff family would have to pay for a lawyer, medical witnesses, and various court costs that could easily exceed $100,000 or more. A typical family could not afford such litigation.

The solution to righting the balance of power between ordinary persons and giant corporations was the development of the class action. Although the concept had existed earlier, the right to bring such an action was severely restricted. A class action is an action brought by one or more individuals on behalf of all persons who were injured by similar acts by the same defendant. Thus, the word class is used in the sense of a group with similar characteristics.

In a class action, plaintiffs can pool their funds and start one action rather than many separate actions. In situations such as the thalidomide case, one parent would be able to sue on behalf of all parents and affected children. This also means that the defendant corporation is facing a large damage award. It also means that many of the expensive issues common to all cases, such as the manufacturer's negligence, would be determined once and for all.

The three major goals of permitted class actions are:

- increased access to the courts
- economy in the conduct of the trial
- deterrence of actual or potential wrongdoers

Expanded Rights to Class Actions

The right to bring a class action exists in all provinces, but is very restricted. British Columbia, Ontario, Quebec, Saskatchewan, and Newfoundland have passed special statutes to give wider grounds for bringing class actions, and it is this more inclusive legislation we look at here. The expanded class action is in use throughout the entire United States.

Certification

In order to be able to bring a class action, the plaintiff who claims to represent the class must first obtain court approval. This is known as certification of the class action. There are two hurdles to be overcome in obtaining certification:

- representation—the person seeking to be certified must be truly representative of all the people on whose behalf the action is brought.
- economy—the action must not be frivolous; it must have common issues so that some economy is achieved. If a person who has a claim does not wish to participate in the class action, that person can opt out and conduct a separate individual lawsuit. If a class action fails to be certified by the court, people can still sue individually.

Bendall et al. v. McGhan Medical Corp. et al., [1993] 14 O.R. (3d) 734

One of the earliest class actions to be certified in Ontario under its new act involved silicone breast implants.

Deborah A. Bendall and Connie Wise claimed they suffered damages arising from breast implants manufactured by McGhan Medical Corporation, Dow Corning Canada Inc., or Dow Corning Corporation. Silicon breast implants had been manufactured and distributed in Canada since the 1960s. However, because of an internal memorandum from Dow Corning staff which indicated concern about the implants, government health agencies in Canada and the United States stopped their sales.

Bendall and Wise claimed that, as a result of the implants, they sustained injuries, including hardening of the breasts, buildup of scar tissue, pain and tenderness throughout the breasts, change of shape, increasing asymmetry of the breast, chronic fatigue, infection, immune system dysfunction, and emotional consequences. This array of symptoms is common to the members of the class of persons who have received silicon gel-filled breast implants. It is estimated that 150,000 Canadian women have received the implants.

The two major components of silicon-gel breast implants are the shell and the filler. The shell is made of silicon rubber. The general purpose of the shell is to determine the shape and contour of the implant in accordance with individual needs and to contain the gel, which acts as a filler to simulate the weight and texture of natural human breast tissue.

Bendall and Wise asked the court for an order that an action be certified as a class proceeding, and that they be appointed as representatives of the plaintiffs for the class. They submitted that the class be defined as "all persons who have had silicon gel breast implants placed in their body, whose implants were manufactured, developed, designed, fabricated, sold, distributed, or otherwise placed in the stream of commerce by the named defendants."

The Court's Decision

The court held that the motion request should be granted. The language of the class proceedings act was mandatory, and it stated that the court shall certify an action if the criteria are met. The court found that it should err on the side of protecting people who have a right of access to the courts. To deny certification at this stage would do a grave injustice to the nameless recipients of implants who have suffered complications, since certification is the only way a large number of women can gain access to possible legal remedies.

Legal Costs

In Ontario, B.C., and Quebec there are agencies that will provide some funding to assist in class actions. In Quebec, it is possible to obtain money for lawyers' fees and disbursements—expenditures necessary to the lawsuit. In Ontario, only disbursements are funded. These costs, however, can be significant since they include the costs of experts' reports.

There is also the question of whether the plaintiffs in a class action will be liable to pay the defendants' legal costs if the plaintiffs lose. In Canada, courts make an award of costs, and the usual principle is that the loser must pay the winner's costs—this does not mean the winner's entire legal bill, but some part of it, usually a third to a half.

The importance of the "loser pay" rule was seen in Quebec where an unsuccessful class action against Canadian Honda Motors resulted in an award of costs of $675,650 against the plaintiffs. As a result of this decision, the Quebec code of civil procedure was amended to provide that costs ordered against an unsuccessful plaintiff in a class action would be limited to what is in effect the small claims court scale—a small sum. In Ontario, if the funding is approved by the class proceedings committee established by the Law Society of Upper Canada, the fund is then responsible for paying the plaintiff's costs.

Recently a private corporation was set up to fund Canadian class actions in return for a percentage of the winnings. The company would finance the substantial legal and expert costs and would be responsible for any costs awarded to defendants if the class action was successful.

Recent Class Actions

- Employees of companies who are downsized in mass layoffs have commenced class actions against employers. Many have been successfully certified, thus giving employees added bargaining power in these situations. Once it has been established that there was no legal cause for the firing, arbitrators are sometimes appointed to assess every individual claimant's specific damages. This saves costs to both employer and employees.
- Class action lawsuits by employees at the CIBC and Bank of Nova Scotia have been started for unpaid overtime. There has been no decision yet in these lawsuits but in the U.S. there have been successful employee overtime lawsuits against WalMart, IBM, Starbucks and Radio Shack.
- There are several class actions against drug manufacturer Merck over use of its drug Vioxx. In one dramatic event in an early Vioxx lawsuit, a plaintiff's lawyer had data on Merck's computers analyzed by using the track changes feature to reveal that a study published in the New England Journal of Medicine had been altered to eliminate data that indicated taking Vioxx could cause heart problems. In another action a Merck memorandum showed if there was a delay in posting warnings about the drug, Merck would make an extra $229,000,000.00.
- In an action against Bayer Inc. it is alleged that the manufacturer hid evidence that a drug Trasylol caused kidney failure, cardiac arrest and stroke in patients undergoing coronary artery surgery.
- A class action seeks compensation in Canada from Dell Computers Inc. arising from alleged soldering problems in certain of its notebooks.
- A class action lawsuit has been filed against Ticket Master for charging amounts that are prohibitive under Ontario's anti-scalping laws. The allegation is that Ticketmaster purchases in advance large blocks of the best seats available for an event and then through a subsidiary re-sells them at grossly inflated prices. Recently Bruce Springsteen joined a fan group that forced Ticketmaster to refund ticket overcharges respecting his concerts. New legislation is sought targeted at this type of scalping.

Apology Act

Several provinces in Canada have enacted an *Apology Act*. The legislation recognizes that some people who have been harmed by a wrong doing are somewhat satisfied by an apology. There is anecdotal evidence of people claiming that if a person had apologized at the beginning, the plaintiff would never have instituted a lawsuit. There is also a belief that an injured party may accept less compensation if there is an apology.

Apology acts have been legislated in other countries and the reports post introduction of this type of legislation have been favourable in that observers believe that plaintiffs have accepted lower compensation if an apology was made at an early stage. In the U.S. this is believed to be particularly effective regarding the medical profession.

Previously lawyers advised their clients never to apologize because it could be an admission of guilt and used against them at a trial. The *Apology Act* specifically states that an apology cannot be used in litigation against the person making it. Businesses may now want to consider having a policy for an early apology if accused of some tort or other harmful act before faced with such a situation.

Alternative Dispute Resolution

Trying to resolve a conflict between parties through the court system can be both expensive and time consuming. Additionally, when one party feels like "the loser," he or she can be, understandably, reluctant to provide the compensation that "the winner" was awarded. In recognition of these difficulties, there has been recent encouragement from the courts themselves—as well as among business people—to try another approach to conflict resolution. This alternative approach is called alternative dispute resolution (or ADR), and normally consists of mediation or arbitration.

Mediation

What is mediation, and how is it different from going to court? The difference is one of both philosophy and process.

Mediation attempts to reach a compromise between the parties, while the court system is adversarial. In other words, mediation allows for the parties to compromise, negotiate, and reach a mutually agreeable solution. The parties themselves decide the outcome. In an adversarial system, both sides present and argue their cases in the best possible light—and then a winner and loser are declared by the third party (usually, a judge, though it could be a jury, too). The judge or jury imposes an outcome on the parties.

The adversarial court process is based on a historic combat model from the Court of Champions, so aggression within the boundaries of the rules is rewarded. There is an all-or-nothing consequence: only one will win. This has a strong effect on making parties settle before a trial, because the courts will not, especially in business disputes, give any compromise solution. As well, the loser will pay not only his or her costs, but quite likely a good portion of the winner's as well (though at the discretion of the judge, the loser is usually ordered to pay a portion of the winner's costs). Because of this all-or-nothing nature of a trial, settlements can be literally concluded on the courthouse steps.

From a process point of view, both methods of conflict resolution involve an impartial third party, but their roles are very different. A mediator is involved in the ADR process. This person is someone both parties can trust. He or she acts as a facilitator, assisting the parties in reaching a solution they can both live with. A judge decides who is "right" and prescribes a solution according to legal principles.

When it comes to actually doing mediation, the process is quite different from that of a trial. With mediation, parties to a dispute meet with the mediator in some neutral setting. Discussions are held until a conclusion is reached. A lawyer may or may not be present. In a court proceeding, witnesses and/or the parties themselves are called upon to present their sides of the story, under oath. Lawyers often (though they do not have to) assist the parties to follow the formal rules of courtroom conduct and to present their cases as favourably as possible. They also present legal arguments to the judge about why their client should win, based on the stories the witnesses and the parties have provided. The judge then decides on the winner and the result.

What about the cost of mediation? It depends on how your case was referred to the process. For example, in Alberta, if you start a case in the Civil Division (popularly called "small claims court"), you are likely to be referred to mediation by the court itself, under the Civil Claims Mediation Project. In this case there is no charge for the service. In Ontario, on the other hand, there is mandatory mediation for some civil actions, but the parties must bear the cost of the mediator. Another option is that you and the party with whom you have a dispute may agree to try mediation before embarking on the court process. In such cases, you would have to agree on how to cover the fees charged by the mediator, as well as any costs associated with the location you chose for the meeting. The cost could be significant, since mediators are trained professionals. Nevertheless, mediation may still be preferable to recourse to the courts, given the cost and time involved in that process.

Note that parties can agree to try mediation in the event of a conflict, prior to any conflict actually arising. As part of the terms of a contract, the parties may include a term that mediation is to be attempted before a court action is started, or that the dispute must go to arbitration and not to court.

Mediation is not without its critics. Opponents to mandatory mediation claim it is not suitable for all cases and will just be another level of bureaucracy and expense in the court process. They also suggest that governments are in favour of implementing mediation so they can download the costs of the administration of the justice system onto the parties involved in a dispute, by making them pay for mediators.

Proponents of mediation claim that its non-adversarial process promotes settlement. The parties meet in the same room and tell their sides of the story personally rather than having lawyers present their cases. The parties are encouraged to find some areas of compromise rather than having a judge impose a final resolution on them.

Arbitration

Another alternative to court proceedings for resolving disputes is arbitration. An arbitrator acts in a manner similar to a judge by hearing the cases of both sides and conducting what is in effect a mini-trial (but without many of the procedural requirements of a formal trial).

An arbitration decision is binding and can be enforced just as a Court Judgment. There are federal and provincial arbitration acts that govern the procedure on arbitration. A clause in the contract agreeing to arbitration means that the parties agree to arbitration under the relevant act, and the procedures given in those acts apply in place of court procedures. In the event of a dispute relating to the contract, the parties must use arbitration to settle it. They cannot use a lawsuit unless, of course, both parties agree to cancel the arbitration clause.

Arbitration is often chosen because it is faster than a court proceeding. In some cases it is cheaper, but the parties must pay for the arbitrator and necessary office space. The parties choose a neutral arbitrator. The arbitrator may be an expert in the business area in dispute. When a party wants to avoid a trial in a foreign court that may be hostile, arbitration is a frequently chosen method to avoid that foreign jurisdiction.

Internet ADR

While the same laws apply to *e-commerce* as to traditional business, the Internet has added new problems requiring new solutions. The customer, retailer, and supplier may speak different languages, and may be located in different countries subject to different laws and cultural customs.

Thus, when conflicts arise, recourse to traditional methods such as lawsuits may be ineffective and too expensive.

Some businesses are supporting on-line mediation. One such business is eBay. It reports the example of a Canadian customer who bought a software package for $320 from a seller in China. When the customer tried to install it, he could not find workable registration codes. The buyer then followed the SquareTrade link from the eBay website. A mediator based in Texas was assigned to the case. The mediator worked with the parties to overcome the anger, frustration, and language problems, and discussed possible solutions. Eventually, the seller agreed to refund the full price of the software and part of the shipping cost to the customer. The cost of the mediation to the customer was minimal. The major cost was born by eBay because it believes that the SquareTrade service makes eBay a better place to trade.

Business Alert!

ADR Options   Governments have recognized that there are significant cost savings not only to the citizens but to the governments by having many disputes resolved using ombudsmen, mediation and arbitration programs funded by governments. There are a number of such programs for banks and other financial service providers such as insurance companies and mortgage companies. There are also some for resolving disputes regarding car purchases and disputes within the franchise industry.

The availability to participate in the procedures vary within each industry and within each province. However, all have information available through an internet search.

Risk Management

People are generally exposed to three types of risks: personal, property, and liability. Personal risks are based on loss of life or income; property risks arise from the property that a person owns; liability arises from obligations to other people which are usually created by laws. This discussion will centre largely on the third type of risk, the one that is created by obligations in law.

With every law there are rights and corresponding responsibilities. These responsibilities translate into risks for businesses. The increasing number of new laws creates more potential liabilities for businesses. Identifying and planning for risks has been compared to putting a fence at the top of a hill to stop a ball from rolling down rather than waiting until it has started to speed down the slope and then trying and catch up with it.

Businesses now have to plan carefully for legal risks. For example, the increase in human rights laws, particularly those regarding sexual harassment, has created rights for employees and responsibilities for employers. An employer may be responsible to an employee who was sexually harassed on the job. There are ways in which an employer can avoid legal liability, however, even if an act of sexual harassment occurs during the employment. You will study methods such as this to reduce the chance that your business will be found liable.

The sinking of the Titanic was one of the early incidents that began to give risk management some credibility as a theory respecting product safety. Prior to that money management, that is, sacrificing safety to profitability, was nearly the sole factor in business decision making.

What may be little-realized outside of engineering risk-management circles is that a ship built less than 50 years earlier than the *Titanic*, the *Great Eastern*, had worse damage from an uncharted rock which ripped a gash in its side longer than the one in the *Titanic*. But it got to shore safely.

The *Great Eastern* was built with safety features that were gradually deleted as too costly in later ships such as the *Titanic* in the shipping business's rush to profitability. The number of lifeboats, for example, was restricted because it was thought to be too expensive to provide a space for each passenger. Suddenly, after the sinking of the *Titanic*, the cost of safety features that previously were too impossibly high, were affordable. Later the *Titanic*'s sister ship, *Olympia*, was fitted with some of them. The *Titanic*'s owner, the White Star Line, was effectively bankrupt because of the consequences of its cost-saving measures; it was absorbed by the Canard Lines. A lesson was learned by some businesses that saving on safety was not necessarily profitable.

It should not be overlooked that an element missing from the *Titanic* disaster, which would be inevitable today, was the class action lawsuit. In the nearly 100 years since the *Titanic* disaster, the courts and governments have made laws that have extended protection to end-users of business products, raised the standard for state-of-the-art safety, and expanded many other areas, such an employee rights. The class action has given consumer groups a way to fund expensive litigation against businesses. The business person who is in an executive capacity must have a general understanding of business law to know the risk created by these laws.

The concept of risk management involves many areas other than product safety. As noted above, many risks are transferred by the fine print in paragraphs that are now standard content in any business contract. Thus, you will be taken through some of the many terms of actual contracts and see the transfer or assumption of risk relating to significant terms.

Risk management will be a theme that runs throughout this text. Sometimes it will be discussed under a topic by that name, but more often it will be contained in the "Business Alert!" feature, giving practical advice on what to do in the situations under discussion.

Risk-Management Plan

Once you become aware of risks and review a business in that light, risks and solutions become more obvious. A legal risk-management program is designed to be an early-warning system for potential legal issues. It identifies areas of business of high risk and high impact.

Risk management involves identifying, measuring, and controlling risk. To identify a risk means to determine which events could occur and result in a loss. To measure the risk means to determine the likelihood that the identified event will occur, its frequency, and the severity of any resulting loss. To control the risk means to deal with it in the most cost-effective manner.

There are both legal and business solutions to risks and often they are linked. For example, a business has to decide on the length of a warranty period for its product. The longer the warranty given in its contract, the more expensive the cost of the warranty. A 30-day warranty may reduce costs but not be competitive because other businesses are giving a one-year warranty. The company could also increase its quality-control program, which would have its own cost but might result in a net reduction in warranty claim payments. The implementation of the quality-control program is a business solution, while the inclusion of a limited warranty or disclaimer term is a legal solution.

A risk-management plan will often consider three possible actions:

- **Elimination or reduction.** A manufacturer may have learned that inexpensive components are available from an overseas supplier in a country that has an unknown judicial system. The manufacturer may not be certain that the delivery deadlines will be met or that the quality will be consistent and so will eliminate or reduce that risk by buying some or all product locally or from a country with a history of enforcing contractual obligations similar to Canada's.
- A retail store, such as a grocery store, may have a significant risk of slip and fall claims. It could create a plan for immediate response to any change in condition on its premises, such as the notorious dropped banana peel, so that this is quickly spotted and removed. The emergency response plan can be combined with video surveillance to make certain that any person who may actually slip did not drop the peel first. The risk of successful slip and fall lawsuits by a customer can be significantly reduced.
- **Transference.** Transference can be accomplished by taking out an insurance policy and hence transferring the risk to the insurance company. A risk-management plan may help to obtain a lower premium.
- The terms in a contract can also transfer risk. As one example, a disclaimer or limited liability clause can limit or reduce the amount a business needs to pay on the

warranty claim transferring the risk to the customer. Disclaimer clauses are subject to a number of rules, as discussed under that topic later.

■ **Self-Insurance.** By this approach, the business decides to retain the risk without purchasing an insurance policy and to pay claims itself. Sometimes a business creates a fund much like an insurance company does to pay any such claims. Increasing deductibles on insurance policies to obtain lower premiums is a way of splitting the risk, that is, some is transferred to the insurance company and some is kept by the business itself.

Business Alert!

There are many sources for advice on identifying and planning for risks. Insurance brokers are specialists in this area. Local fire departments are also willing to do safety inspections for businesses and to give advice about fire hazards.

■ **Business Law** Applied

❸ **John Enman and** Jane Masayana are the sole shareholders and directors of Your Computers? Solutions Inc. Enman is an engineer and Masayana is an accountant. The company designs customized complete business solutions for small businesses, which include computer hardware and software. One of their key advantages over their competitors is that Enman and Masayana custom-design the business systems, and then design software and hardware to implement these systems.

The corporation owns a two-storey building. The bottom floor is mainly retail and the second floor is the workshop for assembly and repairs.

The company had been buying components locally but has learned of a much cheaper source from a country overseas, and is considering using the overseas company as its sole source of components.

Identify all the risks (both legal and business) for this company and create a plan to respond to each risk identified.

In Summation

Laws and the Legal System

■ Laws can be characterized in three main ways: private or civil law (which governs disputes between individuals), criminal or regulatory law (which governs disputes between individuals and society generally), and constitutional law (which governs disputes with governments as lawmakers).

■ One incident may invoke more than one legal proceeding, depending on whether more than one of the categories of law are involved.

The Court System

■ The Canadian legal system is based on both judge-made law—known as common law—which in turn is based on the principle of *stare decisis*, and on government-made law created through the acts of Parliament or the provincial legislatures.

■ Decisions of fact and law are made at the trial-court level, while provincial appeal courts and the Supreme Court of Canada hear only arguments based on issues of law.

■ Whether you will require a lawyer depends on the level of court. Small claims court is designed to allow individuals or businesses to handle the presentation and enforcement of their legal case without the involvement of a lawyer.

- A class action suit is a way for many plaintiffs, who allege harm by one large corporate defendant, to pool resources in bringing a lawsuit. All plaintiffs join in one lawsuit rather than each bringing his or her own.

- Alternative dispute resolution, either mediation or arbitration, is a method to resolve conflict separate from the court system. Mediation is based on a model of negotiated compromise rather than of adversarial "winners" and "losers." Arbitration is conducted similar to a trial but the formal procedures are relaxed. The parties choose the arbitrator(s).

Risk Management

- **Risk** is the possibility of loss. An event might occur that is not favourable to a business.

- Laws create obligations to other people which translate into legal risks for businesses. A business may be responsible for icy sidewalks, a slippery floor, torn carpets, and low overhangs, to list only a few.
    a) elimination or reduction
    b) transfer
    c) retention

risk
the possibility of loss

Closing Questions

1. There is judge-made law and government-made law. If there is a conflict, which governs?

2. Describe the stages of a law suit.

3. What is the difference between a trial court and a court of appeal?

4. What is the standard of proof in a criminal proceeding and in a civil proceeding?

5. a) What are the main pleadings in a civil case?
   b) What is the purpose of each pleading?

6. What is the difference between a barrister, a solicitor, and an attorney?

7. a) Describe mediation and arbitration.
   b) How does each differ from a trial?

8. Match the following:
   1) trial lawyer a) binding precedent
   2) *stare decisis* b) mediation
   3) alternate dispute resolution c) statement of defence
   4) certification d) barrister
   5) pleading e) approval

9. New Era Contractors Inc. has a contract with Bill's Snow Removal Company to clear the snow from the sidewalk and parking area next to the New Era store. The day following a snowstorm, Joan McIver slips on a patch of ice in the parking lot, breaking her hip. McIver was on the way to pay an overdue account at New Era. Now she refuses to pay it.
   a) McIver wants to sue New Era. What is the name of the pleading that she must use to start her lawsuit?
   b) New Era believes that it took reasonable precautions, and it is not responsible for her injuries. The company wants the court action dismissed. What is the name of the pleading that New Era should file?
   c) New Era also realizes that McIver owes on an overdue account. What is the name of the pleading by which New Era can bring a claim against McIver for the amount of this overdue account in the same lawsuit?
   d) New Era feels that Bill's Snow Removal Company was responsible for McIver's injury. What is the name of the pleading by which it can bring an action in the same lawsuit against Bill's Snow Removal Company?

10. Bill Morgan has a judgment against Rita Roman for $5,000. He learns that Roman owns a 1993 Mustang that has a chattel mortgage on it with a balance owing of $5,000. From looking at newspaper ads, Morgan thinks the car is worth $10,000.
    a) Can Morgan seize the car and have it sold? If so, how?
    b) Will he necessarily recover any money from the sale?

11. Small Claims Court Drafting Exercise
    a) Read the following information, and draft a claim against Sure Finance, Inc. with yourself as plaintiff, using any relevant personal data necessary.

       On July 15, 1997, you applied for a loan for your new business in the amount of $5000 from Sure Finance, Inc. You were told by Sure Finance that it would have no trouble getting you a loan, and were asked for a $500 deposit. Sure Finance said the deposit would be refunded if the loan did not go through, as long as you told the truth on your application form. Sure Finance told you on September 1 that it had found a lender, but that a co-signer was required. You cannot get one. That's why you went to Sure Finance in the first place, rather than to a bank. Sure Finance refuses to repay the deposit.

    b) Draft a defence for Sure Finance.
       [Note: There are filled-in precedents and blank forms in the Appendix to assist with this exercise.]

12. a) Attend at a small claims court and listen to one civil case. Do a report on it containing the following:
       - the plaintiff's case
       - the defendant's case
       - the judge's reasons

    b) Find in this text the area of law relevant to the case that you saw. Write a summary of the law. Tell whether you agree with the judge's application of the law or not.

13. From research on the internet find the various types of disputes that can be heard by way of government sponsored ombudsmen, mediation or arbitration in your province.

14. **Internet Research.** Choose a foreign country and do a report about their litigation system.

Class Actions

15. **Internet Research.** Do a report on the thalidomide drug crisis, the related litigation and the effect this case had on class actions and liability. What was the drug supposed to do? Who was the target market and why was the drug uniquely safe for it? Why was the use of this drug a catastrophic problem?

16. **Internet Research.** There have been a number of cases reported in the media where businesses have put a dangerous product on the market and knowingly left it on the market. Find examples of these and do a report on them.

17. **Internet Research.**
    a) Compare the Canadian and U.S. civil (not criminal) litigation procedures. In particular discuss the differences in:
       i)   selection of judges
       ii) cost awards against loser of a trial
       iii) use of juries and control of the amount of jury awards.
    b) Which system do you think is the better?

18. **Internet Research.** Jane Hakim has been involved in a car accident. Her adjuster reviewed the situation and found her 100% at fault. She is unhappy with this decision but does not want to sue the insurance company because it is too costly. Does she have any other option?

Websites

www.nlc-bnc.ca—The site of the National Library of Canada, with links to legal sites.

www.lincon.com—Site dedicated to law of many jurisdictions including Canada. Go to Search Utilities/Foreign/Canada.

www.Canada.justice.gc.ca—Site maintained by the federal Department of Justice. Contains a legal guide to test your knowledge about Canada.

www.paralegalsociety.on.ca—The site provides information regarding the Paralegal Society of Ontario.

www.duhami.org—The site is maintained by Lloyd Duham—many features which include explanations of the trial process and ADR.

www.fco.gov.on.ca—The website of Financial Services Commission of Ontario. It provides information on how to make complaints and an ombudsman for areas such as auto insurance, property insurance, mortgage brokers, motor vehicle accident claims and such.

www.cfa.ca—The Canadian Franchise Association has an ombudsman program regarding disputes between franchisees or franchisors operating in Canada.

www.camvap.ca—The site of the Canadian Motor Vehicle Arbitration Plan. It provides arbitration for dispute between purchasers and manufactures regarding defects in vehicles or administration of new vehicle warranties.

Small Claims Court Claim and Defence

SMALL CLAIMS COURT COMPLAINT FORM (Complete)

WHEN REFERRING TO THIS DOCUMENT PLEASE USE NUMBER IN UPER RIGHT CORNER

PLAINTIFF

Name
NEWCOMP, INC

DEFENDENT(S)

Name		
ROSE TESSA		
Street No. 62 OXFORD LANE	Address	Apt. No.
Borough/City TORONTO	Postal Code M6S 2Z3	Phone No. 888-8800

DEFENDENT(S)

Name		
Street No.	Address	Apt. No.
Borough/City	Postal Code	Phone No.

To the Defendant

The Plaintiff claims from you $ _____ . and costs for the reason(s) set out below

IF YOU DO NOT FILE A DEFENCE WITH THE COURT WITHIN TWENTY DAYS AFTER YOU HAVE / RECEIVED THIS CLAIM, JUDGMENT MAY BE ENTERED AGAINST YOU.

TYPE OF CLAIM

Unpaid account	Contract	Motor vehicle accident	Promissory note	Lease
Services rendered	N.S.F. cheque	Damage to property	Other _____ (describe)	

Reasons for Claim and Details
(Explain what happened, where and when the amounts of money involved.)

1. The Plaintiff's claim is for $3,045.00 for goods sold and delivered.

2. The Plaintiff states that on or about the 1st day of June, 1994, at the request of the Defendant, it supplied and delivered to the Defendant an IBM computer at a price of $3,000.00 plus G.S.T and provincial sales tax, plus interest at 12% per annum on the unpaid balance. On or about the 1st day of June, 1994, the Plaintiff also delivered its invoice No. A101 in the amount of $3,045.00.

3. The Plaintiff states that despite numerous requests for payment, no payment has been forthcoming.

4. the Plaintiff therefore claims:

   a) the sum of $3,045.00;
   b) pre-judgment interest at the rate of 12% per annum from the 1st day of June, 1994 to the date of payment or judgement, whichever shall first occur;
   c) his costs of this action; and
   d) such further and other relief as to this Honourable Court may seem just.

(Where claim is based on a document, attach a copy for each copy of the claim, of if it is lost or unavailable, explain why it is not attached.)

SMALL CLAIMS COURT DEFENCE FORM (Complete)

	Claim No.

PLANTIFF	DEFENDENTS(S)
Name NEWCOMP, INC	Name ROSE TESSA
Address　　　　　　　Postal Code	Address　　　　　　　Postal Code 62 OXFORD LANE　　　M6S 2Z3
City/Borough　　　　　Phone No.	City/Borough　　　　　Phone No. TORONTO　　　　　　888-8800

LAWYER OR AGENT	DEFENDENTS(S)
Name	Name
Address　　　　　　　Postal Code	Address　　　　　　　Postal Code
City/Borough　　　　　Phone No.	City/Borough　　　　　Phone No.

☒ I/We dispute the full claim made by the plaintiff.

❏ I/We admit the plaintiff's claim and propose the following terms of payment.

$ _____ per _____ commencing _____

❏ I/We admit part of the plaintiff's claim amounting to $ _____ and propose the following terms of payments:

$ _____ per _____ commencing _____

❏ I/We dispute the balance claim.

REASONS FOR DISPUTING THE CLAIM AND DETAILS:

1. On June 1, 1994, the Plaintiff delivered a computer to my office which was not the same model as the one which I had ordered. In addition, the top of this computer was badly scratched.

2. Despite numerous requests, the Plaintiff has refused to remove this computer from my office and has refused to deliver the model which I agreed to buy.

NOTE:

If the defence contains a proposal for terms of payment, the plaintiff is deemed to have accepted th terms unless the plaintiff, in writing to the clerk, dispute the proposal and requests a hearing within 20 days of service of a copy of the defence.

If a hearing is requested, the defendant should still make any payments required under the proposal and provide proof of payment at the hearing.

All payments should be forwarded directly to the plaintiff or the plaintiff's representative at the address shown in the bottom left-hand corner of the claim.

IF THE DEFENDANT FAILS TO MAKE PAYMENT IN ACCORDANCE WITH THE TERMS OF PAYMENT PROPOSED, THE CLERK MAY SIGN JUDGMENT FOR THE UNPAID BALANCE WITHOUT A HEARING.

_____　　　　_____
　　　　Date　　　　　　　　　Defendant's Signature/Solicitor or Agent's Name

Drafting A Statement of Claim

A suggested outline that will work for any Pleading in contract, no matter how simple or complicated, is:

a) description of the contract—Who, What, When
b) any relevant terms
c) breach by the defendant
d) damages.

The example given above regarding collection of the amount due on the sale of a computer follows this outline.

The Law of Torts

The Concept of Civil Wrong

A wrong can give rise to two different types of remedy in law—civil or criminal. Sometimes the two occur together, as can happen in the common motor-vehicle accident, when there may be an action in tort for negligence, as well as criminal charges for careless driving. Consider the case of two motorists who get into an angry argument that quickly progresses from fist shaking to heated verbal insults. One of the drivers deliberately rams the other car, severely injuring that driver. The threatening gestures and intentional collision constitute a civil tort of assault and battery. These same actions might also result in criminal charges of assault causing bodily harm, careless driving, or criminal negligence.

Tort   The best definition of **tort** is *wrong*. The word is derived from the Latin *torquere*, to twist. To commit a tort is to do something twisted or crooked—to carry out an action that is wrong. It is a civil wrong, not a criminal wrong.

Two Major Types of Torts

Torts generally fall into one of two main categories.

- **Intentional torts,** harmful acts that are committed on purpose and for which the law provides a remedy. Common ones are assault, trespass, malicious prosecution, false arrest and false imprisonment, defamation.
- **Unintentional torts,** when someone acts carelessly or without thought, and causes unintentional harm to another person or that individual's property. This is called the tort of negligence. Unlike intentional torts, it is a flexible concept, and is not broken up into smaller categories. A doctor who is careless while operating on a patient and thus causes injury, is guilty of the tort of negligence. Someone who drives without proper care or attention—is careless—is also guilty of negligence. The number of situations to which negligence applies is open ended.

intentional torts
harmful acts that are committed on purpose and for which the law provides a remedy

Intentional Torts

Control of Shoplifters

Sometimes a set of actions can give rise to a series of breaches of both tort and criminal law. Shoplifting, for example, normally results in a criminal charge being laid against the offender. But, depending on the response of the business to the incident, it can also lead to one or more of the tort actions described in this section.

The intentional torts affecting the rights of business and customer in a shoplifting situation are:

- false arrest and false imprisonment
- malicious prosecution
- trespass to land
- conversion

Citizen's Arrest and False Imprisonment

One of the most common—and legally uncertain—situations in which a business person may face tort liability is in the handling of persons suspected of shoplifting. The situation generally unfolds as follows. Store personnel either suspect, or see, a person shoplifting. The store personnel, who must call the police, can detain the person until the police arrive (or until they conclude that the person did not commit the offence). The detained person, if shown not to have shoplifted, brings an action for false imprisonment. The store defends itself by saying it had the legal authority to detain the person.

The courts jealously guard an individual's right to liberty. Any time you attempt to deal with a suspected shoplifter, there is an element of legal risk involved. From a practical point of view, the following should be noted:

- citizens do have a right to arrest a person in the act of committing shoplifting
- citizens have no right to search people against their will, but can ask them to permit a search (such as to empty pockets or open a purse)
- if the person objects to a search or to opening purses or parcels, the person should be turned over to the police
- security guards, as persons in authority, when making an arrest, have to warn the person of the right to remain silent and the right to counsel at the point at which they have enough evidence to conclude that the person has committed the offence of shoplifting

What is false imprisonment? There are three requisite elements that must be proven by the plaintiff:

- a deprivation of liberty
- against the will of the person detained
- caused by the defendant

Note that the deprivation of liberty can take several forms:

- physical restraint, in which the shoplifter is actively prevented from leaving the store
- threat of physical restraint, in which no actual touching occurs
- neither physical restraint nor threat of it, but the impression is given that refusing to remain in the store until police arrive will cause the suspect shoplifter embarrassment and public humiliation, or will result in the application of physical restraint

If the plaintiff makes out his or her case on the foregoing elements, it is then up to the defendant store to prove it was justified in detaining the plaintiff (making the citizen's arrest). There is only one way legally to justify such actions, and that is by claiming "legal authority." The onus of proving both these elements is on the defendant store. It will be very difficult to show there was legal authority in the absence of a criminal conviction. Consequently, the store should be cautious in detaining a suspected shoplifter, or else the detained person would likely succeed in an action for false imprisonment. A citizen's arrest for the purpose of investigation only is not permitted.

■ *Critical Concepts of* Citizen's Arrest and False Imprisonment

- Any person (not just police) has a right to arrest, but the circumstances where this is legally justified are fairly limited.
- An arrest may be justified by claiming legal authority, that is:
  a) a crime has been committed by someone
  b) there were reasonable grounds to believe that the detained person committed the offence.
- If a citizen's arrest is not justified, the detained person may succeed in a lawsuit for false imprisonment.
- Security guards have no higher rights of arrest than an ordinary citizen.

Hayward v. F.W. Woolworth Co., [1979] 98 D.L.R. (3d) 345 (Nfld. T.D.)

Hayward went to a temporary table inside the Woolworth store that had been set up for a watch sale advertised for that day. After selecting a watch, the employee at the table told Hayward to pay at the closest service counter because she could not operate the cash register which was at the table. She was suspicious of Hayward's behaviour and alerted security, who began to watch him. Two security officers saw Hayward go to other departments, make purchases, and pay for those, but then leave the store without paying for the watch. The security guards confronted Hayward outside the store, grabbed him by both arms and paraded him to the offices at the back of the store. Hayward produced a receipt for the watch. Hayward then sued the store for false imprisonment.

The Court's Decision

To justify the imprisonment and the assault, the store would have to establish that a theft occurred and that there were reasonable grounds to believe that the plaintiff committed that theft.

The judge found that the security guards had reasonable and probable grounds for believing that an offence had been committed because they kept Hayward under surveillance and did not see him pay for the watch. However, the store could not prove that an offence had actually been committed because Hayward had a receipt for the watch. The judge rejected the store's claim that Hayward may have found a receipt on the floor as speculation and not supported by any evidence.

Consequently, the store could not establish the defence of legal authority. Hayward was awarded $750 in general damages (for "affected nerves" and difficulty sleeping after the incident) and $1,000 in exemplary (punitive) damages.

Evidence at Trial

The question of what evidence will prove an issue at trial such as a reasonable ground for believing that a person committed the offence of shoplifting depends on the circumstances. The trial judge in the *Hayward v. F.W. Woolworth Co.* case above said that the store could not produce any evidence that Hayward had found a receipt for a watch on the floor. The store merely speculated that Hayward had found one of the receipts which the store often found thrown away by others.

Some evidence that Hayward had found a receipt would be that a witness testified that he or she saw Hayward bend down and pick up a piece of paper from the floor near a cash register. Better evidence would be that a witness saw Hayward put that piece of paper in his shirt pocket and the security guards saw Hayward take it out of his pocket. Even stronger evidence would be that a prior purchaser of a watch testifies that he dropped his receipt and saw Hayward pick it up and put it in his shirt pocket.

Business Law Applied

① **Luke Wishart was** shopping at High-Mart Department Store. He went over to the sunglasses department and tried on several pairs. A store security guard, John Picard, saw him look up and down the aisle a number of times, remove the price tag from one particular pair of glasses, and throw the tag under a counter. The tag was large and attached to the bridge of the glasses. Wishart passed several checkout stations and then headed for the door.

Once outside the store, Picard approached him, and asked if he had forgotten to pay for anything. He replied, after a few seconds, "Oh my God, you're right," and handed the sunglasses to Picard, who then escorted Wishart back to the store and called police.

At Wishart's trial for shoplifting, he was acquitted, because the judge believed that he had merely removed the price tag to see better how the sunglasses suited him.

  a) Do you think Wishart will succeed in a lawsuit for false imprisonment?

❷ **Wilfred Wilson was** enjoying some drinks after work at the Roaring Dragon Bar and Grill. He was there for some time and became rather intoxicated. He decided to leave, and so got up and left to walk home. About the time he left, someone went on a rampage in the Roaring Dragon's parking lot, vandalizing several vehicles extensively.

As Wilfred was on his way home, he was jumped from behind by the Dragon bouncer and pinned on the ground until police arrived. It seems that the person who actually damaged the vehicles fit Wilfred's general build, and was wearing jeans and a dark jacket (also like Wilfred).

  a) Will Wilfred be successful in a suit for false imprisonment?

Malicious Prosecution

For an action based on **malicious prosecution** (causing a person to be prosecuted for a crime without an honest belief that the crime had been committed) to succeed, four criteria must be met:

  ▪ criminal charges were laid
  ▪ those charges were later dismissed or withdrawn
  ▪ there were no reasonable or probable grounds for bringing the charges
  ▪ there was an improper motive for laying the charges

malicious prosecution
causing a person to be prosecuted for a crime without an honest belief that the crime had been committed

The last two criteria are very difficult to establish. Actions for malicious prosecution succeed only in the most clear and extreme cases. We commonly say that one person lays a charge against another, but technically this is not correct. The person gives information to the police, who then investigate and decide if charges should be laid. At a later stage, a crown attorney will decide if those charges should proceed. However, all the individuals involved in the incident can be the subject of a malicious prosecution action.

Trespass to Land

Trespass is defined as the entry onto the land of another without the owner's permission, or some lawful right, to do so. For example, a police officer acting under a search warrant has the lawful right to enter without the owner's permission. As well, trespass, a common law tort, occurs if an individual refuses to leave when ordered to do so by the owner or person in legal possession. Standing outside a particular property and throwing a brick through a window also amounts to trespass. There are provincial statutes making trespass a minor criminal matter that can be dealt with by the courts—usually resulting in a fine.

trespass
the entry onto the property of another without the owner's permission, or some lawful right, to do so

The law assumes that a business dealing with the public, such as a grocery store, invites the public to enter with a view to making a purchase. This is permission as required in law. However, a business can refuse entry to a person for any reason, as long as human rights legislation is not contravened. No one can be barred because of race, colour, national origin, and so on.

Businesses who deal with the public are sometimes faced with the problem of trying to control troublesome customers. Although businesses have certain rights to protect their interests, they also have responsibilities to the customers and their rights.

Business Alert!

Trespass and the Control of Shoplifting   Criminal law contains many technical defences to charges of shoplifting. Because of this, and the fact that the trial process is slow and time consuming, stores are sometimes reluctant to press charges against an offender. If the accused individual is eventually acquitted, the store might face a civil action for false imprisonment. There is no defence of reasonable grounds if this happens.

While the use of hidden cameras to catch shoplifters "in the act" is fairly common, another solution that appeals to many businesses is to ban the offender from the store, rather than take the matter to court. A business need not give a reason for preventing anyone from entering the premises, as long as the ban does not violate human rights legislation. If the store is located in a mall or plaza, the individual could be barred from entering the entire property.

Under the provincial trespass acts, the individual must be given notice of the ban, and it is usually best to do this in writing. If a larger area is involved, a formal written notice should be prepared in co-operation with the property manager. Some businesses choose to give a six-month ban initially, following this with a permanent ban should a second suspicious incident take place.

A Typical Written Notice Banning a Troublesome Customer

Westguild Mall, 2244 Willow Street East, Vancouver, BC

TAKE NOTICE that you are hereby banned completely from any part of the premises known as Westguild Mall, and municipally described as 2244 Willow Street East, Vancouver, BC. This notice takes effect immediately.

AND TAKE NOTICE that this prohibition is being made pursuant to the **Trespass to Land Act**. The **Trespass to Land Act** provides for charges, penalties and fines for acts of trespass.

AND TAKE NOTICE that this ban is effective until January 1, 2003.

Dated at the City of Vancouver, in the Province of British Columbia, this 31st day of August, 2002.

Westguild Mall
per:

Janet Fleming

Janet Fleming
Property Manager

Critical Concepts of Trespass to Land

Business premises are private property and no one has the automatic right to enter.

- Businesses that deal with the public by implication give the public permission (licence) to enter to transact business.
- A business can revoke that permission without any reason, subject to human rights legislation. This **revocation**—withdrawal of an offer before acceptance, and communicating the withdrawal to the offeree—makes the customer a trespasser.
- A business can use reasonable force to eject a trespasser, but must first ask the trespasser to leave.

revocation

withdrawal of an offer before acceptance, and communicating the withdrawal to the offeree

Control of the Business Premises

Assault and Battery

Businesses, especially where liquor is served, have to control their unruly customers and protect their premises. To accomplish this, business people must understand not only the tort of trespass to land, but also assault and battery.

The terms *assault* and *battery* are often used interchangeably to mean a physical attack. However, these terms have distinct meanings in the law of tort. And these terms are used with slightly different meaning in the criminal law. In general, **assault** can be thought of as the threat to do harm to a person, while **battery** is physical contact with a person without consent. The freedom to throw a punch ends at the tip of the other person's nose. For example, if two drivers get into an argument at an intersection and one driver shakes her fist menacingly at the other driver but does not hit him, the first driver has likely committed an assault by the threatening gesture.

Battery requires the intention to harm and touching, but the touching can be of two kinds—in anger or not. If the driver in the example above had actually struck the other driver, that act would have had all the elements of a battery done in anger.

In contrast, when a doctor operates on a person without giving disclosure of the risks, that is also a battery, but not one done in anger. Doctors have also been found to have committed a battery if they have given patients experimental medicine without advising them that they are part of an experiment.

When a person who is late for an appointment rushes down a street and accidentally knocks over someone who breaks an arm in falling, a battery has not been committed. The element of intention is absent. However, the person who was running may be liable for the unintentional tort of negligence (which will be discussed later in this chapter).

Self-defence (a response to an assault or battery with as much force as is reasonable in the circumstances) is a complete defence to assault or battery. To establish self-defence, the defendant must prove a genuine fear of injury at the hands of the plaintiff and that the defendant only struck the plaintiff for self-protection. While provocation is not a defence, it may lessen the damage award to the plaintiff. Additionally, as explained further below, a person can use reasonable force (which generally means an assault and/or battery) to eject a trespasser.

assault
the threat to do harm to a person

battery
physical contact with a person without consent

self-defence
a response to an assault or battery with as much force as is reasonable in the circumstances

Spanking Law

The Criminal Code does make an exception for assault permitting teachers and parents to use physical discipline in correcting children or students, provided that the correction is done in the course of providing discipline and the force used is reasonable. The Ontario Court of Appeal recently upheld this section under a Charter challenge by children's rights groups. There was a limitation imposed that an instrument should not be used in administering the punishment.

Critical Concepts of Assault and Battery

- Assault is threatening another with violence, with the ability to carry out the threat causing fear in the victim.
- Battery is the least touching of another without consent and with the intention to cause harm.
- Self-defence is a complete defence to assault and battery.

Cottreau v. Rodgerson and Saulnier, [1965] 53 D.L.R. (2d) 549

Cottreau, a scallop fisherman, was a regular at the Clipper Ship Tavern, owned by Saulnier, in Yarmouth, Nova Scotia. The fisherman was a heavy drinker, and sometimes a quarrelsome customer. Because of a previous incident, he was barred from the Clipper Ship Tavern. He came in one day already quite drunk, and a waiter named Rodgerson told him to leave. Cottreau refused, and Rodgerson physically ejected him onto the sidewalk. Rodgerson turned away, then hearing a movement, turned back. He saw Cottreau moving towards him and, with a closed fist, Rodgerson hit Cottreau in the face.

Cottreau was knocked unconscious, his nose broken, and his forehead fractured. Cottreau sued Rodgerson personally, as well as his employer, Saulnier, for assault and battery. In pleading his defence, Rodgerson stated that he used reasonable force in defending private property. He also claimed provocation.

The Court's Decision

The court stated that the tavern was private property, and that Rodgerson acted quite properly in first asking Cottreau to leave, then ejecting him using reasonable force to do so. The question was whether Rodgerson used reasonable force when he subsequently struck Cottreau while both men were outside on the sidewalk.

The court noted that Rodgerson, aged 23, although a small man at 5'6", was a trained boxer who had fought in the ring. Cottreau was slightly less than average height. Witnesses said that Cottreau was quite drunk, and rushed Rodgerson with his hands at his sides. The court found, after observing both witnesses, that Rodgerson was never in any danger from Cottreau, and that Rodgerson had hit Cottreau out of exasperation. Rodgerson, therefore, used more force than was reasonably necessary in the circumstances.

The claim of provocation also failed. Clearly, Cottreau's behaviour amounted to provocation, but, in law, provocation is not a defence. It can, however, be taken into account in mitigating the award of damages. So, although Cottreau received rather severe injuries, he was awarded only nominal damages of $550, together with remuneration for one day's lost pay, estimated at $250.

The Right to Tow

Parking lots adjacent to businesses are usually private property. In a plaza or shopping centre where a business is a tenant, the tenant may lease only the store space and the lease will contain a right to use common elements, such as parking areas. This area is private property, and a licence is given only to customers of the business. If someone parks a car, not intending to use the business, this is trespass. Signs are normally posted warning that trespassers will be towed, and the business has the right to have the vehicle removed by a private towing company.

The tow truck company normally requests the cost of towing charges from the owner of the towed car, and refuses to release the vehicle until paid. However, the tow truck company has no right in law to make this demand. The business from whose property the car was removed must pay the towing charges. There have been several successful actions in small-claims court—usually by law students—against tow truck companies for recovery of the amounts claimed, and punitive damages.[1]

There is no basis in law on which the tow truck company can collect money relating to the towing charge from the owner. The owner has not committed a tort against the towing company. There is no contract between it and the car owner.

Municipalities make by-laws which regulate towing—for instance, stating that a parked car cannot be towed for a certain period, perhaps two hours. But no by-law does or could give the right to a tow truck company to charge the owner for services.

In contrast, there are laws that permit police-authorized tow truck companies to charge the owner for towing vehicles for certain offences, such as parking on a main street during rush hour.

---

1. See "Law Puts Squeeze on Towing Firms," *The Toronto Sun*, September 21, 1995.

Business Law   Applied

3 **Jennifer Mouty was** refused admission to a bar by a bouncer because she did not have ID. She was of the legal drinking age and objected, before going home and returning with appropriate ID. The bouncer was annoyed, and told her he would not admit her anyway. Mouty stated that, as she was over the drinking age, she had a right to enter.

a) Who was correct?

4 **Sylvia Lieberman,** a contractor, was in the middle of building a large construction project. She experienced some delays in arranging new financing, and several of her subcontractors, anxious about being paid, persisted in visiting her home to demand payment. Sometimes, this happened several times in one day.

a) What could Lieberman have done to prevent the subcontractors from coming to her house?

5 **John Chaytor was** a fashion buyer employed by a department store, Fashions Inc., of London, New York, and Paris. When he and a colleague visited a store of a competing chain in order to compare prices, an employee at the store recognized Chaytor, accused him of being a spy, and exchanged angry words. The store detectives were summoned and told to "watch these people."

Police were called, and two officers arrived shortly afterwards. They were told by the store manager to arrest Chaytor. The officers did so, then escorted him out of the store. When Chaytor started to go in another direction, the police took him by the arm and said, "You must come with us." Chaytor was taken to the police station, but no charges were laid.

a) Was Chaytor rightfully on the business premises of the fashion company? If not, what law did he violate?

b) Did the business have the right to make a citizen's arrest, or merely order him to leave?

c) Did the words, "You must come with us," spoken by the police, equal imprisonment, as there was no physical restraint?

Conversion

This tort is very similar to theft in criminal law, and involves taking the property of another individual, with intent to exercise control over them. Shoplifting is an example.

Conversion (unauthorized use of the property of another) can be committed in two ways. The property might come into an individual's possession by the permission of the owner, but the recipient then refuses to return it. Alternatively, the property might be obtained by false pretences, such as when a customer pays using a bad cheque. In this instance, the owner would either have the goods returned, or would receive their equivalent dollar value.

conversion
unauthorized use of the goods of another

Where one partner, who was in a dispute with his other partners, took a computer purchased and used by the partnership business, that partner was found guilty of conversion and made to pay damages of $50,000.[2]

Conversion is a strict liability offence meaning that innocence and negligence are not a defence. This tort is often used against a bank that pays on a fraudulent cheque even though the bank had no knowledge of the fraud nor could have discovered the fraud with reasonable diligence as the following case demonstrates.

---

2. *Gu v. Tai Foong International Ltd.*, Ont. Sp. Ct., July 18, 2001.

Khosla v. Korea Exchange Bank of Canada, [2008] CanLII 56011 (ON S.C.)

Satwant Khosla was a solicitor who acted for clients who purchased a house. The house was sold using a fraudulent power of attorney. The fraudster was a tenant in the house.

The purchasers borrowed the purchase price of $492,000.00 and had it paid into Khosla's bank account in trust for themselves. Khosla drew a cheque in the name of the true owner of the house. Hence the true owner was the payee named on the cheque.

One month before closing the fraudster, using authentic identification taken from the owner, opened a bank account in the owner's name at the Korea Exchange Bank of Canada ("Korea Bank"). The fraudster deposited the cheque from the payment of the purchase price of the house in that bank account and shortly thereafter withdrew the funds and disappeared.

Khosla's insurer, a title insurance company, paid the purchasers their money, then using its right under the insurance policy [subrogation right] sued the Korea Bank using Khosla's name, for conversion of the cheque.

The Court's Decision

The Court held that there was well settled law that conversion was a strict liability defence. That meant that neither innocence on the bank's part, nor negligence by Khosla was a defence if the elements for conversion were established.

Conversion is wrongful interference with the property of another in a manner inconsistent with the owner's right to possession. The damage amount regarding cheques is the face amount of the cheque. Khosla, as drawer of the cheque, had the right to possession.

A bank commits conversion by collecting, i.e. obtaining the money from the drawer's [Khosla's] bank and then paying it to a person who is not the payee named on the cheque. Here the bank did not pay the funds to the true owner of the property, who was the payee on the cheque, but to a fraudster.

The bank was liable to pay Khosla the full amount of the face amount of the cheque plus interest.

Business Reputation Management

Defamation

defamation

making an untrue statement that causes injury to the reputation of an individual or business, including both libel and slander

Defamation is making an untrue statement that causes injury to the reputation of an individual or business, including both libel and slander. The test of whether harm has been done is the question, "Does it cause others to think less of the person or the business?" The key word to remember is reputation. An insulting comment that injures only pride can be unpleasant and annoying, but it is not defamation. In a very early defamation case, one judge stated, "The best defence to insult is a thick skin."

Eminem wrote a song from his 1999 CD 'Slim Shady LP' which contained lyrics mentioning a neighbourhood acquaintance:

> "I was harassed daily by this fat kid named D'Angelo Bailey,
> He banged my head against a urinal until he broke my nose.
> Soaked my clothes in blood. Grabbed me and killed my throat."

D'Angelo Bailey sued Eminem for $1 million on the basis that the lyrics were untrue and slanderous (*Bailey v. Eminem*, Michigan Trial Court, 2003). Judge Deborah Sarvitto, who appears to have been of the "thick skin" school, decided this case and wrote:

> "Mr. Bailey complains that this rap is trash
> so he is seeking compensation in the form of cash.
> Bailey thinks he is entitled to some money gain
> because Eminem used his name in vain.
> The lyrics are stories, no one would take them take as fact.
> They are an exaggeration of a childish act.
> It is therefore this Court's ultimate position
> That Eminem is entitled to summary disposition."

In short Judge Sarvitto ruled in favour of Eminem.

Defamation has traditionally been divided into two categories:

- **libel**, defamation in which the harmful statement is written or broadcast
- **slander**, defamation in which the harmful statement is spoken

The right to freedom of expression, and the right to protection of reputation, sometimes conflict. Because of this, there are special rules governing such situations as the media's treatment of public figures. The importance of business reputation is also recognized, and, in fact, is given more protection than personal reputation. The right to sue for defamation arises only if the false statement is communicated to a third party. Comments made between two individuals, and not passed on to others, cannot be regarded as defamation. The requirement of communication is called publication of the defamation.

All provinces have either defamation acts or libel and slander acts. In some provinces, the distinction between libel and slander has been abolished, so that all actions for injury to reputation are called actions for defamation.

Sometimes a comment might seem innocent if considered on its own. If another factor, such as knowledge of other information, or of the context in which the remark is made, is added, the innocent phrase can take on a whole new meaning. This is known as **innuendo**, a statement that implies something derogatory about another individual without directly saying it.

Innuendo **Innuendo** derives from a Latin word which means to nod, or to indicate by pointing the head. So *innuendo* means to hint at a meaning, rather than to express it directly.

libel
defamation in which the harmful statement is written or broadcast

slander
defamation in which the harmful statement is spoken

innuendo
a statement that implies something derogatory about another individual without directly saying it

Legalese

Monson v. Tussaud's Ltd., [1894] 1 Q. B. 671

Monson was accused of murder, tried, and acquitted. Some time later, he heard that Madame Tussaud's, a wax museum in London, had created a statue of him to be included in one of its exhibits. Monson visited the museum, where he saw his statue standing next to those of two notorious murderers, just outside the "Chamber of Horrors." There, many gruesome scenes and infamous characters were on display. Monson sued the museum for defamation.

The Court's Decision

The wax museum had to pay damages to Monson, since the act of placing the statue close to the Chamber of Horrors was considered to be libel by conduct. Although the statue by itself was an excellent likeness of Monson, locating it in the context of notorious criminals suggested that Monson was a killer. The wax museum defamed Monson by innuendo.

■ *Critical Concepts of* Defamation

- Defamation involves a false statement that is harmful to the reputation of a person or business.
- The harm caused can be by innuendo.
- The statement must be published, that is, communicated, to a third party.
- Defamation can be either libel or slander.

Libel

Traditionally, libel was defamation in written form. However, libel also includes harm to an individual's reputation that is caused by the conduct, or actions, of another person. More recently, libel has been expanded by statute to include modern methods of communication, including broadcasting, movies, pictures, film, and computer technology.

Monetary damages are presumed by the court in libel cases.

Slander

Slander is defamation in spoken form. The provincial acts state that a slander suit will not be upheld by the courts without proof of actual monetary loss suffered by the individual or business claiming defamation. The exception to this is if the statement made was that the wronged party:

- had committed a crime
- suffered from "a loathsome disease," such as leprosy
- (a woman) had been unchaste
- was unfit to practise a specific calling or profession

Damages

Damages for defamation contain a unique element. Not only is there compensation for ordinary loss, but money is also given for injured feelings, such as humiliation, and to show that the defamed person is innocent.

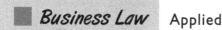 **Business Law** Applied

6 **Igor Taras returned** to his desk one day after a meeting, to find a file folder with "This guy is crazy" written in large letters, right in the centre of the front cover. The file could be seen by everyone who passed by. Taras discovered that the remark had been written by a fellow employee, Gustaf Hermann.

- a) Is the comment libel or slander?
- b) Could the statement be considered to have been published?
- c) Taras suffered no monetary loss as a result of the statement. Could he sue Hermann in tort?

7 **John Nowark and** Peter Youssoff were employed in the same company, and disliked each other intensely. A series of thefts occurred in the office.

On Monday, Youssoff whispered to Nowark, "I know you're the thief."

On Tuesday, Nowark overheard Youssoff say to a fellow employee, "Nowark is a jerk."

On Wednesday, Nowark heard Youssoff comment to their boss, "Nowark is incompetent."

The Monday statement:

- a) Is it libel or slander?
- b) Give two reasons for which Nowark cannot successfully bring an action against Youssoff.

The Tuesday statement:

- c) Is it libel or slander?
- d) Can Nowark successfully bring an action for defamation against Youssoff?

The Wednesday statement:

- e) Can Nowark successfully bring an action against Youssoff?

Defamation on the Internet

How do defamation laws apply to material published over the Internet? Communication over the Internet presents some unique features:

- there is no editor, or intervenor of any sort, filtering potentially defamatory material
- there is the possibility of posting material anonymously
- there is immediate and widespread access to the material (to, potentially, millions of people around the world)

The web gives more people the ability to reach a large audience with ease; but the responsibilities in law are the same. Defamatory statements will bring liability. For example, in a recent case a parent, whose child had Down's syndrome and was a student at a certain elementary school and a child's right activist were engaged in a long dispute over a number of issues with the school regarding the child's educational placement and, in particular, while the parent and activist wanted the child in a French Immersion program, the school placed her in an English class. The parent and child activist posted a "News Release" on a website making several comments which the Court found defamatory including that the Principal was under investigation for criminal conduct, which allegation was false. (*Ottawa-Carlton District School Board v. Scharf*, 2008, ONCA 154 (CanLII))

Libel or Slander

There appears to be no reason why the usual legal principles concerning defamation would not apply to material posted over the Internet. The question is: how will these "old" laws be adapted to cover new situations?

Each time a posting is accessed, it is likely published. But is a message posted on the Internet libel or slander? The division of defamation into libel and slander based on written or spoken form was developed centuries before the Internet. A new situation such as the Internet forces a court to re-examine the situation and develop new principles to determine the categorizations.

First, is there any significance to the difference? The answer is yes. If it is slander, the matter must have resulted in actual damages to sustain a lawsuit in most cases (see the discussion on slander above).

However, if it is libel, a lawsuit can be started without actual damages. Traditionally higher awards have been awarded for libel.

Aspects of libel are that it usually involves a higher level of premeditation and a higher level of permanence than slander. Being in written form, libel will potentially reach a wider audience than slander.

Applying these principles to the Internet, there may be a different result for a statement made in a chat room, than for a statement posted on a website. A chat-room comment may be viewed as less permanent and more spontaneous, and thus similar to slander. A website posting may be seen as more permanent and planned, and therefore more like libel. However, there are also mid-categories: what about postings on a bulletin board? These questions will likely be considered in judicial decisions in the next few years. The Internet may cause a new definition of those terms in place of the test of written or spoken.

Website Links

A recent number of law suits against service providers of websites such as Yahoo and Wikepedia and operators of websites have brought the question of whether the posting of a hyperlink to a website that contains defamatory comments, without any comment, is publication.

In the U.S. there is statutory authority that says there is none (the Communications Decency Act). Under that Act providers are not liable for what users say. In Canada the law is not clear. One of the concerns is that a newspaper's repetition of a defamatory comment is republication and attracts liability. A simple posting of a hyperlink, not repeating the content, may be distinguishable. If the posting is associated with a comment such as, "read this for the true story," that is more similar to re-publication.

The decision to sue in defamation always involves the consideration that the Court action will attract wide attention and prolong the defamation. For example, the Crookes lawsuit, the brief of which follows, attracted wide attention not only from bloggers, on-line and paper newspapers, but also TV news special feature reports: even the BBC ran one on Crookes.

Business Alert!

Crookes v. Wikemedia Foundation Inc., [2007] BC SC 1424 (CanLII)

Wayne Crookes, a former campaign manager of the Green Party of Canada sued a number of persons associated with websites that contained links to websites where alleged defamatory comments about Crookes were posted. One of these actions was against John Newton who operated a website called www.p2p.net which contained commentaries on issues surrounding the Internet as well as other political subjects.

After the first of Crookes' lawsuits against website providers and operators was commenced, Newton published an article on p2p.net with comments on the implications of defamatory actions for those who operate Internet forums. Newton's article included a hyperlink to other sites: www.openpolitics.ca and www.usgovernetics.com. Newton made no comment about the truth of the allegations. Crookes sued Newton in defamation. Newton defended the basis that merely posting a hyperlink was not publication.

The Court's Decision

The Court first found that merely posting a link on a website did not prove that anyone had actually seen the posting, nor had gone to the link and seen the defamatory comment. In particular, it did not prove that anyone who knew the Plaintiff had read the defamatory material because of the posting of this link. That issue would have to be proved by actual evidence.

Secondly, the mere posting of a hyperlink without anything more did not equal publication. Newton had no control over the target website where the alleged defamatory material was published. He did not make any comment on its accuracy nor did he reprint any part of it; therefore, there was no publication.

The Court cautioned, however, that the result might be different if the website host made comments on the accuracies of the statements in the linked article.

Disclosure of Information on Websites

What if you do not know who posted the defamatory material? Courts are ordering Internet service providers to divulge the names of persons who posted defamatory material on their websites. In one highly reported case eBay was ordered to produce information on its Canadian "power sellers" pursuant to sections of *The Income Tax Act.* The Court held that eBay was not foreign-based because it is readily accessible in Canada. Although this latter decision was made under *The Income Tax Act,* it probably reflects the Court's readiness to both assume jurisdiction over foreign located Internet service providers and to require disclosure (*eBay Canada Limited v. Canada (National Revenue),* 2008 FCA 141 (CanLII)).

Defences

Innocent Dissemination

An individual who is in the business of distribution might well be unaware of the contents of a defamatory publication. Bookstores or libraries, for example, will not be held liable if it can be proven that it was not reasonable for them to know of the contents. Bookstores and libraries do not regularly review the contents of every book, magazine, or newspaper they have. However, a publisher does review the contents and often makes changes to the material submitted. So, a publisher cannot claim the defence of innocent dissemination.

Truth

An action for defamation will succeed only if the statement is untrue. The law presumes that a harmful statement is false, and it is up to the individual who made it to prove that it is true, and not harmful to the plaintiff's reputation. Merely claiming that the statement was repeated is not a defence if the statement is untrue. The defence of truth is called justification.

Business Law Applied

8 A library, looking to expand its collection of Canadian heritage books, ordered several volumes from a publisher's catalogue. One of these, called *Towers of Gold, Basements of Clay*, was about the Canadian banking industry. In it, the author falsely claimed that the vice-president of a large Canadian bank had been associated with stock market fraud.

The book proved extremely popular with library patrons, and was often out on loan. One member of the library happened to be a friend of the banking executive mentioned, and told him what was said in the book. The banker sued the book's author, the publisher, and the library.

a) What defence(s) could each claim, if any?

Absolute Privilege

In certain situations, an individual can say anything, even if it is outrageous or untrue. During such proceedings as court trials, or legislative and parliamentary sessions, false statements can be made, and there is no possibility of a successful action for defamation. The comment must, however, be made during the actual proceedings. A member of Parliament can make a defamatory statement about a colleague while Parliament is in session, but cannot repeat that statement outside the House of Commons. **Absolute privilege**—complete immunity from liability for defamation, whereby the defamatory statement cannot be the grounds for a lawsuit—ends at the door of wherever the proceedings take place. You may hear one politician say to another in a debate in the House of Commons: I dare you to repeat that comment outside the house. That Member of Parliament is trying to get the other member to repeat the statement in a place where absolute privilege does not apply.

absolute privilege
complete immunity from liability for defamation, whereby the defamatory statement cannot be the grounds for a lawsuit

Qualified Privilege

Qualified privilege is immunity from liability for defamation when the statement is made in good faith to a person or body which has authority over the person defamed. There are occasions when it might be necessary to report an individual to an organization that oversees a particular profession—the law society, or the college of physicians and surgeons, for example. In such situations, the person who makes the complaint does so out of duty, and does not deliberately set out to harm another's reputation. The statement is made without malice, and is not defamatory.

qualified privilege
immunity from liability for defamation when the statement is made in good faith to a person or body which has authority over the person defamed

Statements made under these circumstances are privileged, and the individual against whom they are made cannot sue. Even if the allegations are later found to be false, a suit for defamation will not succeed. However, if it can be proved that the complainant was malicious, and made the statement for an improper purpose, an action is possible.

A client might be infuriated with his accountant, for example, because of some exchange of insults, and report her to the accountants' professional society alleging fraud, when in fact he knows there is no basis for doing so. Such a motive is improper and malicious—and the accountant could sue her client for defamation. Knowledge that the allegation is false is enough to establish the element of malice.

Fair Comment

fair comment

a defence to an action for defamation in which the harmful statements were made about public figures

Comments on matters of public concern—normally relating to politics or art—can fall under the umbrella of fair comment. **Fair comment** is a defence to an action for defamation in which the harmful statements were made about public figures. Such statements must offer opinions, rather than claim to be a true fact. If a newspaper columnist writes that a well-known rock star is a thief, that is a statement of fact; if the columnist says that the singer's latest CD is a disaster, that is an opinion—a comment on the artist's work. Media frequently rely on this defence. A comment is considered fair if any person could honestly express that opinion on the proven facts.

Vander Zalm v. Times Publishers, Bierman, McLester and Underhill, [1980] 4 W.W.R. 259

While William Vander Zalm was the minister of human resources for the government of British Columbia, he initiated some severe cuts to the province's welfare programs. The defendants published a cartoon depicting Vander Zalm pulling wings from flies, with a smile on his face.

Vander Zalm brought an action against the newspaper for defamation. The newspaper claimed in defence that the fact upon which the cartoon was based was true, that is, Vander Zalm did initiate a program to cut welfare payments. The cartoon was a graphic attempt to express the opinion that the welfare cuts hurt those who could not protect themselves.

Vander Zalm argued that he was just doing his job in good faith and, as he thought, in the best interest of the province. The cartoon went further than depicting a man taking advantage of people who

could not protect themselves. It depicted him as being cruel and sadistic, and enjoying inflicting suffering.

The Court's Decision

The court stated that political cartoons are rhetorical, and the cartoonist makes a point indirectly by use of symbolism, allegory, satire, and exaggeration. Accordingly, readers would not have taken the cartoon literally, and it was not defamatory.

The court further stated that, even if the cartoon was defamatory, the defence of fair comment applied. The test was whether the belief was honestly held—was the cartoonist expressing an honest opinion on a subject of public interest?

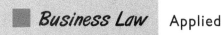

Business Law Applied

❾ **A 12-year-old alleged** that he was sexually abused by a popular rock singer. The allegations were later proven to be untrue.

a) Could the singer bring an action against the boy (a minor)?
b) If the boy states his claims in open court, could he later be successfully sued for defamation?
c) If the boy held a news conference, and said he intended to sue the rock star for abuse, would the boy have a defence against the alleged defamatory statement?
d) If a newspaper reported the statements made in court and at the news conference, would it have any defence against a claim of defamation?

Responsible Communication

The Supreme Court of Canada has recently created a new defence of responsible communication regarding matters of public interest. It will be of most use to journalists, publishers and perhaps even bloggers. The defendant must show, as the term suggests, that he or she acted responsibly in reporting on a matter of public interest. Responsibility can be established by showing due diligence in trying to verify the allegation. Recall that a defence of this type is successful even if it turns out that the "facts" are not true.

The Court also recognized a defence of "reportage". A journalist or publisher will not be liable for (quoting) (repeating) defamatory statements if they are clearly reported as quotes and repeated in order to report what was said in a given dispute (*Grant v. Torstar Corp.* 2009 SCC 61).

Special Recognition of Business Reputation

The laws of defamation not only protect an individual's reputation; they also recognize the importance of the business reputation, particularly in the laws governing slander. Slander is usually not the grounds for a court action, unless there has been some actual monetary loss caused to the defamed person.

However, if the statement is made about the abilities of an individual or a business, damages are presumed and no actual loss must be proved. Successful actions have been brought against persons who have falsely said that a business is **bankrupt**, or declared insolvent by the court, incapable of paying debts. Products and services, too, develop a reputation. Deliberate harm to that reputation is known as **injurious falsehood**, which is a false statement about goods or services that is harmful to the reputation of those goods or services. It is very similar to the tort of the defamation.

bankrupt
declared insolvent by the court, incapable of paying debts

injurious falsehood
a false statement about goods or services that is harmful to the reputation of those goods or services

Attacks by Other Businesses

The business system in Canada is based on free enterprise. Aggressive competition is encouraged, and is thought to be the best way of ensuring efficiency, as well as quality of product, service, and price. Over the years, the courts have developed some controls over business practices they have thought to be unfair. However, faced with a broadly changing economy and expanding business practices, the courts are reluctant to be a source of control over modern business. Hence, most regulations affecting business are passed by federal and provincial governments in the form of statutes, such as the *Competition Act*. Some of the court-initiated controls, developed under the law of torts, are outlined in this section.

Passing Off

This is the business form of plagiarism—taking someone else's work and calling it your own. In everyday language, these products are called "knock-offs," or imitations. Examples of *passing off* include:

- fake Rolex watches
- a garage displaying a sign indicating it is recommended by an automobile association, when it is not
- a singer's name on a CD, when in fact the recording is made by an imitator
- a product displaying the "Good Housekeeping Seal of Approval," when it is not in fact approved

In general, people can use their own name as a business name. The exception to this is when that name has become associated with a particular business or product, and its use elsewhere in the same industry would deceive the public. Two obvious examples are the name McDonald's in the fast food business, or Campbell's in connection with soups or other prepared canned foods. If the business is unrelated, the exception does not apply. Anyone could open up a clothing store called McDonald's Fashions, or Campbell's Creations.

■ *Critical Concepts of* Passing Off

The plaintiff must prove three elements to establish passing off:

- The appearance of the product is well-enough known to indicate the source of the product.
- The defendant's adoption of the similar appearance of its product is likely to cause confusion in the public.
- There are damages to the plaintiff as a result.

Walt Disney Productions v. Fantasyland Hotel, [1994] 154 A.R. 161

Walt Disney Productions objected to the use of the name Fantasyland by the Fantasyland Hotel at the West Edmonton Mall. Disney operates amusement parks in the United States and elsewhere, in which Fantasyland is the name of a theme-park attraction. There are no Disney theme parks in Canada.

In an earlier case, in 1992, Disney was successful in stopping a different company from using the name Fantasyland for an amusement park, also located at the West Edmonton Mall.

The Court's Decision

The court stated that:

While Disney may have a reputation and goodwill in the name of Fantasyland in respect of amusement parks... it does not have a reputation and goodwill... in respect of hotels, nor at large.

A survey undertaken by the defendant indicated that only 3 percent of those questioned thought that the Fantasyland Hotel was connected with Disney. There was, therefore, insufficient evidence to show that a majority of the general public would be misled into thinking there was some connection between the two.

Disney's case was dismissed.

Injurious Falsehood

Defamation deals with untrue statements that harm the reputation of a business or individual; false statements about a business product fall into the tort of injurious falsehood.

There are special defences to this action. As in the law governing defamation, these defences are equivalent to qualified privilege. For example, a consumer group might mistakenly state that a product is defective. As long as the group used reasonable care in investigating the product, and made the comment for the benefit of consumers rather than to injure the business, the "false statement" is not considered injurious falsehood.

Customers who picket stores claiming that they have bought a defective product, or paint their cars yellow, list defects on them, and park the vehicle in front of the dealership, are not liable—as long as the allegations are true. Similarly, the courts are reluctant to become involved in making law in disputes between unions and businesses.

In a recent development a court awarded damages to a competitor for misleading comparative advertising in breach of the Competition Act. Go Travel gave comparative rates with Maritime travel in such away as to give the incorrect impression that Go's rates were cheaper. (*Maritime Travel Inc. v. Go Travel Direct.com Inc.* [2008] N.S.J. No. 224, 66 C.P.R. (4th) 61 (N.S.S.C). A novel approach, it is under appeal at the time of writing but provides another possible remedy to prevent unfair competition from a competitor.

Church and Dwight Ltd. v. Sifto Canada Inc., [1994] 20 O.R. (3d) 484

Church and Dwight Ltd. is the distributor of Arm & Hammer baking soda—a product previously marketed as Cow Brand baking soda. The product has an 80 percent share of the market in Canada.

Sifto Canada Inc., in an effort to increase its share of the market, developed the following advertising copy to appear on the box containing its product:

Sifto Baking Soda—one of the richest sources of naturally occurring sodium bicarbonate is found deep in the Colorado Mountains. The North American Salt Plant at Rio Blanco taps into this vast underground deposit, producing the purest possible baking soda, contained in this box. Sifto Baking Soda has no chemical additives, making it the only naturally occurring baking soda on the market.

100% effective

100% natural

On the front of the box, Sifto Baking Soda is described as "100% pure and natural."

Church and Dwight applied for an injunction to stop the marketing of this new advertising copy, on the basis of injurious falsehood.

The Court's Decision

False advertising is one type of injurious falsehood, and protects a business's interests in being able to sell its products. False statements that attack the reputation of a business, or the quality of its products, are the basis of this tort.

The court found the statement "100% pure and natural" was mere "puffery"—common exaggeration, often used in advertising. However, the statement, "... producing the purest possible baking soda, contained in this box. Sifto Baking Soda has no chemical additives, making it the only naturally occurring baking soda on the market," implied that the competing brand was not natural, and contained chemical additives. This implication was both false and harmful to the reputation of the Arm & Hammer product.

It would be impossible to calculate the actual business loss that would occur until the actual trial—unlikely to take place for several years—so an injunction was granted to stop the offensive behaviour.

Business Law   Applied

⑩ **Angela McGowan had** continual trouble with her new car, which required substantial repairs every few months. The manufacturer honoured its warranty and made the necessary repairs, but refused to take the vehicle back and refund McGowan's money.

After two years of frustration, McGowan painted the car bright yellow, and fixed a large plastic lemon on the roof. She then had "purchased at Fred's Car Dealer" painted in large letters on the side of the vehicle, and for the next few weeks parked it outside that dealership as often as she could.

The manufacturer and the dealer decided to ask for help from the courts.

   a) Did McGowan commit a tort? If so, which one?
   b) Are there any defences she could use if taken to court by the dealer and/or the manufacturer?

⑪ **Shelly McLachlin bought** some software form Macro Hard Inc. She had a lot of trouble with the software but Macro Hard Inc. would not refund her money.

McLachlin created a website called macrohardsucks.com. She posted a page describing her problems with the software and the company's refusal to be of any assistance. She also asked other people to post stories about their experience with the software and dealings with the company.

Assume that Macro Hard Inc. sues McLachlin for injurious falsehood for making statements posted on the website damaging its business's product.

   a) Will Macro Hard Inc. be successful against her respecting her personal complaint or does McLachlin have some defences? If so, what are they?
   b) Will McLachlin be responsible for the comments posted by other people on her website?

Intentional Interference

Competition is encouraged, so businesses are at liberty to attempt to drive a competitor from the market by legal competitive means. There are some limitations on the right to compete; some business practices are considered to be unfair or anti-competitive. One of the legal remedies aimed at controlling unfair competitive behaviour is called the tort of intentional interference with economic interests.

The tort of intentional interference can be committed in a number of ways and it sometimes goes by the names of various sub-categories:

- (intentionally causing one person to breach his contract with another)
- inducing breach of confidential information
- intimidation
- injurious falsehood

inducing breach of contract

intentionally causing one person to breach his contract with another

For example, Volkswagen (Germany) Ltd. lured one of General Motors (U.S.) Ltd.'s key vice-presidents, Josez Lopez, to work for it. General Motors sued Volkswagen for $5 billion, alleging Volkswagen induced Lopez to breach his employment contract with G.M. Volkswagen also, it was alleged, had Lopez bring several boxes of G.M. documents about new car development with him. G.M. claimed Volkswagen thus induced a breach of confidentiality. This dispute was settled privately.

If an employee wants to leave a company for a competitor, this is not a tort. Such transfers occur frequently. But the competitor must not approach the employee and initiate the change in employment. The tort is in the inducement.

67122 Ontario Ltd. v. Sagaz Investments Ltd., [1998] 40 O.R. (3d) 329

Robert Sommers was the head of Canadian Tire's automotive division. Canadian Tire bought its seat covers from the plaintiff. Stewart Lawson of Aim Inc. offered to pay Sommers 2 percent of all purchases by Canadian Tire of seat covers from Aim Inc. Sommers agreed and Canadian Tire stopped dealing with the plaintiff. The bribes were paid to a corporation, controlled by Sommers, called Sagaz Investments Ltd.

Canadian Tire learned of the kickback agreement and fired Sommers, but it continued to deal with Aim Inc. The plaintiff sued Aim and Sommers for intentional interference with economic interest.

The Court's Decision

Both Aim and Sommers were liable on the newly developing tort of intentional interference with economic interest. The essence of this tort is the use of unlawful means to interfere with a business relationship. The plaintiffs claim to have established all elements of the tort:

- there was an existing business relationship between Canadian Tire and the plaintiff
- the defendants knew of this relationship
- the defendants intentionally interfered with it
- the interference was by unlawful means (bribery or kickback)
- the interference caused the plaintiff's loss

The plaintiff was awarded damages of $2 million for loss of business and $50,000 for punitive damages.

Business Law   Applied

⑫ **Volkswagen Canada Ltd.** gave an exclusive franchise for an area in Halifax to Hillcrest Motors Ltd., which was owned by John Spicer and Stephen Gaetz. Because Volkswagen promised delivery of its new Rabbit in November 1994, but only made delivery in 1995, Hillcrest was not successful.

Volkswagen became concerned about Hillcrest and told Hillcrest's bank not to honour any cheques from Hillcrest unless they were also signed by a Volkswagen representative named Baldwin. The bank did return several cheques because of these directions from Volkswagen.

a) Were there any unlawful acts done by Volkswagen?
b) Does Hillcrest have any rights against Volkswagen respecting its instructions to the bank?

Unintentional Torts

The Concept of Negligence

In everyday language, negligence is another word for carelessness. In law, however, the term has a specific technical meaning. Negligence as a tort requires all the elements discussed in the following section.

An automobile accident is probably the most common instance of the tort of negligence. One car driver seldom intends to injure another. But when that individual's attention wanders for a moment and the vehicle fails to stop at a stop sign, slamming into another car, the driver has committed the tort of negligence.

Not every careless act that causes injury is the tort of negligence. There are a number of questions that help decide whether a particular act of carelessness is, in fact, legal negligence. These include:

- Was there a duty to look out for the injured person?
- What was the standard of care that should have been used?
- Was damage caused by a failure to meet that standard of care?
- Was there a reasonably close causal connection between the conduct and the injury (proximate cause)?

The answer to all four questions is "yes" in the automobile accident described above, because:

- The first car driver owed a duty to look out for to the other driver
- The standard of care was to stop at all stop signs
- The failure to meet the standard of care caused the injury
- Compensable damage (to the car) and perhaps injury to the other driver resulted

■ *Critical Concepts of* Negligence

To establish negligence, the courts will ask four questions:

- Was it reasonably foreseeable that the plaintiff would be injured by the defendant's act? (duty owed)
- Did the defendant fail to do what a reasonable person would have done in the circumstances to prevent or avoid injury? (breach of duty)
- Did the failure to act reasonably (carefully) cause the plaintiff's injury? (**causation:** one of the elements of negligence, relating to whether the action produced the damage or injury)
- Did the plaintiff suffer damage or injury as a result, the general nature which was reasonably foreseeable by the defendant (damages)?

causation

one of the elements of negligence, relating to whether the action produced the damage or injury

To Whom Is a Duty Owed?

In the early development of the law of negligence, the courts accepted that a duty was not owed to everyone, but only to those who it was reasonable to foresee could be injured as a result of a negligent act. In recent times, this limitation has been worn away, and the scope of duty is very wide, especially for businesses that deal with the public. A reasonable person is always thinking of the safety of others first. There are very few reported cases today where a business has avoided liability because it does not owe a duty to the person injured. The case, *Donoghue v. Stevenson* on the next page, significantly expanded the scope of duty in the business context.

Example: Unforeseeable plaintiff. A porter at a railway station attempted to assist a man with his luggage. Unknown to the porter the luggage contained fireworks. The porter accidentally bumped into the man knocking down the luggage which caused the contents to explode. A burst of air went down a nearby corridor hitting a scale at the end. The scale was on a platform and fell onto a woman walking below.

The court found that the luggage was not a hazard apparent to the eye of ordinary vigilance but seemingly innocent and harmless (*Palsgraf v. The Long Island Railroad Co.* (1928), 162 N.E. 99).

The Expanding Scope of Duty

As the courts' acceptance of the extent of duty broadens, public awareness of what is possible under negligence laws has resulted in new types of claims, many of which are currently in process. Rape victims have sued police forces for not warning of known rapists in their area.[3]

A son whose father was convicted of hiring a killer to murder his wife has sued the father for psychological trauma after seeing the mother murdered in front of him. Victims of injuries caused by persons ordered deported because of violent criminal records, but allowed to remain in Canada, have sued immigration officials.

Some cases have resulted in findings that people owe a duty to others with whom they had no direct dealings. Psychiatrists, for example, have been found liable to the families of victims killed by patients whose murderous tendencies were known to the doctor, but who did not warn the authorities of the danger. Doctors in general practice have been held liable to victims of traffic accidents caused by patients with epilepsy when the physicians did not report that disability to the driver-licensing authority. All provincial highway-traffic acts require doctors to report patients who are physically incapable of driving.

An interesting area where the law has been developing an expanding duty of care is in the area of liability of commercial enterprises which serve alcohol. The duty of care of these establishments was initially defined as extending to patrons who drink on the premises. Recently

---

3. The case went to trial. The plaintiff was awarded $250,000 against the Metropolitan Toronto Police Commission. See *Jane Doe v. Metropolitan Toronto Commissioners of Police* (1998), 39 O.R. (3d) 487.

the courts have expanded the duty to include persons who could be expected to be on the highways and encounter the person who had been drinking on the premises.[4]

Employers have been held liable for injury to employees who have been served alcohol at work or at a work-sponsored function. Parents were held liable for part of a $2.5 million award for brain injuries resulting from a car crash caused by a teenage driver who had been given drinks at a teen party.

Donoghue v. Stevenson, [1932] A.C. 562 (House of Lords)

Mrs. MacAllister, *née* Donoghue, and a friend went to a restaurant. The friend paid for the meal. One of the items supplied was ginger beer, served in a dark-coloured bottle. When Donoghue finished the bottle, she found the decomposed remains of a snail at the bottom. Donoghue became very ill from drinking the toxic substance.

In looking to sue someone who would be responsible, Donoghue found several problems with the law as it then existed. She did not buy the ginger beer herself, and so could not sue the restaurant owner in contract. The restaurant would not be found negligent, as the bottle was opaque and it was impossible for the snail to be seen, so the restaurant owner was not in breach of what a reasonable person would have done in the circumstances. It was the manufacturer who probably breached the standard of care.

Donoghue therefore sued the manufacturer of the ginger beer in tort, claiming that the company had owed a duty to her as a person who might consume the drink.

The Court's Decision

The case was eventually heard by the House of Lords in England, that country's highest court. There, the decision was that the soft-drink manufacturer had indeed failed to observe a reasonable standard of care, and also had owed a duty towards Donoghue. Lord Atkin, one of the judges, produced what has become the classic statement of the definition of the scope of duty:

> The rule that you are to love your neighbour becomes in law, you must not injure your neighbour; and the lawyer's question, "Who is my neighbour?" receives a restricted reply. You must take reasonable care to avoid acts or omissions which you can reasonably foresee would be likely to injure your neighbour. Who, then, in law, is my neighbour? The answer seems to be persons who are so closely and directly affected by any act, that I ought to have them in contemplation as being so affected when I am directing my mind to the acts or omissions that are called in question.

The test for the scope of duty has become that we owe a duty to anyone we can reasonably anticipate might be harmed by our conduct.

Business Law   Applied

⑱ Easson Seel was returning home around 2:00 a.m., and took a shortcut through the lot belonging to Acupress Inc., a tool-and-die firm. An old wooden shed, badly dilapidated and abandoned for years, stood on one corner of the property. Seel knew the structure was there.

Seel failed to stamp out a cigarette that he dropped as he passed the old shed. The cigarette ignited some dry grass, and the fire quickly spread to the shed. Unknown to Seel, a security guard, Michael Kuz, was asleep in the shed, after having drunk too much before he came on duty that night. The shed was totally destroyed by the flames, and Kuz was killed. Kuz's wife and children brought an action against Seel for the wrongful death of their husband and father.

a) Did Seel owe a duty to Kuz? What is the test the courts will apply to determine the existence of a duty?

b) If he does owe such a duty, is the type of injury foreseeable?

---

4. See *Stewart v. Pettie*, [1995] S.C.R. 131.

⑭ **A car hit** a metal post on a strip of gravel that divided two highway lanes. The post was bent over. A taxicab driver, illegally driving on the gravel strip in order to pass another vehicle, was killed when the post came up through the floorboards of his car and impaled him. His wife and children sued the driver whose car had damaged the metal post.

a) Did the first driver owe a duty to the taxicab driver?
b) Did he owe a duty to the taxicab driver's wife and children?

Expanding Duties and Negligence

The decision in *Donoghue v. Stevenson* opened a very wide scope of duty on all persons for negligence acts, but liability for the negligent use of words, which include advice, opinions and the like both verbal and written, was not at that time actionable. Then, in another landmark case in the law of negligence, the Courts held a bank employee liable to the customer of a second bank for negligently advising that a business's credit was good (*Hedley, Byrne & Co. Ltd. v. Heller & Partners Ltd.*, [1964] AC 465). The liability for opinions and advice is discussed in more detail under the topic 'Business Advisor's Liability'.

The courts were concerned that imposing any responsibility for negligence on advice or information may make certain functions financially unviable. One profession noted was that of auditors of a corporation whose shares were traded publicly. The auditors could be held liable to investors around the world who relied on the company's financial statements to make investment decisions. That would be an unlimited liability to an unlimited class of persons. In order to restrict the scope of this new duty, the Courts formulated a separate test originally called the "Special Relationship" test. Now there were two tests for negligence: one for conduct—reasonable foreseeability; and one for words—special relationship.

Reconciliation of the Two Tests

The two types of negligence: one for words/advice (*Hedley, Berne v. Heller*) and for conduct (*Donoghue v. Stevenson*), had at this point two different tests to establish negligence. The Courts harmonized these two tests by developing a single but two stage analysis usually referred to as the "Anns" test after the British case by the name *Anns v. Merton London Borough Council*, [1978] A.C. 728 (H.L.). The two stages are:

1. Is there a sufficiently close relationship between the parties to testify the imposition of a duty (proximity) and, if so,
2. Are there any residual policy considerations to negate or limit the scope of that duty, the class of persons to whom it is owed, or the damages to which breach may give rise?

In the above two stages, there are policy factors in each stage. These policy factors permit the court to limit or deny liability even though a logical application of a previously established precedent would appear to require a finding of liability. The stage one policy factors are relative to the individuals involved; in stage two they are relative to the interest of society generally. In the *Douglas v. Kinger* case below, there are examples of both types of policy considerations.

Douglas v. Kinger, [2008] ONCA 452 (CanLII)

Brice Douglas hired thirteen year old Mitchell Kinger as a "boat boy" to do menial tasks around his cottage part time for $8.00 an hour. Douglas gave Kinger instructions that included not to use any power equipment unless supervised by an adult.

One day young Kinger went alone to the cottage to cut the grass. The lawn mower gas tank seemed empty but he could not see into it, so he held a lit match in his mouth then peered into the tank. The vapours ignited into flames which consumed the boat house causing a $285,000.00 loss.

Douglas had insurance which covered the loss. However, by the standard terms of most insurance policies, the insurance company has the right to sue in the insured's place (right of subrogation) the wrongdoer. The insurance company sued Kinger in negligence to recover its loss.

The trial judge dismissed the insurance company's claim and it appealed.

The Court of Appeal's Decision

The Court reaffirmed that the "Anns" test had two components, (1) that there be a sufficiently close relationship to establish a duty, and (2) that there were no policy reasons generally to limit the remedy in the circumstances.

The Court held that under the "Anns" test's proximity giving rise to a duty of care would not be determined by foreseeability alone, policy factors relating to the specific relationship had also to be considered. This latter analysis depends on the expectations each party had of the other, here as employer and employee.

The Court found that the employee negligence was contemplated. The employer specifically told the boy not to use power equipment unsupervised. However, employee responsibility for loss was not contemplated. It would have been unreasonable for the employer to expect a thirteen year old boy earning $8.00 an hour at a part time job to reimburse him for a $285,000.00 loss. Additionally, the employer had insured for the loss.

The second stage, residual policy analysis, also favoured a finding of employee exemption from liability. It was of general benefit to the society that employers bear the cost of employee negligence and the cost of insurance as part of the cost of doing business but not to put an impossible burden on individual employees.

The Court upheld the trial judgment and dismissed the insurance company's appeal.

The Standard of Care

The Reasonable Person Test   The **reasonable person test** is a test or standard based on what a reasonable person would have done in similar circumstances. Once it is established that a duty is owed to the person injured, the next issue is to decide the degree, or standard, of care that is owed. In order to decide the standard of care an individual should follow in a particular situation, the courts ask what a reasonable person would have done. This is used to determine the standards to be applied to, for example, a car driver, a skier, and the owner of a business.

reasonable person test
a test or standard based on what a reasonable person would have done in similar circumstances

Reasonable   The word **reasonable** is used often in a legal context, usually along with other words—reasonable foreseeability; reasonable person. *Reasonable* is used, and not *average*. Hence, the reasonable person is more than an average person. The reasonable person is a careful or prudent individual. Reasonable foreseeability is more than just average foreseeability, and implies that some thought has been given to the consequences of an action.

Legalese

Reasonable also means a finding of fact, not of law. Where civil juries are available, it is a question to be decided by the jury, not the judge. The judge will instruct the jury on the law to be applied. For example, in a slip and fall case where a customer is suing a business for not clearing snow from its parking lot one day after the last snowfall, the judge will tell the jury, "The law is—you must decide what the reasonable business person would have done in the circumstances." The jury decides the question of reasonableness, or fact. Did the business act reasonably (with care) in the circumstances of that case?

Business Law   Applied

⑮ A gas station on a local highway had an open cesspool at the back. A family stopped for gas, and the parents went into the gas station building to buy some refreshments. Their 6-year-old son got out of the car, and wandered round to the rear of the gas station, where he fell into the cesspool. The child swallowed some of the liquid, and became seriously ill. The boy and his parents sued the owner of the gas station.

    a) What test would the court apply to determine if the gas station owed a duty to the child?
    b) What test would the court apply to determine the standard of care owed to the boy?
    c) What should a reasonable gas station owner have done in the circumstances?

⑯ A water main burst during a severe cold spell, flooding a nearby residence. The pipe had been installed 25 years previously, at a level that was then thought deep enough to prevent freezing under normal winter conditions.

The homeowner claimed that the pipe should have been buried deeper, and sued the water company. The water company claimed that the pipe was deep enough for normal conditions, and locating it any deeper would have meant considerable additional expense.

    a) Did the water company act as a reasonable contractor?
    b) Freak cold spells happen every so often, and the homeowner brought evidence of one that had occurred 50 years before. Should the water company, knowing of this, have buried the pipe deeper "just in case"?

Higher Standards

The courts impose higher standards on businesses that deal with the public where safety is an issue. The greater the risk, the higher the standard of care. Businesses in the food-service industry, for example, must be certain that every possible safety measure is taken.

Higher standards of skill are placed on persons who claim a higher level of skill or expertise. A surgeon is held to the standard of the reasonable surgeon, not to the standard of any careful member of the public. For more on this issue, see Chapter 4, "Special Business Tort Situations."

Heimler v. Calvert Caterers Limited, [1975] 56 D.L.R. (3d) 613 (Ont. C.A.)

An employee of Calvert Caterers Limited, who was involved in food preparation, was not aware that she was a typhoid carrier. Typhoid is transmitted through food that has been contaminated by the fecal matter of the carrier.

A worker in another company, whose cafeteria was supplied by Calvert, contracted typhoid after eating there. She sued Calvert.

The Court's Decision

Calvert's employee testified that she used the same standards of cleanliness at work that she used at home. The court declared that in such circumstances, "... where the thing is in itself dangerous, the care necessary approximates to, and almost becomes, an absolute liability." Despite her normal care, the employee had not washed her hands sufficiently, so both she and her employer were held liable for the injury.

Presumption of Fault

In a civil action, it is normally up to the plaintiff to prove every element of the case against the defendant. However, in some situations, the incident simply could not have happened without carelessness, and an inference is drawn that the defendant was negligent. For example, a sponge is left in a patient's stomach during a serious operation under anesthesia, and a second major operation is therefore needed. The first surgery was attended by two surgeons and three nurses, but the patient—unconscious at the time—cannot possibly know how the sponge was left in, and who was responsible for the negligence.

The fact that the sponge is found in the patient is some evidence of carelessness by the operating team. An inference can be drawn that some or all of the nurses and doctors have breached the standard of care, and the onus is on each to prove that he or she did not.

This use of circumstantial evidence has benefited consumers in product-liability cases. If a product is unsafe—there is chlorine in a beer bottle, or broken glass in a loaf of bread—the defendant must explain how this could have happened without negligence taking place.

The doctrine, which presumed fault against a defendant, was previously known as ***res ipsa loquitur*** (the facts speak for themselves), but this principle sometimes led to unfair results and so was pronounced "expired" by the Supreme Court of Canada.[5] In that case, a truck had overturned on a highway, killing the driver and the passenger. The passenger's survivors sued the driver's estate for wrongful death. There was no evidence of drinking or speeding or any other act that could be considered a breach of standard conduct. According to a strict application of *res ipsa loquitor*, the driver would be presumed at fault and his estate would have to prove that he was not negligent. Being dead, the driver could not be of much assistance.

res ipsa loquitur
the facts speak for themselves

The court felt that there was no good reason to make the driver liable in the absence of some specific evidence pointing to that fact. It said that what was required, in place of *res ipsa loquitor*, is a situation where the accident itself will provide the basis from which an inference could be drawn, as a matter of ordinary experience, that there was negligence and that the defendant was the person who was negligent.

While an overturned vehicle, without more, would not justify such an inference, presumably finding a decomposed snail in a pop bottle would be sufficient evidence. The use of the rule that presumes a breach of standard conduct by the defendant has been of much benefit to consumers, particularly in product-liability cases. It is not believed that the restatement of this rule will have much effect on any of the business situations where *res ipsa loquitor* was applied in the past, particularly respecting product liability.[6]

■ *Critical Concepts of* Circumstantial Evidence of Breach of Standard

Certain conditions must be met before this rule of circumstantial evidence will apply:

- The situation must be one that could not happen without carelessness.
- There must be some evidence that the defendant was the person at fault.

Causation

It can be difficult to decide what caused a particular incident. Sometimes, two events happen simultaneously, but one is not the cause of the other. For example, if you turned on a light switch and lightning struck the house almost immediately, the one event did not cause the other. The simple fact of an incident happening and resulting in injury does not necessarily mean that the incident caused the injury.

---

5. *Fontaine v. B.C.*, [1998] 1 S.C.R. 424.

6. Allen M. Linden, *Canadian Tort Law*, 7th ed., (Markham, Ont.: Butterworths, 2001), p. 236.

Causation is currently important in cases involving medical questions. If a person who smokes develops lung cancer, was smoking the cause, or might that individual have developed lung cancer anyway?

The Breast Implant Controversy

The issue of causation has become the significant factor in claims against the manufacturers by women who received silicone breast implants. In the United States, several women have won actions in which they alleged the implants caused a variety of symptoms. These cases were tried by U.S. juries.

Each side presented medical evidence to back up its position. The complainants had doctors testify that the implants caused their symptoms. The manufacturers had doctors testify that the implants did not cause the symptoms. The juries accepted the plaintiffs' medical evidence, found a causal connection, and awarded the women multi-million-dollar damages.

As a result, thousands of other women who had these implants in the United States and Canada made claims as a part of class actions based on the victories of these test cases. The manufacturers, fearing overwhelming awards, made a $4.2 billion settlement proposal to all claimants.

After the test-case decisions and the settlement, which was approved by the U.S. courts, several studies done in the United States and Europe by independent researchers—not experts hired by plaintiffs or defendants—concluded there was no causal connection between the breast implants and the medical symptoms.

What originally was a set of "feel good" decisions—awarding a few million dollars to women against multi-billion-dollar corporations—has become very controversial. Newspaper editorials criticize the finding of causation by the juries, and suggest that there is now a significant bias by juries against manufacturers in favour of the "little guy." The suggestion has also been made that "junk" science has begun to influence the trial system. As a result, it is difficult for large business in the United States to obtain a fair jury trial if sued by a consumer.

Many Canadian provinces have abolished the civil jury system. In those provinces where it still exists, complex cases are often taken from juries and tried by judges sitting alone.

The following case discusses whether the failure of a defendant to do something could be the cause of the plaintiff's injury, or whether that injury might have occurred in any event.

JS v. Clement,
[1995] 22 O.R. (3d) 195

Philippe Clement was a dangerous sexual offender serving a life sentence for second-degree murder. Correctional Services Canada (CSC) placed him in Beaver Creek, a minimum-security prison. This was because of a government policy of rehabilitating offenders, including sexual offenders, through a program of gradually decreasing security to help them make the transition from incarceration to community release. Beaver Creek had no fences or other physical obstacles to prevent escape. It depended upon the case-management concept of interaction with inmates to identify unusual behaviour that indicated a security risk.

Early one morning, Clement walked away from Beaver Creek, leaving a partial dummy in his bed. At 8:20 a.m., Clement was called by a corrections officer and, obviously, did not respond. The officer went to a parole hearing without alerting anyone about what had

happened. On leaving the parole hearing at 9:00 a.m., the officer sent two guards to search the cell, and the partial dummy was found. The CSC officials decided not to notify the Ontario Provincial Police (OPP) until after a formal head count, which was finished at 10:10 a.m.

At 7:50 that same morning, a neighbour reported seeing a suspicious person near another house on Winhara Road. The OPP investigated at 8:00 a.m., and patrolled the area until 8:30 a.m., but located no one.

At 10:33 a.m., Clement entered the Winhara Road home of a woman, named only as JS in order to protect her identity in the court action, assaulted her, and stole her car.

JS sued the Canada Correctional Service for her injuries.

The CSC defence was that it did not owe a duty to JS, and that she could not prove that the injury would have been prevented if it had reported Clement's escape to the police earlier than 10:00 a.m.

The Court's Decision

The court held that it was reasonably foreseeable that a known violent sexual offender in the course of his escape posed a significant risk of violence to any woman he met near the prison. A woman living about two miles from the facility, near the major highway that the escapee might use, is close at hand, and the risk to her was foreseeable. Accordingly, the CSC owed a duty of care to JS.

The court also found that the plaintiff established that, but for Beaver Creek's delay in searching Clement's cell and notifying the OPP of his absence, JS would have been warned of the danger. Clement would have remained hidden in the bush east of Winhara Road. It was highly unlikely, knowing of the police presence on Winhara Road, that he would have entered the JS home to steal the car and drive down Winhara Road. Therefore, the failure to warn the OPP caused the injury to the plaintiff.

The court held the federal government liable to compensate JS for her suffering in the amount of $90,000.

Business Law Applied

⑰ **John Linden had** his driver's licence suspended for one year because of careless driving. During the suspension he drove anyway. One day an oncoming car driven by Mary Kwan crossed over the road because Kwan was momentarily distracted. Her car hit Linden's car, causing $10,000 damage to each car.

   a) On learning of Linden's suspension, Kwan wants to sue Linden. Will she be successful? Answer the following questions to justify your conclusion.
     i)   Did Linden owe a duty to Kwan?
     ii) Did Linden breach the relevant standard of care?
     iii) Did Linden's breach, if any, cause the accident?

   b) Linden wants to sue Kwan. Will he be successful? Answer the following questions to justify your conclusion.
     i)   Did Kwan owe a duty to Linden?
     ii) Did Kwan breach the standard of care?
     iii) Did Kwan's breach, if any, cause the accident?

   c) Assuming Kwan was found liable to Linden, would Kwan have any defences?
   d) If Linden was found not to be negligent, would Linden be subject to any other penalty?
   e) What if a bee had flown into the open window of Kwan's car, stinging her and causing her to lose control of the car so that she crossed over the centre lane and crashed into Linden's car? Would Kwan be responsible for the damage to Linden's car? Which element, if any, of negligence is missing?

Damages

There are three types of damages awarded in torts:

- general damages
- aggravated damages
- punitive damages

General damages are usually awarded on the basis that an injured person should be put back in the position that he or she was in before the accident and as if the accident had not happened. They are called compensatory damages because they are to compensate or make up to the plaintiff for the loss.

aggravated damages

compensation for injuries such as distress and humiliation caused by the defendant's reprehensible conduct

Aggravated damages are compensation for injuries such as distress and humiliation caused by the defendant's reprehensible conduct. They are awarded when the defendant's high-handed and oppressive conduct has increased the plaintiff's humiliation and anxiety and so has aggravated the plaintiff's suffering. The defendant must be motivated by malice. For example, if an employer fires someone in front of other employees while making insulting comments, the employer may be made to pay aggravated damages. These damages are meant to compensate the plaintiff for hurt feelings.

Punitive damages are meant to punish the defendant for outrageous conduct. Punitive damages have been discussed under that topic in the part on contracts. Punitive damages are not easily awarded and are given only when the compensatory damages are felt to be inadequate to deter outrageous conduct.

■ *Critical Concepts of* Damages in Torts

There are three main types of damages in torts.

- General damages are to put a person back in a position as if the injury had not occurred.
- Aggravated damages are to compensate the plaintiff for aggravation of injured feelings.
- Punitive damages are to punish the defendant for outrageous conduct and to deter that conduct.

Drawing the Line

What happens if there is a chain of events, one leading to the next, each with its own consequence? The possible unlimited chain of effects has been dramatized in the theoretical "butterfly effect" by mathematicians. Is the person responsible for the first incident responsible for all the following events? The courts have decided that an individual will not have unlimited liability to an unlimited number of people. Some damages will be found too remote. A line will be drawn, but this test may end up being determined on social-policy grounds.

Consider the following example: Helen Orestion drove into a self-service gas station, and got out of her car while still smoking a cigarette. William Klippert was pumping gas into his car at the time. The fumes from this action ignited because of the cigarette, and the explosion caused the following events:

- Klippert's car blew up.
- Klippert was severely burned.
- The gas station caught fire and eventually exploded.
- The gas station was closed for two months, with the resulting loss of profits.
- Klippert's wife was watching from her home, which had a view of the gas station. She knew that her husband was stopping there for gas, and fainted when she saw the gas station explode. She had an unusual calcium deficiency causing thin bones, and she fractured her skull as a result of the fall.
- Tai Sun, a neighbour, saw Mrs. Klippert faint, and tried to revive her. In the panic, Sun fell off the porch, breaking her hip.
- An employee dragged Klippert to safety, but was severely burned on the hands in doing so.
- Glenda Carthy had her car in the gas station for servicing. It was damaged in the explosion, and she had to rent a car for two weeks while she had the damaged car repaired.
- The employees at the gas station lost two month's wages.
- The gas company that supplied gas lost the profits from sales to the gas station.

It is difficult to predict where the courts will draw the line. In the case described here they would not award damages to all of the parties who suffered loss. Instead, they would use a test such as the reasonable foreseeability, or proximate cause, test. Which incident(s) in the long list of events described do you think was (were) reasonably foreseeable? Did any of the events surprise you as not being reasonably foreseeable?

Judges admit that foreseeability is in the eye of the beholder. This means that decisions on this issue will vary because of the individual values of the judge making the decision. Judges are applying value choices, not logic, when drawing the line. At some point they feel "enough is enough." When that feeling will arrive is hard to predict.

Fortunately, most cases fit into common recurring situations or patterns, or deal with rather closely connected events so that remoteness is not an issue. There may be a tendency to make businesses responsible for a larger scope of damages in order to force them to take greater care and to insure for these losses. Thus, businesses are forced to spread the cost of the loss over the their products or services. The loss does not fall on any one individual.[7]

Business Law   Applied

⑱ A 14-year-old boy was careless when he started his father's snowmobile. The machine ran wild, and collided with a defective gas pipe, which projected above the ground. Gas escaped, leaking into a nearby school, where it exploded. The school board sued the gas company and the boy for the cost of repairing the school.

   a) What test would the court use to determine whether the boy should be responsible for the damages to the school, and with what result?
   b) Would the gas company be liable to the school?

⑲ A ship's captain had too much to drink at lunch, and let the vessel run into a bridge that carried traffic over the river. The bridge had to be closed to all traffic, and a doctor on the way to treat a patient suffering from a heart attack was delayed about one hour. The heart-attack victim died. If the doctor had not been delayed, it is very likely that the patient would have survived. The patient's wife and children want to sue the shipowner for their loss.

   a) Did the actions of the shipowner cause the death of the patient?
   b) Is causation sufficient to make the shipowner liable to the wife and children? What test would the court apply, and with what result?

Psychiatric Injury

One of the situations in which the reasonable foresight test has been applied to limit the responsibility for negligence relates to claim for psychiatric injury that occurs alone and not as a result of physical injury. This term includes all forms of mental illness. The Courts were very reluctant to give any award of damages for this type of injury and continue to be cautious in granting relief in this area.

Example. A woman witnessed an accident in which a runaway car killed her husband and several of her children. She was awarded damages for nervous shock. However, the Courts have put limits on responsibility for this type of injury relative to hypersensitive individuals as the next case shows.

---

7. Allen M. Linden, *Canadian Tort Law*, p. 343.

Mustapha v. Culligan of Canada, [2006] CanLII 41807 (ON C.A.)

In placing a bottle of Culligan Water on a dispenser in their home, Mr. and Mrs. Mustapha saw a dead fly and part of a dead fly in the bottle. Nobody drank from the container.

Mrs. Mustapha immediately vomited, had stomach pains and cramps. Mr. Mustapha felt nauseous but did not vomit but felt stomach pains. Mr. Mustapha remained obsessed with the incident. He could not get the image of the dead fly in the water out of his mind. He continually worried about the health of his family who he believed had been compromised and his trust in Culligan had been betrayed.

The Mustaphas sued for damages causing psychiatric injury.

The Trial Judge rejected the claim of Mrs. Mustapha finding that it did not rise to the level of recognized psychiatric injury. However, he found Mr. Mustapha's reaction amounted to a psychiatric illness as a result of the incident and awarded damages to him of about $337,000.00. Culligan appealed.

The Court of Appeal's Decision

The main issue on appeal was whether the test for foreseeability of damages for negligence (remoteness) that causes psychiatric illness is possible or probable.

The Court stated that the test is: whether it was reasonably foreseeable that a person of reasonable robustness and fortitude would likely suffer psychiatric injury that is probable not merely possible harm.

The Court accepted that Mr. Mustapha did in fact have the symptoms that he claimed, but they were not foreseeable on the above test. A person of reasonable robustness would not have had these reactions. The Court of Appeal overturned the Trial Judge's award and dismissed Mr. Mustapha's claim.

Not all psychiatric injury directly caused by the negligent act will be recoverable in an action based on negligence. The courts have developed principles to limit the causation factor. Foreseeability is in itself a limited factor but it is modified by reasonable. In the case that follows the courts discuss how reasonable limits accept foreseeability and applies it to a specific situation.

Thin Skull Plaintiffs

thin skull plaintiff rule

the principle that a defendant is liable for the full extent of a plaintiff's loss even where a prior weakness makes the harm more serious than it otherwise might have been

crumbling skull plaintiff rule

the principle that a defendant may be responsible for increasing a pre-existing weakness

Reasonable foreseeability eliminates the unexpected, if not bizarre, consequences of some acts. However, some consequences that might not be reasonably foreseen regularly result in relief from the courts. While no general principle exists, there are certain recurring situations that, although unforeseeable, are protected by court awards. Two of the most common are those in which people have a pre-existing medical condition—called the thin skull plaintiff rule—and those in which rescuers are injured in the course of their actions. The **thin skull plaintiff rule** is the principle that a defendant is liable for the full extent of a plaintiff's loss even where a prior weakness makes the harm more serious than it otherwise might have been. The nature of the personal injury is foreseeable, but not the extent. Both of these exceptions are illustrated in the exploding-gas-station example above.

A variation of the thin skull plaintiff rule is called the **crumbling skull plaintiff rule** (the principle that a defendant may be responsible for increasing a pre-existing weakness). For example, a person has a medical condition that will eventually result in a complete deterioration of the spine. That person is injured in a car accident and his spine is damaged. Will that person be able to establish that the accident caused injury to his spine? The courts have said yes. Where there are two causes to the injury, some weight will be given to each, but the plaintiff can still recover for the extent that the accident increased the pre-existing injury.[8]

---

8. *Athey v. Leonati*, [1996] 3 S.C.R. 458.

Physical vs Psychiatric Injuries

From the discussions above it can be seen that there is a difference between the responsibility for injury for unusual physical injury (thin skull plaintiff) and injury that is purely psychiatric in nature and which is not as a result of physical injury. For psychiatric injury claims the foresight test is strictly applied; however, for claims relating to physical injuries, an exception is made so that even unforeseen physical conditions attract liability and negligence.

■ *Business Law* Applied

⑳ **Luisa Mammolita held** a yard sale in front of her house. As she moved a table, it collapsed, and a jagged piece cut a visitor, Ambrozine Taylor, on the leg.

Taylor was treated in the emergency ward of the local hospital. The metal that had cut her was rusty, and the doctor gave her a tetanus shot. Unknown to Taylor, she suffered from a rare allergy to tetanus, and her whole leg became paralyzed for life.

    a) Was the paralysis reasonably foreseeable by Luisa Mammolita?
    b) What test would the court apply, and what would be the result?

Limits On Compensable Damage

There are further limitations on some tort damages. The topic of pure economic loss will be discussed in Chapter 6. Traditionally, the courts have been reluctant to give complete damages for pure economic loss in tort because tort law is imposed on businesses by the courts and hence businesses have little ability to reduce this legal risk. In contract law, businesses can protect themselves by contract terms such as limited warranties and disclaimers, and perhaps insure for the risk. This is less possible in tort law. Where liability is unlimited, it is usually impossible to insure.

In the case of *Winnipeg Condiminium Corporation No. 36 v. Bird Construction Co. Ltd.*,[9] a condominium corporation was allowed to recover for defects in residential housing units from the builder because the defects could cause injuries to people. The condominium-unit owners bought the units from a developer. Some owners had bought from other unit owners. Neither the unit owners nor the condominium corporation had a contract with the construction company. The court did allow the plaintiffs to recover damages to repair the condominium but only on the basis that the defect was dangerous and could cause personal injury. To date no case has gone so far as to permit damages for pure economic loss when there has been no danger of personal injury.

---

9. [1995] 1 S.C.R. 85.In the case of *Winnipeg Condominium Corporation No. 36 v. Bird Construction Co. Ltd.*,[9] a condominium corporation was allowed to recover for defects in residential housing units from the builder because the defects could cause personal injuries to people. The condominium-unit owners bought the units from a developer. Some owners had bought from other unit owners. Neither the unit owners nor the condominium corporation had a contract with the construction company. The court did allow the plaintiffs to recover damages to repair the condominium but only on the basis that the defect was dangerous and could cause personal injury. To date no case has gone so far as to permit damages for pure economic loss when there has been no danger of personal injury.

■ *Business Law* Applied

㉑ John Marjorcsak started a dealership to sell harvesters made by the Devlin-Buchanan Company. His first year was very profitable, but in the second year customers began bringing the harvesters back for repair on a regular basis. The harvesters developed a bad reputation. Sales fell off, and Marjorcsak had to close his business.

He discovered that there was a design defect in the harvesters, resulting in the repeated need for repair, and decided to sue Devlin-Buchanan Co. for loss of business. Four employees of Marjorcsak could not find work for one year after the company went out of business, and they, too, decided to sue.

   a) Did Marjorcsak have any grounds in tort law for bringing an action against Devlin-Buchanan?
   b) Could he recover damages?
   c) Would the employees likely be able to recover anything for their lost income?

Defences

A defendant can defeat a plaintiff's claim by showing that the plaintiff has failed to prove one of the elements of negligence outlined above. Additionally, there are two specific defences to a claim in negligence.

Plaintiff's Own Carelessness

contributory negligence

negligence by an injured party that helps to cause or increase (contribute) to his or her own loss or injury

Contributory negligence is negligence by an injured party that helps to cause or increase (contribute) to his or her own loss or injury. The standard of care required of a plaintiff is no different than that demanded of a defendant. In other words, one must act as a reasonable person for one's own safety as well as for the protection of others. The amount of the award will be apportioned according to the degree the incident was the plaintiff's fault. A common instance of contributory negligence is not wearing a seat belt. Contributory negligence is often a factor in auto accidents that happen at an intersection. Consider the following example.

Leonard Bruno was driving a little too fast and failed to see a stop sign until the last moment. He braked, but skidded into the intersection. Stacy Lavery was driving with the right of way, but was adjusting her radio and did not see Bruno until it was too late. She stepped on her brakes, but collided with Bruno. Both drivers were injured.

Bruno would likely be found at fault for causing the accident by running the stop sign. However, it is possible that Lavery would have been able to avoid, or at least reduce, the injury to both drivers had she braked faster. Because her inattention contributed to the severity of their injuries, Lavery's claim would be reduced by the percentage her carelessness contributed to the accident.

Assuming that the court found that the value of Lavery's injuries was $100,000, and that her negligence was 25 percent to blame for the accident, her final award would be reduced accordingly, to $75,000.

■ *Critical Concepts of* Contributory Negligence

- In the case of negligence, both parties may be at fault.
- The fact that the plaintiff was also careless will not be a complete bar to the plaintiff's claim.
- The award of damages to the plaintiff will be reduced in proportion to the plaintiff's own carelessness.

Voluntary Assumption of Risk

In some situations, the courts would consider that the injured person had consented to the risk of injury. If this happens, it is not possible to bring any action for damages. The courts therefore try whenever possible to classify the activity as contributory negligence, so that the plaintiff has at least some chance of receiving compensation.

■ *Critical Concepts of* Voluntary Assumption of Risk

- If the plaintiff has consented to the risk of injury, there is no possibility of obtaining compensation.
- The plaintiff must know and clearly appreciate the nature and character of the risks to be run.
- The plaintiff must have voluntarily incurred the risk.
- The assumption of the risk can be actual or implied by conduct.
- Patrons of a spectator sport are assumed to have consented to injuries that result from normal risks of the sport. A baseball fan, for example, accepts the possibility of being struck by a rogue ball during the game.
- Sports players are taken to consent to injuries they might suffer in the ordinary course of play.
- Car passengers who accept rides from an intoxicated driver, or from one who deliberately engages in extremely dangerous activities, are assumed to have consented to injuries which result from the driving.

Agar v. Canning, [1965] 55 W.W.R. 384 (Man. C.A.)

During a hockey game, Agar hooked Canning on the back of the neck, but left no marks. Canning retaliated by slashing Agar across the face, causing serious injury.

Agar sued Canning for the civil tort of battery. Canning pleaded two defences—provocation, and the voluntary assumption of risk by Agar.

The Court's Decision

The court found that provocation was not a defence to battery, even in a sports situation. Voluntary assumption of risk applies only to negligence, not to intentional torts such as battery.

Mr. Justice Spaston of the Manitoba Court of Appeal stated the bounds of implied consent by an athlete as follows:

Hockey necessarily involves violent bodily contact, and blows from the puck and hockey sticks. A person who engages in this sport must be assumed to accept the risk of accidental harm, and to waive any claim he would have... It would be inconsistent with this implied consent to impose a duty on a player to take care for the safety of other players... Similarly, the leave and license will include an unintentional injury resulting from one of the frequent infractions of the rules of the game... The conduct of a player in the heat of the game is instinctive and unpremeditated and should not be judged by standards suited to polite social intercourse.

But a little reflection will establish that some limit must be placed on a player's immunity from liability. Each case must be decided on its own facts, so it is difficult, if not impossible, to decide how the line is to be drawn in every circumstance. But injuries inflicted in circumstances which show a definite resolve to cause serious injury to another, even where there is provocation, and in the heat of the game, should not fall within the scope of the implied consent.

Canning was held liable.

Business Law   Applied

22 **An 18-year-old spectator** at a hockey game was injured when the puck flew over the boards and struck him in the eye. The hockey rink provided glass screens only at either end of the arena, as is customary.

    a) Would the young man be successful in claiming damages from the hockey club?

23 **A hockey player** got into a fight with a member of the opposing team. The fight took place near the boards, and a spectator was injured by one player's stick.

    a) Did the spectator have a valid claim for negligence against the player?

24 **A golfer was** injured when her partner's club slipped, hitting the first player in the face.

    a) Could the golfer claim damages from her playing partner?

25 **A skier fell** into a gully that had not been properly marked by the ski lodge. The woman broke both legs, as well as both of her skis, and was in traction for four months.

    a) Had the skier assumed the risk of injury when she started to ski down the slope?
    b) Would the court find that she had contributed to her own injury?

Vicarious Liability

vicarious liability

the responsibility of an employer to compensate for harm caused by employees in the normal course of their employment

Vicarious liability is the responsibility of an employer to compensate for harm caused by employees in the normal course of their employment. *Vicarious* means substitute or deputy, and employees are acting as deputies or agents of the employer. If the employee is at fault in normal job duties, then the employer is responsible. The reason for making employers liable, as well as the employee, is that employees often have no funds. In addition, employers are the ones who make the profit and, therefore, must bear the loss. Employers can insure for such losses.

There can be many questions surrounding what it means to do some act in the "scope of employment." Just because you have the opportunity to commit a tort while at work does not necessarily mean it's done in the scope of your employment. The law seems to be developing the concept, particularly in the realm of sexual misconduct by employees.

P.A.B. v. Curry, [1999] S.C.J. 35

A children's foundation ran residential care facilities for emotionally troubled children, ages six to 12. The workers at these facilities were to act as parents would, caring for the children both physically and emotionally. The foundation, after a background check, hired Curry to work at one of its facilities. Unknown to it, he was a pedophile, who then sexually abused a child resident in the foundation's facility. Upon discovery of the abuse, Curry was fired. The issue was whether the foundation should be vicariously liable for the tortious acts committed by Curry. It took the posi-

tion that it was not, since it had done nothing wrong in the hiring or supervision of Curry.

The Court's Decision

The key test for vicarious liability is whether there is a sufficiently close connection between the employment enterprise and the wrong committed. A mere opportunity to commit the tort in the employment setting is not enough to make the employer vicariously liable. To help determine the strength of the connection, factors which may be considered include:

    a) the opportunity that the enterprise afforded the employee to abuse his or her power

    b) the extent to which the wrongful act may have furthered the employer's aims (and hence be more likely to have been committed by the employee)

    c) the extent to which the wrongful act was related to friction, confrontation or intimacy inherent in the employer's enterprise

    d) the extent of the power conferred on the employee in relation to the victim

    e) the vulnerability of potential victims to wrongful exercise of the employee's power

In this case, the foundation was vicariously liable for Curry's misconduct. The act was not merely incidental to the employment setting, but was a product of the kind of relationship fostered by the business enterprise.

Business Law Applied

26 **You run a** small wholesaling outlet. Alf DeVry is your customer-service representative and has been a good employee for several years. One day, Alf is very angry with a particularly troublesome customer, and loses his "cool." Alf punches him, breaking his nose. The customer claims you, as his employer, are liable for this injury. Are you?

In Summation

Torts

- A tort is a civil remedy for the wrongful harm done by one person to another. The harm will either be done intentionally or unintentionally.

Intentional Torts

- Trespass. A business's premises is private property. The **occupier**—any person with a legal right to occupy premises—can prevent anyone from entering or can make someone leave upon being given notice. If the person does not leave on being given notice, that person is a trespasser, and reasonable force can be used to remove the individual. A **trespasser** is one who enters without consent or lawful right on the lands of another, or who, having entered lawfully, refuses to leave when ordered to do so by the owner.

- **False arrest** is causing a person to be arrested without reasonable cause. **False imprisonment** is unlawfully restraining or confining another person.

- Citizen's arrest. If a person is sued for false imprisonment as a result of a citizen's arrest, the citizen can establish the defence of legal authority if:
  a)   the citizen had reasonable grounds to believe the other person was committing a criminal offence, and
  b) the other person actually committed a criminal offence

- Malicious prosecution. If a person gives information to the police so that another is prosecuted but the charge is dismissed, and if that person acted out of malice and did not have proper grounds for the charge, the tort of malicious prosecution has been made out.

occupier

any person with a legal right to occupy premises

trespasser

one who enters without consent or lawful right on the lands of another, or who, having entered lawfully, refuses to leave when ordered to do so by the owner

false arrest

causing a person to be arrested without reasonable cause

false imprisonment

unlawfully restraining or confining another person

- Assault. An assault in tort law is akin to a threat of violence. The actual touching without consent with intent to do harm is a battery.

- Conversion. This is keeping or taking property of another without consent and resembles theft in criminal law.

- Defamation. Untrue statements, made to a third person about an individual's or business's reputation, and that cause harm to that individual or business, are the basis for defamation.

- There are a number of defences for defamation: innocent dissemination, truth, absolute and qualified privilege, and fair comment.

- Injurious falsehood. Slander about a business's product is called injurious falsehood. In addition to truth, the defence of qualified privilege applies.

- Intentional interference with economic interests. There are number of torts under the heading intentional interference with economic interests. These are largely unfair business practices by which one business intends to harm another. These include inducing breach of contract and inducing breach of confidentiality.

Unintentional Torts

Negligence

- Negligence is not merely carelessness, but is a technical term that requires four elements:
  a) scope of duty: was it reasonably foreseeable that the plaintiff would be injured?
  b) breach of standard of care: what would a reasonable person have done in the circumstances?
  c) causation: did the conduct cause the damage?
  d) was the damage proximate (reasonably foreseeable)?

Defences

- There are two defences to negligence:
  a) contributory negligence: the plaintiff may also have been careless and contributed to his or her loss
  b) voluntary assumption of risk: the plaintiff may have known fully of the risk of injury and consented to it

Damages

- General damages are intended to compensate the plaintiff for loss by putting that individual in the same position as if the incident had not occurred.

- Aggravated damages are to compensate the plaintiff because of high-handed conduct of the defendant that increased the injury to the plaintiff's dignity.

- Punitive damages are not compensation to the plaintiff, but punishment to the defendant for outrageous conduct that requires an additional award for deterrence.

Closing Questions

Intentional Torts

1. a) What tort is shoplifting?
   b) Some businesses are suing parents for their children's shoplifting. Are parents liable for their children's torts?
   c) Are children liable for their own torts? Does the *Young Offenders Act* protect them?
   d) If a business does not want to lay criminal charges, what other solutions in law are available for the control of shoplifting?

2. Do you think that the courts are correct in limiting a shopkeeper's right to arrest without legal liability? Should there be special rules for businesses that are vulnerable to loss by shoplifting?

3. Anne Dinnert had been general manager of Tough Attitudes, a dress manufacturer, for 10 years. She quit that job and started her own clothing plant on the other side of the city. Her former boss sent letters to Dinnert's customers saying that she had breached her employment agreement and was under criminal investigation. None of this was true.
   a) Does Dinnert have any remedy in tort law against her former employer regarding these letters? If so, what is it?

4. It was the week before Christmas, and all through the mall it was extremely busy. Frank and Marsha DeValeriote were in the mall parking lot searching for a place to park. They noticed a car leaving in the next aisle, so Frank DeValeriote jumped out of their vehicle and ran over to "stand guard" while his wife drove around to park.
   Before Mrs. DeValeriote could reach the spot, Bruno Greyson drove up and honked at Frank DeValeriote to move so that he could park. Frank DeValeriote explained that his wife was on her way, and refused to move. Greyson decided to force the issue, and two or three times moved his car quickly towards DeValeriote, stopping just short of contact. At this point DeValeriote, who had not moved, shouted some obscene words at Greyson who, infuriated, drove forward until his car touched the other man. Greyson kept moving gently forward. DeValeriote slipped, breaking an arm in the fall. Mrs. DeValeriote had driven up as this was happening, and was so upset that she dropped a fresh cup of coffee in her lap, causing third-degree burns.
   a) What is the nature of the tort or torts which have occurred in this normally quiet shopping-mall parking lot at this joyous time of year?
   b) Is provocation available as a defence for Greyson? If not, why not?

5. A young woman applied for a job. Her potential employer asked one of her previous employers for a reference, and was told that there was suspicion the young woman had been stealing during her time with the company. The woman did not get the job for which she had applied, and later learned about the statement made by her former boss. In fact, the real thief had been caught a few weeks after the young woman had left the company.
   a) Can she sue her former employer for defamation?
   b) Does that employer have any defences?

6. A man is charged with armed robbery and confesses. In order to get out of the confession he falsely alleges that the police beat him while he was held in custody, and shows bruises to prove his claim. The bruises happened as a result of a fight a few hours before he was arrested. An investigation of the alleged police brutality is held, and the officers involved are charged. At the trial of the police officers, the truth is learned, and they are acquitted.
   a) Do the police officers have a remedy against the man for making this allegation?

7. Sun Yat was scheduled to write his final chartered-accountancy exam on Friday at 11:00 a.m. On his way to the exam, he stopped at an office-supply store to pick up some extra pencils and a battery for his calculator. In a hurry, Sun Yat anxiously searched the shelves for the items he wanted, and he was watched by the store manager, who considered the young man's actions suspicious. Suddenly realizing that he was running out of time to make it to his exam, Sun Yat very quickly left the store without buying anything, and began to run through the mall.
   The store manager ran after Sun Yat and stopped him at the mall exit. Quietly, the manager asked Sun Yat to return to the store with him or he would shout so loudly that every security guard in the mall would be there within seconds. Protesting, Sun Yat attempted to get by the manager, who then grabbed him by the arm and called a security guard to help escort Sun Yat back to the store, where he was detained until the police arrived. A search of Sun Yat's briefcase revealed that he had not taken anything from the store, and the store manager promptly apologized.
   Sun Yat was 30 minutes late for the start of the exam and was not permitted to write it. As a result, he did not receive his chartered-accountancy certificate, which he had been fairly certain of obtaining, and is now required to repeat the course—which is only offered every other year. Consequently, Sun Yat lost a job opportunity that had been offered conditional upon him passing the exam and receiving his certificate. The job would have paid him $40,000 a year to start.
   a) What remedy, if any, does Sun Yat have?
   b) Does the store manager have any defence if Sun Yat decided to take him to court?

8. Marion Elliot decided to take a year off work and travel around the world. She terminated her apartment lease, put her furniture in storage, and left a very valuable oil painting she owned in the care of a friend of hers, Ilya Shostakovitch. The friend hung the painting in her living room, and during the year, received many compliments on how good it looked. Shostakovitch came to think of the painting as her own. When Elliot returned and asked for the painting back, Shostakovitch refused, saying, "Possession is nine-tenths of the law. I am very possessive."
   a) What advice would you give Elliot on how she might retrieve her painting?

9. To promote the opening of his new fast-food location, James Kirk stood on the sidewalk at lunchtime, handing out flyers and telling people about the quality of the food available from his outlet. In the course of his statements to passersby, he made the comment that, "In my opinion the cook next door wouldn't know his hand from a spatula, and further, he uses leftovers in the hamburgers." The chef/owner of the restaurant next door happened to be standing near James at the time this comment was made, and the two ended up in a heated argument. The final words were, "You can't say that about me or the food I serve! I'll see you in court."
   a) What is the nature of the statements Kirk has made?
   b) Will the outraged chef be successful in a court action, or is there a defence available to Kirk?

10. a) What is the reason that, in law, a person cannot sue another for slander without proof of actual monetary loss, but a business can sue someone for damage to the reputation of the business or its product without proof of actual loss to the business?
    b) The traditional test for the division of defamation into libel or slander has been whether it was written or spoken. What new tests might be proposed to deal with such categorizations on the Internet?

11. **Internet Research.** Do a short report after Internet research on the Crookes case. If you repeat any of the alleged defamatory comments in your report, are you liable in defamation? Is the mere fact that you are repeating comments a defence? Review all the defences discussed in the text. Do you have any defence?

Unintentional Tort—Negligence

12. Gilbert Sullivan graduated from dental school three months ago, and set up his own dental practice. In his second month of business, he failed to clean out a cavity in a patient's tooth properly before placing a filling in it. As a result, the patient required an extensive, expensive root-canal operation, and lost several days from work.
    a) What must the patient prove in order to succeed in a suit against Sullivan for the injuries suffered?
    b) Which standard must Sullivan meet?
       i) that of a recently qualified dentist?
       ii) that of a reasonable dentist?
       iii) that of the average dentist in that city?

13. Frank's Heating Company was retained to do a heating installation at 21 Flower Street. In writing up the invoice, the salesperson accidentally put down the address as 21 Power Street. Joe Jackson, an employee of Frank's Heating, went to 21 Power Street with all the necessary equipment and supplies. When there was no answer at the door, he left the pipes in front of the garage, along with a note on the door indicating he would return the next day to do the job. Mrs. Hall, the resident at 21 Power Street, arrived home in the dark, and while walking to her garage to open it, tripped over the pipes and broke her leg.
    a) Who should be responsible for Mrs. Hall's injuries?
       i) Jackson?
       ii) the salesperson?
       iii) Frank's Heating Company?
       iv) Mrs. Hall for not taking more care when she was walking?
    b) What must Mrs. Hall prove in order to win her case in court?

14. Gimbo's Circus travelled the rural areas of the province, setting up its tents in the fairgrounds attached to community centres. The circus usually stayed only two or three days before packing up and moving on to the next town.

    When they arrived at Mellenville, they found that the community-centre fairground was not large enough to accommodate the entire circus, and so they had to find another location. They discovered a large, fenced, vacant lot behind an attractive hedge of dense bushes. They asked around and found out that the owner, Virginia Smith, lived in a city a few hundred miles away and rarely came to visit the property. Deciding to seize the opportunity, Gimbo's Circus set up its tents in Smith's vacant lot.

    Smith arrived next day as the show was in progress, and began to argue with the circus manager just outside the tent entrance. She ordered the circus off her property immediately, and the argument was so loud that the performers became distracted. As a result

    - the fire-breathing juggler set fire to one of his juggling balls, which then fell among the crowd.
    - Maria Malloch, who was staying at a friend's cottage in the area for the weekend, was sitting in the crowd when the fireball landed, setting fire to her hair, as well as to the straw on the floor.
    - the crowd panicked, and stampeded out of the tent, knocking down the fence around the entrance to Smith's property, and trampling the expensive bushes she had planted.
    - Malloch was taken to hospital, where it was found she had suffered second-degree burns and would be off work for four weeks. It was also determined that she would require reconstructive surgery to her right ear as a result of the burns.
    a) List the parties you see as having been involved in causing the injuries and property damage in this incident, explaining why you have included each.
    b) List the various legal actions arising from this fact situation, and explain what must be proven.

15. A prostitute entered the Lord Alexander Hotel and solicited a client, who was a guest at the hotel. This action is a crime. While in the guest's hotel room, the woman's heel caught in the carpeting, causing her to trip and break her wrist.
    a) Does the Lord Alexander Hotel owe a duty of care to the prostitute?
    b) If so, what is that standard of care?

16. A passenger on Great Wings Airline became seriously ill from salmonella poisoning. This was traced to the eggs used in the dressing for the Caesar salad that was made specifically for that passenger because she is a vegetarian. The dressing was prepared by Food to Go, the company that does the catering for the airlines. There is no way of detecting the salmonella bacteria, which occur naturally in a small percentage of eggs. It is only possible to destroy the organisms by cooking the eggs, but Caesar salad dressing is made with raw eggs.
    a) Who would the passenger sue for the negligent preparation of her Caesar salad?
    b) Would her action be successful in court?
    c) If unsuccessful in suing for negligence, could the passenger sue under the law of contract? If so, what would be the basis for such a suit?

17. Beryl Mento was waiting for a friend in the lobby of an office building. Suddenly, the large chandelier that lit the lobby fell from the ceiling, striking her a glancing blow. Mento fell, twisted her right ankle, and suffered a fractured leg. The owners of the office tower have no idea why the chandelier fell, and insist it was the chandelier manufacturer's fault. Mento has no way of knowing whose fault the accident was, other than it certainly was not her own.
    a) What rule of law would be useful to Mento and how would it help her in proving her case? (The **rule of law** is established legal principles that treat all persons equally and that government itself obeys.)
    b) Following examination by several doctors, medical evidence indicates that normally when an ankle is twisted in this manner it would result in a sprain. Mento's leg fractured because she suffers from a calcium deficiency causing her bones to be particularly brittle. If it is proven that Mento's fracture is not reasonably foreseeable, would she be unsuccessful in winning her court action?

rule of law

established legal principles that treat all persons equally and that government itself obeys

Defences

18. Branko Dubrovnik had been unable to obtain tickets to a heavy metal rock concert by the group Blow It Out Your Head. He decided to go to the stadium anyway, to see if any last-minute tickets would be available. Because there was no opportunity for a second performance, the stadium manager decided to sell extra tickets, and allow fans into the area that stretched the first 10 feet (3 metres) in front of the speakers, right in front of the stage. Dubrovnik managed to obtain one of these tickets, and when he was told that it was directly in front of the stage and the speakers, he responded, "The louder the better, man. I wanna be taken out of my head."

    For two hours, the young man's ears were subjected to extreme high-volume sound. When he awoke the next morning, he was surprised at how quiet the house was—and then suddenly realized that he had lost his hearing. Over the next several months, his hearing returned, but he had permanently lost 60 percent of the hearing in his right ear, and 30 percent in the left. The young man's hope of becoming a classical flautist appeared to be hopeless now.

    a) If Dubrovnik were to sue the stadium management for his loss of hearing and career opportunity, would either of the defences of contributory negligence or voluntary assumption of risk apply to his action?

19. Lawrence Basset joined the local scuba club to go on a trip to the lovely tropical atoll of Pirogie. Although an experienced scuba diver, Basset had never gone cave diving and thought it would be very interesting to try. The scuba club screened a video of cave diving to the members one evening, showing a full dive, from moment of entry into the water to return aboard the dive boat. Towards the very end of the video there were a few warnings that this type of dive was not for the inexperienced or the faint of heart, but if you persevered, the wonders of the underwater world would dazzle you.

    Next day, Basset asked for a registration form for the dive, and placed his signature at the end of this document—below the clause stating that all divers going into the caves did so at their own risk, and that the club assumed no responsibility for any injuries or difficulties arising from the activity. He was asked if he understood the clause before he signed, and replied, "Oh, sure. I haven't been under water so long that I can't understand plain English."

    On the dive the next day, Basset lost sight of the guide, and became disoriented inside the system of caves, using 15 minutes of the air in his tank as he tried to find his way out. As a result, Basset exited the caves, which were at depths of 100 feet (30 metres), just as he was running out of air. His rapid ascent to the surface brought on a case of the bends, and he was hospitalized for several days. Basset's medical treatment in Perogie was very expensive, and he is now attempting to obtain compensation from the diving club. The club has told him not to hold his breath.

    a) Would the defence of voluntary assumption of risk be successful if Basset were to sue the scuba club for his injuries?

    b) Is the nature of the injuries suffered by Basset covered by the *waiver*?

    c) If the club is found to be negligent in his actions, and Basset had not worn a compass as suggested by the dive master, what would be the argument presented by the scuba club?

Special Business Tort Situations

Professional Liability

Sources of Liability

Professional liability in law, which is rapidly expanding, primarily involves three areas:

- contracts
- torts
- agency

Take the example of an elderly client who retains a lawyer to sell her house so that she can move into a retirement home. She will likely be asked to sign a retainer agreement, which outlines what the lawyer will do for her, and details of billing and payment. This is a+ contract. There is a term implied into that contract that the lawyer will act competently (that is, not negligently).

The lawyer also owes a concurrent duty (a duty existing at the same time as the one in contract) in tort, in particular, under the law of negligence. The lawyer must use the skill of a prudent or careful lawyer. Note that the standard of care required of the lawyer is the same in tort and in contract.

Additionally, the lawyer is her agent and has a fiduciary duty towards her. The client might be quite unfamiliar with current house prices and believe that her house is worth only $100,000, when in fact it is worth $300,000. The lawyer has the ethical obligation, as a person in a position of trust (a fiduciary), not to buy the house for himself at a price below its true value.

Liability in Tort

The differences between liability in tort and liability in contract are fast disappearing. Contractual liability will be covered later; this section will focus on the unique issues that occur in professional liability in negligence.

The same elements are necessary to establish negligence against a professional as to establish negligence generally:

- scope of the duty of care
- breach of the standard of care
- causation
- compensable damage

It is the first two elements, scope of the duty of care and breach of the standard of care, which entail additional issues for professional liability. Scope of the duty of care is of real concern—under the law of negligence, professionals may be liable to people whom they have not even met and who have not paid for their services, a type of client justifiably called a "phantom client."

Business Alert!

Regulation of Professionals   There are no regulations for the use of many professional names, such as psychotherapist, counsellor, financial planner, financial advisor, or even accountant (although there are restrictions on the use of names such as public accountant, chartered accountant, etc.). Anyone can use these terms without any qualifications or training.

Not only is lack of training a concern, but an unregulated professional has no particular rules that must be followed concerning money that you may hand over. If, for example, a business gives a financial planner $100,000 to invest, the planner might use it to pay expenses and then declare bankruptcy. The business would lose its $100,000. In contrast, if a business gave $100,000 to a lawyer, the lawyer must put the money in a trust account for the business (by virtue of law-society regulations). Even if the lawyer declares bankruptcy, that money does not belong to the lawyer, but is clearly set apart as belonging to the business (and would be returned to the business).

Additionally, you may wish to check whether your professional carries insurance for negligence. Real estate agents, for example, are not required to carry such insurance, although they may do so voluntarily.

■ *Critical Concepts of* Scope of the Duty

duty of care

an obligation (in torts) to take care not to injure another

- **Duty of care** is an obligation (in torts) to take care not to injure another. In contract, the liability of a professional is generally limited to persons with whom there is direct dealing (privity of contract) and to those who pay (consideration).
- In tort, the scope of liability can go beyond paying clients and beyond those who have been in direct contact with the professional.

Restricted Scope of Duty of Care

In an earlier time, the courts were hesitant to make a professional liable in negligence for giving information or advice that caused financial loss to the phantom client.

Assume a firm of engineers prepares a report for a publicly traded company. The report advises that, contrary to popular belief (which has lowered stock values), the company's land is not environmentally contaminated. A shareholder visits the company's office and picks up a copy of the report. Then this shareholder posts the report on his website. Persons all over the world buy shares in this company, based on what has appeared on the Web. Creditors also relied on this report in advancing credit to the company.

Now, assume the report proves to be false because of the negligence of the engineering firm. Would the engineers be liable to everyone who would suffer loss in this situation?

The courts have said no. In contract, the scope of obligation is severely limited by the doctrine of privity of contract. Historically, in tort, the scope of obligation has been very wide ranging (based on the test of reasonable foreseeability). That test could effectively result in unlimited liability to an unlimited class of plaintiffs in a situation like the one outlined above. Professionals could not get insurance for such broad liability exposure, and could be driven out of practice. For these reasons, the courts devised a narrower test for defining the scope of the duty of care in negligence when pure economic loss is claimed. That test is "special" or "proximate" relationship. Both terms suggest limits on the scope of liability. Note that the reasonable foreseeability test still applies to personal injury and property damage.

Consequently, if professionals are to be liable to a particular class of plaintiff, they must know that their advice will be given to that person or class of persons who will rely on their advice for a specific purpose or transaction. Actual knowledge of such a potential group or class of plaintiffs will give the professional the opportunity to decline the job if she thinks the exposure is too great, or to take extra precautions (such as an increased fee and/or insurance coverage).

■ *Critical Concepts of* Professional Liability and the Duty of Care

- ■ Under the law of negligence, professionals owe a duty to persons beyond those with whom they deal directly and to persons who may not pay for their services.
- ■ To limit this scope of duty, the test of special or proximate relationship applies to claims for pure economic loss.
- ■ To establish proximity, the plaintiff(s) must have been foreseeable, the reliance by the plaintiff(s) upon the advice given must have been reasonable, and there must not be any policy reason to restrict liability in these particular circumstances.

Hercules Managements Ltd. v. Ernst & Young, [1997] 146 D.L.R. (4th) 577 (S.C.C.)

Ernst & Young performed the yearly audit of Hercules Managements. Because of the negligence of Ernst & Young, the Hercules financial statements overstated its income and assets. Shareholders who relied on the audited statements in buying shares of Hercules sued Ernst & Young for their investment losses.

The Court's Decision

It was admitted that the auditors had breached the relevant standard of practice. So the question before the court was, does the company's auditor owe a duty of care to the shareholders?

Because this was a claim for economic loss, the test of reasonable foreseeability as set out in *Donoghue v. Stevenson* should be restricted by the test of a special or proximate relationship. The test for special relationship or proximity is a two-part test. The first part of the test has two questions:

1) Would the defendants have reasonably foreseen that the plaintiffs would rely on the financial statements? and
2) Was reliance by the plaintiffs in the particular circumstances reasonable?

If the above questions are answered yes, the second part of the test requires the court to consider policy reasons for excluding these particular plaintiffs from the scope of duty of the professionals. The court may consider whether there is a possibility of unlimited liability that would be undesirable.

Here, the plaintiffs' case gave yes answers to both questions which are part one of the test. It was reasonable for the auditors to foresee that the plaintiffs, as investors, would rely on the financial statements in making their decision whether to buy shares of Hercules Managements. It was also reasonable for these plaintiffs to rely on the financial statements, since that's what auditors do— it is within their expertise. In addition, these statements were prepared in a business context; they were not a casual statement passed off in a social occasion.

However, the plaintiffs' case could not pass part two of the test. There were policy reasons to limit the scope of an auditors' duty. If this duty was not limited, auditors would have unlimited liability.

The statements must be used only for the purpose or transaction for which they were created. This was to have them placed before the annual general meeting of shareholders. The shareholders, as a group, could then evaluate how the company was being run, assess the performance of the existing officers and directors, and

decide if they wanted them to remain in office. The statements were not prepared for shareholders to decide whether to buy more shares in the company, nor for new investors to decide on purchasing shares. (The **annual general meeting (AGM)** is the general meeting of shareholders of a corporation that is required by law to be held each year to transact certain specified business, including election of directors. A **general meeting of shareholders** is a formal meeting of shareholders at which they are able to vote on matters concerning the corporation.) The shareholder's claim for investment loss was dismissed.

annual general meeting (AGM)

the general meeting of shareholders of a corporation that is required by law to be held each year to transact certain specified business, including election of directors

general meeting of shareholders

a formal meeting of shareholders at which they are able to vote on matters concerning the corporation

Professional Standards

In professional and business situations, the reasonable-person test becomes more specific. A surgeon, for example, is measured against what a reasonable surgeon would have done in the same circumstances; a lawyer is judged by how another lawyer might have acted. A rural doctor will be held to rural, not urban, standards. The same is true for all professions and businesses.

To help decide what that particular standard should be, the courts will hear evidence from another qualified person in the same field. An act may have been a mistake or caused an injury, but that is not sufficient to constitute a breach of the standard of care. In non-legal terms, the question would be, did the professional act competently? This does not mean a professional must act perfectly. Not every act which causes injury will breach the standard of care.

Cavan v. Wilcox, [1975] 2 S.C.R. 662

Hugh Cavan developed serious pneumonia and was hospitalized. The treating physician prescribed 2 cc of biculin. Cheryl Wilcox was the nurse on duty, and read the doctor's instructions. She had been taught in nursing school that the injection could be given in either the buttocks or the deltoid muscle of the left arm. The patient objected to an injection in the buttocks, and so she gave it in the arm.

The injection was to be into the muscle, and not directly into the bloodstream. However, there is an artery in the deltoid muscle close to the surface. In injecting the drug, the nurse pierced that artery, putting the drug into Cavan's bloodstream. The next day, his arm became gangrenous. Four fingers and most of his thumb had to be amputated.

The patient sued the nurse for negligence in administering the injection.

The Court's Decision

The court held that the nurse had to explain her conduct, and show that it was in accordance with the practice of a nurse with similar experience and qualifications. The nurse had used a standard procedure that was taught in nursing schools, and accepted throughout the medical profession. Even though her act caused the injury and could have been avoided by another practice, such a standard was not the test.

As the nurse had followed the accepted and standard practice, she was found not to be negligent.

Business Law   Applied

❶ An auditor signed the financial statements of a small business that was up for sale. In them, he confirmed that the amount of an outstanding bank loan was $10,000. In fact, the loan was for $150,000.

During the auditing process, the accountant had asked the business for a letter from the bank, confirming the loan amount. He received that letter, typed on plain paper without letterhead, signed by the bank manager, stating that the loan was $10,000. Someone purchased the business, relying on the financial statements. When the error was discovered, the new owner sued the auditor for professional negligence.

The auditor defended by saying he really believed the loan amount to be $10,000, and had checked with the bank.

a) Was the fact that the auditor truly believed the loan amount to be $10,000 relevant to the question of negligence?
b) What test would the court apply to determine if the accountant met the standard of care required? How might the purchaser establish the required practice?

Exemption Clauses

Professionals are increasingly using exemption clauses as a method of protection against lawsuits. Exemption clauses may be individually worded, and so each one must be read carefully. However, in professional liability, disclaimers are normally aimed at either limiting the professional's scope of responsibility, or exempting the professional from claims for negligence. Such clauses are subject to the same principles as discussed in "Exemption or Disclaimer Clauses" in Chapter 6.

However, that part of the disclaimer which attempts to limit the scope of duty of a professional requires a closer look. Here is an example of a clause used by auditors:

> These financial statements are prepared for the use of Newcom Enterprises
> Limited. They are not to be disclosed to any other person, except with the
> consent in writing, of Bean, Counter & Crunchers.

Note that the attempt to limit the scope of duty in this disclaimer is in accord with the court-developed principles of special or proximate relationship. The auditors are saying that it is reasonable to conclude that only Newcom will utilize the statements—is in a special relationship with them—unless they give permission otherwise. These clauses are therefore very often enforced. One such clause was enforced in the case of *Hedley, Byrne & Co. Ltd. v. Heller & Partners, Ltd* [1964] A.C. 465.

Wolverine Tube (Canada) Inc. v. Noranda Metal Industries Limited, [1995] 26 O.R. (3d) 577 (Ont. C.A.)

Noranda Metal Industries retained Arthur D. Little of Canada (ADL) to prepare an environmental audit report. ADL prepared a report which said that there were no environmental problems with the property. The report contained a disclaimer to the effect that ADL would not be responsible for the report to anyone other than Noranda Metal unless ADL consented, in writing, to the circulation of the report.

ADL's report was given to Wolverine Tube (Canada) Inc., which relied on it and purchased Noranda Metal. The report was done negligently—ADL had missed some severe problems with the site. Wolverine had to incur expenses in cleaning up the site and sued ADL for them.

The Court's Decision

The court held that as ADL's report had a disclaimer clause which said that the report could not be given to anyone other than Noranda without ADL's written consent, the plaintiff's action must fail. Professionals must be permitted to curtail the scope of their risk in any project. The disclaimer clause was clear. Any business person should have read the report carefully before relying on it. Wolverine's action was dismissed.

■ *Business Law*   Applied

❷ **An engineer agreed** to design staircases for a business, and told the proprietor he would save a lot of money by using a cheaper covering on them. The business owner agreed. The contract between the business and the engineer contained an exemption clause absolving the engineer of any liability for negligent advice. The cheaper covering was not in accordance with the building-code standards because it was too slippery.

A few months after the new staircases were built, a customer slipped and injured himself. He sued the business and the engineer for the poor covering on the stairs. The business has declared bankruptcy. The engineer claims no liability on the basis of the exemption clause.

a) Does the customer have a contract with the engineer? If not, on what basis could the customer bring an action?
b) Could the engineer rely on the exemption clause?

Business Alert!   Disclaimers   Many professionals, such as lawyers, accountants, engineers, and the like, are prohibited by their professional bodies from using disclaimers that exempt them from negligence. However, many other professions, such as stockbrokers, financial advisors and planners, and real estate agents do not have such restrictions, and often have their clients sign such disclaimers.

If a disclaimer is presented to you by a professional, consider it very carefully before signing it. If it contains an exemption for negligence, you may want to shop around for another advisor who does not use such a disclaimer.

Accountants' and Auditors' Liability

The Enron scandal revealed a serious problem with accounting and auditing practices of corporations that has long been a concern of corporate-reform advocates. Enron auditors, Arthur Andersen, approved financial statements as being prepared in accordance with accepted accounting standards, where the statements were not. For the sake of simplification, one of the things Enron did was to establish a series of partnerships between itself and corporations it fully controlled, and then effectively transfer expenses (losses) to those companies, thus making Enron appear profitable when it was not. The August 2002 issue of *CFO* magazine reported results of a survey which revealed that one of six CFOs said they had been pressured to deviate from accepted accounting practices.

Accountants prepare a company's financial statements and are often its employees. **Auditors** are outside accountants ("watchdogs" over accountants) who review financial statements for a company according to accepted auditing principles to determine whether the statements are properly done. They give an opinion as to whether the financial statements have been prepared according to standard accounting practices. Auditors could be considered as a watchdogs over the accountants. As noted above, the problem is that auditors are not truly independent because they are paid by the very business whose accounting statements they are reviewing.

The concern that the watchmen may become corrupt was dramatized by the Roman satirist Juvenal (1st Century C. E.) in a poem in which a Roman family engaged a watchman to guard the chastity of their daughter. But Juvenal asked, "who will watch the watchman?"

Accountants and auditors are caught in a conflict by the very nature of their tasks. Their client is a business that may be in financial difficulty, and therefore wants its financial reports to look good in order to continue in business and be able to raise money. If the professional does not comply with the pressure to bend the rules, the client will go elsewhere, resulting in the loss of a substantial amount of money to the accounting firm. In the case of a large organization such as a bank, this includes not only a large fee but also spin-off work in receivership and bankruptcy trustee work. On the other hand, if the accountants do comply, they will be personally responsible. Where they are part of a larger firm, they may make the entire firm responsible.

The Enron auditing scandal was not new. Canada had similar situations some years ago. In investigating the causes for the failures of the Canadian Commercial Bank and the Northland Bank, Mr. Justice Esty said of the auditors who acted for the Canadian Commercial Bank:

"It is clear that management did succeed in maintaining an appearance of financial health by its tactics. The financial statements became gold fillings covering cavities in the assets and in the earnings of the bank. By conventional standards of banking and bank accounting, the bank would have been shown as short on assets and earnings."[1]

"As the line of sound and prudential banking went, so did the accounting treatment, until the bank statements and reality no longer coincided. At the end of fiscal year 1984, the auditors had become, and perhaps, unwillingly, a part of the survival tactics of the bank…"[2]

Most of the cases respecting scope of duty of responsibility for economic loss have involved auditors and accountants. The courts have been concerned that if they make auditors and accountants liable to investors/shareholders, no one could prepare or audit financial statements for public companies or even large private ones. No insurance company would give insurance to the professionals for such a large risk.

In the *Hercules Managements* case, the Supreme Court of Canada accepted the above reasoning and effectively gave auditors and accountants immunity from lawsuits for negligence. In the wake of Enron, there has been a call for serious reform of the law in order to restore investor confidence. One suggestion has been to establish an independent board of auditors to monitor the largest of public corporations. These auditors would not be paid directly by the company nor be able to accept other business from it. For discussions on corporate law reform respecting audits and other issues see www.citizenworks.org.

In the U.S. legislation was passed to attempt to make a public corporation's financial statements more reliable especially by increasing the true independence of auditors. It is commonly called Sarbanes-Oxley or for short "SOX". It is referred to by the names of the two U.S. Senators who sponsored the Act.

Auditors

outside accountants ("watchdogs" over accountants) who review financial statements for a company according to accepted auditing principles to determine whether the statements are properly done

---

1. W. Z. Esty, *Report of the Inquiry into the Collapse of the CCB and Northland Bank* (Ottawa: Ministry of Supply and Services Canada, 1984), p. 52.

2. *Ibid.*, p. 83.

Business Law Applied

❸ **Jean Schure was** the accountant for Newform Industries Inc., and regularly prepared the company's annual financial statements. An unexpected business opportunity arose, for which Newform needed new capital. The company approached a group of venture capitalists, showed its most recent financial statements, and obtained a loan of $1 million to finance the new project.

It was subsequently discovered that, because of Schure's negligence, the financial statements were incorrect. The venture-capital group wants to sue Schure, as it would not have lent the money if the statements had been accurate.

a) Would the venture-capital group be successful in suing Schure for negligence based simply on the fact that he was negligent?

b) What type of relationship would the venture-capital group have to establish in order to be successful against Schure? Would they be successful in doing so?

Fiduciary Duty

fiduciary duty

a duty of good faith imposed on a person who stands in a relation of trust to another

The term **fiduciary duty** appears several times in this book—it is one of the most important examples of duty that the courts are imposing in certain types of business transactions. It is a duty of good faith imposed on a person who stands in a relation of trust to another. As it relates to business advisors, fiduciary duty occurs in a situation where the advisor is trusted by a client who is vulnerable, and who is hurt because of reliance on the advice given. The advisor must give up its own self-interest and act solely on behalf of the vulnerable party.

The test is a flexible one, and can be used in a number of situations. It originally was applied to the traditional professions such as lawyers, doctors, or accountants, but today it is also applied to other business advisors such as stockbrokers, real estate agents, and financial advisors.

Fiduciary duty does not mean that the advisor must have additional skill. Rather, it means that there is an obligation of good faith involved in the relationship—fiduciary duty could be thought of as business ethics. In an ordinary business transaction, each party is completely entitled to try to get the best personal deal possible. In a fiduciary relationship, the advisor must always put the client's interests first. Consider the following example.

Example: Steven Ng is known to be looking for a piece of land on which to build a manufacturing plant. Georges Cartier approaches Ng and takes him to see a parcel of vacant land that is ideal for the proposed plant. Cartier agrees to sell the property to Ng for $100,000. What Ng does not know is that Cartier, a speculator, is not the owner of the property, which is currently on the market at $50,000. Cartier buys the property, then resells it to Ng, making a profit of $50,000. There is nothing wrong with this business deal.

If, however, Cartier is Ng's lawyer, he has a fiduciary duty to his client to reveal all the facts of the transaction. If he does not, and Ng finds out afterwards, he can sue Cartier for the secret profit of $50,000.

Some of the most common types of the breaches of fiduciary duty include the following.

Misuse of Confidential Information/Disclosure

This is the use of a client's confidential information for the business advisor's own advantage. For example, a business may ask a real estate agent to search for a piece of property for a new location. During the search, the real estate agent discovers a piece of property at half the market value. The agent realizes it is possible to make a much greater profit by buying the property and reselling it directly to the client.

Conflict of Interest

Conflict of interest arises when the advisor's interests are at odds with those of the client. It can be broken down into a number of categories, including:

- Secret commissions—this amounts to the equivalent of working for two employers. A stockbroker, for example, may charge a client for advice about which stocks to buy. The broker may also be getting paid by that company for selling its shares.
- Secret profit—the business advisor may have an undisclosed interest in the property that is being sold to the client, and thus receive an advantage from the transaction. For example, a stockbroker may recommend purchasing certain shares, and already own shares in the same company. By advising the client to buy the shares, the broker's own shares rise in value.
- Kickbacks—there is no end to the number of ways kickbacks can be made, nor to the number of situations in which they occur. For example, a real estate agent, acting for the buyer of a house, may recommend a certain trust company as having good mortgage rates. The trust company may be paying a kickback to the real estate agent for this recommendation. The kickback may not always come in the form of a cash payment. The agent might receive some type of preferential interest rate or other benefit, such as the right to list all the houses the trust company repossesses under mortgage power of sale proceedings. While these forms of kickback may be the subject of a fiduciary-duty action, they are very difficult for the client to detect. There are usually few regulations in these professions specific enough to catch the various ways that kickbacks can be made. Taking or receiving kickbacks is a criminal offence (secret commissions) under the Criminal Code.

Statutory Liability: Tax Fraud Rules

However, the *Income Tax Act* makes advisors who are involved in the filing of such returns (or assist in the preparation of fraudulent supporting documentation, such as financial statements) liable civilly. If an advisor gives advice that results in a false claim on an income tax return, she may be liable for up to 100 percent of the gross amount of the fraud. So, accountants who give aggressive tax advice should be cautious—if they step over the line from tax avoidance to tax evasion, they may be personally liable.

Additionally, an advisor who provides documents that can be used to support false claims (such as inaccurate financial statements) will be liable for up to 50 percent of the amount of the tax fraud. Accountants are often under pressure from businesses to provide two financial statements, one for the business and one for the government for tax purposes. If accountants acquiesce to such requests, the accountants will now be personally liable in a civil suit, where many of the criminal law protections for the accused are absent.

Occupiers' Liability

The occupier of a property, not the owner, has to take reasonable care that the property is safe. The person who has the right to supervise and control the premises—the right to permit or deny entry to other people—is the occupier. Therefore, in rented premises, the tenant is responsible. The reason for this is that some potentially unsafe conditions can happen very quickly, and need immediate attention. If the owner is absent, it is up to the person on the site to take whatever action is needed.

Few laws are simple, and those surrounding occupier's liability are no exception. Various standards of care, required for different types of persons—customers, paying customers, trespassers, and so on—were developed in earlier times, and have served to complicate a complex issue. As a result, several provinces have passed occupier's liability acts to create a uniform standard of care for lawful users. It is the standard of care required under such legislation that we examine here.

The provinces that have passed occupier's liability acts in an effort to simplify this area of law are Alberta, British Columbia, Manitoba, Nova Scotia, Ontario, P.E.I., and Saskatchewan.

Areas of Responsibility

There are generally four categories of responsibility for the safety of premises:

- physical condition of the property
- safety of customers from attacks by others
- safety of persons injured by drunks after leaving the premises
- safety of people injured as a result of the business of selling alcoholic beverages, and who injure themselves or others on the premises, or after they leave

It is up to the occupier to ensure that the premises are kept reasonably safe for lawful users in all circumstances. If a slippery substance is spilled, for example, it should be cleared up immediately. Similarly, ice and snow must be removed as soon as possible.

The occupier cannot simply put up a notice warning that a danger exists. A large sign saying, for example, "Hole in carpet, watch your step!" is no defence if a customer trips and breaks a leg because of the worn floor covering. If there is a problem, steps must be taken to correct it.

The premises must be maintained in a condition that makes them physically safe for customers. Many retail stores are designed to attract customers' attention to products, displays, and shelf advertising. The floors must be very safe. The occupier is also responsible for making sure that those customers are not likely to be at risk of harm from other users of the premises. This is particularly important in businesses where the sale of alcohol takes place.

The test to decide the care required is "what is reasonable in all the circumstances?" What are all the circumstances? Two cases, in which liability was found in one but not in the other, help illustrate the question.

Case 1

Edwards was a patron of a local bar that ran a strip show. As he was walking down an aisle, on his way to a washroom, he failed to notice a step because he was looking at the entertainment. The court held that in the circumstances—the darkened interior, and the distraction from the stage—the aisle was not reasonably safe. Edwards was held not to be guilty of contributory negligence in allowing the stripper to distract him, because the club owner intended that the entertainment be watched. The club owner was found liable (*Edwards v. Tracy Starr's Shows (Edmonton Ltd.)* (1994), 61 A.L.R. (2d) 233 (C.A.)).

Case 2

A customer in a supermarket where she shopped regularly walked through a cash-register station from the reverse end. She had parcels in her hands, and did not see the chain across the aisle. She tripped over the chain, suffering personal injuries, and sued the supermarket. The action was dismissed, as putting a chain across a cash register aisle that was not is use was a common practice, and so, in the circumstances, the premises were reasonably safe. In addition, the customer was found to be at fault for not taking reasonable care for her own safety (*Rodgers v. Sears Canada Inc.* (1992), 114 N.S.R. (2d) 162 (Ct.) Aff'd cite (N.S.C.A.)).

■ *Critical Concepts of* Occupier's Liability

- Premises must be kept reasonably safe for lawful users in all circumstances. A business must do what a careful person would do to make the property safe.
- The occupier, not the owner, is responsible for making the premises reasonably safe under all circumstances.
- The occupier must take action to make the property reasonably safe. It is not sufficient merely to post a warning of the danger.
- A lower standard of care is required for users of recreational property and trespassers.
- Safety includes not only the physical aspects of the property, but danger from other users.

Occupier's Defence   There are many occupier's liability cases against supermarkets for slip and fall accidents caused by customers falling on an astonishing number of things, from a squashed grape to food sauce. Sometimes the supermarket is held liable and sometimes not. One authority, who reviewed a large number of the cases, suggested that those supermarkets who were successful in defending themselves demonstrated two factors:

Business Alert!

a) the store had in place reasonable policies and procedures to deal with preventative safety, and
b) the policies were actually followed that day[3]

---

3. Allen M. Linden, *Canadian Tort Law*, p. 621.

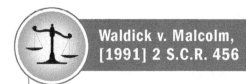

Waldick v. Malcolm, [1991] 2 S.C.R. 456

Marion and Robert Malcolm rented a farm property as shown in Figure 1. A gravel lane led from the road to the barn past the house. At the house, the lane widened to form a parking area for four cars. An ice storm had occurred four days earlier, and was followed by alternate thawing and freezing temperatures. The Malcolms had shovelled the porch and walk, but had done nothing about the parking area.

Mrs. Malcolm, a hairdresser, cut her friends' and relatives' hair without charge, and on February 7, 1989, Mr. Waldick, who was Mrs. Malcolm's brother, visited the Malcolms for a free haircut. After he arrived, Mr. Waldick went back outside to his car to get the U.S. cigarettes he had bought for his sister. On the way back to the house, he slipped and fell, severely fracturing his skull. He admitted that he had known the surface of the parking area was very slippery.

Mr. Waldick sued the owners of the property, and the Malcolms, who were the tenants and sole occupiers. Mr. Waldick later agreed to the dismissal of the action against the owners.

The Malcolms' main defence was that the custom of rural areas should be used in deciding what was a reasonable standard of care. Specifically, this meant that the parking area was not usually cleared,

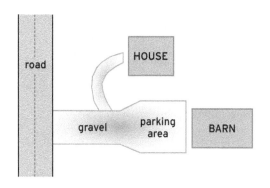

salted, or sanded after a storm. They also claimed that Mr. Waldick could see the danger and, therefore, he assumed the risk of injury. The Malcolms also alleged that he was rushing, while knowing of the slippery condition and, therefore, contributed to the accident.

The Court's Decision

The court stated that the relevant law was section 3 of the *Occupiers Liability Act*, R.S.O. 1980, c. 322, which states:

> An occupier of premises owes a duty to take such care as in all the circumstances of the case that is reasonable to see that persons entering on the premises, and property brought on the premises by those persons are reasonably safe while on the premises.

The court rejected the Malcolms' claim that a rural, not an urban, standard should be applied to this situation. The Malcolms had not presented sufficient evidence to establish such a rural custom. In any event, it was a custom that was below acceptable standards, and would not determine the standard of care in these circumstances.

It was unreasonable to do nothing to deal with the slippery conditions of the parking area close to the sidewalk. The occupiers did not have to salt or sand every inch of the parking area, only that part which they knew would likely be walked on, and which was adjoining the sidewalk.

The court rejected the defence that Mr. Waldick had voluntarily assumed the risk. The court stated that such a defence was very extreme, and should be cautiously applied. Although the Malcolms indicated that Mr. Waldick had gone outside without a coat and, therefore, was likely rushing, this was speculation and was not sufficient evidence to find contributory negligence. The Malcolms were, therefore, held solely responsible for the damages to Mr. Waldick.

Business Alert!   The Premeditated Slip and Fall   Like all laws intended to benefit a particular group of people, occupier's liability laws can be subject to abuse by someone who sees a chance to make easy money. The rise in the number of slip and fall claims has caused some businesses to install video-surveillance systems at the areas these incidents happen most often. In supermarkets, for example, these systems are often found in self-serve meat and fresh-vegetable sections. Cameras have caught individuals tearing off a piece of lettuce, dropping it on the floor, circling around the store, and returning to slip and fall on the lettuce.

An important part of the system is making sure the videotape of the incident is saved for review and possible evidence at trial. There is normally a two-year limitation period respecting slip and fall claims. Thus the retention time of a tape of a known slip and fall accident should be discussed with a legal advisor.

Municipal By-laws Regarding Ice and Snow

There are municipal by-laws requiring the occupiers of property to clear ice and snow from public sidewalks adjoining their property within a certain time limit after a snowfall—usually 24 hours. This, however, is a minimum standard, not necessarily the standard of the reasonable person which the court will apply.

The Role of Insurance   It is absolutely essential for a business to have insurance for occupier's liability. Members of the public are well informed of their rights, or become so if and when required. Thus, if there is an accident on business premises, it is very likely that there will be a claim. Insurance will not only pay for a claim, but will also pay for the cost of defending a lawsuit—a considerable expense in itself. As well, professional adjusters will be involved to help settle the claim. The insurance agent will assist in risk management and inspection of the premises to help the business in loss-prevention practices.

Business Alert!

Safety of Customers

Customers are entitled to assume that they can use business premises without the risk of being attacked by other customers. This is particularly true of places where alcohol is sold, where there must be adequate staff to control and evict troublesome customers. The following two cases describe situations in which liability for failing to control customers was claimed.

Case 1   One evening, while responding to a woman's screams for help, two campers at a government-run conservation area were severely beaten with a baseball bat by another camper. The assailant, who was well known to the conservation authority as a troublemaker, had memos on file about him relating to earlier incidents. Earlier that same evening, he had threatened one of the conservation staff, a 20-year-old recent college graduate, with a piece of firewood over allegations of theft. Nothing was done at that time by the conservation authority to evict or control this camper, and as a result the conservation authority was held to be in breach of its duty of care (*McGinty v. Cook* (1991), 2 O.R. (3d) 283 (C.A.)).

Case 2   Walker was drinking at a hotel when he was struck by another patron. The blow was sudden and unprovoked. There was no evidence that the attacker was drunk, or that he was a known troublemaker. Because it was relatively early in the day, no bouncers were on duty. The court held that the tavern was not liable because the attack was sudden and unexpected, and nothing could have been done to prevent it. The absence of bouncers at that time was not negligence because it was so early in the day (*Walker v. Friesen* (1979), 22 A.R. 431).

■ *Business Law*   Applied

❹ **Peter Giroux developed** a new food product. In order to do some market testing, he arranged with a local supermarket to set up a table inside the store, and give out free samples to customers. One customer dropped some of the food sample on the floor. Giroux was so enthusiastic about the response he was getting that he failed to notice the spill. He had thought about the possibility beforehand though, and decided it was the responsibility of the supermarket to supervise the conditions of the premises.

About five minutes later, another customer walked past, slipped on the piece of food, fell, and broke her leg.

  a) What is the name for the action the injured customer could bring against the relevant business?
  b) Did he take reasonable steps to ensure the safety of the area where his table was set up?

⑤ Bob Klee was a regular customer at a club called the Hot House. He was known to be very aggressive when drunk but, being such a regular, Hot House management tolerated his conduct. Occasionally, Klee would become involved in a fight and would be barred for a week. One night, when his favourite hockey team was eliminated from the playoffs, Klee was drinking at the Hot House and got into a fight with a fan of the other team. Klee stabbed his adversary.

a) Klee has no money, and an action against him would be worthless. Does the victim have anyone else whom he could sue for the injuries? On what basis?

b) What does the victim have to prove regarding the standard of care?

Special Responsibility for Intoxicated Persons

Businesses operating in areas where they are likely to encounter people who are intoxicated, should take this condition into account. This is particularly true if the business makes money by selling alcohol. There are two broad categories involving business responsibility to intoxicated persons. One is when an intoxicated individual sustains personal injury on the premises; the other is when he leaves the premises, and either suffers personal injury or causes harm to a stranger. Taverns that have allowed patrons to leave in a severely intoxicated condition have been liable for injuries to these patrons when they have been struck after falling in front of oncoming traffic.

Buehl v. Polar Star Enterprises, [1989] 72 O.R. (2d) 573

Dr. Frederick Buehl and some friends rented a second-floor room at a fishing lodge operated by Polar Star Enterprises. The lodge was still under construction and, although a sliding glass door was in place, the balcony had not yet been built. The door opened onto nothing, and there was a drop to a cement patio. A large table blocked access to the door.

The owner warned Dr. Buehl about the situation, and advised that the door was locked. The owner offered them another room, which they declined. Later that night, Dr. Buehl came in quite drunk, opened the door, stepped out, and fell to his death.

Mrs. Buehl sued.

The Court's Decision

The court held that Polar Star Enterprises, as occupier, had a duty to make the premises reasonably safe for its patrons. It was reasonably foreseeable that a person might want to open the door for ventilation. It was also foreseeable that a person might be drunk and, in that state, forget a warning given at a time when sober. In the circumstances, a careful business should have put a barricade across the door. This could have been done at a minimal cost, simply using a couple of two-by-fours.

Dr. Buehl was held to be liable for 65 percent contributory negligence. The fact that he was warned of the danger and agreed to use the room was held not to be a voluntary assumption of risk.

Liability to Strangers

Businesses that sell liquor to an individual who is already intoxicated may also be liable to strangers who are injured after the person served leaves the premises. This principle is included in all provincial liquor-control acts, which clearly relate to business situations involving the sale of alcohol (commercial host liability). A judge has said that a host can forcibly take keys away from an apparently intoxicated guest who is likely to drive.[4]

---

4. *Hunt v. Sutton Group Incentive Realty Inc.*, (2001) Ont. Sup. C.J. LEXIS 258. This case was sent back for a retrial because of a flaw in the charge to the jury.

The common law has not traditionally included a provision that makes hosts similarly liable. The open question now is whether a person who supplies alcohol at a private gathering could be liable to strangers for accidents caused by their intoxicated guests after leaving the party (social host liability).

A Toronto judge found parents liable for brain damage to a teenage boy who had been at their children's party. A teen guest had gotten drunk at the party and drove home with the boy as a passenger. The car went off the road and the boy was injured. The court found that the parents failed to supervise the party and prevent drunk teens from driving.[5]

Business Host Liability   If a business is holding a function where liquor is served, a number of precautions should be observed. One judge has said it is permissible to take the keys from an obviously drunk driver and such would not be theft. These precautions may not only prevent an accident but may also be a defence to any claim in negligence.

Business Alert!

- Do not have a self-serve bar. Rather have a bartender who can monitor consumption.
- Hold the event at or near a hotel and arrange for a discounted rooms.
- Have free taxi voucher available.
- Do not announce "last call."
- Stop serving alcohol one hour before the end of the event.
- Serve food at all times that alcohol is served.
- Send an office e-mail advising of the options available so that people do not have to drink and drive.

Hague v. Billings, [1989] 68 O.R. (2d) 321

Kevin Billings and two friends were out on a drinking binge. Over a 10-hour period, while driving around on some back roads, they drank 50 bottles of beer, a bottle of whisky, and smoked some marijuana.

Around 9:00 p.m., they went to a tavern called the Oasis. There, they were served one beer each, before the owner realized they were drunk and ejected them. The three men then went to the Ship 'N Shore Tavern where, during the next 90 minutes, Billings drank four beers.

Some time after Billings left the tavern, he drove his car right across the median, colliding head on with a car coming in the opposite direction. Jacqueline Hague, the driver, was killed, and her daughter was severely injured. Hague's husband sued both taverns on behalf of himself and his family. The injured daughter also sued for her loss.

The Court's Decision

At the trial, the waiter testified that he did not know Billings was drunk, but the trial judge rejected this testimony as unbelievable.

The court reaffirmed that a business which makes its profit by selling alcohol has a very heavy responsibility to its customers, and to anyone who might be injured by them. The judge stated:

> If tavern owners are allowed to sell intoxicating beverages, they must accept as a price of doing business, a duty to attempt to keep the highways free of drunk drivers. The duty to take affirmative action is for the protection of the general public. Society's view of drinking and driving is changing dramatically, and the public has a right to assume that a person or corporation making a profit from the sale of intoxicants will acknowledge and carry out this duty.

The judge found that the Oasis Tavern, by refusing to serve Billings further and ejecting him, had lived up to its responsibility. The judge indicated that it would have been better had the tavern phoned the police.

However, the court held that the Ship 'N Shore Tavern, by serving Billings, had violated its duty to members of the public, specifically, Jacqueline Hague and her daughter. They were held liable, in part, for the $1.8 million damage award made in favour of the plaintiffs.

---

5. *Prebost v. Vetter*, (2001) B.C.S.C., *Lawyers Weekly*, March 30, 2001.

■ *Critical Concepts of* Liability for Intoxicated Persons

A business that sells alcohol should take reasonable steps to:

■ make the premises safe for individuals who are drunk

■ ensure that customers do not become so intoxicated that they suffer personal injury after leaving the premises

■ ensure that customers do not become so intoxicated that they cause injury to others after leaving the premises.

■ *Business Law* Applied

❻ Sam Umali was drinking at the Bull and Bear Tavern from 6:00 p.m. until 11:00 p.m. The waiter, realizing that Umali was getting very drunk, asked if he was driving. When Umali said no, the waiter continued to serve him. Umali left and, in his drunken state, fell directly into the path of an oncoming car. He was killed instantly. Umali was survived by his wife and three infant children. The car driver was not negligent.

a) Did Umali's wife and children have the grounds for an action against the Bull and Bear Tavern for loss of a husband and father?

❼ Kathleen Oakley became very drunk while celebrating at the office Christmas party, held at the Espresso Restaurant and Tavern. When she left, her car would not start, so she flagged down a passing driver and asked for assistance to jump-start it.

Roger Vitali, who was always willing to help someone in distress, stopped and helped her. Oakley said she had cables and would attach them to her vehicle. Because of her drunken state, she attached the positive cable to the negative pole, causing the battery to explode, injuring both her and Vitali.

a) Did Oakley have grounds for an action against the Espresso Restaurant and Tavern?
b) Did Vitali have grounds for an action against the Espresso Restaurant and Tavern?

Risk Management

Think "prevention." Do a formal review with your staff of all possible risks from your operation. Also think "trial." Exaggerate any measures taken for risk prevention. If there is faulty equipment or dangerous areas, place large, simply worded notices; barriers; and the like. Designate one or more staff to be available for immediate response to changing conditions.

Keep good business records of preventive measures. A plaintiff will have a vivid memory of the events, but that day will only be another day to staff. Records of salting, sanding, snow removal, and the like will not only provide evidence that your business took all reasonable precautions but will jog your employees' memory of the day.

Make certain that your business has insurance to cover the risk and the cost of defending lawsuits.

Products Liability

Modern Business Methods

Product manufacture is one of the most important business activities in modern times. Sometimes, these products can be dangerous and seriously injure consumers. Products liability law has been developed to deal with this type of situation. It is primarily aimed at consumers and personal injuries to them, but it has more recently been extended to give some protection to businesses dealing with other businesses.

The complexity of the modern business process means that there may be many companies involved in a chain-like fashion from point of origin to the consumer.

The Supply Chain of a Modern Automobile Business

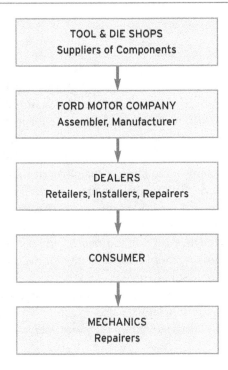

Who Is Liable?

Each of the people detailed in the supply chain could be held liable as the one who caused an injury to a consumer. Where there are many involved, they may all share equally unless they can specifically prove that they were not responsible for the defect. The lawsuit often becomes a fighting match among the businesses in the supply chain, each trying to prove its own innocence, and usually pointing a finger at the others in the process.

Who Can Sue?

This question is answered by the test of reasonable foreseeability as described in the "snail in the bottle" case, *Donoghue v. Stevenson* (see p. 85). The duty of a product supplier has been defined as being owed to everyone who might reasonably be foreseen as a user or handler of the product. This means that the supplier owes a duty not only to the purchaser, but also to someone who uses a product paid for by another, or even to a bystander injured by, for example, an exploding product. In effect, virtually anyone can sue any member of the manufacturer's supply chain.

Grounds for Suing

There are three bases for bringing an action based on products liability principles:

- defects in the manufacturing process
- negligent design
- duty to warn

Defects in the Manufacturing Process   This includes not only defects in the manufacturing process itself, but also in the testing, packaging, and distribution of goods. The courts are very strict in applying liability for such defects. You will recall the case of *Donoghue v. Stevenson* discussed earlier. A manufacturer was held liable for its bottling process. It failed to properly ensure snails did not crawl into its bottles.

Many manufacturers today are also assemblers, in the sense that some of their component parts are supplied by other companies. The car manufacturers, for example, rely heavily on components from outside sources, and make few themselves.

Manufacturers of products that are made from many parts are liable for any injuries caused by defects in the components supplied to them by other firms. This is partly because the manufacturers create consumer reliance on a brand name—usually through expensive, sophisticated advertising schemes. Another reason is the difficulty for the consumer in trying to identify, then find and sue, all the possible suppliers of components.

respondent

the party who defends on an appeal

The manufacturer can claim against the supplier of the component, so that the supplier must ultimately pay. However, the cost of bringing a claim against the supplier must be borne by the manufacturer. This is a large expense saved by the consumer, especially when the supplier is located in a foreign country.

■ *Critical Concepts of* Products Liability

- A manufacturer is liable to a consumer in tort even though there is no contract between them, if fault can be established.
- A manufacturer is liable for all component parts from outside suppliers included in its product.
- If there are several companies involved in the supply chain, and they cannot prove their innocence (that is, they cannot prove how the incident occurred), they will be held equally liable.

Farro v. Nu-Tone Electric Ltd., [1990] 68 D.L.R. (4th) 268

Mr. and Mrs. Farro purchased a ceiling fan from Nu-Tone Electric Ltd. for their second-floor bathroom. The fan was installed by a general building contractor. Shortly after installation, the fan caught fire, and the resulting blaze spread to the rest of the house, causing $60,000 in damage.

The fan was manufactured in Canada, although some parts were supplied by component manufacturers in the United States. The fan was boxed, and installed as a unit. The contractor did not open it, or tamper with it in any way in the installation. The fan was designed with a one-time fuse located in the coil of the motor, so that it would shut off if overheated. The motor was one of the parts supplied to Nu-Tone by a U.S.-based company.

The Farros claimed that the fuse must have been defective or not installed. There was an unusual problem because the fan had been taken by a fire inspector to a Canadian Standards Association (CSA) laboratory for examination. The insurance adjuster, who acted for the company that insured the Farros' home, failed to notify Nu-Tone that the Farros were planning to sue the company, and the fan was disposed of before Nu-Tone had a chance to inspect it.

Nu-Tone claimed that it lost the right to prove its innocence as required under *res ipsa loquitur*. Therefore, the case against it should fail, as the Farros could not prove that Nu-Tone was negligent. In fact, the Farros could not prove any defect in the fan. They could only speculate about possible causes.

The Lower Court's Decision

The trial judge dismissed the Farros' action because of the inability of Nu-Tone to disprove its own negligence because of the destruction of the fan.

The trial judge found as fact that:

- the fire was caused by the fan because of a defect in the overheating protection system (the one-shot fuse). He rejected Nu-Tone's claim that a fire may have started in the bathroom and damaged the fan.

- there was no evidence to support negligent design, or an inadequate system of manufacturing.
- the possible causes of the failure of the protection system were:
  a) forgetting to install the fuse
  b) installing it improperly
  c) installing a defective fuse that was observably defective
  d) installing a defective fuse that was not observably defective

The Court of Appeal's Decision

The Court of Appeal held that Nu-Tone was liable. It squarely placed the burden of disproving negligence on Nu-Tone, and held that the destruction of the fan was not a defence. Nu-Tone could not disprove its negligence, and therefore was found liable. The court stated:

It is not necessary, and it is generally impossible, for a plaintiff to adduce direct evidence that a defect existed when the manufactured product left the factory. It is mere speculation that Nu-Tone had been deprived of an opportunity to prove that they had properly installed a functioning thermal protective device. To give effect to such a speculative defence would undermine the progressive line of cases that place liability on the manufacturer of a defective product. It would be unjust to deprive the Farros of their damages by reason of the failure of the insurance adjuster to notice the **respondent** (the party who defends on an appeal) of a potential lawsuit.

Business Law Applied

⑧ Pseka Mbele, a student, ran a refreshment booth at a beach as a summer job. He sold two cans of pop to Phatima Abdi, who gave one to her boyfriend, Arief Rumi. Rumi drank it and, at the last gulp, saw the partly decayed body of a mouse at the bottom of the can. Rumi became ill, spent three weeks in a hospital, and was off work for five weeks.

   a) Does Rumi have an action against Pseka Mbele even though Rumi has no contract with Mbele?
   b) What if Mbele, a student, has no money? Is the action against Mbele advisable?
   c) On what basis in law does Rumi have an action against the manufacturer of the product?

⑨ Peter Boychuk bought a used brand-name mountain bike from a retailer, Future Cycle, with no mention of any warranties. The bike was manufactured by Euro Cycle Ltd. When Boychuk rode it out of the showroom, the bike lost a defective front wheel and Boychuk hit a pedestrian, Jean Shabot, injuring him.

   a) Does Boychuk have grounds for an action against the dealer for the cost of repair of the bicycle?
   b) Does Shabot have grounds for an action against the dealer and manufacturer of the bike for personal injury?
   c) Shabot has three potential defendants: Boychuk (owner/rider), Future Cycle (dealer), and Euro Cycle (manufacturer). He does not know who is at fault, and has no money to hire expensive experts to prove his case. What principle in products liability law will help him to prove negligence against any or all of these three possible defendants?
   d) What will the result be if the three defendants cannot determine how the accident occurred? How will liability be shared among them?

High Standard of Care

The courts are very rigorous in imposing a high standard of care on companies whose business it is to make money by supplying products to consumers. This is not only to ensure safety and to protect consumers from harm, but also to make the business bear the responsibility for paying for any injury that it causes in the process of earning profits. The cost of product-caused injuries becomes a cost of doing business. The next case is an example of the court's application of a high standard of care in the context of the duty to inspect in the manufacturing process.

Hart v. Dominion Stores Ltd. et al., [1968] 1 O.R. 775

Hart was shopping with his wife in a Dominion store in Welland, Ontario, when he was injured by a bottle of Coca-Cola that exploded in a floor display.

The Court's Decision

The court held that the bottler of a carbonated beverage owes a duty to provide containers of sufficient strength to withstand normal distribution and consumer handling. If bottles are used repeatedly, without proper inspection to determine whether they have been weakened by previous rough handling, and a bottle subsequently explodes, the bottler is liable.

Negligent Design: Duty to Warn

Negligent design of an object is also a basis for breach of the standard of care required by the law of negligence. A design defect is usually more damaging than a manufacturing process defect. Defects of design in a product likely affect every product. A manufacturing process defect, such as a snail in a bottle, may only affect a single user.

A manufacturer is under a heavy obligation to ensure that a product is designed safely to the current state of the art standards, and to warn if there is danger of any use of the product.

Warnings of any danger must be clearly communicated.

Example: A particular house paint was highly inflammable because of its unique composition such that even opening it in a basement where there was a lit pilot light in a furnace was a danger. The user did open a can in his basement and the resulting explosion destroyed his house.

Although there were three labels on the can warning of high inflammability, and the user was an engineer, the Court found that the warnings were not adequate in the circumstances and found the manufacturer liable for the damage (*Lambert et al. v. Lastoplex Chemicals Company Ltd. et al.*, [1972] S.C.R. 569).

One of the most notorious cases in legal lore is that of the U.S. case of an elderly woman who spilled a hot cup of coffee on herself while going through a McDonald's drive-through. She sued McDonald's for failure to warn her that the coffee was hot enough to burn. A jury awarded her $7,000,000.00 at first instance. You might check labels on coffee cups at places where you purchase take-out coffee and see if there is a warning on the label. Do you think it is adequate in that any purchaser would notice it?

Walford v. Jacuzi Canada Ltd., [2007] ONCA 729 (CanLII) (leave to appeal denied S.C.C. 2008-04-03)

At the age of 15¾ years Correna Walford went down a used slide her parents had just installed beside their 4 foot deep backyard pool. She went down on her knees, hit her chin on the bottom of the pool breaking her neck, causing her to float to the surface an instant quadriplegic.

She sued, through her parents as litigation guardians, a number of people who had anything to do with supplying the slide to her parents including the private seller; a retailer, Pioneer Pools, who sold parts for the installation; the manufacturer of the pool, and the manufacturer of the slide (Jacuzi Canada Ltd.).

The Walfords had wanted a slide for their backyard pool. Correna's mother was concerned as to the safety for use with a 4 foot shallow pool. New ones were too expensive, so upon seeing an ad in a newspaper for a used one she bought it and then brought the slide to Pioneer Pools, which company she had been dealing with for two years for pool supplies. She asked employees if the slide could be used in a four foot pool safely and they said there would be no problem. Mrs. Walford gave very strict instructions to all the children about the use of the pool and the slide including going down "only feet first".

However, Correna had gone down slides at Canada's Wonderland on her knees and thought that would be fun. On her second use of the slide she did this. When she hit the bottom she went unconscious and floated to the surface, now a quadriplegic.

The Trial Judge dismissed the action against all of the Defendants. Correna appealed only against Pioneer Pools.

The Court of Appeal's Decision

This Court held that there was a sufficiently close relationship between Pioneer Pools and Mrs. Walford because she had relied on its advice for over two previous years including specific advice with respect to the installation of the slide in question.

The Court held that all manufacturers and suppliers are required to warn all those who may reasonably be affected by potentially dangerous products. This includes not only the original purchaser but any users.

The duty to warn of potentially dangerous products applies only to dangers that are not obvious. The danger of going down the slide on a child's knees was not obvious.

The Court held that the only reference for a standard was the U.S. Consumer Product Safety standard regarding back yard swimming pools. Those standards stated that with a pool four feet or less there was a danger of catastrophic injury if the user did not go down feet first.

The Court reversed the Trial Judge's decision and found Pioneer Pools liable to pay damages of $5,000,000.00 to Correna and her family.

Critical Concepts of Duty to Warn

- Manufacturers must warn customers about dangerous properties of their product.
- If a product can be produced in a safer way, that must be done.
- Manufacturers cannot use the cheaper way of making their product, and rely on warning customers of the danger.
- Manufacturers must also warn of dangers discovered after the product has been sold and distributed.
- The warning must be reasonably communicated.
- The warning should be printed on the label, clearly noticeable, and must describe the specific danger.

Business Law Applied

⑩ **Mr. and Mrs.** Saddlemeyer engaged Bill's Home Renovation Company to refinish the floors on the main floor of their house by sanding and sealing them. The Saddlemeyers planned to be away for the day to avoid the mess, and left a key with Bill telling him to leave the windows open and drop off the key with a neighbour when finished.

Bill purchased a sealer, which displayed the following warning on the label, from Renault Paints Ltd.:

DANGER—FLAMMABLE

Do not smoke. Adequate ventilation to the outside must be provided. All spark-producing devices and open flames (furnaces, pilot lights, spark-producing switches, etc.) must be eliminated in or near working areas. Avoid prolonged breathing of vapours. Wear vapour cartridge mask. Replace cartridge before saturation.

The kitchen was on the main floor of the house, but was not part of the contract work. There was a gas stove in the kitchen, with a pilot light.

After finishing their work, Bill and his helper discussed a recent news article about a liability that had been put on contractors for break-ins when they had left windows open after their work. Bill closed the windows, left the key with the neighbours, and went home. Vapour from the sealer reacted with the pilot light and exploded. Fire damaged most of the main floor of the house, costing $100,000 to repair.

a) What is the liability of the manufacturer, Renault Paints Ltd.? Was the warning on the cans sufficient?
b) Are there any acts from which an inference of negligence can be drawn against the manufacturer in this case?
c) What is the liability of Bill's Home Renovation Company? On what basis could it be held responsible? What if Bill is a fly-by-night contractor and has no insurance? What will be the worth of a judgment against it?

Defences

Defences in the law of products liability are generally the same as in the law of negligence.

Causation

A defendant who can prove it was not careless will be excused from liability. One of the possible methods of doing this is showing that another business in the chain must have been responsible.

In one case, a ketchup manufacturer was sued over a bottle of ketchup that had contained maggots, and made the plaintiff ill. The manufacturer proved that flies and fly eggs cannot live in ketchup during the manufacturing process, because the substance is bottled at a temperature near boiling. As soon as they are filled, the bottles are sealed. The manufacturer also pointed out that the maggots in this case were very young, and must have entered the bottle after it had left the manufacturing plant—probably in the retailer's warehouse. The most likely explanation was that someone had opened the bottle, used a little of the ketchup, then recapped it. The court agreed that the manufacturer had not been negligent, and held the caterer who purchased and sold the bottle responsible.

Contributory Negligence

The plaintiff can be held partially responsible, just as in the law of negligence. It may be that the defect in the product was obvious and the plaintiff should have inspected it. The plaintiff may not have observed warnings or instructions on use.

Voluntary Assumption of Risk

The circumstances of the case may be such that the plaintiff received notice of the defect and should not have used the product. A plaintiff who continued to drink Coca-Cola after realizing that it had a disagreeable odour and taste was denied any recovery.

Nuisance

Like many terms nuisance has a meaning in law that is not necessarily the same as its meaning on the street. The tort of nuisance involves a use by one land owner that substantially and unreasonably interferes with another occupier's ordinary use of the land, but does not include every interfernce.

In day-to-day living because of close contact property owners may often disturb or inconvenience a neighbour. Minimal annoyances do not amount to the tort of nuisance. It is only when the disruptions of the enjoyment of the property are substantial do they become legally unacceptable. Thus the key to understanding when the harm reaches the level that it becomes the tort of nuisance is in the adjectives "substantial and unreasonable". Determining when the interference is substantial and unreasonable is largely a matter of judgment. While there will be some clear areas, there will also be some gray areas where, as it is said, "reasonable people will reasonably disagree".

Unlike many torts it is not the conduct that is the object of the inquiry, but the degree of harm. Individual circumstances will have a significant weight in determining the degree of harm. For example, a rooster crowing every morning at 5:00 a.m. may not be unreasonable in the country but would be in the city. Smoke from an industrial smokestack that blows onto adjoining property causing paint to peel on houses would be a nuisance; however, smoke from a neighbour's occasional Sunday bar-b-q would likely not.

While the tort of trespass involves intrusion on property by a person or an object, nuisance can include intangibles such as smoke or noise. It has been called an early developed common law environmental protection remedy.

The restriction imposed by a nuisance prevent one owner from interfering with the use of the adjoining lands. It is no defence that the offending owner may have been carrying on the business before there was any use of the adjoining land.

The courts have found that temporary construction and demolition would usually not be a nuisance. However, if a cheaper method of construction was used which significantly delayed the construction, there might be a cause of action in nuisance.

Picketing

Picketing by dissatisfied employees, done peacefully, near a business' property disturbs the business' use of its property but is justified on the basis that the employees have the right to inform the public and is not considered a nuisance in law. However, focused or secondary picketing directed at employees' homes, restaurants where employees eat, or hotels or motels where they stay, is an invasion of privacy which is an integral part of the use of land, especially residential land.

Example: Anti-abortionists picketed the houses of doctors who performed abortions. The Court found that the purpose was not to inform the public but to intimidate the occupants of the houses. The right to residential privacy was an important element of the use of residential land (*AJ of Ontario v. Dielmann et al,* (1995), 20 O.R. 3d 229 (Ont.) G.D.).

■ *Critical Concepts of* Nuisance

- Nuisance involves actions on one person's land that cause harm to another neighbour's use of the land or property on the land.
- Not every interference with another's land use will be nuisance; the harm must be substantial and unreasonable.
- It is not the type of conduct by the defendant landowner that establishes nuisance, but the level of harm that the conduct causes.

Sammut v. Islington Golf Club, Ltd., [2005] 16 C.E.L.R. (3d) 66 (Ont.) S.C.J.

The Islington Golf Club ("IGC") had been operating its golf course since 1923. In 2000 developers obtained approval from the Ontario Municipal Board ("OMB") to build houses on the east side of the golf course.

Golf ball spray is a well-known problem for land use adjoining a golf club. The IGC opposed the granting of building permits before the OMB, but the OMB authorized development with a narrow "no touch" zone between the course and any structures on the new development.

The Sammut's house was built close to the line of the no touch zone. Golf balls from the third tee from the golf course frequently hit the house causing damage. The Sammut's could not use that part of the lawn for fear of being hit.

The Sammuts sued IGC seeking damages and a permanent injunction stopping the use of that part of the golf course by golfers.

The Court's Decision

The court held that the Sammuts had made a case for nuisance. The conduct of IGC, while reasonable on its own property, unreasonably and significantly interfered with the use of adjoining land.

It was not a defence that the golf course came there first. An owner could not effectively make adjoining land unusable by starting harmful conduct next to vacant land.

A court awarded the Sammuts damages for the cost of repairs and for inconvenience and annoyance. It also ordered an injunction prohibiting IGC from using that part of the golf course that might result in golf balls being hit on the Sammuts' property. However, the court delayed the enforcement of the injunction for 2 weeks to allow IGC to implement some solution such as screening, landscaping or repositioning the tee or such.

Business Law Applied

Farang Afnam bought a new long distance transport truck from Honest Al's Trucks. The truck manufactured by a large international corporation, Vareva, Inc. It came with a two year warranty. In the first twelve months it broke down fifteen times always at distances hundreds of miles from home.

Afnam contacted a lawyer who advises that there is no lemon law in his province and a battle in a court of law would be too expensive. Afnam's wife, Nadia, decides to go to the court of public opinion. She:

a) Pickets in front of the dealership and hands out flyers telling of the defects in the truck,
b) Puts up a YouTube video telling of the effect of the breakdowns on her family,
c) Goes to Honest Al's home and paces up and down on the sidewalk holding signs complaining about the quality of the truck.

Honest Al wants an injunction to stop her on the basis of nuisance. Will he be successful?

High-Risk Activities

Risk Management

One of the goals of tort law is accident prevention through making the action that caused the injury bear the cost. This is why the tort law of negligence is based on fault. If a business knows that it is going to have to pay a serious amount of money as a result of injuries, it is far more likely to take preventive measures to stop those injuries from occurring. From the business point of view this is seen as being "at risk," that is, at risk of a lawsuit.

Organizations who are at risk now quite regularly form risk-management boards or committees to deal with reducing the problem. These organizations range from standard businesses to government agencies, schools, and so on. Some of the basic concepts of risk management relevant to the sports area are:

- educate all people who have responsibility for the activities in the types of accidents that can occur
- make the participants aware of the dangers of disobeying the rules and taking chances
- make certain that there are properly qualified and trained supervisory staff
- have policies about the supervision, installation, and maintenance of equipment and premises
- have well-rehearsed and clear procedures on what to do when an accident happens, particularly on how to obtain medical help
- ensure that there is proper and adequate insurance coverage
- use exemption clauses where possible, not only to limit liability, but also to give notice to the participants of the dangers of the activities

Waivers

waiver

an agreement not to proceed with the performance of a contract or some term of it

The use of a written waiver is becoming more and more common, especially in sports activities run by schools and athletic associations. A **waiver** is an agreement not to proceed with the performance of a contract or some term of it. It is a type of exemption clause. There are some limitations on these waivers. They are also of doubtful value if signed by a minor, or the parent of a minor. The best use of a waiver form is perhaps not to attempt to limit liability, but to give notice to participants, and their parents if the participant is a minor, of the dangers of the activity. If the document would not normally be considered to contain an exemption clause, the clause must be brought to the notice of the customer before, or at the time of, making the agreement.

There can be no misrepresentation about the enforceability of the clause, and the wording of it will be strictly interpreted against the drafter.

■ *Critical Concepts of* Children

- Minors are liable in tort, though not generally liable in contract for non-necessities.
- Parents are not responsible for their children's torts.
- The standard of care to be applied is whether the child exercised the care expected from a child of a like age, intelligence, and experience.
- Parents may be liable for failing to exercise proper supervision and control.

Waivers in High-risk Activities

Risky activities such as snowboarding and white-water rafting are increasing in popularity. Businesses that run these activities are at high risk for lawsuits in tort. These businesses often use a waiver, an exemption or disclaimer clause to reduce or eliminate responsibility for injury. All of the possible defences to exemption clauses covered in Chapter 6 can be raised in these tort situations. You may recall that the main grounds for avoiding exemption clauses were inadequate notice, misrepresentation as to the legal effect of the clause, and lack of consideration.

While exemption clauses are not usually upheld in consumer purchase matters, they are often upheld where a consumer elects to participate in a high-risk activity. There is a difference in how the exemption clause presents itself in these two situations.

In consumer purchases, the exemption clause is often hidden in the fine print of a long standard form contract. The clause attempts to negate the business's responsibility for loss caused by the products or services—which goes against principles developed by the courts or set out in legislation. The consumer does not truly agree to the contents of the exemption clause, and in fact is often not aware of its existence until there is a problem.

However, in risky sports activities, disclaimers are usually presented on a single page, and not buried in the body of a longer document. As well, even though the clause attempts to negate the business's responsibility for loss caused by participation in the activity, this fits with the court-developed principle that you can voluntarily assume the risk of injury if you wish (in advance of participation in that activity).

IN THE BLEACHERS

For a risk to be assumed, however, the risk must be clear to the customer. If it is not, the clause will be of no effect. For example, an overweight child of 10 bought a ticket to an amusement park. On the back of the ticket and on a sign at the ticket booth there was an exemption clause saying that the amusement park would not be responsible for injury resulting from the use of the equipment. When the child used a tall slide, she broke her ankle on impact at the bottom. She sued and the amusement park set up the disclaimer as a defence. It turned out that the pad at the bottom of the slide was not sufficiently thick for a person of her weight. Thus the court found that the risk was not clear, because the use of the inadequate pad was not clear (*McCarthy v. Royal American Shows Inc.* (1967), 67 D.L.R. (2d) 548 (Man. C.A.)).

It may also be that disclaimers in amusement-park situations will not be as readily enforced because the public generally assumes that all rides in such parks are safe. In contrast, the risk in activities such as white-water rafting is apparent.

executors

the personal representatives of a deceased person named in his or her will

Dyck v. Manitoba Snowmobile Association and Wood, [1982] 4 W.W.R. 318 (Man. C.A.)

The plaintiff, Dyck, was 19 years old, and entered a snowmobile race at Beausejour, Manitoba. Before beginning the race, he signed a form entitled Indemnifying Release. It read as follows:

I have read the supplementary regulations issued for this event and agree to be bound by them. In consideration of acceptance of this entry or my being permitted to take part in this event, I agree to save harmless and keep indemnified the M.S.A. and/or M.S.A., its organizers, and their respective agents, officials, servants and representatives from and against all claims, actions, or damage to may person or property, howsoever caused, arising out of or in connection with my taking part in this event and not withstanding that the same may have been contributed to or occasioned by the negligence of the said bodies, or any of them, their agents, officials, servants or representatives. It is understood and agreed that this Agreement is to be binding on myself, my heirs, **executors** [the personal representatives of a deceased person named in his or her will] and assigns.

The defendant, Wood, was a volunteer who was acting as a flag man. When the first snowmobile came into view for the final lap of the race, Wood stepped about one-third of the way onto the track to show the checkered flag. The second snowmobile passed behind Wood, and so he stepped further into the middle of the track, right into the path of the plaintiff's snowmobile. The plaintiff swerved, but hit Wood, though barely injuring him. The plaintiff's snowmobile went out of control and hit a retaining wall. He was injured, with permanent disabilities assessed by the judge at $90,000.

The snowmobile association and Wood set up the disclaimer as a defence to the plaintiff's claim.

The plaintiff claimed that he did not have notice of the disclaimer, and relied on recent case law in which consumers had defeated disclaimer clauses because they had not been brought to their attention.

The Court's Decision

The court found that the plaintiff had not only read the disclaimer clause, which was on a one-page document, but when he signed it he knew it related to the responsibility of the snowmobile association in the event of an accident.

Wood was entitled to the benefit of the disclaimer clause, as it specifically extended the release to agents of the association. The snowmobile association was acting as Wood's agent in requiring prospective race participants to complete the waiver of liability.

Automobiles

The owner of a car is made liable by provincial statutes, usually called highway traffic acts, for injury done by that vehicle if it is given on consent. If the driver has the car with the owner's agreement and permits another driver to drive, the owner is liable. If, for example, Carol borrowed her father's car and permitted her boyfriend to drive it, her father is liable should the young man be involved in an accident caused by his own carelessness.

In some provinces, the driver is only liable to a guest passenger if the driver was guilty of gross negligence. This requirement has recently been abolished in British Columbia, Ontario, and Quebec. People who ride as passengers in cars as members of drinking binges may be denied any recovery under the voluntary assumption of risk doctrine. Passengers are found to consent to the risk if they encouraged or participated in the drinking. Passengers not found to have consented are usually younger females with older male drivers, dependent on the driver for a ride home.

In Summation

Professional Liability

- The liability of professionals can be based on a breach of contract, a breach of the standard of care required in the law of negligence, or the breach of the duty as an agent (which could include a breach of fiduciary duty).

- A professional may be found liable to a plaintiff even in the absence of a direct contractual relationship between the two.

- Professionals may include exemption clauses in their contracts for service, in an effort to avoid liability.

- A breach of fiduciary duty can be committed by a misuse of confidential information or by acting contrary to the client's interests.

Occupier's Liability

- The occupier of property or premises is the person who exercises control over it. As the party in control of the premises, the occupier is responsible for the physical condition of the property, and the safety of individuals who enter it.

- If the sale of alcohol is part of the business activity on the premises, the responsibility of the occupier extends beyond the door to ensure the safety of intoxicated customers, as well as individuals who are injured by those customers after they leave the premises.

Products Liability

- The aim of tort law is to compensate for injuries caused to the property or person of an individual or business. The liability of a manufacturer for its products has been extended considerably, creating a relationship in tort law with the ultimate consumers of the product, as well as an accompanying duty not to injure.

- The grounds for a tort action for products liability are varied, and include defects in the manufacturing process, failure to warn of inherent dangers from use of the product, and negligent design.

- Defences, such as voluntary assumption of risk, and contributory negligence, are available to the product's manufacturer in defending against liability for the injuries caused.

High-Risk Activities

- A risk of injury is often associated with participation in a sporting event or game. The standard of care to be applied in determining the liability, if any, of the organizers of the sport depends on a number of factors. These include the danger inherent in the particular activity, whether instructions or qualifications for participation are required, and the level of supervision necessary.

Children

- Parents may be found liable for not exercising proper supervision and control over their children's actions that cause injuries to another person, but are not liable for their children's torts.

Closing Questions

Professional Liability

1. Dilip Singh was the accountant for Lyon Steel Ltd. whose regular bank was the Industrial Bank of York. Singh was responsible for preparing the company's annual financial statements. Unknown to Singh, Lyon wanted to raise money for a new project, and approached the Commercial Credit Bank, which relied on the financial statements prepared by Singh in advancing a loan of $150,000. Industrial Bank, where Lyon had an operating line of credit, increased the line of credit to $60,000 after receiving the financial statements. Because Singh had not checked to determine if several of the premises operated by Lyon were owned or leased, the financial statements were wrong. Lyon showed a profit when, in fact, it was operating at a loss. The company went bankrupt, and both banks want to sue Singh for their losses.
   a) Did Singh owe a duty to the Industrial Bank?
   b) Did Singh owe a duty to the Commercial Credit Bank?
   c) Was it reasonably foreseeable that Lyon Steel might raise money for a specific project? Is that the test to determine whether Singh owed a duty to the Commercial Credit Bank?
   d) Did Singh have actual knowledge of either or both of the loans made by the Industrial Bank or the Commercial Credit Bank?
   e) Explain whether it would have made a difference if Singh had placed the following words at the end of the financial statements: "These financial statements are prepared for the use of Lyon Steel Ltd. exclusively."

2. Salton Schnee had bought a rundown ski resort and was now drawing up a business plan for its renovation. In trying to decide whether to invest substantial funds in upgrading the ski lifts from T-bars to chair lifts, he sought advice from the local Chamber of Commerce. Jennifer Schnarr, the representative with whom he met at the Chamber of Commerce, told Schnee that the chamber's tourism statistics indicated that, given past winter traffic patterns, the installation of chair lifts would increase the resort's business by at least 40 percent.
   Based on this information, Schnee placed an order for $300,000 worth of chair-lift equipment. The equipment was installed over the summer, and the ski season began early in October that year. Schnee's happy anticipation quickly turned to anger when his eagerly awaited financial statement showed an increase in business of only 19 percent, during one of the best ski seasons for the area in the past six years.
   a) Do Schnarr and/or the local Chamber of Commerce have a legal problem?
   b) What would Schnee need to prove to obtain a legal remedy?

3. Andy Senza is a promoter and financial advisor in the film industry. While attending an opening night party for the most recent film on which he did the promotion, Senza had a conversation with Gina West. She is a legal secretary who had attended the screening of the new film, and had been invited to the opening-night party by a friend of hers. Impressed by Senza's knowledge of the film industry, West asked him for information about investment opportunities in the industry. As an example, he told her about a film company named Stellar Productions Inc., which was about to begin production on what he anticipated to be a blockbuster hit for release the next summer. What Senza didn't tell West is that he is a 60 percent shareholder in Stellar Productions.
   The next day, West looked up Stellar Productions in the telephone book, and ultimately invested $30,000 in the company's latest project. Because of several technical problems and a leading actor with an attitude, the project eventually fell apart and the investors lost their money. West has since learned that Senza is the majority shareholder of Stellar Productions, and feels that she was manipulated into investing in a failing project.
   a) Advise Gina West, with reasons, whether she has any legal remedy concerning Senza's advice.
   At the same opening-night party attended by West, Jorge Jensen, who had invested in the last film promoted by Senza, asked Senza for financial advice on what to do with the profits expected to be generated by the box-office receipts from the current film. Senza suggested Jensen invest his profits in the same project he had described to West earlier in the evening. Jensen has also recently found out that Senza is the majority shareholder of Stellar Productions.

b) Describe the nature of the duty, if any, owed by Andy Senza to Jorge Jensen.

c) What legal remedies are available to Jensen in this situation?

4. Salim Nehru was a stockbroker who specialized in managing registered retirement savings plans (RRSPs). Jason Walmsley, a single father in his mid-40s with a 3-year-old daughter, had hired Nehru to advise him and to manage his RRSP investments. Walmsley was inexperienced with the stock market, and explained his personal circumstances to Nehru. He told Nehru that he wished to have no more than 10 percent of his portfolio held in medium-risk shares, and that the rest was to be kept in a form that could easily be sold, in case Walmsley needed quick cash.

   Over the course of a year and a half, Nehru made several investment recommendations to Walmsley, who followed his advice. As a result, the value of Walmsley's RRSP portfolio fell from $100,000 to $45,000. When Walmsley realized that he had lost over 50 percent of the value of his RRSP, he investigated the nature of the shares held in it, and discovered to his horror that 80 percent were high-risk or speculative shares. When he confronted Nehru with his discovery, Nehru replied, "We all have good years and bad years—you have to keep an eye on the long term."

   "Exactly what I intend to do," replied Walmsley.

   a) What remedy does Walmsley have?

   b) What would be the basis for his legal action in court against Nehru?

5. Several friends got together and decided to start an investment club, which they named the Pub Night Investment Club. The club members would meet on the third Thursday of every month at a local pub to discuss investment strategies. They decided to hire an accountant to advise them on financial matters, and he agreed to provide them with monthly financial statements and a sheet with investment recommendations on the Monday before their club meeting, so that they could make decisions early before too much beer had flowed across the table.

   One club member, Georgia Smith, decided to share the newsletter on the Internet with a friend who lived in another city. She was unaware that other people had begun to monitor the newsletter which she sent to her friend. At one of the meetings, Smith mentioned to the accountant that she had sent his newsletter over the Internet to her friend in Riverbridge, and the accountant responded that he was flattered she thought so much of his newsletter that she would pass it on. In one of the newsletters, the accountant made a strong recommendation—without having properly investigated the company—and the investment club lost 90 percent of its funds. Several people—non-members of the investment club—began to telephone the accountant, indicating that they too had lost considerable amounts of money as a result of following his newsletter advice. The total losses came to $125,000.

   a) With full reasons, advise the accountant as to the nature and extent of his liability for the negligent advice given by him in the newsletter.

   b) Would it make any difference to your answer if Smith, instead of scanning the newsletter into her computer, had retyped it?

6. Jane Lee saw a note on the personal website of an experienced and well-known investor named Wallace Buffer. The note said Laurentian Gold Mines had just discovered a rich deposit of gold at a drill site in northern Saskatchewan, but that the company was keeping the find secret for a few days.

   Jane immediately called her discount broker and ordered $10,000 worth of shares in Laurentian. Unfortunately, Buffer's information was merely an unfounded rumour, and Jane lost her money. She now wants to sue Buffer.

   a) Is there a contract between Jane and Buffer? If not, in what area of law might Jane find a remedy?

   b) What legal principles apply to determine if there is a legal relationship (duty) between Jane and Buffer? Will Jane be successful in her lawsuit?

Occupier's Liability

7. Ann Rai took her husband's gasoline-soaked clothes to Koziar's Laundromat to wash. The fumes were ignited by electricity in the washing-machine motor and exploded, causing Rai first-degree burns. Koziar rents the store from Cadillac Management Limited. Rae sues Koziar for suffering caused by the burns.

   a) Koziar pleads as his first defence that Rai sued the wrong person because he is not the owner. Would this be a successful defence?

   b) Does Koziar have any successful defences?

8. John Stitt tripped over a paving brick that jutted two inches above the surface of a parking lot, breaking his arm. He sued the plaza owner. The owner says: "If it is big enough to trip over, it is big enough to see."
   a) What is the legal term for the defence that the plaza owner is asserting?
   b) What conduct by the owner might help to defend itself?

Products Liability

9. Yvon Marchand was one of several passengers severely injured when an aircraft experienced a hard landing and collapsed on the runway while still travelling at a high speed. Examination of the plane determined that the cause of the accident had been a bolt in the aileron (the wing flap) which had come loose during the flight, and had jammed the right aileron—making it useless for the landing procedure.

   The aircraft had been manufactured by the Luft Aircraft Company in Canada. That firm had bought the aileron assembly from Nowsky Manufacturing in Yugoslavia. Luft has denied any responsibility, and told Marchand to pursue Nowsky Manufacturing for any injuries she suffered. Nowsky, with no assets in Canada, has sent a reply that, as far as it is aware, the aileron assembly was in perfect condition when it left the manufacturing plant. They suggested that it had been damaged either in shipping or in final assembly at Luft's premises. The aileron assembly had been shipped by Oshiana Transportation Ltd., a company which had been contracted by Luft.
   a) List the potential defendants in an action to be brought by Marchand for her injuries, and explain the principle in products liability law that will help her to prove negligence on the part of the defendant(s).
   b) Assuming the defect was in the original manufacturing of the aileron assembly, and Marchand was successful in her court action, how would the responsibility for her damages be apportioned among the defendant(s)?
   c) Given the cause of the injuries to the passengers on the aircraft, what legal procedure is available to assist them in bringing their cases to court in the most economic and time-efficient manner?

10. Serena Arfred suffered cuts to her mouth as well as digestive-tract injuries as a result of drinking milk from a bottle purchased from Mimo's Variety Store. The milk was found to have small pieces of glass in the bottom of the bottle. It had been bottled by Keewatin Dairies Ltd.

    The bottle had no chips or cracks, and Keewatin prided itself on having state-of-the-art bottling equipment that not only met current provincial standards, but surpassed them. Evidence showed that the bottle had not been tampered with between the time it left the bottling plant and the time it was opened by Serena for use on her corn crunchies. No one could explain how the glass came to be in the milk bottle.
    a) Is Keewatin's ability to show that it exceeds provincial standards in its bottling processes an absolute defence to Serena's court action?

11. Oars Inc. designed and manufactured a rowing machine for use in health clubs. The unique design utilized a wheel, much like that of a bicycle, that rotated on an axle which was propelled by a series of levers and pulleys, which were moved along a rope pulled by the person rowing. A health club member's hand was severely injured when her fingers became caught in the spokes in the wheel and jammed against a pulley. The rowing machine came with an owner's manual, which was located in the manager's office and contained a warning to keep hands away from the revolving wheel when the machine was in operation.
    a) List and explain who the defendants in this action would be.
    b) Decide which of these grounds would be the basis for bringing an action and explain your choice:
       i)   defects in the manufacturing process
       ii) negligent design
       iii) duty to warn
    c) Would it assist the defendant if evidence was available that the club member had filled her water bottle with a measure of four fingers of vodka and some tonic water a half-hour prior to beginning her exercises on the floor of the health club?

12. Alex, a student, created his own summer job by making the rounds of several lakes in a well-known recreational resort area of his province and obtaining contracts to paint docks and boathouses. With contracts in hand, Alex went out to purchase paint that was specifically manu-

factured for a marine environment. Halfway through the summer, Alex's first customers began to complain that the paint was flaking off in large patches from the buildings and docks he had painted earlier. On inspection, Alex discovered to his horror that the paint seemed not to be binding to the material painted, and eventually it would all flake off.

The unhappy customers threatened him with lawsuits if he did not rectify the situation. Alex was forced to purchase a different type of paint, strip all the docks and buildings previously done, and repaint them. A consequence of this was that he had to forgo the contracts that were to be completed during the second half of the summer.

Alex estimates his loss of profit at $10,000, and his cost of repurchasing paint at $2,500. In investigating the problem further, he discovered that the paint manufacturer, Polypaints Inc., and his supplier were both aware that in particularly humid weather, which this summer had been, the chemicals in this paint which cause it to bind to the material painted were affected.

a) Does Alex have any grounds for bringing an action against Polypaints Inc. and the paint supplier for the loss of his summer contracts and the cost of the replacement paint?

b) Failing grounds for bringing an action based on tort, explain with reasons whether Alex has any grounds in contract law for bringing an action against the paint manufacturer and/or the paint supplier.

13. A car driver braked, but failed to stop, and hit a pedestrian. The driver had had his vehicle's brakes repaired by a mechanic only a day before the accident.

The pedestrian sued the manufacturer of the vehicle and the mechanic. Both said the other was at fault. The pedestrian had no evidence, and no idea what went wrong.

a) At trial, the manufacturer and the mechanic relied on the pedestrian's lack of knowledge, saying he had not proved any breach of standard and therefore his action should be dismissed. Do you agree?

b) The manufacturer claimed that the pedestrian was not a user of the car, did not purchase the car, and was not foreseeable. Therefore the manufacturer owed no duty to the pedestrian. Do you agree?

Sports and High-Risk Activities

14. Bart enjoyed the outdoors and had often thought about taking part in one of the war games offered by a hunters' organization in his area. At a promotion meeting, it was explained to the attendees that the organization preferred to refer to their exercises as paintball games, and that a capsule with harmless paint is used as a substitute for bullets in order to indicate when someone had been hit in the course of the game.

Bart decided to sign up for the paintball game to take place the next day. As he paid his money, he was requested to sign an entrance form which included a paragraph absolving the organization from any liability or responsibility for injuries suffered by the participants in the course of the game. The next morning, while preparing the paint pellets, Klaus, a member of the hunters' organization, ran out of the normal paint used and decided to substitute some paint that was on hand for the last 20 pellets. During the game, Bart was directly hit on the side of his nose, next to his eye, by Klaus, who was leading one of the opposing teams.

Half an hour after the game was over, Bart began to experience tingling in his eye and over the next hour lost vision in it. Analysis indicated that the pellet that had hit Bart was one of the last 20 made, using the substitute paint which was found to contain a substance that was highly toxic. As a result of his injury, Bart has lost the use of his eye. This has interfered with his job as a cartographer, in which he needs the use of both eyes for the stereoscopes used for 3-D interpretation of land forms when drawing maps.

a) Will the waiver act as a full defence for the hunting organization if Bart proceeds to court with this matter?

b) Would voluntary assumption of risk be an alternative answer should the waiver not protect the hunting organization?

c) What is the nature of the court action that Bart would bring, and what would he have to prove to be successful?

15. A school held a regular hockey practice Monday, Wednesday, and Friday, immediately after school hours, at a local arena run by Riverside Arena Inc. The school hockey coach was always in attendance.

Bill Smart high-sticked Angus King, catching him in the throat and causing serious injury to his trachea. The young man required several operations over the course of the next two years. King, aged 15, had signed the school's standard form waiver exempting the school from liability in accidents occurring during hockey games and practices. The doctors noticed that the blade on the stick had an unusually sharp edge and were of the opinion that this sharpness had aggravated the injury. The stick had been manufactured by Bower Equipment Ltd. and sold by Sports Distributors Inc. to Bill Smart.

When King was hit, he fell against the glass barrier at the end of the arena. The glass was loose, fell, shattered, and cut a bystander, Robert Gould. Other arena patrons testified that they noticed the glass had been loose for weeks. Riverside Arena admitted that they had no system for regular inspection.

a) Who are the potential defendants?

b) Give the legal term for each basis of possible liability against each of the potential defendants.

c) Which of the defendants do you believe has breached the expected standard of care? Does it have any defences?

d) What is the effect of the waiver signed by King? Which defendant can rely on it?

e) If you were the risk-management consultant for both Bower Equipment and Riverside Arena, what recommendations would you make to those businesses?

f) Who has the best ability to insure for these kinds of accidents? What effect do you think the ability to insure has on judges when making findings against defendants in this type of action?

16. Before taking a two-day course to learn how to ride and jump horses, Dale Gauley was asked to sign a form that exempted the stables from any responsibility for injury suffered by the rider as a result of the riding lessons or jumping.

By that afternoon, Gauley had a pretty good handle on the jumping and had already gone over two metre-high jumps. While approaching the last jump, someone in the parking lot next to the arena honked a horn and Gauley's horse bolted, heading straight for the arena's six-foot fence. As the horse attempted to jump the fence, Gauley fell off, breaking her collarbone, three ribs, and her right hip. She was in hospital for three months as a result.

When she approached the stables for compensation for her injuries, the owner refused to even discuss it. Waiving the form Gauley had signed, he said, "Try getting over this."

a) Assess, with reasons, the likelihood of Gauley's success should she take this matter to court.

17. Roy Smith was staying at a ski resort. After drinking at the bar for most of the afternoon he decided to enter the inner-tube race which the resort held each evening. At the top of the hill, Smith was asked to sign a standard form agreement which included an exemption clause relieving the resort of any liability for damages suffered by him or any other participant in the inner-tube race. Being very drunk and unable to focus well on the form, Smith asked what the paragraphs said and a resort employee explained it was an exemption clause that relieved the resort from any responsibility if Smith injured himself in the race. Smith nodded his head, and the employee then went on to say, "But don't worry: we haven't lost a contestant yet." Smith signed at the bottom of the form and staggered over to his waiting inner tube. In the course of the race he was thrown from the inner tube and hit another contestant. Both of them were severely injured.

a) Will the exemption clause protect the ski resort from being sued by Smith for his injuries?

b) If the exemption clause does not protect the ski resort from responsibility, will the resort also be responsible for the injuries suffered by the other contestant injured by Smith when he fell out of his inner tube?

Multi Issue

18. Match the following:

Assault	Touching
Battery	Theft
Conversion	Threatening
Passing off	Injurious falsehood
Product defamation	Plagiarism

Making Enforceable Business Agreements

What Is a Contract?

A handshake agreement can be a contract. Most of us think of a contract as a formal document, full of incomprehensible legal language, written by a lawyer. But we all make contracts on a regular basis—every time we buy a pen, accept a new job, or have the television repaired, we've entered into a contract.

A **contract** is an agreement that is enforceable in a court of law. A contract normally is an exchange of promises between two or more people that will be upheld by a court. But not every agreement is a contract. For an agreement to be considered a contract, and thus legally binding, it must contain certain factors:

- Contractual capacity. The participants have the **capacity**, that is, the legal capability of entering into an agreement. Some individuals, such as minors, and mentally incompetent or intoxicated persons, are not seen in law as having the capacity to enter into a contract.
- Legality or lawful object. The purpose must be neither criminal nor against the public good.
- Consensus. There must be complete agreement, or consensus, among the participants.
- Intention. The intent must be that legally enforceable obligations will result from the agreement.
- Consideration. All parties must offer a **consideration**, which is the price paid for a promise, something of value promised or paid that is taken to indicate that the person has considered the agreement and consents to be bound by it.

Freedom of Contract

Before beginning a review of contract principles developed by judges or enacted through statutes, it is important to understand a principle called freedom of contract, which means that, generally, people are permitted to vary and even reverse the legal principles that govern contracts by the terms of the specific contract being made. Thus, it is vital to review carefully the precise terms of any agreement, for certain terms may completely displace the legal principle.

contract
an agreement that is enforceable in a court of law

capacity
the legal capability of entering into an agreement; some individuals, such as minors, and mentally incompetent or intoxicated persons, are not seen in law as having the capacity to enter into a contract

consideration
the price paid for a promise, something of value promised or paid that is taken to indicate that the person has considered the agreement and consents to be bound by it

Because of this concern, you will be shown not only the abstract legal rule but how the issue is treated in common contracts and where it is often reversed by reference to these actual agreements and terms.

For example, you will learn a principle called acceptance by conduct, but this rule may be varied by the terms of any agreement. Wayne Gretzky lost a case in which he sued to force a seller to complete a cottage deal: Gretzky alleged that the seller accepted the offer by conduct, which is a well-established legal principle. However, the seller won because the written agreement contained a clause that stated that acceptance could only be in writing.[1]

Working with a Commercial Lawyer

Drafting individual contracts for significant business matters requires cooperation between the business person and the commercial lawyer. The written contract must record the business deal with precision while it protects and advances your business's interest. Thus, the best contracts are a result of cooperation between the commercial lawyer and the business client. For effective communication, the lawyer needs to have some understanding of the business issues, and the business person needs to have some understanding of the legal issues.

In this part of the book you will be familiarized with some of the most common legal issues that affect the modern business deal, which in legal terms is a contract. Such familiarity will assist you in identifying the important elements of the deal for the lawyer who will draft or review the contract on your behalf to ensure that the final agreement accurately reflects the deal. You must be able to communicate what you are really trying to accomplish to your commercial lawyer so that lawyer will be able to help achieve that goal.

You will also review some of the provisions that occur in most agreements and are called "boiler plate clauses," such as entire agreement clauses, liquidated damage clauses, and such. By reviewing both the legal issues and terms that occur in real agreements, you will be well prepared to discuss the legal-business issues in any specific contract with the commercial lawyer.

We now start a review of the elements which are necessary to make a contract. These elements are significant for, if they are not present, the agreement may not be enforceable.

Capacity

The law recognizes that some individuals need special protection when making contracts. Young people under the age of majority—minors—are considered to lack full judgment in business affairs, and therefore there are particular rules to safeguard their interests. People who are mentally incompetent, and individuals who are intoxicated, are also given specific protection at law.

Minors

In the Middle Ages, when a man reached 21 years of age, he was considered strong enough to bear armour and fight for his country. Since he was able to do so he was given full status to conduct his own affairs—he had reached his majority and was legally an adult.

---

1. "No Goal for Gretzky in Cottage Deal," *Toronto Star*, June 12, 1999.

In modern times, many countries, including Canada, have lowered the age at which young people bear full responsibility for their own affairs. In Canadian provinces, the **age of majority**—the age at which a person is recognized as an adult according to the law of his or her province—is not always the same as the age at which a young person is permitted to get married, drive, or drink alcohol.

Province/Territory	Age of Majority
Alberta	18
British Columbia	19
Manitoba	18
New Brunswick	19
Newfoundland and Labrador	19
Northwest Territories	19
Nunavut	19
Nova Scotia	19
Ontario	18
Prince Edward Island	18
Quebec	18
Saskatchewan	18
Yukon Territory	19

In any dispute over a contract, the courts try to balance the interests of both the adult and the minor. If, for example, the contract is for goods that the young person has purchased, the seller might receive financial compensation for taking back a "used" item. A minor who buys a car for $5,000 and drives it for three months could expect to pay rental for its use over that time if the contract is cancelled.

age of majority

the age at which a person is recognized as an adult according to the law of his or her province

minor

a person who has not attained the age of majority according to the law of his or her province, and therefore is not legally an adult

Critical Concepts of Minors' Contracts

- Each province and territory in Canada sets its age of majority. A young person who is legally a minor in one province might be considered an adult in another.
- In general, the courts are unlikely to enforce a contract against a minor.
- It doesn't matter if a minor appears to be over the age of majority and the other party to the contract honestly believes that the young person is an adult. This is true even when the minor has deliberately lied to or misled the adult.
- If a contract is cancelled by the court, the minor is entitled to have any money paid refunded, but must return the goods purchased.
- Parents of a minor are not liable unless they had previously authorized the contract. If a parent co-signs a contract, or persuades the other party that the parents have accepted responsibility for it, they can be held liable.

Repudiation   When parties cancel a contract before it is fully performed, as the minors are doing in the examples in this section, they are repudiating (rejecting) the contract. **Repudiation (anticipatory breach)** is an indication by a party that he or she will not go through with the agreement as promised. It is also called **anticipatory breach.**

Legalese

repudiation (anticipatory breach)

an indication by a party that he or she will not go through with the agreement as promised

Business Law Applied

❶ Sabrina Costa, aged 17, was given $500 by her grandparents to help pay for her future education. On her way to the bank to deposit the cash, she passed an electronics store that had a large sign in the window.

SPECIAL! ONE DAY ONLY! CD PLAYERS regular price $1,000 TODAY'S PRICE $500 (all taxes included) Buy yours now!

Costa did buy hers, telling the salesperson as she handed over her money, "I'm 19 today and this is my birthday present from my grandparents." Later that day, when the CD player was delivered to her house, she was not at home. Her mother refused to accept the delivery and, when her daughter returned, told the young woman to go back to the store and ask for her money to be refunded.

a) Did the business have to return the money?

Minors' Contracts for Necessities[2]

Contracts that involve matters necessary for the young person's survival can be enforced by the courts. Necessities are those goods and services that are needed every day—food, clothing, shelter, education, medical care, job training, and apprenticeship programs.

In deciding whether an item or service is a necessity, the court considers the minor's need for the goods or services, as well as the young person's position, or station, in life. Family and financial background are looked at, and what is seen as a necessity for one individual might not be considered so for another. A full-time student, for example, would likely have no need of a formal business suit; a trainee accountant, on the other hand, could not attend the office every day without one.

Minors must fulfill any contracts they make for necessities. If this were not the law, then no one would be willing to supply them with those necessities.

necessities (necessaries)
the basic goods and services required to function in society

■ *Critical Concepts of* Contracts for Necessities

- A minor has to honour a contract for necessities.
- A minor only has to pay a reasonable price for the necessities. The court will reduce the price if it is not a fair one.[3]
- Apprenticeship and employment contracts are considered necessities if they are to a minor's benefit, and may be enforced against the young person.
- It is up to the other party to prove that the contract is for necessities or, if job related, that it is beneficial to the minor.
- Loans to minors are not recoverable unless they are used for necessities. The *Canada Student Loan Act* specifically provides that minors are responsible for repaying loans granted under that program.

---

2. *The Infants Act*, 1996 R.S.B.C., c. 223 erases the distinction between necessities and non-necessities, and sets out the general rule that contracts with minors are unenforceable (unless otherwise specified in legislation, or ratified by the minor after reaching the age of majority).

3. S. M. Waddams, *The Law of Contracts*, 3d ed. (Toronto: Canada Law Book Inc., 1993), p. 145.

Toronto Marlboro Major Junior "A" Hockey Club et al. v. Tonelli et al., [1979] 96 D.L.R. (3d) 135 (Ont. C.A.)

John Tonelli was a gifted hockey player with great potential. At the age of 17, he signed a contract with the Toronto Marlboro Major Junior "A" Hockey Club, agreeing to play for the club for three years. The document contained a clause that gave the club the option of extending the contract for a further year if it wished, so that Tonelli would be with them till he reached 21 years of age. In another clause, Tonelli agreed to pay the club 20 percent of his salary for three years if he went on to play with a professional hockey team while the Marlboro contract was still in force.

The terms of the contract gave Tonelli a small salary, coaching, and the opportunity to play in the Junior "A" Hockey League.

One year after signing with the Marlboros, Tonelli was offered a salary of $320,000 over three years by the Houston Aeros of the World Hockey Association. Tonelli cancelled his contract with the Marlboros, and signed with Houston. The Marlboros sued Tonelli for damages for breach of contract.

The Court's Decision

The court stated that a contract against a minor was, generally, unenforceable, but that an employment contract could be upheld if it was to the minor's benefit. It was up to the plaintiff to prove that the contract was in fact beneficial.

The Toronto Marlboros claimed that the contract was good for Tonelli, since it permitted him to play in the Junior League, where he could obtain valuable experience. However, balanced against this was Tonelli's exceptional ability as a player, and several terms that were extremely favourable to the Toronto Marlboros. The club had:

- the option to extend the term of the contract from three years to four
- the right to claim 20 percent of Tonelli's salary for the first three years of his professional career
- the right to assign or terminate the contract at any time

The court found that the contract was not beneficial to Tonelli, a minor, and the action brought by the Toronto Marlboros was dismissed.

Proof of Age   If you have a written contract—even a simple sales slip—make sure it includes a term in which the buyer certifies being over the age of majority. This practice will not prevent problems with a minor who decides to lie, but may reduce problems that could occur simply because no one anticipated them.

Your sales staff should not hesitate to ask for proof of age if they have any doubts about the matter. Use the standards set by banks for accepting appropriate proof of age. If the customer is a minor, consider having a parent or guardian co-sign.

When businesses deal with minors, they may use a signature clause, which provides a reminder for staff to check the age of the purchaser. A typical clause of this type is:

Business Alert!

I HAVE UNDERSTOOD AND ACCEPT THE ABOVE TERMS

Elfrida Woods

_____

Signature of Customer or Parent or Legal Guardian

Business Law Applied

2 Afshan Dahl, aged 16, found a part-time job as a receptionist in an office. She needed some new clothes for work, and bought two outfits from a local clothing store. On the way home, she saw something she liked better and went back to the first store to return what she had just purchased. The store refused to let her return the clothes, or to refund her money.

a) Was Dahl able to get out of the contract because she was a minor at law?

3 One of your friends, who was 17 years old at the time, borrowed $200 from you. You knew that he intended to use the money to place a bet in a hockey pool. Your friend did not win and, next day, told you, "Sorry, I can't pay."

a) Could you have made him pay in law?

Mentally Incompetent and Intoxicated Persons

Contract laws give special protection to individuals who suffer from mental impairment at the time of entering into an agreement. The impairment may be due to a variety of causes, including:

- physical disease (for example, stroke or brain tumours)
- mental illness (for example, senile dementia)
- drug use (including both legal and illegal use)
- alcohol use

In order for the incapacitated person to avoid liability on the contract, the other party must have known (or reasonably should have known) of the incapacity. The court will consider circumstances surrounding the transaction, such as the price paid for the goods or services, in assessing what the other party knew (or should have known).

If an individual wishes to avoid liability based on incapacity, he or she must do so promptly upon return to a capable mental state. In cases where individuals suffer from permanent mental impairment, another party may promptly challenge the agreement on their behalf.

One of the most famous claims for mental incompetency was made by Tim Horton's widow, Dolores Horton. She sold the doughnut franchise in December of 1975 for $1,000,000. In 1995 she claimed she could not remember anything about the deal because she had been a drug addict at the time and had, in effect, performed a chemical lobotomy on herself. Now she was clear of the addiction and wanted her interest in the doughnut chain back, which interest was worth about $350,000,000 in 1995.

Unfortunately for Mrs. Horton, the trial judge did not believe that she was unable to understand what she was doing at the time; she lost.

■■■ *Critical Concepts of* Mental Incompetence or Intoxication

Contract laws give special protection to individuals who are impaired by drunkenness, or who are mentally incompetent. A contract made by such a person can be voided by the courts, as long as the following rules apply.

- The contract is not one for necessities.
- The impairment was sufficiently serious that the individual was unable to understand the nature and consequence of what was going on.
- The other party had actual knowledge, or was put on notice (termed constructive notice), of the impairment at the time the contract was entered into.
- The agreement was cancelled within a reasonable time by the person deemed incompetent or drunk. A "reasonable time" means the individual must cancel the agreement promptly after the return to mental competence or sobriety.

■ *Business Law* Applied

❹ Ritchie Brothers, a large firm of industrial auctioneers, specialized in the sale of heavy equipment such as earth movers and road graders. Ron Barr, owner of a construction company, attended an auction and purchased $1 million worth of earth-moving equipment, giving a $250,000 cheque as a deposit. The cheque was drawn on a bank in another city, and Barr was a new customer, so Ritchie Brothers asked that his bank manager confirm the cheque would be honoured. Barr called the bank manager, and then handed the phone to the Ritchie representative, who confirmed the money was on deposit.

The cheque bounced. Ritchie was still in possession of the equipment, and resold it for $50,000, yielding a loss of $200,000. Ritchie Brothers sued Barr for that amount.

Barr claimed that the day before the auction he had been visiting his daughter in Vancouver. He had returned to his hotel room in the evening, where he took medication for a heart condition, and drank two beers. Barr said he remembered nothing after that until he woke up in his own home two days later. During the 48-hour blank period Barr attended the Ritchie Brothers auction, but claimed all he knew of the events of the two days was what other people had since told him.

The Ritchie Brothers' representative said that he was aware of the law of capacity, and therefore had spoken directly to Barr at the auction to make certain that he was competent. The auctioneer had seen no indication of any impairment.

a) Did Barr have to pay?
b) If Barr had been a minor, would the result have been the same?

Legality

Courts will not enforce illegal contracts. **Illegal contracts**—contracts which cannot be enforced because they are contrary to legislation or public policy—fall into either of two situations:

- The agreement involves breaking a civil or criminal statute. This is known as statutory illegality.
- The agreement is against public policy and violates the public interest or the common sense of morality in society.

illegal contracts
contracts which cannot be enforced because they are contrary to legislation or public policy

Statutory Illegality

Within statutory illegality there are also two categories. The first is those acts that are criminal or considered morally wrong. If a hit man successfully carries out his contract and his employer refuses to pay, he could not sue in court. The second category is those acts that are wrong only because a statute makes them wrong. For example, a statute may prohibit the sale of electrical machinery unless it is CSA (Canadian Standards Association) approved. Also, electricians may be prohibited from carrying on business without a provincial licence.

In the second category of illegal acts, those that are wrong only because they are prohibited by statutes, the contract may still be enforced if there was no intention to violate the relevant statute and there is compliance with the statute before performance of the contract is completed. If an agreement was made to sell a machine that at the time had not been CSA approved, this contract would be unenforceable as illegal. However, if before delivery the machine was certified, the contract would be enforced, as the seller had no intention to violate the statute and had complied before completion of the contract.

Workers' Compensation

workers' compensation

a scheme in which employers contribute to a fund used to compensate workers injured in on-the-job accidents, in place of their right to sue in torts

All provinces have what amounts to a government-run insurance plan, under which workers who are injured in the course of their employment receive compensation. **Workers' compensation** is a scheme in which employers contribute to a fund used to compensate workers injured in on-the-job accidents, in place of their right to sue in torts. Just as with a private insurance plan, employers may be penalized by having to pay higher premiums if there are many claims by their employees.

In an effort to avoid this, some employers have included an employment contract clause that says the employee agrees not to make a claim against the employer for injuries caused on the job. But such a clause is illegal and will not be enforced by the courts. The workers' compensation acts in all provinces state that an employee's agreement to give up the right to sue is of no effect. This is an example of an express statutory prohibition of a contract.

Therefore, even if an injured worker has signed a contract containing such a term, the individual still has the right to claim compensation for any on-the-job injury.

Gambling Debts

The Criminal Code of Canada says that gambling is illegal unless it is government run or government licensed. Thus, lotteries, bingo, horse racing, and other forms of gambling that have government approval are indeed legal, although certain restrictions still apply.

Most provinces have legislation that prohibits anyone, including a gambling casino, from lending money to a person for the purpose of gambling. A court would not enforce such a debt made within the province. Curiously, though, Canadian courts will enforce foreign gambling debts if the foreign court has granted judgment against the debtor (see *Broadwalk Regency Corp. v. Malouf* (1992), 6 O.R. (3d) 737).

■ *Critical Concepts of* Statutory Illegality

- Statutory illegality can arise from two different situations: those that are criminal, and those that are wrong only because they are prohibited by civil statutes or regulations.
- Those contracts that are illegal only because they are prohibited by statute may be enforced if there was no intention to violate the statute.
- The court may find that there was no intention to violate the statute if at the time of the performance the illegality was cured.

Mack v. Edenwold Fertilizer Services Ltd., [1996] 3 W.W.R. 731 (Alta. C.A.)

Mack was a farmer who had agreed to buy a supply of fertilizer from Edenwold Fertilizer for $122,000. The agreement and the cheque for payment in full were backdated so that Mack could claim the purchase as an expense in the prior year. Edenwold Fertilizer could not deliver on time, so it agreed to a further agreement for Edenwold to pay interest at 17.5% on the $122,000 until delivery. Edenwold eventually delivered the fertilizer but refused to pay the interest. Mack sued for the interest. Edenwold defended saying the contract and the cheque were backdated for the purpose of cheating on income tax and therefore the agreement was illegal and unenforceable on the grounds of statutory illegality.

The Court's Decision

The court held that there was no doubt that if a contract is found to be for an illegal purpose it is unenforceable. The agreement on its face, that is, to buy fertilizer, was not for an illegal purpose. However, both parties knew that the reason the agreement was backdated was to deceive Revenue Canada. When any party is going to use an agreement for an illegal purpose, such as tax evasion, the entire agreement is tainted by illegality. That tainting of illegality included any agreement made in connection with the main agreement. So here the agreement to pay interest is also illegal and unenforceable. The court stated that it would not help such a plaintiff.

In international business transactions a foreign company will sometimes ask a Canadian company to issue a phony invoice to assist the foreign business in avoiding its country's exchange-control laws. This makes the contract illegal. Any illegal act in performance of the contract affects the entire contract. If the Canadian company finds that it must sue on the contract, it may be left without a remedy because of this illegal act.

Business Alert!

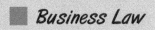   Applied

⑤ **The relevant provincial act** states that a builder must be registered with the provincial Home Warranty Plan office before being able to sell a new home. A builder entered into an agreement of purchase and sale for a house yet to be built. The agreement was to close in eight months. In the sixth month, in compliance with the statute, the builder registered with the plan office. When the time came for closing two months later, the purchaser refused to close on the basis that the agreement was illegal because it violated the *Home Warranties Act*.

a) Was the agreement illegal at the time that it was made?
b) Was it enforceable at the time of closing?

Common Law Illegality

Agreements in Restraint of Trade

There are a number of situations in which the Courts will not enforce a contract as being against public policy, which means against the good of the community generally.

One of the most common situations in business subject to the public policy consideration are agreements that restrict a person's ability to earn a living, which are called agreements "in restraint of trade". The word "trade" was more generally used historically to mean carrying on business or earning a livelihood.

These clauses are usually found in two situations: sale of a business and employment contracts.

Sale of a Business.   A seller agrees not to enter into a similar competing business within a certain distance for a specific time. For example, Idries Shah, who has been running a small food store and who is very popular in the neighbourhood, agrees to sell his business to Farhani Khan. Khan may want a clause in the agreement that Shaw not open up a competing business within a five mile radius for five years. This clause is called a non-competition clause.

Employment Agreements.   An employer may hire an employee who is a super salesman and give him access to confidential lists of his customers scattered throughout not only Canada but other parts of the world. The employer may seek restrictions on the employees right to compete in a similar business after leaving his present employment such as not being able to solicit (approach) customers of his present employers for six months after leaving. This is called a non-solicitation clause.

In reviewing these clauses the Courts start from a premise that such agreements are unenforceable as contrary to public policy because it is in the public interest that everyone be able to earn a living and not need to claim welfare. The clauses will be enforced if the clauses can be considered reasonable. The tests for reasonableness are set out in the critical concepts immediately below.

Although the principle of reasonableness of the restraint (restriction) is the same for both sale of business contracts and employment contracts, it is applied more leniently in the sale of business contracts. The Courts will be more likely to find such terms enforceable in these agreements because there is equality of bargaining power and the seller is getting paid for goodwill (goodwill explained below).

In contrast the Courts are more sympathetic to employees and so more likely to strike down such clauses in employment contracts if they are too wide of scope and not necessary to protect the former employer.

The following two reported cases demonstrate the different application of this one principle to two different situations: business sale and employment contract.

goodwill

the value of the good name, reputation, and connection of a business

Goodwill—the value of the good name, reputation, and connection of a business—can't really be measured in dollars and cents. But when a business is sold, its goodwill is often considered one of its assets, and the selling price includes a sum for it, because when you buy a business, you are also acquiring its location, name, credit rating, reputation, and, most important, its customers—which all add up to that business's goodwill.

Since you have paid for the goodwill of the business you've bought, it might cause your operation a great deal of harm if the seller opened up a new, competing, firm close by. For this reason, a buyer often includes a contract clause that says the seller agrees not to open a competing business anywhere in the same city, or within a reasonable distance of it, for a certain number of years.

But it is in the public interest to make sure that all members of society have the chance to work and thus provide for their own support. If those selling a business agree to severe restrictions on their own ability to work, they could be forced to claim welfare, thus adding to the financial burden on society. Because an employee is seen as being at a disadvantage when negotiating a contract, the courts will, in general, be more likely to strike down restrictive clauses in employment agreements than they would in agreements for the sale of a business.

In any dispute over unreasonable restraint of trade, the courts attempt to balance the two interests—those of the parties to the contract, and those of the public.

■ *Critical Concepts of* Restraint of Trade

The following principles apply to terms that restrain an individual's right to earn a living, in both sale-of-business and employment contracts:

- In general, any contract clause that limits a person's right to earn a living is presumed to be against public policy, and therefore unenforceable.

- This presumption can be overturned if the restraint clause can be proved to be reasonable. To be considered reasonable it must:

  a) be necessary to protect the business

  b) contain restrictions on time, area, and subject matter that are no greater than are needed to protect the business

  c) not be against the interests of the public.

- The person to be restrained must possess some special skill, or knowledge of trade secrets or special techniques. Alternatively, the individual must represent major potential competition to the business sold or to the employment the individual has left.

Misasi v. Guzzo, *Lawyers Weekly*, April 17, 1987

Vince Guzzo and one Misasi were partners in Valles Open Fruit Market. Guzzo sold his interest to Misasi and agreed to a non-competition clause that stated Guzzo would not take a direct or indirect interest in a similar business within a five-mile radius of Valles Open Fruit Market for three years.

A few months after the sale, Amedeo Guzzo, the 19-year-old son of Vince Guzzo, set up a new business called DeVille Produce Limited within the five-mile radius.

Misasi sued on the non-competition clause. Guzzo defended saying that it was his son's business, not his.

The Court's Decision

The court held that the clause was reasonable in terms of subject matter, time and geographic area. However, the court found that the new business was a sham designed to allow Vince Guzzo to avoid his legal obligation not to compete with Misasi. Even though the money for the new store had apparently come from a family friend, the court did not accept that it was likely anyone would advance that amount of money to an inexperienced 19-year-old. Vince Guzzo was found liable for damages for breach of the non-competition clause.

Lyons v. Multari,
[2000] 50 O.R. (3d) 126 (Ont. C.A.) (leave to appeal to S.C.C. denied)

Multari, a recent graduate, went to work as an oral surgeon with Lyons, an established oral surgeon with a five-year practice. They signed a short handwritten employment contract less than a page long, which contained a non-competition clause by which Multari would not operate a competing oral surgeon practice within five miles of Dr. Lyons's office for three years after leaving his employment.

As oral surgeons, they got all patients by referrals from regular dentists. Multari worked for Lyons for 17 months, gave six months' notice, and went to work for a competitor over five miles away. About a year later Multari moved to another office 3.7 miles from Lyons's office, which location was in breach of the non-competition clause.

Lyons sued Multari for loss of business.

The Court's Decision

The court found that Multari had breached the non-competition clause. The question became: was this non-competition clause enforceable? Did the space and time limits go too far and restrict competition generally?

The court observed that in the context of employment contracts, non-competition clauses were drastic weapons compared to non-solicitation clauses.

The court ruled that a non-competition clause should be enforced only in exceptional cases. This was not an exceptional case because Multari had worked only a short time for Dr. Lyons and Lyons was always the main contact with the referring dentists. Lyons did not need this level of protection, and the clause was declared unenforceable.

Business Alert!   Read the Agreement   In a case very similar to *Lyons v. Multari*, a partner at the major accounting firm of Ernst & Young left to go to a rival firm, Arthur Andersen. The Ernst & Young partnership agreement contained a non-competition clause preventing any partner from practicing public accounting within a 50-mile radius of his former office for one year after leaving Ernst & Young.

The court held this clause was unenforceable as being unreasonable. However, the partnership agreement also contained a clause requiring the partner to give one year's notice. The partner did not give any notice and was made to pay damages based on that one-year period in the amount of $250,000.[4]

This case illustrates the importance of not only knowing the relevant common law principles but also closely reading the terms of any relevant agreement.

Effect of Evolving Case Law

Cases such as *Lyons v. Multari* often signal a change in the law and perhaps also in judges' attitudes against wide non-competition clauses in employment agreements. Lawyers watch such cases carefully to see if standard clauses in relevant contracts should be revised.

While employers often try to get the widest terms in an employment contract, lawyers realize that this strategy can backfire as the *Lyons v. Multari* case shows. If an employer wants to make sure that an employee cannot harm the employer when the employee leaves, in light of the evolving case law, it may be better to have an employee sign a clause agreeing, for example, not to work for the employer's three major competitors for a reasonable period of time in place of the traditional clause that restricts area and time. This clause focuses on where the most harm can be done. It is more likely that such a clause will stand up under the court's review in light of cases such as *Lyons v. Multari*.

---

4. *Ernst & Young v. Stewart, Lawyers Weekly*, April 25, 1997.

Business Law   Applied

6 a) In the *Misasi v. Guzzo* case and in the *Lyons v. Multari* case:

   i)   what is the subject matter of the agreements;
   ii) what is the time provision;
   iii) what is the geographic limitation.

   b) The non-competition clause in the *Misasi v. Guzzo* case contained a five mile limitation and so did the clause in the *Lyons v. Multari* case. Why was the clause found reasonable in one case and not in the other?

7 **Frank and Joanna** Demp were the principal shareholders of Fieldstream Arms Co., a small firearms-manufacturing company. The Fieldstream products were only sold in British Columbia.

Frank, a very popular ex-professional football player, was considered a super-salesman. It was mainly through his selling abilities that the firm had grown so successfully over the years. Joanna was the company accountant and business manager.

Fieldstream was sold. A clause in the sale agreement stated that both of the Demps agreed not to carry on or work in any similar business in the province of British Columbia for the next five years.

One year later, Joanna was appointed comptroller of a firm called Target Rifles Inc.; Frank became sales manager of the same company. Target operated out of Vancouver, British Columbia.

   a) Was the restraint clause in the sale agreement necessary to protect Fieldstream Arms?
   b) Did it meet the three tests for reasonableness?
   c) Did Frank represent a potential competitive danger to Fieldstream Arms? Did Joanna? Were there different considerations for each one?
   d) Was the agreement enforceable against either or both of the Demps?

Consensus

Before any contract is finalized, there must be general agreement, or consensus, between the parties involved. There can be several stages in the process before consensus is reached:

- bargaining or negotiating
- **offer** (a promise made by one party that contains all necessary terms so that the other party need only say "I accept" and a contract is formed)
- counter-offer (this stage does not always take place)
- acceptance

Bargaining—An Invitation to Treat

It is through bargaining, or negotiating, that parties to a contract try to reach an agreement that is to their individual advantage. **Invitation to treat** is the technical legal term for the invitation to engage in the bargaining process. Bargaining also involves the making of offers and counter-offers (discussed later).

   The law recognizes the necessity for not interfering with this bargaining process. It is only when a definite offer has been made that some very technical rules come into force. If one party wants to get out of the deal, then these laws must be followed strictly.

offer
a promise made by one party that contains all necessary terms so that the other party need only say "I accept" and a contract is formed

invitation to treat
the technical legal term for the invitation to engage in the bargaining process

If you were seriously considering the purchase of a store, for example, you might write to the owner, saying: "I'll buy your business for the asking price of $100,000. But first I want to speak to my accountants and see if they think it's a good idea." This statement is not an offer; it is part of the bargaining process. Depending on the advice you receive from the accountants, you might want to negotiate for certain terms to be included in the deal. Only when you and the seller have agreed on these terms does the process enter the offer stage.

Merchandise on display in a store usually has the price attached. Is the store making an offer by doing so? In fact, the courts consider that the store is making an invitation to treat, or invitation to buy, rather than an offer. It is the customer who decides to make a definite offer to purchase the goods. This rule is designed to protect the merchant, and is known as the "retail sales exception rule."

The same concept applies to goods in advertisements, catalogues, and price lists. Advertising has become so important that it is the subject of special additional rules under the *Competition Act*.

No Duty to Negotiate in Good Faith

There is no duty imposed upon people negotiating to act in good faith. Rather, each party is permitted to try to get the best deal possible for itself. The conduct of business is based on the competition model, and the courts try to preserve competition in business deals. Even when parties agree to negotiate in good faith, courts have said that such a term is not enforceable because it is uncertain.[5]

However, even in competition there are some restrictions, and so there are rules governing the negotiating process. A party cannot, for example, make a false representation, or take advantage of an obvious mistake, or use undue pressure or influence. The principles which apply to the negotiating process are covered in Chapter 7 ("Defects in a Contract and Remedies").

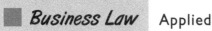

Business Law Applied

⑧ **Fatima DeSouza** was walking along the main street of town, browsing through a sidewalk sale. Outside a bookstore, she saw a bin filled with books, and a large sign above it.

Great bargains!!!!! $1 each

She searched through the books, and found a very old, yellowed copy of *Alice's Adventures in Wonderland*. DeSouza took the book to the cashier. As she was about to pay for it, the owner of the business saw the book, and took it from her hand, saying, "This is an original edition signed by the author. It's worth thousands of dollars. It got into that bin by mistake. I'm sorry. It's not for sale."

DeSouza claimed the bookstore made an offer, and she accepted it, so there was a binding contract.

a) Did the bookstore have to sell her the book?

Offers

Requirement for an Offer

Once the bargaining stage is over, a contract is formed by final acceptance of an offer. "I'll sell you my car for $10,000" is an offer. "It's a deal" is an acceptance. It is only when the process has reached this point that a contract exists, and the court will enforce the agreement. The owner

---

5. EdperBrascan v. 117373 Canada Ltd. (2000), 50 O.R. (3d) 425 (Ont. Sup. Ct.).

of the car must sell it for $10,000, even if the individual has a change of mind or receives a better offer from someone else. The purchaser must pay the $10,000, despite any change of mind. Even if the buyer learns one hour later that the same car is available elsewhere for $5,000, the first contract is binding.

Completeness

The parties to an agreement might genuinely believe that they have passed the offer/acceptance stage of the process and thus have a firm, legally binding contract. However, the law says that all essential details must be included in an offer. It is possible that an offer could seem to be complete with all the essential terms, when in fact it also includes a clause saying that some of these are still open to *negotiation*.

The question of what is an essential term in an offer is a difficult legal problem. If you are involved in a business deal involving a significant amount of money, it is advisable to consult a lawyer before entering into the negotiations, or even have the lawyer assist in the negotiating process.

Offer   The law sometimes uses words in a way that is different from their accepted, everyday meaning. The term **offer** is one such word. For example, when a house is put up for sale, we normally say that the house is offered for sale. While this is quite correct in ordinary language, it is not correct in law. Putting the house on the market is an invitation to treat. Similarly, advertisements in media and displays of merchandise for sale have often been found not to be offers as that term is used in law, but rather mere attempts to induce offers. The study of law involves learning how to classify the same thing using both regular terms and legal terms.

Offeror   The **offeror** is the person who makes an offer. The **offeree** is the person who receives the offer. Iveta Kuz, the offeror, says to Jean Roget, "I'll buy your car for $10,000 today." Roget, the offeree, receives the offer, but need take no further action.

Legalese

offeror
the person who makes an offer

offeree
the person who receives the offer

■ *Critical Concepts of* Offer

- An offer must contain all of the terms that will be included in the contract, so that the other party need merely say, "I accept."
- The essential terms necessary for a contract will vary with the circumstances but they normally are: the parties, the price, the terms of payment, and the subject matter.
- If a term indicates that the party making the offer does not intend to be bound, but may want to negotiate further, there is no offer, but an invitation to treat.

Rossdale v. Denny, [1921] 1 Ch. 57 (C.A.)

Rossdale made an offer to purchase a long-term lease in a property known as Marble Arch. The offer stated:

This offer is subject to a formal contract to embody such reasonable provisions as my solicitors may approve.

The offer was accepted by Major Denny, but later the parties disagreed, and Denny refused to go through with the agreement. Rossdale sued to have the lease declared binding on Denny.

The Court's Decision

The court held that the phrase "subject to a formal contract to embody such reasonable provisions as my solicitors may approve" meant that there were important items left to be agreed upon later by the parties concerned. Thus, no offer had been made, and there was no binding lease. The case was dismissed.

Business Law Applied

❾ **Rychjohn Investments Ltd.** was buying up properties in downtown Calgary as part of a land assembly for redevelopment. The firm wanted to purchase a particular building that had been leased by its owner and was currently occupied. The only way the tenant could be made to vacate the property was by Rychjohn's buying out the lease.

Lawrence Rychjohn, the owner of Rychjohn Investments, negotiated a deal with the tenant, agreeing to pay $125,000 for the lease. Rychjohn paid a deposit of $5,000, and obtained a receipt from the tenant. The receipt made no mention of when the balance of the money was to be paid:

> Received from ___Rychjohn Investments Ltd.___
> ___five thousand___ _____ dollars as down-payment on total
> of ___$125,000___ _____ for purchase of lease from Hunters Bowl Arena as of May 1, 1977, pending
> drawing up of legal document.
>
> ___Ken Hunter___
> Signature

The tenant had his lawyer draw up a contract for the purchase of the lease. It included a term that stated: "… followed by payment of $20,000 on January 15, 2003, and $100,000 on April 1, 2003."

Negotiations with the owner of the building fell through, and Rychjohn Investments was not able to complete the purchase. Thus, the firm was no longer interested in buying the tenant's lease. Rychjohn disputed the tenant's payment dates, and claimed that the offer had been to pay the balance of the sum agreed for the lease purchase in about a year or so, that is, November 2003.

The tenant sued for a declaration that Rychjohn Investments had made an offer to buy out the lease, that the offer had been accepted, and was therefore a binding agreement.

 a) Was there an offer by Rychjohn Investments, as the term is defined legally?
 b) How might the tenant have protected himself against having the receipt declared not to be an offer, and thus losing the deal?
 c) How might Rychjohn have protected itself so that the firm could get out of any agreement to purchase the lease?

Termination of Offers: Acts of the Parties

Offers can be terminated [revoked] by acts of the parties or operation of law. Four ways the parties can end an offer are:

- withdrawal
- written terms of expiry
- rejection of the offer
- counteroffer (which creates a new offer on new terms)

Withdrawing an Offer

An offer can be withdrawn or revoked anytime before acceptance, as there is no consideration paid for keeping the offer open. That is so even if the offeror says that it is open until a certain date, say two days from now. It can be withdrawn before the two days have passed, providing it has not been accepted prior to the withdrawal.

As noted above, even though an offer is put in writing with an irrevocability clause, the offer could still be withdrawn before the date specified. To prevent this from happening, the offer is put "under seal." The use of the seal—refer to the signature page of the Agreement of Purchase and Sale for a Business in the Appendix at the end of this chapter—effectively creates a second contract separate from the contract to purchase the business for money. This second contract is an agreement whereby one party agrees to hold the offer open until the time stipulated in the agreement, based on the assurance of legal enforceability provided by the seal.

Irrevocable **Irrevocable** describes an offer which cannot be revoked or withdrawn. Within the work *revoke* you can see the letters *voke*, which come from *vocal*. *Revoke* literally means to call back. When *ir* is put in front of it, it creates a negative meaning cannot call back.

Legalese

■ *Critical Concepts of* Withdrawing an Offer

- Even though an offer is made, it can be withdrawn, or revoked, at any time before it is actually accepted.
- Even if an offer contains a term that states it will remain open till a certain time and date, it can still be revoked provided that:
  a) the offer is withdrawn before it has been accepted.
  b) the other party is informed that the offer is no longer valid. The information that the offer has been revoked can be communicated directly or indirectly.

Written Terms of Expiry

While the common law gives rules concerning the termination of offers, most standard form contracts contain a specific clause setting out the time the offer expires, which may vary the common law rules. Thus, any agreement has to be read for this clause. See for example clause no. 1 in the Agreement of Purchase and Sale for a Business at the end of this chapter.

The length of time an offer is kept open depends on various considerations. Purchasers often set out a short time frame, such as two days, in the irrevocability clause. The purchaser may be interested in other properties and will not be free to make an offer on those if the offer is left open for a longer time, say a week.

Sellers have similar concerns. If a seller signs back an offer, the seller will usually give only a day or two for acceptance. "Signing back" an offer means altering the offer presented by changing a term, for example, the price, initialing the change(s), and delivering it to the other party. Otherwise, the seller's property is tied up for a long period. A better offer may come in, but the seller cannot accept until the first prospective purchaser declines the offer.

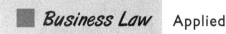

Business Law Applied

🔟 **At 3:00 p.m.** on Monday, Dodd offered to sell Dickenson some property, and stated that the offer had to be accepted before 9:00 a.m. the following Friday. However, on Wednesday morning Dodd sold the property to someone else. Dickenson found out about this sale, and put an acceptance in Dodd's hands before the deadline arrived.

    a) Was Dodd legally entitled to revoke the offer before the stated date?

    b) Was the fact that the offer was no longer valid communicated to Dickenson?

Termination of Offers: By Operation of Law

Offers may also be terminated by operation of law in the following circumstances:

1. After reasonable time, if no time is specified in the offer. What is reasonable will depend on the circumstances of each case.
   Example: A purchase of stocks listed on the stock market—that time may be a matter of a few moments. In a real estate deal it may be two to three days. In other circumstances it could be a week.
2. If the subject matter is destroyed through no fault of either party
3. Prior to acceptance of the offer, either the offeror or the offeree dies or becomes incompetent, and
4. Prior to the acceptance of the offer, the object of the offer is made illegal by statute, regulation, court decision or other law.
   Example: A distributor has agreed to purchase a product from a supplier. Before the shipping of the product, the government passes a regulation prohibiting the sale of products that contain a chemical which this product has.

Counter-Offer

During the course of negotiating an agreement, the parties involved often put several different positions to one another. An individual might offer to sell a car for $20,000, only to have the potential buyer say, "I'll give you $19,000." The $19,000 thus proposed is a **counter-offer**—the rejection of one offer and the proposal of a new one—and the original offer to sell for $20,000 is ended.

    The buyer cannot then insist that the vendor sell at the first offer price of $20,000. The vendor is free to walk away from the deal, as its offer is terminated. Of course, the vendor has a choice and may agree to sell at the first offer price, but it does not have not do so.

    Sign Back   A counter-offer in real estate transactions is a called a **sign back**. A seller might list a property for $500,000—this is an invitation to treat.[6] A purchaser then submits an offer for $450,000, and the vendor makes a counter-offer—signs back the deal—at $490,000.

counter-offer
the rejection of one offer and the proposal of a new one

Legalese

◾ *Critical Concepts of* Counter-Offers

- When an offer is rejected it is put to an end.
- When a counter-offer is made, it ends the previous offer.
- An acceptance that includes any change in terms is a counter-offer.

---

6. The listing is an invitation to treat because some essential terms, such as the closing date, are not usually mentioned in the listing.

Business Law Applied

⓫ Lee Tran bought a new office and warehouse building. It was in a new industrial estate, so the landscaping around the area left something to be desired. He decided to have four 20-foot tall maple trees planted on the north side of the property. He received an offer from Salvia Landscaping that it would supply and plant the trees for $800. Tran replied that he was willing to pay $600.

Salvia Landscaping said that, for $600, it would supply four trees, 15 feet in height.

Tran then said that at that price he would like the four 20-foot tall trees. Salvia Landscaping replied that it was not interested.

At this point, Tran decided that he would accept the offer for four trees, 15-feet tall, at a price of $600.

Salvia Landscaping decided that it didn't want to deal with this client and walked away.

a) Was Tran legally entitled to accept Salvia's offer of $600 for the four 15-foot trees?
b) Was Salvia Landscaping in a position simply to opt out of the deal?

Options

One way to prevent an offeror from being able to revoke an offer is to make it an **option**, which is a new and separate contract to keep an offer open for a specified time in return for a sum of money. Money paid for an option is not considered part of the purchase price if the offeree decides to accept the offer. If the offeree does not accept the offer, the sum paid for the option is not refundable.

For example, the owner of a car advertises the vehicle for sale at $10,000. A potential purchaser says, "Here is $100 to hold the offer open until tomorrow at 12:00 noon." In this case, an option has been paid for, and the offer cannot be withdrawn before noon the next day. However, if nothing is paid specifically to keep the offer open, the offeror can withdraw the offer even if it is open until a certain date.

Stock Options

A form of offer that is playing an increasingly significant role in modern business is the stock, or share, option. In the case of a stock option, a potential purchaser pays the owner of the stock an agreed sum of money. In return, the owner guarantees to keep the buyer's option to purchase open for a given length of time. The money paid is for the option only, and is not applied to the purchase price.

Employers sometimes give employees a stock option on the company's shares as an incentive to encourage good work. If the shares increase in value, the employee stands to gain financially. Stock options such as these are part of an employment contract, and no money is paid for them by the employee.

How Do Stock Options Work?   On January 4, Miller says to Gardi, "Your 500 shares in Apple Computers are selling for $10 each on the stock market today. I'll take a 30-day option to buy your shares at that price, paying you $1000 for the option." Gardi agrees, and Miller hands over $1,000. If, at the end of the 30 days, Miller decides to exercise his option and actually buy the shares, he will pay Gardi $5,000. If Miller decides that he does not want to purchase the shares, he does not receive a refund of his $1,000.

option
a new and separate contract to keep an offer open for a specified time in return for a sum of money

What would persuade Miller to buy Gardi's shares? Consider two possible scenarios:

a) One week after Miller pays for the option to purchase, the price of the shares on the stock market rises to $15. If Miller exercises his option and buys the shares, he will make a profit of $5 a share, a total of $2,500.

b) One week after Miller takes the option, the price of the stock falls to $5 a share. Miller obviously does not buy. He has paid $1,000 for the chance that the stock will go up, and has lost that amount. Gardi has made a profit of $1,000 on the arrangement.

■ *Business Law* Applied

⑫ **Rei-mar Investments** Ltd. offered to purchase a business from Mrs. R. E. Christie. The offer contained the clause: "This offer is subject to inspection and purchaser's financial arrangements on or before October 12, 2003."

Rei-mar had difficulty finding financing, and asked that the date by which the inspection must be completed be extended to November 23; the firm also requested the *closing date* should be November 30. In return, it agreed to pay $2,500.

The company needed a second extension of both dates, to December 21 and 27, 2003, respectively. Mrs. Christie agreed, but received no more money.

On November 27, Mrs. Christie wrote to inform Rei-mar that she had cancelled the second extension and had sold the property to another buyer for a far better price.

Rei-mar sued Mrs. Christie for breach of contract.

a) Was Mrs. Christie entitled to cancel the agreement?
b) How might Rei-mar have protected its interests?

Conditional Offers

Often an offer is conditional on specific criteria first being met. In the Rei-mar case above, for example, the offer depended on the purchaser's finding the property in good condition after inspecting it, and then obtaining adequate financing for the deal. See the Agreement of Purchase and Sale for a Business in Leased Premises in the Appendix at the end of this chapter for similar conditional clauses.

In the Rychjohn Investments case, p. 154, Rychjohn wanted to buy a building and have the tenant out immediately. In order to do so, the company had to purchase two property interests—the building itself and the lease. Rather than negotiating a final agreement with the leaseholder, Rychjohn could have made that deal conditional upon its successful purchase of the building.

In buying a building such as a house or a store, the physical condition of the property is extremely important. For that reason, a purchaser is unlikely to finalize the agreement until the structure is inspected by a competent building contractor. When a business is sold, profitability is of major concern. Thus, the purchaser will only finalize a sale agreement when the books and records have been inspected and shown to support the profit level claimed by the seller.

If the interests of both parties are affected by the condition, it cannot be waived by one party alone. This type of condition is called a true condition precedent. If, for example, an agreement to purchase land is made subject to the purchaser obtaining a zoning change within 60 days, and the change is not made in time, the purchaser cannot waive the condition and conclude the deal without the consent of the seller. The courts have held that the seller in this type of situation has an interest affected because it has not been able to sell its property to others for 60 days.

When a conditional offer is accepted, a conditional contract is created.

Marshall v. Bernard Place Corp., [2002] CanLII 24835 (ON.C.A.)

Mr. and Mrs. Marshall agreed to purchase a home from Bernard Place Corporation for $500,000.00 and gave a deposit of $150,000.00. The Agreement contained the following clause:

"This Agreement is conditional upon the Purchasers obtaining a inspection report satisfactory to them in their sole and absolute discretion."

The Plaintiffs obtained a report that identified several deficiencies which could be repaired at a minor cost. The Plaintiffs refused to close and sued for return of the deposit relying on the above clause. The Defendant claimed that as the deficiencies were minor, the Plaintiffs were not acting in good faith.

The Court's Decision

The clauses drafted gave the Plaintiffs the right to make a subjective decision. There was no restriction saying that minor deficiencies would be acceptable. The wording of the clause permitted the Plaintiffs to assess whether the risks, uncertainties and inconvenience associated with the deficiencies were acceptable according to their own subjective circumstances.

The Defendant was ordered to return the deposit.

While the concept of true condition precedent has been much criticized, it is well entrenched in the law. To give the purchaser the right to waive the condition without the consent of the seller, there must be a phrase to that effect in the contract, for example: "This condition is solely for the purchaser's benefit and can be waived by the purchaser unilaterally." Because it is difficult to tell when the court may find that the vendor had an interest affected by a condition precedent, it is the better practice to add such a phrase to all conditional clauses—assuming the vendor will agree!

Business Alert!

Critical Concepts of Conditional Offers

- An offer can contain a condition which, if not fulfilled, means the contract will not become an enforceable agreement.
- The party who asked for the condition must act in good faith in trying to fulfill it.
- All parties must co-operate in attempting to fulfill conditions.
- Conditions often require the consent of both parties in order to be waived, unless the contract specifies otherwise.

Business Law Applied

⑬ a) Does the *Marshall v. Barnard Place Corporation* decision permit a purchaser to cancel an agreement with such a clause in it because the market price has dropped? What wording in the decision prevents that from happening?

   b) How could a seller protect itself in negotiations respecting a similar conditional clause?

⑭ **Kumar Sharma made** an offer to buy a house. The offer was conditional on his being able to obtain financing. Before the offer expired, he found another house that was more to his liking, and so made no effort to arrange financing for the first property.

On the day the conditional offer expired, Sharma told the seller that he did not have financing and, since the condition was unfulfilled, the agreement was at an end.

   a) Did Sharma make reasonable efforts to fulfill the condition?

   b) Could he rely on the financing condition to escape from the agreement?

Acceptance

When an offer is accepted, a contract is formed. The deal is legally binding, and will be enforced by the courts.

acceptance
an unqualified and unconditional agreement to the terms of the offer

The **acceptance** must be an unqualified and unconditional agreement to the terms of the offer. This unequivocal acceptance requirement is called "the mirror image rule." This metaphor demonstrates the requirement that the acceptance has to reflect the offer exactly as it is made without variation just like a mirror. You cannot say, "I'll accept if my accountant tells me that your records are in order." If you do, you have not in fact accepted the offer in the eyes of the law, and no contract exists.

Silence is not acceptance. Additionally, the person making the offer cannot impose a term such as "if we do not hear from you, we will assume that you have accepted."

While failing to respond will not be acceptance, silence plus use of the goods could be acceptance by conduct. The court may infer from the use of the goods that the party accepted the deal. Assume a seller sends your business some software indicating that the price is $500. If you do nothing, the seller cannot enforce payment. However, if you use the software, that use is acceptance by conduct and you will have to pay for it.

Electronic Acceptance

Some businesses' websites permit persons to create contracts simply by clicking on a graphic. Electronic commerce acts have provided that the "click" is a valid acceptance provided that the software permits the customer to correct any errors.[7]

Business Alert!

Sometimes a debtor sends a cheque to a creditor for a lesser amount and writes "accepted in full settlement" on the back of the cheque. The creditor can cash the cheque and still claim the full amount of the loan. Cashing the cheque is consistent with simply taking a payment on the loan; it is not unequivocal acceptance of the term written on the back of the cheque (see *Brilliant Silk Manufacturing Co. v. Kaufman*, [1925] S.C.R. 249). The creditor would be well advised to write a letter at the time of cashing the cheque indicating that it has accepted the payment as a part payment.

---

7. *Electronic Commerce Act*, 2000, S.O. 2000, c. 17; *The Electronic Commerce and Information Act*, C.C.S.M., c. E150.

■ *Critical Concepts of* Acceptance

- ■ Acceptance must be communicated to the other party and must be unconditional.
- ■ Generally, silence cannot be acceptance.
- ■ Acceptance can be by word—"I'll take it"—or by conduct. Acceptance by conduct might be as simple as using a product rather than returning it immediately.

Negative Option Marketing

In the simplest of terms, negative option marketing means that a firm presents its customers with a product, and says, "You're stuck with this deal unless you notify us you don't want it." Such techniques are illegal in many provinces under censure protection legislation. You can check your provincial government website for the rule in your province.

■ *Business Law* Applied

⑮ Juan Rodriguez, who lived in a province where negative option marketing was legal, signed an agreement with a book club. One term of it read:

Subscriber agrees that the club will send notices of a new book at the beginning of each month. Subscriber must mail rejection by the 15th of the month or subscriber will be deemed to have accepted the book of the month.

a) Was this term enforceable by law?

⑯ A purchaser sends its purchase order to a vendor requesting 50 kilograms of sulphuric acid. On the reverse side of the purchase order, the purchaser says that the vendor is to insure all goods in transit.

The vendor send back its confirmation order form which says (on the back) that the purchaser is to insure all goods in transit.

The purchaser then sends a deposit, the goods are shipped, and the purchaser accepts delivery. Later, it is discovered that the acid strength is weak and unusable because of improper care during shipping.

a) What are the legal terms for the submission of the purchase order, the sending of the confirmation, and the sending of the deposit money?
b) Assume the shipping company has a valid exemption clause absolving it from liability for the damaged acid. Who bears the loss as between the vendor and the purchaser?

Acceptance Scams

Acceptance by conduct has been abused in the past by some firms who sent unsolicited credit cards, books, and other items in the mail. The common law rule is that if these items were in fact used by the recipient, then that use is acceptance by conduct. Consumers were liable to pay for the goods even though they didn't ask for them in the first place.

Some provincial governments have enacted legislation to control this type of marketing. The laws vary greatly from province to province, and some have none dealing with this activity. In Ontario, the law is that the recipient can treat items received in this way as gifts, and is not liable to pay for them. In British Columbia, unsolicited credit cards can be used and the recipient will not be charged for the expenditures made on them.

Contact the consumer affairs branch of the provincial government to find out what the laws are in your province.

Deals Made at a Distance

The Mailbox Rule

Since the acceptance rule requires actual communication to the recipient, what is the result when the parties are not dealing face to face and, for example, a letter is mailed but lost or delayed? Is the receipt effective when the letter is sent or when it is received?

According to a principle called the mailbox rule, acceptance occurs when a letter is put into the Canada Post box if it is reasonable to use mail in the circumstances. This is sometimes referred to as the acceptance-upon-dispatch rule. For example, if an item is advertised for sale in a newspaper ad, which includes a mailing address, then it would be reasonable to use the mail to respond to the ad. This rule is contrary to many people's idea of fairness today. It was developed in 1848 and remains unchanged. That was almost 30 years before Alexander Graham got his first patent on the telephone.

The mailbox rule has not been applied to faxes.[8] These are only "received" when actually received by the intended recipient's fax machine.

The provisions of any contract may specify when communication has been received when any specific method of communication is used. Sometimes the terms of the document may require a certain type of method, such as personal delivery or fax. See for example paragraph 3 of the Agreement of Purchase and Sale for a Business in the Appendix.

The E-mail Rule

When is an electronic document received? There are three possibilities: when it is sent, when it is received by an Internet service provider, and when it is actually opened.

The mailbox rule has been modified by e-commerce acts. They are similar to the model act established by the federal government. The relevant part of the *Ontario Act* is set out below. Note that where a person regularly uses an e-mail system for making contracts, the receipt is deemed to be when the e-mail is received by the Internet service provider (ISP) and not when it is opened by the intended recipient.

"22(3) Electronic information or an electronic document is presumed to be received by the addressee,

---

"(a) if the addressee has designated or uses an information system for the purpose of receiving information or documents of the type sent, when it enters that information system and becomes capable of being retrieved and processed by the addressee; or

"(b) if the addressee has not designated or does not use an information system for the purpose of receiving information or documents of the type sent, when the addressee becomes aware of the information or document in the addressee's information system and it becomes capable of being retrieved and processed by the addressee" *Electronic Commerce Act*, R.S.O. 2000, c. 17, s. 22(3).

---

8. *Eastern Power Ltd. v. Azienda Communale* (1999), 178 D.L.R. (4th) 409 (Ont. C.A.) leave to appeal S.C.C. refused.

■ ■ *Critical Concepts of* The Mailbox Rules

- The parties can agree upon the mode of communication, such as the mail, fax, or personal delivery.
- Where there is no agreement between the parties, the courts may find that it was reasonable to use the mail in the circumstances.
- If the court finds that it is reasonable to use the mail.
  a) acceptance of the offer occurs at the time that the letter is put in the mailbox (assuming that there is correct postage, and that the address is correct)
  b) if the letter is lost or delayed, performance is still fixed at the time the letter was posted
- The mailbox rules apply only to acceptance of offers. They do not apply to withdrawal of offers.

■ *Business Law*   Applied

17 **A life insurance** policyholder was permitted to renew her policy without any medical examination by mailing a notice every five years by June 1 of the relevant year. The policyholder mailed the renewal on June 1 of the fifth year; but the insurance company did not receive it until June 15 and refused to renew her policy.

On June 16 the insured was diagnosed with severe diabetes, and is now uninsurable.

a) Has the insured validly renewed the policy?
b) What rule applies?
c) What proof could the insured provide of mailing the notice if the insurance company has not kept the envelope in which the renewal was mailed?

The Future of the Mailbox Rule

Will the mailbox rule be applied to other forms of communications such as fax and e-mail? This rule decides which of two innocent parties should have their expectation protected. Neither party is at fault if a letter is delayed or lost. Who, then, should have the responsibility to follow up, the person who made the offer or the person who sent the acceptance? Under the mailbox rule, it is the duty of the person who made the offer. All the acceptor has to do is put the letter in the box.

In those days, there was no inexpensive way to follow up. Today, however, with the availability of cheap means of speedy communication such as telephone, fax, and e-mail, the person sending the acceptance may be expected to follow up, since that person alone knows the acceptance was sent and now has the means to check on its receipt. Courts strive to have the law reflect the business practice of the day. It is believed that having the person who sends the acceptance do the follow-up is more in line with current business practices. Thus, recent case law has said that the mailbox rule does not apply to instantaneous communication such as a telephone, telex, or fax.[9]

If you have to give notice under a contract by mail, consider that the opposite party may contest the fact that you did mail the notice. If you end up in court, you may have to prove that you mailed it. The safest practice is to mail such notices by registered mail. Keep proof of any notices that were sent by fax, courier, or e-mail.

Business Alert!

---

9. *Eastern Power Ltd. v. Azienda Communale* (1999), 178 D.L.R. (4th) 409 (Ont. C.A.) leave to appeal to Supreme Court of Canada refused.

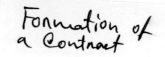

It is also a wise practice to send important notices by more than one way, for example, by both ordinary and registered mail.

The Battle of the Forms

Acceptance by conduct as it relates to a business has resulted in what has been called the "battle of the forms."

Form 1: You own a business and, with legal advice, have created a purchase order that outlines specific terms. Using this form you order goods from one of your suppliers.

Form 2: The supplier sends you a sales confirmation, using its standard sales order. The reverse of this form also sets out a list of terms. The goods are then shipped. You accept them, and place them on display in your store.

Each form was created by lawyers; each described specific terms and conditions. Which set of conditions is legally enforceable?

- When you sent the purchase order, you made an offer for the goods described on it
- The supplier sent a sales confirmation, and thus made a counter-offer
- You received the shipment and put the items on the shelves of your store, thereby showing acceptance by conduct of the counter-offer

So, the terms printed on your supplier's sales confirmation order are the terms of the contract; your purchase-order terms are of no effect under law. The last form that is exchanged usually governs.

The Formation of a Contract

There are four steps to the formation of a contract to sell/purchase a business

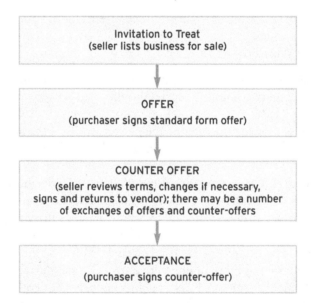

Cooling-Off Periods

cooling-off period
a specified time after a contract is made during which a buyer may terminate the contract by giving written notice to the seller

When an agreement is accepted, it is binding. There is no general rule that allows a party to change its mind and back out of the deal–without, of course, legal consequences. There is no cooling-off period for any business agreement. There are circumstances under consumer protection legislation that permit a person to cancel the contract. A **cooling-off period** is a specified time after a contract is made during which a buyer may terminate the contract by giving written notice to the seller. One cooling-off period relates to contracts made by door-to-door salespersons. The purchaser has a short time to cancel this agreement. The salesperson must give a written copy of the agreement to the purchaser. This cooling-off period applies to contracts for both goods and services. The notice of cancellation must be given in writing.

Unfortunately, there are many small differences among all the provincial consumer protection acts—such as, how long you have to cancel the contract (it varies from two to 10 days), and from when the time period starts. A call to your local consumer affairs department is necessary to check the details for your particular province. You will find these departments very helpful in dealing with consumer law matters.

There is also a cooling-off period, usually of 10 days, for any purchase of a condominium or time-share arrangement in Ontario and British Columbia. Consumer protection laws are relevant if the business deals with consumers. However, when a business deals with another business, the general rule that there is no cooling-off period applies.

Intention

The parties to an enforceable contract must have intended from the start of the process that legal obligations would result from their agreement.

The law does recognize what in former times was called a "gentleman's agreement." This meant neither party would sue if the other broke his promise. So, parties can specify that their agreement is not to be enforced in the courts.

An example of such an agreement is a letter of comfort. A bank may require a parent company to give a letter of comfort to support a subsidiary company's application for credit. The comfort letter is phrased in terms similar to a guarantee but says it is given as comfort only. It is not enforceable. If the subsidiary defaults on its loan, the bank cannot sue the parent on the letter of comfort. For this reason, these letters are often called "cold comfort."

■ Critical Concepts of Intention

- Courts assume that parties to an agreement intend to be bound by it.
- The test to decide whether the parties intended to be legally bound is from the point of view of the promisee (the person who receives the promise). The courts ask, "Would a reasonable person hearing the promise assume that the promissor (the individual making the promise) intended to be bound?"
- Individuals can state in the agreement that they do not intend to be legally bound, and therefore no contract or enforceable agreement has been created.
- In family and social agreements, the court assumes that the parties do not intend to be legally bound.
- Exaggeration has been accepted by the courts as an indication that a person does not intend to be legally bound by the statement. An example of this is advertising where statements are made such as "the best deal in Canada."

Letters of Intent

It is common business practice to use a letter of intent to set out the intentions of both parties involved in an agreement. This document is not itself a contract, but describes what the individuals are willing to agree about. One of the parties, for example, may have to seek budget-committee approval because the arrangement involves a new project. It is understood that neither side has an intention to create legal relations or a contract at that time, but that negotiations might well lead to that end. Probably, it would be clearer if the document were called a "Letter of Intent Only."

NEW DISCOUNT CAR RENTAL

23 Crow Trail Drive
Calgary, Alberta

August 31, 2002

Dear Jim:

Letter of Intent

This letter is an indication by New Discount that it is interested in having you as a franchisee with a location possibly at the Newgate Plaza. The contemplated terms are an initiation fee of $30,000, royalties and advertising contributions of 6% of gross sales, and other terms as set out in our standard franchise agreement.

Please return our confidential questionnaire a.s.a.p. so we can have the usual credit checks, etc. done.

This letter indicates our intent, and is not binding.

Yours truly,

NEW DISCOUNT CAR RENTAL
Per:

Ali Rashid
_____

Ali Rashid
Vice President, Franchising

A letter of intent drafted by a business. It indicates that a contract has not yet been concluded.

■ *Business Law*   Applied

⑱ **Nicole Cormier and** Valentino Torres were at the local variety store. Each of them bought a lottery ticket, agreeing that if either won, they would split the winnings.

Two days later, Torres discovered he had won $1,000,000. When Cormier asked for her share, Torres said that it was just a friendly arrangement and that he did not intend to be legally bound.

   a) Was Torres legally bound to share his winnings?
   b) Would a reasonable person have believed that Torres intended to be legally bound at the time that he made the agreement?

⑲ **Giovanna Genat was** keen to run her own doughnut shop, and signed a franchise agreement with a large organization. The agreement was eight pages long, and contained the following term:

> 23. The franchisee [here, Genat] hereby agrees and accepts that the franchisor does not intend to be legally bound by this agreement and the franchisee relinquishes any right to enforce any **covenants** [terms of agreement] contained in this agreement by action, suit, or other means.

covenants
terms of agreement

Another clause in the agreement said that the franchisor would provide advertising support, paid for in part by a monthly percentage of Genat's business profits. After a few months in operation, she thought that the franchisor was not living up to his side of the agreement to provide advertising, and she decided to sue.

   a) According to the law regarding the intention to create legal relations, could the franchisor rely on paragraph 23, above, to prevent Genat from winning a suit against him?

Objective Test   The phrase **objective test** is frequently used in law. It means that the court does not try to discover the actual intentions of the person at the time in question, but instead asks what a reasonable person might think in similar circumstances.

The decision the court reaches is a matter of fact, not of law. Where juries are available in civil matters, the decision is left to the jury and not to the judge. To see how this works, take an in-class vote to determine how many people think that a reasonable person would have expected Torres (p. 166) to be legally bound by his promise.

The Fine Print   In the franchise case (above), Genat would likely be bound by the term in the agreement that states the franchisor could not be sued on the intention to create legal relations principle. However, this is not the only principle of law that might apply in such a situation. Often, there are several possible remedies available.

The practical point for you as a business person is to recognize that such clauses do exist in these long printed forms. The agreements therefore should not be signed without the advice of a lawyer.

Consideration

Not all agreements or promises are enforceable, since not all are contracts. To be regarded as a contract that is enforceable by a court, the promise must be supported by consideration, or be given in writing under seal.

Consideration is given in exchange for a promise. The consideration must be given by the promisee to the person who makes the promise (the promisor).

What Is Consideration?

The consideration can be anything of value in the eyes of the law—the amount is not important. One early judge said that if the value given was equal to that of a peppercorn, that would be enough to support a contract. An exchange of mutual promises is adequate consideration. Judges will not let a person out of a contract because that individual has made a bad bargain. However, the aggrieved party may have other remedies, such as misrepresentation, duress and the like, discussed in Chapter 7.

A **gratuitous promise** is a promise for which no consideration is given, and is not a contract. Such an agreement will not be enforced by the courts. The requirement of consideration means that courts will more often find promises enforceable in commercial situations than in family or social agreements. For example, if a contractor (the promisor) says, "I'll paint your house," and the owner (the promisee) replies, "I'll pay you $5,000 for the job," the $5,000 is consideration for the promise to paint the house, and the contract is enforceable.

gratuitous promise
a promise for which no consideration is given

■ *Critical Concepts of* Consideration

- Consideration is anything of value given or promised in exchange for the promise sought to be enforced.
- The courts will not inquire into the adequacy of consideration. It need not be fair or equivalent to the value received.

Consideration   **Consideration** derives from the same word as the term *consider*, which means to mentally weigh the merits of an issue, or in other words to take it seriously. The paying of something of value indicates that you have considered the matter and are agreeing to be bound.

■ *Business Law*   Applied

⑳ **Jana Taddeo tells the Red Cross**, "If I pass my final exams, I'll give $5,000 to the Red Cross." In fact, she passed all her exams with excellent marks—but did not give the money to the Red Cross.

   a) Could the Red Cross sue to have the agreement enforced under law?

What Is Not Consideration?

Past Consideration

shrink-wrap rule

contract terms relating to a shrink-wrapped product, often including a limitation-of-liability clause which limits or excludes the manufacturer's liability for damages that may occur from the use of the product

An application of the doctrine of consideration has created a problem for modern marketing, particularly for the software industry, in what has come to be called the **shrink-wrap rule**: contract terms relating to a shrink-wrapped product, often including a limitation-of-liability clause which limits or excludes the manufacturer's liability for damages that may occur from the use of the product. Products may come in a neatly shrink-wrapped package. There is little room on the package for anything other than advertising. The buyer pays for the product, takes it home, and only upon unwrapping it finds a set of contractual terms.

These terms are meant to be part of the purchase agreement. But that agreement is complete at the time of purchase. One party cannot add terms to a contract later unless the opposite party agrees.

past consideration

the consideration has already been given

There is no consideration given by the supplier for any agreement by the purchaser to abide by the terms in the agreement contained within the box. The purchase price has already been paid. It is **past consideration** (the consideration has already been given) and cannot be used again to support terms seen for the first time after opening the package.

To solve this problem created by the concept of consideration, some suppliers who sell shrink-wrapped products have drafted their agreement to allow the purchaser to return the goods if the purchaser does not wish to accept the additional terms. See the excerpt from the Global Village Communication, Inc. software licence agreement below. As noted above, there is no consideration for the terms of the licence agreement, because payment was made at the time of purchase. This payment is now past consideration, which cannot support the licence agreement terms. There are American cases upholding the above type of provision but Canadian case law on point is in an early stage of development.

click-wrap rule

contract terms which are accepted when the user clicks an appropriate icon on a website document

The shrink-wrap concept has been extended to computer software and in that context is often called the **click-wrap rule**: contract terms which are accepted when the user clicks an appropriate icon on a website document. On installing software you will normally be presented with a licence agreement that, among other terms, will likely contain an exemption clause. You have already paid for the product, so that payment is past consideration. However, by giving you the opportunity to disagree with the terms and to return the product for a refund, the software supplier is hoping to avoid the effects of the lack of consideration respecting the licence agreement, particularly the exemption clause.

GLOBAL VILLAGE COMMUNICATION, INC. SOFTWARE LICENCE

IMPORTANT: Before opening the disk package, carefully read the Software Licence Agreement at the back of the *GlobalFax User's Guide*. Opening the disk package indicates your acceptance of the terms and conditions of that Agreement. If you do not agree with the terms and conditions of that Agreement, promptly return the product with the disk package unopened to the place of purchase and your money will be refunded.

Ross v. Alumni Computer Group Ltd., Man. Q.B., Toews (Deputy Registrar), July 26, 2000, *Lawyers Weekly*, August 18, 2000

Ross, a Manitoba resident, purchased computer software from an Ontario corporation. The software came by mail and the package contained a licence agreement on the outside of the reverse side. There was a warning on the front side of the package that the licence agreement was on the back. That warning stated also that the purchaser should read the agreement before opening the package. If the purchaser did not agree with the terms, the purchaser could return the item.

One of the terms was that the law of Ontario should govern any contract dispute. The software was defective and the plaintiff sued in Manitoba and claimed that the governing law provision was ineffective for lack of consideration.

The Court's Decision

The court found that there was no reason why the supplier could not put in a condition in the contract if that term was necessary to make the contract effective in a business situation. The licensing agreement was held to be valid and the governing law term was effective. The lawsuit in Manitoba was dismissed.

Existing Legal Obligations

Additionally, an agreement to continue to perform a contract is not viewed as consideration. This problem has arisen most frequently in the construction industry. For example, an electrical subcontractor may know that a general contractor is desperate to have the electrical system completed so it can get the last payment from the property owner. This subcontractor purposely delays and then demands extra payment to meet the contract deadline. The contractor agrees to pay the extra amount because it will be penalized by the owner if there is a delay.

There is no consideration for this agreement to pay the extra money because the subcontractor was already obligated by its contract to meet the deadline.

Businesses aware of this legal loophole will offer to do slightly more work at minimal cost, which is consideration, or to have the new agreement put under seal. However, this type of agreement may also be attacked on the grounds of economic duress, which is discussed in Chapter 7.

■ *Critical Concepts of* What Is Not Consideration

- ■ Past consideration is not consideration for later terms in a contract.
- ■ A promise to continue to perform a contract is not consideration.

Agreements Enforceable without Consideration

Agreements under Seal

In earlier times even members of the ruling classes were often illiterate; some could not even write their own names, but could indicate that they had agreed to a contract only by placing their seal on the it. The seal was made by dripping red wax on the document. Then the person pressed the seal, often a signet ring, into the wax. Even after people could sign their names, the practice of using a seal on a document continued. The seal was taken as an indication that the person intended to be legally bound. In such a case consideration is not needed. The seal is sufficient evidence of intent to be bound.

You can experience the effect of the legal seal. If a document were put in front of you to sign with a red seal on it, would it make you more cautious about signing it?

The use of a wax seal became obsolete; a small red paper seal replaced it. On today's standard form documents, sometimes the seal is simply shown as a black circle. Even this printed seal is considered a legal seal and will make the document enforceable without consideration.

promissory estoppel

a remedy against a person who made a promise without giving any consideration for it, often used when a creditor waives strict compliance with payment dates and then notifies the debtor in default for not making timely payments

Promissory Estoppel

There is another exception to the concept of consideration in addition to documents under seal. It is called promissory estoppel, and is also known as detrimental reliance or the invisible handshake. **Promissory estoppel** is a remedy against a person who made a promise without giving any consideration for it, often used when a creditor waives strict compliance with payment dates and then notifies the debtor in default for not making timely payments. It was created to prevent injustice caused by the strict application of the doctrine of consideration. It can be formed by words or conduct.

■ *Critical Concepts of* Promissory Estoppel

---

maker

the party who signs and delivers a promissory note

Promissory estoppel has three factors. It is a promise

- which the **maker** (the party who signs and delivers a promissory note) should realize would induce the hearer to rely upon it.
- on which the hearer does actually rely, and
- that reliance is to the hearer's detriment.

Edgar v. Great-West Life Insurance Co., [1982] 42 B.C.L.R. 67 (B.C. Cty. CT.)

William Edgar took out a life insurance policy with Great-West Life Insurance. Edgar sent a letter that was ambiguous but may have been a cancellation of the policy. The insurance company sent out a cancellation notice but continued to automatically deduct premiums from Edgar's bank account.

Edgar died and his estate filed a claim for the death benefit payable on the policy. The company resisted, claiming the policy had been cancelled.

The Court's Decision

The court found that the letter was not clearly a request for cancellation. Even if it was, the insurance company's continuing to deduct the premium was conduct that would induce a person to believe the policy was still in force. Based on this belief, Edgar may not have taken out another policy, to his detriment. This situation contained the factors that are the necessary elements of promissory estoppel.

The insurance company was estopped from denying coverage and had to pay the benefit in full.

The Limits of Promissory Estoppel   Promissory estoppel has certain limits. For example, a creditor may accept a late payment on one occasion. This does not mean that the creditor has created a promissory estoppel and the debtor can pay late again. In a commercial situation, this is considered a mere indulgence on the part of the creditor, and is not assumed to be a promise to waive strict compliance of the contract. Creditors must clearly and unambiguously indicate their intention to waive strict compliance of the contract. While late acceptance on one occasion may not be sufficient, a continuous acceptance of late payments over a period of time may satisfy the conditions for promissory estoppel. If the creditor wishes to resume strict compliance, it would have to give adequate notice to the debtor.

For an example of a clause relevant to estoppel see paragraph 9 of the Purchase Order in the Appendix to Chapter 8.

Estoppel   **Estoppel:** a means to barring or precluding. The word *stop* drives from the same source, *estoper* (Old French), and it can be seen in the term *estoppel*.

Legalese

■ *Business Law*   Applied

㉑ **Refer to the** above case of *Edgar v. Great-West Life Insurance Co.* for the following:

a) Make a summary in outline form of the facts of the case.
b) What are the elements of promissory estoppel?
c) What facts did the court find met the requirement for promissory estoppel?

㉒ **Deluxe French Fries** Ltd. sold frozen french fries and other frozen vegetable products to Maxim Fine Dining, an upscale restaurant. Maxim had been in business for over two years. Deluxe's purchase order required that payment be made on delivery, but Deluxe had never insisted on timely payment during the two years that it had done business with Maxim.

Growing tired of delays in payment, on one delivery Deluxe insisted on immediate payment from Maxim. Maxim's manager did not have a cheque available, because the office was locked, and so Deluxe refused to leave the order. Maxim could not serve any meals that night and sued for the loss of the night's profit and for damage to its reputation.

a) When did the contractual terms require that payment be made?
b) Was there any consideration given by the restaurant to Deluxe for the right to pay late? Why is consideration an important factor?
c) Is there any basis in which Maxim can establish a variation of the contractual term? What elements must be established?
d) What could Deluxe have done, if anything, to legally require payment on delivery on the occasion mentioned in the question?

Risk Management and Contracts

The law respecting conditional clauses was discussed above under "Conditional Offers." Now this type of clause will be reviewed from the risk-management perspective.

Often when a contract is made, there is an assumption or a shifting of risk by various terms. Take again the situation where you want to purchase a new building worth $200,000 for your business. You have enough for a down payment of $100,000 and expect to be able to borrow the balance from a bank on a mortgage. If you sign the agreement to purchase the building and later find out that you cannot get an approval for the mortgage loan, you will be in breach of the contract. At the very least, you will lose your deposit. You have assumed the risk that you will be able to get the loan. If you ask the bank for pre-approval, it may refuse because it may want to get its own appraisal to verify that the property you want to buy is worth what you think it is. However, banks do not readily give pre-approvals in business situations.

A common solution for this problem is for a purchaser to put a conditional clause in the agreement. A typical financing clause follows:

> **Subject to Financing.** This agreement is conditional upon the purchaser being able to raise suitable financing for the balance of the purchase price within 30 days of the acceptance of this offer. If the purchaser is unsuccessful in arranging this financing, then this agreement is null and **void** (never formed in law) and the deposit money is to be returned in full forthwith together with interest, if any, upon receipt of written notice by the purchaser.

void
never formed in law. You can refer to the Agreement of Purchase and Sale for a Business in the Appendix to this chapter for a similar clause.

You can refer to the Agreement of Purchase and Sale for a Business in the Appendix to this chapter for a similar clause in Schedule "A".

The risk for the 30-day time period has shifted to the seller. The property is tied up and the seller cannot accept any other offers, even unconditional offers or offers with a higher price, for that period of time. Thus, before accepting a conditional offer, the seller will want to be as certain as possible that the purchaser is serious about wanting the property and has the creditworthiness to obtain the required financing.

Such a conditional offer is also a risk for the real estate agents (if any): if the purchaser is unsuccessful, the agents probably will not get any commission. The seller gets some assistance from the common law in this situation. There is a duty of good faith in carrying out terms of contracts, so the purchaser must take reasonable and honest steps to obtain financing. The purchaser cannot use this clause as an excuse to get out of the deal, just because, for example, the purchaser has found another property that is more appealing.

This same risk analysis can be applied to many of the terms of contracts. As you review the clauses in specific terms, try to think of the risk factors associated with each term.

In Summation

The Contract

▪ A contract is an agreement containing certain key factors which, if present, make it enforceable in law. Those factors are:

Capacity

▪ An individual must be able to understand the nature of the business agreement being entered into. In certain instances, the law recognizes that a person may lack this capacity, and will not allow the contract to be enforced against that person. These instances include:

a) Minors. A contract with a person under the age of majority is generally not enforceable, whether the other party to the contract is aware of the minor's age or not. An exception to this rule exists if the contract is for necessities. In this situation, the minor will be responsible for paying a reasonable price for the goods or services received.

b) Mentally incompetent and intoxicated persons. A contract will be unenforceable if the impairment is serious enough to affect an individual's understanding, and the other party was aware of the incapacity at the time the contract was signed. The condition of being impaired is the key, and not the means by which the impairment has been caused. An exception exists for contracts providing necessities to the impaired person.

Legality

- A contract will be considered illegal and unenforceable if its purpose is contrary to the interest of society (public policy) or the result will break the law (statutory illegality).

- Illegal contracts are divided into two categories: those that are wrong in and of themselves (criminal wrongs), and those that are wrong only because they are prohibited by statute.

- If the contract involves a matter that is only wrong because it is prohibited by statute, the contract may be enforced if the party who violated the statute shows that it had no intention to do so and corrects the violation before the contract is completed.

- Contracts involving restrictions on a person's ability to earn a living often arise on the sale of a business or when an individual is employed, and are considered contrary to public policy. Contracts of this nature may be enforceable provided the restriction is reasonable, based on factors of time, geography, and content.

Consensus

- Consensus means the parties have reached a final agreement and a contract is created. Consensus is arrived at through the bargaining process of negotiation, offer, and unconditional acceptance of the offer. (**Negotiation** is direct communication between the parties to agree on a contract, or efforts to resolve disputes without third-party intervention.)

- Unless a separate contract is made to keep an offer open for a particular period of time, an offer must come to an end at some point. This may occur in one of several ways, including lapse of time, expiry of a time limit, the making of a counter-offer, or the withdrawal of the offer prior to unconditional acceptance occurring.

- In general, a contract is not completed until acceptance is communicated to the person who made the offer.

negotiation
direct communication between the parties to agree on a contract, or efforts to resolve disputes without third-party intervention

Deals at a Distance

- Communications in a business deal may be in whatever form the parties agree to, but failing a specified form, the test is what method was reasonable in the circumstances.

- Where communication by mail is required or reasonable, acceptance occurs when the letter is put in the mailbox, regardless of whether it is delayed or even fails to reach its destination.

- If communicating by mail, a registered letter is best for purposes of evidence.

Intention

- It is assumed that parties to a contract intended to create an enforceable agreement. Whether the intention was present or not is viewed from the eyes of a reasonable person receiving the offer. It is presumed that in circumstances such as advertisements and family agreements, such intention is lacking.

- Parties can put a term into an agreement indicating that it is not to be enforced as a contract. The courts will then not enforce the agreement.

- For door-to-door sales, there is a cooling-off period, the length of which varies by province. During this time, a contract may be cancelled without legal consequences.

Consideration

- Consideration is anything of value. It is the price for which the promise or act of the other party is bought.

- The courts will not look at the adequacy of consideration and will not let a person out of a contract because of a poor bargain.

- Past consideration and a promise to perform an obligation under a contract are not viewed as consideration for a new term or contract.

- Consideration will not be required in documents under seal or where promissory estoppel can be established.

- Promissory estoppel occurs when one party to a contract does or says something that it should realize that the other party may rely upon, and upon which that other party does rely, to its detriment.

- Promissory estoppel may occur when a party waives strict compliance with the terms of the contract, such as the terms of payment. But a mere indulgence will be assumed in commercial situations.

Closing Questions

Capacity

1. Boris Ivanovich, aged 17, was accepted as a student at the Cabbage Town School of Welding. Tuition was $3,000 for the term. Because Ivanovich had limited funds, the school agreed to let him pay $200 at the commencement of the term, with the balance to be paid on completion of the course. At the end of the term, Ivanovich refused to pay the balance of the tuition, and requested the return of his $200 because he was a minor.
   a) Would the Cabbage Town School of Welding be successful if it sued Ivanovich for the balance of the tuition owing?
   b) Would your answer be any different if Ivanovich could produce evidence that two other welding schools in the same city have an average tuition fee of $2,200?
   c) If the manuals and textbooks for the welding course had cost $300, and the same books were used by the other welding schools, would Ivanovich be required to pay that amount over and above the tuition?
   d) If instead of the Cabbage Town School of Welding, Ivanovich had attended the Northern School of Origami (Japanese Paper Folding), would the school be successful in suing for the balance of his tuition?

2. Eighteen-year-old Vadim Maclinsky had spent the early part of the afternoon in a Vancouver park drinking half a bottle of scotch, and watching people in-line skate along the paths. After leaving the park, Maclinsky wandered into a sporting goods store, where he saw a wall display of in-line skates. When a salesperson approached, Maclinsky explained, his speech slurred, that he lived four miles from where he worked, and there was no direct bus connection between his apartment and workplace. He thought the skates would help him get to work faster, probably cutting his travel time in half, and he wouldn't have to pay bus fare anymore.

   The salesperson handed Maclinsky a roll of mints, said, "Do something about your breath," and suggested he try the $900 pair of skates. Maclinsky slumped into a chair, his eyes glazing over, while the salesperson fitted the skates and tied up the laces. The young man staggered to his feet, shakily rolled 10 feet across the floor and into a wall, and then said: "This is gonna be great. I'll take them." He handed over his credit card and the salesperson completed the transaction.

   Next day, Maclinsky was at the store's door when it opened and handed the skates back to the salesperson. He demanded a credit be put on his credit card, saying, "I took law in high school and I didn't have the capacity to make this contract."
   a) On what grounds would Maclinsky argue that he did not have capacity to enter into the contract?
   b) Which of these would you recommend he use? Why?

3. Could an 18-year-old living in Halifax, owing $600 to a book-of-the-month club, be successfully sued by the corporation sending her the books?

4. Lorraine McDonald rented a snowmobile from Til-then Snowmobile Rentals Limited. She was 17 years old at the time. The rental contract for the snowmobile contained a clause that said the driver agreed to stay within the boundaries of Til-then's own park, and follow marked trails at all times. Another clause stated that the snowmobile would be returned in good condition. The young woman signed the contract.

   McDonald set off with a group of friends to explore the winter sports park. One friend urged her to drive off the marked trail, and follow what seemed to be a path through a wooded area. She did so, and promptly collided with a tree. The young woman was not injured, but the snowmobile sustained $5,000 in damages.

   The rental company brought an action against McDonald and her parents for the cost of repairing the snowmobile.
   a) Did the company win its case?

5. Sandros Markan, aged 17, ordered a tailor-made suit at a price of $450. It was necessary because of his station in life as a trainee bookkeeper. Before the suit was finished, he discovered that an identical suit was available at another store for $125. Markan cancelled the order from the first tailor. The tailor sued.
   a) What was the result?

6. Benito Lucas, aged 16, dropped out of school and obtained work as a door-to-door salesman. The job required that he visit various areas of the city. At first, he was very successful and, on the strength of his money-making record, persuaded Jorge Panza, a neighbour, to sell him a car for $2,500. Lucas paid a deposit of $600, and agreed to pay the balance in monthly instalments over the next year. Three weeks after purchasing the car, Lucas lost his job. He took the car back to his neighbour, and demanded a refund of his $600. Jorge Panza refused, and sued the young man for $1,900, the balance owed.
   a) Was Panza able to have the contract enforced?
   b) Was the car a necessity or a convenience?

Legality

7. Assume an unmarried woman signs an agreement to be a "gestation mother" for a married couple that cannot have a child. A gestation mother carries another woman's fertilized egg to birth. The "mother" is implanted with an egg from the wife which has been fertilized by her husband's sperm in a test tube. The married couple agreed to pay the woman $10,000 for the service, and they actually paid the money. After birth the gestation mother does not want to give up the child to the couple. The couple wants the court to order that she do so, or return the $10,000.
   a) What principle of contract law would be applied and with what result?
   b) Do you think matters such as custody of a child should be determined by contract law?
   c) Should gestation-mother contracts be enforceable? What problems might occur? Do you think women in low-income groups or in Third World countries might be exploited?

8. Apprentice Industries has replaced much of their office equipment and have agreed to sell the used equipment to Kurtz Liquidators for $20,000. Kurtz has given a deposit of $5,000. Both parties have agreed that nothing would be put in writing and the deal would be all cash to avoid paying the GST. Apprentice Industries has found a use for its used equipment and now does not want to go through with the deal. It refuses to return the money and Kurtz wants to sue for his deposit.
   a) What legal defences can Apprentice Industries raise?

9. Arc Industries wants to buy a used truck from the Depot of Reliable Repos. It obtains a six-month complete warranty. The sale price is $20,000, but the Depot sales rep says, "Arc can have it for $15,000, if $5,000 is 'under the table' money."
   Arc agrees. One month later, the truck has serious problems and the Depot refuses to honour its warranty. Arc wants to sue. What defences might the Depot raise and with what result?

10. Thelma Eisenstein and Louis Leforge had been arguing for several months over who had the faster car. Feeling absolutely certain of his ability to win, Leforge proposed a race from Saskatoon to Nanaimo, B.C.—the winner to receive ownership of Leforge's vintage 1965 Mustang convertible. Eisenstein agreed, and the race took place.
    Eisenstein won, and asked Leforge to transfer ownership of the Mustang. He reneged on the agreement, believing that Eisenstein could not enforce it, in spite of her threats to take him to court.
    a) Explain the arguments that would be presented by both Eisenstein and Leforge about the enforceability of this contract.
    b) Which argument do you think would be successful?

11. Contracts that are illegal, and those that are against the public good, will not be upheld by the courts. Decide which category each of the following falls into. A contract:
    a) to employ an illegal immigrant
    b) for the sale of a business in which the seller agrees never to enter into a competing business
    c) in which an employee agrees never to work for any competitor of the current employer
    d) in which an employer agrees not to report to the police acts of theft by his employee

12. While she was standing at a major intersection waiting to cross the road, Marion Eliot saw Ken Ainsworth's car run a red light and hit the passenger side of a car being driven by Barb Smart. As the three young people waited for the police to arrive, Ainsworth approached Eliot and introduced himself, leaving a $100 bill in the palm of her hand after they shook hands. Ainsworth then said, "There's another nine of them to follow if you don't act as a witness in court about this accident."

    Eliot wrote down Ainsworth's address, then slipped into the bushes at the side of the street and away from the scene of the accident. She later learned the matter had been settled, and no charges brought against Ainsworth because there were no witnesses to the incident. Eliot contacted Ainsworth, and asked him for $900—the balance of the $1,000 owing under their arrangement. When Ainsworth had stopped laughing long enough to catch his breath, he looked seriously at Eliot and said, "You must be wacko, and by the way, I'm calling in the $100 loan that I made to you."
    a) Can Eliot enforce the contract that she made with Ainsworth?
    b) Could Ainsworth successfully sue Eliot for the return of the $100?

13. Sylvia Park owned a very successful retail clothing store, located on a main street in Sydney, Nova Scotia. On selling the business she signed an agreement that contained a term stating she would not become involved in a similar business anywhere in Canada for a period of five years.
    a) Which principles of the law relating to restraint of trade should be applied here?
    b) Is this restrictive clause valid?

14. Rasa Persaud, a professional engineer, was an estimator with Foundation Consulting Engineers in the borough of Alandale. Her job was to predict the cost of certain construction projects, which involved calculating the cost of supplies such as steel and concrete, as well as the cost of labour.

    Her work meant she learned how to complete the estimates, and which were the best sources of supply for various types of materials. Persaud worked exclusively in the firm's offices and had no direct contact with the suppliers or clients. Her employment contract stated that for a period of five years after she left the firm she would not "engage in the professional practice of an engineer either alone or in association with, or as an employee of any persons within Alandale, or two miles thereof."

    Alandale has a mix of industrial parks and residential areas, and is part of the largest metropolitan area in the province. There were two other firms of engineering consultants in the borough, and 100 more in the whole metropolitan area.

    Persaud decided to open her own business as a professional engineer, specializing in estimating. Her firm would be based in Alandale. Accordingly, she advised her former employer that she did not view the restrictive clause in her contract as being enforceable. Foundation Consulting Engineers sued Persaud to obtain a court order to stop her from breaking the contract.
    a) Does the law initially presume that the restrictive clause in Persaud's contract is valid?
    b) What factors must the employer prove to have the restrictive term upheld.
    c) What case discussed in the text could Persaud rely on to support her position?

Consensus

15. Sally Bernstein went into a clothing store where she had never shopped before. Immediately, she saw a dress—exactly what she was looking for—lying on a chair among several other outfits. Another woman, obviously a very fussy but long-time customer whom the assistants knew well, was examining them. When the first customer went into the changing room, Bernstein took the dress she liked to the cashier, and said she wanted to buy it.
    a) Is the store required in law to sell the dress to her?

16. Marilyn Stein's mail carrier delivers a book with a letter enclosed. The letter states that the book is on sale for half its normal price and, if she doesn't want it, she must return it by a certain date or be billed for it.
    a) Does Stein have any obligation, either by common law or statute, to pay for this book?
    b) Do her rights change if she starts to read the book, and then decides she doesn't want it?

17. Which of the following brings an offer to an end? (There may be more than one correct answer.)
    a) the given time period has expired
    b) the offer is revoked
    c) the vendor sells it to another person without you knowing about it

18. Ben Letterman agreed to purchase a building from Robert Zimmer for $200,000, and gave a deposit of $20,000. Letterman also had Zimmer sign an agreement showing a sale price of $250,000, which Letterman would show to his credit union. The credit union would only lend up to 75 percent of the value of the property, and Letterman needed the extra money.

   The agreement was also made subject to Letterman's being able to obtain financing from the credit union in 30 days. It had a clause saying that Letterman could waive this condition.

   Property values have dropped drastically so Letterman wants to get out of the deal and have his deposit back. He does nothing about attempting to arrange financing, and so the condition is not fulfilled. Letterman now wants to sue for the return of his $20,000, as Zimmer refuses to return it.

   a) What various legal defences can Zimmer raise?

   b) Does it matter that Letterman did not actually apply for financing from the credit union and did not give the credit union a copy of the phony agreement?

Deals at a Distance

19. On July 1, Uma Mile sent a letter to Oy Yen Chan offering to sell a rare hairpin for $40,000. On the same day that Chan received the letter, July 2, she mailed her acceptance. The acceptance letter was delayed in the mail.

   Mile changed her mind and sent a letter revoking the offer on July 4. On July 11, Mile received Chan's acceptance letter.

   a) Assuming that the offer was not accepted, could Mile revoke the offer to sell the pin?

   b) Did Chan validly accept the offer to sell? If so, what was the date of the acceptance, July 2 or July 11?

   c) If Chan's letter had been lost in the mail, would that make any difference to the final result?

   d) If Mile had agreed to sell the pin to John Ancores with delivery to take place in August, who could successfully claim the pin as between Chan and Ancores?

   e) What remedy would Ancores have against Mile, if any?

20. Chris Benoit owns a gym that he agrees to sell to Fit Finley. Benoit agrees to stay on for three years to help with the changeover. Among other clauses, the sales agreement contains the following:

   i) Chris Benoit agrees that he will not be involved directly or indirectly in the business of a gym or a similar business that is carried on within five kilometres of the present establishment for five years after leaving the employ of Fit Finley

   ii) Benoit agrees not to make any claim against the Workers' Compensation Fund while in the employ of Finley

   iii) This agreement is conditional on Fit Finley's obtaining a zoning change to allow the running of a restaurant on part of the gym premises

   Finley decides that he wants out of the deal, and so he does not apply for the zoning change.

   a) What is the legal term for the first clause?

   b) What are the three legal criteria that will be applied to determine whether the first clause is enforceable, and with what result?

   c) Is the clause not to claim against the Workers' Compensation Fund enforceable?

   d) Can Finley rely on the fact that the condition was not satisfied to get out of the deal?

Intention

21. At Christmas dinner your brother told you that if you could get the second week in March off, he would take you with him to the Bahamas for a holiday. On your return to work in January you made arrangements for that week off and, at the end of January when your holiday time was confirmed, you contacted your brother to get information about the trip. Your brother's response was, "Get real: you took me seriously?"

   a) Will you be successful in getting to the Bahamas on your brother's money, and why?

22. Which of the following legal doctrines allows both sides in a business deal to be able to settle all the terms of the agreement without triggering contract law and thus making the deal legally binding?
    a) Failure of consideration
    b) Lack of capacity
    c) Lack of consensus
    d) Intention to create legal relations

Consideration

23. Read the limitation of liability clause from Global Village Communication, Inc.'s software licence on p. 169. Assume that one of the terms of the licence agreement states that Global Village Communication, Inc. is not responsible for the failure of the fax software, for any cause.
    a) What legal principle is this clause written to avoid? What are the consequences to the supplier if this principle applies?
    b) What legal principle is Global Village attempting to use to make the exemption clause effective? Will the clause as drafted avoid the problem that the exemption terms were not shown to the purchaser at the time of the purchase?
    c) What types of loss might the failure of fax software cause? What are some of the most extreme cases?
    d) Do you think a supplier of software should be permitted to limit or exclude its liability in this way?

24. Is consideration required in a contract under seal?

25. A contract is a legal idea that has been developed mainly for use in commercial situations. The element that makes it more likely that a court will find a contract existing in a commercial rather than a social situation is called:
    a) mutuality of promises
    b) consensus
    c) intention to create legal relations
    d) consideration

26. While walking along the edge of the river, Meredith Drew suddenly heard someone calling out for help. Unravelling a rope she kept for just such occasions, she threw it to Franklin Morris in the water and pulled him to shore. Morris repeatedly thanked Drew for saving him, and then told her to come to his house later and he would give her a reward of $100.

    When Drew appeared at Morris's door that evening, he was feeling much less shaken by the incident. Advising Drew not to walk too close to the riverbank, he said he had no intention of paying a reward and closed the door.
    a) Can Drew successfully sue Morris on his promise to pay her the reward?

27. Sylvan Corporation was in financial trouble and approached one of its major suppliers, Bolts R Us Inc., to see if some arrangement could be made to extend payment for the material Bolts supplied. Bolts was worried that Sylvan would switch to a cheaper plastic material available from its competitors, and so it agreed to extend the payment from its usual 30 days following delivery, to 120 days, in order to assist Sylvan in its refinancing.

    At the end of the year, Bolts R Us presented Sylvan with an invoice for the interest due on the payments that were made after the 30-day period. This was a substantial amount of money, and when Sylvan complained, Bolts replied that it had received no benefit from the extension of the payment dates and, as far as it was concerned, the money was due and payable immediately.
    a) The president of Sylvan Corporation has asked you to write a memo explaining in detail whether Sylvan must pay the money claimed by Bolts R Us Inc.

Multi Issue

28. On June 1, Maria, aged 17, a child-prodigy entrepreneur, agrees to buy a job-search website business called Big Bucks for Young Turks from Bill, aged 21, for $5,000. The website permits employers to post jobs suitable for entry-level positions for a small advertising fee, which allows job seekers to search for free.

Bill tells Maria that the basis for success is that many job seekers from other countries find out about jobs and come as illegal immigrants hoping to get landed-immigrant status if they can stay long enough before getting caught.

Maria gets Bill to agree that he will never again open a job-search or similar business in competition with her. Bill agrees but says, "This is just an agreement between you and me and we agree neither can sue the other; we are honest people and do not want lawyers and courts involved." Maria agrees and gives a deposit of $500. The deal is scheduled to close in 30 days.

The next day, Sally, aged 21, hears of Maria's deal and asks Maria to sell the deal to her for $7,000. Maria is delighted about making $2,000 profit in one day and signs an agreement to give the deal to Sally for $7,000, which Sally pays to Maria immediately.

a) Identify all the legal issues raised in the above question.

b) Can Bill enforce the June 1 agreement against Maria?

c) Can Maria sell her deal to Sally? What is the legal term for the selling of this deal? What steps, if any, must Maria take to make certain that the sale to Sally is proper in law?

29. Find a standard form contract that you, or someone you know, has signed recently. When this part of the text on contracts has been completed, identify three clauses in the agreement that were covered in this part and discuss the legal issues involved.

Websites

www.legalhumour.com—Site by a Canadian lawyer with humorous stories, news, articles relating to law.

www.duhaime.org/ca-con1.htm—Duhaime's Contract Law Centre. Good general information on contract law.

Agreement of Purchase and Sale for a Business in Leased Premises

AGREEMENT OF PURCHASE AND SALE
FOR A BUSINESS IN LEASED PREMISES

PURCHASER _____ JOHN CONVISER _____ , agrees to purchase from
<small>(Full legal names of all Purchasers)</small>

VENDOR _____ JENNIFER CARTHY _____
<small>(Full legal names of all Vendors)</small>

all the assets of the business known as _____ URBAN ATTITUDES _____
(including the chattels, fixtures and inventory of the business set out in schedule "A" as are now located upon the premises and inspected and approved by Purchaser)

situated at _____ 345 MAIN STREET _____ (the "Business")
together with the lease of the premises, and the trade name and goodwill of the business (the "Assets").

PURCHASE PRICE: _____ TWO HUNDRED AND FIFTY THOUSAND _____ Dollars (CDN$ 250,000.00)

which total Purchase Price include the amount of $ _____ ONE HUNDRED THOUSAND _____ in respect of inventory of the Business.

DEPOSIT:
Purchaser submits (_____ TWENTY-FIVE THOUSAND _____ Dollars (CDN$ 25,000.00)
<small>(Herewith/Upon acceptance)</small>

cash or negotiable cheque payable to _____ FIRST CORPORATION REALTY, INC. _____ to be held in trust pending completion or other termination of the Agreement and to be credited toward the Purchase Price on completion. Purchaser agrees to pay the balance as follows:

SCHEDULES(S), A _____ attached hereto form(s) part of this Agreement.

1. **IRREVOCABILITY.** This Offer shall be irrevocable by _____ VENDOR _____ until _____ 5:00 _____ p.m. on the _____ 1ST _____ day of _____ JULY _____, _____ 2004 _____
    <small>(Vendor/Purchaser)</small> <small>(year)</small>
    after which time, if not accepted, this Offer shall be null and void and the deposit shall be returned to the Purchaser in full without interest.

2. **COMPLETION DATE:** This agreement shall be completed by no later than 6:00 p.m. on the _____ 1ST _____ day of _____ SEPTEMBER _____ 2004,
    <small>(year)</small>
    on which date possession of the Business and Assets is to given to Purchaser, title to the Assets shall be conveyed to Purchaser and Purchaser shall pay or satisfy the total Purchase Price.

3. **NOTICES:** Vendor hereby appoints the Listing Broker as Agent for the purpose of giving and receiving notice pursuant to this Agreement. **Only if the Co-operating Broker represents the interests of the Purchaser in this transaction**, the Purchaser hereby appoints the Co-operating Broker as Agent for the purpose of giving and receiving notices pursuant to this Agreement. Any notice relating hereto or provided for herein shall be in writing. This offer, any counter offer, notice of acceptance thereof, or an notice shall be deemed given and received, when hand delivered to the address for service provided in the Acknowledgement below, or where a facsimile number is provided herein, when transmitted electronically to that facsimile number.
    FAX No _____ 532-6691 _____ (For delivery of notices to Vendor) FAX _____ 392-7742 _____ (For delivery of notices to Purchaser)

4. **NON-COMPETITION:** Vendor and the undersigned _____ jointly and severally covenant not to carry on or be engaged in or concerned with (either directly or indirectly in any manner whatsoever including without limitation as a principal, agent, partner or shareholder) any business competitive with or similar to the Business as presently carried on, within a radius of _____ 5 _____ miles of the premises for _____ 36 _____ months after completion. The aforesaid covenant shall survive the completion of the transaction provided for herein.

5. **VENDOR REPRESENTS AND WARRANTS** that:
    (a) the Assets are now and shall at the time of completion be owned by Vendor free and clear of all encumbrances, liens or charges and no other person has now or shall at the time of closing have any interest in the assets except
    (b) Vendor is not now and shall not at the time of completion be a non-resident person within the meaning of section 116 of the Income Tax Act (Canada);
    (c) the Business has been carried on in the ordinary course and all financial statements and other information provided to Purchaser are true, accurate and correct in all material respects and have been prepared in accordance with generally accepted accounting principles applied on a consistent basis and Vendor shall, at the time of completion, have no liabilities, contingent or otherwise, except as reflected therein or in the statement to be delivered pursuant to the Bulk Sales Act (none of which shall be inconsistent with past practice or materially adverse);
    (d) no expenditures shall be made out of the ordinary course of business prior to closing and the Business shall be carried on up to the time of completion in the ordinary course and in a commercially reasonable manner with a view to preserving the goodwill of the Business;
    (e) the tangible Assets are now and shall at the time of completion be in good condition, subject only in the case of equipment to reasonable wear and tear;
    (f) Vendor is not in default of any agreements related to the Business and there are no actions, suits or proceedings against or on behalf of the Vendor, pending or threatened, which may affect the Business, and the Vendor is not aware of any existing grounds on which any such action, suit or proceeding might be commenced;
    (g) there is a good, valid and subsisting lease of the premises for a term of _____ 2 _____ years at a monthly rental of $ _____ 2,000.00 _____ expiring on the _____ 1ST _____ day of _____ SEPTEMBER _____ (a copy of which lease is attached hereto);
    <small>(year)</small>
    (h) there are not now and shall not at the time of completion be any employees of the Business except the following, all of whom can be dismissed on the minimum applicable statutory notice period without further liability: _____ N/A _____

6. **VENDOR COVENANTS:**
   (a) to comply with section 5 of the Retail Sales Tax Act;
   (b) to comply with the Bulk Sale Act;
   (c) to deliver to Purchaser at or before the time of completion the written consent of the lessor to the assignment of the lease of the premises to Purchaser;
   (d) to indemnify and save harmless the Purchaser from and against all liabilities, claims and demands in connection with the purchased business existing or incurred as at the time of completion and not shown on the financial statements provided to the Purchaser or in the statement delivered pursuant to the Bulk Sales Act or expressly agreed to be assumed by the Purchaser in this Agreement.

7. **PURCHASER REPRESENTS AND WARRANTS** that Purchaser is not now and shall not at the time of completion be a non-eligible person within the meaning of the Investment Canada Act.

8. **PURCHASER COVENANT** to pay all applicable retail sales tax and federal sales tax on completion (or furnish appropriate exemption certificates) eligible in respect to this transaction.

9. **THE OBLIGATION OF PURCHASER** to complete this transaction shall be subject to satisfaction of the following conditions (which may be waived in whole or in part by Purchaser without prejudice to any claim for breach of covenant, representation or warranty):
   (a) the representations and warranties of Vendor shall be true at and as of completion as if given at that time;
   (b) Vendor shall have performed all covenants to be performed by Vendor at or prior to the time of completion.

10. **INVENTORY:** Prior to completion, either party may elect by written notice to the other that the inventory shall be physically counted after the close of business on the day prior to completion and valued at Vendor's cost thereof in which case the total Purchase Price shall be increased or decreased to the extent that the valuation so obtained is greater than or less than the amount set for inventory stated above. Failing such an election, neither Vendor or Purchaser may dispute the amount of valuation of inventory.

11. **ADJUSTMENTS:** Any business taxes, insurance, rent, hydro, water, fuel, employee's wages and vacation pay and usual prepaid items being transferred to Purchaser, as applicable, shall be apportioned and allowed to the day of completion, the day of completion itself to be apportioned to the Purchaser.

12. **THE BILL OF SALE** and other transfer documents are to be prepared at Vendor's expense and any security documents are to be prepared at the expense of Purchaser, and each party is to pay the costs of registration of their own documents.

13. **AGENCY:** It is understood that the brokers involved in the transaction represent the parties as set out in the Confirmation of Representation below.

15. **TENDER:** Any tender of documents or money hereunder may be made upon Vendor or Purchaser or their respective lawyers on the day set for completion. Money may be tendered by bank draft or cheque certified by a Chartered Bank, Trust Company, Province of Ontario Savings Office, Credit Union or Caisse Populaire.

16. **AGREEMENT IN WRITING:** This offer when accepted shall constitute a binding agreement of purchase and sale, and time shall in all respects be of the essence of this Agreement. There is no representation, warranty, collateral agreement or condition affecting this Agreement other than as expressed herein. If there is conflict between any provision added to this Agreement (including any Schedule attached hereto) and any provision in the standard pre-set portion hereof, the added provision shall supersede the standard pre-set provision to the extent of such conflict. This Agreement shall be read with all changes of gender or number required by the context. The heirs, executors, administrators, successors and assigns of the undersigned are bound by the terms herein.

DATED at _____ this _____ **30TH** _____ day of _____ **APRIL, 2004** _____

SIGNED, SEALED AND DELIVERED   IN WITNESS whereof I have hereunto set my hand and seal:
in the presence of:

_____   _____ **John** _____ (Affix Seal) _____
                                                    (Purchaser)   (Date)

_____   _____ (Affix Seal) _____
                                                    (Purchaser)   (Date)

VENDOR accepts the above Offer and agrees with the Agent above named, in consideration for his services in procuring the said Offer, to pay him on the date above fixed for completion, a commission of ____ **6** ____ % of the Total Purchase Price, which commission may be deducted from the deposit. I hereby irrevocably instruct my solicitor to pay direct to the Agent any unpaid balance of commission from the proceeds of the sale.

DATED AT _____ this _____ **1ST** _____ day of _____ **JULY, 2004** _____

SIGNED, SEALED AND DELIVERED   IN WITNESS where of I have hereunto set my hand and seal:
in the presence

_____   _____ **Jeniffer** _____ (Affix Seal) _____
                                                    (Vendor)   (Date)

_____   _____ (Affix Seal) _____
                                                    (Vendor)   (Date)

(THE UNDERSIGNED _____ in consideration of Purchaser
entering into this Agreement, hereby executes this Agreement for the purpose of paragraph 5.

DATED at _____ this _____ _____ day of _____ 19 _____

SIGNED, SEALED AND DELIVERED   IN WITNESS whereof I have hereunto set my hand and seal:
in the presence of:

_____   _____ (Affix Seal) _____
                                                    (Vendor)   (Date)

SCHEDULE "A"

1. This offer is conditional upon the Purchaser's approval of the gross weekly sales figure which shall be not less than $4,000.00 upon expiration of the one (1) week inspection period. In this respect, the Vendor agrees to allow the Purchaser to inspect the operation of the business during the normal business hours and assist the Purchaser in familiarizing with the daily operation of the business for the period of one (1) week after the acceptance of this offer, such one week period to be determined by the parties hereto.

2. It is a further condition of this offer that the Purchaser will have the right to continue the use of the business name, "Urban Attitudes" and in that regard, the Vendor shall register the Declaration of Dissolution of the partnership name.

3. All conditions in this offer are for the benefit of the Purchaser only and may be waived at any time or times at the option of the Purchaser.

4. This offer is conditional upon the Purchaser arranging satisfactory financing on or before July 1, 2004; otherwise this offer shall become null and void and the deposit is to be returned to the Purchaser without any deduction or penalty.

Important Terms in Business Contracts

The Age of the Standard Form Contract

Contract law was developed in an age when both the purchaser and the seller usually knew and dealt with each other on a face-to-face basis. The seller often made the product or supplied the service, and all the terms of the sale were specifically negotiated. One hundred years ago, if you wanted to buy a dresser you would have gone directly to a cabinetmaker. There, you might see a model of the exact dresser that you wanted. You would be able to talk to the maker, a skilled craftsman, about the quality, and you would be able to bargain about the price. The contract would be custom made to your purchase.

Today, if you want to purchase a DVD player at an electronics store, you will probably deal with a salesperson who may or may not know much about these units, or about electronics at all. That salesperson will work for a dealer who purchased the unit already boxed from a wholesaler or a distributor. The distributor will have obtained the product from the manufacturer. Even the manufacturer may have obtained components from other suppliers. The price is not negotiable, and you will pay whatever is asked. The terms of the contract are also not negotiable.

Mass-production and mass-marketing techniques have created standardized approaches to all aspects of the business process. Just as the transactions are standardized or similar, and the marketing approach is standardized, so too are the contractual terms. This modern business contract has come to be known as the **standard form contract**: an offer presented in a printed document, the terms of which are the same for all customers, and which becomes a contract when signed (accepted) by the customer.

The standard form contract has proven to be a great advantage to business, and is in harmony with mass-marketing approaches. However, it has also created inequalities for those who are purchasing goods or services according to such an agreement.

Standard form contracts are drawn up by teams of lawyers employed by large business organizations or special interest groups. For example, the standard form agreement for the purchase and sale of a car (see Appendix) is prepared by an automobile dealers' association. New—and used—car dealership associations use forms adapted from a similar precedent. If you are going to be buying or selling a car through a dealership, this is the type of agreement that you will likely be asked to sign. Similarly, the common printed contract for the purchase of a small

standard form contract
an offer presented in a printed document, the terms of which are the same for all customers, and which becomes a contract when signed (accepted) by the customer

business (see Appendix to Chapter 5) is not only drawn up by the real estate brokers' associations, but is also often filled out by the real estate agent and not by a lawyer.

In a consumer retail sale the salesperson who presents the agreement may have absolutely no understanding of what the form actually means. The contract is put in front of the purchaser, who is told, "Sign here," and neither the salesperson nor the customer realizes the implications of many of the terms.

Business Alert!

Business Protections   It cannot be overstressed that many of the protections that are developed by both courts and legislatures respecting the abuse of standard form contracts are focused on the consumer. A business person does not necessarily have these protections. As a general rule, it is better to assume that you will be held to any agreement that you sign.

Agreements That Must Be in Writing

Only some contracts must be in writing. Contracts can be oral, written, or inferred from conduct such as a handshake. They may consist of a series of letters and conversations. Though many business contracts are on printed forms, these agreements are in fact not always legally required to be in writing. However, there are often very good reasons, other than the legal requirement, to have agreements set out in writing.

The first requirement for written contracts was enacted by the English Parliament in 1677, in an act called the *Statute of Frauds*. This is the oldest statute that remains largely unchanged as part of many provincial statutes. Under it, the contracts that must be put in writing that you will most frequently encounter in business are:

- leases for periods of longer than three years
- contracts for the sale of land (such as a house), or for an interest in land—such as mortgages
- a collateral promise by one person to pay the debt if the primary debtor defaults; this is technically called a **guarantee**, but is usually referred to as "co-signing"[1]

guarantee

a collateral promise by one person to pay the debt if the primary debtor defaults

The requirement is that the contract be "evidenced" in writing. This does not mean that the entire agreement has to be in writing, only that the major terms must be written down. Therefore, an agreement that is partly oral and partly written will comply with the *Statute of Frauds* if the main terms are in the written form.

A fax copy of a letter signed by the person who was sued in contract was held to be sufficient to satisfy the requirement of evidence in writing.

Statutory Requirements

All provinces have minimum thresholds for contracts to be in writing. The requirements vary with the acts but $50.00 is a typical amount. In some provinces this requirement is included in the Sale of Goods Act and applies only to goods. In other provinces, it is found in consumer laws that set out minimum thresholds for the purchase of certain consumer goods and services. Although the law on this point is changing, government websites have easily accessible information on this issue.

---

1. The *Statute of Frauds* has been repealed in Manitoba and British Columbia. British Columbia, however, has retained a requirement of writing for certain contracts, specifically those relating to land, guarantees, or indemnities (see *Law and Equity Act*, 1996 R.S.B.C., s. 253).

Business Law   Applied

1 **Joan Fairgreif agreed** to be the housekeeper for John Ellis on agreement that his house would go to her when Ellis died. This agreement was never put in writing, but it was the clear understanding to them both.

Ellis reconciled with his wife, and Fairgreif was required to leave. Ellis promised to pay her $1,000 to replace the previous agreement. Fairgreif agreed to this, but when the money was not paid she sued for the sum.

    a) Was the original agreement about the transfer of the house enforceable?
    b) Was the agreement to pay the $1,000 enforceable?

2 **Arthur Wellington agreed** to buy a CD player for $200 from an electronics store. He paid a $10 deposit, promising to pay the balance in two weeks. The salesperson tore off a piece of tape from the cash register, showing the sum of $200, and wrote "less $10 deposit—balance $190" as a receipt so that Wellington could prove that he paid the $10 deposit.

A week later, Wellington changed his mind and did not want the machine. Because he had studied business law, he told the owner that this is a sale of goods and the contract must be in writing or it is not enforceable. The store owner threatens to sue.

    a) Who is correct?

Electronic Contracts

Are contracts stored in a computer in electronic binary code contracts in writing? E-commerce acts have removed any ambiguity in that area by making them the same as written contracts, provided they are accessible in the same format for later reference. The act does not apply to certain documents, for example, those required to be registered (such as a deed for land), or a negotiable instrument (such as a cheque).

An electronic signature also satisfies any requirement that a document be signed. An electronic seal is the equivalent of a paper or wax seal.[2]

Verbal Contracts

Because of the law requiring certain contracts to be in writing, it is a common belief that *all* contracts must be in writing, or that the word contract refers to a written document. This is not true. Verbal contracts, which are frequently used in daily life, are enforceable. For example, many landlords rent apartments based on oral agreements. These agreements are usually monthly tenancies, meaning that it is understood that they will automatically be renewed every month until either party terminates the tenancy. Also, many employment contracts are oral.

Verbal Contracts   While verbal or oral contracts are often enforceable in law, they are not a wise way to do a business deal. Be particularly careful of the person who says nothing needs to be put in writing. If a disagreement develops, you will have only "one person's word against another." One of the founders of the movie studio Metro-Goldwyn-Mayer, Sam Goldwyn, was often heard to say, "An oral agreement is not worth the paper that it is written on."

Example: Verbal Contracts   The difficulty in proving a verbal contract was demonstrated in the case *Miller v. Carley* (2010), 98 O.R. (3d) 432. The trial judge rejected the Plaintiff's claim that he lent the Defendant ten dollars ($10.00) to buy a winning lottery ticket on the basis that they would share the winnings. However, in the *Chamberland* case, a brief of which follows, the trial judge did accept the Plaintiff's testimony as truthful.

Business Alert!

---

2. *Electronic Commerce Act*, 2000, S.O. 2000, c. 17; *The Electronic Commerce and Information Act*, 2000 C.C.S.M., c. E150.

Chamberland v. Provincial, [2008] CanLII 67399 (ON S.C.)

A group of five employees at the Waste Management Department of the City of Sudbury won a lottery of $13 million on July 9, 2005. As with many such groups, the parties participated in a pool for a number of years by contributing a sum such as $5. While there was a core of regular contributors, some joined for certain periods or certain draws only.

All agreements regarding participation were oral. It was agreed that all would contribute equally and all would share equally.

The Plaintiff had been a regular member but when transferred to another division for about a year, he did not participate. Shortly before the win, he returned to the same division as the other defendants.

The Plaintiff testified that on the morning of July 8, 2005 he drove the organizer of the pool, Mr. Provincial, to work and asked if he could "spot" (lend) the Plaintiff the $5 to participate in the pool and Provincial agreed. Provincial denied this conversation.

The Court's Decision

On a review of the evidence the Court found that the conversation had taken place and that the Plaintiff had proved a contract to share equally in the proceeds.

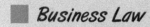

Business Law   Applied

❸ a) In the *Chamberland v. Provincial* case above was the consideration for the participation in the contract the actual payment of $5? If not what was it? Why was it held by the Judge to be adequate consideration?
b) How could both the Plaintiff and the Defendants have protected themselves?
c) Assume you are in a group of several employees who want to participate in a lottery pool. Outline points for an agreement regarding participation in the pool.

Interpretation of Terms

It is difficult to think of every detail when making a contract. Many terms and meanings are often understood without the need of saying them. For example, if you tell a clerk in your business to buy a box of new file folders because supply is running low, you do not have to tell the clerk all the details. He will know many of them (such as colour, kind, price, and supplier) by customary usage. It may be that the office uses only manila-coloured folders, buys one box of 100 folders at a time, and buys them from Business Supplies R Us. Common sense will tell the clerk whether he should fill your order immediately or as soon as his present task is finished. If he sees a sign advertising a sale at half price at a different store, he knows he has the authority to buy at that store without having to check first. If you specifically mention all these details to the clerk, he would be insulted. And where would the need for such particularity end?

So it is with contracts. There are aspects that are seemingly ambiguous or incomplete, but the courts strain to fill in the gaps to give effect to the contracts either by interpretation or by reading extra terms into a contract even though they may not be expressly included (implication of terms).

The potential for genuine misunderstanding between parties is very real. A host may look out the window and say, "It has stopped raining." A guest may take that to mean that she should leave. A bystander overhearing the comment may conclude that the host was only commenting on the weather and nothing more. Can you tell which interpretation is correct?

The courts always begin contract-interpretation cases by saying that they are trying to find the true intention of the parties. But they don't ask the parties to get into the witness box and testify as to their understanding at the time the contract was made. If they did, of course, each party would likely give an interpretation that would help that individual win. The courts apply an objective test; they try to determine what a reasonable person would have thought the words used in the agreement meant.

The courts do not apply special legal meanings to the words in the contract, but use meanings that business people would give to those words. It may appear that legal terminology is being employed, but the term is likely a business word from a past era. The courts will also look to dictionary definitions to see if standard meanings contained there will solve the problem. As well, a contract often provides definitions of terms within the contract.

Additionally, the courts consider specific meanings used within a particular type of business. For example, in the baking industry it is widely accepted that a dozen means 13 (a baker's dozen). An order by a bake shop from a supplier for a dozen croissants will mean 13 croissants are to be sent, not 12.

Businesses frequently use long standard form contracts. There is a rule of interpretation that applies to this type of contract which gives some relief to the other party. If there is an ambiguity in a term so that it has two or more meanings, that term is construed so as to give any benefit of the doubt to the non-drafting party—or *contra proferentem*, which literally translates as "against the one who offers" (proffers) the contract. But as the one who offers is usually the drafter, the phrase is thought of as meaning "against the one who drafted."

This rule applies only to standard form contracts. It does not apply to contracts that are custom drafted with input from both sides to meet individual situations.

■ *Critical Concepts of* Interpretation

- The meaning of a term is that which a reasonable person would understand.
- A dictionary meaning may be accepted to establish the commonly understood meaning.
- If a term has a special meaning within a particular trade, expert evidence by a member of that trade will be used to determine that special meaning.
- If one party drafted the document, ambiguities will be construed against that party and in favour of the other party. This applies to standard form contracts, which are usually presented to the other side simply for signature.
- All words will be interpreted in context. So if the word is not clear standing alone, reading other provisions in the contract may clarify the meaning.
- The context of the business and any prior course of dealings may be considered in interpreting the terms.

Shafron v. KRG Insurance Brokers Western (Inc.), [2009] SCC 6 (CanLII)

Morley Shafron was an insurance agent who signed an employment contract with KRG Insurance Brokers (Western) Inc. The contract contained a clause that restricted his right to compete with his employer after leaving its employ for three years within the "Metropolitan City of Vancouver".

Morley left that employer and within the three year period started to work in the same business in Burnaby, in British Columbia, which is a separate city from Vancouver. KRG sued Shafron for breach of this covenant claiming the term "Metropolitan City of Vancouver" meant to include the nearby City of Burnaby. The matter went through three levels of court.

The trial judge found that the term was not a specifically defined term and hence the clause could not be enforced for ambiguity.

On appeal by KRG, the British Columbia Court of Appeal said that the clause could be read to mean "City of Vancouver, University of British Columbia Endowment Lands, Richmond and Burnaby".

The Supreme Court of Canada found that the term "Metropolitan City of Vancouver" was uncertain and ambiguous. There was no evidence that demonstrated a mutual understanding of the parties to the definition of that term when they entered into the contract and it was inappropriate for the Court of Appeal to rewrite the covenant. KRG lost.

■ *Business Law*   Applied

❹ Franklin had a lump-sum snow-removal contract with Neige Geht Inc. for the parking lot, driveway, and sidewalk areas of the hotel he owned in Prince George. The short written contract was drawn up by both. It required Neige to remove snow from the specified areas "until the end of the winter season." April that year was cooler than usual and there were two unexpected snowfalls at the end of that month. Neige gave an invoice to Franklin for extra snow removal for April. Franklin objects, claiming that winter means until the last snowfall of the year.

   a) Is there an ambiguous or uncertain term in the snow-removal contract?

   b) Would the court apply the contra proferentem rule?

   c) Assume the dictionary definition of winter says: "coldest season of the year, December–February." Assume the astronomical definition is: "from the winter solstice (December 22nd) to the vernal equinox (March 20th)." What argument can you make for the owner and what argument for the contractor to support each party's position?

   d) What test would the court apply if asked to interpret the contract between Franklin and Neige?

   e) Is that test objective or subjective? Would the judge ask each of the parties what the term meant to them?

Adding Terms

Terms Added by Parties

A party may claim that there was a term agreed upon that was not written down. However, the parol evidence rule may prevent any changes to the written agreement by adding terms that vary or contradict the written document if the written document appears to contain the whole contract. Evidence of any kind, whether oral or written, that contradicts or varies the written term will likely be excluded.

One reason for this exclusion is that the courts mistrust oral evidence. When things go wrong, parties are apt to make up a story that varies from the written document. Also, some terms agreed upon in negotiation might have been replaced by later terms. Only the written document represents the final agreement.

There are exceptions to the parol evidence rule. For example, sometimes a contract is partly oral and partly written. Additionally it may consist of an exchange of letters or telephone calls. There may even be a situation where the parties actually form two contracts relating to the same transaction—one oral and one written. Only when the court decides that the document contains the entire agreement does the parol evidence rule apply.

To soften the harsh effects of the parol evidence rule, it has been restated as a presumption. A presumption means that a thing will be assumed until the contrary is proven. It will take clear evidence to displace this presumption and a simple statement by a party will not likely be sufficient. An example of clear evidence might be a letter written by the party now objecting to the term, but which letter contains the alleged term in writing. See the *Corey Developments v. Eastbridge Developments* case discussed under "Entire Agreement Clauses" below for another example of clear evidence of an additional term.

Even under the restated rule where there is contradictory evidence amounting to merely one person's word against another, the written term will likely govern. Thus it is important to have written evidence of every statement relied upon in every agreement. Commercial lawyers have experience in drafting clause to capture in writing these terms that might otherwise go unnoticed.

■ *Critical Concepts of* Parol Evidence Rule

- Where evidence is sought to be admitted to contradict a term in a written document, there is a strong presumption that the written terms govern.
- This presumption will be stronger where the parties produce an individually negotiated document than where a printed form is used.
- This presumption will be less strong where the contradiction is between a specific representation and a general exemption clause in a standard form contract.

Gallen v. Butterley, [1984] 9 D.L.R. (4th) 496 (B.C.C.A.)

A sales representative told a farmer that buckwheat would smother weeds. The farmer purchased the buckwheat seed, but the buckwheat did not smother the weeds and the entire crop was lost. The farmer sued for loss of profits because of the crop failure. The seed company defended by relying on a clause in its standard form purchase order that said the seed company gives "no warranty as to the productiveness or any other matter pertaining to the seed sold to the producer and will not in any way be responsible for the crop."

The Court's Decision

The court said that the assurance that the buckwheat would smother weeds contradicts the written term that the seed company did not give any guarantee of the productiveness of the seed and would not be responsible for the loss of the crop.

The parol evidence rule does not prevent the introduction of such evidence but merely creates a strong presumption in favour of the written term.

However, the presumption is weakest when a standard form contract is involved. Here the evidence of several farmers clearly established that the oral assurance had been made, and so the presumption was displaced. The seed company was found liable for the loss of profits relating to the failed buckwheat crop.

Terms Implied by the Court

express terms

actual stated terms, written
or oral

The parties will have agreed on certain terms of an agreement. These are called **express terms**: actual stated terms, written or oral. However, at times there are gaps left in the contract, and the parties or the courts must try to determine how those gaps should be filled in. Sometimes statutes provide that certain terms must be included in every contract of a particular kind. For example, statutes such as the sale of goods acts and the partnership acts are a collection of terms that were implied by courts into agreements based on the practices of the businesses of the day. For example, the courts accepted that, by custom, a term should be implied into an agreement to sell products that the seller owned the goods and had the right to sell them. This term and other terms implied by custom were collected together to form the *Sale of Goods Act*. Additional terms may also be added by custom and usage of a particular business, though not expressly implied by a statute.

The courts will imply terms which are based on the parties' expectations and which are necessary to give effect to the agreement. For example, when a business engages the service of a lawyer or an accountant, there is usually no express term that the professional will act competently. However, the court will imply such a term on the basis that it is so obvious a term that it was understood to be agreed between the parties. In oral employment contracts there is usually no agreed term that an employee will be given notice for a period of time if fired without a good reason. The courts imply this term into such agreements.

In an early case a tenant leased a house by way of an oral lease agreeing only to a price and the length of the lease. The house was infested with cockroaches. The court implied a term that the house be habitable and free of noxious insects, and set aside the lease.

However, the courts will not necessarily imply a term just because one of the parties wants it. The principle is meant to be used only to repair an obvious oversight.

The test for when a court will imply a term was expressed by a judge of the U.K. Court of Appeal as follows:

> If it is such a term that can be confidently said that if at the time the contract was being negotiated someone had said to the parties, "What will happen in such a case?" they would both have replied, "Of course, so and so will happen; we did not need to say that; it is too clear."[3]

Thus, it can be seen that the court will only add a term that it feels *both* parties would have readily agreed to if it had been suggested to them at the time that they negotiated the contact. Another judge phrased the above test to the effect that if an officious (meddlesome) bystander were to have suggested some provision in the agreement, the parties would have responded, "Oh, of course."[4]

So the test for a court-implied term based on both parties' fair expectation is sometimes called the "officious bystander" test. The purpose of the implication of a term is to give business efficacy to the agreement. Efficacy in this sense means to produce the effect intended.

Duty to Act in Good Faith

One term that is implied into agreements with an increasing frequency in the modern business context is a duty to co-operate in carrying out the contract. This is sometimes expressed as a duty to act in good faith. For example, a bank was a landlord of a large office building. Its

---

3. *Reigate v. Union Manufacturing Co. (Ramsbottom),* [1918 1 K.B. 592 per Sutton L.J. p. 605.

4. *Shirlaw v. Southern Foundries Ltd.* (1926), [1939] 2 K.B. 206.

Nickel Developments Ltd. v. Canada Safeway Ltd., [2001] 1999 D.L.R. (4th) 629

Nickel Developments Ltd. owned a shopping centre and leased a supermarket building to Safeway, which was the anchor tenant. Nickel agreed to a non-competition clause such that during the lease Nickel would not lease to any competing businesses that sold similar supermarket products. The lease was for a 20-year term, providing for renewals every five years according to market rates.

After operating its supermarket for 13 years at that location, Safeway closed down its operation and let the store stand vacant. Safeway continued to renew the lease and pay the rent. Safeway did this because it had a more profitable store a short distance away and did not want a competitor to lease the closed store.

Nickel sued Safeway for breach of contract. Safeway defended saying there was no express term in the lease requiring it to continue to operate a store at that location. It was paying its rent and that was all that was necessary.

The Court's Decision

The court found that Safeway had received benefits from Nickel, particularly the non-competition clause. Safeway was the anchor tenant and a closed supermarket would obviously affect other businesses in that shopping plaza.

Even though there was no actual term requiring continuous operation of the supermarket, the court implied one to give the effect to the arrangement that the parties must have intended. Here the court found that it was reasonable that the parties intended, at the time the contract was made, that Safeway would continue to operate the business. Because Safeway had not done so, it was in default and the lease was terminated.

tenant was also its bank customer. The tenant/customer successfully sued the bank over the cashing of a fraudulent cheque. When it came time to renew the lease the bank would not co-operate, in retaliation for the tenant's lawsuit. The court held that the bank had a duty to act in good faith and co-operate in renewal of the lease. It could not use this opportunity to retaliate against the tenant. The tenant was a good tenant by all criteria.

Similarly, the court will often imply duties on sellers to co-operate so that the sale can take place. The seller of an export business was held to have an implied obligation to assist the buyer with the transfer of the export license. There was no express term regarding this transfer. The failure to include such a term was an obvious oversight and it was a term that was necessary to give effect to the sale agreement.

While a duty to act in good faith will be implied in carrying out a contract, recall that such a duty will not be implied in the negotiation process.

Business Law   Applied

❺ **Haroun Rashid agreed** with Calgary Lumber Ltd. to sell lumber for the lumber mill on commission. After the agreement, the mill raised its prices by 25 percent. Rashid made no sales and blamed the increase in prices. Sales reps for other companies netted about $60,000 in that year, but Rashid sold nothing. Assume Rashid's failure to earn commissions was, in fact, due to the increase in prices by Calgary Lumber.

a) Was there a term in the agreement between Rashid and Calgary Lumber that it would not raise its prices?

b) Is there any basis on which Rashid could sue Calgary Lumber? What could he recover?

Exemption or Disclaimer Clauses

Exemption clauses (disclaimers)

clauses in a contract that limit or completely eliminate the damages or other relief that the court would normally award against a party who has breached a contract

Exemption clauses (disclaimers), often called limited liability clauses, are clauses in a contract that limit or completely eliminate the damages or other relief that the court would normally award against a party who has breached a contract. For example, the *Sale of Goods Act* would normally imply a condition of merchantability (good condition) into the contract for the sale of a used car. A used-car dealership may want to buy a car that has been repossessed by a bank. The bank may not want to give any guarantees about the condition of the car, and so it has a term in the agreement that the car is being sold "as is," in order to exclude the condition of merchantability. (See term number 2 of the used-vehicle bill of sale in the Appendix for a typical "as is" clause.)

The dealer/purchaser then must decide if it wants the risk of buying a car without a warranty. Repossessed cars normally are sold for below market value. One of the reasons is that the vendor will usually insist on an "as is" exemption clause. The lower price is some compensation for the risk.

Exemption clauses are not only contained in long written contracts but may also appear in shorter documents that you do not sign, such as the receipt that the dry cleaner gives you when you hand over your clothes for cleaning. At the entrance to a public parking lot you will invariably see a sign that says something like "Charges are for use of parking space only. Not responsible for loss or damage to vehicle however caused." Airline tickets usually contain restrictions on responsibility for loss of luggage, as well as other exemption clauses. Even concert, theatre, and coat-check tickets may contain exemption clauses. Computer software will typically contain a limitation of liability clause on an early screen in the installation process. The screen will say that if you click on "continue" and use the software, you have accepted the terms of the limitation clause.

Risk Management and Exemption Clauses

A business normally wants to limit its liability for its products or services. A combination of business practices and contractual clauses can assist. These clauses can range from limitations on liability to complete exemptions from any liability.

As an example of a business practice to reduce risk, let us consider a security company that offers a monitoring service. It may decide to eliminate the risk of employees missing signals by having two employees monitoring instead of one. Or it may add a supervisor who would make surprise visits to its various locations to ensure that the employees are awake and at their stations. But the business must add the costs of such actions to the price it charges its customers.

An example of a legal means to reduce the risk would be to add a term in the contract that the security company is not responsible for damage caused by the negligence of its employees. The cost of adding this exemption clause would be minimal. Of course, marketing considerations, such as whether customers would be willing to accept such a clause as part of their service agreement, must be taken into account.

Businesses can also use insurance or self-insurance to cover certain types of risks assumed under a contract. If it chooses self-insurance, the business sets up its own fund to provide for payment of any claim resulting from the risk.

Controls over Exemption Clauses

A reader's initial response to the topic of exemption or disclaimer clauses is often that the business that uses them is "getting away with something." Exemption clauses are a necessary part of business and are fair to both sides if there is equal bargaining power and both fully understand the effect of the clause and the risk each is assuming.

Exemption clauses are fair when bargaining power and knowledge of the law are equal between parties. For example, Chrysler Canada Limited might purchase steel from Dofasco Steel Company Limited, agreeing to an exemption clause, and thus obtaining a lower price for the product. Both parties will have the risks assessed by lawyers, and be well aware of all possible eventualities.

But when the parties do not have equal knowledge or bargaining power, the scenario can be very different. In small-business or consumer transactions, for example, the purchasers cannot afford to have a lawyer examine every deal. A business that uses standard form contracts containing many detailed terms has a distinct advantage over its usual customer. The customer might be quite knowledgeable about competitive pricing and drive a hard bargain, but frequently has little or no expertise in legal matters.

Thus, exemption clauses can be abused. Both the courts and provincial governments have put restrictions on the use of exemption clauses. The court-developed principles, which are set out in the next Critical Concepts, depend largely on findings of fact. Facts may change with every situation, and so it is hard to make general statements as to whether exemption clauses are enforceable in a particular situation. It appears that they will be enforced in deals between businesses, but that they will very likely not be enforced against retail customers or consumers. This can cause some difficulty for the business person, who often knows how to negotiate for a good price but may fail to realize the legal and financial impact of exemption clauses. These court-developed principles for control of exemption clauses apply to any clauses that are unusual or onerous.

Provincial legislation makes exemption clauses in contracts for the sale of goods and services unenforceable. These consumer contracts are discussed later under the topic "Retail Sales". The following case involves providing a service and would now be decided under consumer protection legislation, which likely would give the same result. Yet the principle stated in this case is important because there may be other unusual and onerous clauses in standard form agreements that the court will strike on any of the bases discussed under the heading judicial control over exemption clauses.

However, in reading the two following reported cases, *Trigg v. MI Movers* and *Fraser Jewelers v. Dominion Electric Protection,* note that *Trigg* involves a consumer and *Fraser Jewelers* involves a business dealing with another business. The courts may treat the two situations quite differently because of the presence, or lack of, unequal bargaining power, i.e., the courts may be more willing to strike down onerous clauses in consumer standard form contracts than in business contracts.

■ *Critical Concepts of* Judicial Controls over Exemption Clauses

- Adequate notice: the exemption clause must be brought to the attention of the person signing the agreement.
- Timing: notice of the clause must be at the time of purchase.
- Misrepresentation: If a salesperson misrepresents the effects of the clause, this could be grounds for making the clause unenforceable.
- Interpretation: The exemption clause will be narrowly and strictly interpreted. If damage occurs in a way not expressly stated in the clause, the clause will be ineffective.
- Fundamental breach: A **fundamental breach** is a breach of the whole contract or of an essential term that is so serious that it means that the contract is not fulfilled in a fundamental manner, and the defaulting party cannot rely on an escape clause to avoid liability.

Trigg v. MI Movers International Transportation, [1991] 4 O.R. (3d) 56 (Ont. C.A.)

Daniel Trigg signed a standard form contract with MI Movers International Transportation Services to ship his 1971 Rolls-Royce and 1979 Ferrari from Ontario to Britain. At the time of signing the contract, the shipper's sales agent told Trigg that the company was responsible for damage caused by its own negligence, but not for "acts of God," such as a lightning strike. Because of this statement, Trigg did not purchase insurance for the cars on the voyage. The vehicles were damaged in transit, because of the shipper's negligence. The shipping contract in fact contained a clause effectively limiting liability for all damage to 10 cents per pound weight for each car, a total of $940. The clause was printed on the back of the contract, and was not drawn to Trigg's attention at the time of signing. He had not read the clause.

6. The amount of any loss, damage, or injury for which the carrier is liable, whether or not the loss results from negligence, shall be computed on the basis of and limited to the lesser of

   a) the value of the goods at the place and time of shipment including the freight and other charges if paid; or,
   b) 10¢ per pound per article.

The Court's Decision

The court held that where one party raises a defence based on a limitation or exemption clause, the issue is whether that term is part of the contract. The general rule is that it is not, unless the clause is so obvious that the individual signing the agreement must be presumed to have seen it.

It is up to the party seeking to benefit from the clause to prove that adequate notice of it was in fact given to the other party. If a standard form contract is used, then the **burden of proof**—the requirement that a party who claims a fact to be true must lead evidence to establish it in a court proceeding—is even greater.

The court noted that Trigg did not have to rely on the misrepresentation by the sales agent, as the shipper could not prove that the limitation clause had been brought to Trigg's attention. Trigg was awarded $54,000, the cost of repairing his vehicles.

Fraser Jewelers (1982) Ltd. v. Dominion Electric Protection Co., [1997] 148 D.L.R. (4th) 496 (Ont. C.A.)

The owner of Fraser Jewelers signed a contract on behalf of the company for a burglar alarm system and monitoring. The monitoring system cost $75 per month. An alarm button was installed in the jewelry store that would send a signal to the security company's office. The security company would notify the police.

The contract contained the following clause:

It is understood that ADT is not an insurer, that insurance if any, shall be obtained by the customer and that the amounts payable to ADT thereunder are based upon the value of the services and the scope of liability is herein set forth and is unrelated to the value of the customer's property or the property of others located in the customers premises... That if ADT should to be found liable for loss, damages or injury due to a failure of service or equipment in any respect, its liability shall be limited to a sum equal to 100 percent of the annual service charge or $10,000 whichever is less as the agreed upon damages not as a penalty... and that the provisions of this paragraph shall apply if loss, damages or injury... result from negligence of ADT, its agents or employees.

One day burglars entered the store. The owner pressed the button but the police were not called by the security company for

10 minutes. It was admitted that if the police had been called immediately, the burglars would have been caught. The security company had been negligent.

The jewelry company sued the security company for its loss of $40,000. The security company pleaded the exemption clause in defence and claimed its liability was limited to $900. The jewelry store responded by saying that the owner had not read the contract before signing and had no notice of the exemption clause.

The Court's Decision

The court rejected the response by the jewelry company that it did not have notice of the clause. It said, "A business man executing an agreement on behalf of a company must be presumed to be aware of its terms and to have intended that the company be bound by them."

The court further found the term to be fair in the circumstances. The owner admitted that insurance rates were so high that he decided not to take out insurance. The courts said that it is unreasonable to make the security company an insurer at the rate of $75 per month. The security company was quite entitled to limit its liability by a clause in the agreement. If it had intended to be an insurer, it would have charged a significantly higher rate.

■ *Business Law*   Applied

6 **Review the** *Trigg v. MI Movers* case above and then answer the following:

a) What were the critical facts of the case?
b) What was the legal issue?
c) Who won? Was the disclaimer enforced?

7 **Review the** *Fraser Jewellers v. Dominion Electric* case above and answer the following:

a) What were the critical facts of the case?
b) What was the legal issue?
c) Who won? Was the disclaimer enforced?

8 **Kathy Nelson made** a New Year's resolution to get fit and lose 10 kilograms by Easter. She joined Curves-R-Us Spa and on January 5, 2000, signed its standard form contract taking out a one-year health-club membership requiring monthly payments of $50. Nelson's resolve cooled by March of that year. She had made payments for January, February, and March and then stopped going and making payments.

At the end of the second year (2001) of the contract term, she started to receive nasty calls from the spa's collection manager claiming she owed almost three years worth of payments. He told her to read the contract. Unlikely as it seemed, she was able to find a copy of her contract and read with horror the second last paragraph on the reverse side that said:

> Renewal. This contract is automatically renewed every year for a one-year period unless the customer gives written notice of cancellation 90 days before the anniversary date of the contract and any renewals thereof.

a) If the renewal clause is effective, how much does Nelson owe?
b) Does Nelson have any defence to the claim?
c) Why do you think the spa waited until the end of the second year to contact her? Why didn't it begin collection immediately within 30 days after the first default?
d) Why do you think the cancellation term was set at 90 days before the end of the anniversary date of the contract?

Are Exemption Clauses Enforceable?

This is a complex area and one of the "hot topics" in the area of contract law. In consumer purchases for sale of goods, these clauses are absolutely ineffective in most provinces. For most business transactions, there is no absolute prohibition of these clauses. Instead, the courts have developed principles that always depend on the individual circumstances of each case. The courts will ask the following questions. (The person who signs the standard form contract prepared by a business is called the weaker party.)

■ Was the existence of the clause made clearly known to the weaker party? (Adequate notice.)
■ Was the notice given at the time of the making of the contract? (Timing.)
■ Was anything said to the weaker party to create the belief that the exemption clause did not apply? (Misrepresentation.)
■ Did the clause precisely cover the event? The language of the clause will be strictly construed against the stronger party. (Strict interpretation.)

Entire Agreement Clauses

In standard form contracts you will inevitably see a clause that says that the written document contains the whole agreement between the parties and that there are no other obligations by way of representations, warranties, terms, or collateral (side) agreements.

entire agreement clause

a term in a contract in which the parties agree that their contract is complete as written

An **entire agreement clause** is a term in a contract in which the parties agree that their contract is complete as written: it seems similar to an exemption clause but it has a completely different purpose. Entire agreement clauses are primarily aimed at any oral statements that are made before a contract is signed. They are an attempt to ensure that the parol evidence rule will be upheld. The classic example of this situation concerns the sales rep who tells a customer that the car was owned only by a little old lady who drove it to church on Sundays. After purchasing the car, the purchaser learns that there were a number of prior owners and none of them were little old ladies or churchgoers. However, the entire agreement clause says that there were no such statements relied upon by the purchaser. See paragraph 3 of the Used Car Bill of Sale (in the Appendix to this chapter) and paragraph 13 of the Purchase Order (in the Appendix to Chapter 8) for examples of entire agreement clauses.

In contrast, exemption clauses are aimed at reducing or eliminating liability for damages that may result after the contract has been formed and during performance.

For a complete understanding of the rules respecting entire agreement clauses, some knowledge of the law of misrepresentation is also necessary, and so you will see entire agreement clauses discussed further under that topic in Chapter 7. There you will learn that, as with exemption clauses, there are special statutory rules that protect consumers by nullifying the entire agreement clauses in certain consumer retail transactions. However, no such special statutory rules exist to nullify entire agreement clauses for business-to-business transactions.

In some cases it may be possible to establish that an entire agreement clause is invalid on any of the bases discussed above in "Judicial Controls over Exemption Clauses."

The Enforceability of Entire Agreement Clauses

Sometimes entire agreement clauses are very strictly enforced and sometimes they are ignored. It is hard to find a principle that accurately predicts when entire agreement clauses will be enforced. One commentator suggested that entire agreement clauses are used by judges to avoid having to make a finding against a party's credibility. When a judge really does not believe the additional evidence, the judge relies on the entire agreement clause and says the evidence is excluded. When however, the judge does believe the evidence, the judge finds that the entire agreement clause is ineffective.[5]

In comparing the *Hawrish* and *Corey Developments* cases, a distinguishing feature may be that Hawrish had no concrete evidence to corroborate (back up) his version of the events, while Corey Developments could point to a written note by the defendant's lawyer.

---

5. Paul Perrel, "A Riddle Inside an Enigma: The Entire Agreement Clause," *Advocates' Quarterly* 28 (March 1998), p. 287.

Hawrish v. Bank of Montreal, [1969] S.C.R. 515

Andrew Hawrish, a lawyer, was a shareholder in a new company called Crescent Dairies Limited. When the company was formed, it applied for a line of credit from the bank. The bank insisted on a personal guarantee from Hawrish, who signed the usual bank guarantee form containing a continuing guarantee clause covering present and future indebtedness. The company failed, and the bank sued Hawrish on this guarantee.

Hawrish claimed that before he signed the guarantee, the bank manager told him that he would be responsible only for the present bank loan, and not for any future advances. The bank manager had also told him that, when the bank had the guarantee of the two directors of Crescent, Hawrish himself would be released from the guarantee he had given. Two directors did give their personal guarantees later.

When the bank brought its case to court, Hawrish wanted to introduce the statements by the bank manager but the bank resisted, relying on the entire agreement clause.

The Court's Decision

The court held that the entire agreement clause was effective in preventing Hawrish from introducing the bank manager's statements into evidence. The entire agreement clause stated that there were no representations relied on except those expressly in writing. To allow Hawrish to introduce the bank manager's alleged statements would be to contradict the clear meaning of the entire agreement clause. The parol evidence rule states that evidence cannot be admitted to establish a term that would vary the written term. The written terms stated that there were no additional terms.

Corey Developments Inc. v. Eastbridge Developments (Waterloo) Ltd., [1997] 34 O.R. (3d) 73 Aff'd (1999) 44 O.R. (3d) 95 (C.A.)

Corey Developments agreed to purchase a parcel of real estate from Eastbridge Developments for $2,015,000. The agreement was conditional upon Eastbridge obtaining permits for water and sewage services for the land. Corey put up a deposit of $201,500, which was not to be held in trust but to be used for development costs of the land. Because the deposit was not to be held in trust, Corey wanted the personal guarantee of well-known Calgary developer Nader Gerhmazian, who was a principal of Eastbridge, such that the deposit would be returned if the deal was not completed. Nothing was said about the personal guarantee in the agreement of purchase and sale.

The condition was not satisfied and Eastbridge was by then insolvent and so it could not pay back the deposit. Corey claims that he had the personal guarantee of Nader Gerhmazian. Gerhmazian denied giving it and pleaded the parol evidence rule and the entire agreement clause in defence.

The Court's Decision

The trial judge found that Gerhmazian's assertion that he had not given a personal guarantee was "preposterous" on the evidence.

There was documentary evidence that Gerhmazian's lawyer had given a written undertaking to Corey on Gerhmazian's behalf stating that Gerhmazian would give the guarantee, among other evidence.

The legal issue was whether the evidence could be admitted in light of the Supreme Court of Canada's decision in *Hawrish v. Bank of Montreal* (above). The entire agreement clause stated that there were no additional terms apart from the written terms. The parol evidence rule states that no evidence can be admitted to contradict this term, which says that there are no additional terms.

The court quoted a judge in the *Gallen v. Butterley* case (above), who said that the "principle in *Hawrish* is not a tool for the unscrupulous to dupe the unwary." The court applied the restatement of the parol evidence rule as set out *Gallen v. Butterley* to say that in exceptional circumstances external evidence may be introduced to vary the written terms of the agreement. Those exceptional circumstances occurred here. Gerhmazian was held liable on the guarantee.

9 a) **What was the** key factual issues in the *Corey Developments* case and how was it decided?

b) What was the key legal issues in this case and how was it decided?

c) Why might the combination of the entire agreement clause and the parol evidence rule exclude the evidence that the plaintiff wanted to introduce at the trial?

d) How did the trial judge avoid the rigid application of the principle in *Hawrish v. Bank of Montreal*? Did she strictly follow *stare decisis*?

10 **Pat Monteiro agreed** to sign a bank guarantee for her husband's business's term loan for $100,000. The clause on the guarantee form said that she was guaranteeing the business's debts to the bank from all sources. The form also contained an entire agreement clause.

Monteiro said she wanted to make it clear that she was responsible only for the term loan. The bank manager told her not to worry; the wording was a mere formality, but he couldn't change the bank's standard form. However, the bank would never enforce the guarantee except for the term loan.

Five years later the husband's business went bankrupt. Fortunately, the term loan had been fully paid off, but his business owed $50,000 to the bank from a mortgage on the store that it owned. The bank now sues Monteiro for the $50,000 based on the wording of the guarantee form that she would guarantee all of the business debts to the bank from all sources.

The bank manager says he cannot remember details about a transaction from five years ago, but he very much doubts he would have said what Monteiro now alleges.

a) Can Monteiro rely on the statements by the bank manager that she would be responsible only for the term loan at trial? What clause in the guarantee is relevant and what rule of evidence?

Overview of Misrepresentation, Parol Evidence Rule And Entire Agreement Clauses

Judges wanted to make a rule that simplified contract dispute so that at least the contents of a contract would not be in question. Thus where a contract was in writing and appeared to be complete, i.e. if dealt with all essential terms and perhaps a few other terms, the parties would not be allowed to introduce evidence of additional terms that they allege were agreed upon except in very narrow circumstances. That is the *parol evidence rule* which for simplification purposes could be thought of as the "only the written terms" rule.

However, a strict application of this rule did not always bring about fair results. Parties may have been told untrue things before a contract to get them to sign the contract. These early statements were not made part of the final contract. The introduction of standard form contracts made the problem worse. There were only a few places to fill in the blanks. The pages of fine print were not negotiable. There was no realistic opportunity to put in any clauses regarding the pre-contractual statements.

The judges developed the existing law of misrepresentation to meet this problem. The remedy of misrepresentation is an exception to the parol evidence rule. Statements made before the contract, which persuaded the person to sign the contract, but were not made a term of the contract, could be introduced into evidence.

Then drafters added entire agreement clauses to most standard form contracts. These clauses patched up the misrepresentation loophole, which the judges had developed as an exception to the parol evidence rule. The entire agreement clause stated clearly that there were "no representations". This type of clause was held effective to bar evidence of a misrepresentation in the case of the *Bank of Montreal v. Hawrish* (see the topic "Entire Agreement Clauses"). The law of misrepresentation would be completely nullified where a contract contained an entire agreement clause. All standard form agreements began to contain this clause.

Governments acted to completely overwrite entire agreement clause in consumer contracts.

Judges saw that the strict application of *Hawrish* and the use of the standard form agreements which automatically contained entire agreement clauses were causing unfair results in business cases. Thus the judges acted to adapt and soften the parol evidence rule according to different types of agreements. They then softened the strict application of the entire agreement clause so that when an evidence of another term or representation was strong, that evidence would be admitted to establish the representation. (*Corey Developments v. Eastbridge*).

In *Hawrish,* the guarantor had only his verbal testimony to allege an agreement that he would be released when a new board of directors was approved for the corporation. In *Corey Developments,* there was evidence by the guarantor's own lawyer that the guarantor agreed to give the guarantee and that the lawyer had signed the commitment to that effect.

In summary, for consumers the law of misrepresentation governs. Consumer protection statutes nullify entire agreement clauses.

However, for businesses the exception to the entire agreement clause are limited to circumstances where there is a very strong, probably written, evidence to overcome the entire agreement clause.

Miscellaneous Clauses

Agreements to Specify Damages

The innocent party in a breach of contract suit might be awarded damages as monetary compensation for the loss suffered. Some contracts contain terms specifying **liquidated damages**, which are the amount of damages (in cash, or liquid, form) to be paid should the agreement be breached. The term in the contract might contain an exact dollar figure, or it could give a formula that sets out how the damages will be calculated.

The courts have developed strict rules surrounding this type of clause because of possible abuse by businesses that hold a superior bargaining position. Such firms have been able to force other companies to accept damages clauses out of proportion to any realistic estimate of loss. In reality these are **penalty clauses**—terms specifying an exorbitant amount for breach of contract, intended to force a party to perform—included to make sure that the contract is met.

The principle the courts have developed to guarantee fairness in damages clauses is: the liquidated damages clause will be enforced only if, at the time the contract is made, the amount is a genuine pre-estimate of the damages that a court would award.

Consider this example:

A contractor agrees with a mine owner to dig a shaft by June 1. The mine owner calculates that his loss, if the shaft is not completed on time, will be $10,000 a day.

If the mine owner insists on a clause setting damages at $100,000 per day after June 1, this is not a reasonable pre-estimate of damages, and will be struck down by the court.

If the mine owner sets the damages at $10,000 per day in the contract, this is a reasonable pre-estimate, and will be enforced without proof of actual loss. The mine owner might in fact lose only $1,000 a day. On the other hand, if the real loss was actually $100,000 a day, he would still receive only the $10,000 a day specified in the contract.

liquidated damages
the amount of damages (in cash, or liquid, form) to be paid should the agreement be breached

penalty clauses
terms specifying an exorbitant amount for breach of contract, intended to force a party to perform

See paragraphs 7 and 9 of the Used Car Bill of Sale in the Appendix for examples of clauses that attempt to specify damages.

■ Critical Concepts of Liquidated Damages and Penalty Clauses

- Liquidated damages are genuine pre-estimates of the amount the courts would award.
- Penalties are estimates of damages unrelated to the real damages.
- The fact that a term is called liquidated damages in a contract is disregarded by the court. The courts will apply the genuine pre-estimate test to determine whether the estimate is valid.
- If a liquidated damages clause is struck down, the innocent party can still sue for its real loss.

■ Business Law Applied

⑪ New East Manufacturing Company ordered a quantity of steel from Cansteel Inc. The contract contained a clause that put the manufacturing company's loss estimate at $10 per unit should the supplier fail to deliver. Cansteel did breach the contract. New East Manufacturing discovered that its actual loss was in fact close to $50 per unit, rather than the $10 specified in the agreement.

a) What is the name for this type of clause?
b) What test would the courts apply to decide whether the term was enforceable?
c) Could New East claim the full $50 per unit loss?

Deposits

A deposit is an amount paid at the beginning of the contract as a sign of good faith. It suggests that the purchaser is serious about the agreement, and intends to follow through with it. The amount of a deposit must also be based on a pre-estimate of damages.

The Used Car Bill of Sale specifies in several places what happens to the deposit paid by the purchaser. Should the purchaser fail to complete the agreement, the deposit is forfeited, or lost. Clauses 7 and 10 deal specifically with the purchaser's deposit. While most standard form agreements specifically deal with what happens to a deposit under various possible circumstances, some do not. If this is the case, common law rules apply.

In studying the law of contracts, it is not safe to draw conclusions about the law based on retail business practices. For the sake of good public relations, businesses often waive compliance with the law. Businesses often permit customers to take back a deposit or return goods for a refund. In law, the business may not legally be required to do so.

■ Critical Concepts of Deposits

- A deposit is forfeited if the deal is not completed by the fault or choice of the depositor.
- The loss of the deposit can be attacked as a penalty if that deposit was larger than a genuine pre-estimate of damages.
- The innocent party who holds the deposit must accept it as the complete payment, or remedy, for damages, and cannot sue for more, even if damages actually are greater.
- There is an exception for real estate transactions. The innocent deposit holder can retain the deposit and sue for any additional actual loss.
- It is common practice for retailers to refund deposits, but this is business practice, not law.

Real Estate Transactions

An example of a deposit and a down payment in the same transaction can be seen in the normal real estate deal.

A real estate deal is normally completed in two stages. First, an offer is presented on a standard form, along with a deposit. When the offer is accepted, it becomes the agreement for purchase and sale. The second stage may not happen till several weeks or months later, when the final amount is paid and the purchaser receives the deed (or is registered on *title* as owner)—the deal is closed. A house sale might involve amounts such as:

Deposit	$10,000
Down payment	$40,000
Mortgage to seller	$150,000
TOTAL	$200,000

Deposits   Be careful in giving any deposits. The business receiving them may not be able to refund them. It is a common complaint by purchasers of franchises that they have given large deposits in the order of $100,000 for initiation payments, but the franchise company has gone bankrupt. If giving a large deposit, have a credit check done on the company. Credit bureaus such as Dunn & Bradstreet will do credit checks for members of the public. Also, make certain the deposit is acknowledged to be held "in trust" for your purpose so it can't be used in the business generally. If the deposit is held in trust and the business goes bankrupt, it cannot be used to pay off other creditors and will be returned in full. Try to get a personal guarantee of the return of the deposit from the owner of the company. If that individual won't give a personal guarantee, be cautious!

> **Business Alert!**

Down Payments

The court will determine if the payment in advance is a deposit or a down payment (also called a pre-payment) by examining the circumstances surrounding the making of the agreement, and what the parties said at the time. A **down payment** is a sum of money paid by the buyer as an initial part of the purchase price, and not completely forfeited if the contract is breached. If a contract specifies that a payment in advance was in fact a deposit, this will be of some influence on the court.

The key difference between a deposit and a down payment is that if the agreement is breached, the holder can deduct any actual loss from the down payment, but must refund the balance. With a deposit, the holder can keep the entire amount no matter what the actual loss is.

down payment
a sum of money paid by the buyer as an initial part of the purchase price, and not completely forfeited if the contract is breached

■ *Business Law*   Applied

⑫ **Silverio Ranieri paid** a deposit of $1,000 while the landlord of a retail store had a written lease prepared. The next day, as he was on his way to sign the lease, Ranieri saw a location that he liked better, and rented it. He returned to the first landlord and asked for his deposit back. The retail store was located in a busy area, and it was likely that the landlord could re-let it easily without suffering any actual loss.

a) Did the landlord have to return the deposit to Ranieri?

b) If Ranieri had paid first and last months' rent on the first unit, would the landlord have to return that amount?

Interest Charges

The rate of interest to be charged is a significant factor in the decision to give or accept credit in business. Interest costs, and the way they are calculated, can add considerably to the principal involved. There are both federal and provincial statutes governing the charging of interest. Violation of these provisions could mean that you would not be permitted to charge interest at all, or could do so only at a much lower rate.

The Criminal Code prohibits interest rates above 60 percent per annum. This provision is commonly referred to as the "loansharking" section. All sums payable for the granting of credit are to be included as part of the interest calculation. So, sums called bonuses or finder's fees may be included in the calculation of the effective interest rate.[6]

■ *Critical Concepts of* Interest

- The right to charge interest is a matter of contract, and must be included as a term at the time the agreement is made. It cannot be added by one party later.
- Interest must be expressed in an annual form, such as 24 percent per annum. If it is put in any other way, the *Interest Act* states that only 5 percent per annum can be charged. It can be put as a daily or monthly charge as long as the per-annum rate is also stated.
- In consumer contracts, in addition to the annual interest rates, all costs associated with the credit—such as administration costs, fees, bonuses, insurance, and the like—must be disclosed.

■ *Business Law* Applied

⑬ **Sookraj Deva needed** some extensive dental work. It was to cost $2,000, and he arranged with his dentist to make monthly payments on the total amount.

The work was performed and the dentist sent his bill. Printed at the foot of the invoice was: "2% per month on the unpaid balance."

Deva complained to the dentist that there had been no agreement to pay interest, and that the rate was too high anyway.

a) Does he have any grounds to challenge the interest charges?

Business Alert!

Credit Card Interest Charges   Consumer groups frequently warn that credit card interest rates are unnecessarily high. A user, unaware of the effect of interest charges, can easily become caught in an inescapable trap of spiralling debt.

Most bank credit cards charge interest at about three times the prime rate. Retail credit cards are even higher. It is good business sense to pay any credit card balance in full every month. If this is not possible, and a purchase is absolutely necessary for the business, a bank loan can usually be negotiated on a short-term basis, at less than half the credit card interest rates.

---

6. Canadian Criminal Code, s. 347.

Stating Interest Charges

This excerpt from a Bell Canada statement of account shows the correct way to indicate interest charges:

> **Late Payment Charge Increase**
>
> Due to an increase in the prime interest rate, effective June 26, 2002, Bell Canada increased the amount it charges on overdue accounts to 1.25 percent per month or 16.07 percent per year.

Cancellation Charges

Some businesses attempt to claim an administrative charge at the time of cancellation. Amounts claimed will vary. Amounts of $100 to $200 are common, but some businesses claim much larger sums. There are two common legal issues involving cancellation charges:

- They may not be part of the contract, but are added on at the time of cancellation. These are not enforceable for lack of consideration. One party cannot add a term without the consent of the other party.
- They may be made a term of the contract, but the courts could regard them as a penalty clause, and therefore declare them unenforceable (see p. 133).
- To be enforceable, a cancellation fee must be a genuine pre-estimate of the damages that a court would award. If the amount is excessive, the clause will not be enforced.

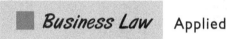 **Applied**

⑭ Accucomp Computers Inc. had a fire-insurance policy on its premises. The company found a new insurance broker, who offered a much lower rate, and as a result Accucomp wrote to its current broker to cancel the existing policy. The broker replied that there would be a $100 cancellation fee. Accucomp does not want to pay this.

a) What two rules about cancellation fees might help Accucomp avoid having to pay?
b) What facts would make the cancellation charge enforceable or not?
c) If the broker can establish that the administrative costs involved in cancelling the policy were $100, would this affect the situation?

Forum Selection Clauses

Venue refers to place: a venue clause determines in which place a trial over a contract dispute will take place. Since the growth of international trade and especially since NAFTA (the North American Free Trade Agreement), Canadian businesses are increasingly making contracts with foreign-based companies. For example, an English wholesaler purchases bananas from a Columbian farmer. The English whole-seller resells these bananas to an American distributor and directs the Columbian farmer to ship directly to the U.S. using a ship registered in Liberia. The American distributor has by this time resold the bananas to a Canadian business located in Ontario. The ship sinks in international waters. There is a serious problem determining which country or province has jurisdiction and which law applies Thus, businesses are cautioned to have governing law and venue clauses in any contract. See paragraph 10 of the Purchase Order in the Appendix to Chapter 8 for a governing law and venue clause.

The importance of this issue was dramatized by the case of Canadian funeral franchise company Loewen Group Inc. A Florida franchisee sued Loewen in a dispute over a franchise agreement. The matter was heard before a Florida jury. The plaintiff's counsel made a point of the defendant's being a foreign company. He referred to foreign companies' taking advantage of simple Florida folk and even mentioned the sneak attack on Pearl Harbor by foreigners.

In a case that most observers felt was of doubtful merit, the jury awarded punitive damages of $500 million against Loewen. It appealed, but the Florida Appellate Court was of no help. That court ordered Loewen to post a bond for the full $500 million or the appeal would be dismissed. Loewen could not raise that amount of money and was forced to settle with the plaintiff by paying him $150 million.

Canadian companies can avoid foreign courts, especially American jury trials, by insisting on a venue clause that names a province in Canada where the company carries on business as the place of trial.

Alternatively, if the foreign company will not agree to a Canadian jurisdiction there can be an arbitration clause so the matter can be heard before an international arbitration tribunal.

Online Agreements

Online agreements typically use forum selection clauses as users may live in any part of the world. Here is an example of Facebook's forum selection clause.

> "You will resolve any claim, cause of action or dispute ("claim") you have with us arising out of or relating to this Statement or Facebook in a state or federal court located in Santa Clara County. The laws of the State of California will govern this Statement, as well as any claim that might arise between you and us, without regard to conflict of law provisions. You agree to submit to the personal jurisdiction of the courts located in Santa Clara County, California for the purpose of litigating all such claims."

Rudder v. Microsoft Corp., [1999] CanLII 14923 ON

The Plaintiff started a class action on behalf of an estimated 89,000 users of MSN in Canada against Microsoft Corporation claiming damages in the amount of $75 million primarily for breach of contract relating to charges for use of MSN services.

The contract is an electronic one called a "Membership Agreement". It contains the following provision, which is called a Form Selection or Venue clause.

15.1   This Agreement is governed by the laws of the State of Washington, USA, and you consent to the exclusive jurisdiction and venue of courts in King County, Washington, and all disputes arising out of or relating to your use of MSN or your MSN membership.

The representative Plaintiffs, two law students, claim that the clause was obscured in the Agreement and that terms of Agreement should be treated as "fine print" requiring specific notice of such a clause.

The Court's Decision

Microsoft moved for an order staying this action so it could not proceed in Canada on the basis of the Form Selection clause.

The Court found that Canadian courts would enforce Form Selection clauses unless there was a strong case to override the Agreement.

The MSN membership contract was shown in its entirety twice and the reader required to click "I agree" on each occasion before proceeding.

The fact that it was on separate pages did not make it "fine print" or obscure the Form Selection clause. As the two Plaintiffs were law students, this point was particularly indefensible. The Court stayed the action.

There are often "governing law" clauses in international agreements. Such a clause may say, for example, that any disputes are to be governed by the laws of Alberta. This is not protection from a foreign court. A Florida court, for example, would still hear the trial but apply Alberta law. Experts from Alberta would be called to testify as to the relevant Alberta law.

Privity of Contract

Privity of contract is the principle in law that since a contract is created by two or more people exchanging promises, it is generally only those individuals who are direct parties to the agreement who are subject to its obligations and entitled to its benefits.

Exceptions to this general rule exist for certain situations. An example is a contract for life insurance. Referred to as an insurance policy, such a contract is entered into by the insurance company and the **insured** (the one who buys insurance coverage). However, if the insured individual dies in circumstances that require a payment to be made under the terms of the policy, it is an outside party—the **beneficiary**—who is the person who enforces the contract against the insurance company and receives the benefits.

Privity   **Privity** comes from the Latin word *privatus*, which means private. Thus, privity refers to a private arrangement. Only those who are part of a contract have rights connected with it; outsiders have none. Privity is the legal expression of the "one on one" concept.

Limitations of Privity

The concept of privity developed at a time when supplier and purchaser dealt directly with each other. (If you wanted a dresser, you went to the cabinetmaker and made the deal directly with him.) Today there is often a chain of businesses between the manufacturers and end-users.

The retailer is usually the last link in the chain and deals directly with the end-user. The contract for sale is between the retailer and the end-user. By the doctrine of privity, the end-user can sue the retailer only for any loss because of a defect in the product.

However, it is the manufacturer who is responsible for quality control, length of warranties, and the like. The retailers are little more than a conduit for the product. The customer, however, has no contract with the manufacturer, and so cannot sue it in contract.

This inadequacy in the law has been the subject of much discussion but little action. To date, only Saskatchewan (*Consumer Product Warranties Act, R.S.S. 1978, c. C-30*) and New Brunswick (*Consumer Product Warranty and Liability Act, S.N.B. 1978, c. C-181*) have passed legislation that gives consumers (but not businesses) a direct right to sue manufacturers for loss caused by defective products.

privity of contract
the principle in law that since a contract is created by two or more people exchanging promises, it is generally only those individuals who are direct parties to the agreement who are subject to its obligations and entitled to its benefits

insured
the one who buys insurance coverage

beneficiary
the person who enforces the contract against the insurance company and receives the benefits

Avoiding the Limitations on Privity

Generally, a party who is not a party to a contract cannot take legal action on it. Nevertheless, there are exceptions to this general rule, though they are not wide ranging. For example, if a transaction is based on an agency relationship (see Chapter 6) or the contract has been assigned, a person who was not part of the original agreement may be able to enforce it through the legal process.

Tort

Whereas in contract, the doctrine of privity only allows a party to sue another party, tort law, which you will study shortly, allows a person to bring a lawsuit against a wider range of defendants. In one of the most dramatic cases in legal history, a person who became sick after drinking a soft drink containing a decomposed snail, but who did not purchase the product, was permitted to sue the manufacturer, but only for personal injury and related loss, not for financial loss. Tort law is now developing to allow persons to bring actions in tort against non-parties for financial loss, but on a restricted basis.

For example, a condominium corporation, which is the legal vehicle used by the individual owners, brought an action against the general contractor who renovated the building, because a large piece of the external wall fell. However, only the developer, who converted the building to a condominium, had the contract with the general contractor. To avoid the problem of lack of privity, the court allowed the condominium corporation to sue the builder in tort.

The loss was recoverable but only because it related to repairs that were a substantial risk of injury to the health or safety of the occupants. The court stated that claims relating to poor quality of work would not qualify for this remedy in tort.[7]

In a tort case such as one arising from a car accident, the injured party may have a broken arm (personal injury) and also lost wages from not being able to work (economic loss). In tort remedies, the economic loss was always a result of personal injury. Thus, the concept of awarding financial loss unrelated to personal injury was historically not recognized in tort, as this was given only in contract.

Legalese

Pure Economic Loss   **Economic loss** means financial loss and covers losses that are usually awarded in contract claims, such as the cost of repair or replacement of an item or loss of profits. The word pure refers to the fact that these losses are not connected with personal injury.

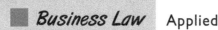 **Business Law**   Applied

⑮ **Your company manufactures** automatic spray booths for use in painting products as part of the manufacturing process. You sell a unit to TAP Technologie, which you know as a distributor for various suppliers. TAP Technologie sells the unit to Biscoe Inc. for use in its plant. Biscoe Inc. pays TAP Technologie in full, but TAP Technologie is insolvent and uses the money to pay other creditors. Now Biscoe Inc. has the unit and your company has been paid nothing for it.

   a) Can your company bring an action against Biscoe Inc. for the value of the unit?
   b) Would it make any difference if Biscoe Inc. had not paid TAP Technologie?
   c) Could you sue Biscoe Inc. in tort?
   d) How could your company have better protected itself?

Collateral Warranty

The courts have also found a legal relationship in contract between remote parties by the legal fiction called collateral warranty. Advertising and promotional literature which is intended to induce end-users to purchase the product has often been the foundation for finding a warranty between the manufacturer and the consumer. The consideration for the collateral warranty is the consideration paid on the main contract.

This principle of collateral contract has been criticized as an unnecessary legal fiction that should be avoided in favour of other remedies. However, the terms collateral contract and collateral warranty appear in most disclaimer and entire agreement clauses, and so the business person needs to be familiar with their meaning in a general way.

---

7. *Winnipeg Condominium Corporation No. 36 v. Bird Construction Co. Ltd.* [1995] 1 S.C.R. 85.

Assignment

Contractual rights can be assigned. Assigning means transferring the contractual rights to another person who then stands in the place of the original party and can enforce the contract in the same way. **Assignments** frequently occur in business. For example, when a business applies for a bank loan, it will often be asked to assign its accounts receivable as security for the loan. **Accounts receivable (book debts)** are amounts owed to a person which can be sold, usually at a discount, or pledged as security for a loan. Accounts receivable are contracts. Assume a furniture store has sold some items on credit to a customer who agrees to pay in monthly installments for a year. The agreement to purchase and pay over the year is a contract. The right to collect on this contract is assigned to the bank as security for the loan—in other words, the bank can collect the debt from the customer if the furniture store defaults on the loan.

accounts receivable (book debts)
amounts owed to a person which can be sold, usually at a discount, or pledged as security for a loan

Statutory Assignment

The court of equity developed rules to permit the assignment of contractual rights. But these rules are very technical. To simplify the law of assignment, most provinces have passed statutes which set out the procedure for assigning contracts. Assignments which meet the requirements of the statute are called statutory assignments—to distinguish them from *equitable assignments* (which are explained below). A **statutory assignment** is an assignment that complies with statutory provisions enabling the assignee to sue the debtor without joining the assignor to the action. The safest procedure is to adhere to the statutory requirements. The policy reason behind the statutory procedure is protection of the debtor. The debtor must know with certainty whom to pay: the debtor cannot be put at risk of having to pay twice. For that reason, it is the creditor or **assignor**—the party that assigns its rights under a contract to a third party—who must sign the notice of the assignment.

statutory assignment
an assignment that complies with statutory provisions enabling the assignee to sue the debtor without joining the assignor to the action

assignor
the party that assigns its rights under a contract to a third party

factoring
the business of buying accounts receivable, usually at a discount, and then collecting directly from the customer

Businesses that sell on credit often need cash. For this reason, they sell their rights to collect their own account to businesses that specialize in taking such assignments and collecting on them. This way, they can obtain immediate cash rather than having to wait for their customers to pay their accounts. The businesses that take assignments of accounts are usually finance companies. The older name for this is **factoring**: the business of buying accounts receivable, usually at a discount, and then collecting directly from the customer. The essence of the factoring business is that it buys at a substantial discount, say about 30 to 50 percent, but it assumes the risk that the account may not be paid at all.

Take the example of a car dealership that sells about 10 cars per week by lease. The dealership may want cash; it may not want to wait three to five years for the lease payments to be made. The dealer will sell the leases at a discount to a factor—for cash.

■ *Critical Concepts of* Making Statutory Assignments

- The assignment must be complete and unconditional (that is, absolute)—except in Manitoba and Saskatchewan; see *Law of Property Act*, R.S.M., s. 31, and *Choses in Action Act*, R.S.S., s. 2.
- The assignment must be in writing.
- Notice of the assignment must be given in writing to the debtor and must be signed by the person making the assignment (again, except in Manitoba and Saskatchewan).

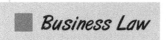 **Business Law** Applied

> **⑯ Nelson Markelj sold** his car to Helen Zawada for $10,000, to be paid in monthly installments of $1,000. When only the first payment had been made, Markelj decided that he wanted to travel around the world. He assigned the balance of the payment in writing to Norman Richler. Markelj phoned Zawada and told her of the assignment; he then got on a plane to Papua New Guinea. Zawada refuses to pay, and Richler wants to sue.
>
>   a) Identify the transactions and the parties. What is the contract and who are the parties to it? What is the assignment and who are the parties to it?
>   b) Can Richler alone enforce the assignment against Zawada?

Equitable Assignment

equitable assignment

an assignment, other than a statutory assignment, which does not require that the assignment be absolute, unconditional, in writing, or that notice, written or oral, be given by the assignor

If there is a defect in any of the procedures required for a statutory assignment, it will likely still be valid as an equitable assignment. An **equitable assignment** is an assignment, other than a statutory assignment, which does not require that the assignment be absolute, unconditional, in writing, or that notice, written or oral, be given by the assignor. However, in this case the assignor retains an interest in the contract and must be part of any settlement and a party to any litigation. This can create extra problems and significant expense if the assignor (the creditor) leaves the country (as in the above question), dies, or refuses to co-operate.

Competing Claimants

A dishonest creditor may assign (that is, sell) the debt twice or more to separate purchasers. The assignment that governs will be the one of which the debtor received notice first. The other assignment(s) will be completely ineffective.

For example, Elizabeth Raymer buys a VCR from Home Electronics Inc. on credit. In July, Home Electronics sells the right to collect the debt for $2,000 to Sure Finance Company for $1,500. Home Electronics gives a signed notice of the assignment to Sure Finance, but does not mail it to Raymer until October of that year. Home Electronics then sells the same rights to collect Raymer's debt to Canadian Collections Corp. in August. That same day, Canadian Collections Corp. sends the notice of the assignment signed by Home Electronics to Raymer. Raymer need pay only Canadian Collections Corp., even though that assignment was made after the one to Sure Finance. She received notice of the assignment to Canadian Collections first. It is the time that the debtor receives valid notice of the assignment that determines which of the competing creditors can collect.

Debtor's Defences

assignee

the third party to whom rights under a contract have been assigned

The **assignee** (the third party to whom rights under a contract have been assigned, Sure Finance and Canadian Collections in the example above) cannot acquire a better interest in the contract than the person who gave the assignment. In law this is called taking the assignment "subject to the equities." Equities here means the rights of the original parties. This applies to both statutory and equitable assignments.

In the above example, assume that the VCR needed repairs—which were Home Electronics' responsibility—costing $150. That $150 could be deducted from the amount Raymer has to pay Canadian Collections.

■ *Critical Concepts of* Assignments

- ■ When the same contract is assigned several times, the first date on which the debtor received valid notice of the assignment determines which assignment is enforceable.
- ■ The debtor can set up any defences against the person who makes the assignments that could be asserted against the assignor (the creditor).
- ■ Even if the assignment does not comply with statutory procedures, it will still likely be valid as an equitable assignment, but the original party to the contract must be a co-plaintiff, or a defendant if he or she refuses to co-operate in any lawsuit.

In Summation

Printed Contracts

- ▦ While verbal contracts are enforceable, statutes such as the *Statute of Frauds* require certain agreements to be in writing.

Interpretation

- ▦ The courts do not apply legal meanings but interpret contract terms according to what a reasonable person would think the terms meant.
- ▦ The parol evidence rule prevents parties from testifying as to their understanding of the terms.
- ▦ In making an interpretation, the courts will consider various factors including:
  a) dictionary meanings
  b) custom and usage in the trade
  c) prior dealings
  d) the context in which the contract was made
- ▦ If one party drafts a standard form contract, any ambiguities will be interpreted against the drafter (*contra proferentem*).

Attempts by Parties to Add Terms

- ▦ Even though a long, printed contract is signed, a party may claim there were additional terms not written down.
- ▦ An aspect of the parol evidence rule raises a presumption that where a document appears to contain the entire agreement, there are no other terms, verbal or written.
- ▦ There are many exceptions to this application of the parol evidence rule, such as when a series of documents as an exchange of letters constitutes the contract. Then no single document appears to contain the entire agreement.

Terms Implied by the Courts and Legislature

- ▦ Some terms of a contract may be statutorily implied. These are terms which must be included in a contract because legislation requires that they be.
- ▦ When it is necessary to add a term to give effect to an agreement, the court will imply one only when it concludes that both parties would have readily agreed to it at the time the contract was made.
- ▦ A term that is being implied with greater frequency today is the duty to act in good faith in carrying out obligations undertaken in the contract.

Exemption Clauses

- An exemption or disclaimer clause is an attempt by a business to limit or completely exclude liability that would normally flow from the breach of a contract.

- The courts have developed several principles that control the abuse of exemption clauses, such as interpretation *contra proferentem* and ineffectiveness in the case of misrepresentation or inadequate notice. Inadequate notice has been the most successful ground for avoiding the effects of exemption clauses.

- Courts are less likely to enforce exemption clauses in retail consumer transactions, but more likely to enforce them in business-to-business transactions.

Entire Agreement Clauses

- An entire agreement clause states that all terms are contained in the agreement in writing and that there are no other terms, verbal or written.

Agreement to Specify Damages

- A term in a contract can set out how the damages are to be quantified, such as $1,000 per day until construction is complete.

- If the amount is not a reasonable estimate of the damage that a court would award (a liquidated damages clause), it will be viewed as a penalty and not enforced.

Deposits

- A deposit is a sum of money given at the time a contract is entered into as a sign of good faith that the person who gave the deposit will go through with the deal.

- A deposit is not refundable if the contract is not completed through the fault of the person giving the deposit.

- A down payment is a part payment on the contract and usually is made when the deal is closed.

- Businesses may elect to refund deposits as a gesture of good will, even though they are not legally obligated to do so.

Miscellaneous Clauses

- A cancellation clause must be included at the time the contract is made. A cancellation charge cannot be added by one party.

- Interest charges must state the annual rate and be included as part of the contract. Effective annual rates over 60 percent are prohibited by the Criminal Code.

- A venue clause states in which jurisdiction (that is, country, province) a trial over a contract dispute will take place.

- An arbitration clause determines that disputes over the contract will not be heard in court but before a private arbitrator chosen by the parties.

Privity

- Generally, only those individuals who have been involved in the creation of the contract can receive the benefits and be subject to the obligations which have been agreed to by them.

- The limitations of the doctrine of privity may be avoided in some situations where agency, tort, or collateral warranty apply.

- Assignment of contractual rights to another party will also avoid the doctrine of privity.

Assignment

- The privity of contract rule restricts enforcement of contractual rights to those parties who entered into the original contract.

- An exception to the privity of contract rule permits contractual rights to be transferred (assigned), allowing the party receiving the rights (the assignee) to enforce the terms of the original contract.

- Statutory assignment requires the assignment of rights under a contract to be unconditional and in writing, with written notice of the assignment being given to the debtor.

- Where the statutory assignment requirements are not met, the assignment may still be a valid equitable assignment.

- If a debtor received two or more notices of assignment, the debtor need honour only the first one received.

- The assignments are "subject to the equities" between the original parties.

Closing Questions

Exemption Clauses

1. **Internet Research.** Find the complete decision of the *Chamberland v. Provincial* case on an Internet website and answer the following questions:
   a) Did the case involve the finding of fact and an application of well-established law, or did it involve the creation of a new principle of law.
   b) Does this case stand for the proposition that anyone who alleges participation in a lottery pool will be successful in a lawsuit against the winners? If not, what limitations are there on the application of this case to persons who claim to be part of a lottery where other participants deny that claim.

2. Dewey, Cheatem and Howe is an accounting firm which is considering using an application service provider (ASP) to do its on-line billings and to store its back-up data from all computers.
   a) What business risks is the firm facing if it uses the services of the ASP as contemplated?
   b) What terms in the ASP's service contract would likely cover that risk and with what result?
   c) How could the firm protect itself with the legal or business solutions respecting this contract? Which is likely to be the more effective, the legal or the business solutions?

3. In the case of *Trigg v. MI Movers International Transportation* the exemption clause in the contract was not enforceable against Mr. Trigg because he had not read the clause. In the case of *Fraser Jewelers (1982) Ltd. v. Dominion Electric Protection Co.*, the president of Fraser Jewelers also claimed he had not read the exemption clause, but it was enforced against him. Are these cases reconcilable. If so, how?

4. Identify some of the situations where you have seen a disclaimer, limited liability, or exemption clause. Where they are contained in written documents, bring them to class and study the language that is used.

5. You have designed a complete small-business accounting software package that can be operated on a computer the size of a calculator, and you want to market it.
   a) What possible claims might purchasers make against you?
   b) Draft in your own words (that is, ignore legal terminology) an exemption clause that would reduce the risks associated with such possible claims. Compare your clause with clauses found in agreements that came with a calculator, personal organizer, or accounting software that you may have purchased.

6. When asked to sign a contract in which the exemption clause had been pointed out, Ralph replied: "Sure, no problem. They're not worth the paper they're written on anyway."
   a) Discuss whether his attitude towards exemption clauses is an accurate one.
   b) What further information would you require in order to determine whether Ralph's assessment of this clause is accurate or not?

7. Vesna Yevtoshenko purchased a colour printer for her computer, which she used in her business of making advertising flyers for retail stores. The printer was advertised as being able to print five pages per minute, with clear colour separation, and laser-quality letters.

   In the course of the first month of using the new printer, Yevtoshenko found that it printed at a rate of two pages per minute, and the colours were constantly bleeding into each other, making the flyers appear messy and unprofessional. The store that sold the printer to her attempted to correct the problems three times. After the third visit, they advised Yevtoshenko there was nothing more they could do unless she wanted to use this machine as a trade-in for a much more expensive piece of equipment.

   At this point, Yevtoshenko had lost three contracts totalling $5,000, and her business reputation was suffering as a result of her being unable to meet her contract deadlines. When she pointed this out to the store, it replied that the contract contained an exemption clause protecting the store from any damages suffered by a purchaser of the printer, and the store had done all it needed to do in assisting her with correcting the problems.

   a) Yevtoshenko has come to you for advice on her situation. Outline the issues involved and advise whether she has the right to return the printer to the vendor and demand a refund of her money, as well as the damages suffered by her from the loss of the printing contracts.

   b) If Yevtoshenko bought the printer for personal use and experienced the same problem, what legislation would apply to the sale?

   c) Yevtoshenko bought the printer for personal use and experienced the same problem. She used the machine to print her résumé, and a letter applying for a job as a computer technician, at an annual salary of $40,000. She didn't get the job, and heard later that it had been given to another, less-qualified, applicant, because the firm thought the poor quality print of Yevtoshenko's résumé meant she did not have the necessary skills. Does Yevtoshenko have any remedy?

8. Joan Spetz took her white satin wedding dress, trimmed with beads and sequins, to a dry cleaner for cleaning. When the clerk gave her a receipt to sign, Spetz asked why she had to do so. The reply was that the form exempted the dry cleaner from liability for damages to the beads and sequins on the dress. In fact the clause read: "The company is not liable for any damage, however caused."

   When Spetz picked up the dress after it was cleaned, she discovered a large stain on the satin. The beads and sequins were not damaged at all.

   a) If sued for the replacement cost of the dress, could the dry cleaner rely on the exemption clause?

   b) If the receipt form had contained an entire agreement clause, would the result be the same?

Interpretation

9. a) What is the name of the rule that prohibits parties generally from testifying as to their interpretation of what a term in a contract means? What justification is given for this rule?

   b) If a term in a contract is ambiguous, what types of evidence would a court admit to assist in resolving the ambiguity?

   c) What is the name of the rule of construction (interpretation) that applies especially to standard form contracts respecting ambiguity, and what is its effect?

10. Protagoras was a sophist in Greece during the 5th century B.C. A sophist was someone who used his skill at logic and reasoning for practical purposes. The lawyers of the day sought him out as a teacher. He put the following question to his lawyer students.

    > "A student asked a law teacher to teach him for a fee. The professor refused to take the money, saying, 'You can pay me after you win your first case.' The student readily agreed. After a short time went by, the law professor approached the student and said, 'You owe me your fee.' The student replied, 'But I haven't won my first case yet!' Said the professor, 'Pay or I'll sue.' "Who wins?"

Parol Evidence Rule

11. John Conrad was negotiating with Marney Lansky for the sale of Conrad's house, for which he asked $300,000. Lansky counter-offered $280,000, but said, "Okay to $300,000 if you throw in that grand piano."

They signed a standard form agreement of purchase and sale of a house at the sale price of $300,000. No mention was made of the piano in the contract, in order to avoid paying GST. Lansky moved in to find out that Conrad had moved out with the piano. She now wants to sue for it. What two principles of law will assist Conrad in defending any lawsuit brought by Lansky?

12. a) What does *parol* mean in the parol evidence rule?
    b) What are the two situations to which it applies?

13. One application of the parol evidence rule prevents parties from giving evidence to add or vary terms to an agreement that appears to be the entire agreement between the parties. Why does the strength of this presumption differ between an individually negotiated agreement and a standard form agreement?

Deposits, Down Payments, and Damages

14. Lalka Industries buys a delivery truck for $100,000 from Gibraltar Manufacturing on credit and gives a $25,000 deposit on signing, then a down payment of $5,000 on delivery. Lalka Industries cannot complete the purchase. Gibraltar Manufacturing repossesses it and sells to another customer for $90,000 for a loss of $10,000.
    a) Can Lalka Industries recover any money from Gibraltar Manufacturing?
    b) If your answer to a) is yes, how much?
        i) $5,000
        ii) $10,000
        iii) $20,000
        iv) $25,000
        v) $30,000

Venue

15. Gibraltar Services sold personal accounting software over the Internet. When Gibraltar sends the software by courier to the purchaser, the package contains a licence agreement that has an exemption clause limiting Gibraltar's responsibility for damages, however caused, to $1,000. It also has a clause saying that the law of British Columbia governs any disputes with respect to the contract.

    One unit was bought by a California customer. There was an error in his bank account resulting in a $10,000 loss to the customer. The software did not detect this error, and the 30-day limitation period contained at the bottom of the customer's bank statement expired, so the customer has no recourse against the bank.

    The customer sues Gibraltar in California for the $10,000 and punitive damages of $1,000,000, and requests a jury trial.
    a) Which law applies, B.C. or California?
    b) Can Gibraltar Services successfully require that the lawsuit be held in British Columbia? If the lawsuit takes place in California, how can that court apply the law of B.C.?
    c) Will the exemption clause be effective?
    d) What could Gibraltar have done with its contractual terms to better protect itself?

Interest

16. Joseph Pereira has opened his own retail home-computing store and sells computers, giving customers two years to pay at 5 percent interest. He gives the customers a one-page bill of sale that says only, "Computers sold at $2,000 at 5 percent interest to be paid in equal installments over two years." In fact, the computer's normal sale price is $1,700 and the balance of the price consists of administration charges and fire and theft insurance.
    a) Has Pereira complied with all the laws regarding charging interest?
    b) What should Pereira have done?

Privity and Assignment

17. A business purchases a recycling machine from a retail environmental-products store. The machine cleans oil so that it can be reused. The retailer purchases the item from a distributor, who in turn purchased the item from an importer, who obtained the item from a Mexican manufacturer.

   The machine completely exploded in the third month of use, because of a defect in design. The explosion seriously injured a workman.

   The business wants to claim a refund of the purchase price, and for business loss because of the shutdown of the plant for one week resulting from the explosion. The workman wants to sue for his injuries (assume that any workers' compensation legislation does not bar this type of lawsuit).

   The retailer is insolvent and has no money to pay a judgment.
   a) Identify all of the contracts in the above scenario, and the parties to each. What lawsuits will have to be started to involve the manufacturer? What problems does the doctrine of privity of contract create in this type of situation?
   b) Are there different considerations for the business and its employee?
   c) Would your answer to the above be different if the purchase was made in New Brunswick or Saskatchewan?
   d) What changes would you suggest for the simplification of the law respecting the doctrine of privity?

18. Which of the following statements is correct? (More than one may be correct.)
   a) The assignor is the party transferring the contractual rights.
   b) If a creditor assigns a debt twice, the debtor has to pay only the party who received the first assignment.
   c) If a creditor assigns a debt twice, the debtor has to pay the party who first gave notice to the debtor.
   d) A person taking an assignment takes it subject to the equities between the original parties.

19. In this question, all events take place in the same year:
   a) On July 1 a creditor gave written assignment of a debt to a first assignee.
   b) On July 2 this creditor gives a written assignment of the same debt to a second assignee.
   c) On July 3 the second assignee delivers notice of the assignment to the debtor.
   d) On July 4 the first assignee delivers notice to the debtor.

   The creditor, the first assignee, and the second assignee all demand payment from the debtor. Which of the following statements are true?
   a) The debtor must pay half of the amount to the first assignee and half to the second assignee
   b) The debtor need only pay the first assignee as that assignment was made first
   c) The debtor need only pay the second assignee because that assignee gave notice of the debt first
   d) The debtor need not pay either of the assignees because the debtor did not consent to the assignment

20. Joe Creditor sold a computer to Amy Jones on a two-year lease. Creditor assigned the lease in writing to Factor Finance Company. Creditor telephones Amy and tells her to start making payments to Factor Finance. Amy objects, saying that she did not consent to paying Factor. Anyway, the computer needs $200 in repairs. Factor says repair cost is a matter between her and Joe Creditor, as he sold her the computer.
   a) Is the assignment by Creditor to Factor Finance a valid statutory assignment? If not, is it a valid assignment in law?
   b) Does Amy have the right to set off the costs of the repair against the lease payments? If so, what is the name of the legal principle that permits her to do so?

Multi Issue

21. Review the Used Car Bill of Sale in the Appendix to answer the following questions.
    a) Identify the following clauses in that agreement:
       i)   any entire agreement clause(s)
       ii) any disclaimer clause(s)
    b) Review clause number 7. What are the consequences if the purchaser refuses to take delivery? Could this clause be attacked as a penalty clause? What is the legal test for a penalty clause?
    c) Review clause number 9. What are the consequences if a purchaser defaults in payment? Could this clause be attacked as a penalty clause? Again, describe the legal test and the consequences in your opinion.

22. a) Why do you think the courts give little weight to the parties' versions of what a term means in a contract when the meaning of that term is disputed in a court proceeding?
    b) Why do you think the courts will not impose a duty to act in good faith in negotiations but will imply that duty on parties when carrying out a contract?
    c) What is the difference in meaning of an express term and an implied term of a contract?
    d) What type of evidence is excluded by the parol evidence rule when the court is interpreting a contract?

23. John Lindner is the vice-president for marketing of a company that wants to launch a new product. Lindner wants to be certain of several things:
    a) that the sales representatives do not make any promises that will result in liability to the company;
    b) that the product guarantee is only three months;
    c) that any product guarantee is limited to replacement cost and not for any financial loss or business downtime;
    d) as he will probably be selling on credit, that if any payment is missed, he has the full range of legal remedies available;
    e) as he will be dealing with people overseas, that the disputes will be settled according to his own provincial laws and any trial will take place in his own area;
    f) that if he accepts a late payment, he can still insist on strict compliance with future payments.

    Identify and name each of the clauses from standard form agreements contained in this text that would satisfy Lindner's concerns.

24. Do a search to find websites that give examples of standard form contracts for businesses that a business can download and use. Download one of the contracts that you think would be useful in a business and bring it to class for discussion. Identify the clauses that relate to issues that have been discussed in the text so far.

25. Find three stories in newspapers about a business civil lawsuit. Do not select any that involve fraud or criminal matters. Write a report on them and attach the articles. Search newspaper databases at the library or on the Internet in addition to looking at current editions of newspapers.

26. Review the Business Sales Agreement in the Appendix to Chapter 5 and find the following clauses, all of which have been discussed in the text so far:
    1. consideration
    2. deposit in trust clause
    3. irrevocability
    4. non-competition
    5. condition on financing
    6. acceptance

Used Car Bill of Sale

	DAY	MONTH	YEAR

PURCHASER'S INFORMATION

PURCHASER'S NAME: FIRST   MIDDLE INITIAL   LAST

PURCHASER'S ADDRESS

CITY/TOWN	PROVINCE	POSTAL CODE

HOME TELEPHONE NO.	BUSINESS TELEPHONE NO.

DRIVER'S LICENCE NO.	EXPIRY DATE

TERMS OF SETTLEMENT

SELLING PRICE	
ADMINISTRATION FEE	
TRADE-IN ALLOWANCE (IF ANY)	
NET DIFFERENCE (ADD LINES 1 AND 2 AND DEDUCT LINE 3)	
P.S.T. ON NET DIFFERENCE	
LICENCE FEE	
GASOLINE	
PAYOUT LIEN ON TRADE-IN	
G.S.T. PAYABLE ON TRADE-IN	
BALANCE DUE	
DEPOSIT: ❑ CHEQUE ❑ CASH ❑ CREDIT CARD	
PAYABLE ON DELIVERY (CERTIFIED FUNDS ONLY)	
INSURANCE: ❑ LIFE ❑ ACCIDENT ❑ LOSS OF INC.	
P.S.T. ON INSURANCE	
LIEN REGISTRATION FEE	
BALANCE FINANCED SUBJECT TO APPROVAL	
NET AMOUNT TO BE FINANCED	
COST OF BORROWING %	
TOTAL BALANCE DUE $	

CAR INFORMATION

YEAR	MAKE	MODEL	COLOUR	STOCK#

SERIAL OR V.I.N. #

DISTANCE TRAVELLED	❑ KMS ❑ MILES	PURCHASER'S INITIALS	IF MANUFACTURER'S WARRANTY APPLICABLE; TIME IS MEASURED FROM:

THIS CAR WILL BE DELIVERED WITH
A SAFETY STANDARDS CERTIFICATE ❑ YES _____ ❑ NO
CERTIFICATE NUMBER

DEALER GUARANTEE

IS THERE A DEALER GUARANTEE ON THIS CAR? ❑ YES ❑ NO
IF YES, COMPLETE THIS SECTION.

_____ DAYS OR _____ KM
(WHICHEVER COMES FIRST)

DESCRIPTION _____

TERMS OF THE CONTRACT

1. **PURCHASER'S OFFER:** By signing this form I have made an offer to purchase the car described above ("the car"). I understand that this offer becomes a binding contract between the dealer and me when it is accepted by the signature of an authorized official of the dealer.

2. **CAR SOLD "AS IS":** I agree that if the appropriate space below is initialed by me, the car is sold "As Is" and is not represented as being in a road worthy condition, mechanically sound or maintained at any guaranteed level of quality. The car may not be fit for use as a means of transport and may require substantial repairs at my expense.

   _____   If this space is not initialed by me, this clause
   Purchaser's Initials   does not form part of this agreement.

3. **ACKNOWLEDGEMENT OF TERMS:** I acknowledge having read all terms of the contract, including those on the reverse. I understand that they form part of this agreement. I also agree that no verbal promises have been made to me by the dealer or its employees. The dealer and I agree that the written terms contained in this contract make up the entire agreement between us.

SIGNATURES:

Purchaser's: _____

Co-Signer (If any) _____

TERMS ON BACK FORM PART OF THIS CONTRACT

VENDOR'S ACCEPTANCE

DATE REGISTRATION No.	NAME OF OFFICIAL (PLEASE PRINT)
ACCEPTOR'S REGISTRATION No.	TITLE
DATE	SIGNATURE

Used Car Bill of Sale (continued)

4. **WARRANTIES:** I understand that there are no warranties or representations given by the dealer regarding the car or affecting my rights or those of the dealer, other than those contained in this agreement or set out in any applicable legislation or manufacturer's warranty.

5. **TRANSFER OF OWNERSHIP:** Legal ownership of the car shall not pass to me until the entire purchase price has been paid in full. I agree that until that time, I shall:

    (a) maintain insurance on the car with the dealer as the named beneficiary in the event of a loss;
    (b) not sell or transfer the car to anyone else;
    (c) not allow any lien or other interest to be taken in or against the car;
    (d) not allow the car to be used in the commission of any illegal act; and
    (e) reimburse the dealer for any costs the dealer may incur due to may failure to comply with any of (a), (b), (c), or (d) above.

6. **CREDIT DISCLOSURE:** I authorize the dealer to obtain credit information on me from any credit reporting agency or any credit grantor and to disclose credit information on me to any credit reporting agency or to any credit grantor with whom I have financial relations.

7. **ACCEPTANCE OF DELIVERY:** If I refuse to take delivery of the car when it is made available to me, or on the delivery date specified in this agreement, the dealer shall notify me, by registered mail, sent to my last address known to the dealer, that the car is available for delivery. If I fail to take delivery of the car within seven (7) days of signed receipt of this notice, or if the notice is returned to the dealer unclaimed, the dealer may resell the car with no further notice to me.

    When the dealer resells the car, I agree to pay the dealer the difference between the agreed upon purchase price and the amount obtained on the resale ... as well as any expenses incurred by the dealer in reselling the car. Any deposit or car traded-in may be kept by the dealer to apply against any loss suffered by the dealer. If the loss is greater than the total of the amount paid as a deposit and the value of the trade-in, I agree to pay the difference to the dealer.

    The dealer agrees to provide me with a detailed accounting of the resale and a list of expenses incurred. These expenses may include, but may not be limited to, advertising, insurance, daily interest, etc. The dealer shall maintain the right to use any legal means available to collect any sum owing by me under this agreement.

8. **SECURITY INTEREST:** If the entire amount owing by me is not paid at the time I take delivery of the car, or if any car traded in by me contains an encumbrance of any sort, so that I cannot pass clear title to the dealer, I grant the dealer a security interest in the car being sold to me up to the amount owing, and understand that the dealer may register this interest under the Personal Property Security Act.

9. **DEFAULT IN PAYMENT:** If I miss any payment due under this agreement, then the entire purchase price shall immediately become due and payable. The dealer, or anyone assigned by the dealer, shall then have the right to repossess the car without notice to me.

    On seven (7) days notice to me by registered mail, sent to my last address known to the dealer, the dealer may resell the car by private sale or public auction. The dealer shall have the right to make whatever repairs are deemed necessary to put the car in adequate condition for resale.

    I agree to pay the dealer the difference between the balance of the purchase price still owing by me and the amount obtained on resale ... as well as any expenses incurred by the dealer in repossessing and reselling the car.

10. **CANCELLATION OF AGREEMENT:** This agreement may not be cancelled by me. If by mutual consent, the dealer and I agree to cancel the contract, the dealer shall return any deposit or cars traded-in as part payment of the purchase price. Should any cars traded-in by me be sold prior to the mutual cancellation of this agreement, the dealer agrees to pay me the amount of the trade-in allowance shown on the front of this agreement.

Defects in a Contract and Remedies

Defects

None of us would agree to a contract without being aware of all it contained—unless we were mistaken as to its nature, deliberately misled by the other party, or forced into the agreement. If any of these situations did occur, it would cancel consent—the intention to create legal relations—and could be seen as a legal reason for getting out of a contract. Some may call these grounds loopholes in a contract.

The laws governing when a contract can be set aside are very restricted, and differ greatly between consumer and business transactions. There are consumer protection laws that do not apply to deals between businesses. Courts have traditionally been very reluctant to set aside agreements, and it is not easy to get out of a business contract once it has been made. Courts will not help a business get out of a bad deal if it was fairly negotiated.

The reasons that a court would consider are:

- Misrepresentation. During the bargaining process, one party states a fact that is untrue, and the other party relies on this fact when entering into the contract.
- Mistake. The parties make an error in the agreement. However, a legal mistake is a very limited ground for relief.
- **Duress.** Actual, or threatened, violence, or unreasonable coercion is used to force agreement. This threat or coercion can be economic.
- **Undue influence.** An individual, such as a lawyer or accountant, who holds a position of trust because of specialized knowledge, takes advantage of the other party. It is the misuse of influence and the domination of one party over the mind of another to such a degree as to deprive the latter of the will to make an independent decision.
- ***Non est factum***. One party is misled as to the type of document being signed. *Non est factum* ("it is not my doing") is a plea that a person didn't know what he or she was signing.

A contract can be made up of both oral and written statements. However, a court will not accept evidence of any verbal statements that change or contradict the terms of a final written contract. Terms that have been agreed to verbally must be consistent with those that appear in the actual written document. This is known as the parol evidence rule.

duress

actual, or threatened, violence, or unreasonable coercion used to force agreement

undue influence

the misuse of influence and the domination of one party over the mind of another to such a degree as to deprive the latter of the will to make an independent decision

non est factum

("it is not my doing"), a plea that a person didn't know what he or she was signing

Misrepresentation

What Is a Representation?

Misrepresentation is one of those words that is used differently in law than in ordinary use. A representation, as the term is technically used in law, usually refers to statements made before the contract is formed. For example, a salesman tells a customer that the car dealership will provide a courtesy car related to any repair work necessary during the warranty period. The customer then signs the standard form Used Car Bill of Sale (as found in the Appendix to Chapter 6). Nothing is written into the agreement about the courtesy car. That matter is not then a term of the agreement. The purchaser may not have thought to have it included because she has the salesman's assurance and her mind was satisfied on the point. In addition, she is more concerned about price, warranty period, and such.

When she comes for her first repair under the warranty she asks for her courtesy car. The service manager looks puzzled and asks where she got that idea. He pulls out the contract and shows her that there is nothing in it about a courtesy car. She tells her story. Of course, the sales rep has moved on and is not present to confirm it.

In this example the statement regarding the courtesy car is called a representation. If it is false, it is a misrepresentation. If it had been part of the contract, it would have been a term of the type that is called a warranty.

Usually, the law says we must live up to our agreements or face the legal consequences. Therefore, you had better know what you are getting into when you enter into a contract—"let the buyer beware!" However, the courts have developed special rules to give relief to innocent parties who have relied on misrepresentations in entering into a contract. If the criteria outlined in the Critical Concepts (which follow) are present, the person who made the misrepresentations could be liable for them.

Of course, it is easy to make up a misrepresentation after the fact, so the courts are reluctant to ignore the written document. The person asserting the representation may have some difficulty in proving that it was made. The evidence may simply be one person's word against another. It will be difficult to predict which version the court will believe. That is why it is advisable to have every promise in writing.

Representations are usually restricted to statements of fact. However, if the maker is an expert, then opinions can be the basis for a representation. For example, one person may tell a purchaser that there will be no difficulty in getting a zoning change respecting the property. This statement is a matter of opinion and not of fact and the purchaser cannot hold the seller liable for it based on misrepresentation. However, if the maker is an expert in the field, such as a lawyer, the maker may be held responsible.

Types of Misrepresentation

There are three types of misrepresentation:

- innocent—one party to a contract makes a statement without being aware that it is incorrect or untrue
- negligent—facts are misstated because of carelessness
- fraudulent—one party deliberately misleads the other

Critical Concepts of Misrepresentation

- A misrepresentation is a statement of fact made during the bargaining process that is untrue.
- It concerns a fact that was sufficiently important to persuade an individual to enter into a contract.
- It is not made a final term of the contract.
- An expert may be liable for statements of opinion.

Queen v. Cognos Inc., [1993] 1 S.C.R. 87

Douglas Queen was an accountant with a secure, well-paying job in Calgary. He began discussions with officers of a large Ottawa computer software company, Cognos Inc., regarding a job. The officers of Cognos told Queen that Cognos was going to develop a new software accounting package and Queen would be hired to work on it. Queen left his old job and joined Cognos in Ottawa. He signed an employment contract with Cognos that said Cognos could terminate his employment on one month's notice.

After only two weeks on his new job, Queen was told that Cognos's senior management had not approved the financing nor conducted a feasibility study for the project. They had decided not to go ahead with it. Queen was transferred to several fill-in positions and let go after 18 months of employment. He was given one month's notice according to the contract.

Queen sued Cognos for misrepresentation concerning the approval of the software project. Cognos defended by saying that the contractual term allowed the company to terminate on one month's notice and replaced any rights Queen might have regarding statements made in negotiations.

The Court's Decision

The statements made by the officers of Cognos to Queen while he was still employed at his Calgary job and before he signed the employment contract with Cognos were representations. These statements fulfilled all the requirements of a representation:

1) the maker knew the listener would rely on them
2) it was reasonable that the listener rely on the statements
3) the listener suffered damages by relying on them

The court dismissed Cognos's argument that the later term of the contract governed and replaced any statements made before the contract. The representation made was that this project would go ahead. This was untrue. Although the Cognos officers believed it would proceed, they were negligent in telling Queen that it was definite. They should have revealed that the project still needed approval at higher levels.

The term in the contract which provided one month's notice related only to length of notice on termination if the project had been approved. It did not in any way indicate that Queen had assented to a job for which the project had not been approved. The court ordered Cognos to pay $67,224 plus interest to Queen.

■ *Business Law*   Applied

1 **Lesley and Philip** Sand are thinking of purchasing a house. They see one they particularly like, and arrange to view it. The current owner, Arthur Keye, shows them around the house, stating, "I've owned this house for 20 years, and it's completely sound. There are no problems." In fact, as the Sands later discover, the house is infested with termites.

There are three possible explanations of Keye's making the statement he did:

  i) Over the past few months he has noticed some droppings of sawdust in his basement. No one has been sawing wood, and so there is no reason for the sawdust to be there. However, he hasn't bothered to find out the cause of the sawdust.
  ii) He does not know that there are termites in the building.
  iii) He's seen the termites, but tells the Sands the house is problem-free since he's desperate to sell it so that he can move to Florida.

  a) Decide which of the three types of misrepresentation would apply to each of the above situations.

2 **Relying on Esso's** estimate that he would sell 800,000 litres of gasoline annually, John Mardon signed the lease for a filling station.

However, Esso's company accountant had made a mathematical error, and this estimate was totally wrong. In fact, annual sales at this particular station were approximately 240,000 litres. The lease agreement that Mardon signed made no mention of the projected annual sales.

  a) If Esso claims as a defence the fact that the statement about annual sales was not in fact part of the contract, is that valid?
  b) The gasoline company did not intentionally mislead Mardon. It was simply a mistake. Is that a valid defence for Esso if he were to sue Esso?

Silence

caveat emptor

let the buyer beware

In most contracts, the seller does not have any legal duty to disclose facts that might affect the buyer's decision to purchase. This rule in the sale of products is expressed in the phrase *caveat emptor*, let the buyer beware. A more modern translation of the Latin is "let the buyer be well informed." If I buy a car from Shady Sam's Used Cars, and discover that it gets terrible gas mileage, that is my problem. Sam does not have to tell me that the car is a "gas guzzler," even though he may be well aware of that fact.

There are exceptions to the usual right not to disclose any information harmful to your interests:

  ■ If there is a special position of trust between the parties, or where the contract is based on good faith, creating a fiduciary duty (see Chapter 4). One of the limited types of contracts where there is a requirement of complete disclosure is an insurance contract. The applicant must reveal any circumstances that might affect the insurance company's decision to grant a policy of insurance or the amount of the premium. The insurance company also has a duty of good faith to the customer. If it fails to pay a claim without a valid reason, it will have to pay damages for breach of this duty in what is called a bad faith action.
  ■ If there is a statutory requirement of disclosure. For example, if you solicit investment funds through the sale of franchises or shares, legislation requires disclosure of certain relevant information.

- In the sale of land, there is an obligation to reveal defects that may cause injury to health. For example, if the vendor knows that there are toxic wastes buried in the land, the vendor must reveal this.

- If you elect to give information (assuming there is no position of trust, or statutory obligation to disclose), it must be complete and accurate. The law recognizes that a half-truth is the most dangerous of lies. For example, a landlord told a prospective purchaser that the premises were currently rented to a reliable tenant. The landlord did not reveal that the tenant had given notice to terminate the tenancy. This was held to be a misrepresentation.

- If a party makes a statement believing it to be true at the time but later discovers facts that make it untrue, that individual must tell the other side of the change. For example, a company charged an employee with stealing money from it. Some friends of the employee offered to replace the money. The company later learned that the employee had not stolen the money, but it accepted the repayment from the friends. The company was held to have had an obligation to reveal the true state of affairs and therefore had to return the money.

Putting a positive spin on damaging information has become a well-honed skill of the modern business person. However, this practice may come into sharp conflict with the laws regarding accuracy in making a statement. For instance, when a business is in financial difficulty, the rule requiring accurate and complete information in statements may cause difficulties for the officers of that company in dealing with its bank.

■ *Critical Concepts of* Accuracy in Statements

- There is no duty to reveal harmful information to the opposite party, unless there is a relationship of trust between the parties or a statutory obligation to disclose.

- If any statement is made, it must be full and complete.

- If any statement is true when made but later proves to be untrue, the change must be revealed to the other party.

N.B.D. Bank (Canada) v. Dofasco Inc., [1997] 34 B.L.R. (2d) 209 (Ont. Gen. Div.)

The National Bank of Detroit agreed to give a rotating line of credit to Algoma Steel. As part of that financing arrangement, the bank required detailed timely financial information from Algoma before each advance. The time came for a $4,000,000 advance. The bank asked for the agreed financial information from two of Algoma's officers and directors. Algoma had just settled a difficult strike. The chief financial officer of Algoma told its board of directors at a meeting that in addition to the problems caused by the strike, the price of world steel had fallen so that the Algoma plant could not produce steel at a competitive price. The company was insolvent.

When speaking to the bank, both Algoma officers, who had been at the board meeting, told the bank that Algoma was in difficulties because of the costs in delays of start-up after the strike. They said nothing of the opinion of the Algoma CFO. One of the officers forgot to send a part of the Algoma financial information requested by the bank. The bank did not notice that this information was missing.

The bank advanced the $4,000,000 and when Algoma went bankrupt, the bank sued the two officers personally for fraudulent and negligent misrepresentation.

The Court's Decision

The court found that silence is normally not a basis for misrepresentation; however, if something is said, it must be complete. Cleverly selecting words that might be literally true by themselves can be a misrepresentation. The maker of a statement must make certain that the listener is not misled. The statement that Algoma was experiencing difficulty because of the strike was true, but it was only part of the story. The failure to provide some of the financial statements was also held to be deliberate. If the bank had seen these statements, it would have made further inquiries before advancing the money.

The trial judge noted that Algoma's officers were "in a box." However, he said that the officers "had a duty of care to give highly relevant information made relevant by the circumstances of the case."

The officers were found personally liable to the bank on the basis of negligent misrepresentation.

Business Alert!   Caveat Emptor   Sellers are rarely obligated to disclose defects in an article being purchased. You must undertake your own research, and calculate the possible risks before entering into any business deal. The courts will not set aside a transaction simply because one side had more—or better—information than the other.

For major purchases, it's always best to have the item inspected by a professional:

- houses and other buildings—a contractor or certified inspector should inspect the condition of the structure
- businesses—an accountant should verify the profitability of the business
- vehicles—a mechanic should inspect for mechanical soundness
- property in commercial areas—the purchaser should inspect for possible contaminated land

Business Law   Applied

3 Christopher Clause owned a motel located at the midway point of a highway connecting two large cities—an excellent situation for an overnight stop when travelling between the two. Clause discovered that the government planned to construct a superhighway north of the old road. When it was completed, most traffic would bypass his motel.

Clause immediately put the motel up for sale, and it was bought by Karl Gustaffson at fair market value. One month after taking over the business, Gustaffson learned about the proposed new highway. He sued Clause to have their contract set aside.

a) Does Gustaffson have a valid claim in court?
b) Were the facts misrepresented by Clause before the sale agreement was signed?
c) Did Clause have a duty to reveal the plans of the highway to the purchaser?
d) What, if anything, could the purchaser have done to protect himself?

Advertising

Advertising is a powerful tool in influencing people to purchase goods. Representations made in a particular advertisement might not, in fact, be included in the agreement to purchase. Courts have found that false statements made in advertising can also be regarded as misrepresentations.

Deception in advertising has become such a problem in modern business that special rules for misleading advertising have been made part of the *Competition Act*.

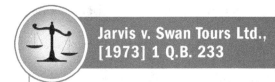

Jarvis v. Swan Tours Ltd., [1973] 1 Q.B. 233

Jarvis decided to take a holiday in Europe. In a brochure published by Swan Tours Ltd., he found this description of a trip to Switzerland:

> House party centre with special resident host... Morlialp is a wonderful resort on a sunny plateau... Up there you will find yourself in the midst of beautiful Alpine scenery, which in winter becomes a wonderland of sun, snow and ice with a wide variety of fine ski-runs, a skating rink, and an exhilarating toboggan run... Why did we choose the Hotel Krone? Mainly because of the *gemütlich* and friendly welcome you'll receive from Herr and Frau Weible... Mr. Weible, the charming owner, speaks English... All of the arrangements are included in the price of your holiday... Welcome party on arrival. Afternoon tea and cake for seven days. Swiss dinner by candlelight and yodeller evening. Chalet farewell party in the Alphutte bar.

Jarvis booked a 15-day holiday. During the first week of his stay, there were only 12 guests in the hotel. For the second week, Jarvis was the only guest. Mr. Weible could not speak English. The yodeller was a man from the village, who sang four short songs. The skiing was terrible, and the "cakes" served with afternoon tea were potato chips. Jarvis sued the tour company.

The Court's Decision

The court awarded Jarvis a refund of his money, as well as damages because his vacation had been ruined. The statements in the brochure were held to be misrepresentations, or statements made before the contract in order to persuade Jarvis to enter into the agreement.

Jarvis was awarded damages for financial loss such as the cost of his ticket, and also for a non-financial claim for loss of enjoyment.

Unjustified Claims of Fraud

Fraudulent misrepresentation is based on the action of *deceit* in tort. The tests the courts use to establish whether fraud has taken place are very strict.

Emotions can run high in civil actions, and one party may be absolutely certain that the other was fraudulent. The wronged person tends to see fraud where a more dispassionate observer might not. Because of the level of feelings that can be generated, the individual being sued might well feel unjustly accused and refuse to settle the matter out of court. In an effort to ensure that only valid fraud cases are heard, the courts usually award substantial costs against an individual who unsuccessfully alleges fraud, even if that party eventually wins the court action on other points. The amount of money involved can be a large percentage of any final court award, and is a serious deterrent to allegations of fraud without strong supporting evidence.

In a recent case that went to arbitration, a group of Pizza Pizza franchise owners sued the parent company for using incorrect accounting methods that inflated the amount of such items as royalties that were due to the parent company. The franchise owners also alleged fraudulent accounting practices by the parent company.

The judge who arbitrated the matter awarded $2.7 million to the store owners because of the incorrect accounting practices, but found that they had not proved their allegation of fraud. As a result, they were ordered to pay $500,000 in costs to the mother company as compensation for the legal fees it had incurred in defending the fraud issue.

Tort and Contract

Unfortunately, the law respecting misrepresentation is complicated because innocent misrepresentation developed under the law of contract, but both negligent and fraudulent misrepresentation developed under and remain part of the law of tort. **Negligent misrepresentation** (an incorrect statement made without due care for its accuracy) derives from the tort of negligent misstatement (*Hedly, Byrne & Co. Ltd. v. Heller*, [1964] A.C. 64) It was first called negligent misrepresentation in the case *Esso Petroleum Co. v. Mardon* [1976] 2 O.E.R. 5 (C.A.). **Fraudulent misrepresentation** (an incorrect statement made knowingly with the intention

negligent misrepresentation

an incorrect statement made without due care for its accuracy

fraudulent misrepresentation

an incorrect statement made knowingly with the intention of causing injury to another of causing injury to another) derives from the tort of **deceit** established in the landmark case of *Derry v. Peek* (1889), 14 Pa.P.P. 337.

These two torts occur in a contractual context and so are often, incorrectly from a technical point of view, considered part of the law of contract. Curiously, then, a large part of the law regarding the negotiation stage of a contract is governed by the law of tort.

Remedies for Misrepresentation

The court's approach to awarding damages varies by the type of misrepresentation. There are two possible remedies a court can give for misrepresentations: rescission or damages.

Rescission means the cancelling of the contract, with both parties put back into their original positions. One party must give back the money; the other must return the goods.

Damages are monetary compensation in a lawsuit for the loss suffered by the aggrieved party. The early courts did not want to award damages against a party who made an innocent misrepresentation, but in effect said to the aggrieved party, you have a choice to go through with the contract or to get out of it. In other words, you can take it or leave it!

For example, in the private sale of a car a seller honestly believes it to be a 1999 Mustang and sells it for $15,000. On reading the car manual the purchaser discovers it is a 1998 car worth $2,000 less. The purchaser can either keep the car or return it and get his money back. He cannot keep the car and sue for the $2,000. There has been some flexibility to this remedy particularly in small claims court, but the traditional response has been no damages for innocent misrepresentation.

For negligent misrepresentation only damages are awarded, and on a tort basis, as misrepresentation is a tort.

Because fraud is so serious, the innocent party is permitted to choose rescission or to claim damages, and sometimes is permitted both.

Bars to Rescission

In some circumstances the court will not grant the relief of rescission. One of the most frequently encountered situations where there is a bar to rescission involves a resale. If the property was resold at fair market value to a purchaser who had no notice of the misrepresentation, ownership would pass to the innocent purchaser even if the misrepresentation is fraudulent. Thus, selling an item on credit or accepting an uncertified cheque in payment may not be wise. For example, you sell your car to a purchaser who gives you a false identity. You take an uncertified cheque which bounces. The purchaser immediately resold the car to a second and innocent purchaser who has no notice of the fraud. You get nothing for your car, but you cannot get it back from the innocent purchaser either.

Rescission may also be denied if there is delay in claiming the rescission. Courts may view delay as a sign that the party claiming rescission is not acting in good faith but seeking to get out of the contract on a technicality. It is always safest to claim rescission immediately upon discovering the grounds for it.

Misrepresentation and Theft

The case of misrepresentation must be distinguished from theft. If a car is stolen and resold, the true owner can recover the car. There is a governing legal maxim that no one can give what he hasn't got. The thief has possession but not ownership. Many a sad car purchaser, who got a great deal on a private sale through the newspaper, has awakened early one morning to the sound of a bailiff's tow truck repossessing the car on behalf of the true owner. So, buying from an unknown vendor can be risky. At the very least, obtain and keep verified information about the seller's identity (such as a driver's licence).

Rescission **Rescission** is derived from Latin. *Re*, used in this context, means back, as in return; *scission* comes from the Latin verb *scindere*, to cut, (*scissors* comes from the same word). Thus, when a contract is rescinded, it is "cut back," so that it never existed.

rescission

the cancelling of the contract, with both parties put back into their original positions

damages

monetary compensation in a lawsuit for the loss suffered by the aggrieved party

Legalese

■ *Critical Concepts of* Remedies for Misrepresentation

- ■ Not all remedies can be given for all types of misrepresentation.
- ■ Innocent—rescission, only
- ■ Negligent—damages, only
- ■ Fraudulent—rescission and/or damages and sometimes both

Stolen Cars   One of the most frequent misrepresentations concerns the sale of stolen cars. One pattern for stolen car sales is for the car to be stolen in one province, brought to another province, and registered there. This is easy to do. In many provinces there are no checks by the government ownership-permit office on the accuracy of the information given on the transfer registration.

Business Alert!

Even where there are checks, these may not be effective. Chop shops buy wrecked cars to obtain valid V.I.N. (vehicle identification numbers) and then have one stolen to match for year, model, and such. The stolen car gets the wreck's V.I.N. and this one will not show up on police stolen-car lists!

So beware of buying cars advertised for sale in newspapers or in ads posted on a bulletin board, especially if you are getting a fantastic deal on a very popular model. Consumer protection laws will give no value against a sophisticated criminal who will likely be difficult to find.

■ *Business Law* Applied

❹ **Angelo Bolatta advertised** his Mustang car for sale at a price of $16,500. A man who introduced himself as Roland Berry called on Bolatta one evening, tried the car, and said he liked it. In the course of general conversation, the prospective purchaser represented himself as being connected with professional hockey. Roland Berry was well known as a coach at the time.

The purchaser wrote a cheque for $16,500, signing it "Roland Berry." Bolatta asked for identification, and was shown a pass to the local stadium. This carried a photograph of the purchaser, along with an official-looking stamp. Bolatta registered the change of ownership, and allowed Berry to take the car. Two days after Bolatta deposited the cheque, his bank advised him that it had been forged, and that the credit in his account was cancelled.

A few days later, Muriel Gibson, who had advertised for a car of this type, received a visit from a man who said his name was Angelo Bolatta. He showed her a motor-vehicle permit bearing Bolatta's name and address. The car was exactly what Gibson wanted, and she bought it for $14,800. Within the next three or four days, Gibson discovered that the usual driver's manual was missing from the glove compartment, and telephoned Bolatta to ask for further information about the car. The whole story was then revealed in an excited conversation.

Her telephone call proved a fateful one for Gibson, because Bolatta brought an action against her for return of the car.

   a) What were the two contracts involved, and who were the parties to each?
   b) What type of misrepresentation was made by Berry to Bolatta and Gibson?
   c) What steps did Bolatta take to protect his interests? Were they what any reasonable person would have done under the same circumstances?
   d) How else might Bolatta have safeguarded his interests?
   e) How did Gibson attempt to protect her money? Were the steps she took reasonable?
   f) What else might Gibson have done?
   g) Which particular remedies for misrepresentation were available to Bolatta?
   h) Which principle would the court apply to decide the case? What would be the result?

Protect Your Interests   The courts sometimes apply one particular principle when deciding a case, but another principle, though unexpressed, can also be presumed to be relevant. In actions involving fraudulent misrepresentation, in which two innocent parties are suing each other, the unexpressed principle often appears to be which party might have best protected its interests according to the normal practice.

In the Bolatta case above, the usual practice before accepting a cheque from a stranger would have been to ask for two or three pieces of identification, including photo ID and a driver's licence.

Alternatively, a certified cheque would have safeguarded the seller's interests. The standard form Automobile Purchase Agreement states that "certified funds are required upon delivery" (see Appendix).

Entire Agreement Clauses

It will be useful to recall entire agreement clauses now that you have seen concrete examples of misrepresentations. The parol evidence rule does not exclude misrepresentations, that is, statements made before the contract was formed. However, entire agreement clauses do exclude these (mis)representations. Review the entire agreement clauses in the contracts in this text. You will often see wording such as "there are no representations . . . ," which language is directed at excluding the remedy of misrepresentation that you have just been studying.

However, when these clauses occur in standard form contracts, they may be subject to defences for entire agreement clauses discussed in Chapter 6, as well as those discussed respecting onerous and unusual clauses under the topic "Exemption or Disclaimer Clauses" in Chapter 6 as well.

Representations and Terms

A representation is a statement made before the contract is made, while a term is part of the contract. If a sales rep says during the sales pitch that the car had only one owner, and nothing is written down in the agreement, then the statement is likely a representation. If the statement proves to be false, the other party could seek damages or rescission (depending on whether the sales rep knew or ought to have known the statement was false). However, if the contract states, for instance, "The vendor warrants that this car has had only one previous owner," then the statement is a term. If the statement proves to be false, the other party could seek damages for breach of contract. Sometimes there are significant consequences to this fine distinction.

For example, condominium purchasers were told by the sales rep that a second tower was to be built. This statement was significant to the purchasers for it would mean that the unit being bought would keep its value. The purchasers bought a unit relying on this statement. However, the developer had business problems and could not build a second tower. The purchasers sued based on misrepresentation for the loss in value of their unit.

The court held that the statement was not a statement of an existing fact, but of an intention relating to a future event. The statement was true at the time as the developer fully intended to build a second tower but could not do so for reasons out of its control. It was therefore not a misrepresentation.

If the purchasers had made the statement a term of the contract, they could have had their damages. The term may have read something like "the vendor warrants that it will build a second tower."

If the purchasers had proposed such a term it is questionable whether the vendor would have agreed to it. The legal test for finding that a statement is a term is that the maker must have intended to warrant (guarantee) the statement. It was not clear in the circumstances that the maker was intending to guarantee the building of the second tower: the vendor was merely stating his honest belief that he would do so.

Special Consumer Rules

Most provinces have enacted special rules to control misrepresentation in consumer transactions. The various acts, usually called unfair trade acts or business practices acts, differ in detail. In dealing with misrepresentation, however, each is similar. Each, in effect, makes the representation govern over the written contractual provisions. Any entire agreement clause is nullified.

Each act also provides that a representation is a term of the contract and therefore the normal contract remedies can be given for any type of representation. The above common law restrictions of different reliefs for different types of misrepresentation have therefore been simplified for consumer transactions.

In addition, these acts make misrepresentation an offence punishable by a fine or imprisonment. The government official responsible for prosecuting such offences is usually called the director of the act. In some provinces these laws have been put into part of its *Consumer Protection Act*. Any statements made by a business prior to the contract that might be excluded by the parol evidence rule or an entire agreement clause are made admissible at a trial. Here is an example of the clause in an act that makes such evidence admissible.

Here is an example of a section which is typical of this type of statute. It makes a wide range of statements deceptive practices.

Consumer Protection Act, 2002, S.O. 2002, c. 30, Sch. A

Evidence

18 (10) In the trial of an issue under this section, oral evidence respecting an unfair practice is admissible despite the existence of a written agreement and despite the fact that the evidence pertains to a representation in respect of a term, condition or undertaking that is or is not provided for in the agreement.

Scams Aimed at Students

Individual misrepresentations such as the representation by the car salesman about the availability of a courtesy car (given at the beginning of this chapter) are governed by these acts. However, so are the many schemes for fraud, such as those that supposedly offer job positions as movie extras, models, positions for children in TV advertising, and the like.

The essence of these scams is that the business appears to be giving something but grossly overcharges for pictures, lessons, and so forth. The promised jobs never materialize. For example, one scam that promises jobs for movie extras begins with a personal interview. The interviewer is enthusiastic and praises the victim. The interviewer says that he has a client from New York who would "just love" the victim. However, the victim will need professional photographs.

The photographs will cost $800. In fact they are worth about $100. After the photographs are paid for, the victim will need "composition cards" at a cost of $500. These are merely business cards available for about $14 per 1000 at a print shop. The interviewer will continually assure the victim of job opportunities that will more than pay for the expenses.

However, after all the money is handed over, the interviewer will begin making excuses as to why there are no immediate jobs, but promise a change in the near future. Soon the victim will get a "no longer in service" response to telephone calls. These scam artists will have moved to another city.

Where there is a business or trade practices act in the province, this type of scam should be reported immediately to the provincial consumer affairs department, which will undertake the prosecution of the offenders. Scam artists get away with these scams only because most victims do not know of the correct place to complain. Unfortunately, the police will usually not investigate such complaints and they often do not know of the business practices act in their own province.

■ *Critical Concepts of* Consumer Rules

Rules that apply to retail consumer transactions change the law respecting representation and entire agreement clauses.

- Any verbal statements are deemed to be terms of a contract.
- Entire agreement clauses are nullified.
- Normal contractual remedies in damages as well as criminal sanctions apply.

The Most Popular Consumer Frauds

Thousands of Canadians get taken every year in consumer scams. There is usually an up-front payment. The victim is promised a job, loan, or whatever, but must first pay.

"Earn up to $10,000 every year without leaving your home!"

"$25 per hour guaranteed, no experience necessary!"

"Trouble getting a loan? We'll get you one, bad credit no problem!"

Telemarketing frauds often begin with the following qualifiers—an approach that sifts out those individuals who are likely to disbelieve the scam. The principle involved in the qualifier is, if they believe this, they just might believe the whole scam.

"I'm doing an advertising survey."

"I'm not selling anything, this is part of an advertising promotion."

"You just won a free, all-expenses-paid vacation" (or car, free gift, large sum of money, etc.).

"We want to place a vacuum in your home as part of a promotion."

If you are contacted on the phone or see advertisements for any similar types of offers, contact the RCMP phone-fraud investigation unit, and check out the people behind the offer before you send any money. Also check with provincial government consumer affairs departments, which specialize in tracking such frauds and may recognize a new scam before the police do. You can get information on the Web by visiting the RCMP site and clicking on "Economic Crime Prevention," or you can check out businesses on the Better Business Bureau website.

Business Law   Applied

⑤ **Bertram bought an** air conditioner in August during Aircontrol Inc.'s end-of-season sale. Concerned that he would not be using it until the next season, Bertram asked Patricia, the salesperson, if the unit would be covered for any problems that might occur during the next year. Patricia responded the unit would be covered up to the next September.

All went well until July of the next year, when the unit developed a strong vibration noise. Aircontrol examined the air conditioner and told Bertram it would cost $400 to make the necessary repairs. When Bertram complained, the store referred to the sales contract, which said there was a six-month warranty. The sales contract also contained a clause saying that the sales contract represented the entire agreement and that there were no other promises made.

a) What is the name in law for the statement made by the salesperson that the unit would be under warranty until next September?

b) Does the entire agreement clause in the sales contract deal with the statement made by the sales rep? If so, how?

c) Does Bertram have any remedy to insist that the warranty period extends until September of the relevant year?

d) If Bertram had bought this air conditioner for his business, would he be able to rely on the same legal principle?

e) What must business persons do to protect themselves in this type of situation?

Mistake

The legal concepts surrounding mistake are complex, and are not dealt with in detail here. There are certain cases in which the courts will give relief because of mistake, but these are few and far between. Instead, the courts tend to preserve business deals, on the basis that businesses need to be able to rely on their transactions, rather than having them reopened later. Mistakes that could have been avoided by due care will not usually result in relief from the court.

To begin to understand the scope and complexity of the law of mistake, consider the following cases. Each falls into a different legal category.

- A purchaser agrees to buy a vacant lot, described in the agreement of purchase and sale as an area of 100' x 200'. When the deed is typed, a mistake is made, and the area is given as 10' x 200'. No one involved in the transaction notices this, and the deed is properly registered. Ten years later, the owner wishes to sell the land, and the prospective purchaser realizes the mistake. In this instance, the error was in the recording of the agreement, and the owner would be permitted to have the deed corrected. (Mistake of fact—the parties are unaware of a fact that is important to the contract.)

- Two business partners agree to end the partnership. One is to stay in the same office, and keep the original telephone number. There is a contract with Bell for a full-page advertisement in the Yellow Pages with one year still to run, and the partners agree to share the expense of this equally. After they agree to do so, the partner who moved from the office discovers that Bell will cancel the advertisement if the telephone number is given up. She therefore claims she was mistaken in making the agreement to pay, and wants her ex-partner's number changed. The other partner wants to keep the number, because it is well known by clients. The courts would consider this particular agreement to be binding, despite the innocent, but mistaken, assumption of one partner. (Mistake of law—one party, knowing all the relevant facts, comes to the wrong conclusion about their legal effect.)

- A retailer agrees to sell a customer a used chair for $100, and deliver it in one week's time. Before delivery, an antique collector happens to visit the store, and tells the retailer the chair is a rare piece, worth $10,000. At the time of the sale, both retailer and customer believed the chair to be worth $100. The contract is binding. (Mutual mistake—the parties have a common intention, but this is brought about by a shared misunderstanding.)

- A decorator enters into an agreement with a dentist to redo all the office furnishings and fixtures. The contract says that all new materials are to be in a colour called "stonecrop." When the decorating job is completed, the dentist is angry to find his offices a cheery shade of yellow. The decorator says that is indeed the colour "stonecrop," which the dentist insists is a neutral greyish colour. (Mistake as to interpretation of terms—the court tries to determine what the term means by asking how the reasonable person would interpret it. If this is possible, and the contract was breached, damages will ensue to the wronged party. If it is impossible to determine a meaning, the contract will not be binding.)

- An entrepreneur is setting up a small business. She did not realize that the lease governing the space she rented made her responsible for the cost of insurance and certain other maintenance costs. She admits she did not take the time to really understand the lease before signing, and claims she would have never entered into the agreement had she realized the full extent of her obligations. The contract is binding. (Mutual mistake of fact—Both parties agreed orally to a term, but by mistake [e.g., a typo] a different term was put into the written agreement. The disadvantaged party would be able to claim rectification [correction of the error].)

AMJ Campbell Inc. v. Kord Products Inc., [2003] CanLII 5840 (ON S.C.)

AMJ Transportation Inc. ("AMJ"), a transportation company, sold its subsidiary, Kord Products Limited, which made transportation containers, to ITML Inc. ("ITML") for $13,688,000.00 subject to adjustments depending on evaluation of the inventory.

One of the items for evaluation was "average selling price" which was defined in a non-binding letter of intent as "net of taxes, freight rebates and discounts". At the Purchaser's lawyer's request the phrase was changed to "net of taxes, freight, rebates and discounts".

The change was highlighted in the track changes feature during the exchange of drafts of the final agreement.

The difference in interpretation was that under the first reading only freight rebates (estimated at ten percent of the freight charges) would be deducted. Under the second version, all payments for freight charges plus freight rebates would be deducted. This was a difference, including interest, of about $1 million.

AMJ sued for rectification of the contract based on mistake.

The Court's Decision

The Court found there was no ambiguity in the final version of the phrase.

Only AMJ was mistaken as to the effect of the phrase. ITML was not mistaken, so the mistake was unilateral (one-sided).

While relief of rectification could be granted for unilateral mistakes if certain conditions were met, the Court was influenced by the fact that by highlighting the track changes, AMJ's attention was drawn to the change. The Purchaser did not and could not reasonably be taken to know that AMJ was mistaken. The Purchaser relied on the final version in agreeing to the deal.

AMJ's action for rectification was dismissed.

■ *Critical Concepts of* Unilateral, or One-Sided, Mistake

This is probably the most frequent category of mistake encountered in business. In it:

- Only one party is mistaken.
- If the other party knows of the mistake, that party cannot take advantage of it.
- If the transaction is still in the offer stage, it can be withdrawn, providing it meets the rules governing offers.

Proving that the opposite party knew of the mistake, and took advantage of it, may not be an easy task.

E & OE   Businesses often include the notation *E & OE* (errors and omissions excepted) at the bottom of invoices and statements. This is an attempt to say that the transaction can be set aside if it later proves to contain a mistake. It has no effect in law.

Business Alert!

■ *Business Law* Applied

⑥ **Stephen's Travel Agency** sent a firm quote to a corporate client of $7,500 for a package deal. The client accepted the quote and paid.

One week later, the agency discovered that it had forgotten to include one item for $10,500. Stephen's informed the client of the error, and requested payment. The client refused, claiming it had not known of the mistake, and had paid in good faith.

a) On what legal remedy could Stephen's rely?
b) What would the travel agency have to prove in order to be successful in its attempt to secure payment?
c) Would the size of the error be sufficient to establish that the client must have been aware of it?
d) What circumstances might indicate whether the client knew of the mistake?
e) If the invoice had contained the notation E & OE, could the travel agency rely on this fact?

Duress

Entering into a contract "under duress" has a fairly limited meaning in law. Duress is not succumbing to a high-pressure sales pitch, nor is it renting a truck at a high rate because there is one rental company in town. Duress is an overt threat inducing someone to enter into a contract.

Actual or threatened violence cannot be used to force an individual to enter into a contract. Duress might also be in the form of blackmail, or the threat of criminal prosecution. Someone who has been forced to consent to a contract can have that agreement set aside by the courts. The threat of force means there is no true consent.

Economic Duress

One form of duress is economic duress. Sometimes, one business is aware of another company's financial difficulties, and uses unfair methods to obtain better terms in a contract. The following case is an example of such a practice.

The Canada Life Assurance Company v. Stewart, [1994] 118 D.L.R. (4th) 67

Beverly Stewart, aged 43, purchased a small business, the Manhattan Gourmet Hot Dog Stand, in a shopping mall near Porter's Lake, Nova Scotia. The previous owner owed the mall proprietor $3,600 in overdue rent. The landlord, the seller, and Stewart agreed that as new owner she was not liable for the arrears.

Shortly after Stewart took possession, the landlord began to pressure her for payment of the previous owner's rent arrears. When Stewart herself fell into arrears for one month, the landlord had a bailiff seize the premises, and lock Stewart out. She was allowed back in only after signing a new lease in which she agreed to be responsible for the previous tenant's overdue rent. Stewart signed the new lease without taking legal advice on it, because of

the time constraints involved and the fact that she was afraid of losing her business entirely if she did not regain immediate possession.

Some time later, a dispute arose over the amount of arrears, including those owed by the previous tenant, and Stewart withheld rent for several months. The landlord evicted Stewart, then allowed the previous tenant to seize the business equipment and set up operations once again at the same location.

The landlord sued Stewart for rent arrears. She lodged a counterclaim, asking for $28,000 damages for business loss, a declaration that the lease was invalid, and an appropriate sum for aggravated damages.

The Court's Decision

The court found that Stewart, although a capable and hard-working woman, was a naive and inexperienced business person. The landlord was aware of this, and used the fact to advantage in imposing terms it knew Stewart must accept or else suffer serious financial loss. This was economic duress, and negated Stewart's consent to the lease.

Stewart was awarded $28,000 for loss of her business. The landlord was awarded $24,000 as reasonable rent for the months Stewart had withheld payment.

The court stated that the landlord's conduct had been so at odds with accepted business practice in the community that aggravated damages were appropriate. However, none were given, since the $28,000 for business loss was considered sufficient to serve also as punishment and deterrent.

Business Law   Applied

❼ Direct to the Net Inc. became a great success in only four years after start-up and it decided to go public. About one week before making the announcement of its initial public offering (IPO), it was served with a statement of claim by a former shareholder who alleged the company had used his ideas without paying for them four years ago.

The Directors of Direct to the Net Inc. believe that there is no merit in the claim and feel that they are being blackmailed, but do not want to report a lawsuit of this type on the corporation's disclosure material for the public offering. They agree to pay one million dollars to settle the claim.

  a) Is there any ground in law by which the corporation can have the settlement set aside by a court after the IPO? If so, what is the name for this course of action?
  b) What business considerations are relevant to the decision to sue and the timing of any lawsuit to set aside the settlement?

Undue Influence

Undue influence is that type of influence which prevents a party to a contract from exercising independent judgment or decision making in signing a contract. It is of two types, actual and presumed, and it occurs in two types of situations: firstly, where there is no special relationship between the parties, and secondly, where there is a special relationship.

Actual

One example of actual undue influence was a case in which a person claimed to be a medium giving a message from a dead relative that large amounts of money should be paid to the medium to conduct a ritual to save the deceased from suffering in the next world. In another case, a bank manager threatened to lay criminal prosecutions against a son who forged his father's name on a promissory note, unless the father signed a personal guarantee of the son's loan which was then in default. This threat of criminal prosecution against the son was considered actual undue influence by a person (the bank manager) not in a special relationship with the aggrieved party (the father). Thus actual undue influence appears to require an element of express coercion.

Actual undue influence is often an abuse of bargaining power and akin to duress. In the two examples above there was no special relationship and the aggrieved party must prove the undue influence.

Presumed

Sometimes, trust or confidence exists between certain individuals in traditional relationships such as lawyer-client, accountant-client, doctor-patient, and the like. The person who is in the position of trust cannot use that influence to gain a personal advantage at the expense of the other party. This rule is akin to fiduciary duty and abuse of trust. A fiduciary relationship is one in which a weaker or more vulnerable person places trust and confidence in a stronger or more skilled person (see a more complete definition of agency in Chapter 6). In such a relationship undue influence is presumed. That means it does not have to be actually proved. There does not have to be any express coercion or threat. Instead, the presumption would have to be **rebutted** or proven to be false to avoid liability.

rebutted
proven to be false

There is a second type of special relationship that is not a traditional one but is open-ended. Thus, it is based on the particular facts of a case; one person may in fact give trust and confidence to another and this trust is abused. Because this type of relationship is based on the facts of a case, it is called a *de facto* special relationship. A common example is marriage. A married woman today is, generally, not presumed to be under the influence of her husband. However, in a traditional marriage, if the wife does leave financial matters to her husband and has no business experience, these facts may well support a finding that there was a special relationship, which in turn raises a presumption of undue influence.

Legalese

Presumption   A **presumption** in law is something assumed to be true without the necessity of proving it to be so. For example, if a lawyer buys a house from a client, and a client wants to set aside the transaction claiming the price was too low, the court will presume that the lawyer used undue influence, that is, took advantage of the trust that the client put in the lawyer.

The lawyer has the right to rebut (disprove) the presumption. Usually this is done by showing that a fair price was paid, and that the lawyer had therefore not taken advantage of the weaker party.

◾ *Critical Concepts of* Undue Influence

- Undue influence means that some unfair advantages have been taken of a weaker person by a stronger person.
- Actual undue influence requires some overt act, and it compares to duress.
- Presumed undue influence arises from a special relationship which is similar to a fiduciary relationship.
- Special relationships can be traditional ones (such as lawyer-client) or ones formed on the individual facts of the case.
- Generally there is no special relationship between a bank and a customer; a bank may not know that a borrower (for example, a husband) has a special relationship with a proposed *guarantor* (his wife).

Guaranteeing Debts

Undue influence has been extended to apply to situations in which a person co-signs a loan for another at a bank. This is a three-party transaction. Assume for the purpose of this explanation that the lender is a bank, the primary debtor is a husband, and the co-signer is his wife.

In this case, the undue influence is not that of the bank, but the influence of the husband. While there is no special relationship between the bank and the wife, there may be one between the husband and the wife.

However, this special relationship will be found only if the wife entrusted financial affairs to the husband. The bank may be on notice of this special relationship, and knows that there is a presumption of undue influence of the husband over the wife.

Since many wives today are independent and have business experience, they are not subject to their husband's influence in financial matters. Therefore, there is no recognition of married women as a specially protected class when signing a guarantee for their husband's debt. For example, if a woman is a housewife with no business experience, she might well put her confidence in her husband for her financial affairs and then be in a special relationship which establishes undue influence.

The above discussion has used the terms *husband* and *wife* but the rule likely includes anyone in a close relationship, such as a parent and child, or persons living in common law relationships, including same-sex relationships.

One method the bank uses to defend against allegations of undue influence is to insist that the cosigner have independent legal advice (I.L.A.).

Bank of Montreal v. Duguid, [2000] 47 O.R. (3d) 737

Ann Duguid was a real estate agent. She signed a guarantee to a bank for a loan that her husband used to purchase a parcel of real estate as an investment. She gave the bank a net-worth statement that she had prepared herself. Her husband was a high-school principal.

The investment failed and the husband declared bankruptcy, so the bank sued Mrs. Duguid on the guarantee. She defended claiming undue influence of her husband, which she pleaded should be presumed in the circumstances of any wife signing a guarantee for husband's indebtedness.

The Court's Decision

The relationship of bank to guarantor is not one of the traditionally recognized relationships that gives rise to a presumption of undue influence. Neither is the relationship of husband and wife generally such a recognized category. However, the latter may be in the open-ended *de facto* category of special relationships if the wife does actually entrust her, or their, financial decisions to the husband.

While this fact puts a particular marriage into the category of a special relationship, the bank must be put on notice (called constructive notice) that this is one of those special relationships. The bank will only be on constructive notice if:

a) the relationship is a close one such as husband and wife, parent and child, and the like
b) the transaction is manifestly (obviously) disadvantageous to the co-signer

Even if there is a presumption of undue influence and the bank is on notice of it, there is a third element. The bank can rebut the presumption by showing:

a) the wife received I.L.A.
b) the bank had a private meeting with the wife and explained the transaction to her, and
c) the wife made an independent decision free of the husband's influence

The bank can establish that the wife made an independent decision by facts such as the wife's sophistication in business.

Here Mrs. Duguid did not entrust financial decisions to her husband, so the presumption did not arise. If it had arisen, the bank could have successfully rebutted the presumption because Mrs. Duguid was experienced in business.

The guarantee was found valid.

❽ **Mary Row was** a school teacher married for 15 years to James Row, who was a lawyer. Mrs. Row left all decisions on financial matters to her husband and did not even have a credit card in her own name.

Mr. Row wanted to invest in hi-tech stocks and arranged for a bank loan. The bank insisted on a guarantee from Mrs. Row. Since Mr. Row was a lawyer, the bank did not require that she have I.L.A.

The stock investments were a complete loss, the husband became depressed, could not practice law, and eventually went bankrupt. The bank sued Mrs. Row on the guarantee.

a) What facts must Mrs. Row establish to raise a presumption of undue influence? Will she likely be successful in doing so?

b) Was the bank on constructive notice of any special relationship in these circumstances?

c) What possible defence can a bank raise? Will it be successful?

d) If you believe the result would be different in this case than in the Duguid case above, why do you believe so?

Business Alert!

Spousal Guarantees for Loans   Banks and large financial institutions are well equipped to cope with changes to the law affecting how a spouse's guarantee of a partner's loan is treated. Most small businesses, however, have not yet realized the dangers involved in giving credit using spousal guarantees.

Assume, for example, that you are the sales manager of a publishing company. One of your salespersons places a large order for a new bookstore. The store is run by a corporation, in which the only shareholder is a man whose principal asset is a house, registered in *joint tenancy* with his wife. Any other assets he possesses are affected by *liens*.

The bookstore wants to take delivery of this large shipment on credit, paying in instalments over the course of a year. You decide that the business is a risk, and you cannot grant credit without some security. Accordingly, you ask the owner to sign a guarantee agreeing that he is personally liable for the debt. Of course, a half-interest in a matrimonial home is difficult to realize upon, so the wife also must sign and at this point you encounter the law of undue influence.

The safest course for a business to follow in accepting a guarantee from any person not actually involved in the business—such as a spouse or parent—is to insist on that person's obtaining independent legal advice. Simply having individuals sign a statement that they have been advised to obtain legal advice, but do not wish to do so, may be ineffective. If necessary, build the cost of obtaining I.L.A. into the cost of the transaction. The choice of lawyer should always be left to the individual who is giving the guarantee.

Non Est Factum

The defence of *non est factum* is not usually available to business people. It was developed in a much earlier time, when a large percentage of the population was illiterate. Sometimes, a document was put in front of a person who could neither read nor write, and a signature—an X was sufficient—requested. The individual might be told that the document was a simple letter, when in fact it was really a guarantee of a debt, or a deed to the ownership of land. To have such an agreement set aside by the courts, the illiterate party could plead there was no intention of signing that type of document, and that it was understood to be something entirely different.

For example, an elderly widow is told that she is signing a mortgage renewal, but she is actually signing over the deed to her house. A mortgage renewal is a different type of document from a deed to a house. This is the basis of the plea *non est factum*. It does not apply if only some of the terms are different from what the assignor thought (for example, a different price).

In modern times, it is reserved for people the court feels need protection, but who do not technically fit into the legal category of those who lack capacity. Most reported cases have involved very elderly persons who are clearly taken advantage of by unscrupulous relatives or financial institutions. It has also recently been applied to set aside spousal guarantees.

Discharge and Remedies

Discharge of Contract

All things must come to an end—including a contract. At some point, the contract must be discharged, and the promises made by the parties brought to an end. Usually, **discharge of contract** occurs when all the parties have done exactly what they were required to do under the terms of the agreement: the promises have been completed and the parties have no further obligations to each other.

For example, a manufacturer agrees to supply a fleet of delivery vans by September 11 of a given year. It does not supply the vans until December 1 of that year. This is a breach of contract. If the person suffered damages because of the delay, the manufacturer will likely have to pay the purchaser for the loss.

Should it happen that circumstances, not created by the parties, have made it impossible, or virtually impossible, for one of the parties to do what was promised, the contractual performance is considered to be frustrated. All the parties are discharged from their obligations under the contract. An example of this would be if a stand-up comic had a contract to perform at a night club, and the club was destroyed by an arsonist the night before the comic was to appear.

The circumstances that give rise to frustration occur after the contract has been made. **Frustration** is an outside event that makes the performance of the contract impossible, and excuses a party from performance. The grounds that are necessary to establish frustration are narrow. They are sometimes considered as unforeseeable.

Many contracts, especially international agreements, contain a *force majeure* clause, which widens the scope of grounds for not performing a contract because of radically changed circumstances. The following is a common *force majeure* clause:

> St. Anne warrants and represents that its requirements under this contract shall be approximately 15,000 tonnes a year, and further warrants that in any one year its requirements for Secondary Fibre shall not be less than 10,000 tonnes, unless as a result of an **act of God** (the violence of nature), the Queen's or public enemies, war, the authority of the law, labour unrest, or strikes, the destruction of or damages to production facilities, or the non-availability of markets for pulp or corrugating medium.

Yet another way in which a contract could be discharged is for the parties to the contract to mutually agree to their obligations being brought to an end, even though the promises made have not been completed.

Sometimes the parties agree to end the present contract and completely replace it with a new contract. The process of substituting a new contract for an old one is called **novation.**

Force Majeure and Novation   **Force majeure:** the term comes from civil law (France). *Force* has its usual meaning of strength or power. *Majeure* means superior or irresistible. Hence, it refers to an overwhelming power such as a hurricane or an enemy army.

Novation is a term derived from the Latin *nova*, meaning new. *Nova Scotia* means New Scotland.

discharge of contract
occurs when all the parties have done exactly what they were required to do under the terms of the agreement: the promises have been completed and the parties have no further obligations to each other

frustration
an outside event that makes the performance of the contract impossible, and excuses a party from performance

act of God
the violence of nature

novation
the process of substituting a new contract for an old one

Legalese

Remedies

breach

failure to live up to the terms of a contract

The courts have devised several remedies to make good the losses to the victim of the **breach**, or failure to live up to the terms of a contract. The main remedy is to award damages.

Damages

Damages awarded under the law of contract are a sum of money calculated as a dollar figure equal to the loss caused by the breach. There are two steps in the process of determining damages. The first is to decide if the damages are the kind of damages that the plaintiff is entitled to recover, or are these the type of consequences for which compensation should be provided? This issue is discussed under the topic "Drawing the Line" below. If the damages claimed meet the first test, then the question becomes how to put a money value on the claim. This issue is discussed under the topic "Putting a Dollar Value on the Loss."

Written contracts often specify how damages are to be calculated; where such a contract is involved the terms have to be reviewed carefully, as they may displace the contract law principles.

Business Alert!   Contracts   People enter into contracts thinking that they will be performed. In every contract, you must fully consider what remedies you have and their impact on you if the contract is not performed. Sometimes including certain terms in a contract, such as the right to repossess goods if there is a default in payment arrangements, will save you from serious loss.

Drawing the Line

> ... for want of a nail, the shoe was lost; for want of a shoe, the horse was lost; and for want of a horse, the rider was lost.
>
> *Poor Richard's Almanac*, Benjamin Franklin (1758)

Courts will not award damages for every type of loss that results from the breach of a contract. In a 17th-century case, a blacksmith was negligent in repairing a horse's shoe. Because of this defective shoe, the rider was delayed, arriving late for his wedding to an heiress. When the intended bridegroom did not appear on time, the heiress married another man. The rider had lost the opportunity of a lifetime, and sued the blacksmith for damages. The courts held that the blacksmith was responsible for the consequences of his poor work.

Later judges considered this type of loss too remote, and developed principles to draw the line in deciding when damages are appropriate. Now, damages will be awarded only for losses that are reasonably foreseeable. Such losses can be divided into two types:

- Those that happen in the normal course of business
- Those that arise from special circumstances, such as a one-time-only large deal. This type of loss can only be foreseeable if it is actually told to the other party at the time of the contract.

reasonable foreseeability

the test of what a person could have anticipated would be the consequences of his or her action

This principle of **reasonable foreseeability**—the test of what a person could have anticipated would be the consequences of his or her action—was first stated more than 100 years ago, when economic conditions were less complex than they are today. Court decisions over the years have modified it, but most court judgments on damages begin with this principle and its two types. The second of these—awareness of special circumstances—has been said to involve not just knowledge, but also an undertaking by the other party to assume responsibility for those circumstances. The courts feel that the other party must be given the right to decide:

- if it wants to assume the obligation
- that it can perform as requested
- whether it needs to increase the price in order to insure, or self-insure, for the extra risk

The first cases that developed the restriction of reasonable foreseeability involved transportation companies. These companies typically charge a low fee relative to the damages that might occur for breach of contract. For example, a courier company might charge $20 for delivery of an envelope. This envelope might contain a winning tender bid for a job that would net a profit of a million dollars. If the courier delivers the letter one day late, should it be responsible for paying the loss of $1 million that directly results from the delay?

The principle of reasonable foreseeability or remoteness requires that the courier company be told that the envelope contains a tender and, knowing this, it specifically undertakes to deliver on time. Because of the experience with this problem of a potentially large loss relating to a small service charge, all transportation companies, courier companies, and the like have limitation of liability clauses in their contracts (bills of lading) which restrict their liability unless a higher value is declared. These clauses are discussed under the topic of couriers in "Bailment" (Chapter 8). At present, this risk is usually managed by insurance. By the terms of the shipping contract, it should be clear to the customer that either it or the transportation company has assumed the risk of loss or delay during carriage and must insure for it. However, most courier companies have a policy not to accept tenders.

See the Limitation of Liability clause and term 3 in the Courier Bill of Lading in the Appendix to this Chapter. Term 3 refers to the declared value. Additionally, the courier may refuse to take the item if the declared value is high.

Hadley v. Baxendale, [1854] 9 All E.R. Rep. 461

The shaft in a mill grinding machine broke. All other machinery in the mill depended on this piece of equipment, and so the mill came to a full stop. The mill arranged to send the shaft by carrier to the manufacturer for repair.

It should have taken three days for the shaft to reach its destination. However, because of the neglect of the carrier, it took a month. The mill lost its profits for that one-month period, and sued the carrier for damages.

The Court's Decision

The court stated that the rule governing the award of damages for breach of contract was that the guilty party must pay the innocent party the damages that would arise in the usually course of things, or arising out of special circumstances told to the breaching party at the time the contract was made.

In the present case the only circumstances told to the transportation company at the time of the contract were that the article to be carried was the broken shaft of a mill and the plaintiffs were the owners of the mill. The transportation company should have known that there would be loss of normal business profits because of delay.

However, the court found that these facts were not enough to put a transportation company on notice that the entire mill was shut down and waiting for the return of the shaft. Often mills send shafts for repair but the mill is not closed down. The millers may have had a second shaft.

The transportation company was not liable for the total loss of profits for the one month. [Note: the case was sent back to a jury for assessment of the damages based on losses in the ordinary course of business, assuming the mill could still function. Unfortunately no report was ever made of the assessment. It is possible that the parties settled the case.]

Business Law   Applied

⑨ Paul Xuereb knew a collector who wanted a 1957 T-Bird and was willing to pay a premium if it was delivered on or before June 1. In late May, Xuereb found a suitable vehicle in Danny Samutt's garage. This type of car was currently selling on the open market for about $25,000. Xuereb agreed to pay Samutt $20,000, and pick up the vehicle on June 1.

The day after he had made his agreement with Samutt, Xuereb visited the collector and arranged to resell the car to him at a price of $40,000, guaranteeing delivery on June 1. However, when Xuereb went to collect the vehicle, Samutt had changed his mind and decided not to sell. Xuereb would certainly be able to find a similar car elsewhere, for about $25,000, but not by the June 1 deadline. The collector bought from another source.

Xuereb sued Samutt for breach of contract.

a) Which test would the court apply to decide what type of loss, if any, Xuereb can recover from Samutt?

b) If Samutt was liable for damages, would he have to pay $5,000 or $20,000?

Putting a Dollar Value on the Loss

The law does not assume that a loss has been incurred simply because a contract has been breached. The non-breaching party must prove that it has suffered a loss directly as a result of the contractual non-performance.

The principle that generally determines how damages are expressed monetarily is called the expectation interest, because the victims of the breach receive what they expected, an amount of money that places them in as close to the same position as possible as they would have been in if the contract had been performed.

For example, if Bill Jensen agreed to sell his 1999 Mustang to Beverly Martins for $15,000, but then refuses to go through with the deal, how can Martins be put in the same position as if the contract had been performed? Assuming another similar car is available for $20,000, having Jensen pay her the difference of $5,000 will put her in approximately the same position as if the contract had been performed.

Mitigation

As well, when a contract has been breached, there is an obligation on the part of the "innocent" party to mitigate his loss—in other words, to keep the losses to a minimum. If you fail to do so, the court may take this into account when awarding damages, and reduce the amount accordingly. To sit back, relax and let the losses pile up could have serious legal consequences.

For example, let us say you ordered 50 metres of special fabric for a renovation and decorating project. Shortly before completion of the project, you found out that your supplier could deliver none of the fabric on time. You would be obligated to try to find another supplier, in order to complete your contract for the renovations (and thereby avoid losing the profit you would make on that project). If you paid more to obtain the fabric from the second supplier, you could claim the additional amount in damages against your first supplier.

■■ *Critical Concepts of* Quantifying the Loss

- A claim for damages for breach of contract must be proven.
- Under the expectation interest principle, damages should place the victim in the same position as if the contract had been fulfilled.
- Business losses are for loss of profit, and normal expenses incurred to earn that profit must be deducted from the gross income.
- The victim must take reasonable steps to reduce the loss. This is called mitigation.

Terminology

Damages can be classified by different names. You'll need to know the terminology because you will see different names associated with the term damages in written contracts, especially in exemption clauses. Consider the example of a business that buys software for $10,000. The software proves defective, but can be fixed for $2,000. Loss of profits because of delays caused by the breakdown of the software can be calculated at $50,000. However, there will be future losses as well.

The cost of repair is called direct damage. The loss of profit flowing from (or, as a consequence of) the software defect is called consequential damage. The cost of repair and the business loss that can be quantified at the time the lawsuit is started are called **special damages** (damages to compensate for expenses and quantifiable losses). The future loss of profit that can only be estimated is called **general damages** (damages to compensate for estimated losses).

special damages
damages to compensate for expenses and quantifiable losses

general damages
damages to compensate for estimated losses

■ *Business Law* Applied

⑩ **A theatre retained** a heating contractor to repair its heating system. The contractor agreed to do so, but the work was negligent, and the system broke down one night, leaving the building without heat. The water pipes froze and had to be replaced. The theatre had to cancel a one-night contract, losing the profits related to that event.

The theatre's average gross sales for one evening are $50,000. Its average expenses for one evening are $40,000. The cost of replacing the pipes was $8,000.

a) What damages would the court award to the theatre in an action against the heating contractor?

⑪ **Keanu Carlton was** the vice-president of International Marketing Company, Ltd. He was let go because of the company's downsizing policy. His lawyer advised him that the company would have to pay him the equivalent of one year's salary as monetary damages because the firing was not for a justifiable reason in law.

Carlton learned of another job opportunity that he could apply for immediately upon his termination, but he decided to wait one year before taking on new employment. He then sued International Marketing for one year's salary.

a) Would he be successful?
b) What defence could the company raise? What is it technically called?
c) What would Carlton have to do to be able to claim the one-year salary equivalent?

Punitive Damages

punitive damages (exemplary damages)

compensation for damages beyond the plaintiff's actual losses, awarded to punish the wrongdoer

Punitive damages (exemplary damages) are compensation for damages beyond the plaintiff's actual losses, awarded to punish the wrongdoer The courts have been extremely reluctant to make such awards in contract cases. To obtain an award of punitive damages a plaintiff's case must pass two hurdles:

- there must be a separate actionable wrong
- the damage award already given must not be sufficient to deter such conduct

Sometimes in a contract situation a tort is committed. This occurred in the next case, *Performance Industries Ltd. v. Sylvan Lake Golf and Tennis Club Ltd.* One of the corporation's principals committed the tort of deceit during the negotiation of a contract. This tort is a separate wrong that could give a rise to lawsuit (court action) and hence is a separate actionable wrong.

The second hurdle is called the test of rationality. There must be a reason why the award of damages already given was not sufficient to deter this type of conduct. In *Performance Industries* (below) the test of rationality was not met; however, in *Whitten v. Pilot* (see Chapter 15) it was met. In *Performance Industries* the court said the combined award was large enough to deter people from doing what Performance Industries did. However, in *Whitten v. Pilot* the award of damage was mere compensation for loss of the plaintiff's house, and an additional award was necessary to deter insurance companies from using their superior wealth and bargaining position against individual claimants.

Legalese

Exemplary **Exemplary** comes from *example* and it means to use a damage award to set an example to deter similar conduct.

Performance Industries Ltd. v. Sylvan Lake Golf and Tennis Club Ltd., [2002] S.C.C. 19

Sylvan Lake Golf and Tennis Club Ltd., whose principal was Frederick Bell, signed a deal to develop a part of a golf course with Performance Industries Ltd., whose principal was Terrence O'Connor. A picture of a double-row housing project was used as the basis for their oral agreement. O'Connor had his lawyer prepare the deed, which described the dimensions of the property as 180 yards × 110 feet.

The trial judge found that the oral agreement was for 110 yards, which was necessary for a double row of houses. The trial judge also found that O'Connor knowingly had the deed prepared with 110 feet in order to slip one over on Bell. This amounted to fraud.

Further, the trial judge found that O'Connor did everything to obstruct the lawsuit:

... O'Connor swore false affidavits, refused to produce relevant documents, gave false testimony in the course of two separate trials and did everything in his power to prevent the truth from coming to light ...

The trial judge awarded *rectification* of the agreement so that "feet" was replaced by "yards"; gave full **expectation damages**—an amount awarded for breach of contract based on the expected results if the contract had been properly performed—as if the housing project had been completely and flawlessly completed and made a profit of $620,000; gave punitive damages of $200,000; and ordered that O'Connor pay Bell's complete legal bill (called solicitor and client or complete indemnity costs). The corporate veil was pierced and O'Connor was made personally liable for the sums awarded jointly with his corporation.

O'Connor appealed to the Supreme Court of Canada.

The Supreme Court's Decision

The court held that punitive damages would not automatically be awarded where there was a finding of fraud. The test in *Whitten v. Pilot* (Chapter 15) required additionally that there be a test of rationality before punitive damages would be awarded.

The test for rationality meant that punitive damages would be awarded only if the compensatory damages were not sufficient to deter the wrongful conduct. Here the court found that compensatory damages were generous; nothing further was needed for deterrence. The punitive damage award was disallowed, but O'Connor was not given any award of costs on the appeal event though he won on this issue.

■ *Business Law* Applied

⑫ An employee sued an employer for wrongful dismissal. The employer claimed that he found marijuana in the employee's desk and reported this to the police. The police investigated and concluded that the employer planted the substance. The police charged the employer with obstruction of justice. The employer pleaded guilty and was fined $20,000.

The employee wins the wrongful dismissal action and is awarded one year's salary plus benefits. Then the employee asks for punitive damages of $100,000.

a) What must the employee establish to be entitled to an award of punitive damages? Will he be able to meet the test?

b) What defence can the employer assert to the claim for punitive damages? What case law that you have studied could it rely upon for its position? What if the employer had been given a conditional discharge by the criminal court, or fined $100,000? Would either of these circumstances have an effect on the employer's defence to the claim for punitive damages?

Other Types of Damages

Different forms of damages may be awarded by the courts.

Mental Suffering

The loss in a breach of contract is not always an economic one. For example, if an individual who works full time and receives only two weeks' vacation a year paid for a disastrous trip on which accommodation and services were unacceptable, the vacationer has lost more than just the money given to the travel agency. In this case, the courts would award a sum for loss of enjoyment. Damages for mental suffering are awarded very cautiously, and often supported by medical evidence.

Expenses

In some cases, potential profits may be speculative, and therefore difficult to determine. Here, the courts might award expenses to the innocent party for preparing for the contract. For example, an architect hired to design a new building could have spent time and money acquiring books and taking training courses to get to know the particular needs of a new client. If the contract was cancelled before any actual work on the project had begun and the architect accepted another contract, there could be no claim for loss of profit. The architect could, however, claim the value of all the preparation work. The principle the courts use to award damages in this type of case is called the reliance interest. The architect relied on the contract, and incurred expenses because of this.

Double Compensation

If the architect in the previous example was unable to obtain a substitute contract, the courts would allow a claim for loss of profit. It would not be possible to claim both types of damages—the courts would assume that the general preparation expenses had been included in calculating the profit.

expectation damages
an amount awarded for breach of contract based on the expected results if the contract had been properly performed

Quantum Meruit

In some situations the "guilty" party might benefit from breaking the contract. Consider the example of a construction contract that is to be paid in stages according to the progress of the work:

completion of basement	$10,000
completion of first floor	$10,000
completion of roof	$10,000

The owner of the new building might breach the contract when the basement has been excavated, but the concrete has not yet been poured, so the first payment is not due. If the contractor has other work available and cannot claim loss of profit for the balance of the contract, the court will award damages for the benefit of the work done—the value of excavating the basement.

Quantum meruit is based on the principle called restitution. The courts restore a benefit given to the defendant by the plaintiff. The plaintiff relies on the defendant's promise (in the above example, this is the promise to pay for work done) and the plaintiff gives value (does the work). So the defendant is considered to be unjustly enriched—he got something for nothing. The courts make the defendant pay the value of the benefit. **Quantum meruit**, "as much as is merited," is the amount a person deserves to be paid for goods or services provided to another person requesting them, even if some of the elements of a contract are missing.

quantum meruit

"as much as is merited," the amount a person deserves to be paid for goods or services provided to another person requesting them, even if some of the elements of a contract are missing

Other Remedies

The courts have developed other remedies for breach of contract in situations where damages are not appropriate. Originally, these remedies were developed by the courts of equity. But as the court of law and court of equity have merged, all courts can apply these remedies.

Specific Performance

Sometimes, the court will order a **specific performance**: an order requiring the defendant to undertake a specified task, usually to complete a transaction. This is normally done only if the item is unique. If, for example, a plaintiff arranges to purchase three adjacent pieces of land to build a manufacturing plant, but the vendor of the middle lot refuses to close the deal, damages are of little value to the plaintiff. In these circumstances, the court will make an order forcing the vendor of the middle lot to convey the land. A specific performance order is not given in personal-service contracts.

specific performance

an order requiring the defendant to undertake a specified task, usually to complete a transaction

Injunction

The court can issue an **injunction**, an order instructing one party to halt a particular process or action. A landlord, for example, might wish to force a tenant out because someone else has offered to pay a much higher rent. The current tenant is a furniture distributor, whose loading dock is at the rear of the building and can be accessed only by a lane at one side of the property. The landlord begins to leave his own vehicles blocking the access lane for long periods, thus disrupting the tenant's business. The tenant can obtain an injunction ordering the landlord to stop parking his vehicles in the lane.

injunction

an order instructing one party to halt a particular process or action

Interlocutory (Temporary) Injunction

Sometimes the plaintiff needs immediate relief and cannot wait two or three years for the matter to come to trial. In this case, the plaintiff can sue for an **interlocutory injunction**, a temporary injunction which lasts only until trial.

Mareva Injunction

If the court believes that the defendants might move their assets from the jurisdiction before the case comes to trial, and thus avoid paying a court judgment, it can order them not to do so. If, for example, the defendant is a foreign-based shipowner whose only asset is a ship currently anchored in Vancouver harbour, the court will make an order restraining removal of the vessel.

The court must be satisfied that the plaintiff has a reasonable case, and that the defendant has no other assets within the jurisdiction to satisfy the judgment. As a practical matter, the defendant will be allowed to post a bond, or **letter of credit**—a written promise by one person's bank to pay another person when specified conditions are met—for the value of the plaintiff's claim, and then remove the ship.

Civil Search Warrant, or Anton Piller Order

In certain cases the court will issue an **Anton Piller order**, which is an order that the defendant must permit its premises to be searched without informing the defendant, made without notice to the defendant if giving notice would defeat the plaintiff's ability to obtain the remedy. For example, if an employee who has signed a confidentiality agreement leaves the job, secretly taking confidential information, the employer can obtain an Anton Piller order to search the employee's home, car, garage, and so on, to locate these documents.

Rectification

A **rectification** is a court order which corrects a written document to reflect accurately the contract made by the parties. It is most often done when the aggrieved party can prove the terms of an oral agreement, and that there was a mistake made when putting the oral agreement into written form. For example, two parties agree that one will purchase from the other part of a vacant lot having a measurement of 1,000 ft × 1,000 ft, but the written document, because of a typo, describes the lot as 100 ft × 100 ft. One party misses the typo and signs the written document with the mistake.

Accounting

A court can order that one party must produce its private books and records, and then permit an expert chosen by the other party to examine these and prepare a report. For example, two people might set up a small business together, with one taking all responsibility for the bookkeeping. After a while, the other party begins to suspect that the profits are not being divided as they should, but cannot gain access to the books. The remedy is then to sue for an accounting.

interlocutory injunction
a temporary injunction which lasts only until trial

letter of credit
a written promise by one person's bank to pay another person when specified conditions are met

Anton Piller order
an order that the defendant must permit its premises to be searched without informing the defendant, made without notice to the defendant if giving notice would defeat the plaintiff's ability to obtain the remedy

rectification
a court order which corrects a written document to reflect accurately the contract made by the parties

In Summation

Defects in a Contract

▪ A contract is based on the assumption that each party has freely given consent to perform the promises contained in it. If this is not the case, there are five main areas of concern the courts will consider in deciding whether to allow a claim by one party that consent was not freely given.

Misrepresentation

▪ This is a statement, made by one party at the time of contracting, which is designed to persuade the other party to enter into the agreement, but which does not appear in the final contract. The misrepresentation may have been innocent, negligent, or fraudulent in nature. Each type of misrepresentation will result in a particular remedy or choice of remedy for the party who cannot be considered to have freely consented to the agreement because of the misrepresentation that was made.

▪ Most provinces have passed special consumer protection legislation to guard consumers against misrepresentations or unfair business practices, and there are standard form contracts that contain clauses stating that no representation has been made other than those contained in the contract.

Mistake

▪ A remedy is sometimes available for the parties where a contract has been based on a mistake. The courts will attempt to determine if the mistake was made by one or both parties, and whether the mistake related to an important element that the parties relied on in creating the contract. This is a complex area of law and not easily proven.

Duress

▪ Consent obtained through force, whether by threatened violence, blackmail, or economic duress, will result in the contract being treated as though it never existed.

Undue Influence

▪ Undue influence may be actual or presumed.

▪ Where there is a special relationship, there is a presumption of undue influence.

▪ Special relationships may be traditional ones such as lawyer-client, or also relationships of trust based on the facts of the particular situation.

▪ Where there is a presumption of undue influence, the alleged wrongdoer must prove that undue influence was not used.

Non Est Factum

▪ This defence to non-performance by one of the parties to a contract is based on that party not having understood the true nature of the document that was signed. Not normally used by a business person, it usually involves an individual who, through some infirmity, was not able to understand the nature of the document.

Ending a Contract

▪ The obligations or promises undertaken by the parties to the contract might be brought to an end in one of several ways, the most preferable usually being performance.

Remedies

- A contract is breached if a party does not perform according to its terms. A number of remedies arise from such a breach, their purpose being to compensate or assist the non-breaching party.

Damages

- Damages are an award of money that the court has ordered the breaching party to pay as compensation to the non-breaching party for the loss of the bargain represented by the contract. Damages are intended to place the non-breaching party in the same position as if the breach had not occurred, by awarding monetary compensation for any reasonably foreseeable loss caused by the breach.

- What would be reasonably foreseeable as a loss arising from a breach will depend on what was in the minds of the parties at the time of contracting. Certainly those losses, including loss of profit, that would occur in the normal course of business could be anticipated, as well as any losses arising from special circumstances that were brought to the attention of the breaching party at the time the contract was made.

- The courts will consider several factors in calculating the damages to be awarded, including whether the non-breaching party has mitigated its damages by taking whatever reasonable steps are necessary to minimize the losses experienced from the breach.

- Punitive damages are not easily awarded. There must be a separate actionable wrong and the other damages must not be sufficient to deter the wrongful conduct.

Other Types of Damages

- Monetary damages may be awarded for reasons other than putting the party in the position as if the contract had not been breached. These awards will be based on such considerations as pain and suffering (mental suffering) or expenses incurred.

Other Remedies

- In cases where damages are not sufficient to meet the needs of the non-breaching party, various other remedies may be brought into play. Usually these remedies involve a court order requiring the breaching party to complete, or refrain from, some action.

- Various types of injunctions are available to stop the breaching party from pursuing a particular course of action that has caused, or will cause, harm. The injunction may be temporary or permanent in nature.

- The courts may order the breaching party to proceed with the contract and specifically perform the promises made in the agreement.

- Remedial orders allowing a party to obtain information or evidence through a search of the breaching party's property (Anton Piller order), or granting access to financial records for an accounting of profits, are a few of the orders available to the court to assist in situations where a contract has been breached.

- The remedy of *quantum meruit* is available if the parties have not included a means to determine the value to be exchanged under the contract, and ensures that a reasonable price will be paid for the work done.

Closing Questions

Misrepresentation

1. Grouse Nest Resorts Ltd. arranged to borrow $1,250,000 from the First National Mortgage Company to build on two pieces of vacant land. The hotel company gave the mortgage on each of the properties as security for the loan.

    Under the terms of the building loan agreement, the mortgage company was to advance the money in instalments, over several months. The standard form mortgage document contained a clause stating that the mortgage company could refuse to make any further advances for whatever reason it chose. The president of Grouse Nest Resorts complained to the mortgage manager of First National that the clause could place Grouse Nest into bankruptcy if a loan instalment should be refused. The mortgage manager replied, "Don't worry, that clause is only used to prevent borrowers from taking off to Las Vegas." He reassured the president of the hotel company that if the development proceeded, the money would be advanced. On the strength of this representation Grouse Nest signed the mortgage. The first instalment was paid on time, but the mortgage manager was overruled by his superiors and no other advances were made.

    a) Could Grouse Nest Resorts Ltd. rely on the oral representations made by the mortgage manager in order to enforce the loan agreement?

2. Computer Aces Inc. sells a computer system to A.J.M. Leasing Ltd., whose business is financing car purchases by taking the leases as security. The sales representative tells A.J.M. that accounting software for the leasing business worth $10,000 will be supplied with the computer. When the officer from A.J.M. notes that nothing is said in the purchase order about the software, the sales rep explains that the software is in development and will not be ready for three months.

    A.J.M. buys the computers. Three months later when it asks for the software, a new sales rep, who has replaced the previous one, says he does not know anything about this.

    a) Is there an express term regarding the accounting software in the contract?

    b) Will the courts imply a term into the contract saying Computer Aces must supply the software?

    c) What would the results be if this were a consumer purchase? What is the reason for the difference in the laws governing consumer and business transactions?

3. Examine the entire agreement clause in the Agreement of Purchase and Sale for a Business in the Appendix to Chapter 5.

    a) What do the terms *representation* and *warranty* mean? Why are they included in this clause?

    b) Give an example from your own experience, or that of a relative or friend, where an oral statement has been made in the purchase of something and the statement was not written down as part of the contract, and that statement turned out to be false.

    c) Bring a copy of a contract that you or someone you know has signed recently, and note the clauses in it that you have studied in this course.

4. In the *Queen v. Cognos* case, what was the conflict between the representation made by the employer and the term of the contract?

    a) What were the elements of misrepresentation that Queen had to establish? Was he successful in establishing them, and was there a misrepresentation? Why was it not a fraudulent misrepresentation?

    b) There was a written employment contract between Queen and Cognos Inc. Why didn't Queen, who was an accountant, have a term written into the contract guaranteeing that the project would go ahead?

5. Robert Goddard and Norm Chomsky were friends and worked together as accountants in the same company. Chomsky found what he thought was a great bargain—one acre of vacant land on the edge of the city, selling for $50,000. Chomsky told Goddard, "I can't believe this deal. This property is worth $200,000. We can sell it within three months, and make a ton of money." Goddard agrees to put up $25,000 and the property is purchased. After months of trying to resell it, it becomes clear that the property is of little value because of its bad location, downwind from a mushroom farm. Eventually, the men sell the property for $25,000. Goddard wants to sue Chomsky for his loss of $12,500.

   a) Is Chomsky's statement about the value of the land, or its prospects for resale, a misrepresentation?

   b) Could it be a collateral warranty, or a term of the contract?

6. Ronald Dale advertised his dog-grooming salon for sale at $60,000. He wanted to complete the transaction quickly, and retire to Florida on November 2, in two weeks' time.

   Hector Hermitage, a young man who had recently received an inheritance, contacted Dale, inquiring what the gross monthly billings were for the salon. Dale stated they had averaged $8,000 a month for the past six months. When Hermitage asked to see the financial records, Dale told him they were with the accountant who was on holiday until November 12. Dale added that he could not wait until then to complete the sale of the business, and had other people currently interested as well.

   Hermitage decided Dale looked honest, so he offered $60,000 cash, which Dale accepted. The deal closed on October 31. When the accountant returned, Hermitage discovered to his horror that the average gross monthly billings for the previous six months were $5,800. Dale was still in the city to sell his house, and when Hermitage demanded his money back stated: "A deal's a deal, kid."

   a) On what legal basis could Hermitage argue for the return of his money?

   b) Would it make any difference if Dale had a well-known reputation for being terrible at paperwork, so that he relied on his bookkeeper and accountant to do all his financial paperwork?

   c) One of the reasons Hermitage is so angry is that he has already invested time and money in having a business plan drawn up and an advertisement campaign begun. If all goes according to the plan, the salon's business will increase by 60% within the next five months—generating a profit, though not as large as anticipated. Assuming Dale's statements were deliberately fraudulent, identify the various remedies available to Hermitage and decide which you would recommend to him.

7. Before signing the sales agreement for the software package Accounting for You, version 5.3, Alicia Marakovna asked the salesperson if it was the most recent version. He assured her it was. Later that day she saw a newspaper advertisement for the same software package, version 6.0, to be offered by the same store the next day.

   Marakovna returned to the store in fury, and was told by the salesperson that the 6.0 version had been in the backroom when she was there earlier, but was not to be sold before the advertised date. He then went on to point out a clause on the back of the agreement that Alicia had signed that contained the words "This agreement constitutes the entire agreement. No representations or warranties other than those in written form constitute the agreement." Marakovna replied: "Who ever reads the back of these things?"

   a) Will Marakovna be able to get a court to set aside this contract?

   b) Would it change your opinion if the statement that version 5.3 was the most recent version available had been in a brochure on the counter of the store?

   c) If the salesperson had told Marakovna that she could return the software if she was not satisfied with its performance, but the written agreement stated no returns allowed, would Marakovna be able to use the salesperson's statement as evidence in court?

8. Mary Cunningham was considering buying an antique lamp from Jay Scott, an antiques wholesaler. Cunningham, an antique retailer, said, "This must be a Victorian lamp." Scott did not reply, and Cunningham bought the lamp. Some time later she discovered it had in fact been manufactured in the 1960s.
   a) Is there a misrepresentation?
   b) Are there any circumstances where Cunningham could rely on misrepresentation?

9. Maurice Bullen, a mover, is considering buying a van for his business. The salesperson tells him that the model he is interested in will not be a "gas guzzler," and that given the current cost of gas to travel 1,500 kilometres should cost no more than $50. Bullen decides that he wants this model and signs a sales agreement that contains the words:

   > This agreement constitutes the entire agreement. No representations or warranties other than those in written form constitute the agreement.

   Bullen did not see this clause because the print was small and it appeared on the back of the document. In his first week of using the van, Bullen drove 1,000 kilometres, and spent $60 on gas. Checking his receipts, he determined that the price of gas had not increased since his discussions with the salesperson, but that a recent federal budget would put gas up five cents a litre in three weeks' time.
   Bullen is no longer a happy customer.
   a) Can Bullen get a court to set aside his contract? Why or why not?
   b) If the term regarding gas consumption was in a brochure, would this change your opinion?

10. During construction of an office building, Jackson Silvermann signed an agreement to rent premises on the main floor for use as a restaurant. He expected the building to be 100 percent occupied within five months of his restaurant opening. For various reasons, businesses were slow to rent in this location and six months after his restaurant opened the building was only 30 percent rented.
    Silvermann wants out of his lease. The landlord admits he knew there would be difficulties in renting this location but claims he never discussed this element with Silvermann when they signed the restaurant lease, and that he knew nothing of the restaurateur's expectations.
    a) On what legal remedy will Silvermann rely?
    b) Will Silvermann's claim be successful? Why or why not?
    c) On what legal principle will the landlord rely?

11. Jorge Mendocino was an independent contractor who made his living by purchasing vacant parcels of land, building residential houses on them, and reselling the houses at a profit. One day while driving through a heavily populated area of Toronto, he saw a piece of vacant land for sale that would be perfect for two Victorian townhouses. He immediately telephoned the agent and put in an offer on the property. The offer was accepted and four months later the transaction was completed.
    Mendocino proceeded to build the two houses and to landscape the properties before selling them. He was known in the trade for the excellent landscaping of the properties he sold. However, whatever plant material he put in—grass, trees, shrubs, flowers—all would wither and die within a week of planting. One day, Mendocino was talking to a neighbour at the building site, who said she too experienced similar problems with her plants on that side of her property ever since the gas station that used to be there had been taken down two years ago. Mendocino then had the soil tested and discovered the ground was so toxic that nothing would grow, and he probably would not be able to sell the houses. Angry, Mendocino confronted the vendor and demanded his money back as well as damages for the loss of profit from the sale of the houses. The vendor suggested Mendocino go hoe a row of beans.
    a) Explain whether Mendocino will be successful in having the court set aside the contract and award him damages.
    b) From the sample Offer to Purchase provided by your instructor, identify the clauses that the vendor would rely on for his defence and explain fully if they would be an answer to Mendocino's court action.

Mistake, Duress, Undue Influence, Non Est Factum

12. Bill Graham owned his own truck, and entered into a contract with Voth Bros. Construction. After the work was completed, Voth Bros. alleged that the loads were short. Knowing that Graham was in financial trouble, Voth refused to pay anything unless Graham reduced his charges. Graham, unable to pay his subcontractors until Voth paid him, complied with the demand and sent an amended invoice which Voth paid. Graham then sued for the difference between the original invoice and the amended one.
    a) What grounds support Graham's action?
    b) Will he be successful?

13. Eddie Giordano was in the middle of a recession. His business was down, and he needed help. Giordano went to his accountant, who told him he could lend him $20,000 but only if he signed over a 25 percent interest in his business.
    a) Is there a problem of duress or undue influence?
    b) If there is a problem, how should Giordano and his accountant plan for the transaction?

14. Bill Simco was 84 and almost blind. He had two children who, being greedy, wanted his money *now*. They produced what they called a letter of thanks to the grandchildren for taking care of him during his recent illness and told him to sign it. Simco instead signed a promissory note for $50,000.
    a) Is this a case of undue influence or *non est factum* or neither?
    b) If there is a problem, what is the solution for Simco?

15. Tara Olsen responded to a newspaper advertisement that read "10-foot fibreglass Sunfish for sale, $400 firm." She telephoned Ben Bartollini, the owner, and told him that she had just finished a sailing course and wanted to buy her own boat. She arranged to meet him the next day with the cash. Olsen arrived at Bartollini's house, handed over the $400 and opened the garage to discover a 10-foot fibreglass Sunfish canoe. When she tried to get her money back Bartollini refused.
    a) On what legal basis might Olsen argue her position and what difficulties might she encounter?
    b) If successful, what would be her remedy?

16. For several years, Geraldine Kikuta had managed Drew Mair's art store. During that time Mair had slowly withdrawn from the business side of the store to pursue his personal interest of creating unique sculptures from discarded junk. Mair had come to rely on Kikuta exclusively to handle the business affairs of the store and to act as his personal *agent* for the sale of his artistic creations. As a result of Kikuta's promotion of his work, Mair was now a well-known name in the contemporary art world.

    One day, Kikuta presented Mair with an ultimatum—either he sold her 60 percent of the store for $10,000 or she would not be back to work the next morning and she would advise the art world that she could no longer in good conscience act as agent for Drew.

    Mair was at a loss. He had become so totally dependent on Kikuta to run the store that he had no idea as to the state of the financial books, business orders, or even where the office coffee machine was located. And, if Kikuta were suddenly to stop acting as his agent in the circumstances she suggested, his reputation and sales would probably drop to nothing. He signed the contract, and accepted the cheque Kikuta just happened to have with her.
    a) Can Mair use duress as a reason to avoid this contract? If so, what is the nature of the duress?
    b) Would Mair be able to raise undue influence as a means of avoiding the contract?

17. You are the manager of a branch of a major bank. Giancarlo and Gina Romero, successful entrepreneurs, have come to meet with you to arrange the financing for the purchase of their latest business venture. You have indicated that before the bank advances funds it requires a guarantee for the loan. The couple shows you the deed to a cottage property registered in the name of Gina Romero. She offers to sign the guarantee today so that they can obtain the funds immediately.
    a) What concerns about this situation, if any, come flooding into your mind?
    b) If you see a problem in this transaction, what steps would you take to avoid it?

18. Gordon Thompson had worked as an engineer with Foundation Consultants Ltd. for ten years. Without any warning, he was called into a supervisor's office to be told that the company was downsizing, and that day would be his last on the job. Thompson was offered three months' salary ($15,000) if he would sign a form releasing the company from any other financial obligation to him. The release exempted the employer from any court action over the firing. The cheque was already made out—it was handed to him along with the release form.

    Thompson had not expected to be fired. Last year he had bought a house, and now had a large mortgage. He also obtained a loan to renovate the house, and his wife had just taken six months' maternity leave without pay. Thompson was worried about surviving financially while looking for employment, so he took the $15,000 and signed the release.

    It took Thompson over a year to find another job. During this time, he sought legal advice. His lawyer told him that the employer would have been liable for one year's salary, approximately $60,000, had Thompson not settled the matter but instead had taken the employer to court. Thompson wants to sue and have the release set aside.

    a) What is the technical name for the grounds Thompson could plead to have the agreement set aside?

    b) Could he plead undue influence? There is a relationship between him and the employer, but is it a special relationship as used in the law of undue influence?

    c) Will he be successful in having the release set aside?

19. The Bank of Credit and Commerce tried to enforce a loan guarantee against Christine Macdaid, who was married to William Macdaid, a farmer. The bank's lending officer visited the farm while the husband was on a business trip, and demanded that Mrs. Macdaid guarantee a loan made for a barn that was currently under construction.

    The bank's officer stated: "These papers have to be signed or the work on the barn will be shut down."

    The woman signed the papers because she did not want the construction to stop, since the barn was needed for the farm operation.

    The loan went into default, and the bank sued Christine Macdaid personally.

    a) Did Christine Macdaid have any grounds in law to attack the guarantee? If so, what are they?

    The bank argued that the statement made by the lending officer was "ordinary business pressure."

    b) Was this an ordinary business transaction?

    c) Who do you think would succeed and why?

20. Create a fact situation that clearly illustrates the elements of *non est factum*.

21. Gerhard Gertler left his reading glasses in his car. Because he was late for his next meeting he asked Barney Naismith, his bank manager, what the interest rate was on the promissory note he was signing at that moment. Naismith said it was 5%, but wrote down 8% before Gertler signed.

    a) Is this an example of *non est factum*?

    b) If not, does Gertler have any other remedy available?

22. Kerr Shipping Company sent a cable through the RCA telegraph service. The cable was to the captain of one of the Kerr vessels, at that time in the Philippines, instructing him to pick up and deliver certain freight to New York.

    The message cost $26.78, and was sent in code so that competitors could not learn of Kerr's plans. Because of an error by RCA, the cable never reached its intended destination.

    Kerr sued RCA for $500,000, the loss of profits that would have been made from the shipment.

    a) Would the action be successful?

    b) What steps might Kerr Shipping have taken to safeguard its interests in these circumstances?

Undue Influence

23. Direct to the Net Inc. became a great success in only four years after start-up and it decided to go public. About one week before making the announcement of its initial public offering (IPO), it was served with a statement of claim by a former shareholder who alleged the company had used his ideas without paying for them four years ago.

The directors of Direct to the Net Inc. believe that there is no merit in the claim and feel that they are being blackmailed, but believe they cannot report a lawsuit of this type on the corporation's disclosure material for the public offering. They agree to pay one million dollars to settle the claim.

a) Is there any ground in law by which the corporation can have the settlement set aside by a court? If so, what is the name for this cause of action?

b) What business considerations are relevant to the decision to sue and the timing of any lawsuit to set aside the settlement?

Remedies

24. June Colwood had an e-mail account with Canada On-line (COL). She did not pay her last instalment. Instead of shutting down her mailbox, COL left it open and let e-mails accumulate. Colwood asked for these e-mails but COL refused to release them until she paid. There was no term in the contract dealing with the consequences of non-payment.

One of the e-mails which Colwood did not receive was a response to a job application telling her that she successfully got a job at a salary of $50,000 per annum, but that she had to reply in 24 hours. Because COL did not release her e-mail, she did not learn of the acceptance until a week after the deadline. Because she missed the deadline, the job was given to someone else.

Colwood wants to sue COL for one year's pay for the loss of the job.

a) If there is no express term covering the retention of e-mails, is there any basis on which Colwood can sue?

b) What defences respecting damages would COL raise and with what result?

25. Scientific Feed Diets Inc. sells Cattle Feed "Super Grow" to a rancher. Unfortunately, it is laced with strychnine, because of the carelessness of Scientific Feed Diets Inc. The rancher is a health-diet nut and reads that Cattle Feed contains all the needed nutrients for humans. He decides to experiment with the diet for thirty days, but after the first mouthful of the poisoned cattle feed, he becomes violently sick and cannot work for six months.

He wants to sue Scientific Feed Diets Inc. for damages for breach of contract.

a) What principle of contract damage law would Scientific Feed Diet raise in its defence and with what result?

26. Shelina Memarbashi paid an art gallery $50,000 for what she believed was an unknown work by Picasso. However, her judgment was wrong. A few weeks later, an art-critic friend saw the painting and told her that it was created by a minor student of Picasso, and as a result was worth only $10,000. The friend had been present at another auction where the art gallery had bought the piece for about $2,000.

a) Could Memarbashi successfully sue the art gallery for a refund of the $40,000 excess payment?

27. Ping Lok had a contract to paint the Allensons' house for $5,000. The money was to be paid upon completion of the job. Ping Lok stripped all the paint from the exterior walls, and prepared them for painting. He had completed one wall when the Allensons changed their minds and decided to put up aluminum siding.

Because the job had not been completed, the Allensons refused to pay Ping Lok any money under the contract.

Ping Lok's remedy is:

i)   specific performance
ii) interlocutory injunction
iii) mareva injunction
iv) *quantum meruit*
v)   rectification

a) Explain the nature of the remedy available to Ping Lok, and the approximate dollar amount he might expect to receive as a result of his court action against the Allensons.

28. Theo Stakis had a contract to purchase a thoroughbred racing horse named You Betcha from Brad Taylor, the breeder. The contract was to be completed following the Kentucky Derby, in which the horse was entered to race.

When You Betcha won the Kentucky Derby, Brad Taylor refused to sell the horse to Stakis. Stakis had intended to use You Betcha for breeding, and anticipated huge profits as a result of the breeding program.

a) What remedy would you suggest Stakis pursue?

29. Roland Clelland negotiated a contract to provide leather bracelets to Bracelets R You, a high-fashion store. The store would pay Clelland $2 for every bracelet he delivered on June 15, in time for the summer bracelet parade in the shopping mall.

On January 31, Clelland arranged with Max Weill to have 3,000 strips of leather delivered to Clelland's house on April 30, at a cost of 25 cents a strip. Clelland intended to use these strips of leather to make his artistic bracelets by June 15. At their meeting, Clelland told Weill all about his deal with the store. He added that, if the contract with Bracelets R You worked out, another chain of fashion stores was prepared to place a three-year order with Clelland, who anticipated an income of $40,000 a year from that contract.

Clelland left Weill's warehouse with assurances the leather would be delivered on time. On April 17, Weill phoned Clelland and said he would not be able to deliver the leather strips after all, but he was sure that Clelland could make other arrangements.

If Clelland does not have the leather by April 30, he will lose the contract with Bracelets R You and all profits he would have made.

a) Advise Clelland as to his remedies and obligations and make a recommendation on what action he should take.

30. Aly Hamada agreed over the telephone to purchase Judie Home's electric treadmill for $1,500 at the end of the month. She then sent a contract to Home, which Home promptly signed and sent back.

At the end of the month Hamada presented Home with a cheque for $1,000 and asked for the treadmill. When Home checked the contract, she found a mistake had been made in typing and the purchase price was shown as $1,000.

Home's remedy is:

i)   rescission
ii) accounting
iii) rectification

a) Explain the nature of the remedy that Home will obtain based on your choice of remedy.

31. A retailer ordered 10 television sets, at a cost of $5,000, from a supplier. Normally, these particular appliances would all be sold in one month, for gross sales of $10,000, and a profit after expenses of $3,000. However, the supplier failed to deliver.

    The retailer sued for breach of contract.

    a) How much would the court award in damages for breach of contract?

    b) If the retailer had been able to obtain the televisions from another supplier at the same price, but chose instead to sue the usual supplier, what damages would the court award?

32. A supplier delivered defective sugar to a brewery. As a result, one entire month's production of beer was contaminated and had to be destroyed. Rumours spread throughout the hospitality industry that the brewery was supplying defective beer, and its long-term sales were affected.

    The brewery sued the sugar supplier for damages for loss of profit (sales minus expenses) of $100,000, as well as $2 million for damage to its reputation. The sugar company claimed that it should be liable only for $50,000, the replacement cost of the destroyed beer.

    a) Could the sugar supplier reasonably have foreseen that delivering defective sugar would result in the loss of one month's profit for the brewery? Was the damage to the brewery's reputation reasonably foreseeable?

    b) Should the damages be limited to the replacement cost of the beer?

33. An equipment dealership buys 10 harvesters from General Machines Ltd. for inventory of the dealership. As the harvesters have a design defect that costs $1,000 per unit to repair, it has to repair the five units sold. Word spreads so it cannot sell the remaining five units on which it would have earned a profit of $2,000 per unit. Also, future business will be lost because its reputation will be damaged.

    a) What losses are recoverable from General Machines Ltd.?

    b) What are the terms in the law of damages for the various types of damages suffered by the dealership?

34. Read the Limitation and Remedies clause from a Masu Inc. software license agreement which is reproduced below.

    > Masu Inc. shall have no liability for any indirect or speculative damages (including, without limiting the foregoing, consequential, incidental, and special damages) arising from the use of or inability to use this product, whether arising out of an action in contract or tort, including, but not limited to, negligence, or under any warranty or condition, irrespective of whether Masu Inc. had advance notice of the possibility of any such damages, or such damages are foreseeable, including, but not limited to, loss of use, business interruption, and loss of profits. Notwithstanding the foregoing, Masu Inc.'s total liability for all claims under this agreement, whether in respect of a single occurrence or series of occurrences, shall not exceed the price paid by you for the product. These limitations on potential liabilities were an essential element in setting the product price. Masu Inc. neither assumes nor authorizes anyone to assume for it any other liabilities.

    a) Select all the terms in this clause that you have studied in this book. Identify the related topics in the text (by page number), review them, and then discuss the significance of each term.

    b) What types of damage claims might business customers make against Masu Inc. resulting from failure of its software?

    c) Why does the limitation clause contain the sentence "These limitations on potential liabilities were an essential element in setting the product price"?

35. In the law of damages, it is said that a loss due to a subcontract, that is, a resale to a third party at a higher price, is too remote since it is not the normal result of a failure to deliver goods.

    a) What does the above mean?

    b) What case mentioned in the text established this principle?

    c) What can be done to make a vendor liable for loss of profits on a subcontract?

36. The plaintiff agreed to purchase a used hydraulic blade for the front of his tractor from the defendant for $1,000. At the time the plaintiff had a contract to do work at a gravel pit. The hydraulic pump was defective and the defendant tried unsuccessfully to repair it. Because of the delays in repairing the pump, the gravel pit owner cancelled the plaintiff's contract.
    a) What damages could the plaintiff claim?
    b) What would the plaintiff have to prove to make the defendant responsible for loss of profit respecting the work at the gravel pit?

37. Joe's Tavern learns of a new beer glass that contains a microchip which signals the bartender when the glass is nearly empty, permitting the bartender to direct a waiter to that table. It orders 100,000 units of the item from a manufacturer at $10 per glass. The manufacturer completes and ships half of the order and is paid in full to that point. Suddenly the market price for these products drops to $5. Joe's Tavern tells the manufacturer that it wants to cancel the contract. The manufacturer advises Joe's Tavern that the manufacturer intends to complete the contract by making the parts, shipping them, and billing in full.
    a) Is Joe's Tavern's cancellation a breach of contract?
    b) What damages, if any, would the manufacturer be able to claim and why? Would the manufacturer be able to get punitive damages against Joe's Tavern based on the fact that it intentionally breached the contract?
    c) Do you think the legal principle achieves an economic result?

Multi Issue

38. a) Identify the clauses which affect or determine how damages will be calculated in the:
        i)   Used Car Bill of Sale (Chapter 6)
        ii)   Purchase Order (Chapter 8)
        iii) Courier Bill of Lading (Appendix in this chapter)
    b) The Courier Bill of Lading contains a clause limiting its liability to $2 per pound (or $4.41 per kilogram). Is this provision consistent with the principle respecting remoteness of damages set out in *Hadley v. Baxendale*? (**Remoteness of damages** is the principle of whether the damages are too far removed from the original negligent act.)
    c) The car purchase agreement sets out the formula for calculating damages if a customer fails to accept delivery. What principles of law determine if such a clause will be enforced and with what result?

remoteness of damages
the principle of whether the damages are too far removed from the original negligent act

Websites

www.rcmp-grc.gc.ca/scams/ecbweb.htm—The Economic Crime Prevention site. RCMP website includes the latest scams, business frauds, etc.

www.scambusters.com—Internet ScamBusters. Avoiding scams via Internet commerce.

strategis.ic.gc.ca/sc_consu/engdoc/homepage.html?categories=e_con—Industry Canada, Consumer Information. Includes tips to avoid consumer scams.

www.phonebusters.com—Information on the latest fraud schemes.

Courier Bill of Lading

CANADA FAST

WE WANT TO BE YOUR COURIER

BILLING COPY
1116999

MONTH	DAY	20		CONFIRMATION No.		

FROM	CHARGE TO	TO
ADDRESS		ADDRESS
CITY	POSTAL CODE	CITY	POSTAL CODE
SHIPPER'S SIGNATURE	PIECES	PHONE NUMBER	PLEASE PRINT SIGNATURE	RECEIVED IN GOOD ORDER

10 ▶ SHIPMENT/DETAILS/EXPED. ACCOUNT No.

| NO. OF PIECES | WEIGHT | **LB** |
| | SUBJECT TO CORR. | **KG** |

DECLARED VALUE (FOR INSURANCE PURPOSES)
$ SEE TERMS

LIMITATION OF LIABILITY IMPORTANT. PLEASE READ

THE AMOUNT OF ANY LOSS OR DAMAGE FOR WHICH THE CARRIER MAY BE LIABLE, SHALL NOT EXCEED $2.00 PER POUND (OR $4.41 PER KILOGRAM) COMPUTED ON THE TOTAL WEIGHT OF THE SHIPMENT UNLESS A HIGHER VALUE IS DECLARED ON THE FACE OF THE BILL OF LADING BY THE CONSIGNOR (SENDER).

N.B. NOTE CAREFULLY CONDITIONS BELOW HEREOF INCLUDING LIMITATIONS AND EXCLUSIONS OF CARRIER'S LIABILITY, WHICH ARE HEREBY ACCEPTED.

TERM 1 RECEIPT & FREIGHT

Received at the point of origin on the date specified, from the consignor mentioned herein, the property herein described; in apparent good order, except as noted (contents and conditions of contents of package unknown) marked, consigned and destined as indicated herein, which the carrier agrees to carry and to deliver to the consignee at the said destination, if on its own authorized route or otherwise to cause to be carried by another carrier on the route to said destination, subject to the rates and classification in effect on the date of shipment.

It is mutually agreed, as to each carrier of all or any of the goods over all or any portion of the route to destination, and as to each party of any time interested in all or any of the goods, that every service to be performed hereunder shall be subject to all the conditions not prohibited by law, whether printed or written, including conditions on back hereof, which are hereby agreed by the consignor and accepted for himself and his assigns.

TERM 2 NOTICE OF CLAIM

No carrier is liable for loss, damage or delay to any goods carried, under the Bill of Lading unless notice thereof setting out particulars of the origin, destination and date of shipment of the goods and the estimated amount claimed in respect of such loss, damage or delay is given in writing to the originating carrier or the delivering carrier within sixty (60) days after the delivery of the goods, or, in case of failure to make delivery, within nine (9) months from the date of shipment.

The final statement of the claim must be filed within nine (9) months from the date of shipment together with a copy of the paid freight bill.

TERM 3 NO SPECIAL AGREEMENT

The parties agree that notwithstanding any disclosure of nature or value of the goods, the amount of any loss or damage, including consequential, incidental or indirect damages, loss of earnings or profits, resulting from the loss of or damage to the goods and/or misdelivery, failure to deliver or delay in delivery of the goods, shall not exceed the maximum liability of the carrier aforesaid.

TERM 4 PAYMENT GUARANTEE

The shipper agrees to pay the carrier all shipping charges in the event the receiver, on a collect shipment or the third party on a third party billing shipment, refuses to pay the carrier.

TERM 5 GOVERNING LAW

The contract for the carriage of goods listed in the bill of lading shall be deemed to include and be subject to the terms and conditions prescribed by law of the jurisdiction where the goods originate which if Newfoundland, Nova Scotia, New Brunswick, Prince Edward Island, Saskatchewan and British Columbia, the regulations made pursuant to the Motor Carrier Act of each Province; Quebec, the bill of lading form and terms and conditions approved by the Quebec Transport Commission; Ontario, the Truck Transportation Act and Regulations thereto; Manitoba, The Highway Traffic Act and Regulations thereto; Alberta, The Motor Transport Act and Regulations thereto.

TERM 6 ENTIRE AGREEMENT

This bill of lading constitutes the entire contract between the carrier and the shipper, and no agent, servant, or representative of the carrier has authority to alter, modify or waive any provision of this contract.

Special Business Contracts

Operating a Business Website

Nearly all businesses, even small start-ups, have websites. Some are merely for advertising or are online catalogues, but some sites permit sales to be made. Sales are contracts, and so the law of contract applies. However, new technology has changed some of the ways of doing business and has created uncertainty in certain areas of the law of contract. The law of contract was formed in era when people primarily dealt face to face. The electronic commerce acts are responses by governments to meet the challenges posed by advancing technology.

The law, particularly the law of contract, applies to e-commerce transactions equally as it does to traditional transactions. However, some of the unique features of technology require some adaptation of the older rules. These adaptations are described here.

The Need For Standardization

Electronic commerce is global. Websites can be easily viewed in many countries and products may be ordered and shipped to countries that have a wide range of different legal laws and systems. It would be impossible for a business to know all of these rules and have certainty that business transactions would be binding. Businesses would not know when they have a binding contract, one that would be enforced by the courts, and when not.

Accordingly, the United Nations Commission on International Trade Law ("UNCITL") has a model statute called the United Nations Model Law on Electronic Commerce. Although it uses the term 'law', it is not a binding statute. It is meant to be a model so that all countries will adopt it for a uniform code for international e-commerce business transactions.

Canada's Uniform Electronics Commerce Act

To avoid any arguments over the division of powers in our Constitution and to attempt to achieve uniformity in every province throughout Canada, the government has followed the UN's initiative and also passed a model act, which has no legal force, and which was intended to and has formed the basis of provincial legislation. Most provinces' legislation has adopted this model in whole or in part. While most provinces have adopted the element discussed below, if you are doing business across provincial boundaries, you will have to check the rules for any specific province—the *Uniform Electronic Commerce Act* ("UECA").

Scope: E-Commerce acts govern most business contracts. They exclude only documents such as wills, deeds to land and the like.

Consent: E-Commerce acts provide that electronic documents and methods cannot be used without a person's consent. However, that consent can be implied by reason of a person's conduct. What is implied consent has not yet been defined. For example, if you put your email address on a business card, is that sufficient to imply consent for the use of email for notices under a contract?

Forum Selection and Governing Law

Even if you can determine the seller's physical location, will you be able to sue if it is in a foreign country, and will you be able to afford the cost of doing so? The laws which determine the governing law and place of trial are complex.

Because of the complexity of these laws, some countries are proposing legislation that an on-line contract will be subject to its laws and jurisdiction if the website can be viewed from that country.

Example: If a website was put up by a British Columbia company on a server in British Columbia which was viewed in California, and goods were ordered by a resident of California from the British Columbia website, the laws in California would govern the transaction and the venue of any trial would be California. If such laws are enacted, they will require careful consideration by Canadian businesses who sell products on their websites.

When purchasing on-line, refund policies should be checked carefully, including the cost of shipping charges and who pays them. Some purchasers prefer to buy on-line from a business which also has a bricks-and-mortar store within easy access for returns and warranty problems. The location of a physical store in your jurisdiction will lessen the probability that you will have venue and governing law issues.

E-commerce legislation permits the formation of contracts by electronic agents. These are created by interactive software that is used on websites to take orders. Previously, contracts were always made between two humans; now contracts can be made between a human and a machine.

Mistake

Some rules of contract are more applicable than others to e-commerce: one of these is the law of mistake. The need for precision in using any computer system and the speed of the transaction makes mistake an important consideration. This applies to both businesses and consumers.

Example: Mistake by Business. United Airlines mistakenly posted a discount round trip ticket to Paris return from New York for $30. Six hundred customers clicked on the "I accept" before management discovered the mistake. Chat lines spread the word of these "deals" faster and wider than previously possible. Transactions such as the above raise the question as to whether posting information on a website is an invitation to treat (such as listing a product in a catalogue) or is an offer.

United Airlines decided to settle this case for public-relations reasons. Many businesses, especially in the travel industry, have been subject to this type of mistake.

Example: Mistake by Customer. A retail business might intend to order 50 DVD players for its store, but the employee types in 500 and does not notice. E-commerce statutes require that electronic agents give the customer an opportunity to correct any errors and permit cancellation if, on becoming aware of the error, the customer promptly notifies the vendor.[1]

Mistake   Because mistake is a great risk to businesses and customers alike, special considerations must be given to it.

- Include a notice on the website page that the information is not an offer in law but an invitation to customers to make an offer
- Use software that identifies unusual transactions. For example, an unusually large number of purchases from one customer may indicate an error on the part of the customer. Also, an unusually large number of purchases, such as the sale of the round trip from New York to Paris, may indicate an error on the part of the business.
- Purchasers might institute controls on e-mail orders, such as requiring that a second person approve the e-mail before it is sent.

■ *Critical Concepts of* Mistake

The common law respecting **mistake** has been varied by e-commerce statutes.

- The error must be material.
- The electronic agent must give the customer the opportunity to correct the error.
- The customers must promptly notify the business of the error on becoming aware of it.
- The customer must return or destroy the consideration as required by the business, or deal with it in a reasonable manner.
- The customer must not benefit if the contract is not enforced.

Domain Names

The address of a website is called a **domain name.** For example, www.leasing.com. The right-hand side, which is usually .com, .net, .ca, or the like, is called a high-level domain name. The registration for high-level domain names is controlled by the International Corporation for Assigned Names and Numbers (ICANN). Country names such as .ca are controlled by national authorities.

domain name
the address of a website

The domain name is a new type of business name. Previously, protection of business names was done by registering the name as a trademark in any country in which it was used. However, a trademark registration is not sufficient to automatically stop domain registration because the latter is done by a separate organization.

There has been significant misuse of domain names. Some businesses register names that are very similar to large business names, hoping to divert traffic to their site. Pornography sites are famous for this. For example, if you go to www.nasa.com you would not, at least at the time of writing, be able to find any information about rocket launchings.

Cybersquatting is another problem. It is the registration of a domain name containing a business name of another person, with the intention of selling the domain name to that business. Individual people register any number of names that are similar to the names used by large organizations or governments, in an attempt to force the large organizations or governments to pay a fee to buy the right to use the name.

cybersquatting
the registration of a domain name containing a business name of another person, with the intention of selling the domain name to that business

Example: An Australian man registered www.universityofoxford.co.uk. The university registered the domain name www.ox.ac.uk. However, a search for the term Oxford University always put the Australian man's site at the top of the list. So, Oxford objected and won this dispute.

---

1. *Electronic Commerce Act*, R.S.O. A2000 S21.

ICANN delegated the domain-name registration process to several organizations, one of which is the World Intellectual Property Organization (WIPO). These organizations oversee the formation of arbitration tribunals to hear the domain-name disputes. There is a choice of a single arbitrator or a panel of three arbitrators. Users have to pay, so they often use single arbitrators. However, commentators have suggested that there may be a bias in the decisions of single arbitrators in that they tend to favour larger businesses. Even though it is more costly, it is recommended that smaller businesses or individuals choose the three-arbitrator-panel arbitration option. The smaller party is able to choose one of the panel members directly.

Legalese

Bad-Faith Registrations   Bad-faith registration is generally considered to be a registration by a person who does not have a legitimate interest in actively using it, and who intends to resell it (cybersquatting) or to mislead the public to his or her site (an act similar to passing off).

Example: Jim Carey complained to WIPO alleging bad faith registration because a business called BWI Domains registered "JimCarey.com". Fans searching his name came to that site and were directed to another site where the fan had to pay on a "pay-per-click" basis. The WIPO ruled in Carey's favour saying that the BWI Domains had no legitimate interest in this famous name (WIPO case number D2009-0563).

■ *Critical Concepts of* Bad-Faith Registrations

While the law is developing on the rights to have exclusive use of a domain name, there appear to be three principles that are applied in claims that attack domain-name registration on the basis that the registration was done in bad faith:

- The owner of the challenged name has no legitimate commercial interest in the name other than reselling it.
- The name is similar to the name of another business such that it would mislead the public into believing that the challenged name is the same business as the business bringing the complaint.
- Where both businesses can establish a legitimate interest, the right to registration would probably be decided on a first-registration basis.

. Sucks Websites

Disgruntled consumers have resorted to retaliation towards business they feel have treated them badly, or have not stood by the product sold, by creating websites airing their grievances and inviting others to do the same. These sites are often given the business' name followed by ".sucks.com". The business' name is usually a registered trademark and a registered domain name.

Under domain name jurisdiction the business can ask the arbitrator under WIPO to have the right to use that name, transfer it to the business exclusively and thereby prevent the dissatisfied customer from using it.

There are also a number of traditional legal remedies to protect a business name and reputation such as trademark infringement, passing off, defamation, and injurious falsehood, all of which are described elsewhere. Case law developed under each of these remedies makes allowances for consumer complaints so in the usual case would be of little use to the business.

The new issue raised by the domain name arbitration jurisdiction was whether under this regime, a business could have the exclusive right to use that name as a website transferred to it and thereby prevent the use by an aggrieved consumer. The answer in an early arbitration case went against the business and in favour of the consumer as the next case brief, the decision of an arbitrator under WIPO, demonstrates.

Wal-Mart Stores Inc. v. <walmartcanadasucks.com> and Ken Harvey, WIPO Arbitration and Mediation Centre Case No. D2000-1104

Ken Harvey registered the domain name "Walmartcanadasucks.com" and started a webpage with a page stating "this is a freedom of information site set up for dissatisfied Wal-Mart Canada customers". The message went on to invite customers to tell their horror stories relating to dealings with Wal-Mart Canada. Wal-Mart made an application under WIPO for arbitration asking that the rights to use the name in question be transferred to it exclusively.

The Arbitrator's Decision

The Arbitrator ruled that the dispute resolution process under WIPO respecting domain names is to protect against bad faith and domain name registrations not provide a remedy for alleged misconduct involving domain names. The name "Walmartcanadasucks.com" was not confusingly similar to Wal-Mart's trademark name. Further Harvey did not register the domain name in bad faith. Harvey had a legitimate interest to use it as a foundation for criticism of the complaint. Wal-Mart's application was dismissed.

Website Development Contracts   If you plan to have a technology company design your website, there are certain terms of the contract that are critical:

Business Alert!

- you should include a precise description of the site specifications
- the scope and the length of warranties should be spelled out
- the remedies for non-performance should be specified
- there should be provisions for ongoing support
- there should be a clear understanding of who owns the content and any technology developed or licensed for the site, including all the rights to the text, graphics, images, software and databases

The contract with the business hosting or operating the site should include:

- a description of the service to be provided
- a performance guarantee
- a clear statement of who owns the information on the site
- protection of any confidential information gathered through the site

E-commerce and E-crime

Although it seems to be counterintuitive, it appears that it is safer to make purchases by a credit card on-line than by a cheque.

Most fraud on the Internet is done by small operators who do not wish to have a relationship with a credit card company because it would reveal too much about them. Also, credit card companies and valid businesses are often anxious to ensure consumer confidence in the use of credit cards on the Web, and so they resolve problems by absorbing losses rather than by passing them on to consumers.

Also, beware of website ratings. Many scammers rate their own businesses very high. There is no way of checking on who is giving these rave reviews.

Virtual "fencing" is common. Where is a better place to sell a stolen item than through the anonymous Internet auction houses? However, remember that a purchaser does not get ownership of a stolen item and will have to give it back to the true owner if the item is traced.

Criminal charges may sometimes be effective. A 20-year-old Kingston, Ontario man was found guilty of fraud for listing a pickup truck for sale on eBay. A man from Indiana agreed to buy the truck and sent a cheque. There was in fact no truck and the purchaser complained to local police, who arrested the seller.[2]

Business Alert!

Safe On-line Buying   Because of new challenges raised by the Internet, some practices are safer than others.

- Pay by credit card. If you do not get the product, you can challenge the charge with your credit card company. Do not deal with cheque- or cash-only sellers.
- Encrypt. Do not give your credit card number on-line unless the latest security protocols are in place.
- Check your statements. Always review your credit card statements for billing errors or unauthorized purchases, and notify your credit card company immediately if there are any.
- Do business with companies you trust. Deal only with companies you know and find reliable.
- Print out the purchase contract. You need to have a paper record in case there are any problems.

Privacy

Canada's need for privacy has been dramatized in newscasts of employers opening employee e-mails, Internet service providers withholding e-mails to force payment of accounts, and biometric face scanning at the Super Bowl and at airports.

What if a principal of a company, which has a demand loan with a bank, takes a medical for his insurance company and the medical shows he has developed a serious heart problem? The next day, although his financial statements are favourable and the loan is in good standing, the bank manager calls him at the office and demands an immediate payment of the loan. The bank manager does not have to justify calling the loan because it is a demand loan, and does not tell the business person why. However, the bank and the insurance company share data as marketing partners.

There have been allegations in newspaper articles of abuse of data collection. In one such article, a woman had just successfully completed a one-year diet program and lost 75 pounds (35 kilograms). One month later, she got a free box of chocolates in the mail promoting a discount direct-mail candy business. The allegation was that the dieting firm and the candy business exchanged information on customers because of mutual self-interest.

The use of computers and the Internet has made it increasingly easy for businesses to collect a wide range of data about every person in Canada. Some businesses specialize in doing just that.

These advances in technology permit businesses to collect data with the consumer's knowledge and often without. Businesses frequently use their websites to collect information about customers. Every time a form is filled out, the information is preserved in a database.

Information can also be gathered without the visitor's knowledge. As one example, "cookies" are small computer files placed on the user's hard drive without the user's knowledge or permission (though you can also set your browser to notify you before any cookie is added to your hard drive). They can display advertising such as banner ads personalized for that user's preferences as determined by information collected about that purchaser from many sources, including tracking which website that purchaser visits and with what frequency. This explains

---

2. See "eBay Buyer Pays $18,000 for Non-Existing Pick-Up Truck," *National Post* on-line, September 13, 2000 (www.nationalpost.com).

"We put all new employees on probation."

why when one user goes to a website, the banner ad displays the latest about upcoming wrestling matches and when another user goes to the same website, the banner ad on that user's computer promotes the latest Harlequin romance novel.

To address these privacy concerns the federal government has enacted the *Personal Information Protection and Electronic Documents Act* (PIPEDA). It was enacted in three phases to allow provinces to enact their own similar legislation, which will displace the federal legislation for matters under provincial jurisdiction. However, if a province has not enacted similar legislation, the federal legislation will govern for that province.

Scope

PIPEDA was drafted to apply to all forms and types of personal information collected, with very limited exceptions, such as a business title, address, phone number, and information that is already public, for example, in a listing in a telephone directory.

Obligations

Two core principles of PIPEDA are knowledge and consent. A consumer must be given full knowledge of the intended use of the information and the opportunity to consent or refuse the disclosure. That consent, however, can be expressed or implied.

Expressed consent is needed for health and financial information; but implied consent will suffice for other information. For example, a business might send a letter to its current customers saying that it would like to provide their names and addresses to another marketing firm after a specified date unless the customer informs the business of an objection.

The disclosure notice must be in clear, simple language so that the consumer can understand the purpose for which the information will be used. A good practice for a website is to have a disclosure notice with a check box or "click through" to obtain the consent of the individual or to permit that person to refuse to have the information used for any named purposes or at all.

There is no "grandfathering," that is, a business cannot use personal information already in its possession without a new consent.

Individuals can withdraw their consents, and so a business will have to keep accurate records that can be updated to delete names of people whose consents are withdrawn.

An interesting example of a privacy issue occurred in the U.S. Disney owned ToysMart Inc., which was an online toy company that went into bankruptcy. As an online business it had few hard assets. One of its assets of major value to other online businesses, especially toy companies, was its customer list. ToysMart had collected that data with the express policy that it would be kept confidential. However, in bankruptcy it listed its customer list as an asset for sale. It later withdrew that offer under protest. The case did not go to a hearing but is described on the U.S. Federal Trade Commission website.

Social Networking Sites

Social networking sites have become immensely popular boasting millions of users worldwide. They often have lengthy online membership agreements that contain consents to the use of private information without restriction, perhaps even the resale of it for profit.

Canadian users should be aware that the U.S. does not at the time of the publication of this text have privacy law as does Canada and many European countries. The U.S. has federal and state privacy acts which apply only to government agencies. The regulation of the use of private information is in the control of the individual website operators and depends on both their policy and terms of service.

Users upload a significant amount of confidential personal information including birth dates, phone numbers, race, religion, sexual orientation, daily schedules, etc. While it may be made accessible only to authorized persons, hackers may be able to view it.

The concern is that this information can be used by:

- criminals for identity theft
- employers for background checks
- employers for finding cause for dismissal
- government agencies
- insurance company defendants in law suits for personal injury

The concerns about privacy have been turned into a warning slogan by privacy advocates: Does what happens on Facebook stay on Facebook?

Facebook, for example, warns users that it will collect information about them from other sources. Privacy advocates warn that if you put anything on a networking website you should consider that you are publishing it just as if you published it in a magazine.

To use Facebook again as an example, its licence states:

> "By posting User Content to any part of the Site, you automatically grant, and you represent and warrant that you have the right to grant, to the Company an irrevocable, perpetual, non-exclusive, transferable, fully paid, worldwide license (with the right to sublicense) to use, copy, publicly perform, publicly display, reformat, translate, excerpt (in whole or in part) and distribute such User Content for any purpose on or in connection with the Site or the promotion thereof, to prepare derivative works of, or incorporate into other works, such User Content, and to grant and authorize sublicenses of the foregoing."

Again to take an example from Facebook it warns that privacy is not guaranteed:

> "We cannot and do not guarantee that User Content you post on the Site will not be viewed by unauthorized persons. We are not responsible for circumvention of any privacy settings or security measures contained on the Site."

Use of Facebook information against the interest of the users continues to surface. A court ordered a Plaintiff claiming as a result of injuries in a car accident that he suffered loss of enjoyment of life. He was ordered to disclose his Facebook postings to the defendant. (*Leduc v. Roman*, 2009 CanLII 6838 [ON S.C.])

Opt-Out Consent

An opt-out consent is one in which customers must indicate to a business that they do not wish their information to be collected, used, or disclosed by other business. If the customer fails to check that box, the business then infers consent for the proposed use of the information.

The federal Privacy Commissioner has indicated that he has a very low opinion of opt-out consent, which he considers, at best, token observance of privacy protection.

In one finding the commissioner notified Canada Post that it violated the *Privacy Act* by selling new home addresses of Canadians using Canada Post mail-redirection services to business mailers. The commissioner found that Canada Post's opt-out feature did not make it clear that Canada Post was going to sell the information on the change of address card to brokers, mass mailers, or direct marketers. He also found that it would not be reasonable to expect that a person signing a notification of change of address form would be giving consent for the disclosure of personal information to these entities.[3]

Exemptions

The act uses a number of exemptions, most of which will not be of use to businesses. These exemptions include information gathered for academic research, journalism, and the like. However, information collected for debt collection is exempt.

Administrative Obligations

The act imposes a number of administrative obligations on an organization that collects personal information, so as to make that organization responsible for that information. These businesses must:

- designate a personal-information supervisor and adopt policies to give effect to the act
- maintain the accuracy of personal information
- retain the personal information only as long as required for the purpose identified at the time of collection
- put security safeguards in place to protect that information from loss, unauthorized use, hacking, etc.
- provide access and the right to amend incorrect information
- apply procedures to receive and respond to inquiries and complaints concerning compliance with the act

Enforcement

The commissioner responsible for PIPEDA will be the Privacy Commissioner under the *Privacy Act* (Canada). Complaints can be made to the commissioner, who has the power to review the organization's information-management practices and assess penalties for breach of the act, including making the businesses' personal-information practices public, and levying fines from $10,000 to $100,000, for which directors, officers, or employees may also be personally liable. The commissioner may also order the business to correct its practices and pay damages to the complainant, including damages for humiliation.

---

3. Privacy Commissioner Decision, January 14, 2002, *Lawyers Weekly*, June 14, 2002.

Employee Privacy

The definition of personal information includes data collected by employers regarding employees from all sources: employment applications, health claims, and performance reviews, to name a few.

Because the equipment belongs to the employers, they can probably monitor e-mail to see if employees are sending personal e-mails at work. Employers will want to have clearly worded policies about personal use of e-mail, or whether a personal use is permitted at all. Employers will need employee consent to review the content of e-mails: they will likely require that consent as a condition of employment.

The employer's interest is that e-mail contains "click stream data" which identifies its source. If the employee e-mail contains defamation, pornography, or an infringement of intellectual-property rights, the employer may be affected.

Breaches of Privacy

Personal data is of great value to marketing and advertising firms. Hackers often target businesses. An alarming occurrence of a data breach occurred in the U.S. with Heartland Payment Systems. This Company processes payments for major credit card companies. Hackers used keyboard loggers and then "sniffers". Sniffers are simple pieces of malwar that collect information as it passes across a network. As of this date there is no legislation requiring businesses to notify customers of breaches of data. There are proposals for legislation. There are voluntary disclosure guides issued by various privacy commissioners in Canada, both federal and provincial, available on their websites.

Court Documents   If you are employed in a law firm or the business that has to file documents with the government you should take care to review any documents filed for the disclosure of critical information such as social insurance numbers which may be contained on documents filed in the court proceeding particularly if income tax returns are filed. There is no need usually to have such information made publicly available. That information can be blacked out or a ceiling order can be obtained so that the public cannot have access to it. Identity thieves can use a social insurance number with other information easily available on social networking sites to create a complete set of false documents.

Buying and Selling Products

There are a variety of legal rules that govern liability for sale transactions in addition to those of general contract law. The rules are different, depending on whether one is dealing with **real property** (land, buildings, and fixtures; land and anything attached to it), **intellectual property** (personal property in the form of ideas and creative work, created by the intellect) or personal property (tangible items or goods that are not real property). This section will focus on liability when buying and selling this last type of property.

real property

land, buildings, and fixtures; land and anything attached to it

intellectual property

personal property in the form of ideas and creative work, created by the intellect

Buying and Selling Goods

Much of modern business centres on buying and selling goods, so that it is not surprising that there are special laws aimed at goods. Every time a retailer purchases from a supplier and resells the item to a customer, specific rules of contract govern the transaction. Different rules apply to buying and selling between businesses than to transactions that take place between businesses and consumers. This distinction is important for the small-business retailer who buys according to business laws, but sells under consumer protection laws that tend to make the retailer primarily liable. Whether the retailer has a realistic right to recover liability from the supplier depends on the terms of the arrangement. If the supplier is located in a foreign country that does not have consumer protection laws, or the supplier goes out of business, the retailer may be left solely responsible.

How Did the Laws Originate?

Laws relating to land developed during the Middle Ages, when business as we know it today was almost non-existent. With the onset of the industrial age, the sale of goods became the centre of economic activity and so laws governing the practices involved were developed. These laws were collected (codified) and set out in an English statute, the *Sale of Goods Act*. This act has been adopted by all Canadian provinces in essentially the same form, but with different section numbers.

After World War II, other changes took place in society that culminated in an explosion of new consumer protection laws, particularly in the 1960s and 1970s. These laws included provisions making businesses liable for the quality and safety of the goods that they market. In addition, they restricted the ability of businesses to use written contracts as a way of avoiding liability with consumers.

Therefore, in addition to terms agreed to in a contract of sale, a seller's legal liability for the quality, safety, and usefulness of personal property which is sold can be governed by one or more of the following set of legal rules:

- *Sale of Goods Act*
- consumer protection legislation
- products liability in tort

The *Sale of Goods Act*

All provinces and territories have legislation which holds the seller of goods responsible for minimum guarantees concerning the quality of the goods they sell. This legislation is often known as the *Sale of Goods Act*. It also sets out rules concerning when items sold actually belong to the purchaser and no longer the seller, and rules concerning what action buyer and seller can take if terms of the sale contract are not fulfilled by the other party.

In buying and selling, people often forget to specify some terms of the contract, and may even forget vital items. So, the courts developed special rules for the sale of goods that would apply if the parties forgot some essential terms. For example, in buying an item, if the parties forgot to specify the price, that omission would be fatal and there would be no enforceable contract. However, the *Sale of Goods Act* provides that if the price is not agreed upon, then the price will be a reasonable price.

The *Sale of Goods Act* provides, in effect, a type of standard form contract for the sale of goods where parties omit certain terms. The act is drafted so that the terms are implied only if the parties do not specify them. If the parties agree to specific terms, those, and not the *Sale of Goods Act* terms, are legally enforceable.

The first important thing to notice, however, is that this act applies only to "sales" of "goods."

What Are Goods?

The first step in considering whether the *Sale of Goods Act* applies to any given business transaction is to determine whether that transaction is actually a "sale of goods." If it is not, then the rules in the act will not apply.

A sale can be described as an exchange of goods for money. This is to be distinguished from:

lease

a contractual arrangement where the owner of property (the landlord) allows another person (the tenant) to have possession and use of the property for a certain period in return for the payment of rent

goods

are items such as televisions, clothes, and cars

- a **lease**, which is a contractual arrangement where the owner of property (the landlord) allows another person (the tenant) to have possession and use of the property for a certain period in return for the payment of rent. Note, however, that British Columbia has extended its legislation so that the implied conditions discussed below apply to leases as well as to contracts of sale.
- barter or trade, which is an exchange of goods or services for other goods or services.

Goods are items such as televisions, clothes, cars, and so on. These are to be distinguished from:

- services
- real property, such as a house
- work and materials

Historically, goods were treated differently under contract law from other subjects such as services or land. Different considerations relate to goods as distinct from services. For example, if someone sells you a car, you want to know that that person is the legal owner and therefore has the authority to sell the vehicle. Such a question does not arise in the sale of services.

More recently, however, it has been thought that there are many similarities between goods and services, and that they should be treated the same. Nowadays, legislation, particularly consumer protection acts, often specifically includes both goods and services—the goods and services tax (GST) is one example. However, separate contract rules did evolve for goods alone and this distinction must be remembered in reading the *Sale of Goods Act* principles that are discussed in this chapter.

ter Neuzen v. Korn, [1995] 3 S.C.R. 674

Mrs. ter Neuzen could not have a child and went to Dr. Korn for artificial insemination many times between 1981 and 1985. She was later diagnosed as HIV-positive, the probable cause being the artificial insemination. She sued the doctor both for negligence and for breach of the condition of merchantability under the *Sale of Goods Act*.

The Court's Decision

The court found that the doctor was primarily rendering a service, and not supplying a good, and therefore the *Sale of Goods Act* did not apply in this situation. The tort of negligence was a possible grounds of liability, but the doctor was found not liable, given that there was no test to detect HIV prior to January 1985.

Business Law Applied

❶ **Louise Yang was** a dog breeder who bought a shipment of champion stock sperm from Nick Shep, who was a well-known breeder in the area. Louise had her female dogs inseminated, but none of the dogs had pups. It was subsequently discovered that the sperm was infected with a virus that rendered it infertile.

   a) Is Louise's situation covered by the *Sale of Goods Act?*

❷ **Car-lease arrangements** are becoming a very popular means of acquiring new vehicles. This is an arrangement whereby you acquire possession and use of the vehicle for a period of time (usually two years), and then either return the car, or purchase it for a predetermined price.

   a) Does the *Sale of Goods Act cover this type of acquisition?*

The Requirement of Writing

Except in Ontario and British Columbia, where legislation differs, the *Sale of Goods Act* provides that a contract for the sale of goods (over $40-50, depending on the province) is not enforceable unless one of three conditions is met:

   ■ it is in writing, or
   ■ the buyer has received and accepted the goods, or a portion of them, or
   ■ the buyer gave something in partial payment for the goods when the contract was formed

The courts have been flexible on what will be sufficient to satisfy a statutory requirement of writing. (See Chapter 5 for more on the requirement of writing in contract law.)

Conditions and Warranties

The *Sale of Goods Act* implies certain terms into every contract of sale. In other words, the act automatically makes certain terms a part of every contract of sale.

The terms in a contract are not all of equal importance. The law recognizes this, and divides those terms into two categories:

   ■ conditions
   ■ warranties

Conditions are major, essential terms which, if breached, give the innocent party the right to terminate the contract and claim damages, while **warranties** are minor terms which, if breached, permit only a claim for damages but not the refusal to complete the contract. If the conditions in a contract are broken, the courts will usually set aside the agreement, as its purpose has become pointless. The buyer can reject the goods. If, for example, you order a dark-blue Chevrolet sedan and the dealer delivers a bright-pink Chevrolet convertible, the conditions of your agreement have been violated and you would be legally entitled to refuse the car. You would be permitted to choose to cancel (repudiate) the contract and obtain a refund of any money paid, such as a deposit.

If the warranties in a contract are broken, the courts will consider a claim for loss caused by the breach, but will not cancel the agreement. If the car delivered to you was a dark-blue Chevrolet sedan, but the turn signals were not working, you could not refuse the car and cancel the deal. You could, however, claim the cost of repairing the turn signals. You would have to perform the contract by paying for the car and seeking a reduction in price by claiming for the cost of repair.

The parties can agree when a contract term is a condition, so that if it is violated, the innocent party can cancel the agreement if it wishes. If the parties to a contract have not specified which terms are in fact conditions, the courts will decide the issue. A contractual term will be found to be a condition if the breach deprived the innocent party of substantially the whole benefit of the contract.

conditions

major, essential terms which, if breached, give the innocent party the right to terminate the contract and claim damages

warranties

minor terms which, if breached, permit only a claim for damages but not the refusal to complete the contract

The act specifies that some terms of a sales agreement are conditions, while others are warranties. For example, a condition of a sales agreement is that the seller has the right to sell the goods, either as its owner or on the owner's authority. Also, the act places a condition that the seller has a duty to deliver the goods, transferring possession of the correct quantity, of the right quality, at the proper place and time, provided that payment has been made or credit terms have been agreed.

Similarly, the seller guarantees—gives a warranty—that the goods are free from any charge, lien, or mortgage in favour of a third party. If they are not, this must be revealed at the time of the transaction. The time of payment agreed to by the purchaser is also a warranty, and not a condition. If the purchaser refuses to pay for goods already delivered, the only remedy is to sue for damages. The agreement cannot be cancelled, nor the goods seized.

Business Alert!

Certification   Often, goods are purchased with a "certification." This does not provide the same measure of protection as the implied terms under the *Sale of Goods Act*. Certification only guarantees compliance pursuant to a specific safety code or regulation—it is not an assurance of general quality. For example, a vehicle may have its brake system overhauled and certified according to certain transportation safety regulations. However, there may be serious problems with other parts of the car, such as the engine. The condition of the engine is usually not guaranteed by a certificate of safety. *Certified* does not mean fully warranted.

■ *Critical Concepts of* Conditions and Warranties

- The court will decide whether a term is a condition or a warranty.
- The *Sale of Goods Act* specifies certain terms to be conditions or warranties when the agreement involves selling goods.
- The parties to the agreement can specify terms to be conditions or warranties. Such an agreement supersedes the court-made principles and the *Sale of Goods Act*.
- If there is a breach of a condition, the agreement can be cancelled.
- If there is a breach of a warranty, the victim can claim damages only.

The Condition Concerning the Right to Sell the Goods   In regular business transactions, we generally assume that a person selling us goods has the right to do so. However, if this is not so, it can lead to harsh consequences for the innocent purchaser. The *Sale of Goods Act* tries to protect an innocent third-party purchaser by implying a term that the seller has the right to sell the goods into the sale contract.

Consider a situation where stolen property has made its way through several parties:

Ned's car → stolen by "X" → ends up at 123 Car Sales Ltd. → bought by Albert → sold to Pauline

After the car was stolen, no one had the right to sell it. The true owner, from whom the car was stolen, can have it repossessed from Pauline, because in law you cannot give what you haven't got. So the thief gave possession of the car (which he had), but not ownership (which he did not). He also gave only an improperly issued certificate of ownership.

Each "innocent" person in the chain has a remedy against the person from whom they bought the car. This is because the *Sale of Goods Act* implies (adds in) a condition that the seller has the right to sell the goods, even if nothing was specifically said about having this right when the deal was made. Unfortunately, the last "innocent" person in the chain, in this case 123 Car Sales, will likely be unable to seek recourse (unless they can find "X" and he has money to pay).

The Condition Concerning the Right to Sell Goods

Sale of Goods Act, R.S.A. 1980, h. S–2, s. 15

In a contract of sale, unless the circumstances of the contract are such as to show a different intention, there is
(a) an implied condition on the part of the seller
   (i) that in the case of a sale he has a right to sell the goods, and
   (ii) that in the case of an agreement to sell he will have a right to sell the goods at the time when the property is to pass

---

Car Theft   The Insurance Bureau of Canada runs an insurance-crime-prevention bureau that gives helpful information on its website regarding the prevention of car theft. For example, it reports that most cars are stolen with the keys in the vehicle, so it is important for employers to give specific instructions to employees not to leave keys in vehicles. Contrary to popular belief, the bureau reports that criminals go for the easiest opportunity. Thus, any theft-prevention device is better than none in reducing the risk of theft. The most frequently stolen cars are not the expensive cars but the easiest ones to steal.

Business Alert!

The insurance bureau says that auto theft is an attractive source of income because it is relatively easy to do and the criminal penalties are low. As technology expands, so do the techniques of professional car thieves. However, one preventive innovation is a computer chip that freezes the car if it is started without a key. See www.ibc.ca.

General Use

Merchantability   Merchantability means that the product is both saleable and useable for its normal purpose. Is the product of such a quality that a customer would pay the asking price without seeking a deduction? In other words, the product cannot have any defects, and must be able to be used as it should be. A lawn mower must cut grass; a refrigerator must be able to preserve food.

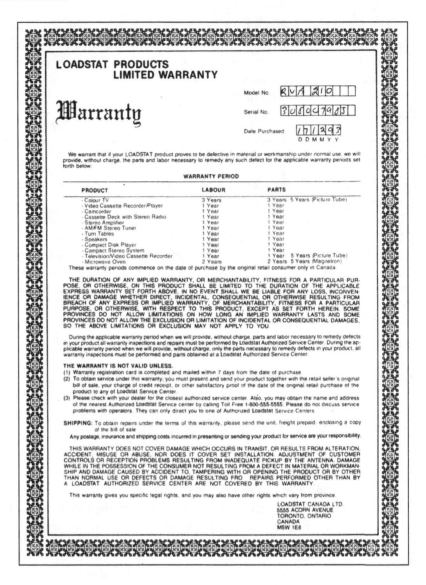

Although called a condition under the act, this term is usually called a warranty or a guarantee in everyday speech. It has been said that a warranty is an indication of a manufacturer's faith in its product. Note that the Goldstar Products Limited Warranty refers only to warranties and not to conditions. Such clauses are construed *contra proferentem*. The quality, or merchantability, warranty applies only to goods sold by description—as most consumer purchases are. Any retail purchase of items in a package or container is a sale by description. There is really no opportunity to inspect the product and determine its quality. For example, a bottle will be labelled "shampoo" and be identified with a brand name. The word *shampoo* is a description of the product. So the bottle must contain usable shampoo. If a shirt label says "100% cotton," the shirt must be cotton and not polyester—the use of the word *cotton* is a description of the goods.

Historically, the laws surrounding the sale of goods dealt only with quality, and remedies for repair or replacement. Regulations governing the safety of goods developed under the law of torts. Recent judgments, however, have applied the *Sale of Goods Act* in such a way that it includes safety, and have awarded damages for personal injury.

The significance of this change in the law is that all businesses in the supply chain will be liable for defects that injure, without regard to whether the businesses was at fault—that is, negligent. The concepts of negligence and product liability are reviewed in depth in Chapter 4.

Condition of Merchantability

Although the section numbers differ among most provincial *Sale of Goods Acts*, they are all very similar. The warranty of merchantability also applies to the sale of used goods, but the requirement of merchantability is that of a used product, not a new one.

The Sale of Goods Act, R.S.O. 1990, c. S1, s15 (2)

2. Where goods are bought by description from a seller who deals in goods of that description (whether the seller is the manufacturer or not), there is an implied condition that the goods will be of merchantable quality, but if the buyer has examined the goods, there is no implied condition as regards defects that such examination ought to have revealed.

Condition   Implied terms regarding merchantability or quality are called **conditions** in sale of goods acts.

The word *condition* is technically used to describe the term of a contract that allows the innocent parties to cancel an agreement, return the goods, and get their money back (see p. 273). Its use developed historically and, although confusing today, it is so entrenched in the law that there is little hope of it being changed to reflect modern usage.

Legalese

Business Law   Applied

❸ **FabFoods Ltd. ran** a small grocery chain. It purchased a large order of jam from a distributor's catalogue by filling in an order form and sending a payment in advance to take advantage of an offered discount. When the jam arrived, the labels were completely discoloured. FabFoods contacted the distributor, requesting a refund of its money in return for sending the goods back.

The distributor refused, saying that the discoloration was not that firm's fault, but the fault of the manufacturer. The distributor pointed out that there was nothing in the purchase order about any guarantee of the quality or the appearance of the labels, and that FabFoods must take up the problem with the manufacturer. In addition, FabFoods purchased the product at a considerable discount, and should not therefore expect first-rate merchandise.

a) Since there was no agreed term regarding quality in the contract between FabFoods and the distributor, is there any law that would put such a term into the purchase order?
b) Does the fact that the jam was sold at a discount affect any right to a warranty of merchantability?
c) Does FabFoods have a contract with the manufacturer?

❹ **Don Mackenzie bought** a bottle of tropical fruit punch from Pal Paik's variety store by taking the bottle to the cash register and paying $1. After drinking the bottle, Mackenzie became very sick and was hospitalized for several weeks. When he recovered, Mackenzie sued Paik for compensation. Paik claimed that she only put the bottle on a shelf, and the state of its contents was not her fault. She suggested Mackenzie should sue the supplier.

a) Did Mackenzie have any possible remedy against the variety-store owner? If so, what is the basis for this claim in law?
b) Was the fact that Pal Paik's Variety did not bottle the drink a valid defence?
c) Would Paik have any remedy against the supplier? What if the supplier is from Taiwan and refuses to compensate Paik's Variety? What practical problems does Paik face?

Special Use   The *Sale of Goods Act* also provides an implied condition that goods will be suitable or fit for a particular purpose if that purpose is made known to the seller and it is in the seller's line of business to supply such goods. Imagine, for example, that a paint contractor has a project to paint a refinished church that has used a new drywall, made in part with recycled newspaper. The contractor advises his supplier of the new drywall, and asks for a paint that will cover it. The supplier recommends a certain paint, but when the contractor applies it, it streaks. The *Sale of Goods Act* puts an implied term of fitness for this special use in the contract for the sale of the paint. An **implied term of fitness** is a term implied into the contract that the goods are of a type that is suitable for any special purpose for which they are bought. The supplier, who is in the business of selling paint, knows that the contractor is relying on the supplier's skill and judgment in supplying goods that are fit for the purpose. This implied condition is called fitness for use or purpose.

implied term of fitness

a term implied into the contract that the goods are of a type that is suitable for any special purpose for which they are bought

As well, the *Sale of Goods Act* stipulates that the purchase cannot be made by trademark, which means brand name. However, in line with modern commercial practice, that requirement has been interpreted so as not to have as much effect. It will not be a defence for a retailer to claim that an article is sold by a brand name in order to escape liability in a fitness for use situation.

Condition of Fitness for Special Use

The Sale of Goods Act, R.S.O. 1990, c. S1, s15

b) Where the buyer, expressly or by implication, makes known to the seller the particular purpose for which the goods are required so as to show that the buyer relies on the seller's skill or judgment, and the goods are of a description that it is in the course of the seller's business to supply (whether he is the manufacturer or not) there is an implied condition that the goods will be reasonably fit for such purpose, but in the case of a contract of a specified article under its patent or other trade name, there is no implied condition as to its fitness for any particular purpose.

MacDonald v. Kennedy, [1983] 43 Nfld. & P.E.I. R. 235

William Kennedy was a farmer, and as a sideline repaired and sold used farm equipment. He had sold only five tractors in the year preceding the following incident.

Kennedy put an ad in a newspaper for the sale of a Massey Ferguson tractor "in perfect condition." The plaintiff, MacDonald, and a friend, Stewart, who was also a farmer, went to Kennedy's farm to look at the tractor. MacDonald wanted the tractor to operate a snow blower. Kennedy told MacDonald that the tractor was 20 years old and had been recently painted, but he thought it would be up to the task of operating a snow blower. Stewart drove the tractor to test the gears, but did not test the lifting qualities of the hydraulics that were necessary to the running of a snow blower.

MacDonald and Kennedy agreed on a price of $3,500 for the tractor. Two months after it was sold, the tractor developed clutch and hydraulic problems. Kennedy refused to do anything about it. MacDonald brought an action for a breach of an implied term of fitness for use as a snow blower, under the Prince Edward Island *Sale of Goods Act*.

The Court's Decision

MacDonald did not claim that he had an express warranty that the tractor would be useable as a snowblower, but relied on the *Sale of Goods Act* to imply such a condition of fitness or suitability. Mac-

Donald then had to prove all of the elements necessary to make that section applicable. Kennedy was not in the business of selling tractors. It was clear that this was simply a sideline, and that he was a farmer. This was a case of one farmer selling a tractor to another.

MacDonald did not rely on Kennedy's skill and judgment with respect to the tractor's suitability for use as a snowblower. There was an opportunity to test the tractor, and this was done, though no test was made of the hydraulics. The facts did not therefore fit the second test of reliance on the vendor's skill and judgment.

The implied warranty of fitness for a particular purpose did not apply. The seller was not in the business of selling tractors, and the purchaser did not rely on the seller's skill and judgment in making a decision as to whether the tractor would be suitable for use as a snowblower. MacDonald's action was therefore dismissed.

■ *Business Law* Applied

⑤ Lars Larsson, a farmer, designed an apparatus for lifting bales of hay from his truck to the second storey of his barn. He purchased a large quantity of strong metal clothesline wire from the local hardware store for use in the lift. After a few weeks of use, the line snapped. Larsson returned to the hardware store and demanded a refund for the cost of the clothesline wire. The hardware store refused.

   a) Was there an implied term of fitness for use in the agreement for the use of these goods?

⑥ Elsa Petherham needed a packaging machine for the assembly line of her plant. From a manufacturer, she purchased a repossessed machine that was designed to use 1.3-mm-thick plastic. Petherham used that thickness as well as thinner plastic in her plant, and the salesman said that there would be no problem—the machine could use anything thinner, but not thicker.

On installation, Petherham found that the machine would not use the thinner plastic. Half of the packaging to be done in her operation required the thinner size. She complained to the manufacturer, who replied that they had offered no guarantees, merely an honest opinion. There was nothing in the contract guaranteeing that the machine would work with thinner plastic. The manufacturer pointed out that it was a repossessed, used machine, and suggested that if Petherham had wanted a guarantee, the manufacturer would have sold a new machine at three times the price.

   a) Given that the written purchase order contained no terms regarding fitness for use, did the contract for sale contain such a term?

The Condition Concerning Correspondence to Description   There is also an implied term that goods sold by description will correspond to that description. For example, if you agree to purchase "one dozen aluminum snow shovels" from a catalogue, you will not receive one dozen plastic snow shovels.

A sale by description has generally been held to be any sale where you set out in descriptive terms the goods to be subject of the contract. This is in contrast to a sale by sample, or situation where one points out goods on display and orders some of whatever is presented.

It should be noted that sales of motor vehicles, including used motor vehicles, are viewed as sales by description. The justification for this is that vehicle sales are either new or used. This is no doubt stretching the interpretation of the word *description*. However, it is done by the courts to give consumers the benefit of the *Sale of Goods Act* implied terms when purchasing cars.

It is usually easy to determine whether the goods delivered conform to the description in the contract of sale. However, this issue can be more difficult if the non–compliance with the description relates to quality.

Condition of Correspondence to Description

Sale of Goods Act, R.S.O., 1990, c. S.1, s14

Where there is a contract for the sale of goods by description, there is an implied condition that the goods shall correspond with the description and if the sale by samples as well as by description, it is not sufficient that the bulk of the goods corresponds with the sample if the goods do not also correspond with the description.

The Condition Concerning Correspondence to Sample   When a seller provides samples of goods for inspection prior to purchase, the act provides that:

- the goods provided will correspond to the sample in quality, and
- the buyer will be able to compare the goods provided with the sample, and
- the goods provided will be free of any unapparent defect making them unsaleable without a discount (unmerchantable)

■ *Business Law* Applied

❼ **Raj Gamba ran** a retail greenhouse. In the fall, he visited Nori Nedlov's plant and tree farm, to place an order for delivery the following season. He spent a lot of time examining Nori's stock. The stock looked terrific and healthy, so Raj placed a large order for delivery to his greenhouse in the spring. When the delivery date finally arrived, Raj happened to be tied up with a big client. He took a quick glance at the items, and thought they looked fine. After a few weeks in the greenhouse however, he noticed some growth problems, and some disease damage, which could only have occurred before being shipped.

a) Is Raj's order a sale by sample or a sale by description?
b) If it is a sale by description, which of the implied terms have arguably been breached?
c) If it is a sale by sample, which of the implied terms have arguably been breached?

Exemption Clauses   The *Sale of Goods Act* implies certain terms in contracts for the sale of goods if the parties forget to include them. However, the act also permits parties to agree that those implied terms are excluded. So, in a sale, a warranty of quality that would be implied by the *Sale of Goods Act* could be excluded by an exemption clause. For example, if a company buys a machine for its plant without any mention of warranties, the *Sale of Goods Act* implies certain warranties in the purchase contract. However, if the contract contained a term stating that all warranties implied by law were excluded, then the *Sale of Goods Act* warranties would not apply.

Exemption Clauses

The Sale of Goods Act, R.S.O. 1990, c. S.1, s53

Where any right, duty or liability under a contract of sale by implication of law, it may be negated or varied by express agreement or by the course of dealing between the parties, or by usage, if the usage is such as to bind both parties to the contract.

Hunter Engineering v. Syncrude, [1989] 1 S.C.R. 426

In early 1975, Syncrude ordered some mining gearboxes from Hunter Engineering. These were to be used to drive conveyor belts at Syncrude's tar-sands project in northern Alberta, and had been specially designed and built for Syncrude, based on specifications it had provided. The contract with Hunter contained a clause limiting its liability for the equipment to 24 months from the date of delivery or 12 months from the date of start-up (whichever came first), but said nothing further concerning liability.

Subsequently, Syncrude entered into a contract for similar equipment with Allis Chalmers Canada Ltd. However, the contract with Allis Chalmers contained a clause excluding any warranties (including the implied *Sale of Goods Act* warranties) other than those found in the agreement.

The gearboxes from both Hunter and Allis Chalmers developed cracks and were unable to do the job required of them. The issue for the court's consideration was whether the *Sale of Goods Act* condition of fitness for a particular purpose applied to either or both of these contracts.

The Court's Decision

The *Sale of Goods Act* conditions applied to the contract with Hunter, but did not apply to the contract with Allis Chalmers. The former had not expressly excluded the *Sale of Goods Act* provisions, while the latter had.

Exemption Clauses   The *Hunter v. Syncrude* case proves that exemption clauses can be effective in business transactions. Failure to clearly state that statutory conditions (that is, contractual terms implied into a contract by virtue of legislation) are not applicable to a given transaction can lead to expensive consequences in the event of product defects.

Business Alert!

■ *Critical Concepts of* Implied Conditions

The *Sale of Goods Act* provides that certain terms are included in every contract of sale, unless the parties agree otherwise:

- guarantees (called conditions) that the seller has the right to sell the goods
- guarantees (called conditions) that the goods will be fit for general use (merchantability) and for a special purpose made known at the time of sale (fitness for use)
- guarantees (called conditions) that if goods are purchased by description, the goods delivered will correspond to that description
- guarantees (called conditions) that if goods are purchased by sample, their quality will correspond to that of the sample and will not have any latent defect making them of unsaleable general quality

Business Law Applied

8 **Anand Singh bought** a used car "as is" and did not inspect it. The next week the car developed serious problems, and Singh wanted to return it and get his money back.

   a) Does the warranty of quality or merchantability under the *Sale of Goods Act* apply to the contract for the sale of the car?

   b) If not, what steps could Singh have taken to protect his interests?

9 **Adolph Gostonyi bought** a used computer from a classmate. Gostonyi knew very little about computers, and visited a branch of a major retailer—High-Comp Inc.—to purchase disks for his new system. Gostonyi had heard about a new disk, with the brand name Digico, that was reputedly of better quality than other disks on the market.

Gostonyi explained to a salesperson that he was a computer novice, had just bought a used machine that had originally been supplied by High-Comp, and wondered whether the Digico disks would be suitable for his computer. The salesperson replied that the disks were the best on the market and would indeed work. In addition, the disks were currently on sale at $5 less than their usual price. Gostonyi bought a box of 10 disks.

When he got home and tried them on his computer, they would not work. A friend advised him that these were high-density disks, and that Gostonyi's computer could read only double-density disks. Gostonyi returned to the store and complained. The store manager stated that Gostonyi had specifically asked for Digico disks and the box was clearly marked in large letters "high-density." So, said the manager, the young man knew what he was buying, and the store was not responsible.

   a) Is there any provision in the *Sale of Goods Act* that would assist Gostonyi?

   b) What are the facts necessary to bring a situation within this section of the *Sale of Goods Act*?

10 **Julie Vanderhoof bought** a used car from Ed McMotors Ltd. A sign on the car described it as a six-cylinder Mustang. There was a clause in the sale contract stating that "all conditions, warranties, and liabilities implied by statute, common-law or otherwise, are hereby excluded."

A few weeks after the car was delivered, Vanderhoof discovered that it had only four cylinders.

   a) Does the exclusion clause that excludes all statutory warranties prevent Vanderhoof from obtaining her remedy in court?

   b) Does the fact that the car is a used vehicle mean that the *Sale of Goods Act* does not apply?

Rules Concerning the Transfer of Ownership

The *Sale of Goods Act* also sets out rules concerning when purchasers of goods become the actual owners of those goods. They are often referred to as rules concerning the transfer of **title**—a legal concept roughly equivalent to ownership.

title
a legal concept roughly equivalent to ownership

   In law, the owner of an item usually has the risk of loss. If an item is damaged or destroyed, it is the owner who has to pay for the repair or suffer the complete loss. For example, if you buy a television set, take it home yourself, and drop it when unloading your car, you must pay for the repair.

There are a number of rules under the *Sale of Goods Act* that determine when a person becomes an owner. As was the case with the conditions discussed above, these rules are implied into every contract of sale, unless the parties agree otherwise. As many of these were developed from the practice of merchants of a much earlier age and are contrary to the expectations of today's business person, businesses normally prefer to use purchase orders. An example Purchase Order is given in the Appendix to this chapter. The terms of the standard purchase orders usually displace the antiquated rules under the act. Common variations include:

- **F.O.B.**—free on board, a designation for goods when the seller must arrange and pay for transportation to the shipper, and the goods remain at the seller's risk until delivery
- **C.I.F.**—cost, insurance, and freight, a designation for goods, making the seller responsible for arranging the insurance (in the buyer's name) and the shipping charges, with the goods remaining at the seller's risk until delivery to the purchaser
- Ex Works—from the supplier's place of business: the purchaser is responsible for the goods from the time they leave the supplier's property

Because of the great importance of understanding whose responsibility it is to pay for insurance during transportation, there are **Incoterms:** a set of standard contractual terms commonly used in purchase orders, and adopted by the International Chamber of Commerce. Purchase orders may simply refer to a term such as "ex works according to I.N.C.O. 2000." Definitions for commonly used terms can be seen on the International Chamber of Commerce website at www.iccwbo.org/incoterms/preambles.asp.

The separation of ownership and possession is the significant concept in this area. For example, a person may own an item before possessing it. Assume a business has purchased a used machine for its factory from another manufacturer. The business pays for it and arranges to pick it up the next day. That night a fire destroys the building where the machine is kept, ruining it. Who bears the loss?

In this case, ownership passed on to the purchaser. Even though the purchaser did not have possession, it had ownership and hence the risk of loss. The purchaser had to take steps to protect the machine such as making sure that it was covered on its insurance policy.

Management of transportation risks is one of the important business concerns in relation to the passing of ownership. Goods shipped either locally or overseas are at risk. It is therefore important to know who owns the goods at what time so that proper arrangements for insurance can be made.

The Rules The precise wordings of the *Sale of Goods Act* rules are given in a box on page 285. Here are simplified statements of the rules with examples of each:

Rule 1
Ownership transfers to the purchaser when the contract is made even though the goods are not paid for.

Example:

Alpha Company orders a computer, which is in inventory, from Computers Inc., by faxing a purchase order (this is an offer). Computers Inc. faxes a confirmation of the order (this is an acceptance). The contract is made on the communication of the acceptance to Alpha Company.

F.O.B.

free on board, a designation for goods when the seller must arrange and pay for transportation to the shipper, and the goods remain at the seller's risk until delivery

C.I.F.

cost, insurance, and freight, a designation for goods, making the seller responsible for arranging the insurance (in the buyer's name) and the shipping charges, with the goods remaining at the seller's risk until delivery to the purchaser

Incoterms

a set of standard contractual terms commonly used in purchase orders, and adopted by the International Chamber of Commerce

Alpha Company becomes the owner of the computer even though it has neither paid for nor taken delivery of it. If the computer is damaged, Alpha Company must still pay full price. The item is at the risk of the owner.

Rule 2

If the item is not completed, ownership does not pass to the purchaser until the item is completed and the purchaser is notified of the completion.

Example:

Alpha Company wants to buy a computer but it must be configured to meet certain requirements. Computers Inc. makes the necessary changes and notifies Alpha that the computer is now ready. At this point Alpha Company becomes the owner.

Rule 3

The goods are completed and ready for delivery but something must be done to determine the price. Ownership passes to the purchaser when the price has been determined and the purchaser has been notified of it.

Example:

Alpha Company needs cable for all of its computers. A representative goes to a liquidator's warehouse and sees a pile of cable that seems of the right kind. A sign says $1 per metre. Alpha Company agrees to buy the whole lot. The liquidator says it will have the pile measured that evening and call Alpha Company with the price.

Ownership passes when Alpha Company is notified of the price.

Rule 4

When goods are sent "on approval," ownership passes when the buyer signifies acceptance, or upon the expiry of an agreed time period (if none has been agreed to, then upon the expiry of a "reasonable" time period).

Example:

Alpha Company ordered some computers "on approval" for 60 days, to see if they could keep up with the demands of the business. Ownership passes when Alpha says it will accept the computers, or at the end of 60 days.

Rule 5

When there is a sale of unascertained or future goods by description, ownership passes when those goods are in a deliverable state, and are unconditionally set apart for the contract.

Example:

Alpha Company ordered some computers, but Computers Inc. has to get them from a warehouse across town. The computers become Alpha's when they are irrevocably set aside for their purchase order.

It can be difficult to ascertain when items are irrevocably set aside for a specific order or customer. In one case, the court held that items being placed on a pallet and marked with the purchaser's name meant that the goods were irrevocably set aside. Courts in other cases have suggested that more is required, because at this point you could still remove the goods from the pallet and send them to somebody else.

Rules Concerning the Transfer of Ownership

Sale of Goods Act, R.S.O. 1990, c, S.1, S19

Rules for ascertaining intention

(1) Unless a different intention appears the rules set out in this section are the rules for ascertaining the intention of the parties as to the time at which the property in the goods is to pass to the buyer.

(2) When there is an unconditional contract for the sale of specific goods in a deliverable state, the property in the goods passes to the buyer when the contract is made and it is immaterial whether the time of payment or the time of delivery or both be postponed.

(3) When there is a contract for the sale of specific goods and the seller is bound to do something to the goods for the purpose of putting them into a deliverable state, the property does not pass until the thing is done and the buyer has notice thereof.

(4) When there is a contract for the sale of specific goods in a deliverable state but the seller is bound to weigh, measure, test or do some other act or thing with reference to the goods for the purpose of ascertaining the price, the property does not pass until the act or thing is done and the buyer has notice thereof.

(5) When goods are delivered to the buyer on approval or "on sale or return" or other similar terms, the property in them passes to the buyer

    (a) when he signifies his approval or acceptance to the seller or does any other act adopting the transactions, or

    (b) if he does not signify his approval or acceptance to the seller but retains the goods without giving notice of rejection then if a time has been fixed for the return of the goods, on the expiration of that time, and, if no time has been fixed, on the expiration of a reasonable time, and what is a reasonable time is a question of fact.

(6) When there is a contract for the sale of unascertained or future goods by descriptions and goods of that description and in a deliverable state are unconditionally appropriated to the contract either

    (a) by the seller with the assent of the buyer, or

    (b) by the buyer with the assent of the seller, the property in the goods thereupon passes to the buyer.

■ *Critical Concepts of* Risk and Ownership

- The usual legal rule is that "risk follows title," or, whoever owns the goods assumes the risk of loss or damage.
- The *Sale of Goods Act* sets out rules governing when ownership changes hands.
- The *Sale of Goods Act* rules concerning when ownership changes can be altered by agreement between the parties.

Re: TK-IDM Distribution Inc., [1990] B.C.J. no. 2269

Axel and his partners smuggled computer chips into Canada. TK-IDM ordered 400 of these, but before it could take delivery, Canada Customs seized 399 of the chips. The one chip that was not seized was sent to another customer. The court had to determine whether ownership of the chips had passed to TK-IDM at the point when they were seized by customs officials.

The Court's Decision

Title (ownership) had not passed to TK-IDM, because the chips— **unascertained goods**, which are goods that have not been set aside (identified and separated from a group) and agreed upon as the subject of a sale—were not "unconditionally appropriated" to the contract with TK-IDM. In other words, they were not irrevocably earmarked as being owned by TK-IDM. This was shown by the fact that at least one of the chips had been sent to someone else. As well, the court found some evidence to suggest that the parties had agreed that the chips would remain at the seller's risk until delivery to the purchaser, since the purchaser was to have the right of inspection and acceptance or rejection at the time of delivery.

■ *Business Law* Applied

unascertained goods
goods that have not been set aside (identified and separated from a group) and agreed upon as the subject of a sale

⑪ **Many coffee vendors** now utilize a self-serve system, where you fill your own cup from any one of several pots offering a variety of coffee selections. If you knock your cup on the floor after filling it, but before paying for it, whose coffee is it?

⑫ **Gustav Harcourt bought** a vehicle from People's Vehicles Ltd. He wanted the tires upgraded to a special high-tread all-season radial. The cost of the upgraded tires was worked into the purchase price and financed over three years. People's was going to call Gustav when the tires were changed and the car was ready to pick up. On Thursday, at 6:00 p.m., the service manager from People's left a message on Gustav's voice mail saying that the car was ready to pick up. At 3:00 a.m. on Friday, the car was severely damaged in a hailstorm. Gustav got the message to pick up the car at 8:00 a.m. Friday.

a) Who will have to cover the cost of repairs to the car?

Remedies

If a seller or purchaser breaks one or more of the terms contained in the contract of sale, the usual remedies for breach of contract are available—that is, suing for damages or attempting to back out of a deal without legal liability (rescission). Remember that you can always sue for damages, but whether you can avoid the contract without legal liability will depend on the seriousness of the term breached.

In addition, the *Sale of Goods Act* adds some additional remedies, chiefly for the benefit of an unpaid seller. What makes many of these particularly useful is that they can be implemented on short notice, without recourse to the formal court process.

- suing the purchaser for the purchase price of the goods (which can be different from suing for damages)
- retaining any deposit made
- holding the goods until payment is made (in the absence of credit arrangements being in place, or if the buyer is insolvent)
- **stoppage in transit**—reclaiming possession from the carrier of the goods while in transit, in order to stop delivery to the buyer, if the seller discovers that the buyer is insolvent
- exercising the right of resale, if either of these last two measures is utilized

stoppage in transit
reclaiming possession from the carrier of the goods while in transit, in order to stop delivery to the buyer, if the seller discovers that the buyer is insolvent

insolvency
the inability of a business to pay debts as they come due

Insolvency is the inability of a business to pay debts as they come due. It does not necessarily mean a formal bankruptcy. It can be difficult to determine whether a purchaser is in this position. A seller should think carefully before using the remedies based on insolvency, because if he is wrong, he would be liable for any loss resulting to the purchaser.

Of course, the buyer also has remedies for a breach of contract under the *Sale of Goods Act*. The buyer may sue for damages for non-delivery, sue for damages for breach of warranty or condition, reject the goods for breach of condition, or sue for specific performance. Note that this last option is one that would be used fairly infrequently. The courts generally do not make people specifically live up to the terms of a contract, since money damages are generally adequate compensation. However, if the goods to be delivered have some unique quality, specific performance may be an option.

■ *Critical Concepts of* Remedies

- The usual contractual remedies are available for breaches of contracts covered by the *Sale of Goods Act*. An aggrieved party can sue for damages or reject the deal if the breach is a breach of condition.
- In addition, the *Sale of Goods Act* offers the seller additional ways to protect his interest, including keeping deposits, keeping the goods until payment is made, and reclaiming the goods while in transit.

■ *Business Law* Applied

⑬ **Abdi Omar was** the distributor of computer hardware that was sold at retail much more cheaply than the competition's hardware. Omar delivered a large order to Discount Computer Warehouse, granting the firm 60 days' credit.

Discount did not settle its account within the 60-day period. Omar drove by the store and noticed a sign in the window advertising a clearance sale, with some of the items he had supplied being sold at below cost. Omar wondered whether the owner was clearing out his stock, intending to close the business and keep the money personally. He drove straight to his lawyer's office to find out what his options were. The questions he asked his lawyer included the following. How would you have answered them? What other questions might he have asked?

    a) Does the *Sale of Goods Act* apply to my agreement to supply the hardware to Discount Computer Warehouse?
    b) Is Discount's failure to pay its account a breach of a warranty or a condition?
    c) What can I do? Can I take back the goods?
    d) How could I have safeguarded my interests better right from the beginning?

⑭ **Nicole LaRue owned** a wholesale fruit-merchandising company called Great Grapes and Such. She had dealt with Arnie's Caverns, a small winemaker, for many years. She always billed Arnie on a net 30-day basis. Last week, Arnie placed an order for some chardonnay grapes. Nicole boxed up several cases of her best grapes, worth $20,000, and had Northwest Transport come to pick them up. Just after Northwest left Nicole's premises, she received a phone call from a competitor, who mentioned that Arnie had not paid for any merchandise he had shipped in the last three months. The competitor also said he had heard a rumour that Arnie was "going under." Nicole was concerned, and wanted her grapes back until she could secure payment in advance from Arnie.

    a) Assuming it is practicable, could Nicole reclaim possession of the grapes while on the truck?
    b) What would be the consequences if Nicole reclaimed possession of the grapes, but was wrong about Arnie's financial situation?

Retail Sales

Consumer Protection Legislation

As the face of society has changed, so too has the nature of consumer sales. The business situation of the 1990s is very different from what it was when the *Sale of Goods Act* was first enacted in 1893.

The Manufacturer's Role When the *Sale of Goods Act* rules were developed, the customer often dealt directly with the person who made the item. Today's seller is often a retailer who, thanks to prepackaged goods, is little more than a conduit for the manufacturer. Yet, the *Sale of Goods Act* rules place responsibility on the seller, not on the manufacturer. This is also true in common law rules of contract, under which only parties to the deal are liable on the agreement.

Standard Form Contracts The use of printed form contracts and mass-marketing techniques means that there is little or no negotiating over the terms of a contract. If terms are printed on the back of a sales invoice, the purchaser might be unfamiliar with the language, and unable to assess the risks involved in agreeing to them. The purchaser might not even be aware of unusual terms that are completely at odds with how the deal was perceived.

Prepackaged Goods: Complex Technology   Both packaging and the complexity of certain high-tech goods mean that purchasers can no longer inspect many items for themselves, but must accept the quality of the goods as described.

Advertising   The power of advertising to influence purchasers is undisputed. That advertising can be misleading and deceptive has been equally demonstrated.

International Trade   Manufacturers are often not located in the same province or country as the consumer. Consumer protection laws may be much more lenient in the manufacturer's place of business. It is also very costly to try to bring a lawsuit in a foreign country.

The Legislation

In the 1960s and 1970s, federal and provincial governments enacted a number of consumer protection laws. These laws are update frequently so they should be checked regularly. Fortunately, most governments have websites with summaries of the current legislation and information material along with help lines. However, there are differences among the various provincial acts.

What is a Consumer Transaction?

Consumer protection acts govern only transactions for personal use but not for business use. The transactions protected include purchase of goods, services and leases.

Example: Asha buys a clock for her home. That is for personal use and consumer protection acts govern the transaction. She buys the identical model clock for her business; that is not a transaction covered by consumer protection acts.

In this section we look mainly at laws that add warranties regarding quality and performance to consumer transactions and prevent exclusion of these warranties by the use of exemption clauses. Because the number of consumer protection laws is so vast, and is increasing, a summary of major issues and rules is contained at the end of this section. Consumer protection laws are also set out in various chapters as they relate to the relevant subject matter.

Manufacturer's Warranties   Virtually every new consumer item sold in Canada today comes with some sort of product warranty. The Goldstar Warranty (p. 276) is typical of these, containing provisions that:

- give very specific warranties about product quality and the length of that warranty
- limit the repair or replacement obligations
- give specific remedy or complaint procedures
- limit the extent of the manufacturer's liability in the event of defect or loss

Consumer Act Preservation of Warranties   Most consumers believe that the express warranty card or brochure that is included with their new purchase outlines the supplier's entire obligation. Few are aware that most consumer products sold in Canada today also come with certain non-excludable statutorily implied warranties of fitness and merchantability. The warranties of fitness and merchantability are a result of the *Sale of Goods Act* discussed previously in this section. The fact that they are non-excludable in consumer transactions comes from consumer protection legislation.

These acts typically provide that the implied conditions and warranties of the *Sale of Goods Act* cannot be waived in the case of a sale to a consumer. In other words, in the case of a sale to a consumer, the parties are prohibited from agreeing that the implied conditions and warranties will not apply. The following is a typical section from such an act.

Consumer Protection Act, 2002, S. O. 2002, c. 30, Sch. A

Quality of services

9. (1) The supplier is deemed to warrant that the services supplied under a consumer agreement are of a reasonably acceptable quality. 2002, c. 30, Sched. A, s. 9 (1).

Quality of goods

(2) The implied conditions and warranties applying to the sale of goods by virtue of the *Sale of Goods Act* are deemed to apply with necessary modifications to goods that are leased or traded or otherwise supplied under a consumer agreement. 2002, c. 30, Sched. A, s. 9 (2).

Same

(3) Any term or acknowledgement, whether part of the consumer agreement or not, that purports to negate or vary any implied condition or warranty under the *Sale of Goods Act* or any deemed condition or warranty under this Act is void. 2002, c. 30, Sched. A, s. 9 (3).

■ *Critical Concepts of* Ineffective Exclusion of Warranties

Businesses attempt to exclude or limit warranties of quality in retail consumer contracts. Consumer protection laws make these exclusions ineffective and the legal process to reach this result entails three:

■ warranties implied by the *Sale of Goods Act*
■ these warranties excluded by retail sales contract
■ the exclusionary terms made ineffective by consumer protection laws

Hazardous Goods   There is also an extensive regime of federal legislation designed to protect consumers from potentially harmful goods—as distinguished from goods that may be substandard or not useful, but which do not necessarily pose a threat. *The Food and Drug Act*, R.S.C. 1985 c. F-27, and the *Hazardous Products Act*, R.S.C. 1985 c. H-3, are two important federal acts of this type. They generally prohibit the sale of certain items unless certain qualifications have been met.

■ *Critical Concepts of* Consumer Protection Legislation

■ Legislation prohibits parties to a consumer sale from agreeing that the implied conditions of the *Sale of Goods Act* will not apply. In other words, those conditions cannot be waived by the parties.
■ Legislation varies from province to province, and may imply terms in addition to those in the *Sale of Goods Act*, as well as extend liability for the products beyond the immediate parties to the contract.
■ There is also a regime of federal legislation concerned chiefly with safety protection.

■ *Business Law* Applied

⑮ **Lisa Desoto had** a swimming pool installed in her back yard. The pool came with a warranty card that guaranteed materials and workmanship on the pool itself for two years, excluding the filtration system. There was also a clause stating that there were no other warranties or conditions, expressed or implied by common law statute or otherwise.

The filtration system broke down the first day and had to be completely replaced. Desoto claimed the replacement cost of the filtration system from the pool manufacturer. The manufacturer pointed to the warranty card and said that the filtration system was not included in the warranty.

   a) Was this a consumer sale?
   b) Was there an express guarantee? Was there a limitation in the express warranty with respect to the filtration system? Was it effective?
   c) What law would imply a warranty (condition) of quality to the filtration system?

⑯ **Alfredo Vincenzo bought** a stain remover, sold under the brand name Stain Out, from a retail store. He tried to remove a stain from a suit coat, and the stain remover discoloured the garment. The instruction sheet inside the box contained the following statement printed in small letters at the bottom:

Not responsible for any loss or damage or injury however caused by the use of Stain Out. Vincenzo demanded a refund of the cost of the stain remover and the replacement cost of his coat.

   a) Were there any expressed warranties in the contract of sale of the stain remover? Were there any implied conditions?
   b) Was there a breach of any implied conditions?
   c) Was the exclusion clause effective?
   d) If the retailer refuses to pay Vincenzo and says it is the manufacturer's fault, as the retailer received the stain remover in a package and did nothing to it, does Vincenzo have any remedy against the retailer?
   e) What if the manufacturer's place of business is Mexico City and the manufacturer refuses to pay? What practical problems does the retailer face in recapturing money paid to the customer from the manufacturer?
   f) If the sales-confirmation order of the manufacturer contains a limitation of warranty clause similar to the one on the instruction clause, can the retailer claim successfully against the manufacturer? What are the practical and legal problems that the retailer faces in trying to bring an action against the foreign manufacturer?

Products Liability in Tort

The complexity of the modern business process means that there may be many companies involved in a chain-like fashion from point of origin to the consumer. When something goes wrong with a product, causing serious injury or harm, the offending party may be at any point on the manufacture and supply chain. There may be no direct contractual link to the injured party, and so remedies based in contract law would be unavailable for use by that injured party. Product liability law has been developed to deal with this type of situation. It provides a means of legal recourse in the absence of a contractual link between the responsible party and the injured party. For a more thorough discussion of the basis for such legal action, see Chapter 4.

Motor Vehicle Sales

Remember that almost all car salespeople are paid a commission based on profit—the more the dealership makes on a car, the more the salesperson gets paid. Since a "good" deal for a buyer is a "bad" deal for the salesperson, a number of tricks are often used to help sell more cars for higher profits. The most common tricks used by salespeople (and their managers) are described in this chapter; make sure you understand how they work before you start negotiating.

The Trade-in Buyer   If a car salesperson identifies you as a "trade-in buyer," you are in big trouble. Once you say (or even hint) that you will buy a new car *if they offer you enough on your trade-in*, you are marked as a sucker who can be taken advantage of in many parts of the transaction and not even notice it as long as your trade-in price is acceptable.

How this scam works is fairly simple—John Smith knows his trade-in is worth only $800 (retail), but he tells the salesperson that he will buy a new car today if they will give him $2,000 for his old car. The salesperson will then figure out a way to make $3,000-$4,000 profit from John's new car purchase even after "giving" him $2,000 for his trade-in.

John will end up paying the sticker price (MSRP) on the new car, his interest rate will be higher, there will be a number of overpriced or worthless ("back-end") options added to the car, he'll pay $180 for "processing," $400 for "dealer prep" and "transportation," $900 for an extended warranty (that's only worth $400), $350 for paint sealer and fabric protection, etc.

When it's all over, and John has been thoroughly fleeced, he will tell all of his friends what a shrewd negotiator he is because the dealer paid him $2,000 for his old clunker. (Before he left, the salesperson probably said to John, "Mr. Smith, don't tell anyone how much we paid for your old car—we wouldn't want everyone in town to think we're pushovers." Yes, they would!)

The Payment Buyer   The "payment buyer" sets himself up for a rip-off similar to that of the trade-in buyer. After learning that someone will buy a new car as long as the monthly payment doesn't exceed a specific figure, the salesperson structures the deal to wring the maximum amount of profit out of the buyer—all around the specified monthly payment. A larger down payment is required, the length of the loan is extended to five or six years, the monthly payment is raised "just a little bit more," the purchase price of the car is as high as possible, numerous overpriced and/or worthless options are added, etc. The buyer doesn't even notice that he's been fleeced—he's just happy his payment is "affordable."

Consumer Protection: Issues and Laws

- There are a significant number of rights and responsibilities for consumers and businesses governed by consumer protection acts. The have become so numerous only a summary is attempted here. There may be variations within the various provinces.
- a consumer is defined as an individual who is acting for personal, family or household purposes
- a person who is acting for business purposes is not included
- The act applies to both goods and services
  - covers such service-based businesses as health and fitness clubs, motor vehicle repair services and credit repair agencies
- does not apply in an area of exclusive federal jurisdiction, such as banking
- outlaws negative-option billing
  - consumers can refuse to pay for goods or services that they did not request
- prohibits misleading estimates for home renovations and moving services
  - the final cost cannot exceed the original estimate by more than 10 per cent, unless approved by the consumer
- requires businesses to deliver goods or services within 30 days of the date specified in the agreement; the failure to do so entitles consumers to a refund

- doubles the cooling-off period for cancelling agreements for timeshares, vacation clubs, fitness memberships, dance clubs and most door-to-door sales worth more than $50, for any reason, to 10 days after receiving a written copy of the agreement
- increases to 10 days the time to cancel agreements for credit repair
- ensures consumers receive written contracts for goods or services worth more than $50 to be delivered or paid for in the future
- treats Internet purchases the same as all other consumer purchases
  - in Internet transactions, the business must disclose detailed information to the consumer, including policies on cancellations and exchanges, and deliver a copy of the agreement within a specified time
- prohibits motor vehicle repair shops from charging for work without giving an estimate—the only exception is where an estimate is offered, the consumer declines the estimate and authorizes a maximum amount, and the final cost does not exceed that maximum amount
- extends to the buying or leasing of services the same protection as when consumers buy or lease goods
- requires full disclosure of the cost of long-term leases and interest on purchases
- outlaws advance payments for loan brokering and credit repair
- gives consumers one year to rescind agreements due to unfair business practices
- increases the maximum fines for contravening the Act
  - the fine for individuals doubles to $50,000
  - the fine for corporations more than doubles to $250,000
  - individual offenders also face the risk of imprisonment for two years less a day

Bailment

In personal-property law, there is a distinction between ownership and possession. When you deliver something to someone, you do not necessarily give ownership; you may wish to give only possession. This is the essential concept of **bailment**—transfer of possession of personal property without transfer of ownership. When you hand over your TV set to the repairman for a week, you give the right to possession, but you do not transfer ownership. The repairman is merely the custodian of the TV set for a specific purpose for a limited time. Whenever a person gives possession of an object to another but does not transfer ownership, the legal term for the transaction is "bailment." Bailment can occur in a number of situations:

bailment
transfer of possession of personal property without transfer of ownership

- repair—leaving a car or VCR with a repair person
- storage—leaving furniture in a warehouse or storage unit
- leasing—renting a car or a fax machine
- couriers—giving a letter or parcel for delivery
- freight—shipping a parcel with a trucking company

Bailment **Bailment** derives from the French word *baille*, meaning custody. Releasing someone on criminal bail is giving custody of the accused to the person who signs the bail. That person must keep track of the accused and make certain he or she appears for trial, or lose the money put up for bail. *Bail* also occurs in the word *bailiff*. A bailiff seizes goods or takes them into custody to be sold for payment of judgments. The person who owns the goods and gives up possession is called the *bailor*. In this book, such a person will be called the *owner*. The person who receives temporary possession of the goods is termed the *bailee* in law, but will be called the *custodian* in this chapter.

Legalese

Bailment As a Business

Bailment may or may not be for payment. For example, leaving your car parked at a friend's house for a couple of weeks while you are away on vacation is an example of a bailment without payment. This kind of bailment is known as a gratuitous bailment. This chapter deals only with bailment in a business situation, which is normally contractual bailment. It is technically referred to as bailment for hire or reward.

What Is a Bailment?

A bailment consists of three elements:

- Delivery of an item. This is where possession of the object changes hands, but the ownership of the item has not changed. As well, delivery generally requires that the custodian have some awareness that he or she now has possession of the item—or could have possession of the item (such as a coat rack in a reception area, with a sign saying "please leave coats here"). It is often easy to tell whether delivery of an item has occurred, but occasionally it can be more difficult. This is particularly the case if the item is very large (making physical delivery difficult), or if the custodian does not actually know he or she has an item in his or her care.
- Delivery for some purpose. There can be a variety of reasons for which items may be given to another party in a bailment situation. Some of these are noted in the introduction to this section.
- Delivery with the intention that the item be returned at some later time. This is consistent with the essential concept of bailment, which is that possession changes hands without the intention that ownership should change hands.

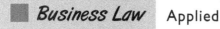 **Business Law** Applied

⑰ **Ken Kristov's car** broke down one evening on the way home from work. He had been working late, and his favourite car repair shop, Jasper's Fixit and Repair, was closed. Ken had the tow truck driver drop his car in Jasper's fenced parking lot, and Ken dropped his car keys in Jasper's mail slot.

a) Has there been a bailment of Ken's car?

Custodian Responsibilities

Certain concepts affect every commercial bailment relationship:

- The custodian has no ownership right, only a temporary right to possession
- The custodian has a duty to care for the object with the skill of a reasonable and careful person in that particular business
- If the goods are damaged, the burden is on the custodian to show that he or she was not negligent

The following example illustrates the extent of the duty of care for a custodian in the business of operating a warehouse or storage facility. A thief broke into a warehouse facility and stole some of the goods stored inside. The thief got in by breaking a glass pane in one of the warehouse's doors. It was found that the warehouse operator should have realized how easy it would be for a thief to break and enter, and was therefore liable to the owner of the goods. The courts impose a very high standard on these custodians who are in the business of bailment. They say, in effect, if you are going to make money by having possession of goods, you must take every precaution to safeguard those goods.

However, if a VCR was left with a friend for a few weeks and a thief broke in by smashing a glass pane in the residential house door, the homeowner would likely not be held negligent for having a glass pane in his door. The extent of the duty of care in this situation is lower, because of the "business" of the custodian.

While the courts put a high duty of care on the custodian, the custodian is not liable for damage to the goods from all causes. A custodian is not an insurer of the goods. There is no requirement at law that the custodian even carry insurance on the goods. So if your goods are damaged by a natural disaster, such as a flood or lightning, the custodian would not be responsible for that damage, unless the custodian had specifically assumed such responsibility by the terms of the bailment contract.

Insurance   Many insurance companies will not cover loss relating to goods put in storage, especially in the small, self-serve-style storage units. Before putting goods in storage, make certain the storage company carries insurance for all risks. If not, check with your own insurance company before signing a contract. If you sign a contract for storage that recites that you are to take out insurance yourself, ascertain that you are, indeed, able to get that insurance.

Business Alert!

Use of Exemption Clauses in Contracts of Bailment

Those businesses which routinely become custodians of items often attempt to limit their liability for loss or damage to those goods through the use of exemption clauses. Exemption clauses, which read something like the following, are regularly found on dry-cleaning claim checks, on signs hung in coat checks, and the like:

> Not responsible for loss or damage, however caused, including by any negligence on the part of the company's employees.

As noted in Chapter 6, the courts are generally reluctant to enforce these clauses against consumers, but may be more inclined to do so in business-to-business transactions.

Notice of the exemption clause is key to whether it will be enforced by the courts in bailment situations. If the owner has actual notice of the exemption clause, it has a greater likelihood of being effective. However, if the owner did not actually know about the exemption clause, its enforceability becomes more questionable. If the custodian can successfully argue that she took reasonable measures to draw the clause to the owner's attention, the clause may yet prove effective. For example, a large sign at eye level, well lit and easy to read, may provide the owner adequate "notice" of the exemption.

As well, in order to be effective, the clause must exclude or limit liability for the precise way in which the loss or damage occurred. If a sign posted in a coast check says "Not responsible for lost articles," and a leather jacket was damaged by knife slashing, the clause would not be effective.

Fundamental breach may also apply to nullify the exemption clause. Recall that fundamental breach is a total failure to do what was promised. For example, in a courier contract, delay in delivery would not be a fundamental breach but mere negligence; failure to deliver the item at all may well be a fundamental breach.

If there is a fundamental breach, the exemption clause will not apply unless the court finds that it was reasonable to have the exemption clause in spite of the fundamental breach.

Hogarth v. Archibald Moving & Storage Ltd., [1991] 57 B.C.L.R. (2d) 319 (C.A.)

The defendant, Archibald Moving & Storage Ltd., was in the business of operating a warehouse and storage facility. The plaintiff stored goods in the defendant's warehouse. A fire, which was found to be accidental, destroyed the warehouse, including the plaintiff's goods. Investigations revealed that the building had no smoke detectors, sprinkler system, fire doors, or fire alarms. Also, there were no security personnel to monitor the facilities.

Under the by-laws for the city of Vancouver (where the warehouse was located) and the provincial fire code, the defendant was not required to have sprinkler systems, fire alarms, or detection systems. An expert witness for the plaintiff stated that a sprinkler system would have either contained or extinguished the fire.

The Court's Decision

The court found that a bailment for reward (payment) existed between the plaintiff and the defendant. In the circumstances, the defendant was found to be negligent in failing to provide appropriate fire-detection methods. The court pointed out that, in a bailment relationship, the burden is on the custodian to show there was no negligence on its part, and the defendant, in failing to provide fire-detection methods, had not done that.

The court found the defendant liable to the plaintiff for the loss of the goods.

■ Business Law   Applied

⓲ **Quan Li has** just bought a Store-It-Ur-Self franchise. He rents out a unit to his first customer, John Gould. Gould stores some house furniture in it while he is building a new house. The sewer backs up and floods the unit, ruining Gould's furniture. There is no written contract, only an oral agreement to pay $100 in storage fees.

Li had heard that there were special traps that could be put in sewers. Because only a very few storage businesses had them, Li did not have them installed.

Gould wants Li to pay for the damage. Li claims he did nothing wrong and is not responsible.

a) Who has to bear the loss, Li or Gould?

■ Critical Concepts of Bailment

- Bailment involves a change of possession of items, but not a change of ownership.
- There must be a delivery of an item in order for a bailment to arise.
- A custodian of an item must use the care and skill of a reasonable and careful person in his particular business when looking after goods in his possession.
- Businesses attempt to limit their liability for goods they hold as custodian through the use of exemption clauses. These may or may not be effective, depending on whether the owner was aware of them at the time the contract of bailment was entered into, and how comprehensively the clause is drafted.

bill of lading

a receipt signed by a carrier or transportation company acknowledging that certain goods have been given to it for shipment

Courier and Transportation Companies

When a customer gives a package to a courier for delivery, this is a bailment. The courier has possession of the package, but it does not own it. On taking the package the courier normally has the customer sign a document called a **bill of lading**, which is a receipt signed by a carrier or transportation company acknowledging that certain goods have been given to it for shipment. It is one type of contract, and so both bailment and contract laws apply to a bill of lading.

Bill of Lading   **Bill** simply means *document*. For example, an account from a doctor may be called a doctor's bill. **Lading** comes from an Old English word meaning load. It is a receipt for goods loaded on board and is sometimes called a waybill. The word *way* is used in the ordinary of sense of *on the way*, again meaning loaded on board.

Concerns of customers regarding couriers and transportation companies usually centre on damage to (or loss of) goods, theft, and delay. The terms for couriers' bills of lading are determined by federal and provincial statutes that govern transportation companies. These terms are normally written on the reverse side of the bill of lading. Usually one of these clauses is an exemption clause that limits a courier's responsibility to a very small amount unless the customer declares a higher value. A sample Courier Bill of Lading is provided in the Appendix to Chapter 7.

Because this limitation clause is implied by statute, one of the defenses to an exemption clause, inadequate notice, does not apply. A customer cannot claim that it did not have notice of the term in order to avoid a statutory exemption clause.[4] This rule applies to all statutorily implied exemption clauses of which the one in courier bills of lading is an example.[5] Also, as the term is drafted by the government legislature, the rule that exemption clauses are to be interpreted against the interests of the drafter (*contra proferentem*) does not apply.[6] Nevertheless, courts have found that the bill of lading must be signed by the customer in order for the exemptions to be effective.

One note of warning must be stated. There were early cases making couriers liable for delay. However, in these cases the courier companies' staff were explicitly told by the customer that the document contained a tender and verbally warranted that the tender would be delivered on time. Courier companies have learned from such cases. They will now usually not accept tenders at all. Additionally, they carefully instruct their staff not to make any verbal warranties and merely to tell the customers to read the bill of lading.

International Transport Inc. v. Imperial Paving Ltd., [January 19, 1987] Doc. 841961, B.C.S.C. (unreported)

International Transport Inc. transported equipment from Kansas to Burnaby, British Columbia, for Imperial Paving Ltd. International Transport did not secure the equipment properly, and so it fell and was damaged beyond repair.

The customer sued the transportation company for damage to its property. The transportation company set up the limitation of liability clause in the bill of lading as a defense.

The Court's Decision

The bill of lading provides statutory limitations to its liability. However, in order to be able to take advantage of this provision the bill of lading must be completed at the time that the goods are received by the transportation company and signed by the customer. Here the bill of lading was completed but it was not signed. The transportation company did not have the benefit of the exemption clause and had to pay for the loss in full.

4. *Cornwall Gravel Co. v. Purolator Courier Ltd.* (1978), 18 O.R. (21)551 Aff'd [1980] 2 S.C.R. 118.

5. *B.G. Linton Construction Ltd. v. C.N.R. Co.*, [1975] 2 S.C.R. 678; and Rui M. Fernandes, *Transportation Law*, vol. 2 (Scarborough, Ont.: Carswell, 1991), pp. 35-37.

6. *Maddill v. Chu*, [1977] S.C.R. 400.

■ *Critical Concepts of* Defences to Statutory Exemption Clause

- Inadequate notice is not a defence to an exemption clause in a courier's bill of lading, as the clause is implied by statute.
- If the bill of lading is not both completed *and* signed by the customer, the exemption clause is not enforceable.

Business Alert!

subrogation

the right of an insurer who has paid a claim to "step into the shoes" of the insured and sue the person responsible for the loss Out of caution, some businesses send critical documents by several modes to ensure delivery.

Transportation Protection   The law regarding the responsibility of transportation companies and couriers is complex, and so it is difficult to predict with accuracy whether such a company will be responsible for loss in the carriage process. It is far better to have a term with your insurance company that covers loss because of carriage than to have to make a claim against the transportation or courier company. The insurance company then will have to decide whether it will pursue the claim in a subrogation action against the carrier. A **subrogation** is the right of an insurer who has paid a claim to "step into the shoes" of the insured and sue the person responsible for the loss.

■ *Business Law* Applied

⑲ **Wicked Knits was** a sweater manufacturer operating outside of Calgary. It wanted to ship its new line of sweaters to an annual trade show in Vancouver for distributors in western Canada, which was held every year from August 1 to August 3.

Cannex Couriers ran extensive ads saying "Guaranteed overnight delivery or it's free." Wicked Knits sent its shipment by Cannex on July 26, telling the driver that the shipment must arrive before August 1. Wicked Knits signed a bill of lading which contained a term on the reverse saying that Cannex's liability, even for negligence, was limited to three times the cost of the freight charges. This term is set by the provincial statute governing courier and transportation companies.

Because a Cannex employee mistakenly sent the shipment to Montreal, the goods did not arrive until August 3. Wicked Knits claimed that it had lost its opportunity to do business in western Canada for one year and claimed $100,000.

- a) Was the Cannex employee negligent?
- b) Does the exemption clause cover negligence?
- c) Does the advertisement "Guaranteed overnight delivery or it's free" increase Cannex's liability for loss? What does the ad say Cannex will offer as specified damages if it breaches its guarantee?
- d) Is the exemption clause effective, or will Wicked Knits succeed in its claim for loss of business?

Innkeepers

innkeeper

a person who maintains a business offering lodging to the public

Hotel and motel businesses were singled out for special restrictions by the courts. An **innkeeper** (a person who maintains a business offering lodging to the public) was made responsible for damage to items left in his or her care, whether because of negligence or not. All provincial governments have enacted innkeepers acts to diminish the harshness of these rules. Under the

Innkeepers Act, if a business providing accommodation posts a notice on the back of the room door, the liability of the innkeeper will be limited to the amount under the act. Various provinces have different amounts, and amounts can vary from time to time, but a limit of $50 to $100 is not unusual. Innkeepers must also provide a safe for guests' valuables. If the guest deposits valuables in the safe, the innkeeper is strictly liable for them and must have insurance to cover their loss.

Custodian's Remedies

What options are available to the custodian who does work on an item, but then does not receive payment? The businesses of bailment are based on contracts, so the custodian has the usual contractual remedies (such as suing for any amount owed). However, many different acts, such as the *Repairman's* (or *Garagemen's*) *Lien Act*, the *Transportation of Goods Act*, the *Warehouseman's Act*, and the *Public Vehicles Act*, working together with common law and standard form contracts, also apply and give the custodian the right to a lien for unpaid work and the sale of the item if the lien is not paid. The owner must be given written notice of the sale and the opportunity to pay the amounts owing and get the item back.

If the item is sold after seizure, the proceeds of the sale are applied first to the cost of the sale, and then to the custodian's fee; the balance, if any, is paid to the owner. If there is a shortfall, the custodian can sue the owner for that amount.

Seizure is always subject to the qualification that it can be done without a court order only if there is no breach of the peace. For example, a car owner pays by cheque for the repair of his car and takes his car home. But the cheque bounces. Assuming the garage has the right to a non-possessory lien, the garage can send a bailiff to seize the car if the car is sitting in the owner's driveway. If it is in a locked garage, the bailiff cannot break the lock to seize the car.

If the owner disputes the amount or the quality of the work, the owner can apply to the court and post security in the form of a bond or letter of credit for the amount of the custodian's claim. The court will order the release of the item pending resolution of the dispute between the owner and the custodian. The court application, however, may cost a significant amount of money and may not be cost effective, because most disputes over personal property involve less money than the court costs. Therefore, the right to retain possession of the goods gives the custodian a significant bargaining advantage.

■ *Critical Concepts of* Custodian's Lien

- The custodian has a right to retain the object until paid.
- The costs of the services performed regarding the object are a lien on the object. Such a lien is called a possessory lien.
- If there is a term in the contract, or in applicable legislation, the right to a lien may survive even after the object is taken back by the owner. Such a lien is called a non-possessory lien.
- If payment is not made, the custodian can sell the item after giving notice to the owner and after a period of time, usually about ten days. The owner receives what funds are left after payment of costs and the amount owing to the custodian.

Mullin v. 897634 Ontario Inc. cob: Allied Bailiff Services, [1996] 27 O.R. (3d) 145

The plaintiff's husband brought the plaintiff's car to a garage for repair and signed a work order for the repair. He later picked up the car and gave a cheque for payment. The cheque bounced, and the garage hired a bailiff to seize the car. The plaintiff paid the bill and the cost of seizure under protest, and then sued the bailiff for loss of the use of the car.

The bailiff defended by saying that it was acting properly as agent for the garage. The garage had the right to a non-possessory lien on the car under the applicable legislation.

The plaintiff replied by saying that the act required a signed acknowledgment of debt. The owner had not signed the work order herself, and so the garage had no right to a non-possessory lien.

The Court's Decision

The work order was a signed acknowledgment of debt sufficient to satisfy the requirement of the act. The fact that it was not signed personally by the owner herself was not a defence. The owner had clearly authorized her husband to sign on her behalf. The bailiff was acting properly on behalf of the garage.

There was no dispute as to the quality of the work; therefore, the plaintiff had to pay for it. The action was dismissed against the bailiff with costs to be paid by the plaintiff car owner.

 Business Law Applied

⑳ Barbara Shuster takes her car into a garage to have her transmission fixed and signs a standard work order to this effect. When she picks up the car, she listens to it and feels that the transmission has not been repaired correctly. She says she wants to get another mechanic's opinion on whether the repair work is adequate. The garage refuses to release the car until payment is made. Shuster is outraged; she refuses to pay and leaves. A few days later, she is served with a notice saying that the mechanic will sell the car in 10 days if she does not pay the bill in full.

   a) Does the mechanic have the right to hold the vehicle until payment is made even when the customer questions the quality of the work?
   b) Can the owner recover the car without paying the mechanic?
   c) If the owner does nothing after the notice of intent to sell, can the mechanic actually sell the car? What will be done with the proceeds of the sale?

Restrictions on Motor Vehicle Repair

The most common complaints to all provincial ministries that deal with consumer affairs concern the repair of motor vehicles. By virtue of the possessory and non-possessory lien rights, car-repair garages have powerful bargaining and enforcement tools. In Ontario, for example, this is offset by new consumer protection legislation that requires the repairer to comply strictly with a number of procedures, or the repair is free. This legislation applies to all vehicle repairs, even business vehicles. The definition of vehicle is wide and includes many types of construction equipment. The legislation is a very direct attempt to control abuse by garages.

In Summation

Operating a Business Website

- E-commerce acts make the law of contract apply to e-sales with few changes.

- There are important changes regarding mistake. Customers must be given an opportunity to correct errors at the point of ordering.

- Customers are permitted to cancel a contract even after delivery on the basis of mistake if they notify the business immediately upon discovering the mistake, return the product, and do not benefit from the cancellation.

Sale of Goods Act

- The terms of a contract fall within two categories. Conditions are terms essential to the actual performance of the contract, while warranties are terms of a minor nature which, if not met, allow a claim for damages but not cancellation of the contract.

- A contract for the sale of goods contains certain terms that are automatically included, even if the parties do not mention them, because of the operation of the *Sale of Goods Act*.

- The *Sale of Goods Act* details several conditions and warranties that are to be considered present as an implied part of the contract. These include terms concerning fitness for use, merchantable quality, and correspondence of the goods delivered to their description in the contract.

- The parties to a contract may agree to exclude the implied conditions and warranties set out in the *Sale of Goods Act*, by using an exemption clause specifically stating this intention.

- The *Sale of Goods Act* details when the ownership of goods changes hands, unless the parties agree otherwise. Generally, the owner of goods bears the risk of loss or damage to them.

- There are special protections for an unpaid vendor, which are set out in the *Sale of Goods Act*.

Privacy

- Privacy legislation balances the need to protect individual privacy with the desire of businesses to collect personal data.

- Privacy legislation is based on:
  a) informed consent: businesses must clearly indicate how the information will be used, and stick to that use only
  b) consent: businesses must obtain consent to collect, use, or disclose personal data
  c) access: individuals must have access to their personal data and be permitted to correct or withdraw consent
  d) accountability: individuals can complain to the privacy commissioner, who can apply a variety of remedies against an offending business

Retail Sales

Consumer Protection Legislation

- Consumer protection is a specific area of law aimed at the sale of goods to an individual for personal use. Conditions and warranties are implied as part of the consumer transaction, but exemption clauses attempting to exclude these implied terms are not enforceable under consumer protection legislation.

Products Liability in Tort

- There does not need to be a direct contractual relationship between parties in order for the seller to be liable for products sold. Liability may arise in tort law.

Bailment

■ Bailment leaves ownership of an item with its owner (the bailor) while possession is passed to another person (the bailee) for various reasons, such as repair or storage.

■ In order for a bailment to arise, there must be delivery of an item, for some purpose, with possession to be restored to the owner at a later time.

■ Bailment for hire or reward is usually for a business purpose and places a duty on the custodian to care for the object with the skill of a careful and prudent person in that particular business. If damage occurs to the item during the bailment, the onus is on the custodian to prove there was no negligence.

■ Exemption clauses are often used by custodians in an attempt to limit liability for loss or damage to the goods they hold. To be effective, these must be drawn to the attention of the owner and expressly cover the way in which loss or damage occurred. These will also not be effective in the case of a fundamental breach of contract.

■ Certain businesses involving bailment are subject to terms and exemption clauses imposed by legislation. In such circumstances as a consumer transaction and complicated standard form contracts, the exemption clause may be unenforceable.

■ A custodian can retain an item until paid and is entitled to a lien under which the item may be seized and sold. Funds received from the sale may be applied against the outstanding account.

■ In some circumstances, provincial statutes have created a right to sell the item upon which work has been done, even if possession has been given up. This is possible if there is a written acknowledgment of debt for services related to the item.

Closing Questions

Operating a Business Website

1. Jason Bullen is designing a website for his employer, a retail business. Bullen knows that it is important to bring very fast closure to impulse buying. His proposed website displays the product with a button entitled "I buy" immediately next to it. The customer merely enters a credit card number and clicks on the button. Immediately, a message flashes saying the purchase has been successful. The product is shipped the very next day.
   a) Are there any concerns about this site under common law contract rules or e-commerce legislation? Is there a difference in application of these rules? If so, what is it?
   b) What changes would you suggest to the website?

2. **Internet Research.** Find advice on careful practices for purchasing online particularly if a vendor is not a long established business. Make a list of the suggestions that you think are the most important and discuss them in class.

3. **Internet Research.** Do a report on complaints to Canadian Privacy Commissioners, federal or provincial, regarding Facebook's use of personal data. Describe the complaint and Facebook's response. What do you think is the proper solution?

Conditions and Warranties

4. Identify each of the following terms as either a warranty or a condition of the contract, and indicate the remedy available if the contractual obligation is not met.
   a) Payment for goods to be made within 30 days
   b) Seller has good title to the goods
   c) Goods are free from defects making them unmerchantable
   d) Goods are free from any lien or encumbrance
   e) Goods are to be delivered on the first day of March
   f) Seller will deliver 10 boxes of photocopy paper

5. Lila Dhaliwal operated a giftware shop. She ordered 100 plates with a pattern of blue and gold concentric circles. Her wholesaler delivered 100 plates with blue and yellow concentric circles.
   a) Was this a breach of condition or warranty under the contract and what would Dhaliwal's remedy be?
   b) Would it make any difference if the purchase contract between Dhaliwal and the wholesaler contained a clause agreeing that colour differences were warranties?
   c) If Dhaliwal refuses to pay for the plates, what could the wholesaler do?

6. Morawa ordered some stationery from Precise Envelope Company. The stationery was delivered with the name *Morawa* misspelled as *Morewe*. Morawa wants to refuse delivery and have the contract cancelled. The printer claims that this is a minor mistake and wants Morawa to complete the contract but pay a reduced amount.
   a) What type of term is the spelling of a business name on stationery?
   b) Does a breach of this nature permit rescission of the contract?

7. Jennifer Wu had a contract for #1 Grade Kentucky Blue Grass seed for her mini-golf operation. In the agreement was a clause stating that the parties agreed to treat the quality of the seed as a warranty of the contract. The seed delivered was #3 Grade, and when Wu discovered this, she looked in the *Sale of Goods Act* and discovered that the quality of the goods is considered a condition of the contract. When she raised this issue with the vendor, he told her she should have rooted that out before signing the contract. "The seeds are yours."
   a) What would you advise Wu concerning her position in this matter?

8. **Internet Research.** Do a report on privacy concerns regarding the use of confidential information on social networking sites.

9. **Internet Research.** Do a report on the ability of hackers to invade and collect personal and business confidential information and trade secrets. Refer to the report of the Monk Centre for International Studies of the University of Toronto and its inquiry into Ghostnet.

Consumer Sales

10. Sunjee experienced a number of problems with the new computer system he had bought from Delta Electronics. When he opened the CPU, he discovered that the disk drives were reconditioned units.
    a) What legislation applies to this transaction?
    b) Is Sunjee entitled to rescind the contract and obtain a refund of the money he paid for the computer system?
    c) Would it make any difference if the disk drives could be easily removed and replaced by new units, and if so what would be the result for Sunjee?
    d) What is Sunjee's legal position if the sales contract contains a clause excluding all warranties except those given in the contract, and the contract states there is no warranty of fitness for use?

11. Samantha always felt awkward asking customers at the store where she was employed to sign the store's standard form agreement containing an exemption clause releasing the store from responsibility for any injuries that might occur. Whenever a customer asked what the form was for, Samantha would reply: "Oh, you know, just the usual stuff about use of the product and things like that. The stuff that stores normally get you to sign." Nine times out of 10 the customer would sign.
    a) Is Samantha creating a problem for her employer, and if so what is the nature of that problem?
    b) What would be the effect if, instead of having the customer sign the standard form contract, Samantha was simply required to tell the customer, just before she entered the sale in the cash register, that the store will not be responsible for any injuries?
    c) Samantha forgot to tell the last customer about the store's policy before she entered the sale in the register. Thinking quickly, she shouted after him, "By the way, the store will not be responsible for any injuries from using the product!" What is the result of her action—other than to have everyone in the store stare at the customer?

Sale of Goods Act

12. Calla Lilli wanted to develop a landscape plan for her back yard. She decided to buy a computer program called Green Thumbs Up to help her do this. The promotional material on the box read: "... design the garden of your dreams—everything you need is right in this box!" Unfortunately for Calla, the program was little more than a listing of plant names. Is the purchase of a computer program a purchase of a "good"?

13. a) Look at clause number 8 in the Used Car Bill of Sale located in the Appendix to Chapter 6. Why does the car dealership want that clause included? What *Sale of Goods Act* rule does it vary?
    b) Look at the Purchase Order reproduced in the Appendix in this chapter.
        i) Review paragraph 3. What is the meaning of the term *FOB*?
        ii) Assume a purchaser is located in Toronto. What is the probable difference in ultimate cost to this purchaser between two products of identical price, both of which are sent FOB port of departure? One supplier is in Taiwan and the other is in Montreal.

14. Meadowview College central supply placed a standing order for Inkblot brand dry-erase whiteboard markers from PaperClips Stationers. Until the year 2004, 1,000 boxes were to be delivered to Meadowview at the start of each term (that is, in September and January of each year). After the first month of use in the classroom, the janitorial staff reported difficulties cleaning the whiteboards and corrosion of whiteboard surfaces where the ink had been left on the boards for more than a day. When contacted about the problem, PaperClips said that whiteboard markers where meant to be erased within a reasonable time after use, and that they could offer no resolution to the problems Meadowview was experiencing.
    a) Does Meadowview have any claims pursuant to the *Sale of Goods Act*?
    b) If so, what remedies are available to Meadowview? Which would be preferable, and why?

15. Harold Mertma was a wood crafter who made furniture by special order. He worked in a workshop out behind his house. Alison Snodgrass had placed an order with Harold for an oak bookshelf/entertainment unit. She wanted specially crafted hollow shelving, so that the unit would not be exceptionally heavy. Alison lived in an older home, and had some concerns that the floor might not be able to bear the weight of a solid wood unit.

    When Harold finished the unit, he had Alison come over to the shop to inspect it. She was happy with the work. The next day, Harold delivered the unit to her house, and set it up. However, after two weeks, Alison noticed the floor sagging. She called a building inspector, who confirmed that the unit was at least 50% too heavy for her floor support, and that it would cost some $10,000 to repair the damage already done. Alison called Harold and told him to take the unit back, and to provide a cheque for the $10,000 it would cost her to fix the floor.
    a) Does Alison have any legal basis for the claim she is making against Harold?
    b) What arguments does Harold have to defend Alison's claim?
    c) Who would bear responsibility for the cost of the unit if Harold's workshop burned to the ground after Alison inspected the unit, but before Harold delivered it?

Retail Sales

16. a) Is a retailer under any legal obligation to take back, or exchange, clothing which is bought but does not fit?

    b) Does it make any difference if there is a sign posted by the cash register which reads "All goods satisfactory, or money refunded"?

17. Frank Flude bought a used car from Gorjeta Used Cars. At the time of the purchase Gorjeta offered Flude a one-year warranty through a warranty company for $1,000. Flude refused.

    Two days after delivery, the car had problems and these continued for three months. Gorjeta has refused to pay for the cost of the repairs, claiming that Flude had the opportunity to buy a warranty and refused, and so Gorjeta had no responsibility to pay for the repairs.

    a) Is Gorjeta correct?

18. **Internet Research.** Sasha Eskandarian heard a rattle in her family car and brought it in to Joe's Reliable Repair Shop for repair. Joe gave a written quote of $500.00. When Sasha came to pick up her car Joe said sorry, he had encountered unexpected problems and the charge would be $1,000.00. Sasha checked with other mechanics and that was a valid charge for the work done.

    a) Find a statute in your province that governs the repair of motor vehicles and give the name of the statute. [HINT: In law the term car is never used, only the term motor vehicle is].

    b) Find a section or sections in that act which would govern the contract between Sasha and Joe's Reliable Repair Shop and give your opinion as to whether Joe can charge Sasha for the additional amount.

Bailment

19. Gobindhar Arbib stored some household furniture with Safe-Store Inc. When Arbib picked up the furniture, some of it had mould and watermarks on it, indicating a flood. The business denies any flood. Arbib wants to sue the storage company, but is concerned that he doesn't have any way to prove how the damage occurred.

    a) Is there any rule in the law of bailment that will assist Arbib?

20. A bailor is:
    a) the possessor of the item bailed
    b) the owner of the item bailed
    c) the cup used to remove water from a boat
    d) the person who seizes goods for payment of judgments

21. A bailment for hire:
    a) involves payment for the services rendered
    b) is a gratuitous bailment
    c) is the opposite of bailment for reward
    d) is the remedy provided by the court when a party does not pay for the services rendered

22. Wanda owned a rare and expensive painting by a well-known artist. It was her pride and joy. When she decided to leave on an extended one-year vacation overseas, Wanda sublet her apartment and arranged to leave her oil painting with her friend Fred, who, because he operated an art galley, would know how to properly take care of it. In return, Fred could enjoy having the painting on his wall for a year.

    Several months later, Fred decided to hold an exhibit of oil paintings. Wanda's painting was to be the featured attraction and Fred advertised far and wide. Unfortunately, the exhibit also caught the eye of Skylight Sam, who dropped in one night after the show was closed and took Wanda's painting for his private viewing pleasure.

    When Wanda wandered back home and asked Fred for her painting, all he could give her was the picture from the newspaper that had accompanied the report on the theft.

    a) Describe the nature of the relationship outlined in this situation and, using legal terms, define the various parties to the relationship.

    b) Explain, with reasons, whether this relationship was based on friendship or for value.

    c) If Fred has no money, what other source of funds might Wanda look to, assuming she has established the right to recover the value of the painting from Fred?

23. Cathcart Services Limited sent a tender by Purolator Courier Limited. Cathcart clearly indicated on the bill of lading and told the Purolator employee who picked up the package that it was a tender that had to arrive on time. The bill of lading contained the terms limiting liability for loss or damage to $250.

    The tender was not delivered. The tender was the lowest one and would have been accepted. If Cathcart had gotten the job it would have made a profit of $37,000. Cathcart wants to sue Purolator for its loss. Purolator says it has lost the records relating to this delivery.

    a) Since Purolator cannot find its records regarding the delivery, will Cathcart be able to prove negligence by Purolator? What bailment rule will help?

    a) Are there any grounds in contract law that would assist Cathcart in avoiding the limitation of liability to $250,000?

24. Ivan Firchuk put his home-entertainment system in for repair with Electronic Edge Repairs Inc. Electronic Edge did the repair work but, unfortunately, went into bankruptcy. The trustee in bankruptcy claims that the home-entertainment system is an asset of the business and is going to be sold to a liquidation company.

    a) What is the legal term for the transaction whereby Firchuk gave the home-entertainment system to Electronic Edge?

    b) Does the trustee in bankruptcy have the right to sell the home-entertainment system?

    c) Does the trustee in bankruptcy have any rights over the home-entertainment system?

25. Alison Frizelli was attending a business luncheon at Chez Alphred, a trendy downtown restaurant. She pulled up to the entrance and noticed a sign which said "Please allow our parking attendant to assist you." She got out of her car . . .

    a) and handed her keys to a well-dressed young man she assumed was the parking attendant. In fact, he had just been forcibly removed from Chez Alphred for disruptive behaviour. The real attendant was off parking another car. The ejected patron took Alison's car for a joyride and crashed into a ravine, causing several thousand dollars in damage.

       i) Can Alison use bailment to recover damages against Chez Alphred?

       ii) Can Alison use any other legal principles to recover damages from Chez Alphred?

    b) and handed her keys to the Chez Alphred parking attendant. On the way to the parking garage, the attendant swerved to avoid hitting a young child who ran across the street. He consequently hit a light pole, causing several thousand dollars in damage to Alison's car.

       i) Can Alison use bailment to recover damages against Chez Alphred?

    c) and handed her keys to the Chez Alphred parking attendant. As the attendant drove away, she noticed that the bottom of the sign said "We are not responsible for loss or damage to vehicles." While in the parking garage, Alison's car was vandalized by parties unknown, resulting in several thousand dollars in damage.

       i) Can Alison use bailment to recover damages against Chez Alphred?

Websites

www.fraud.org—This is the National Fraud Information Center site, dealing with scams against businesses, telemarketing fraud, credit card fraud, Internet fraud, and other scams.

strategis.ic.gc.ca/SSG/ca01168e.html#laws—Industry Canada, Consumer Connection. Links to federal consumer protection acts, and essays on frauds and other issues.

cbc.ca/consumers/market—Marketplace. Product information of interest to consumers, based on CBC's *Marketplace*.

www.bbb.org—Better Business Bureau. Includes information on buying on-line.

www.innovationlaw.org—A site operated by Bell Laboratories to consider new challenges to traditional law brought about by technology.

cyber.law.harvard.edu/node/5211—The website of the Berkman Centre for Internet and Society at Harvard University containing articles on latest issues respecting the Internet including privacy and social networking sites.

www.mgs.gov.on.ca/english/releases/nr072005-b.htm—See Ministry of Government Services, Backgrounder, "The New *Consumer Protection Act*" (July 20, 2005), for Ontario consumer protection laws.

www.computingcases.org—A site dedicated to reviewing issues on the Internet and the law.

Purchase Order

GAHZAIN CHEMICALS INC.
Purchase Order Terms

---

1. **INCLUSIONS/DISCOUNTS.** The price shall be fixed and shall include the cost of the Goods, storage, transport and installation. Invoices shall be paid within 30 days of receipt of the Goods. Periods established relative to discounts shall be calculated as of the date of receipt of the relevant invoices. However, if the invoice is received before the Goods, the starting point of the discount period shall be the date the Goods are received.

2. **PACKAGING/SHIPPING AND SHIPPING NOTICE.** All Goods must be properly packed in boxes or otherwise prepared for shipping, so as to prevent any damage during shipping, handling and storage. The Supplier shall be liable for any damage resulting from poor packing. All packing charges shall be paid by the Supplier. Immediately when the shipment of Goods is dispatched, a copy of the shipping notice, packing slip and bill of lading shall be forwarded by Supplier to Purchaser identifying the Goods to be shipped, the Purchase Order Number, carrier, carrier number and routing. Routing shall be by the most economical and expedient route. The Purchase Order number shall appear on all shipping documents, as well as on the packaging and the delivery order. The Purchaser reserves the right to return, at the Supplier's expense, all Goods that do not bear the required inscriptions.

3. **DELIVERY.** Delivery shall be FOB Port of Departure. Delivery shall be performed on the date and according to the delivery method provided for herein. If the Supplier fails to deliver the Goods by the date specified herein, the Purchaser may claim as liquidated damages the sum of 5%, of the total amount of the Purchase Order, for each business day the delivery is delayed, notwithstanding the causes of such delay. Both Purchaser and Supplier agree that 5% of the total amount of the Purchase Order for each business day delivery is delayed is a fair and reasonable estimate of the damages that Purchaser would suffer if the Goods are so delayed. The liquidated damages shall be payable by Supplier to Purchaser as of the first day of the delay without formal notice and at the simple request of the Purchaser, or, Purchaser may at its sole discretion hold back the said amount on the balance owing under this Purchase Order. The liquidated damages are payable in addition to any other recourse the Purchaser may have with regard to the Supplier.

4. **TITLE/INFRINGEMENT.** The Supplier warrants that the delivered Goods are free and clear from all encumbrances and liens and that all Goods shall be free of any claim, whether rightful or otherwise, of any person by way of infringement of any patent, copyright, trademark or industrial design or the like, and shall indemnify, hold harmless and defend Purchaser from any and all such claims and legal proceedings arising thereon and from all expenses and costs resulting or claimed to have resulted from any and all such claims and legal proceedings.

5. **WARRANTY.** The Goods shall be of a merchantable quality and of the best grade of their respective kinds. Supplier warrants to Purchaser that the Goods shall be suitable for the service and performance intended and of the quality specified and shall conform to the specifications, drawings, or samples, and other descriptions contained under this Purchase Order. Supplier guarantees the Goods against any and all defects in workmanship and materials for a minimum of twenty-four months following acceptance of the Goods by Purchaser and if the Goods are to be operated on-site, for twenty-four months following the successful installation of the Goods.

Supplier agrees to repair or replace any and all defects in the Goods or the performance of the Goods in a good, workmanlike manner to the satisfaction of Purchaser and without cost to Purchaser, and such work relating to the

Goods shall commence no later than ten (10) days upon receipt of notice to this effect from Purchaser. The Goods are ordered by Purchaser in reliance of each and all of the warranties and guarantees specified in the Purchase Order and Performance Guarantee and implied by law or usage of trade, and unless otherwise expressly stated in the Purchase Order, these warranties and guarantees shall control. The Supplier acknowledges that the Purchaser has made known the purpose for which the Goods are being supplied and performed and that Purchaser relies upon the Supplier's skill or judgement such that the implied warranty of quality of fitness applies to the Goods.

6. **INSURANCE.** The Supplier undertakes to conform to the written directives of the Purchaser relative to the types of insurance policies required, where applicable.

7. **COMPLIANCE.** Supplier warrants that the Goods supplied hereunder shall have been produced, sold, delivered and furnished in strict compliance with all applicable laws, regulations, labour agreements, working conditions and technical codes or requirements to which the Goods are subject. Supplier shall executive and deliver such documents as may be required to effect or evidence compliance. Any and all laws and regulations required to be incorporated into agreements of this character are deemed incorporated by reference.

8. **TERMINATION OF AGREEMENT**. Either party may terminate this agreement when the other party breaches an obligation hereunder and fail to remedy such breach within 30 days of receipt of a written notice to that effect.

9. **NON-WAIVER.** Failure of the Purchaser to insist upon strict performance of any of the terms or conditions under the Purchase Order or failure or delay to exercise any rights or remedies provided hereunder shall not be deemed a waiver of any of Purchaser's rights under this Purchase Order.

10. **GOVERNING LAW.** The parties agree that this agreement shall be governed by the laws of Alberta. The parties further agree to submit to the courts of Alberta.

11. **CANCELLATION.** The Purchaser reserves the right to cancel this order or any part of it if the order is not delivered within a reasonable time period and upon such cancellation may procure substitute goods similar to those to which the order is cancelled, or complete the finished Goods by whatever method it chooses. Purchaser may then withhold further payments to Supplier and Supplier shall be liable for the difference between the cost of such substitute Goods or the cost of finishing such Goods and the price set forth in this Purchase Order for such Goods.

   In the event of rejection for any or all non-conforming Goods, the Purchaser may, at its sole option, grant additional time for Supplier to correct the non-conformance. Should Supplier fail to do so within such additional time, or should additional time not be granted, Purchaser may, at its option, either cancel the order as to the non-conforming Goods and retain the same rights with respect to substitute Goods as are set out in the preceding paragraphs and, in addition, recover the costs incurred by Purchaser in removing the non-conforming Goods and installing substitute Goods, or cause the non-conformity to be covered at the Supplier's expense.

12. **CHANGES.** Purchaser may, by written change order, make changes in, including additions to, or deletions from, the Goods. If any such changes affect the amount due or the time of performance under the Agreement, an equitable and reasonable adjustment shall be made.

13. **ENTIRE AGREEMENT.** The Purchase Order, including these Purchase Order terms and conditions, any Schedules attached hereto and any additional terms and conditions incorporated in writing and attached to the Purchase Order constitute the sole and the entire agreement between the parties. No other terms or conditions shall be binding upon the Purchaser unless accepted by it in writing. Supplier may not subcontract or assign all or any part of its obligation under the Purchase Order without Purchaser's prior written consent.

The Organization of a Business

Initial Considerations

Choosing a Name

A name is a valuable asset for a business, and choosing a creative name is often a difficult task. It is legally acceptable to use your own name, unless it has become widely associated with another business in the same industry. Doreen McDonald, for example, could not open a fast-food restaurant called McDonald's. She could, however, quite legally set up a clothing store with that name.

Once a name is found for the business, the next step is to make sure that its use will be legally permitted. There are several legal restrictions to consider. A business cannot:

- adopt a name similar to one already in use by another well-known firm in the same industry, if doing so is likely to deceive the public. This action is known as **passing off**—misrepresenting goods, services, or a business in order to deceive the public into believing that they are another's goods, services, or business. The provincial government might refuse to approve registration of such a name.

- use a name that is a registered trademark of another business. *McMuffin*, for example, is a registered trademark of McDonald's, and so it would be illegal to open a muffin shop called McMuffin's.

- employ terms, such as *Limited*, *Ltd.*, or *Inc.*, to suggest that it is incorporated, unless it actually is a corporation.

passing off
misrepresenting goods, services, or a business in order to deceive the public into believing that they are another's goods, services, or business

Trade Names

Sometimes a business uses a name other than the one it first registers with the government. This is a **trade name**—a name used by a business, often in addition to the registered or incorporated name. *The Bay* is a trade name of the Hudson's Bay Company Canada, Ltd., and *Panasonic* is a trade name of Matsushita Electronic of Canada, Inc.

trade name
a name used by a business, often in addition to the registered or incorporated name

Numbered Companies

Since choosing the right name is sometimes a difficult and slow process, there is a procedure for incorporating a business without having to register a name at that time. When the incorporation is approved, the government simply assigns the next number in line to the new corporation, so that it becomes known as, for example, 76324 Canada Limited. The corporation's name could be changed later by a formal application to the government, but this would involve additional legal expense. Often, therefore, numbered companies simply use a trade name, and are described as "76324 Canada Limited, carrying on business as Confidential Management." The short forms, *COB* and *O/A*, are often used in place of *carrying on business* and *operating as*.

The Liabilities of a Business

- The source of potential claims against a business can be roughly divided into two categories, arising from contract and tort law.
- Contract—this includes money owed to suppliers, employees' wages, taxes, rent, and bank loans.
- Tort—such liability generally relates to members of the public. Some of the most common tort areas important to business are:
    a) occupier's liability (e.g., slip and fall)
    b) vicarious liability (e.g., injury done by an employee driving a company delivery van on business)
    c) products liability (e.g., selling a defective bicycle that subsequently injures a pedestrian)

Protection of Personal Assets

A serious concern that faces everyone who sets up a business is how best to protect personal assets. This is an important point to consider when deciding the form a business will take. In sole proprietorships and partnerships, the business owner's personal assets can be seized by business creditors. Only incorporation will ensure that business assets and personal assets remain separate.

The owner of a typical small business would be able to categorize assets as follows:

Personal Assets	Business Assets
House	Inventory
Car	Equipment
Life insurance	Delivery van
Bank account	Accounts owed by customers

There are three common ways of protecting personal assets:

- transfer to spouse
- incorporation
- insurance

Transfer to Spouse   Transferring ownership of personal assets to a spouse is acceptable, as long as it is not specifically done to avoid creditors. If potential claims from creditors exist at the time the assets change ownership, the transfer can be set aside on the legal grounds of fraudulent conveyance. When a business is just starting, and there are no creditors threatening legal action, a conveyance to a spouse would likely be permissible. The transfer of property to a spouse is final, in that the person making the transfer loses complete control over the assets. It is possible that there may be unwelcome consequences to such a transfer.

Incorporation Incorporating involves forming a separate company. Only the assets of the company are then available to creditors. However, in the case of a small business this may be of little protection, as creditors may well demand personal guarantees by the owner and spouse before granting any loan or credit.

Insurance Insurance can cover tort liability, as well as such areas as providing income if the owner becomes sick and providing money to pay employees during the time of sickness. It cannot assist in protecting against business trade debts.

Choosing the Form of the Business

The law divides all businesses into one of four categories:

- sole proprietorship
- partnership
- limited partnership
- **corporation**—a business organization that is a separate legal entity (person) from the owners

There are other ways of carrying on business—such as franchises and joint ventures, which are also called strategic alliances—that are not separate legal forms. (A **joint venture** is an agreement between two or more independent businesses to cooperate on a particular project only.) Many people believe that the best form of business is always incorporation. This is not necessarily true, especially in the beginning stages of a business. The best form of business can be determined only after considering many factors, and obtaining the advice of a lawyer and an accountant.

Should I Incorporate?

Incorporation is not automatically the best form for a one-person business. Advice should always be sought from lawyers and accountants, as there are many factors that could influence the decision. One tax consideration is that a small business usually operates at a loss for the first year or two. If it is not incorporated, that loss can be used by the owner against personal income to reduce tax liability. If the business is incorporated, the loss stays with the company and can be used only against corporate income. As a business progresses and becomes more profitable, then perhaps incorporation should be considered.

corporation
a business organization that is a separate legal entity (person) from the owners

joint venture
an agreement between two or more independent businesses to cooperate on a particular project only

---

■ *Critical Concepts of* Setting Up a Business

- Choose a name.
- Select the form—sole proprietorship, partnership, limited partnership, or incorporation.
- Register or incorporate.
- Obtain a municipal or professional business licence, if applicable.

Sole Proprietorships

Sole proprietorships, or one-person businesses, have become increasingly common today as more and more people set up "work from home" businesses. Many people believe that there are numerous legal hurdles to leap before setting up a business. In fact, you can start a one-person business or a partnership very simply. Merely choose a name and register it. If you use your own name as a business name, you do not even have to register—just start doing business.

Business Alert!

Protecting Personal Assets   In a sole proprietorship, there is no protection for the owner's personal assets. Both business and personal assets can be seized by creditors if the business owes debts, which amounts to unlimited liability.

Business Names

There are a number of possibilities when it comes to naming a sole proprietorship or a partnership. These include:

- the owner's name—Milo Melan's Bakery
- a personal name other than that of the owner—Milo Melan carries on business as Jean Savarin Bakery
- coined words—Milmel Bakery; Kopy-Katz Kopiers
- names that suggest more than one owner—The Gibson Group; Milo & Sons; Milo and Company
- generic or general names—Fresh Bakery; Sunshine Fruit Stand
- names of places—Vancouver Video; Front Street Bakery

The ending *and Company* can be used, but not *Milo Company*. The latter suggests a corporation.

Registration

If the sole proprietor uses a name other than a personal first and last name in the business, that name must be registered with the appropriate provincial government office. This is a very easy process that does not require the advice of a lawyer. The business owner need only visit the office, fill out a short form, and pay a small registration fee. The form is then put on public file, and anyone can search to discover the owner of a particular business. The registration must be renewed every five years.

Not registering a name means that the owner of a business may be fined. In some jurisdictions, such as Ontario and Nova Scotia, the owner cannot sue in the business's name unless it is registered. If a customer does not pay, for example, the owner of the business cannot take action to collect the debt until the business is registered.

Partnerships

The Formation of a Partnership

A **partnership** is the relationship between two or more persons carrying on a business with a view to profit. Normally, the advantages in sharing control of a business with others—being able to pool knowledge, experiences, and resources—far outweigh the disadvantages. Therefore, groups of people co-operating have become the method of carrying on business that tends to support the greatest growth potential. Sometimes such groups of business people will form a corporation. If they do not, then the joint business is usually run as a partnership (referred to as "firms").

Small corporations are often run very much like partnerships. Thus, many of the problems encountered in maintaining co-operation among partners are also discovered among the shareholders of a corporation.

Many partnerships survive for years with few or any problems. Others run into difficulties within a very short time—choose your business partners carefully! Some of the common problem areas in partnerships have typically been:

- disagreements about how to run the business
- dishonesty by one of the partners—for example, taking partnership money secretly and leaving the country
- incompetence, such as poor performance of a contract, so that the partnership does not get paid or is sued

Critical Concepts of Partnerships

- Two or more individuals can agree to become partners, orally or in writing.
- The law will find two or more persons to be partners—even in the absence of their express agreement—if they carry on business together with the intention of making a profit.
- Not all business arrangements are found to be partnerships. The courts use three tests in deciding whether a partnership exists even if there was no intention that it should. The court will ask if there was
  a) a joint contribution to the capital to start a business
  b) an intention to share profits and losses
  c) joint participation in the management of the business.
- The court need be satisfied that only one of the tests is met to find that a legal partnership exists.
- All partnerships must register their partnership name and list the partners with a provincial business name-registry office, or suffer the same penalties as sole proprietors for failure to register.

Legal Partnerships   It is possible to be part of a legally binding partnership even though there was no deliberate intention of doing so. The legal finding of a partnership has serious consequences: the personal assets of any partner will be liable for all partnership debts should the partnership assets be insufficient to cover them.

Business Alert!

Business Law Applied

❶ **Two Vancouver bakeries** pooled their orders of wheat from Alberta in order to take advantage of lower freight rates available when a larger volume is shipped. There was no intention of forming a partnership between the bakeries.

a) Are the bakeries legally partners?
b) What if both bakeries are corporations? Can they form a partnership if they want to?
c) Does it matter that the businesses have no formal partnership agreement?

❷ **Two students decided** that, as a summer job, they would run dances every Saturday night from June until September. They rented a local hall, and paid the owner a $500 deposit, each contributing $250 of this amount. The students agreed that any profits they made would be split equally between them, and that they would consult each other about all aspects of organizing the dances. The thought of partnership never crossed their minds.

a) Would the courts find the two students to be partners?

❸ **Simone and DiCarlo** started a business together, naming it Mega Fitness Health Club. No partnership agreement was signed, and little discussion of the organizational aspects of the business took place. Simone advanced $10,000 as start-up capital, while DiCarlo put in $5,000, promising another $5,000 as soon as he could.

Simone proved to be a good salesperson, and signed a large number of patrons for yearly memberships. DiCarlo worked the same number of hours, but generated a far smaller amount of business. At the end of the first year, the business earned a profit of $100,000.

Simone claimed that, because he contributed twice as much capital and generated twice as much business, he was entitled to 75 percent of the profits. DiCarlo disagreed, and insisted the profits be evenly divided.

a) Who was legally correct?
b) How might Simone have safeguarded his interests?

❹ **Assume the same** facts as in the previous question, except that the business is a variety store. There is frequent employee absence, and Simone always has to fill in, averaging about 60 hours a week.

DiCarlo has another job and is rarely available to do extra work, averaging about 40 hours a week in the store.

At the end the year, Simone wants some salary compensation for the additional 20 hours he has worked every week. DiCarlo refuses.

a) Is Simone entitled to the extra compensation on a merit basis?
b) What could Simone have done to protect his interests?

❺ **A real estate** brokerage firm has four partners—A, B, C, and D. There is no partnership agreement of any type. Partners A, B, and C want X admitted as a new partner, but D does not.

A, B, and C call a meeting and vote in favour of X as a partner. D votes against the proposal.

a) Is X a new partner?

The Consequences of Partnership

The consequences of entering into a partnership are serious. An individual who does so will have liability to outsiders for conduct of the other partners and employees of the partnership.

A Partner's Responsibilities to the Partnership

Courts place strong obligations of trust on business partners, and a partner owes a fiduciary duty (see Chapter 4) to the other members of the partnership. One partner could not, for example, take advantage of the others by stealing a business opportunity in the same type of business in which the partnership is involved. It is up to the partnership to decide whether the opportunity is good or not. If the partnership declines to act on any business opening, an individual partner is free to take full personal advantage of it. In such circumstances, it is advisable for that partner to obtain a written release from the other partners.

Similarly, the courts would find a partner in breach of fiduciary duty if that individual failed to reveal business opportunities to the other partners. Consider a case in which the partnership is having difficulty selling a piece of real estate for $100,000, and decides to reduce the price. One partner knows that a potential buyer is in fact willing to pay the original asking price. That partner cannot keep this knowledge a secret, buy the property at the lower price, and resell it to the buyer later at the full price.

■■ *Critical Concepts of* Responsibilities to the Partnership

- Business partners owe a fiduciary duty to each other.
- The duty applies to business opportunities within the same area of business only.
- Partners can decline any business opportunity and consent to an individual partner's using it for personal advantage.

Fiduciary   Hi-fi (high fidelity) is a precise, or faithful, reproduction of sound, and derives from *fides* (faith), the same Latin source for **fiduciary**. Fiduciary duty, then, is an obligation to show the *utmost good faith* in dealing with others. The highest standard of good faith is to be applied once a fiduciary relationship is established. The other party's interest must be put above your own. You must do unto your partner as you would have your partner do unto you. This includes the relationship between:

Legalese

- business partners
- directors of a corporation and the corporation
- applicants for insurance on application forms given by the insurance company
- professional advisors, such as accountants and lawyers, and their clients

■ *Business Law* Applied

⑥ Harris and Tweed agreed to set up an accounting firm together. Harris was introduced to Armroster at a party, and said he would be happy to do a little "moonlighting," looking after Armroster's firm's books in the evenings after normal business hours. Harris did not tell Tweed about the agreement, and kept all of the money that Armroster paid him.

Tweed later found out about the arrangement, and demanded half the fee.

   a) Did Tweed have any right to a share in the fee?

A Partner's Responsibilities to Outsiders

Perhaps the greatest liability that a partner faces is being responsible for the acts of fellow partners. If one partner enters into a contract in the partnership's name, all members are individually held to that agreement, as well as the partnership itself. Partners can restrict the authority of any one of their members, but unless outsiders are made aware of that limitation, they are not bound by it.

Partners are generally regarded as having the authority to sign contracts on behalf of the partnership (apparent authority). Any private restrictions on this usual or normal authority are not binding on outsiders unless they are specifically told of the limitations. This is sometimes called the **indoor management rule**—"indoor," or private, management restrictions do not affect outsiders. It is the principle that a person dealing with a corporation is entitled to assume that its internal rules have been complied with unless it is apparent that such is not the case.

Limitations of a Partner's Rights

There are two limitations on a partner's right to bind the partnership to any agreement. Contracts that are made outside the normal course of business will not be binding on the partnership. For example, a partner in a clothing store orders a large supply of books on gardening—an action not in the normal course of running a clothing store. The book supplier could not enforce this contract against the partnership.

Similarly, unless specific restrictions on a partner's authority are made known to outsiders, the partnership can be held to any agreement that a partner makes on behalf of the business. If, for example, the partners in a clothing store inform the Arrow Shirt Company that no partner can place an order for an amount over $10,000, the store cannot be held liable should one partner in fact order $15,000 worth of inventory. If the shirt company had not been previously told of this policy, it could enforce the contract for $15,000.

---

indoor management rule

the principle that a person dealing with a corporation is entitled to assume that its internal rules have been complied with unless it is apparent that such is not the case

---

■ *Critical Concepts of* Responsibilities to Outsiders

- ■ A partner is personally responsible for contracts related to the partnership business entered into by all other partners.
- ■ All partners (and the firm) are liable for any tort, especially fraud, perpetrated by any partner, such as misappropriations of client trust money.
- ■ Each partner is responsible for acts of any employee which injure anyone (vicarious liability).
- ■ All partners are equally responsible for the above liabilities. This equal responsibility is called **joint liability** (a liability shared by a number of persons, each of whom is personally liable for the full amount of a debt).

joint liability

a liability shared by a number of persons, each of whom is personally liable for the full amount of a debt

---

Legalese

Vicarious   **Vicarious** derives from the Latin word *vicarius*, or substitute. In the term *vicarious liability*, *vicarious* means that you have deputized someone, or given that person authority to act on your behalf. In a partnership agreement, you have deputized all the partners to act on your behalf, and so you are responsible for any of their actions taken in the normal course of business.

■ *Business Law* Applied

❼ **Singh and Ghandi** were partners in a travel agency. The firm specialized in package tours, for which customers always had to pay a deposit of 10 percent of the full cost when the tour was booked. On August 1, the travel agency had $100,000 in its bank account, all of which was owed to a tour organizer. On August 2, Singh withdrew the money and left the country. No one knows where he is now.

The travel agency's customers sued the firm for the return of their deposits.

   a) Was Ghandi liable to repay the money?

❽ Mike Pappas and Chris Christopolous were partners in a record shop called More Music. While Pappas was on vacation in Banff, Christopolous ordered 1,000 copies of a CD by an unknown artist he believed would soon be famous. Christopolous also felt that the business should diversify, and so ordered 100 expensive cameras.

There was a downturn in the business, and More Music was unable to pay anything on either of these two contracts.

a) Was Pappas personally liable on the contract with the supplier of the CDs?
b) Was Pappas personally liable on the contract with the supplier of the cameras?
c) If Pappas and Christopolous had a written partnership agreement, specifying that all contracts must be signed by both partners, would Pappas's liability be any different?

❾ More Music's troubles have only just begun. The company that supplied the CDs submitted an invoice for $10,000. Full payment was requested immediately, or it would sue More Music for breach of the contract that Christopolous had signed.

After other secured debts were paid, More Music had assets of only $2,000. Pappas had personal assets consisting of:

- a half-interest in More Music
- a house
- a car

a) Which, if any, of Pappas's assets could the record company seize to satisfy its claims?

Disputes in a Partnership

The potential for discord in a partnership is great. Some of the areas that frequently cause problems are:

- breakup of a partnership
- one partner wanting out of the agreement
- death of a partner
- finding money to pay the deceased partner's estate
- unequal contribution of work or money to the partnership
- new partners
- deciding whether a new partner can join the firm
- expanding into new types of business
- deciding if a new business opportunity should be undertaken

The Partnership Act

Partnerships were one of the most common ways of carrying on business until corporations took over that role in the 20th century. In 1890 in England the many laws regarding partnership were collected in one act called the *Partnership Act*. All Canadian partnership acts are based on this act and the sections remain largely unchanged from the original drafting.

Ownership Agreements   Small businesses should make sure that the following vital matters are dealt with in an ownership agreement.

Business Alert!

- The contribution expected from each partner, in money as well as in work
- Banking arrangements for the firm
- Requirements and responsibilities for signing cheques
- How profits are to be divided
- What draws are permitted against future profits
- How the partnership's books are to be maintained, and when/where they will be open for inspection by partners

- How disputes will be settled
- Admissibility of a new partner
- Provisions for a partner wishing to retire from the firm or to sell that interest to an outsider, for the death of a partner, or for the expulsion of a partner
- Mechanisms for evaluating a retiring or deceased partner's interest in dollar terms
- An option for surviving or remaining partners to purchase that interest
- A non-competition clause in the event a partner withdraws from the firm

If a partnership does not have a partnership agreement, then any disputes may have to be settled by the *Partnership Act* if it contains relevant sections. As the act was effectively drafted in 1890, some of the principles contained in it may not correspond to a 21st-century reader's idea of fairness.

A typical set of sections from a partnership act is given next, followed by questions that will help you understand how disputes will be resolved by the application of that act. If you don't like the results, you may want to ensure that you have a partnership agreement with terms that will change the effect of the relevant sections of the partnership act.

The Partnership Act

24. The interests of partners in the partnership property and their rights and duties in relation to the partnership shall be determined, subject to any agreement express or implied between the partners, by the following rules:

1. All the partners are entitled to share equally in the capital and profits of the business, and must contribute equally towards the losses, whether of capital or otherwise, sustained by the firm.
2. The firm must indemnify every partner in respect of payments made and personal liabilities incurred by him or her,
    (a) in the ordinary and proper conduct of the business of the firm; or
    (b) in or about anything necessarily done for the preservation of the business or the property of the firm.
3. A partner making, for the purpose of the partnership, any actual payment or advance beyond the amount of capital that he or she has agreed to subscribe is entitled to interest at the rate of 5 percent per annum from the date of the payment or advance.
4. A partner is not entitled, before the ascertainment of profits, to interest on the capital subscribed by the partner.
5. Every partner may take part in the management of the partnership business.
6. No partner is entitled to remuneration for acting in the partnership business.
7. No person may be introduced as a partner without the consent of all existing partners.
8. Any difference arising as to ordinary matters connected with the partnership business may be decided by a majority of the partners, but no change may be made in the nature of the partnership business without the consent of all existing partners.
9. The partnership books are to be kept at the place of business of the partnership, or the principal place, if there is more than one, and every partner may, when he or she thinks fit, have access to and inspect and copy any of them.

Partnership Agreements

One of the best methods of dealing with disputes in a partnership is to make sure that an agreement among the owners is made at the time the business venture is started. This **partnership agreement**—an agreement between persons which creates a partnership and sets out its terms—will deal with how disputes are to be settled. Shareholders in a corporation have similar concerns. In a corporation, such agreements are known as shareholders' agreements.

partnership agreement
an agreement between persons which creates a partnership and sets out its terms

The Death of a Partner

Why insist on a partnership agreement at the start of a business venture? Consider just one of the items listed in the "Business Alert!" on p. 319–320—provisions for the death of a partner. What happens to a legal partnership when one member dies?

When they first begin operations, few business people consider the potentially devastating effects that death—their own, or their partner's—can have on the firm. A deceased partner's heirs are entitled to demand payment of the full value of that individual's share of the partnership. The partnership itself dies with the partner, but in actuality the business continues—unless there is no money to pay for the claims against it. You might want to be in business with your partner, but you may not want to end up in business with your partner's spouse.

Corporations have a separate legal existence apart from their owners, and do not cease to exist when a shareholder dies. But, for small corporations with only one or a few shareholders, the situation is similar to a partnership. If a shareholder was in a key management position, the surviving owners are faced with problems such as:

- purchasing the deceased's shares (the holder's proportionate interest in the assets of a corporation) to avoid control of the corporation going to people the surviving shareholders do not want
- finding the money to pay for the shares
- establishing the least expensive, but fairest, way of determining the value of the shares

---

Critical Concepts of The Death of a Partner

- When one partner dies, the partnership is dissolved.
- When a shareholder dies, the corporation continues to exist and is not dissolved.

Planning by Agreement

The law stating that the partnership dissolves on death can be varied by a term in the partnership agreement. Such a clause specifically sets out that the partnership will not be dissolved on the death of one member, and determines how the deceased partner's estate will be paid.

Usually, a careful business plan involves a combination of the following factors, plus personal wills that deal specifically with the transfer of the interest in the partnership on death.

Insurance

Life insurance can be obtained for each partner, with the surviving partners the beneficiaries of the policy. In some large businesses, rules insist that not all key personnel, including partners, travel on the same aircraft, so that a situation in which all critical managers die at the same time—thus making continuation of the business impossible—never occurs.

Self-Insurance

The partnership can choose to set aside a percentage of the annual profits in order to cover buying out a deceased partner's interest or shares.

Valuation

The value of the deceased's shares or interests in the business is determined by a formula that is usually contained in a buy-sell clause in the agreement.

Buy-Sell Clauses in a Partnership Agreement

There are many situations in which the owners of a small business might decide to end their association, including one partner's wish to leave, personality conflicts, death, retirement, or long-term disability. Under such circumstances, a buy-sell clause provides a method for determining the value of the business and each owner's share in it. The four usual methods of fixing value are by:

- expert appraisal
- a fixed-priced formula
- arbitration
- a shotgun clause

The appraisal method of evaluation is often avoided because of the potential costs involved. There are people—usually chartered accountants—who specialize in estimating the value of businesses, and their fees can be significant.

A fixed-price formula might value a partner's holding as, for example, "three times earnings." Earnings would then be defined as the average of that partner's share in the business over the past five years. The average over a five-year period is used to prevent an atypical or unusual value being caused by the partner dying in either an exceptionally good, or an unusually poor, year.

The cost of arbitration can be underestimated. Both sides in any dispute might have to retain lawyers. As well, they will have to agree to, and appoint, an arbitrator and pay that individual's fee. Arbitration will likely be held as a mini-trial, at which both sides present evidence of the value of the partnership, including evaluations by two sets of estimators.

A common method of evaluating a business without a formal appraisal is a shotgun buy-sell, named after the shotgun wedding because of the similarity of the do-or-die consequences. Imagine that Smith and Wesson are sole partners, or the only two shareholders in a private corporation. Smith wants out, and so, under the terms of the buy-sell clause in their partnership agreement, he must offer to buy Wesson's shares at a certain price. Wesson has the right to buy Smith's shares at the price first named. If Wesson does not buy Smith's shares at this price, then Smith has the right to buy Wesson's shares at that same price. Thus, Smith is forced to offer a fair price because, if the price is too low, Wesson will purchase Smith's shares for less than they are worth. The weakness in this types of transaction is that, if Smith is currently cash rich and Wesson is suffering a period of being without cash or credit, Smith can offer a low price, knowing that Wesson is not in a position to purchase Smith's share even for that sum.

Forced Buy-Sell Clauses

These clauses are worded so that when a specific event—such as the death of a partner—takes place, the partner (or the heirs) must sell that individual's shares, and the other partners must purchase them. There is no choice. The purchase price is often set out as a fixed-price formula in the partnership agreement.

Voluntary Buy-Sell Clauses

These clauses are usually of the shotgun variety, and allow a partner to end the partnership at will. One partner might simply want out of the partnership agreement.

A Typical Buy-Sell Clause

If either partner desires to sell her share in the business, she shall be at liberty to do so, and shall first offer such share to the other partner at a price to be agreed upon or fixed by arbitration, and if the other partner shall not, within seven days, accept such offer, then the selling partner shall be at liberty to sell her share to any other person or persons.

■ *Business Law* Applied

⑩ **Michael Bereskin worked** loyally for a small grocery store for 20 years. The business was owned by two partners, Parr and Manza. Parr liked Bereskin and told him that, next year, he would sell him his share of the business and retire. Unfortunately, Parr died six weeks later. Manza does not want Bereskin as a partner.

  a) Does Bereskin have the right to become a partner?

⑪ **Castellian and Lynkowski** are equal partners in a boat-rental business. There is a written partnership agreement containing a shotgun buy-sell clause. Castellian wants to retire, as he has become tired of the business. He believes the business is worth $50,000. Castellian is thinking of offering Lynkowski $10,000 to see if he can get Lynkowski's half-interest for a bargain price, then sell the entire business at a profit, and retire.

  a) Would you advise Castellian to take this course of action?

Limited Partnership

Before the widespread use of corporations, the only way to limit liability was through use of a **limited partnership.** This is a partnership in which some of the partners limit their liability to the amount of their capital contributions and are not active in conducting the business. An investor who does not want to take part in the day-to-day running of the business can still give advice, and be at risk only for the amount of money put into the business. The personal assets of a **limited partner** (a partner in a limited partnership whose liability is limited to the amount of his or her capital contribution) cannot be seized.

There are two types of partners in a limited partnership—the general partner and the limited partner. A **general partner** is a partner in a limited partnership whose liability is not limited, and who usually runs the business. It is only the limited or silent partners who are prevented from taking part in day-to-day management.

To obtain protection as a limited partner, the business must register as a limited partnership under relevant provincial legislation. Most provinces have an act specifically called the *Limited Partnership Act*, which usually requires certain information to be given on the public registration form. This generally includes:

limited partnership
a partnership in which some of the partners limit their liability to the amount of their capital contributions and are not active in conducting the business

limited partner
a partner in a limited partnership whose liability is limited to the amount of his or her capital contribution

general partner
a partner in a limited partnership whose liability is not limited, and who usually runs the business

- the firm's name
- the name and address of each general partner
- the name and address of each limited partner
- the date the partnership commences
- the date the limited partnership is to end

Limited partners become liable as general partners if:

- the partnership is not registered as set out above
- the partnership continues beyond its expiry date without a renewal certificate being filed showing the intention to extend the limited partnership
- false or misleading statements are given on the certificate of registration
- a limited partner takes an active part in the management of the business
- a limited partner's name is used in conjunction with the firm's name, or a limited partner claims to be a general partner

Though less common than they used to be, limited partnerships are being used in some new forms of business organizations. In the world of franchising, for example, Journey's End Motel uses a limited partnership in the structure of its business organization.

Business Law Applied

⑫ **A creditor has** a $100,000 judgment against a certain partnership. The business is valueless. The partners have a written partnership agreement making A and B general partners, and C a limited partner whose contribution is $10,000. C has a house worth $100,000, but A and B have no personal assets.

The creditor searches, and finds no registration of the limited partnership.

   a) What right has the creditor against C?
   b) Is C's liability limited to $10,000 because he is a limited partner?

Limited Liability Partnerships

limited liability partnership

a partnership in which partners who are not negligent are not personally liable for losses caused by the negligence of another partner or of an employee directly supervised by another partner

Both Alberta and Ontario have passed amendments to their partnership acts which permit a new type of partnership called a **limited liability partnership**—a partnership in which partners who are not negligent are not personally liable for losses caused by the negligence of another partner or of an employee directly supervised by another partner. To have this limitation, the partnership must be registered as such and the term "limited liability partnership" must be clearly shown on letterhead and signs so that clients are made aware that they are dealing with a limited liability partnership before they engage that partnership. The partnership name must contain a notice of the limitation of liability such as, "Smith and Jones, LLP."

The partnership as a business continues to be liable for the negligence of any partner or employee, and so the firm's assets remain at risk.

Ending a Partnership

Most partnership agreements have terms that set out the requirements for ending the partnership. One common term is that if one partner wants out, the partnership is not dissolved, but that partner's share is purchased by the remaining partners under the conditions of a buy-sell clause.

In the absence of a partnership agreement, the association is still very easy to bring to an end. This is an advantage to a party wanting to do so, but it is a great disadvantage to partners who want to continue the business. Dissolution of a partnership means the business, including the assets, must be sold, all creditors paid, and, if there is any money left over, it must then be divided among the partners.

A partnership can be dissolved, unless the terms of the partnership agreement provide to the contrary, when:

- Any partner gives notice of intention to withdraw and dissolve the partnership.
- A partner dies, declares bankruptcy, or becomes insolvent.
- A date is specified in the partnership agreement to bring the partnership to an end.
- A court order is issued under the provincial partnership act. The court might make this order on several grounds:
    a) the business is operating continually at a loss
    b) the business is engaged in some illegal activity
    c) one partner becomes mentally incompetent, or is unwilling or unable to perform partnership responsibilities
    d) dissolution is just or equitable

Franchises

What Is a Franchise?

A franchise in law is a special kind of licence, granting the right to use trademarks, trade names, and a business system for products and services.

A franchise agreement is made between the founding company—the franchisor—and the small business outlet—the franchisee. Because of the extreme difficulty in differentiating between these two terms, the founding company is usually referred to as the parent company.

Franchising, adaptable to a wide number and variety of companies, is a $90 million business in Canada. Some of the currently most successful franchises are McDonald's and Canadian Tire.

Franchising has many advantages. To the founding company it offers expansion without expenditure of capital. It also offers the large multinational corporations the chance to imitate small business patterns within their large organizations. One of the current theories is that small businesses are more flexible and sensitive to customer demands. The franchise arrangement seems to combine the best of large and small business—the small-business person has access to sophisticated marketing and design that only a large corporation can afford, as well as a complete system that has been tried and proven successful. As well, the franchise arrangement provides working systems that can be inspected.

Business entrepreneurs often assume that purchasing one of these working systems means their business is more likely to succeed. While this is frequently true, franchising is a trouble-fraught area. Many small businesses are unhappy with their situation, and several large litigation matters are in progress against franchise corporations by groups of their franchisees.

The Standard Franchise Agreement

These agreements are governed by normal contract law. There are standard form contracts that contain many of the terms that appear in other standard form agreements. Some of the terms that are unique to franchise agreements are as follows.

- Initiation fee/franchise fee—an up-front payment that varies with the prestige of the franchise. The franchise fee for a McDonald's outlet, for example, can be $500,000.
- Royalties—these are usually paid monthly to the parent company, and are based on a percentage of sales or profits.
- Advertising fee—this is usually expressed as a flat rate, and is a contribution to advertising taken out by the parent company for the benefit of all franchises on a regional basis.
- Optional advertising fee—sometimes, the parent company undertakes localized advertising that benefits only a small number of franchisees.

Common Terms of the Standard Form Franchise Agreement

Some clauses are found in the standard form franchise agreement. The following are among the most important.

- Non-competition—the franchisee will agree not to be involved in a competitive business during the franchise agreement term, and for some time after it expires. The validity of this term depends on the reasonableness of the restrictions as to time, geographic area, and subject matter.
- Confidentiality—much of the success of the franchise organization will be internal business systems that it has developed and published in training manuals. Franchisees will have to agree not to reveal these techniques. This will extend after the franchise agreement has been terminated.
- Tied selling—the agreement may require that the franchisee purchase supplies only from the parent company or suppliers that the parent company approves. This arrangement may result in volume discounts; however, unscrupulous parent companies have been suspected of abusing the power given by this type of arrangement and receiving kickbacks. This is a reviewable transaction under the *Competition Act*.
- Exclusivity—this clause prohibits the parent company from selling the rights to another franchise within a defined area without the written consent of the franchisee.
- Right to sue—many franchise agreements contain a clause in which the franchisee acknowledges that the parent company does not intend to be bound by the franchise agreement. In this way, the parent company cannot be sued if it violates the agreement. If you see such a clause in an agreement, you should be very wary of dealing with this parent company, and investigate very thoroughly.

Complaints by Franchisees

The most common complaint by franchisees is that they are not earning the profits that they expected. A franchise agreement is not a guarantee—success depends on many factors, and any business always has risks. It is important to investigate the parent company before signing any franchise agreement. The following complaints are not presented here as facts, but as **allegations** (statements made that have not yet been proved) commonly made by dissatisfied franchisees. The parent companies involved always deny the allegations.

allegations
statements made that have not yet been proved

- The parent company makes its money by taking initiation fees, making it impossible for the franchisee to carry on business, and then closing the franchise. The business is then resold to a new franchisee, who in turn pays a large initiation fee.

- The parent company takes out the lease on the site (head lease), and leases the site in turn to the franchisee (sublease). The parent company adds a secret amount on to the rent, above that set by the owner. For example, the rent from a plaza owner might be $5,000 a month, but the parent company charges the franchisee $6,000 per month. This increase is not disclosed to the franchisee.

- The franchisee pays rent directly to the parent company and, sometimes, the royalty payments are expressed as part of the rent. This gives the parent company exceptional power over the franchisee, because commercial lease law is very strict, with none of the protection found in a residential tenancy. Unsophisticated franchisees, relying on their experience of residential tenancy law, may not realize that being late in paying rent permits the parent company to send in a bailiff and lock out the franchisee. No notice or warning need be given.

- Volume rebates are obtained from original suppliers, but these are not passed on to the franchisees. Sometimes, the franchisees allege that the owners are receiving kickbacks from the suppliers, and are not finding the cheapest supplier of the same quality.

- The parent company inflates average sales figures during sales presentations. Sometimes, it is not revealed that it can be many years before the average is achieved.

Giving a Deposit   It is always very dangerous to give money up front without concurrently obtaining something of equal value in exchange. Many franchisors (parent companies) ask a large deposit or initiation fee on the signing of the franchise agreement. A **deposit** is a sum of money paid by the buyer to the seller, to be forfeited if the buyer does not perform its part of the contract. Not infrequently franchisees have given over their life savings in such an arrangement only to find that the franchise company went bankrupt and the money was used to pay its normal business expenses. While this situation occurs more frequently with start-up franchises, it can happen even with established ones.

At a minimum, franchisees should insist that any money paid to the franchisor corporation be held in trust until the individual franchise unit is completed and turned over to the franchisee. If the franchisor agrees that the money is to be held in trust, then that money cannot be used for any other purpose. The directors of the corporation would likely be personally liable for the amount. Of course, if the directors do not have personal assets, this precaution is of no help to the franchisee.

Unfortunately, franchisees often sign 40-page franchise agreements in the excitement of a franchise trade fair. In their enthusiasm they don't consider the very real need for independent investigation of the franchise and legal and accounting advice.

Buying a Franchise

The purchase of a franchise is a contract, and so all the remedies in contract law apply. But these protections cannot be a substitute for careful business judgment based on very thorough investigation of the intended franchise purchase. Sometimes purchasers do not fully understand the risk involved and incorrectly believe that a franchise is a guarantee of profitability. If a purchaser is relying on statements made by the franchisor, those statements should be in writing, as the next case shows.

Legalese

deposit
a sum of money paid by the buyer to the seller, to be forfeited if the buyer does not perform its part of the contract

447927 Ontario Inc. v. Pizza Pizza Ltd., [1987] 62 O.R. (2d) 114

This case involving Pizza Pizza provides an example of frequent complaints made by franchisees. You will have to judge whether you think the complaints are justified, or a result of unrealistic expectations. The case demonstrates that exemption clauses can be effective. While there are some bases for attacking the clauses and making them ineffective, it is not wise to allow yourself to be put in a position where you have to rely on these legal technical arguments.

Khursheed Hamidani and Mohammed Khan decided to purchase a Pizza Pizza franchise, located in a shopping centre at Jane and Alliance in Toronto. The two had seen the business advertised in the local newspaper.

There were several meetings between Hamidani, Khan, and Pizza Pizza officers about the sale of the franchise. Before signing the agreement, Hamidani and Khan retained a lawyer to negotiate on their behalf. The lawyer made several changes to the agreement. The franchise initiation fee was $30,000.

After taking possession of the business, problems began to develop, and Hamidani and Khan defaulted on the agreement. They were locked out by Pizza Pizza as a result, and the franchise was subsequently sold by the parent company to another franchisee. That franchisee was able to run the business successfully and meet average sales figures for Pizza Pizza operations.

The franchise agreement signed by Hamidani and Khan contained a standard form exemption clause.

Hamidani and Khan sued Pizza Pizza for misrepresenting the profitability of the outlet during the pre-purchase negotiations.

The Court's Decision

The court found against Hamidani and Khan on all issues. It identified four issues of fact and law to be decided.

1. Did any of the statements made in the negotiation process amount to representations in the legal sense—that is, pre-contractual statements of fact, and not of opinion?

There was a conflict in the evidence, in that Hamidani and Khan claimed they were told that the business would earn daily sales of between $4,500 and $5,000 from the outset. Pizza Pizza Ltd. said Hamidani and Khan were told that these were sales averaged over all Pizza Pizza outlets, and were only estimates for an individual unit.

The court found that Pizza Pizza's evidence was more credible, and more consistent with the written material that was also supplied to the plaintiffs before the contract was signed. The statements made by Pizza Pizza were not representations in the technical sense, but were merely estimates.

2. Was there misrepresentation in the sense of any inaccuracy?

The average figures stated for Pizza Pizza outlets were accurate, and the two franchisees did not offer any evidence to the contrary. The fact that the outlet did not achieve the average store results may have been due to the plaintiffs' lack of business skills. Very condemning evidence was the fact that the franchise was resold, and the new owners achieved the average Pizza Pizza outlet earnings.

3. Was there negligence?

There was no fault proven on the part of Pizza Pizza Ltd. in calculating the figures.

4. Was the exemption clause valid?

The franchise agreement contained an exemption clause stating that there was no representation or warranty, unless expressed in writing as part of the agreement. As Hamidani and Khan had retained a lawyer to negotiate the agreement for them, and changes had been made at the request of this lawyer, Hamidani and Khan were not able to establish any of the grounds holding the exemption clause to be ineffective.

Business Alert!

Buying a Franchise While franchising is a very common, and often successful, form of doing business, not all franchisees are happy with their parent companies. In the Ontario legislature, an MPP criticizing the lack of legislative protection for franchisees said, "Franchising is beginning to look like the Wild West of business."

Franchisees often allege that failure is not because of business factors, but because of unfair advantages taken by the parent company. It is wise to be very careful in selecting a franchise operation. Before signing any franchise agreement or handing over any money, make sure you do each of the following.

- Check with several other franchisees—not selected by the sales personnel of the parent company.
- Check with the local Chamber of Commerce, Better Business Bureau, and provincial consumer and commercial affairs department yourself.

- Retain a lawyer and an accountant early in the proceedings.
- Ask your bank manager to check into the parent company.

Law Reform

Several provinces have instituted special legislation to protect franchisees. Other provinces have discussed such legislation, but have not as yet enacted it.

This legislation usually requires that parent companies:

- file financial statements publicly
- give a history of any bankruptcy or criminal records of their officers and directors
- list all past and current lawsuits alleging deceptive business practices
- list all franchisees, current and past

The disclosure requirements are enforced strictly by the courts. The disclosure must be complete in that all information must be contained in the disclosure documents and they must be delivered before the purchaser commits to buy the franchise.

1490664 Ontario Ltd. v. Dig This Garden Retailers Ltd., [2005] CanLII 25181 (ON C.A.)

Ms. Bellinger, through her numbered company, entered into a Franchise Agreement with Dig This Garden Retailers Ltd. paying a franchise fee of $30,000.00. She received some disclosure and went through a training program in Vancouver before opening her store.

She quickly found that it was not profitable and gave notice of rescission of the franchise agreement suing the Franchisor for damages including return of her initiation fee and set up costs totaling $172,000.00. She also sued the two shareholders of the Corporation who were also its directors and officers and who were directly involved in negotiating the agreement.

A Trial Court found for Ms. Bellinger. The Franchisor appealed.

The Court of Appeal's Decision

The Court of Appeal found that although Dig This Garden Retailers did make substantial disclosure in that they complied with about 70% of the Act, that was not sufficient. An additional failure was that they gave it in bits and pieces. The Act required complete disclosure of all the information listed in it and that it be in one document before signing the franchise agreement. Ms. Bellinger was therefore entitled to claim recession.

Dig This Garden Retailers alleged that if she claimed rescission she could not also claim damages. The Court stated that this might be the position at common law, however, the statute gave her a statutory right to rescission and also gave her a right to damages so that she could claim both.

In addition the Act made anyone associated with the franchise liable. Association was defined to include anyone who controlled the Corporation or who participated in the negotiations. The two individuals sued as defendants met both of those qualifications in that they were shareholders, officers, directors and participants in the negotiation. They were jointly liable with the corporation for the damages.

The Statutory Duty of Good Faith—Franchise Agreements

While in most contracts made between businesses the competition model of "every person for themselves" governs, there are some exceptions. For example, where there is a contractual relationship with an adviser such as a lawyer or an accountant, that advisor owes the client, even a business client, a fiduciary duty.

However, there are some relationships, once a contract is formed, into which the law, either by common law or statute, imposes a middle level duty of good faith.

For example, an insurance company does not have a fiduciary duty to the insured policy holder in paying a claim, but does have a common law duty of good faith to pay out a valid claim and not, for example, to refuse to pay a valid claim, force the insured to sue and use the cost of litigation to make that insured take a lower settlement. Breach of that obligation alone would result in an award of damages relating to bad faith conduct (discussed in Chapter 15: Insurance). Franchise agreements have this duty imposed by statutes in provinces where they have been passed.

■ *Critical Concepts of* Good Faith

■ A party may act in self-interest but must have regard to the interest of the opposite party which means he must deal honestly and reasonably with the opposite party.

■ Good faith is a minimal standard, in the sense that the duty to act in good faith is only breached when a party acts in bad faith. Bad faith is conduct that is contrary to community standards of honesty, reasonableness or fairness.

1117304 Ontario Inc. (Harvey's Restaurants) v. Cara Operations Limited, [2008] CanLII 56704 (ON.S.C.)

The Plaintiff operated a Harvey's Hamburger franchise restaurant pursuant to a License Agreement with the owner of the Harvey's trademarks, Cara Operations Limited. The parties also entered into a License Agreement with Cara for a Church's Chicken restaurant to be operated at the same site.

In July, 2000, with two years of the Church's Chicken license left, Cara terminated that license due to supply problems and offered a rebate of $12,500.00 to the Plaintiff, which was not accepted.

The Plaintiff sued for breach of the statutory duty to act in good faith claiming damages for the present value (i.e. depreciated value) of the equipment used for the chicken operation and for loss of profits.

The Court's Decision

The Court found that all Ontario franchise agreements are governed by the Arthur Wishart Act which states in Section 3:

(1) Every franchise agreement imposes on each party a duty of fair dealing in its performance and enforcement.

(2) A party to a franchise agreement has a right of action for damages against another party to the franchise agreement who breaches the duty of fair dealing in the performance or enforcement of the franchise agreement.

(3) For the purpose of this section, the duty of fair dealing includes the duty to act in good faith and in accordance with reasonable commercial standards.

The court reviewed the statutory duty of good faith and noted that in franchise relationships, a party may act self-interestedly; however, in doing so, that party must also have regard to the legitimate interests of the other party. As long as that party deals honestly and reasonably with the other party, the other party's interests are not paramount. Good faith is only breached when a party acts in bad faith; bad faith conduct is conduct that is contrary to community standards of honesty, reasonableness or fairness.

The duty of good faith can be contrasted with the concepts of unconscionability and fiduciary duty. When a party acts unconscionably, it engages in excessively self-interested or exploitative conduct. A fiduciary party, on the other hand, acts solely in the interests of the other party. Such action is entirely selfless. Good faith can be seen as embodying a middle ground between these two categories of selfish and selfless behaviour.

There was no termination provision in the chicken license. The offer of $12,500.00 was not reasonable and was given in a "take it or leave it" manner both of which were seen as a breach of duty to act in good faith.

The Plaintiff was entitled to damages. The Plaintiff could prove the loss of the value of the equipment purchased originally at $70,000.00 but having a remaining present day value of $20,000.00; but could not prove any loss of profits. The Court awarded the Plaintiff damages of $20,000.00 for the loss of the present value of the equipment.

Franchise ADR

Even with profitable franchise business concepts and best practices, there will be problems to overcome and disputes to settle. To meet the challenge of how to establish cost effective dispute resolution mechanisms to avoid both the skyrocketing costs of litigation and the damaging consequence to the franchise brand of public trials, the Canadian Franchise Association has initiated an ombudsman program. The project was spearheaded by McDonald's Canada.

In Summation

Starting a Business

Restrictions on choosing a name come from several areas of law:

- The name cannot trade on another person's or business's reputation so as to deceive the public. This is known as passing off.
- A name cannot be similar to a registered trademark, whether it deceives the public or not.
- The words *Limited* or *Inc.* cannot be used unless the business is a corporation.

Protection of Personal Assets

- The form of a business is an important consideration to a business person from the point of view of protection of the owner's personal assets from business creditors.
- The forms of business are:
  a) sole proprietorship
  b) partnership
  c) limited partnership
  d) corporation

Sole Proprietorship

- This is a one-person business. There are very few legal restrictions, but if the owner's first and last name is not used, it must be registered publicly so that the public will know who is behind the business name.

Partnership

- A partnership is an association of two or more people for business purposes, with a view to profit.
- All partnership names must be registered.
- A partnership can be intentional, but it can also be unintentional—that is, implied by the court.
- While partners can decide how various matters are to be resolved by a partnership agreement, in the absence of such a document, the *Partnership Act* will be used to settle matters which are often disputed, such as division of profits, the right to take part in management of the business, and the right to salary for work done by a partner for the partnership business.
- Partnership agreements can vary the *Partnership Act* provisions and also deal with other matters, such as specifying events when one partner can buy out another (buy-sell clauses), and setting out a means for establishing the value of each partner's share of the partnership (shotgun buy-sell clause.)
- The consequences of entering into a partnership are serious:
  a) Partners have a fiduciary duty to each other
  b) Partners are responsible to outsiders for the acts of other partners and employees:
     i)   for contracts made within the usual course of a partnership business
     ii) for torts of partners committed in the course of the partnership business
     iii) for torts of employees by vicarious liability
  c) All partners are jointly responsible for the above liabilities.

Limited Partnerships

- To restrict the above liabilities a limited partnership can be formed.
- The limited partner will not be responsible for the liabilities of the partnership beyond the investment of capital.

- The limited partnership must be registered as a limited partnership.

- The limited partner cannot take an active part in the business.

- In Ontario it is possible to form a limited liability partnership, which permits a partner to be active in the business but restricts her liability to her own torts and those of employees she supervises directly.

Franchises

- Franchises are not treated as a separate legal form. They are a collection of various rights that permit the use of the parent company's business advantage—brand names, logos, confidential recipes and formulas, and so on.

Closing Questions

Partnerships

1. Kathryn Cameron, who has just inherited $1,000,000, is considering going into the travel-agency business with Amy Jones as a partner. Jones has considerable ability, especially in accounting, and will supervise all bookkeeping staff, but she owns only her car and owes $5,000 on credit cards.

    The partnership will have $200,000 in a working capital as a result of a loan from the bank. It will have about $500,000 normally on deposit from customers.
    a) What are the partnership's assets and liabilities? What are the partners' personal assets and liabilities?
    b) What risks are associated with this business?
    c) What are the risks for the partnership and for each partner?
    d) What advice would you give to each partner to limit her exposure?
    e) Assume that Amy cannot pay the amount owing on her credit card. Can the bank sue the partnership for this debt? Assume further that the bank eventually obtains a judgment against Amy. Is there any way that the bank can collect on that judgment against the partnership?

2. The section of the partnership act given in the text states: "… subject to any agreement express or implied between the partners…"
    a) What does this phrase mean and what effect does it have?
    b) What value does it reflect regarding freedom of contract versus control by legislation?
    c) Will this value always work to the benefit of a weaker party? Do you know of legislation which prohibits varying its terms by contract? Does it relate to consumer situations or business situations?

3. On a website, find the section of the *Partnership Act* for your province which is similar to the one given in the topic on disputes in a partnership in the text. If you don't know of a website with this information, try a search with the name of your province followed by the word *statute*. Bring it to class and determine if there are any significant differences between it and the one in the text.

4. Harris Investments Inc. specializes in land speculation, buying land for the purpose of reselling it at a profit. From time to time, Harris Investments finds itself short of cash, and enters into an arrangement with Mitsu Enterprises Ltd., whereby each corporation puts up some money to buy the land.

    In one deal in which Harris Investments and Mitsu Enterprises agreed to buy a piece of land, it was Mitsu Enterprises that signed the agreement. Mitsu Enterprises began to find itself in financial difficulties, and did not close the deal. The market price of the property has dropped, and the vendor wants to sue for his lost profits. Unfortunately, Mitsu Enterprises' efforts to refinance did not work out, and it went into bankruptcy.

    a) Does the vendor have any grounds for suing Harris Investments, even though it did not sign the agreement of purchase and sale?

5. Which of the following would constitute a partnership?

    a) Hank and Rick pooled their money to buy a 1965 Mustang, which they intend to repair and resell.

    b) John and Juan bought a cab together. John drives it during the day, while Juan drives it at night. They split the cost of maintenance.

    c) Karin and Ricki both have delivery services. Whenever one of them has a delivery, she checks with the other to see if she has anything that needs delivered in that direction. The delivery charge for the item is split between them.

    d) Ellis and Joe purchased an old house, which they renovated. When renovations were nearly completed, they purchased another house described as a "handyman's delight," using the first house as collateral for the purchase of the second. The first house is now on the market and renovations are underway on the second house.

6. Alicia Armstrong worked in a pet shop for an hourly rate. One day, she suggested to Ron Briggs, the owner, that they add a dog-grooming saloon at the back of the shop, where Armstrong could wash, trim, and groom dogs. Briggs agreed, and the arrangement was made that he would do the bookings and the pickup and delivery of the dogs, while Armstrong did the grooming. Ron was to receive $5 from the fee for each dog.

    It was agreed that the store sign would be changed to read Pet Shop and Dog Grooming Salon. All went well until the day a valuable show dog that had been sent for a grooming prior to a local kennel show escaped out the back door of the store. When the owner threatened to sue Briggs for the value of the lost dog, Briggs pointed to Armstrong and said, "It has nothing to do with me— she's the one who operates the dog-grooming salon." Armstrong held up her electric dog clippers and her scissors and responded, "You're looking at my assets."

    a) Would the dog owner be successful in establishing that a partnership exists between Armstrong and Briggs?

    b) If Armstrong is not a partner, but is an employee of Briggs, what legal principle might make Briggs responsible for the actions of his employee in allowing the dog to escape?

7. Ally, who is 17, and Taiko, who is 20, decided to set up a partnership to provide costumes to local theatre groups. Ally was an excellent seamstress and would take care of that side of the operation, while Taiko would look after sales. Taiko was an excellent salesperson and, before long, the two of them were extremely busy. It became necessary to acquire two more sewing machines under a lease-to-buy arrangement over a 24-month period.

    A friend of Taiko's provided a loan of $20,000 to the partnership at 10 percent interest to purchase a large quantity of material that would be used to make the costumes. Ron was recently hired as a part-time employee at a rate of $15,000 a year to help Ally with the costume creation. A partnership agreement, which requires the two partners to split any depths or profits, had been created at the time the lease and loan were taken out. Ally has now decided that she wants to leave the partnership.

    a) Is Ally bound by the partnership agreement, and if not, why not?

    b) Since Taiko had entered into the lease, loan, and employment contract on the understanding that these things were partnership contracts, is she in any way obligated to live up to the contracts?

8. Two fishermen in Nova Scotia decided to form a partnership for the purpose of supplying fish to a local cannery. All went well until a dispute arose between the cannery and the partners as to the amount of money owed on a catch that had been delivered. When the cannery refused to issue a cheque, the partners decided to sue. The lawyers for the cannery conducted a partnership-registration search, and found that the fishermen had not registered their partnership as was required under the *Nova Scotia Partnership Act*.

    a) Explain the arguments available to the cannery and the fishermen, and the likely outcome.

9. A hotel operation was owned by a partnership consisting of one general partner, and 10 limited partners who had each put in $100,000. Over the last couple of years the hotel business had fallen off, and it continued to operate at a loss.

   Concerned at how the hotel was being managed, the limited partners asked for a meeting with the general partner, and an accounting of how operations were handled. At the end of that meeting, the limited partners decided to begin meeting quarterly, and requested that the general partner provide them with financial reports to be reviewed at that meeting. The general partner was expected to attend the meeting in order to answer any questions.

   a) Are the limited partners running any risk in the actions they have decided to take?

   b) What recommendations would you make to the limited partners that would help to meet their needs, while retaining their limited liability?

10. Beverly, Jordy, and Will formed a partnership to sell articles and memorabilia related to various futuristic science-fiction movies and television shows. On a holiday to the Far East, Will attended a manufacturers' convention, where he saw excellent reproductions of a medallion worn on a very popular space TV show, and which was to be made available to the market in the next year.

   On his return home, Will raved about the sights he had seen on his holiday, but said nothing about the item that he had come across. He then set up a separate proprietorship under the name Loxana Sales, and placed an order for 2,000 of the medallions, which he intended to sell at $20 each.

   a) Since Will came across the medallion on a personal holiday, is he under any obligation to tell his partners about it?

   b) What would be the result if Will did have a duty to his partners concerning this item?

strategis.ic.gc.ca—Industry Canada. General business information site, including information on trade and investment, business financing, licences, legislation, and regulations.

www.netnation.com—NetNation Communications. Search for free to ensure your website name can be the same as and/or include your business name.

www.betheboss.com—Be the Boss. Information on franchising.

www.franchise-update.com—Franchise Update: The Ultimate Resource for Franchise Opportunities.

www.worldbusinessreview.com—Website for World Business Review. Explores latest trends in business, especially designed for education.

Corporate Law

The Concept of a Corporation

The idea of an artificial legal personality dates back to the time of the Phoenician traders. In medieval times, artists and craftsmen would meet and discuss matters of common interest over a meal, usually dinner. The groups thus became known as *cum panis*, or "with bread." The word *company* derives from this phrase.

In England, merchants and craftsmen formed business organizations known as guilds. It was recognized as important that these organizations should carry on even after current members died, and so the sovereign would issue a royal charter, granting the guild many of the rights of an actual person. This included the power to enter into contracts, and the right to own property and to conduct lawsuits. Thus, the guild survived any change in membership, and would cease to exist only if the monarch cancelled the charter.

The world's oldest corporation is a Canadian company. The Hudson's Bay Company received its charter on May 2, 1670, from Charles II of England. The original name of the company was "The Governor and Company of Adventurers of England Trading into Hudson's Bay."

Separate Legal Person

A corporation is considered to be an artificial person, and has a separate legal existence from its owners. A **legal person** is an entity (a corporation or a human being) recognized at law as having its own legal personality. This distinction has led to the awkward use of the terms *corporate person*, and *natural person* or *individual*, to distinguish between the two. When the word *person* is used on its own, both types of persons are meant. The corporation has been called a legal fiction, as it is only a concept and has no physical existence—therefore, it never "dies." One of the great influences on the formation of the common law, Sir Edward Coke, said of Corporations in 1612: "Corporations cannot commit treason, nor be outlawed nor excommunicated for they have no souls."

The concept of a corporation has become far more accepted and familiar since Lord Coke's day. In 1993, a senior executive of the General Electric Company described that corporation as "having a small company soul in a large company body."

Corporation **Corporation** derives from the Latin word *corpore*, meaning body. A corporation is a group or body of people who join together to form an organization that acts as one person. Of course, a single individual can also form a corporation.

legal person

an entity (a corporation or a human being) recognized at law as having its own legal personality

Legalese

Limited Liability

limited liability

the principle that a corporation can shield owners, directors, and managers from liability for many obligations of the corporation

The concept of a separate legal entity or person is the foundation for **limited liability**, which is the principle that a corporation can shield owners, directors, and managers from liability for many obligations of the corporation. Creditors of a corporation can seize only the corporation's assets—not the shareholders' personal assets, as in a partnership or sole proprietorship. The shareholder loses only the amount of money paid for the shares.

Salomon v. Salomon & Co. Ltd., [1897] A.C. 22 (H.L.)

Joseph Salomon had a successful shoe-manufacturing business and wanted to incorporate. He therefore formed a corporation called Salomon & Co. Ltd., and sold the shoe-manufacturing firm to it. Since the newly formed corporation had no money, Joseph Salomon personally took back a mortgage from the corporation, with the assets of the shoe-manufacturing business as security.

The new corporation continued in the old line of business and, over time, incurred debts from suppliers. Unfortunately, the business ran into many problems and became insolvent. The creditors all brought claims for unpaid accounts. Joseph Salomon was one of those creditors, and sued the corporation for payment of the mortgage. The problem with this was that there was so much owing under the mortgage, Salomon would take all of the assets of the business, leaving nothing to pay the other creditors.

The creditors cried foul, claiming that Joseph Salomon and Salomon & Co. Ltd. were really one and the same. He therefore should not be able to take money in priority over other creditors.

The Court's Decision

The court noted that, in law, a corporation is a separate legal entity from its owners. They affirmed that this concept had a real meaning, and therefore a corporation could give a mortgage to its shareholder (owner) just as if the shareholder were a stranger. Accordingly, Joseph Salomon could enforce his mortgage and take the assets of the business.

Business Alert!

Corporate Assets   The Salomon case was decided at a time when the use of a corporation, and all it implied, was not widely known. Today, before offering credit, sophisticated creditors always search the assets of a corporation to determine if there are any free assets. Normally, small businesses such as Salomon have few assets. Those they do possess are usually subject to a lien from the bank. So, when a person gives credit to a corporation, that person is relying on the fact that the business is sound and able to pay its bills from its income.

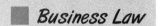

Business Law Applied

❶ **Three shareholders formed** a corporation to carry on their business. To celebrate the end of their first successful year, they went on a fishing trip together, leaving the company in the control of its manager. The aircraft in which the three were travelling crashed on the way to their destination. There were no survivors.

A creditor who had not been paid by the corporation obtained a judgment against it for $10,000. On hearing of the death of all three shareholders, the creditor claimed that the corporation had ceased to exist, and sought to seize the deceased shareholders' personal assets.

a) Was the creditor correct under law?

Incorporating a Business

The process of incorporation is a simple one that involves obtaining the proper form, filling it out, filing it with the appropriate government office, and paying a filing fee. Some stationary companies carry legal forms: incorporation forms sell for about $10. The filing fee will vary but it is usually around $250.

The process of filling out the forms is not that difficult; however, choosing whether incorporation is the correct form of business, and the consideration of problems and dispute resolution by way of a shareholder agreement, are both matters of some complexity and require professional advice from a lawyer and an accountant.

An example of **Articles of Incorporation** (the basic document creating a corporation in most Canadian jurisdictions) for an Ontario corporation is shown in the Appendix to this chapter. This is a one-person company. The particular clauses are worded generally so that they can be used by most small businesses.

The common shares have voting rights. The directors can determine later whether any class of preference shares has voting rights or not. The incorporator (owner) will issue voting common shares to himself and may decide to issue non-voting preference shares to give to family. This transfers any increase in value of the corporation to them, but does not give them a right to run the company.

Articles of Incorporation
the basic document creating a corporation in most Canadian jurisdictions

Keeping the Protection of the Corporate Form

The limited liability of a corporation affords no protection unless it is clearly indicated on every contractual document that the document is being signed on the corporation's behalf. Merely signing an agreement could make the individual personally liable, even if the contract or promissory note states in the body of the document that the agreement is with the corporation. All documents signed on behalf of the corporation should contain a clause such as the following:

The Systems Co., Inc.

Per: _Claire La Mort_____

Claire La Mort, President

You will sometimes see the phrase "authorized to bind the corporation" below the title of the corporate officer. This is required by various provincial registry acts when signing documents that relate to land. It is not necessary to use that phrase in normal business transactions.

Pre-incorporation Contracts   A business might find it necessary to sign a contract before incorporation is granted by the government. In order to avoid personal liability of the individual signing such an agreement, there should be a clause immediately above the signature, expressly stating that the signer does so on behalf of a corporation and without personal liability. This is effective so long as a corporation is in fact subsequently formed.

Business Alert!

Claire La Mort, on behalf of a company to be incorporated, and without personal liability

Dated at Vancouver this 20th day of November, 1997   _Claire La Mort_____
                                                              signature

---

Bank of Nova Scotia v. Radocsay, [1981] 33 O.R. (2d) 785 (C.A.)

John Radocsay went into partnership with one other man, in a business called Classic TV & Sound. Five days later, Radocsay had another company incorporated, under the name Radocsay Televisions Ltd.

Two years later, Radocsay signed a demand promissory note in favour of the bank for $12,500.

The bank sued Radocsay personally when the note was not paid.

Radocsay defended saying he signed on behalf of the corporation, and that as the bank was notified of the new corporation, the bank should have realized that he was signing in this capacity.

I promise to pay on demand the sum of $12,500.

Dated: July 20, 1976

John Radocsay
_____

J. Radocsay

The Court's Decision

The court stated that the incorporation of a firm enables a merchant to carry on that business much as before, but with the advantage of not being liable for the debts of the business if things go wrong. But the merchant must be careful that the debts are those of the corporation and not personal debts. The merchant is the one to reap the advantages of this wonderful new creation, and so is the one who must demonstrate that old contractual relationships have been severed, and new ones created.

It was the duty of the person signing the note to make certain that the note, on its face, clearly showed that it was being signed in a representative capacity, on behalf of a corporation. As the note was signed by Radocsay without anything more, Radocsay was personally liable.

Business Alert!

Signing Corporate Documents   The case of *Bank of Nova Scotia v. Radocsay* demonstrates the need for clarity in signing a corporate document. A number of cases have found the opposite, and have held that a person signing a note on which the corporate name appears somewhere is signing as a representative of the corporation. However, you do not want to be in a position where that is left for a court to decide. The best protection you can have is to make certain all corporate documents are clearly identified as being signed on behalf of the corporation.

■ *Business Law*   Applied

❷ **Eleanor Marathon negotiated** a loan with a small finance company for her new business, Marathon Fashions Inc. The loan was to be used to purchase a new computer system for cash, accounting, and inventory controls. Eleanor Marathon was clear that she did not want to sign a personal guarantee for the loan, and the finance company agreed. As part of the security documentation, Commercial Finance Company asked Marathon to sign a loan repayment agreement which read in part:

> In consideration for a loan by Commercial Finance Company to Marathon Fashions Inc., the undersigned hereby agrees to make the monthly instalments.

> Dated at the City of Edmonton in the Province of Alberta this 26th day of September, 1999

a) In signing this loan agreement, did Marathon take on liability personally, or on behalf of the corporation?

b) What alteration should she make to the agreement to ensure that she does not assume personal liability?

Modern Creditor-Proofing Schemes

The corporate form has been used to protect individuals from liability to creditors in a number of ways. Here is one example of a creditor-proofing scheme used to protect a small-business person from liability on a lease and from trade creditors.

Two corporations are incorporated. One is the parent, in this case called a holding company ("Holdco"). It owns all the shares of a subsidiary, which is the operating company and which is named Perfect Jewelers Inc. Assume the operating company makes a profit of $10,000 in a given year. These profits from Perfect Jewelers could be used to purchase inventory and other assets. Instead, they are sent to the parent company by a way of **dividends** (sums declared by the board of directors as payable to shareholders). The dividends go tax-free from the subsidiary to the parent. The parent then lends the subsidiary the same $10,000 back. The subsidiary, in turn, gives the parent security for the loan by way of a **lien** (a claim against property) on its assets to the extent of $10,000. This security agreement will have priority over claims of creditors to the assets of Perfect Jewelers to the extent of the $10,000.

This transaction can be done any time there is profit in the operating company. After a time, all the assets of the operating company will be subject to a lien in favour of the parent. If the profits had been left in Perfect Jewelers and used to buy assets, these assets could be seized by creditors.

dividends

sums declared by the board of directors as payable to shareholders

lien

a claim against property

A Creditor-Proofing Scheme

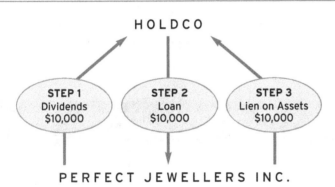

Creditor-Proofing Schemes   Many people believe that if they are dealing with a corporation, they are dealing with a business of substance that can pay its debts. However, the opposite is true for many corporations, especially small companies. In the majority of cases either a creditor (such as a bank) will have liens upon all of the assets, or the owners will have a creditor-proofing scheme in place.

If you are extending credit to any business, you should, at an early stage, obtain advice from an accountant or a lawyer to understand the risks involved and what steps can be taken, if any, to reduce those risks. Learn what a bank does in similar circumstances and take the same precautions.

Business Alert!

Piercing or Lifting the Corporate Veil

The concept of the separate legal identity of a corporation is firmly entrenched in our business law. But the law also recognizes that the corporate form can be abused. There are two well-recognized situations where the corporate veil will be pierced and the persons controlling the corporation will be made liable.

One of these situations is agency. This is governed by principles you studied in Chapter 6. For example, A Corporation may agree with B Corporation to find investors who will buy the shares of B Corporation. A Corporation sells some shares of B Corporation to Mr. X. It turns out that some of the statements made by the A Corporation representative are inaccurate. Mr. X may well have an action directly against B Corporation on the basis of agency law.

Additionally, if the corporation is not a valid operating agency but merely a device or sham used to avoid liability, and fraud or conduct akin to fraud is involved, the corporate form will be penetrated.

It must be emphasized that the corporate veil will not be lifted merely on the basis that it seems fair to do so. The grounds for lifting the corporate veil are very narrow and difficult to establish. However, while the courts have been reluctant to expand the law respecting lifting the corporate veil, both the courts and the legislatures have widely increased directors' liability (a topic reviewed shortly) so often that there are remedies against directors even when there are no grounds to lift the corporate veil.

subsidiary corporation

a separate corporation owned or controlled by a parent corporation

Only the veil of the subsidiary is pierced, thereby making the parent corporation liable. The veil of the parent is *not* pierced, and so the individuals who are shareholders of the parent are not personally liable.

■ *Critical Concepts of* Piercing the Corporate Veil

The corporation is a separate legal entity. That separate form will be pierced on the basis of:

- agency;
- complete control of the corporation by the persons sought to be made liable, and the use of the corporation for fraud or like conduct.

Transamerica Life Insurance Company v. Canada Life Assurance Co., [1996] 28 O.R. (3d) 424 (Ont. Ct. Gen. Div.)

Canada Life was an insurance company that invested the premiums paid by its customers in mortgages. It found more investment opportunities that it could use, and so it decided to incorporate a wholly owned **subsidiary corporation**—a separate corporation owned or controlled by a parent corporation—called Canada Life Mortgage Services Limited (C.L.M.S.), to make these mortgage investment opportunities available to other investors for a fee.

The plaintiff, Transamerica Life Insurance Company, made 54 mortgage loans which were arranged by C.L.M.S. Many went into default. The plaintiffs sued C.L.M.S. on the basis that C.L.M.S. had agreed to underwrite the mortgage loans, which meant investigating and doing a risk assessment. C.L.M.S. responded that it had only agreed to act as a broker, that is, to bring the plaintiff into contact with a potential borrower, which the plaintiff had to assess for itself.

The plaintiff also sued Canada Life as the parent company, claiming that the corporate veil should be pierced.

The Court's Decision

The corporate veil cannot be pierced merely because it would be "just and equitable" to do so. The court can only look behind the separate corporate existence of C.L.M.S. and attribute liability to its sole shareholder, Canada Life, if there is such complete control of the subsidiary that it is a mere conduit for the parent, and the corporate form is used for fraud or conduct akin to fraud.

Complete control does not mean complete ownership, but control to the extent of domination so that C.L.M.S. did not function on its own. The evidence indicates that the relationship between C.L.M.S. and Canada Life was that of a typical parent and subsidiary. While C.L.M.S. was completely owned by Canada Life and its directors were officers of Canada Life, it did operate a business separate and distinct from its parent. The plaintiff's case did not meet this element of the test for piercing the corporate veil.

The plaintiff also did not meet the second element: the controlling mind (shareholder) must be involved in fraud or similar conduct. While the plaintiff alleged fraud on the part of officers of C.L.M.S., there was no allegation of fraud on the part of any officers of Canada Life. The fraud must be on the part of the dominating person and not on the part of the subsidiary corporation alone. The plaintiff's claim failed with respect to that element of the remedy of piercing the corporate veil as well.

❸ Larry Loophole discovered a piece of real estate that had been a landfill site many years ago. Quite deep under the landfill was a swamp. It was otherwise an excellent site for a residential condominium tower. Larry was an experienced builder and knew that problems would not surface for at least twenty years. He incorporated a business called Value Condominiums Limited of which he was the sole shareholder and director.

Value Condominiums sold all of its units quickly, but the problem also surfaced more quickly than Larry anticipated. The purchasers want to sue Larry personally because Value Condominiums has no assets. All of the profits of Value Condominiums were paid to Larry as dividends.

a) Is the fact that all of the dividends of Value Condominiums were paid to Larry sufficient to establish personal liability on Larry? What is the name of the legal remedy that the purchasers will rely on in these circumstances?

b) It is clearly not fair that Larry be permitted to use the corporate veil to escape personal liability. Can the corporate veil be pierced on the grounds of unfairness?

c) Are there any grounds for piercing the corporate veil in the above situation? If so, what are they?

Miscellaneous Matters

Two Jurisdictions

An organization can incorporate under either federal or provincial law. All provinces have a *Corporations Act* governing the incorporation of companies. While there are some technical differences among three types of corporations—Letters Patent, **Memorandum of Association** (a document setting out the essential terms of an agreement to form a corporation), Articles of Incorporation—these are being eliminated by changes in the law. For our purposes, we will assume that all firms are incorporated under the articles of incorporation process.

> **memorandum of association**
> a document setting out the essential terms of an agreement to form a corporation

The scope of the business decides whether incorporation should be at the federal or provincial level. If a company is going to be operating Canada-wide then, obviously, incorporation should also be Canada-wide. The Bay is an example of a Canadian corporation with branches in most areas of the country.

If a business will operate only locally, within one province, then that company should seek incorporation under the appropriate provincial act. A ski resort that is going to operate only in British Columbia would incorporate under the *British Columbia Corporations Act*; a grocery store that will operate solely in Toronto should incorporate under the *Ontario Corporations Act*.

The various corporations acts outline a set of rules that govern the operation of corporations. In one way, these acts are similar to the partnership acts in content and purpose, but the corporations acts are far more complicated.

Public and Private Corporations

There are two types of corporations—public and private. In some provinces, public companies are technically called offering companies, since they sell their shares to the public; they are also known as reporting companies, as they must file additional financial information to government agencies that oversee the sale of shares in the stock market. Public companies, such as International Business Machines (IBM), are also referred to as **broadly held corporations**, because they are corporations whose shares are publicly traded on the stock market and who have a wide range of shareholders; private companies are referred to as **closely held corporations** (corporations which do not sell shares to the public).

> **broadly held corporations**
> corporations whose shares are publicly traded on the stock market and who have a wide range of shareholders
>
> **closely held corporations**
> corporations which do not sell shares to the public

Private companies do not sell shares, and are thus known as non-offering, non-reporting, or non-distributing companies. For ease of reference, we refer to companies as either public or private.

Corporate Securities

Advantages of the corporate form of business include the flexibility in raising money, combined with possible protection of the personal assets of the owners of the business. The corporation has two unique ways to raise money—selling part of the right to share in profits (shares/stocks) or by loans (bonds). These are called corporate securities. These two forms of investment are best known in public companies, and can be seen in the financial sections of daily newspapers, where market prices are listed.

Corporations can also raise money by private arrangement with banks and other financial institutions.

Shares

Most of us think of a company shareholder as an owner, but there are important restrictions on the rights of the shareholder, who, for example, has no entitlement to the use of the assets of the company. A shareholder has a right to share in the corporation's assets on the **winding up** of the corporation (dissolving, ending a corporation) if there are any assets after all creditors are paid. A shareholder of Bell Canada cannot walk into a phone centre and take a phone, saying, "I'm an owner, I have a right to this, it's an asset of Bell Canada."

A shareholder is an investor who has a right to share in the profits of a company only if a dividend is declared. The shareholder takes a risk on whether the company will make a profit. There is no automatic right to a dividend, even if a profit is declared by the board of directors. Nor is there automatic distribution of all profits to shareholders, as some may be retained for other uses (such as new-product development). The directors face two competing interests—keeping profits for business use and expansion, and pleasing shareholders so as to maintain the company's image as an attractive investment.

There are two ways that a **share** (the holder's proportionate interest in the assets of a corporation) can give a return on the investment:

- capital increase—the value of the share price has increased because the worth of the company and its potential for profit have increased
- dividend—this is similar to the payment of interest on a loan. It is income to the shareholder, and is paid as a share in the profits of the company

The Pros and Cons of Issuing Shares

The advantage of raising money by issuing shares is that there is no need to make any repayment in the early years of a business. This is a distinct benefit, because a new company is unlikely to earn a profit for several years. If the money were raised by bonds, the corporation would have to make regular payments, even though it did not earn any profit.

On the other hand, shares usually contain voting rights. The more shares sold, the greater the chance of control going out of the company founders' hands. Apple Computer is an example of this. The inventors lost control of the company, were removed from the board of directors, and were fired as employees.

Types of Shares

There are generally two types of shares—common and preferred—but there are many sub-categories within each. Preferred shares are usually given priority in payment of dividends and

---

winding up
dissolving, ending a corporation

share
the holder's proportionate interest in the assets of a corporation

of a share in the corporation's assets if the company is wound up. **Common shares** are shares carrying no preferential right to distribution of assets on breakup, but usually carrying voting rights.

Issued/Authorized Share Capital

The organizers of the corporation decide how many shares to issue, having first considered both present and future monetary needs. The **authorized share capital** is the maximum number (or value) of shares that a corporation is permitted by its charter to issue. It is difficult to change this figure once incorporation is granted, and so most companies provide for flexibility in the amount right from day one. Authorized share capital determines how many shares a corporation can issue. Issued or allotted shares are the shares the corporation actually does issue.

Voting/Non-Voting Shares

Shares can be either voting or non-voting. The holder of non-voting shares has the right to participate in corporate profitability but not control. In a family business, parents might give non-voting shares to children at any early age to provide an investment income for them. In this way, adults keep all the voting shares—and hence control of the corporation—to themselves.

A corporation might have:

Authorized share capital	1000
Issued share capital	
Common	100
Preferred	200
Total	300
Unissued share capital	700

Proxy   In the context of shares in a public company, **proxy** means agent or delegate. It has to come to mean informally the form a shareholder signs, authorizing someone else to vote the shares. Management of public corporations usually circulates proxy forms with the announcement of the annual shareholders' meetings. Many such annual meetings are poorly attended, and shareholders typically sign over their voting rights by proxy to management. This means that senior management virtually controls the election of the board of directors—the people who decide management salaries.

Bonds

Corporations can also raise money by borrowing. By issuing a document called a **bond** (a certificate of a debt owed by a corporation), the corporation acknowledges that a certain amount of money has been lent to it, and will be paid back with interest at stated times. Unlike shares, the amount due under the bonds must be paid even if the company shows no profit or no dividend is declared.

Canada Savings Bonds are perhaps the best-known form of bonds. By buying them, a person is contributing to the funding of the federal government, which promises to pay a fixed rate of interest each year. Corporate bonds work in the same way.

Bonds may include more than an acknowledgment of debt; they also may include mortgage-type security. This mortgage is a charge on the corporate assets.

The advantage of issuing bonds is that they do not carry voting rights; thus, there is no danger of loss of control of the corporation. The disadvantage is that regular payment must be made. If the company is not profitable, it might not be able to meet the payments and could be put out of business by the bondholders.

common shares
shares carrying no preferential right to distribution of assets on breakup, but usually carrying voting rights

authorized share capital
the maximum number (or value) of shares that a corporation is permitted by its charter to issue

Legalese

bond
a certificate of a debt owed by a corporation

Consider the following example. An investor pays $100,000 for a corporate bond that requires annual payments of $10,000 principal, plus 10 percent interest. (To simplify matters, ignore the annual reduction in principal.) Each year the corporation will be required to pay the investor $10,000 principal and $10,000 interest, for a total of $20,000. If the corporation does not make a profit, it will not be able to pay.

If shares were sold for $100,000, and the company was not profitable, no payments would have to be made to the shareholders. The advantage to a new company of selling shares is obvious. The shareholders not only participate in the profits, they also share the risk. New business ventures are not usually profitable in the first few years, and so raising money through the sale of shares relieves the burden of having to make debt payments. On the other hand, there is the risk of losing control of the corporation.

Convertible Bonds

Shares and bonds represent two extremes of the types of securities a corporation can offer when raising money from private sources. There are many combinations of shares and bonds, as varied as the ingenuity of financial experts. Some securities are convertible into another form. For example, some bonds have provisions that they can be converted to voting shares if the corporation fails to make a payment. The terms of each series of shares or bonds must be examined to see the rights associated with each.

The Structure of a Corporation

A corporation is divided generally into three areas:

- shareholders—the people who have power to elect members of the board of directors
- **board of directors**—the governing body of a corporation, responsible for the management of its business and affairs
- officers—the executives who carry out the day-to-day management of the corporation

board of directors

the governing body of a corporation, responsible for the management of its business and affairs

Corporate Structure Versus Government Structure

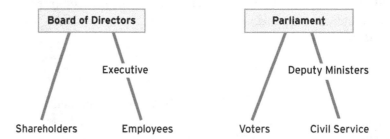

Shareholders

The same sections of the corporations acts apply to shareholders' rights for both public and private companies, but different sections are usually most relevant to the different shareholders' disputes.

The main problem for shareholders in public corporations is that they have a very limited right to information and no real control or influence over how the company operates. The separation of management and ownership in a corporate structure means that the shareholder, who is really an investor and not an owner, has little to do with the running of the company.

The concerns of shareholders in private companies are similar to those encountered in partnerships, including disagreements among the owners.

Shareholders in a Public Corporation

Shareholders are entitled only to certain confidential information of the corporation. They do not have the right to know the daily business of the company—such as new deals in the making, or trade secrets. An investor could not, for example, buy shares in Coca-Cola Limited, and then demand to know the secret formula for the making of Coca-Cola.

Shareholders do not owe a fiduciary duty to the corporation. A shareholder can own shares in Loblaws and the Bay, and owe no duty to either. Indeed, that shareholder can start a rival retail department store in competition with both. This is one reason why shareholders have a very limited right to corporate information.

Critical Concepts of Shareholders' Right to Information

Shareholders have the right:

- to see the **financial statements** (annual accounting statements that normally consist of a balance sheet and income statements) of the company, but not to see the day-to-day accounting books, business files, and business transactions.

- to apply to the court to appoint an **inspector** (a person appointed by the court to investigate the affairs of a corporation) if it can be shown that there is a serious concern about corporate mismanagement. However, the corporations acts require a certain minimum percentage of shareholders (the lowest being 5 percent in B.C.) to make this application. It is hard to obtain the required percentage of shareholders in large public corporations.

- to know whether directors have been purchasing shares of the corporation, if it is a public company. This is one type of **insider trading** (the use of a corporation's confidential information to buy or sell its securities). Directors must report their purchases or sales of shares, so that shareholders can tell whether they have been using confidential information to make personal profits.

financial statements
annual accounting statements that normally consist of a balance sheet and income statements

inspector
a person appointed by the court to investigate the affairs of a corporation

insider trading
the use of a corporation's confidential information to buy or sell its securities

---

Business Law Applied

❹ **Sandra Keho is** a shareholder of Estate Best Development Corporation Limited, a large public real estate development company. She learned of a rumour that this corporation may be buying a particular piece of real estate for development. Keho thought this a bad idea, and asked the president of the corporation if the rumour was true. The president refused to answer. She then asked certain directors of the corporation, but they too refused to tell her.

The annual shareholders' meeting does not take place for another nine months, and Keho considers this too long to wait to ask any questions.

a) Does Keho have the right to call a meeting of the corporation before the annual meeting?
b) Does she have a right as a shareholder to force the corporation to reveal the information that she seeks?

Control in a Public Corporation

The separation of powers and functions in a corporation is roughly similar to that of voters in a democracy. People who are familiar with small corporations where the same people are shareholders, directors, and officers might not realize that shareholders have very limited control in a public company. Although there are additional remedies for shareholders, the only real control they have over the corporation is the ability to vote out board members—just as voters have only that remedy and control over Parliament. The large public corporation functions more like a small monarchy than a democracy. Often it is senior management that controls the corporation—not the shareholders.

This control is done by use of the proxy form. Management, in co-operation with the board of directors, controls the mailing out of the notice of the shareholders' annual meeting, and the proxy forms are sent in the same package. In the accompanying correspondence, management usually suggests whom they want the shareholders to nominate for their proxies—normally management itself. By doing this, senior management is, in effect, controlling who is elected to the board of directors. Therefore, senior management significantly influences the election of the very people who set the size of management salaries.

Most shareholders are unaware of the consequences of signing the proxy form, and do so according to management's recommendation as a matter of course.

Because of this use of proxies, public corporations most often act as autonomous bodies run by management, whose acts are rubber-stamped by directors over whom shareholders have little control.

In 1997 the shareholders of the Bank of Nova Scotia had an item put on the agenda of its annual general meeting (AGM) to discuss putting limitations on senior-executive compensation. Merely getting such an item on the agenda was viewed as a great step forward for shareholder power in a public corporation. The shareholders, of course, had no expectation that any resolution could be passed to limit executive compensation—and no such resolution was.

Executive Compensation

Various security commissions have passed regulations that require the compensation for top-level executives to be revealed each year. Some governments require disclosure of compensation of senior civil servants. There is no requirement that union leaders reveal their compensation and union leaders have usually refused voluntary disclosure.

The issue of out-of-control executive salaries came to a head in Canada with the firing of Eleanor Clitheroe of Hydro One, an Ontario crown corporation. Clitheroe was fired as CEO of that corporation by a new board of directors alleging that she had received excessive perks and misspent the company's money. At a time when Hydro One had a massive debt of $22 billion, her alleged compensation in 2001 was:

    a) salary and bonuses: $1.6 million
    b) expenses for chauffeur-driven limousines: $330,000
    c) car allowance to buy a Mercedes-Benz: $214,000
    d) vacation pay in lieu of vacation: $172,484
    e) memberships in several exclusive clubs, some with entrance fees of $60,000

Clitheroe sued Hydro One for wrongful dismissal, alleging that her compensation was legal because it was approved by the Hydro One board of directors.

A study by the *Financial Times* published in the *National Post* (July 31, 2002) revealed that out of the 25 largest U.S. companies that had declared bankruptcy in the preceding six-month period, the top executives made more than $3.3 billion from these companies in the year before bankruptcy by way of salary, bonuses, and share sales.

■ *Critical Concepts of* Shareholders' Control

Shareholders have the right:

- to receive notice of, and to attend, annual general meetings of the corporation.
- to call special meetings of the corporation to deal with a particular problem when the board of directors refuses to call one. (A **special meeting** is any meeting of shareholders other than the annual general meeting.) However, a certain percentage (usually unobtainable in large public corporations) of the shareholders must agree to it, and so the right is rarely exercised.
- to vote at shareholder meetings to elect or replace directors, and to confirm or reject what directors have done during the past year (one vote per share).
- to assign voting rights to a proxy.

special meeting
any meeting of shareholders other than the annual general meeting

Business Alert!

Shareholders' Remedies   Because the remedies available to shareholders in a corporation are inadequate, as well as expensive to obtain, shareholders who are unhappy with management are normally advised simply to sell their shares. There have been some successful actions in which shareholders have organized support and replaced the board of directors and, consequently, management. However, such cases are rare and involve considerable expense.

Takeover Bids

A takeover bid is an attempt by a group of investors to acquire a sufficient number of shares so that they can control the corporation and replace the board of directors with the group's own nominees. Ordinarily, obtaining approximately 10 percent of the shares of a public corporation will allow this to be done. If management becomes inefficient, and the business could be run more profitably, an outside group of investors might attempt to gain control of the corporation, replace the board of directors and, in turn, fire current management.

The rules for takeover bids require that if any investors do obtain control, they must then offer to purchase all other shareholders' shares at the same price paid to acquire control.

Shareholder Power   Businesses are often accused of putting profits above all else. Increasingly, shareholder groups are organizing to persuade the corporation's board and management to take social responsibility into account—such as refusing military contracts, showing environmental responsibility, and avoiding discriminatory hiring and promotion practices.

During the Vietnam War, shareholder groups of certain firms in the United States tried to stop these corporations from taking part in business deals that supported the American war effort. In a widely reported incident at a General Motors (U.S.) shareholder meeting, a group of shareholders calling themselves Shareholder Power questioned the board of directors as to why no minority groups were represented on the board. The next year, Dr. Leon Sullivan, a black Baptist clergyman, was appointed to the General Motors board.

Shareholders in Private Corporations

Private corporations are usually run along the same lines as small partnerships, and the most common dispute is a disagreement among the owners. However, there are no rules similar to a partnership act governing disputes among shareholders. Thus, a shareholder of a private corporation may simply be squeezed out of any active part in the business, and be unable to sell the shares because there is no market for them. It is difficult to sell shares of a small corporation, since a potential investor must be interested in the specific business, and willing to co-operate with the remaining shareholders.

An attempt by one group to take unfair advantage of another single shareholder or group of shareholders in a corporation is called oppression, and special sections of the *Corporations Act* are called shareholder oppression sections.

In private corporations, the founders usually have an understanding that the shares will be split equally, that each individual will be on the board of directors and have a position as an officer of the corporation, and that all business will be done by agreement. While this happens in the early stages, problems may arise, and one group of shareholders may change this balance of power arrangement. Courts have extended the concept of oppression so that it includes inability to co-operate resulting in a deadlocked company.

The **oppression remedy**—a statutory procedure allowing individual shareholders to seek a personal remedy if they have been unfairly treated—has been called a charter of rights for shareholders because it gives the court very wide powers to remedy oppressive conduct. Both federal and provincial acts contain oppression remedies.

oppression remedy

a statutory procedure allowing individual shareholders to seek a personal remedy if they have been unfairly treated

Shareholder Oppression

The relevant section of the federal *Corporations Act* is typical of how legislation deals with this problem across the country. In reading this section, remember that shareholder is included in the term *security holder*.

---

241 Canada Business Corporations Act, R.S.C.

---

(1) Application to Court Re Oppression.—A complainant may apply to a court for an order under this section.

(2) Grounds.—If, upon an application under subsection (1), the court is satisfied that in respect of a corporation or any of its affiliates

   a) any act or omission of the corporation or any of its affiliates effects a result,

   b) the business or affairs of the corporation or any of its affiliates are or have been carried on or conducted in a manner, or

   c) the powers of the directors of the corporation or any of its affiliates are or have been exercised in a manner, or

   d) that is oppressive and unfairly prejudicial to or that unfair disregards the interests of any security holder, creditor, director or officer, the court may make an order to rectify the matters complained of.

Remedies for Shareholder Oppression

The powers given to the court under this section are very wide, and able to be adapted to a great number of situations.

---

241 (3) Canada Business Corporations Act, R.S.C.

Section 241 (3) Powers of Court.—In connection with an application under this section the court may make any interim or final order it thinks fit including, without limiting the generality of the foregoing.

   a) an order restraining the conduct complained of;

   b) an order appointing a receiver or a receiver manager;

c) an order to regulate a corporation's affairs by amending the articles or by-laws or creating or amending a unanimous shareholder agreement;

d) an order directing an issue or exchange of security;

e) an order appointing directors in place of or addition to all or any of the directors in an office;

f) an order directing a corporation, subject to subsection 6, or any other person, to purchase securities of a security holder;

g) an order directing a corporation, subject to subsection 6, or any other person, to pay a security holder any part of the monies paid by him for securities;

h) an order varying or setting aside a transaction or contract to which corporation is a party and compensating the corporation or any party to the transaction or contract;

i) an order requiring a corporation, within a time specified by the court, to produce to the court or an interested person financial statements in form required by section 149 or an accounting in such other form as the court may determine;

j) an order compensating an aggrieved person;

k) an order directing rectification of the registers or other records of a corporation under section 236;

l) an order liquidating and dissolving a corporation;

m) an order directing an investigation under a part XVIII to be made;

n) an order requiring the trial of any issue.

Tilley et al. v. Hails et al., [1992] 7 O.R. (3d) 257

The oppression remedy has often been used to break a deadlock among shareholders when it becomes apparent that the shareholders can no longer co-operate, and the business cannot survive without court intervention.

Alexander J. Tilley founded Tilley Endurables Inc. in 1980. The initial product, a hat designed by Tilley, soon became very popular. The product line was expanded to include a wide variety of sports clothes for men and women, sold in the firm's retail outlets in several Canadian cities.

The marketing success and product recognition of Tilley Endurables has been based on Tilley's close personal identification with the company, and the publicity he has generated on its behalf. The company's catalogues and advertisements contain photographs of Tilley and members of his family and staff wearing the company's products. The logo of Tilley Endurables bears Tilley's likeness. He and the company have been the subject of

many newspaper and magazine articles. To the buying public, Tilley Endurables is closely connected with Alex Tilley.

Tilley met Dennis Hails, who operated Dennis H. Hails Interiors Limited, when Hails undertook interior design work for some of Tilley's stores and for his personal residence.

In 1987, Tilley Endurables was experiencing significant financial difficulty, and Tilley could pay neither Hails nor a number of other creditors. Tilley had unusual skill in product design and marketing, but was weak in the financial management of the company. Hails offered to try to place the company on a proper financial footing, and to inject some capital by way of a loan of $200,000. He later contributed about $1 million in loans to the corporation.

Tilley was initially so grateful to Hails for his help that he offered to give him 50 percent of the company's shares for nothing. By doing so, Tilley was giving up control of the corporation—from that time on, decisions could be made only on agreement between Hails and Tilley. Hails admitted that he did not insist on 50 percent, but would have accepted fewer shares in exchange for the assistance he had offered.

The two men entered into a shareholder agreement, by which Tilley agreed to transfer 50 percent of the shares to Hails, and the board of directors would consist of Tilley and Hails. As well, Tilley was to be president, while Hails was vice-president of the corporation. In practice, Tilley took over product development and related areas, while Hails took over financial management. The shareholder agreement provided for the sale of shares, but only on the death or disability of Hails or Tilley. It did not include provision for the forced sale of shares, or for any other events. Tilley and Hails agreed that they had discussed the matter previously, and Hails had said that he would sell his shares back to Tilley if Tilley demanded.

As time went on, Tilley and Hails found that they were quite incompatible and their relationship became hostile. Hails took several actions that were calculated to drive Tilley out of the business. Tilley complained of a long list of items, but two of the most significant were that Hails published a Tilley Endurables catalogue that, for the first time, did not contain photographs of Tilley or his family wearing the company's clothing. Secondly, Hails caused Tilley to be charged with possession and unsafe storage of an unregistered handgun, contrary to the Criminal Code. As a result, the police came to Tilley's office, placed him under arrest, and took him to the police station where he was photographed and fingerprinted. The gun was an 1890s revolver, part of Tilley's collection of outdoor and military memorabilia.

The charges were withdrawn by the Crown Attorney but, since that incident, Tilley and Hails have not spoken directly, communicating only by memos or through company employees.

Hails had several complaints against Tilley, including Tilley's telling employees and the bank that Hails was leaving, causing the bank to reduce Tilley Endurables' line of credit.

Both Tilley and Hails made applications under the shareholder oppression sections of the relevant provincial corporations act, each asking for a court order that one be required to sell his shares to the other.

The Court's Decision

The court found that a private corporation should be viewed in the same way as a small partnership. Whenever the shareholders could not co-operate, the court could make an order that one of the shareholders sell the shares to the other. Therefore, it was necessary to determine whether it was Tilley or Hails who was responsible for the deadlock in the affairs of Tilley Endurables.

The court found that it was Hails who was responsible. The most important ground was the finding that it was Hails who had Tilley charged and arrested for the weapons offence. If convicted, Tilley would have acquired a criminal record. The charges were groundless, as shown by the Crown Attorney's decision that they be withdrawn. The court found that Hails's conduct was intended to remove Tilley from the management of Tilley Endurables, contrary to the terms of the shareholders agreement, and to force him out of the company—this was a clear case of oppression.

Hails had sought to take unfair advantages of Tilley's— perhaps misguided—generosity in giving him 50 percent of the company's shares. If Hails were permitted to purchase Tilley's shares, it would allow Hails to succeed in his goal of driving Tilley out of the business and obtaining ownership of it for himself. While Tilley had engaged in some conduct that was not in the best interest of the company, it was clearly in retaliation against Hails's actions.

Hails had contributed significant capital to Tilley Endurables by way of loans, and could still claim against Tilley for the return of this money.

Hails was therefore ordered to sell his shares of Tilley Endurables to Tilley at a value to be established by an arbitrator, who was to be chosen by the parties or appointed by the court. In this way, Hails would not walk away empty-handed, but would receive full value for his shares in the company.

■ *Business Law* Applied

⑤ John Cole, a chemical engineer, devised a process for producing an industrial chemical in a completely automated plant. Because he did not have enough money to set up business himself, he took Randy Palsar and Sylvia Kim as financial backers and partners. A new corporation was formed, and all three received equal shares, and were appointed as the only members of the board of directors.

Palsar and Kim became employees of the new corporation—president and vice-president. For tax reasons, Cole became an independent consultant, holding a contract with the corporation. A term of the contract was that it could be cancelled with 60 days' notice by either side.

Bickering soon began. Palsar and Kim were on one side of the arguments; Cole was on the other. At the next shareholders' meeting, Palsar and Kim voted that Cole should not be reappointed to the board.

The new board—consisting of Palsar and Kim—cancelled Cole's consulting contract, giving him 60 days' notice. The board then appointed another technical consultant to become its third member.

Cole feels that he has been squeezed out of the company that was his idea.

   a) Does Cole have any remedy? If so, what is the name of that remedy?

   b) What powers of the courts set out in section 234 (3) above might assist Cole?

❻ Montgomery is a shareholder in Comp-lex Realty Corporation. He is a passive investor, in that he lent $100,000 to the corporation for a specific land-development project and took back shares in return. Kitchener and Clive are the only other shareholders, and the only directors of Comp-lex. They manage the day-to-day affairs of the business.

Comp-lex purchases a piece of land from Kitchener and Clive for $100,000. Montgomery learns that the land is worth only $50,000, and wants to take some action against the corporation, as well as against Kitchener and Clive.

   a) Does Montgomery have any remedy?

   b) What items in section 234 (3) might be of assistance?

Shareholder Agreements

Although the shareholder oppression remedies set out in the acts are extensive, they still depend on obtaining a judge's opinion that there has been some oppression. Therefore, shareholders are well advised to enter into a **shareholder agreement** (see "Ownership Agreements," Chapter 9), an agreement between two or more shareholders, similar to a partnership agreement. A shareholder agreement is a type of ownership agreement and, coupled with an employment contract, is considered the best protection for a shareholder against the problems of dispute. The employment contract ensures that the shareholders cannot be unjustly fired from the corporation.

> **shareholder agreement**
> an agreement between two or more shareholders, similar to a partnership agreement

Shareholders' agreements usually deal with the following common areas of dispute:

- The right to sit on the board of directors
- A right that the other shareholders will not sell to outsiders without giving the right of first refusal
- The right to buy the shares of the other shareholders, or force them to buy the dissident shareholders' shares, when certain events happen
- The method of valuation for the shares, either by formula, arbitration, or a shotgun-style clause

Directors

The directors of a corporation have the power to manage or run the corporation in the sense that they set the policies and make major decisions. The day-to-day management is carried out by the executives, such as the president and vice-president, who are called officers in corporate law. These executives may also have other titles, for example, chief executive officer (CEO) or chief operating officer (COO). The directors' functions are similar to those of Members of Parliament, and the executives' functions are similar to those of senior civil servants. The directors have the power to fire the president and other executives.

In large corporations, the directors choose a management committee to make most decisions, referring only major ones to the full board.

◼ *Critical Concepts of* Directors

- ◼ A private corporation need have only one director, but a public corporation must have at least three.
- ◼ A public corporation must have at least two outside directors, that is, directors who are not officers or employees.
- ◼ Decisions are usually made by a simple majority vote, but the corporate by-laws or the incorporating documents filed with the government at the time of registration may require more than a majority on certain issues.

Directors' Duties

Competence and Fiduciary   Directors have the ultimate control of a corporation, but with that power comes great responsibility. Both the common law, which is developed by judges, and the statute law, which is passed by the legislatures, are increasing the obligations of directors. A well-known article on directors' responsibilities in corporate governance is entitled "Why No Sane Person Should Be a Director of a Public Corporation." While the corporate shield has been maintained to protect shareholders (investors), that shield has been removed respecting directors and officers in many areas.

Canada Business Corporations Act, R.S.C. 1985 G. C-44

117 (1) Duty of Care of Directors and Officers.—Every Director and Officer of a corporation in exercising his powers and discharging his duties shall:

a) act honestly and in good faith with a view to the best interest of the corporation; and

b) exercise the care, diligence and skill that a reasonably prudent person would exercise in comparable circumstances.

◼ *Critical Concepts of* A Director's Duties

Directors must exercise the skill of a reasonable person in performing their duties. If there are any breaches of this standard by the directors, they are subject to the usual tort remedies.

Directors owe a fiduciary duty to the corporation and must:

- ◼ disclose any interest, direct or indirect, on any contracts made with the corporation, and refrain from voting respecting such matters
- ◼ not take personal advantage of business opportunities related to the corporation.

If directors breach their duty, they can be removed from office. Directors cannot pay dividends to shareholders if doing so would make the corporation unable to pay its debts as they come due.

Canadian Aero Services Ltd. v. O'Malley et al., [1974] S.C.R. 592

Canaero was in the business of making maps for mining explorations projects. The president and executive vice-president of the company, who were also directors, were planning and negotiating a mapping contract with the government of Guyana. The project was awaiting Canadian government foreign aid before finalization.

Before approval was received, the two directors resigned, formed their own company, bid on the Guyana deal, and won the contract. The directors, even as employees, had signed no written employment agreement, and so there was no confidentiality or non-competition clause involved. Canaero brought an action against the two former directors, based not on breach of contract, but on breach of a fiduciary duty to act in the company's best interest.

The Court's Decision

The court held that the directors and senior officers of a corporation owe a fiduciary duty to act in the best interest of the company in spite of the absence of any contractual term. The two former directors/officers knew of the Guyana deal because of their position in Canaero. They could not spend a number of years on the Canaero payroll developing a project for that company and then, just as the opportunity was about to be realized, form another corporation and seize the chance for themselves.

The court further held that if the directors wanted to take advantage of an opportunity that the corporation rejected, the directors must still disclose their intent to do so and obtain prior approval.

Business Law Applied

❼ Wilson Arnott was one of three directors of a small manufacturing company. He had recently become friends with a vice-president from a competing firm. They often went away on weekend fishing trips, and frequently played golf together.

The other directors were unhappy about Arnott's contact with a competitor and the possibility of his leaking confidential business plans and information. Arnott maintained it was none of the company's business, since it was part of his personal life.

The other directors tried to remove Arnott from his position on the board.

a) On what grounds could they base their action?
b) Would it be successful?

❽ Harold Elliot was the director of a paint-manufacturing company, Enviro Chemicals Ltd., operating in British Columbia. The firm discovered a new process for making mercury-free paint that was a lot less harmful to the environment than competitors' products.

Enviro Chemicals Ltd. decided that it would not patent the new process, preferring to keep it confidential—as Coca-Cola does with its formula. Before Enviro went into production of its new product, Elliot and a lab employee left the company and moved to Ontario, where they set up their own paint-manufacturing firm. There was no written confidentiality clause with either Elliot or the lab worker.

Enviro Chemicals brought an action to stop Elliot and the employee from producing this new product in Ontario.

a) Would they be successful?
b) Elliot also contacted Enviro Chemicals' long-standing customers in Ontario and made contracts with them for the sale of other paint products. Could Enviro Chemicals stop Elliot's new company from dealing with these customers?

Statutory Liability: Wages, Taxes

The concept of the corporation as a separate entity, which was established in the case of *Salomon v. Salomon*, above, has been firmly upheld in the law. Yet there are an increasing number of situations in which the human agents of a corporation, the directors, officers (senior management), and even employees, may incur personal liability for acts done on behalf of and in the best interests of a corporation.

Businesses are required to collect many taxes and similar items on behalf of the federal and provincial governments. For example, businesses must deduct income tax from employees' paycheques and remit this to the federal government. Businesses also must collect GST and remit it to the federal government. Such sums are considered trust money for the government in the hands of the business. The money taken from employees' salary is a tax credit of the employee. The statutes which require companies to make the various deductions that must be remitted to governments invariably now make directors personally responsible if the funds are not in fact sent to the government.

Directors have the defence of due diligence. This defence, in effect, puts the onus on directors to prove that they have taken precautions to ensure that the money deducted is sent to the government. This defence provides a very narrow window for a director to escape liability. It means that the directors must take action to ensure that the money reaches the government, or the directors will likely pay themselves.

When a business is in good financial shape, there's little concern for directors respecting liability of this type. It is when the business is approaching insolvency that problems occur. The businesses' managers will be desperate for cash, and there will be a nice sum of money in its general bank account because of payroll deductions and taxes collected. However, the fact that these sums are used for valid business expenses, even to keep the business alive, is not a defence. Directors are personally liable if the money doesn't reach the government and they cannot establish a due diligence defence.

Likewise, directors are personally liable under most provincial and federal corporations acts for wages, including vacation pay, owed to employees up to the time of the corporation's bankruptcy. All provinces except the Atlantic provinces impose such liability on directors. Directors are not liable for future wages after the date of the bankruptcy such as termination or severance pay or wrongful dismissal claims.[1]

The time limit respecting the length of responsibility for unpaid wages varies with the acts, but most acts restrict the liability to six months' wages prior to the bankruptcy.

There is at present no due diligence defence in the corporations acts respecting claims for unpaid wages. However, business lobby groups have been requesting that such a defence be added, so the corporations acts may be amended to include one.

Under the Canadian Labour Code, which applies to federally regulated corporations only, directors are liable for severance pay (future wages) as well as unpaid wages to the date of the bankruptcy.

Note that the above liability is imposed by statute and is imposed on the directors by reason of their status alone. A director is liable in this situation simply by having the position. It is not necessary for the director to be personally involved or even have any knowledge of the acts in question. A director can't say as a defence, "Hey, I wasn't at the meeting where that was discussed," and escape responsibility.

---

1. *Barrette v. Caltree*, [1993] 1 S.C.R. 1027.

Directors may also be liable under statutes such as the many environmental-protection acts. These types of statutes are passed for the benefit of the public generally and in that sense are called public welfare statutes. This type of liability is discussed in Chapter 17.

■ *Critical Concepts of* A Director's Statutory Liability

- If the corporation deducts amounts for income tax, PST, GST, unemployment insurance, and the Canada Pension Plan from employee salaries and does not forward that money to the relevant government agency, the directors will be personally liable for those sums.
- Directors have the defence of due diligence if the corporation fails to remit the above deductions.
- Directors may be personally liable under the various provincial corporations acts for six months' unpaid wages for employees if the company goes bankrupt.
- Many public-welfare statutes make directors personally liable for any corporate act that violates these laws. This includes human-rights and environmental-protection legislation.

Directors of Insolvent Corporations   If you are a director of a company that is experiencing financial difficulty, you would be well advised to consult with a lawyer immediately. You may need to resign promptly to avoid personal liability (as described above) which will derive from activities beyond your control. Additionally, in order to prove the defence of due diligence you should leave a paper trail of your efforts to make certain the relevant funds reach the government. For example, send memos to key employees such as bookkeepers, accountants, and the like, insist that deductions be put in a separate trust account, and review cancelled cheques proving sums were remitted.

Business Alert!

Soper v. The Queen, [1998] 1 F.C. 124 (C.A.)

In October 1987, Soper became a director of Ramona Beauchamp International (1976) Inc., which operated a modelling school. In November 1989, he was given a copy of RBI's balance sheet, which indicated a net loss of $132,000. He resigned from the board in February 1988.

However, during the period of his directorship, RBI had not withheld taxes and other deductions, and remitted them to Revenue Canada. Under section 227.1 of the *Income Tax Act*, Soper would be personally liable for those amounts from October 1987 to January 1988, unless he could show he exercised skill, care, and diligence to prevent the failure to remit.

The Court's Decision

A director is expected to act reasonably to fulfill his or her obligations, having regard to his or her level of skill and experience. Here, the director was an experienced business person who became aware of the serious financial difficulties of the company shortly after joining the board. An experienced business person would have wondered about the status of remittances due to Revenue Canada, especially since the financial problems were ongoing. Doing nothing, in these circumstances, does not meet the standard of acting with skill, care, and diligence.

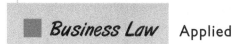

Business Law Applied

⑨ Alice Williams was a director of Hi-Tech Promotions Inc., a Manitoba corporation. The company was experiencing financial difficulty. Williams, a skilled business woman, recommended severe cost-cutting that would have saved to the business. Unfortunately, the other directors would not accept her advice and spent money recklessly. The company went bankrupt.

Revenue Canada made a claim against Williams for $100,000 respecting sums deducted from employees' paycheques for income tax. Williams claims that she was not negligent in acting as a director: it was the other directors who were negligent. Also, when the business was set up she had ensured that there was a system in place so that any money deducted from employees' salaries was sent immediately to the government. She had no idea that the system was not being followed. Additionally, the money was used to save the business and hence kept the employees working longer.

a) Is the fact that she was not negligent a defence for Williams?
b) Is the fact that the money went to try and save the business, and not to her or to any director personally, a defence?
c) Is the fact that Williams honestly believed that the money was being sent to the government according to the system that she set up a defence?
d) Does Williams have any defence?

Personal Liability in Tort

Directors are protected from personal liability when conducting a corporation's business properly. For example, if the corporation breaches a contract, the aggrieved party cannot sue the director who signed the contract on behalf of the corporation. Directors are protected respecting contracts that they sign on behalf of a corporation.

However, a tort is a civil wrong. If a director commits a tort, even if acting in the best interests of the company and within the scope of her authority as a director, she will be personally liable. The torts of most concern to directors are the economic torts. These torts include ways of doing business that are considered unfair in the sense of being beyond what is acceptable competitive behaviour.

For example, the directors of Alpha Shipping Builders Ltd. learned that Beta Designs had spent a lot of money on the research and development of a new very efficient hull design. These directors approached Beta's chief engineer and lured him away from Beta with an offer of much higher pay. The engineer joined Alpha and brought the knowledge of the new design and used it at his new job, thereby saving Alpha considerable research costs. This is the tort of inducing breach of contract. Alpha Shipping is liable, but so are any directors or officers who actually took part in the tort.

There is some protection given to directors. Directors are not liable for matters that arise from concurrent (dual or parallel) liability in tort and contract. If the matter can give rise to a contract claim, that claim must be pursued in contract, where directors have no liability, and not in tort.

For example, a person who had purchased a valid ticket to a theatre was refused admission by the manager because of a personal squabble. The ticket holder sued the manager personally, claiming that the manager had induced the company to breach its contract (thereby committing a tort). But the court held that the real nature of the claim was for a breach of contract by the theatre. It refused to honour its obligation to let the purchaser in to see the show. The purchaser could not use the tort of using breach of contract to obtain personal liability against the manager.

The term "director's liability" is often used. But the same rules apply with respect to officers or employees of the corporation. This liability is usually only of importance if the corporation is insolvent. Since the corporation is liable for acts done by directors, officers, and employees on its behalf, full recovery can be made against it if the corporation has assets.

The case *ADGA Systems International Ltd. v. Valcom Ltd.*, below, is a decision of the Ontario Court of Appeal on directors' liability in tort. It has generated much controversy. Critics ask what is the use of having a corporation if the directors are liable in tort? Supporters of the decision reply that directors are protected from all valid business risks; it is only when a director is personally involved in committing a civil wrong (a tort) that the director is liable.

Will *ADGA Systems* become law across Canada? It may be worth noting that the law in the U.S. on directors' liability in tort has been the same as set out in the *ADGA Systems* case for over 20 years.

Critical Concepts of Director's Liability in Tort

- Directors are not liable for contracts made on behalf of a company.
- Directors are liable for torts they commit on behalf of a corporation.
- Directors must have been personally involved in the tort. It is not sufficient that they were directors at the time that the tort was committed.
- It is not a defence that the directors were acting in the best interests of the corporation or within their scope of authority for the corporation.
- A plaintiff cannot use a tort claim to obtain personal liability of a director when the claim is possibly a contract claim (concurrent tort/contract liability matter).

ADGA Systems International Ltd. v. Valcom Ltd., [1999] 168 D.L.R. (4th) 351 (Ont. CA)

ADGA Systems was in competition with Valcom in the security-systems industry. For several years ADGA Systems held a substantial contract with Correctional Services Canada for technical support and maintenance of security systems in federal prisons. On a call for tenders on renewal of the contract, Correctional Services Canada required all tendering parties to list 25 senior technicians and their qualifications.

Valcom had no such employees but interviewed ADGA employees and used their names on the Valcom tender. Curiously the tenders of ADGA and Valcom had the same names. Valcom got the award. ADGA sued Valcom's sole director and two of its senior employees for inducing breach of contract.

The Court's Decision

The court held that officers, directors, and employees of a corporation are personally responsible for their tortious conduct even though that conduct was directed in a *bona fide* matter in the best interests of the corporation, provided that the conduct was "tortious in itself."

The phrase "tortious in itself" means that the plaintiff cannot use a concurrent liability matter to obtain liability in tort when it would be unsuccessful in contract. For example, if a corporation refuses to pay on a contract, the directors cannot be sued in court for conspiring with their own company for directing that it not pay on the contract. That issue is one of contract only.

Here the conduct was tortious in itself. Valcom had made agreements with employees at ADGA to leave the employment of that company and come to Valcom if it was successful on the bid. This is the tort of inducing breach of contract. The directors of Valcom who participated in making this arrangement with the ADGA employees were personally responsible for the loss to ADGA.

Business Alert!

Directors' Liability   If you are asked to be a director of a corporation of which you are not the controlling shareholder, you should investigate the options given below for your personal protection. In some jurisdictions there are restrictions on directors' obtaining indemnification for personal liability.

- obtain an indemnity from the corporation or its shareholders
- have the corporation take out and pay for directors' liability insurance
- have the corporation set up a trust fund for legal fees to defend actions against directors
- obtain legal advice and consider early resignation if the corporation is in financial difficulties
- perform and document due diligence respecting all government remittances and employee wages

■ *Business Law*   Applied

⑩ **Joel Shuster and** Janet Russell were directors of Lion Corp. Inc. It made a special industrial-strength tape, sold only to manufacturing companies. Shuster was lucky in the gene-pool lottery of life and had inherited considerable wealth. Russell had the more usual luck and was born and remains penniless, living largely on her credit cards.

Russell learned that Fasteners Inc., a new company, was entering into competition with Lion Corp. Russell told the only supplier of the raw film, which is needed for making tape of this particular type, that the people behind Fasteners Inc. had been involved in scams in the U.S. As a result, Fasteners Inc. could not get raw product from this crucial supplier and had to cease operation. Several months later, Fasteners Inc. learned that it was Russell's interference which prevented them from getting supplies. Assume that the acts of Russell are the tort of intentional interference with economic interests and Fasteners Inc. wants to bring an action based on that tort against as many defendants as possible.

a) Has Lion Corp. committed the tort? If so, why?
b) Fasteners Inc. wants to bring a claim against Joel Shuster because Russell has no money. Is Shuster liable? If so, on what basis?
c) Is Russell liable? Does she have a defence that she was acting only as a director of Lion Corp. Inc. and in the best interests of that company? What is the downside of suing Russell?

In Summation

Corporations

- A corporation, in law, is considered a legal person with a separate identity from its shareholders.
- The fact that a corporation has a separate legal existence is the basis of the concept of limited liability. Creditors can look only to the corporation's assets, not to the assets of the owners of the corporation.

- Any contracts signed clearly by an individual on behalf of the corporation and a third party are made between the third party and the corporation.
- This separate identity can be lost in certain circumstances:
  a) the corporate representative does not make the other person aware that he/she is acting in a corporate capacity
  b) the corporate veil is pierced because of agency, or because of fraud or similar conduct by a person who dominates the corporation
- An individual can sign a contract on behalf of a corporation that is not yet incorporated if the correct language is used to notify the opposite party, and the corporation is later actually formed and then adopts the contract.

Corporate Securities

- A corporation can raise money by the issuance of securities. These can have various terms but are divided generally into two types:
  a) equity—shares, stock
  b) debt—bonds
- A share is an interest in the net assets of the corporation (capital).
- A shareholder has a right to a portion of the profits of the corporation, but only if the dividend is declared by the board of directors (income).
- A bond is evidence of a loan and must be repaid with interest at fixed times.

The Structure of a Corporation

A corporation provides a flexible structure for carrying on business. That structure is composed of:
- board of directors
- executive (officers/senior management)
- shareholders

Shareholders

Technically, shareholders are investors with very limited control over a corporation. In a private corporation, shareholders appear to be owners, but that is because the same person or persons are often shareholders, directors, and officers.

- While the same laws apply to all shareholders, some laws are more relevant to shareholders in public corporations and other laws are more relevant to shareholders in private corporations.
- In public corporations, the shareholders' rights that are most pertinent are:
  a) the right to certain limited information, such as the corporation's annual financial statement
  b) the right to vote and elect directors if the shares are voting shares
- In private corporations, a shareholder's usual concerns are that the other shareholders and directors may use the corporate assets for personal gain and against the interests of that shareholder.
- Corporations acts contain shareholder oppression remedies that give shareholders the right to apply to the court in situations where they have been unfairly taken advantage of by the abuse of control in the corporation.

Directors

- Directors have the power to run the company; officers carry out these policies. Directors have certain duties and liabilities.
- Directors' duties are to manage the company's affairs with due care and skill (not be negligent), and to put the company's interest above their own (fiduciary duty).

- Directors' fiduciary duties includes a duty:
  a) to disclose any personal interest in the contract made by the corporation with an outsider
  b) not to take a corporate opportunity for personal benefit
  c) not to compete with the corporation

- Directors' liability, stemming from statute law, includes personal responsibility if amounts deducted from employees' salary (e.g., income tax) or taxes collected (GST, PST) are not sent to the government. This liability is imposed on the basis of status alone. The directors need not have been negligent or even aware that the sums were not remitted.

- Directors have a defence of due diligence to the above liability.

- Directors (except in the Atlantic provinces) are liable for unpaid employee wages if the corporation goes bankrupt.

- Directors are liable for torts committed on behalf of the corporation, but only if they were personally involved in committing the tort. They are not liable on the basis of their status as directors alone.

Closing Questions

Corporate Form

1. Jane Rowe forms a corporation called Jane Rowe Ltd. She then wants to form a partnership between herself and her company called Rowe and Partners. Can she do this?

2. Ben Lee bought a two-storey building consisting of a store on the first floor with an apartment above. An offer to lease signed "Joc's Appliances Ltd., per: Joe Smith, president" was presented to Lee.
   a) Who is liable on the lease if there is a default? This is a company: will it necessarily have enough money to pay on a judgment?
   b) What precautions should the landlord take?

3. Brown Corp. Inc. manufactures bricks. It owns all the shares in White Corp. Inc., which is the sales arm of the business. The members of the board of directors of White Corp. Inc. are all officers of Brown Corp. Inc.

   A salesmen on the staff of White Corp. Inc. negligently told Systems Inc. that a certain type of cement block was suitable for a retaining wall. It wasn't, and the wall collapsed, damaging expensive machinery. Systems Inc. learns White Corp. Inc. has no assets. Any profits are sent to Brown Corp. Inc. immediately by way of dividends.
   a) Diagram the corporate structure and the contract involved. Will Systems Inc. be successful in claiming its loss against Brown Corp. Inc.?
   b) If the statements by the sales representative of White Corp. Inc. had been fraudulent, would that make any difference?

4. Eugene Summers has just gotten a job in another city and wants to sell his home as soon as possible. He hears that the market may be going up, but he can't wait. He lists his house for $200,000 and gets a signed offer for the full asking price the very next day.

   The purchaser is 928316 Alberta Limited. The president drove up in a new Lincoln to present the offer personally. Summers was suitably impressed by the president's expensive silk suit and Rolex watch. The offer came with a $1,000 deposit; it contained a clause saying that it was subject to the purchaser being able to arrange satisfactory financing in 60 days, and that the closing date was in 90 days.
   a) Evaluate the agreement and the risks involved for Summers. Should he sign it as it is? Are there any terms that you might suggest that he put into a counter-offer?

5. a) Which of the following is/are considered person(s) in law?
  i) Wilfred Corbin
  ii) Jane Smart & Daughters, Antiques
  iii) Bill and Company
  iv) Microsoft Inc.

  b) Which of the above is termed an "individual" in law? What is another legal term for "individual" in this context?

6. Mario and Grace decided to start an amusement arcade. They each contributed $5,000 for expenses, and they rented a location and purchased five Virtual Reality Helmets (interactive technology games). The arcade has been open only for one month but is already a huge success. They have now hired a manager who would like to invest some money, and they are looking at renting the premises next door in order to expand their operation.

Four days ago, a customer attempting to fight off his 3-D attackers lashed out with his hand and struck the person waiting next in line, knocking out one of that individual's teeth. Yesterday a young woman became so engrossed and agitated by the activity that she fainted, striking her head on the floor.

A friend told Mario that the arcade should incorporate in order to get more investment capital and to protect Mario and Grace from any lawsuits. Grace believes they should set up a partnership instead.

  a) What issues should they consider in deciding which form of business would be appropriate for their operation, considering both benefits and liabilities? Which method of operation would you recommend?

  b) What is the nature of the business operation that they are currently running?

7. Vera Marques, a single mother with three children, signs an agreement to buy May Ling's house. Relying on this agreement, Ling purchases a new house for herself. Marques must sell her own home to complete this purchase. She sells it to Madison Construction Limited, which is a small one-man company. The sole shareholder, officer, and director is Rick Madison. The purchase agreements is signed "Madison Construction Ltd. per: Rick Madison, president."

Marques has barely enough money to make ends meet, so she checks out Madison's record carefully and learns he has been successfully buying old homes and renovating them for resale for over 20 years.

Unfortunately, before closing the deal, Madison has a heart attack and can't arrange financing. The series of agreements falls like a chain of dominoes: Ling can't close her deal; Marques can't close her deal. Ling sues Marques for her loss of $50,000, and Marques claims against Madison Ltd. and Rick Madison personally. Assume that Madison Ltd. has no assets; however, Rick Madison does have considerable personal wealth.

  a) Draw a diagram of the above contracts and then determine the liability of all concerned and indicate which party will get a judgment against another party. Who will ultimately bear the loss?

  b) Are there any grounds to pierce the corporate veil and make Rick Madison personally liable to Marques? Is it fair that Marques bears the loss and that Rick Madison keeps his wealth and contributes nothing to the loss? Is fairness a grounds for penetrating the corporate veil?

  c) Assume that at the time that the agreement was signed, Madison Ltd. had not actually been incorporated. Rick Madison had been carrying on business as a sole proprietor and had only recently instructed his lawyer to apply for incorporation. The incorporation of Madison Ltd. was in effect a few days after Madison signed the agreement to purchase the house from Marques as described above. Is there now any ground to obtain personal liability against Rick Madison?

  d) What could Marques have done to obtain personal liability against Madison?

  e) In a situation such as the above sale of a home, is there any difference in risk in selling to a small company such as Madison Ltd. and to a couple with children?

Shareholders

8. Wally and Barry are equal shareholders, officers, and directors of Walbar Ltd., which operates a pool hall. There are several pool tables in the establishment, but one table in particular is not used very often by the patrons. Wally decides to take it home and set it up in his basement. When Barry objects, Wally replies, "Look, it's my company, too; I have a right to take the pool table."
   a) Is Wally correct?

9. Edmond wanted to involve his family in his corporation and decided to give 20 percent of the shares to each of his two sons, retaining 60 percent in his own name. Each son was appointed a director and vice-president, and took an active part in the business.

   Edmond's oldest son, Adam, began to follow a lifestyle of which his father did not approve. There were late-night clubs and excessive drinking and gambling. When Adam married a woman who called his father "Popsy," Edmond could not stand it any longer. He promptly removed his son from the board of directors and fired him from his position as vice-president, giving him sufficient notice to meet the requirements for dismissal.
   a) Does Adam have any remedies?

10. Wanson Chung gets Bill Kim to invest in his company in return for 30 percent of its shares. In 1998 Chung had signed an employment agreement with this corporation by which he became president. If his employment was terminated for any reason, he would receive a severance package valued at $1,000,000.

    Kim and another shareholder, who also has 30 percent of the shares, arranged to have Chung fired. Chung claims the million-dollar golden parachute. Kim says that he didn't know of this employment agreement when he invested, and didn't even think to ask about such an arrangement.
    a) Is the agreement between Chung and the corporation a valid contract?
    b) Does Kim have any remedy to possibly set aside the termination provision?

11. The Pagannini Corporation has authorized capital of 600 shares, of which 500 are issued. Antonia Dvorak wishes to obtain control of the company, as she thinks it has a great unused potential. She has specific ideas of how to run it. Dvorak buys 251 of the issued shares, which gives her control of the corporation by one share.

    As soon as Dvorak purchases the shares, the board of directors, which is made up of the only other three shareholders apart from Dvorak, announces a need for new capital and proposes to issue the balance of the 100 shares—giving 25 to each shareholder. The resulting share structure is as follows.

	Current	Proposed
Other Shareholders	249 plus 75	324
Antonia Dvorak	251 plus 25	276

    a) What will be the result of the proposed new share issue as far as control is concerned?
    b) Dvorak is a majority shareholder—does she have a remedy?

Directors

12. UCM Plastics Ltd. was given the right of first refusal for a new biodegradable-plastic technology in its experimental phase. The five-member board of directors met, and the vote was three to two against the purchase of the new technology. Subsequently, Al Manian, one of the directors who had voted against the purchase, incorporated a provincial corporation and bought the new process. Six months later, the technology was perfected, and the first year's sales totalled $6,000,000.
    a) Has Manian acted properly in this situation, or is there a remedy available for UCM Plastics Ltd.?

13. Soleil Systems Inc. was a computer-software company whose reputation depended primarily on the work of Francesco Dietmar. He was a senior officer and a director of the company, but had no written employment contract.

Agrisif Ltd. purchased the shares of Soleil Systems Inc. and proceeded to make a number of changes in the style of management. Right from the start, Dietmar did not get along with the executives of Agrisif and, four months after the purchase, he resigned, along with several key employees. They immediately started a business in direct competition with Soleil.

a) Are there any grounds on which Agrisif would be able to sue Dietmar?

b) Are there any unknown elements in this situation that might change your answer to a)?

14. Which of the following, if any, owe a fiduciary duty?

a) partner in a partnership

b) the president of a corporation

c) a shareholder of a corporation

d) a director of a corporation

15. Gareth Thomas was a director of Middleton Manufacturing Inc. The company put out a call for bids from suppliers for a multimillion-dollar order of the raw materials needed for the coming year.

Fiona Ferguson, Thomas's wife, owned and operated a small independent bookstore. Business was excellent, and she planned to expand, taking over the premises next door. A few days before the Middleton board was due to make a decision on its contract, Ferguson was contacted by George Hammond, one of the suppliers who had submitted a bid to Middleton.

Hammond offered Ferguson a loan of $30,000 at 2 percent interest, to be repaid over 10 years. "That'll give you room for a book or two!" he said.

a) Does this loan create any legal problems for Thomas and, if so, do they depend on whether Hammond's bid is the successful one?

16. New Inspiration Mines Inc. was in negotiations with a prospector over a possible gold claim. This claim was low on New Inspiration's priority list, and negotiations were stalled.

Michel Lebois, a director of New Inspiration, approached the owner of the claim and bought it for his own company, Successful Mines Ltd. The claim turned out to be a good one, and Successful made a profit of $5 million.

a) Did Lebois have any duty to New Inspiration Mines Inc.? If so, what is the technical name for this duty?

b) What could New Inspiration do about this situation?

17. Joan Compeau, a recent graduate, has been offered a directorship on the board of directors of three corporations. Each will have business cards printed for her, saying "Joan Compeau, Director." She is elated!

a) What advice would you give Compeau?

18. David Sherman was a director of Empower Corp Inc. The president of this company, Joan Galway, induced the chief researcher officer of a competitor to join their company and bring with him vital, confidential market research. However, it was all to no avail, as Empower Corp went bankrupt with no assets.

GST, which had been collected, had not been sent to the government and employee wages had not been paid for three months. The government, employees, and the competitor have sued Sherman and Galway.

a) For which of the following, if any, is Sherman responsible, and why?

i) unremitted GST

ii) employee wages

iii) damages to the competitor for inducing breach of contract

b) For which of the above, if any, is Galway responsible, and why?

19. What is the difference between the remedies of piercing the corporate veil and directors' liability in tort? Give the elements necessary to establish each remedy. Which is easier to establish?

20. Compare the results in *Salomon v. Salomon & Co. Ltd.* with the results in the *ADGA Systems International Ltd. v. Valcom Ltd.* Why was the separate identity of a corporation upheld in Salomon? Why were the directors made liable in the other case?

Multi Issue

21. Match the technical word in the first column with the closest synonym in the second column.

Franchise	Substitute
Fiduciary duty	Owner
Vicarious	Trust Relationship
Corporation	Licence
Proprietor	Person

Websites

www.incorporate-it.ca—Incorporate-It Services. Help for incorporating a company in Canada.

www.canadaone.com—Tips on registering a small business and getting a GST number, and over 700 articles on starting a small business.

Articles of Incorporation

ARTICLES OF INCORPORATION
STATUTS CONSTITUTIFS

Form 1.
Business
Corporations
Act.
1982
Formule
numero 1
Loi de 1982
sur /es
compagnies

1. The name of the corporation is: Dénomination sociale de la compagnie:

| T | , | J | , | | M | O | R | G | A | N | I | N | C | . | | | | | | | | | | | | | | | | |

2. The address of the registered office is: Adresse du siège social:

(Street & Number or R.R. Number & if Multi-Office Building give Room No.)
(Rue et numéro ou numéro de la R.R. et, s'il s'agit d'un édifice a bureaux, numéro du bureau)

Newmarket, Ontario | M | 1 | H | 5 | J | 9 |

(Name of Municipality or Post Office)   (Postal Code)
(Nom de la municipalité ou du bureau de poste)   (Code postal)

Town of Newmarket   in the / dans le/la   **Regional Municipality of York**

(Name of Municipality, Geographical Township)   (County, District, Regional Municipality)
(Nom de la municipalité, du canton)   (Comté, district, municipalité régionale)

3. Number (or minimum and maximum number) of directors is: Nombre (ou nombres minimal et maximal) d'administrateurs:

Minimum of One – Maximum of Ten

4. The first director(s) is/are: Premier(s) administrateur(s):

First name, initials and surname Prenom, initiales et nom de famille	Residence address, giving street & No. or R.R. No. or municipality and postal code. Adresse personnelle, y compris la rue et le numéro, le numéro de la R.R. ou, le nom de la municipalité et le code postal	Resident Canadian State Yes or No Résident Canadien <u>Oui/Non</u>
Terrence J. Morgan	**1234 Main Street** **Newmarket, OntarioM1H 5J9**	**Yes**

5. Restrictions, if any, on business the corporation may carry on or on powers the corporation may exercise	Limites, s'il y a lieu, imposées aux activités commerciales ou aux pouvoirs de la compagnie.

None

6. The classes and any maximum number of shares that the corporation is authorized to issue.	Catégories et nombre maximal, s'il y a lieu, d'actions que la compagnie est autorisée a émettre:

The Corporation is authorized to issue an unlimited numher of shares of one class designated as common shares, and an unlimited number of shares of a second class designated as preference shares.

7. Rights, privileges, restrictions and conditions (if any) attaching to each class of shares and directors authority with respect to any class of shares which may be issued in series:	Droits, privilèges, restrictions et conditions, s 'il y a lieu, rattachés à chaque catégorie d'actions et pouvoirs des administrateurs relatifs à chaque catégorie d'actions qui peut être émise en serie:

1. the preference shares may be issued in one or more series;

2. the directors are authorized to fix the number of shares in and to determine the designation, rights, privileges, restrictions and conditions attaching to the shares of each series;

3. the preference shares of each series shall, with respect to priority in payment of dividends and in the return of capital in the event of liquidation, dissolution or winding up of the Corporation, be entitled to a preference over the common shares of the Corporation and over any other shares ranking junior to the preference shares;

4. the holder of each common share has the right to one vote for such common share at all meetings of shareholders other than meetings of the holders of another class of shares and to receive the remaining property of the Corporation upon dissolution.

8 The issue, transfer or ownership of shares is/is not restricted and the restrictions (if any) are as follows:	L 'émission, le transfert ou la propriété d'actions est/n 'est pas restreinte. Les restrictions, s'il y a lieu, sont les suivantes:

The right to transfer shares of the Corporation shall be restricted in that no shares shall be transferred without either:

(a) the previous consent of the directors of the Corporation expressed by a resolution passed at a meeting of the directors or by an instrument or instruments in writing signed by a majority of the directors; or

(b) the previous consent of the holders of at least 51% of the shares for the time being outstanding entitled to vote expressed by resolution passed at a meeting of the shareholders or by an instrument or instruments in writing signed by such shareholders.

9. Other provisions if any, are:	Autres despositions, s'il y a lieu:

1. that the board of directors may from time to time, in such amounts and on such terms as it deems expedient;

(a) borrow money on the credit of the Corporation;

(b) issue, reissue, sell or pledge debt obligations (including bonds, debentures, notes or other similar obligations, secured or unsecured) of the Corporation;

(c) to the extent permitted by law, give a quarantee on behalf of the Corporation to secure performance of any present or future indebtedness, liability or obligation of any person; and

(d) charge, mortgage, hypothecate, pledge or otherwise create a security interest in all or any of the currently owned or subsequently acquired real or personal, movable or immovable, property of the Corporation, including book debts, rights, powers, franchises and undertakings, to secure any debt obligations or any money borrowed or other debts or liability of the Corporation.

The board of directors may from time to time delegate such one or more of the directors and officers of the Corporation as may be designated by the board all or any of the powers conferred on the board above to such extent and in such manner as the board shall determine at the time of each such delegation;

2. that the number of shareholders of the Corporation, exclusive of persons who are in the employment of the Corporation and exclusive of persons who, having been formerly in the employment of the Corporation, were, while in the employment, and have continued after the termination of that employment to be shareholders of the Corporation, is limited to not more than fifty (50), two (2) or more persons who are the joint registered owners of one (1) or more shares being counted as one (1) shareholder; and

3. that any invitation to the public to subscribe for any shares or securities of the corporation is hereby prohibited.

| Nom et adresse des fondateurs | Full residence address or address of registered office or of principal place of business giving street & No. or R.R. No., municipality and postal code |
| First name, initials and surname or corporate name
Prénom, initiale et nom de famille ou dénomination sociale | Adresse personnelle au complet, adresse du siège social ou adresse de l'établissement principal, y compris la rue et le numéro, le numéro de la R.R., le nom de la municipalité et le code postal |

<table>
<tr><td>Terrence J. Morgan</td><td>1234 Main Street
Newmarket, Ontario
M1B 5J9</td></tr>
</table>

| These articles are signed in duplicate | Les présents statuts sont signés en double exemplaire. |

Signatures Of incorporators
(Signature des londaleurs)

_____

TERRENCE J. MORGAN

Dealing with Banks and Other Financial Institutions

Types of Financial Institutions

There are a number of organizations from which a business can borrow money—banks, trust companies, finance companies, leasing companies, credit unions, and so on.

In borrowing from these organizations, you will likely be asked to sign a personal guarantee and put up collateral. This chapter will explain what the various financial institutions are, how they operate, and what the normal lending practice involves.

Banks

Many of the functions carried out by today's banks can be traced back almost to the beginning of recorded history. In the 12th century, the Knights Templar, a religious and military order, regularly sent money and supplies from Europe to Palestine. Thus, they developed an efficient banking system, gradually becoming bankers for a large part of Europe.

The first banks as we know them were the Riksbank in Sweden, established in 1656, and the Bank of England, which began business in 1694. These were modeled on the practices of 17th-century goldsmiths. Their trade meant that these men had to keep large quantities of precious metals on hand and, as a result, they built secure vaults for its storage, and maintained private guards—all as part of the cost of doing business. Other people could store their precious metals in a goldsmith's vault on payment of a fee, and the vault's owner naturally gave a receipt. Rather than face the risks of moving the gold if it was later used in payment to someone else, the goldsmith's receipt was often simply signed over to the new owner. This was how paper currency began.

The goldsmiths realized that, because their depositors were using the receipts in this way, only about 10 percent of the gold was actually removed from the vaults every year. Therefore the goldsmiths could issue paper receipts for 10 times the amount of gold that they had in storage—effectively creating money. As long as the goldsmiths could meet the demands for turning over the actual gold, there would be confidence in the paper currency.

The practice of issuing receipts for what one does not possess was soon made legal under the bank acts. The gold that was held in storage, and represented by the receipt, was called the reserve. And, since the amount of gold existing in the reserve could be less than the quantity of gold represented by receipts, the system was called the fractional reserve system. Because the amount of receipts—the quantity of currency—was related to the amount of gold on reserve, the system was called the gold standard.

In the early years of this century, the words "will pay to the bearer on demand one dollar in gold" were printed on every Canadian dollar bill. At no time, however, did the banks hold one dollar in gold for every dollar note issued. Today, paper currency simply says "legal tender," and the gold standard is no longer the basis of the banking system.

Banks Today

Banks today work on the same principle as they did in the 17th century. We no longer use the gold standard, but instead employ a more complicated system, in which a government-run central bank—in this country, the Bank of Canada—controls the money supply.

The banks realize that most customers, particularly businesses dealing with large amounts of money, use cheques rather than cash in most transactions. Again, therefore, only some 10 percent of the banks' money in hard cash is in demand at any one time. The *Bank Act* sets out the amount of cash reserves any financial institution is required to have available—usually approximately 10 percent of the bank's assets. The remaining 90 percent is working—earning income for the bank—which is, after all, simply another business that must make money to survive.

If a bank makes a loan—say $100,000—it does not give cash. Instead, a number is entered in a ledger book or a computer system, and a cheque may be issued. When the loan is paid off, normally by cheque, the entry is cancelled—there has been no cash involved. The bank has created $100,000 in money and then extinguished that money, all with the stroke of a pen or a tap on a keyboard. It is the ability to create money that makes banks and trust companies unique among all businesses. Other financial institutions do not have this capacity.

The Size of the Banks

In 1983, Walter Stewart wrote in his book *Towers of Gold, Feet of Clay*:

> In terms of assets, the Royal Bank of Canada is 22 times the size of General Motors Canada. The Canadian Imperial Bank of Commerce is 4.5 times the size of Bell Canada. The Toronto-Dominion Bank—the smallest of the "big four" banks—is almost 2.5 times the size of Canada's top four oil companies lumped together.

This is still true today.

The *Bank Act*

Federal legislation—the *Bank Act*—governs all banks within Canada. The act divides banks into two broad categories—Schedule A and Schedule B. Canadian banks fall into the first class; foreign banks are considered Schedule B institutions.

Schedule A Banks

There are no restrictions on the size of Schedule A banks, but they must be public companies, Canadian controlled, with no individual shareholders possessing sufficient shares to control the bank.

Schedule B Banks

There are restrictions on the size of the assets that foreign banks can have, effectively limiting the amount of money they can create and lend. This is done to protect Schedule A banks from foreign competition.

Foreign banks can enter retail banking, dealing with customers through "ground level" banks, but typically only deal with businesses. Schedule B banks are a common source of business loans, and are sometimes willing to approve business ventures that have previously been turned down by Schedule A institutions.

Trust Companies

Trust companies, like banks, can lend money and offer mortgages. They can also take deposits from the public, and must maintain certain reserves to meet demands from customers. The big difference between banks and trust companies is that trust companies can be privately controlled—they can even be one-owner companies.

Current Issues

Because of the unique laws allowing Canadian banks to create money and giving them monopoly protection, there have also been regulations prohibiting the banks from expanding into other financial areas.

The current issue in banking law is deregulation. Banks and trust companies are pressing for the further removal of government restrictions on their activities. The banks are moving away from their traditional roles of simply receiving deposits and making business loans, to what they call the financial supermarket, a place where all financial needs can be supplied. These include traditional banking services, investment advice, stockbroking, and insurance.

Insured Deposits   All deposits with banks and trust companies that operate in Canada are insured by the Canada Deposit Insurance Corporation (CDIC). Currently, deposits are insured to a maximum of $60,000 per customer, per institution. The insurance fund is paid for by banks and trust companies, who pass on the expense to customers as a cost of doing business. If your assets total more than $60,000, it is a good idea to spread various deposits among different financial institutions, thus gaining maximum insurance protection.

Business Alert!

Credit Unions

Credit unions are another option for those seeking financial services. They grew out of a movement among a group of German farmers in the 1850s, who pooled financial resources to buy supplies at a lower cost. This original idea still forms the basis of the modern credit union, where persons with some common bond (usually a profession or community) pool resources to provide financial services for one other. Key features of credit unions include:

- Member ownership and control: the credit union operates by a board of directors chosen by and from the membership. In order to become a credit-union member, you must meet certain criteria, usually a placing a minimum deposit and being a member of the group the credit union is desirous of serving.
- Non-profit: profits of the credit union are shared with members, as opposed to being returned to shareholders.

And like banks, the following are features of credit unions as well:

- Deposits are insured to limits set out in the relevant legislation. For example, in Alberta, the Credit Union Deposit Guarantee Corporation, set up under the *Credit Union Act* R.S.A. 1980, c. C-31.1, insures 100 percent of deposits with a credit union.
- They are closely regulated via complex legislation (enacted provincially).
- They offer a broad range of financial services.

Finance Companies

There are many private institutions, such as small mortgage companies, that lend money to private individuals and businesses. These are not connected with any banks, but are brokerage types of businesses, specializing in bringing together people who have money to invest and those who are looking to borrow.

Finance companies can be very large. Some, such as Trans Canada Credit, not only make consumer loans but often take over financing from other businesses. For example, if you buy a car, the dealership will arrange financing for you on the spot. However, even if the documents are drawn up in the name of the dealership, that firm will usually assign the loan to a finance company. You are then given notice to make your payments directly to the finance company.

Borrowing from Banks

A significant source of financing for most businesses is by way of bank loans. There are several different types of loans. The bank may also ask for security, often called collateral, which pledges property which a bank can cease if the loan is not paid. The common types of security are discussed in the next chapter.

You, your spouse, your friend or relative may be asked to sign a guarantee. As demand loans and guarantees are very commonly used in business loans, they are discussed next.

Demand Loans

Business loans are often made on a demand basis, to be repaid when asked by the bank. The important question is, when the bank makes a demand, how long does the business person have to come up with the money? Does *demand* mean *demand*? One judge said that a business person has the time it takes to open a desk drawer and take out a cheque book to pay a loan when demanded. Later courts have not been quite so strict. The following case illustrates the way a court will determine the time period in a demand situation.

Mr. Broadloom Corporation (1968) Ltd. v. Bank of Montreal, [1984] 44 O.R. (2d) 368 (C.A.)

Mr. Broadloom had been dealing with the Bank of Montreal for 13 years. The bank became concerned when Mr. Broadloom's financial statements were six months late, and revealed that the company was in financial difficulty. The bank gave Mr. Broadloom's financial statements to an independent accounting firm, which advised the bank to call its demand loan immediately.

The bank had the two owners of Mr. Broadloom into the bank for a meeting, and told them that the bank loan was called. The firm was required to pay $1.5 million at once. The owners were surprised. They had been negotiating with the bank to clear up the company's problems, and were not prepared for such a sudden change in the bank's attitude.

Mr. Diamond, one of the owners, asked the bank how much time he had to pay, and was told, "None." When the corporation couldn't come up with the money, the bank sent in a receiver. Forty minutes after the meeting, Mr. Broadloom was closed down and in the possession of the receiver.

The owners were able to repay the entire bank loan of $1.5 million in three months; however, the firm was out of business. The owners sued the bank for the loss of their business.

The Court's Decision

The court realized that it had to balance two factors. The banks had a right to take relatively fast possession of assets and appoint a receiver, because it was well known that when a business was going broke, the assets could quickly disappear—often with the collusion of the owners.

On the other hand, the owners must be given some chance to keep their business alive. Here, the owners did pay the bank loan within only three months. So the bank was hasty, and should have given the owners some time to come up with the money.

The bank was ordered to pay damages to Mr. Broadloom's owners equivalent to the value of their lost business.

Reasonable Time

How long do you have to pay up if the bank calls a demand loan? Unfortunately, no specific period, such as 10 days or 15 days, can be given. The often-recurring word *reasonable* is the test. What is reasonable will vary with the circumstances, but in the normal case, the bank cannot demand a cheque before you leave the bank manager's office. Unless there are circumstances which justify urgency, 10 days is probably a good rule of thumb.

Lines of Credit   Businesses often negotiate operating lines of credit on a demand basis. Because of the problems of an unexpected demand, businesses are now trying to negotiate term loans. A term loan has the advantage that it cannot be called on demand, and need only be repaid by the fixed date set by the term.

Business Alert!

Bank Loans   Don't be shy negotiating about interest rates when you apply for a bank loan. Bank officers take this as a good sign. It shows that you are somewhat sophisticated in financial matters. It also is an indication that you intend to repay the loan. People who default on loans are almost never concerned with interest rates.

Business Alert!

Newspapers and a number of websites often list comparative interest rates for banks and other financial institutions. There is a difference in rates, and so shopping around can be beneficial. As a rule of thumb, 1 percent difference in interest on $100,000 results in a difference in payments of $100 per month.

Loan Guarantees

A guarantee for a loan is often called co-signing. Co-signing is one of the most frequent contracts used in credit arrangements. You will encounter co-signing arrangements both as a borrower and as a business giving credit to customers. There are two types of co-signing agreements:

- guarantee—an agreement in which the third party is usually liable only if the main debtor defaults on the loan
- **indemnity** or surety—an agreement in which the third party undertakes to be equally liable for the loan owed by the main debtor

indemnity

an agreement in which the third party undertakes to be equally liable for the loan owed by the main debtor

There are two levels of legal relationship in a guaranteed lending agreement. The first is between the lender and the borrower; the second is between the lender and the co-signer.

The Guarantee Triangle

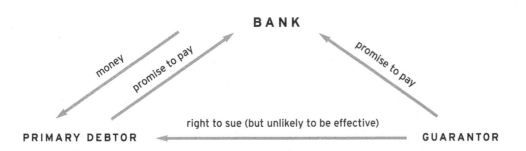

Why a Guarantee?

In business, there are three reasons a guarantee is normally required when a corporation obtains a loan:

- The corporate form implies limited liability; therefore, the owner's personal assets cannot be seized to satisfy the loan on default. The corporation might not have sufficient assets of its own.

- Even if the corporation does have assets, it may also have many other creditors. If the loan goes into default, all assets might have to be shared among creditors. The secured creditors—those who hold mortgages and other securities—will more than likely be able to seize most of the corporate assets.
- In attempting to avoid creditor lawsuits, the corporation may have tried to hide its assets through a series of complicated transactions.

If a co-signer is required to pay the loan amount, that individual can seek recovery of the sum involved from the primary debtor.

Co-signer Beware   A co-signer is required when a lender wants some reassurance that the loan will be paid and does not have full confidence in the principal borrower. This is an important consideration if you are asked to co-sign a loan. Many people agree to do so without taking into account that, if the lender does not have full confidence in the borrower, there may be good reason for this. Co-signers often do not appreciate the very real risk that they may have to pay the full amount of the loan. Such a document should be signed only after careful consideration of the consequences.

If you have signed a continuing guarantee and no longer wish to be responsible for future loans, you can likely terminate your liability for future advances, but not for current loan amounts. This is a technical question depending on the wording of the guarantee and requires legal advice.

Standard Guarantee Terms

guarantor

a co-signor, a person who signs a guarantee

The basic terms of the standard form bank guarantee set out that the **guarantor** (a co-signor, a person who signs a guarantee) will pay if the primary debtor fails to pay. However, there are other terms that govern many situations that can occur and which the average business person does not consider when signing a guarantee. It is perhaps easier to understand the terms of a guarantee if it is first understood that the courts have developed a number of rules which give safeguards to the guarantors. The terms in a bank guarantee are drafted in response to these judge-made laws and are often an attempt to vary or nullify these principles.

■ *Critical Concepts of* Guarantees

Some of the most frequently relevant common law rules regarding guarantees are as follows:
- The guarantor is responsible only for the loan being guaranteed.
- The guarantor is to be given credit for all payments made against the loan. New advances are not the responsibility of the guarantor.
- A guarantor is responsible only for the debts that can be legally enforced against the debtor. If the debtor has a defence to the loan, even a technical one, the guarantor is released.
- If the bank is negligent in dealing with other security relating to the loan, the bank must give the guarantor a credit for the amount of the security.
- A bank cannot materially vary the arrangement with the primary debtor without the consent of the guarantor. This prohibition against material variation includes, for example, increasing the interest rate on any renewal.

Major Terms of Guarantees

All Debts Are Guaranteed

Review the opening clause in the standard Bank Guarantee Form in the Appendix to this chapter. Note this wording: "guarantees payment to the Bank of all debts and liabilities, present or future . . . at any time owing by the Customer to the Bank."

This phrase means that the co-signer has agreed to guarantee all loans or amounts of any kind owed by the primary debtor (the customer) to the limit stated, and not merely the particular loan being guaranteed. For example, if the customer who had a loan also defaulted on a credit card debt owed to the bank, the guarantor would be responsible for both the loan and the credit card debt to the limit of the amount set out in the guarantee.

Material Variation

At common law the bank could not vary the terms of the loan agreement with the primary debtor in any material way without the consent of the guarantor. Lenders have attempted to nullify this right of the guarantor and give themselves the freedom to make any variation of the original arrangement without the consent of the guarantor. (Review clause 8 of the example Bank Guarantee Form in this respect.) However, the courts have frequently overruled these clauses by interpreting them very restrictively.

The material variation rule is one that is of particular use to business people in defending against claims on guarantees. The next case is an example of how the courts struck down one such material variation clause.

Royal Bank of Canada v. Bruce Industrial Sales Ltd., [1998] 40 O.R. (3d) 307 (Ont. C.A.)

BF and BB were employees of Bruce Industrial Sales. They signed guarantees for a revolving line of credit for their employer corporation for the principal amount of $128,000 with interest at prime plus 1.5 percent. A revolving loan means that the customer can pay down the loan and then withdraw as needed up to the limit of the loan. The guarantee form contained a material variation clause similar to clause 8 in the Bank Guarantee Form in the Appendix.

BF and BB resigned from the company at a time when the revolving loan was at $95,000. They gave notice to the bank to have their liability determined (fixed) at that amount so no further principal could be added to that sum.

Very shortly after the bank received this notice from the guarantors, the corporation renegotiated its credit. The bank converted the revolving line to a fixed loan and increased the interest rate to prime plus 2.5 percent. When the corporation defaulted, the bank sued the guarantors for the $95,000 plus interest and was successful at trial. The guarantors appealed.

The Court's Decision

The guarantors claimed that the increase in the interest rate from prime plus 1.5 percent to prime plus 2.5 percent was a material variation of the original guarantee agreement, which nullified the guarantee. The court agreed that a change in interest by a full percent was material. In this situation, that increase added about $10,000 per year to the debt. The court stated further that any change to the detriment of the guarantor was a material change.

The bank countered by saying that its material variation clause permitted it to make whatever arrangement the bank "may see fit" with the customer, and so the guarantors had agreed to permit the bank to increase the interest rate on renegotiating the loan.

The court held that broad, imprecise language such as "may see fit" could not support the bank's position that the guarantors had intended to give the bank unlimited discretion to vary the loan terms. As the change was material, the entire guarantee was unenforceable.

The next set of questions will assist you in understanding certain of the guarantee clauses, the situations they cover and how these clauses relate to the common law principles respecting guarantees.

Business Law Applied

❶ Bernard Conway guarantees a bank loan in the amount of $10,000 for a friend, Carl Chernos, and signs a standard form guarantee containing a continuing guarantee clause. Chernos pays the loan down to $5,000, but soon runs short of money and borrows another $5,000 so that the loan is back up to $10,000.

Some months later, the bank advances another $5,000, so that Chernos now owes a total of $15,000. Chernos goes out of business and defaults on the loans. The bank sues Bernard Conway.

   a) Does Conway have to pay $5,000, $10,000, or $15,000?
   b) What would the result have been at common law?

❷ Natasha Keyes was one of four shareholders of Telcorp Inc. She was asked to co-sign for Telcorp's loan of $100,000. She wasn't concerned because the bank had a lien on Telcorp's assets which were easily worth $200,000 even on a forced-sale basis.

Telcorp went belly up. Its trade creditors successfully had the lien set aside because the bank had registered it improperly. The bank now wants Keyes to pay the full $100,000. Review clauses 3 and 7 of the Bank Guarantee Form in the Appendix to answer the following questions.

   a) Can Keyes successfully defend against the bank on the basis of its negligence in registering the lien?
   b) What would have been the result at common law?

Defences

Guarantees are one type of contract, and so all contractual defences can be used in relation to guarantees. Some of the most frequent defences raised are:

- misrepresentation
- *non est factum*
- undue influence between borrower (not the lender) and guarantor

Misrepresentation

Often bank staff themselves do not understand the terms of the bank guarantee form and tell the guarantor, for example, that the guarantee is only for the loan being negotiated and not for all debts owed by the borrower to the bank. Sometimes a well-meaning bank manager may say something to the effect that the guarantor need not worry because there's lots of other security, that the guarantee is a mere formality, or that the guarantor will be let off the guarantee if he resigns from the company.

Unfortunately, when trouble arises that bank employee is no longer on the scene to confirm the statement in question. And even if that employee is available, the matter is now in the hands of a person at a higher level of the bank who insists on strict enforcement of the guarantee. Strict enforcement will mean relying on the entire agreement clause to exclude any oral statements made (see the example Bank Guarantee Form in the Appendix).

You may recall that in the case of *Hawrish v. Bank of Montreal*, discussed in the section on entire agreement clauses in Chapter 6, because of the entire agreement clause, statements made by a bank manager to a guarantor were not permitted to be put before the court to contradict the written terms of the bank guarantee form.

Non Est Factum

This is a defence if the person who cosigns does not know that the document being signed is a guarantee. This defence is usually restricted to persons with disabilities such as visual impairment, a low education level, and the like.

Undue Influence

This critical influence is by the primary debtor over the guarantor. If the bank knows, or the circumstances are such that the bank should realize, that the guarantor is not making a free choice, the guarantee may be invalid because of undue influence. This situation most often occurs where a spouse, often a husband, is the primary debtor and has his wife, who has no business experience, sign as guarantor. This ground has given rise to the requirement to have the guarantor get independent legal advice (I.L.A.).

However, I.L.A. is not generally required respecting a guarantee. Where a business person executes a guarantee, no I.L.A. is required because a business person is considered sophisticated enough to understand the risk involved in signing a guarantee. Similarly, a wife signing to guarantee a husband's business loan may have business experience, or clearly be of a sufficient educational level so that she must understand the risk she is assuming. Lack of I.L.A. would likely not be a defence to such a person.[1]

Merchants Consolidated v. Team Sports & Trophies (1984) Inc., [1995] O.J. No. 84 (O.C.J. Gen. Div.)

Peter Brill was the principal of Team Sports and an experienced businessman. He signed a guarantee for the loans to his corporation. He later sold his interest in the corporation and severed all ties with it.

The business did not fare well under new management. The bank sued Brill on the guarantee. Brill defended, saying that he believed that the guarantee would end when he left the corporation, and that he had not obtained independent legal advice before signing the guarantee.

The Court's Decision

The court found that Brill was bound to the continuing guarantee. Brill was a sophisticated businessman who was quite familiar with the company's operation and with the concept of giving a guarantee for a loan. There was no possibility of any undue influence. I.L.A. was not necessary for a knowledgeable guarantor.

I.L.A. Required

The question of when I.L.A. is necessary is a difficult one. The Supreme Court of Canada said the question is twofold: whether the persons signing the guarantee can understand the risks being assumed, and whether they can freely choose to accept the risk (*Gold v. Rosenberg*, [1997] 3 S.C.R. 767).

I.L.A. is of most concern where the co-signer gets no direct or indirect benefit from the loan and is unsophisticated in business.

Under the *Alberta Guarantees Acknowledgment Act*, all guarantees must be notarized. This means that the guarantee must be signed before a **notary public**, a person (usually but not

notary public
a person (usually but not necessarily a lawyer) authorized to take sworn testimony such as an affidavit

---

1. *Bank of Montreal v. Featherstone* (1989), 68 O.R. (2d) 541 (Ont. C.A.).

necessarily a lawyer) authorized to take sworn testimony such as an affidavit. The notary must be satisfied that the person signing understands any potential legal liability.

Loan Insurance   Banks often require a borrower to take out insurance and have arrangements with an insurance company to provide that insurance. The rates are often higher than the market rates.

Most consumer protection acts provide that the lender must permit the borrower to arrange for insurance with its own insurance company. The lender must clearly disclose that right in writing.[2]

Business Law Applied

❸ Bill Cohen agreed to sign a guarantee in the standard form for a bank loan to Dillip Singh. The bank manager told Cohen that it was only a formality, as Singh had sufficient assets to cover the loan. Singh suffered major business losses and declared bankruptcy. The few assets he had at the time were immediately seized by creditors.

The bank sued Cohen for payment of the loan that he had guaranteed. Cohen wants to raise the statements made by the bank manager to prove a defence of misrepresentation.

a) Could he do so?

Family Law Considerations

Family law reform has added a series of technical defences to guarantees. As changes in family law are rapid, and vary from one province to another, we can only underline the need for legal advice if a business is giving credit secured by a guarantee. There are two main points to consider—because a spouse may have an unregistered interest in the guarantor's personal assets, it is wise to find out:

- whether the guarantor has a spouse. If so, the spouse should also sign the guarantee form.
- if the spouse received independent legal advice (see p. 377) in which the guarantee was properly explained.

Consider the following case. Terrific Togs, a clothing manufacturer, wants to ship $200,000 worth of goods on credit to Best Dressed Clothes Store. Before the items are sent, Terrific Togs has Best Dressed's owner sign a personal guarantee, relying on the fact that he has a house in his name alone, free and clear of any mortgages, and valued at $200,000.

But he also is married. Some time later, the owner and his wife divorce, and she is awarded a half interest in the matrimonial home. As a result, the security for the guarantee to Terrific Togs is reduced by half.

If the house had been registered in the name of both husband and wife, the wife's signature would have been necessary on the guarantee, since it is very difficult to sell a half interest in a matrimonial home.

A certificate of independent legal advice is recommended, as many recent court decisions have released a wife from a guarantee because of undue influence and duress by the husband.

---

2. See, for example, section 27 of the *Consumer Protection Act*, R.S.O. 1990, c. C.31.

It is difficult for a creditor, with no knowledge of any marital problems, to anticipate these defences.

Further, in most provinces a spouse's consent is necessary for the transfer of any interest in the matrimonial home. The matrimonial home can be not only a city residence where the couple normally lives, but also a recreational property, such as a cottage which is used as a family normally uses cottage property. In such a case there would be two matrimonial residences, the city house and the cottage. Hence, if the cottage was inherited by a husband and the title was in his name alone, a bank could not accept a mortgage on that property as security unless the wife also signed, even though she is not showing on the title as an owner.

■ *Business Law*   Applied

❹ **You have recently** gotten a job in a bank as an account manager. One of your better clients, John Harris, inherited a cottage from his parents about five years ago. John is married and he and his wife use the cottage on most weekends, weather permitting.

John applies to you for an increase for his business loan and agrees to put up a mortgage on this cottage for security for the increase.

  a) Will this mortgage by John to the bank be good security given to the bank? John's wife is not shown on the title and has not paid anything towards the purchase or maintenance of the property. Does she have any claim against this property?

Negotiable Instruments

Banks, trust companies, credit unions, and other financial institutions all use cheques, which are one form of **bill of exchange**, or negotiable instrument—a written order by A to B (usually a bank) to pay a specified sum of money to a named party or to the bearer of the document. A promissory note is another. There are other types of negotiable instruments, but they are less common. All negotiable instruments are governed by the *Bill of Exchanges Act*.

bill of exchange
a written order by A to B (usually a bank) to pay a specified sum of money to a named party or to the bearer of the document

Cheques

A **cheque** is a bill of exchange drawn against a bank and payable on demand. The bank holds money on deposit for the person who signs the cheque (the **drawer**, the party who draws up or signs a bill of exchange). The bank (the **drawee**, the party required to make payment on the bill of exchange) technically owes the depositor the money, and must obey the depositor's orders respecting its use. A cheque is an order to the bank to pay on demand a specific sum to a named person (the **payee**, the party named to receive payment on the bill of exchange).

The bank is given an opportunity to tell the payee whether the bank can make the payment. There are many reasons the bank will not honour a cheque—insufficient funds, a stop-payment order, a stale-dated cheque, and so on. The cheque must be presented to the bank, which must then indicate if it will pay. This process is called acceptance. Once the bank has accepted the cheque, it cannot refuse to pay. Acceptance is one form of certification.

cheque
a bill of exchange drawn against a bank and payable on demand

drawer
the party who draws up or signs a bill of exchange

drawee
the party required to make payment on the bill of exchange

payee
the party named to receive payment on the bill of exchange

Forged Cheques

The bank is liable to the customer if the bank cashes a forged cheque. However, there is a situation in which a bank will not be liable for forged cheques. The bank will not have to pay if the customer's account documents contain a limitation clause, and the forgery is reported to the bank after the time period specified in that clause.

The Parties to a Cheque

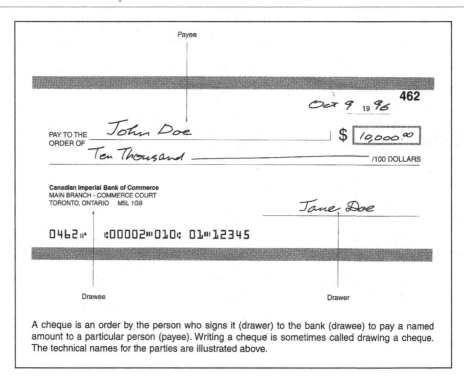

A cheque is an order by the person who signs it (drawer) to the bank (drawee) to pay a named amount to a particular person (payee). Writing a cheque is sometimes called drawing a cheque. The technical names for the parties are illustrated above.

Aero Transfer Company Limited v. The Royal Bank of Canada et al., [1972] S.C.R. 45

The chief accountant of Aero Transfer Company Limited forged the signature of the company's authorized signing officers on 73 cheques, totalling $165,109.03. The cheques were drawn on the company's account at the Royal Bank between April 1963 and April 1968. Aero's auditors only discovered the fraud in May 1968, when the audit revealed that a cheque for $9,077.14 was a forgery. Notice was immediately given to the bank about all 73 forged cheques.

The bank refused to repay the total amount to Aero, and relied on its account verification form which read, in part:

... The undersigned hereby agrees with the Bank ... to verify the correctness of each statement of account received from the Bank ... and within 30 days ... to notify the Bank in writing ... of any alleged omissions from or debits wrongly made to or inaccurate entries in the account ... and that at the end of the said 30 days

the account as kept by the Bank shall be conclusive evidence without any further proof that except as to alleged errors so notified ... the Bank shall be free of all claims in respect of the account.

The Court's Decision

The court upheld the verification agreement. As notice was given for the last cheque in the amount of $9,077.14 within the 30-day period, the bank had to reimburse the customer for that sum. However, notice was not given within the required 30 days for the previous 72 cheques. Although the bank had a responsibility to reimburse the customer for forged cheques, the verification agreement meant that the bank was not liable for those cheques outside the 30-day period.

Embezzlement   What's the difference between **embezzlement** and **theft**? Both terms involve stealing and are criminal offences. Embezzlement occurs when an individual has legal possession of the goods. A bank teller, for example, has legal possession of the cash in that individual's drawer, but has no right to use it personally. If the teller steals that money, it is embezzlement.

Legalese

If a customer takes the money from the teller's cash drawer, it is theft. If that individual uses force or threat in the process, then a robbery has been committed. If a weapon is used, armed robbery has taken place.

Forgery   In order to safeguard its interests against forgery, a business should take certain precautions.

Business Alert!

- Have bank reconciliations done as soon as they are received, so that notice of any discrepancies can be given within the period specified in the verification agreement (usually 30 days).
- Make sure that internal controls are in place.
- Have employees who have access to accounting records bonded with a fidelity bond. These are issued by insurance companies, who will then repay the money should the employee steal from you.

Business Law   Applied

⑤ **Chris Louie was** a bookkeeper for Newvest Company. He had no authorization to sign cheques for the firm. Newvest had an account agreement with the bank, containing a clause requiring notice of any discrepancies in the bank statements within 30 days, or the bank was released from liability.

Over a two-year period, Louie forged the signature of Newvest's president on 10 cheques to a phony supplier, and cashed the cheques himself. Newvest's auditor caught the last (the tenth) cheque, and the firm gave notice to the bank, within 30 days of that final cheque, that all 10 cheques were part of a fraudulent scheme.

Louie was by this time known to be a severe alcoholic, and had no ability to repay the amounts taken. The bank refused to reimburse Newvest for the 10 cheques.

- a) Was the 30-day verification agreement effective for the bank?
- b) Could the bank refuse reimbursement of all 10 cheques?
- c) What should Newvest Company do to protect itself regarding possible forged or unauthorized cheques in the future?

Stop-Payment Orders

A cheque is an order to the bank to pay. The customer can cancel that order before the cheque is cashed—accepted—by the bank, by making a stop-payment order. If the customer issues such instructions, the bank must obey them, or must reimburse the customer if it wrongly cashes the cheque. However, the customer must have a legitimate reason for stopping payment, or the bank will not be liable for a mistaken payment.

Remfor Industries Ltd. v. The Bank of Montreal, [1978] 21 O.R. (2d) 225 (C.A.)

The president of Remfor Industries Ltd. called the account manager of the Bank of Montreal and advised him to **stop payment** (an instruction from the drawer of a cheque to the bank not to pay the cheque) on a cheque for $10,853, postdated September 12, 1972. All information about the cheque was correct, except that the amount was actually $10,800.

The bank's computer system identified cheques by cheque number and amount. Because the amount was wrong, the bank cashed the cheque, and refused to reimburse Remfor. The company sued the bank for the return of its $10,800.

The Court's Decision

The court held that the bank had a duty to inspect cheques subject to a stop order, and inquire if a cheque with very similar particulars was found. The fact that the bank used a computer system that did not permit that this type of examination was not a defence. As part of its duty to inquire, the bank must put a system in place that can carry out that duty in full. The bank had to reimburse Remfor for the full amount of the mistakenly cashed cheque.

stop payment

an instruction from the drawer of a cheque to the bank not to pay the cheque

The customer must supply sufficient, accurate information so that the bank can identify the cheque. What happens if the information is reasonably close, but slightly inaccurate? Is there a duty on the bank to check with the customer if it sees a close, but not identical, cheque being presented for payment?

Stop-Payment Agreement

Since the Remfor decision (above), banks have used a standard form stop-payment agreement that customers wishing to halt a cheque must sign. Thus, placing a stop-payment order involves a visit to the bank, and cannot normally be done over the phone.

The standard form stop-payment agreement contains the following clause:

… the Bank is under no obligation to inquire as to any discrepancy between particulars described on this form and any particulars of any cheque presented to it, and the undersigned hereby waives and holds the Bank harmless from any claim relating to such a discrepancy.

There are court decisions that say this exemption clause is not effective because the bank has given no consideration for it. The bank is under a legal duty to stop payment, so that carrying out that duty is not consideration. After these cases, some banks began putting this exemption clause in their account opening forms as well. The consideration then would be the opening of the account.

Other Concepts Concerning Cheques

Stale-Dating   Although in law the right to sue on a cheque extends to six years, banks as a matter of policy will not honour a cheque six months after its date.

postdated

dated later than the time when it is given to the payee

Postdated Cheques   Cheques can be signed, and dated for payment in the future. A stop-payment order can be applied to a **postdated** cheque (one which is dated later than the time when it is given to the payee), as long as the cheque is still in the hands of the payee. A stop-payment may be ineffective if the cheque has been signed over to another party—**endorsed** (signed with one's name on a negotiable instrument, e.g., on the back of a cheque).

At Sight/On Demand Some bills of exchange are made payable at sight, meaning that three days' grace will be allowed to find the money to pay. On demand, however, means immediate payment is required.

The normal cheque is dated, and is payable on demand on or after that date, within a reasonable period of time. The bank must pay on the same day that a cheque is presented, provided that takes place on or after the cheque date. There is no grace period.

So, if a business gives a cheque dated January 31 to a supplier, and then calls the bank and asks that payment be held up for a day until the business gets the money to cover the cheque, the bank cannot so do. It must mark the cheque NSF (not sufficient funds) and return it on the same day.

Endorsements Signing the back of a bill of exchange is technically an endorsement, and may mean that the person so signing has accepted liability for payment of the bill. However, signing the back of a cheque at the bank is also an acknowledgment of receipt of the money.

Restrictions on Cashing One type of endorsement permitted in law is to put restrictions on the cashing of a cheque. A **restrictive endorsement** is an endorsement with a limitation. A common one is to specify that the cheque can be deposited only to a particular account in the name of the payee. If you are writing a cheque for a large sum it is advisable to write "for deposit only" on the reverse. This way, if it is stolen, the cheque cannot be cashed.

Bad Cheques Knowingly writing a cheque without sufficient funds in the account can be the criminal offence of obtaining goods by false pretenses. If you write a cheque which is returned NSF, and you did so when there was no money in your account, nor the possibility of any being there by the time the cheque was likely to be presented for acceptance by the bank, the Criminal Code presumes that you intended to obtain the goods by false pretenses.

Letters of Credit

A letter of credit is a document in which the bank guarantees to pay a stipulated sum when a specified event takes place. When the event happens, the bank has to pay. In order to maintain the letter of credit's reliability as a business transaction, banks will make payment, and will not become involved in any disputes between the customer and the person to whom the letter was granted. Fraud, of course, is always a ground for refusal to pay. However, the banks will probably insist that the customer obtain a court order—an injunction—to stop the bank from making payment.

A letter of credit could read, for example, that the bank guarantees to pay $1 million to Photomat Corporation when the purchase of its assets by Entrepreneurial Investments Limited is completed, if Entrepreneurial Investments doesn't pay. Once the sale is completed, Photomat need only advise the bank that this has happened, and that Entrepreneurial Investments has not paid, and the bank will pay the money to Photomat. Entrepreneurial Investments cannot stop the payment by the bank for any reason short of fraud.

Letters of credit are used as a means to guarantee payment, especially in international transactions. But there can be disadvantages.

For example, a Canadian distributor makes arrangements with a Taiwanese manufacturer for the supply of kitchen utensils (knives, forks, and such). As part of the contract, the Canadian distributor agrees to post a letter of credit with a bank for $100,000 against shipment of the product. Shipments usually amount to $50,000. This arrangement means that the Taiwanese company only has to provide an invoice signed as received by the Canadian distributor to the bank and the bank has to pay the amount of the invoice to the limit of the letter of credit.

endorsed
signed with one's name on a negotiable instrument, e.g., on the back of a cheque

restrictive endorsement
an endorsement with a limitation

The first two shipments are satisfactory. But the third shipment worth $50,000 contains many defective items to the value of $25,000. The Taiwanese company can still obtain a full payment from the bank on the letter of credit for $50,000. While this is a breach of warranty, there is no fraud. The Canadian distributor is left with trying to negotiate a settlement or suing, probably in a Taiwanese court, for the value of the loss.

Thus, experienced Canadian business people will not easily post a letter of credit for a large amount. Additionally, they order small shipments in the beginning to be assured of quality and performance.

■ *Business Law*   Applied

⑥ **The Farah Company** gave a postdated cheque, no. 357, dated September 1, 1997, to a supplier for a shipment of inventory in the amount of $500. Farah did owe the money, but was short of cash, and therefore told the bank to stop payment on the cheque well before its due date. However, the cheque had been identified to the bank as no. 358, not 357, and it was paid when the supplier presented it.

a) Can a stop-payment order be put on a postdated cheque?
b) Did the bank owe a duty to the Farah Company to screen for the cheque even though the detail was inaccurate?
c) Does the bank have to reimburse the Farah Company for the mistaken payment?

Promissory Notes

promissory note

a written promise to pay the amount stated on the instrument

When obtaining a loan, you will almost certainly be asked to sign a promissory note as part of the security for the transaction. A **promissory note** is, quite simply, a written promise to pay the amount stated on the instrument, and is usually required as part of a loan or purchase that is to be paid in instalments. The note might also outline the instalments and interest charges involved in the transaction.

An IOU is not a promissory note, but is only an acknowledgment of debt.

Transferability

Banking developed based on the use of paper receipts for gold deposited in a secure vault. The receipts were evidence that the gold existed, and could be transferred from merchant to merchant in a chain of transactions, never needing to be reconverted to the actual gold. The documents were freely transferable—negotiable—between one owner and the next.

Today's concept of money is the best example of negotiable paper. If you give a friend $20, and ask her to buy you a book, but she goes to a record store and buys a CD for herself, that store owner does not inquire about the purchaser's right to the money. Your restriction on the money's use has no effect on the store owner, who accepts the $20 bill at its face value.

Holder in Due Course

third party

a stranger to the agreement, a person who is not one of the parties to a contract

Free transferability of negotiable instruments is what sets them apart from contracts. Because negotiable instruments are freely transferable, a **third party**—a stranger to the agreement, a person who is not one of the parties to a contract—may acquire greater rights to them than the immediate parties. This party is called a **holder in due course**: an innocent third party enti-tled to collect on a negotiable instrument in spite of any defences of the original parties.

In the case of your $20, the record-store owner has acquired a greater right to the money than the friend to whom you gave it. Technically, you could enforce the agreement not to buy a CD against your friend, but not against the store owner. Another example of a holder in due course is a business which pays a roofing contractor a $500 deposit by cheque for work to be completed; that contractor signs the $500 cheque over to a building supply company as pay-ment on a previous account. The building supplier is a third party, or holder in due course of the cheque, a negotiable instrument.

What happens if the roofing contractor does not in fact carry out its agreement with the business that paid the deposit? The business demands repayment of the $500, to which the roof-ing contractor replies that it no longer has the cheque, and is about to declare bankruptcy. The building supplier maintains that it received the cheque on account of a valid debt, and intends to cash it. The building supplier, as a holder in due course, can cash the cheque even though the roofing contractor defaulted on its contract with the business. The legal status of the parties is:

- the business is the drawer
- the roofing contractor is the payee
- the building supplier is the holder in due course

Great care must be used in giving cheques (especially postdated ones) and promissory notes in a business transaction as the next case brief demonstrates.

> **holder in due course**
>
> an innocent third party entitled to collect on a negotiable instrument in spite of any defences of the original parties

---

■ *Critical Concepts of* Holder in Due Course

- Bills of exchange such as cheques and promissory notes are negotiable, or transferable, instruments.
- The party to whom the bill of exchange is transferred is called a holder in due course.
- A holder in due course is not affected by any defences the person who signed the bill may have against the payee, unless the holder has notice of the defences at the time the holder takes the note.

Raymond Bibaud v. Banque de Montreal, [1975] C.A. 186 (Que.)

Pine Lake Development Corporation sold Raymond Bibaud a lakefront lot and agreed to build a cottage on it for $31,850. Bibaud gave Pine Lake a promissory note in the amount of $2,817. The note stated that it was payable in 36 monthly instal-ments of $78.26. Bibaud gave postdated cheques for the 36 monthly instalments. Pine Lake immediately transferred the note and all cheques to the Banque de Montreal for value.

Pine Lake went out of business and did not even begin con-struction. Bibaud stopped payment on the cheques, and the Banque sued, claiming it was a holder in due course.

Bibaud replied that the Banque was not an innocent third party, as Pine Lake was its customer and it should have known at the time it took the note that the firm was in such financial diffi-culties that it could not fulfill its contact to Bibaud.

The Court's Decision

The court held that the Banque was a holder in due course of the note and the cheques. The issue became whether Bibaud had a defence that the Banque was not innocent, and should have known of Pine Lake's almost certain default on the build-ing contract. The court held that the fact of the customer rela-tionship did not in itself prove that the Banque knew that Pine Lake could not fulfill its obligations. The court stated that the business of banking would be impossible if a bank, on taking a negotiable instrument from a regular customer, was obliged to conduct an inquiry to determine what obligations its customer had incurred, and whether the customer was in a financial posi-tion to meet them.

Business Alert!   Not Negotiable   In the Bibaud case, the buyer could have safeguarded his interests by endorsing the back of the note and each cheque with restrictive words such as "not negotiable."

Business Law   Applied

❼ **Raj Vong Associates** Inc. bought a computer system from Acu Computers Inc. at a cost of $20,000. Raj Vong did not want to get a bank loan, and so gave Acu Computers four postdated cheques for $5,000 each. Acu Computers signed these cheques over to its bank, to be applied against its loan.

There was a problem with the computer system, and Acu Computers denied liability. The bank demanded payment on the cheques from Raj Vong, who does not want to pay until the computer problem is sorted out. The bank sued on the notes.

   a) What is the bank's status in relation to the cheques?
   b) Can Raj Vong claim the problem with the computer as a defence to payment on the cheques?

Business Law   Applied

❽ **Pentagon Construction Maritime** Ltd. gave two postdated cheques for $20,000 each to Miramichi Glassworks Ltd. for installation of windows in a new building. Pentagon knew Miramichi was in financial difficulties, and made it clear to Miramichi and to its bank, the Royal Bank, that the cheques would not be honoured unless the contract was performed. Miramichi signed the cheques over to the bank to be applied against its loan.

Miramichi went into bankruptcy and did not fulfill the contract. The bank sued Pentagon on the cheques.

   a) What special status could the bank rely on in bringing the lawsuit?
   b) Does Pentagon have any defences?

Consumer Notes

Holder in due course status has been much abused because people today are unfamiliar with it. In consumer car sales, for example, a dealership would sometimes finance the car purchase and have the consumer sign a promissory note or give postdated cheques. The dealer would then assign those cheques to a bank or finance company. If the car broke down, the buyer still had to pay the bank in full, because it was a holder in due course.

Accordingly, the *Bills of Exchange Act* was amended to provide that, in a consumer transaction, a promissory note or bill which includes a cheque must be marked "consumer note" on its face. **Consumer notes** are promissory notes arising in a consumer credit sale. Cheques postdated more than 30 days are included as consumer bills, and must be so marked. Consumer notes are subject to the defences that could be raised by the original parties. In other words, the special status of the holder in due course does not apply to consumer notes. In the car-sale example, if the vehicle broke down, the consumer could plead that mechanical defect as a defence against payment to the bank.

If the note or bill is not stamped "consumer note" even though it is a consumer transaction, the innocent third party has holder in due course status. The person who failed to mark it will be subject to criminal prosecution, but if that individual is insolvent or has left the juris-

consumer notes
promissory notes arising in a consumer credit sale

diction, that remedy will not help the consumer. The act also provides that failing to mark a consumer note as such will make it unenforceable by the payee. The onus, then, is on you as a consumer to make certain any such note or bill is clearly marked.

In most situations where you will be asked to sign a consumer note, you will also be asked to sign other security. The *Bills of Exchange Act* consumer note provision applies only to the promissory note or postdated cheques. For Constitutional reasons, the federal government cannot enact laws dealing with personal-property security. If, for example, a **chattel mortgage**—a mortgage of personal (chattel) property—is given at the same time, the consumer-note provision does not apply to that chattel mortgage. To cover this gap in consumer protection, many provinces have legislated requirements that all security instruments involved in consumer credit transactions be marked in the same way as consumer notes, so that a holder in due course status cannot be claimed.

chattel mortgage
a mortgage of personal (chattel) property

Holder in Due Course Status   A business person can obtain the same protection as is afforded an ordinary consumer by endorsing any postdated cheque or promissory note on the reverse with the words "not negotiable." This prevents a holder in due course from taking the promissory note or cheque free of defences that could be raised between the primary parties.

Business Alert!

Business Law Applied

⑨ **Raj Patel purchased** a used car from New Era Cars. Patel signed a promissory note and gave a chattel mortgage on the car. The note read:

September 15, 1997

The undersigned promises to pay New Era Cars Ltd. on demand the sum of thirty thousand dollars ($30,000) with interest at the rate of 10 percent per annum before and after maturity and default.

New Era assigned the note and chattel mortgage to Secure Financial Company Ltd. for value. It turned out that the car's speedometer had been turned back, and Patel wanted out of the deal, based on fraudulent misrepresentation concerning the mileage. Secure Financial Company claimed it knew nothing of the fraud, and sued on the note. New Era has gone bankrupt.

a) What type of transaction is this?
b) What special protection does the maker of a note normally have in this type of transaction? Does the above promissory note qualify for that protection?
c) Would Secure Financial Company be successful in its lawsuit?
d) What remedies does Patel have against New Era? Are they of any practical value?

In Summation

Financial Institutions

- There are a number of lending institutions through which a business might finance its operations.
- In Canada, the federal *Bank Act* divides all banks into Schedule A (Canadian banks) and Schedule B (foreign banks), and governs all activities carried on by those institutions. Neither type of bank may be privately owned or controlled.
- Trust companies are also available for financing operations, and may be privately owned or controlled.

- Credit unions are another option for financial services. They are member-owned and controlled, and are non-profit.

- Finance companies, usually private institutions, are another source of financing, and may operate either by financing the transaction itself or by acting as go-betweens, connecting those with the need for capital to those with money to invest.

- Deposits with banks and trust companies are insured under the Canada Deposit Insurance Corporation (CDIC) to a maximum of $60,000 per customer, per institution.

Co-signing for Loans

- Co-signing for a loan will be done through either an indemnity or a guarantee.

- If you co-sign an indemnity agreement for someone receiving financing from a lending institution, you agree to be equally liable for the repayment of the debt with the person who has taken out the loan.

- A guarantee agreement will make you liable for repayment of the loan only if the person who has arranged the loan with the financing institution has defaulted. A financial institution lending money to a corporation will often require a personal guarantee from a shareholder before the loan will be made.

- A lending institution's standard form of guarantee will often include clauses that attempt to exclude any defences that might be raised by a party to the loan. Examples are continuing guarantee clauses, used to ensure future loans are covered (not just the funds advanced at the time of signing the guarantee), and entire agreement clauses, aimed at excluding any oral representations made at the time the guarantee was signed, and which may alter or contradict the terms of the guarantee.

- Exemption clauses and issues related to family law may also enter the picture in determining the defences or extent of the responsibility incurred by a third party co-signing for a loan.

Demand Loans

- Financing is often done by means of a demand loan. This type of loan does not have a particular date set for its maturity. Instead, it must be repaid within a reasonable period after a demand for repayment of the loan is made by the financial institution.

Negotiable Instruments

- Although there are several types of negotiable instruments, including promissory notes and letters of credit, the cheque is the most common form used by financial institutions in their transactions.

- A customer who becomes aware of a forgery or theft involving a cheque is obligated to give notice of the situation to the financial institution. As well, a financial organization that has paid out under a forged or stolen negotiable instrument will incur obligations.

- Stale-dated cheques, postdated cheques, cheques payable on sight, and endorsements of various types all create restrictions or rights that attach to the negotiable instrument and its use.

- Other types of negotiable instruments, such as letters of credit and promissory notes, may be used depending on the nature of the financial transaction and the customer's requirements. Promissory notes and letters of credit may be transferred or negotiated between parties, and may ultimately lead to a situation in which a third party which has acquired a negotiable instrument possesses greater rights as a holder in due course than the party from which the negotiable instrument was obtained.

- To protect consumers, a negotiable instrument, such as a promissory note or cheque, that is used in a consumer transaction must be marked on its face with the words "consumer note." Negotiable instruments involved in consumer transactions are also made subject to the defences available to the original parties in the transaction. This avoids the possibility of a situation arising in which a third party becomes a holder in due course, and is able to enforce payment on the negotiable instrument when the debtor has a good defence against having to make payment under the consumer transaction.

Closing Questions

1. Maxine Mair sold her house for $190,000. After keeping $10,000 for living expenses, she divided the remaining $180,000 into three amounts of $60,000 which she placed in three separate accounts with the Credit Trust Company.
   a) Why has Mair deposited her money in this way?
   b) If the Credit Trust Company were to collapse and declare bankruptcy, what amount of money would she be able to claim?
   c) Would it have made any difference if Mair had made the same arrangements with a bank rather than a trust company?
   d) How could Mair have maximized protection for her money on deposit?

2. Claudette Foster runs a small promotional business that specializes in making plastic figurines of well-proportioned men and women. These are sold to health clubs as promotional items. The main assets of the business are the moulds, which Foster designed and created.
   When she receives an order from a health club, she contracts out the actual manufacture of the figurines to various plastic companies which use her moulds and then return them to her along with the completed figurines. Foster has arranged a business loan of $60,000 with Andre Fernandez.
   a) Advise Fernandez of the various types of security instruments that could be used in making his loan to Foster, and recommend which would best fit his purpose in these circumstances.
   b) Fernandez has come to you for advice. He tells you that Foster has defaulted on her loan repayments because of her poor management skills. He also tells you that the business itself would be a good one in the right hands, but Foster is making noises that if he does not drop the interest rate on the loan by half and restructure her monthly payments, she will relocate to Batavia, New York, where her cousin has a small plastics company. Restructuring the loan does not make economic sense for Fernandez. Explain to him the alternatives available in these circumstances, and what procedures would be necessary to put them in place.

3. The Konstabul and Nikakolakos families lived next door to each other in a small Canadian town; they had also lived close by in the same home town in the old country. Their friendship went back many years.
   Nikki Nikakolakos asked Kostos Konstabul to sign as a personal guarantor of a $20,000 bank loan for Nikakolakos's son, Peter. The loan was to enable Peter to buy a car, and Nikakolakos assured Konstabul that the young man had recently started a well-paying job at a factory and, playing on the Old World connection, said that she would do the same for him if he ever needed it.
   Konstabul finally agreed to go to the bank with Peter, and there he signed a guarantee containing an entire agreement clause. The loan was to be secured by a chattel mortgage registered against the car. On the day Konstabul signed the guarantee, the bank manager said, "Don't worry: the bank has a chattel mortgage on the car, which is worth far more than the loan amount."
   For several months Peter Nikakolakos made payments on the loan. However, the factory laid him off, and eventually he defaulted on the loan. The bank seized the car. Unfortunately, the vehicle had severe mechanical problems and brought only $5,000 at auction. The bank then demanded $15,000 from Konstabul, who complained that he had signed the guarantee only because the bank manager had said the car was worth more than $20,000. Konstabul asked Nikakolakos to speak to Peter and to the bank, reminding her that their families were from the same town in the old country. She replied, "Kostos, this is Canada, a new country full of opportunity; you've got to leave the Old World behind. Sorry, nothing I can do. You know what sons are like."
   a) What is the technical name in the law of contract for the defence Konstabul would raise to the bank's demand for the $15,000?
   b) Can Konstabul successfully rely on this defence? Why or why not?
   c) Does Konstabul have any remedy at law concerning Nikki Nikakolakos and/or her son Peter?

4. Andrew Brown was a director of a corporation. He signed a bank guarantee for a term loan of $100,000 on the standard Bank Guarantee Form (see Appendix). A few months later Brown resigned and left the corporation. The next month the corporation became insolvent.

The loan had been paid down to $50,000 when Brown resigned. Later it was increased to $60,000 and remained at that amount at the date of insolvency.

The bank had a lien over the assets of the corporation but failed to register it properly. If the lien had been registered properly, the bank could have realized $30,000.

The corporation had an overdraft of $20,000.

The corporation's lending by-law was invalid, and so the loan between the bank and the corporation was not enforceable.

The corporation is owed $10,000 by a customer, but the bank refuses to attempt to collect this debt even though the bank has a valid assignment of all of the corporation's accounts receivable.

The corporation owes Brown $15,000 for unpaid wages for work done for the corporation.

The corporation's credit card with the bank has an outstanding balance of $15,000, but $10,000 of this amount was used by the president for personal expenses.

a) Is Brown liable for the term loan at $50,000 or $60,000? Could Brown have done anything to limit his liability?

b) Can Brown claim a credit for $20,000 because of the bank's negligence in improperly registering the lien?

c) Can the bank claim the corporation's overdraft of $40,000 against Brown?

d) Since the original loan agreement between the primary debtor (the corporation) and the bank was unenforceable, is the guarantee of that same loan unenforceable against Brown?

e) Can Brown claim a credit for the $10,000 account receivable which the bank refused to collect?

f) Can Brown claim a credit for wages owed him by the corporation?

g) Can the bank claim the $15,000 on the corporate credit card account against Brown? Can Brown set off the $10,000 used by the president of the corporation fraudulently for personal expenses?

5. Barry and Denise Grierson have agreed to jointly and severally indemnify Frobisher Trust Company for a loan made to their small business, Barden Ltd. If Barden were to default on its payments under the loan, which of the following could the bank do?

a) Frobisher Trust Company must first attempt to collect the money from Barden Ltd. before contacting the Griersons.

b) The bank must sue both Barry and Denise Grierson for the default on the loan.

6. Loans officers normally require a shareholder as a guarantor whenever a loan is being made to a small corporation because:

a) they prefer dealing with real people rather than legal fictions

b) limited liability means that only the corporation's assets are available if the loan goes into default

c) the guarantee would allow the lending institution to step around other creditors of the corporation to obtain its money directly from the shareholder

(More than one answer may be correct.)

7. Karen Stauffer guaranteed a loan for Gloria Fogel to the Bank of Credit and Commerce, and signed a continuing guarantee form. The bank agreed to lend Gloria Fogel $100,000, to be paid in two instalments of $50,000, one on January 1 and one on June 1. The first $50,000 was advanced, and then Gloria Fogel declared bankruptcy on May 31. The bank did not learn of this and, on June 1, paid the remaining $50,000.

Fogel's trustee in bankruptcy used the money to pay Fogel's creditors. Having done so, there was nothing left to pay the bank, which then sued Karen Stauffer on the guarantee.

a) Could Stauffer use the bank's mistaken payment after the bankruptcy as a defence to the claim on the guarantee?

b) What would the position have been at common law?

8. Xavier Bosnovich wanted to start a business, and arranged a $25,000 loan with the Bank of Credit and Commerce. Bosnovich asked his mother to sign a guarantee for the bank. She did so, putting her signature on a personal guarantee contained in the bank's standard Guarantee Form (see Appendix).

Xavier paid the loan down to $5,000, and then increased it back to $25,000. Xavier went bankrupt and the bank demands payment of $25,000 from his mother.

a) Does she have to pay $5,000 or $25,000?

b) What would the result have been at common law? Was there anything the mother could have done to limit her responsibility to $5,000 under the terms of the standard bank guarantee?

c) If the original bank loan had been at 6% and the new loan was at 7%, would the mother have a defence? If so, what is the name of the defence and what result? Can you cite a legal precedent that supports your position?

9. Rules for the use of cheques are made under the *Bank Act*. True or false?

10. Dominik Borgia is an accountant. When his secretary took a three-week leave of absence for an operation, Borgia called a placement agency and arranged for a temporary secretary. Part of the job of Borgia's regular secretary was to prepare cheques to pay for office expenses.

Six weeks after Borgia's regular secretary returned to work, it was discovered that the temporary secretary had forged and cashed two cheques totalling $15,000. Borgia has advised the bank that he expects it to reimburse him for the forged cheques. The bank replied it had no interest in his claim.

a) What further information would you want to know to determine whether the bank's position is a valid one?

11. Which of the following are negotiable instruments?

a) a cheque

b) a promissory note

c) a bill of sale

d) a **certified cheque** (a cheque on which a bank has indicated that it will be cashed when presented for payment)

e) an IOU

f) a bill of exchange

certified cheque

a cheque on which a bank has indicated that it will be cashed when presented for payment

12. Gabe Rufo and Muriel Napier operated a partnership that specialized in installing new drains. The firm was called Down the Tubes. Napier and her crew had completed a drain installation for an elderly gentleman, who was bedridden. When giving the customer a quote for the installation, Napier had placed a piece of paper in front of him, saying, "This is a work order—sign here." The elderly man, who was a friend of Napier's family, had misplaced his reading glasses and relied on the young woman to tell him the contents of the paper before he signed.

In reality, what he signed was a promissory note obligating him to pay $10,000 on demand. Napier later endorsed the promissory note to Quickin Finance Co. When Quickin presented the note to the old gentleman for payment, he refused to pay it, claiming he had never signed a promissory note.

a) What is the legal status of Quickin?

b) Would Quickin be successful in enforcing the note against the elderly gentleman?

c) If the promissory note had been endorsed to Rufo as an individual, instead of to Quickin, what would his status be?

d) Would the elderly gentleman have a defence to payment on the promissory note if Rufo was the person seeking to enforce it against him? If so, what is the nature of that defence?

13. Who has the responsibility for marking "consumer note" on a promissory note used in a consumer transaction?

a) the vendor

b) the purchaser

c) the bank

d) a holder in due course

e) a third party receiving the promissory note endorsed by the vendor

14. Identify the following clauses from the example Bank Guarantee Form in the Appendix.
    a) entire agreement clause
    b) governing law clause
    c) acceleration clause
    d) interest default clause
    e) material variation clause
    f) mailbox rule clause

15. Mrs. Grande signed a personal guarantee for the debts of her husband's business. She held 10 percent of the shares of that company and was a director. She was a traditional housewife, took no part in the business, and signed whatever documents the husband told her were necessary for the business. She didn't read the documents before signing, as she trusted her husband. The business failed and the bank now sues her on her personal guarantee.
    a) Can Mrs. Grande successfully defend against the bank's claim on the basis of *non est factum*?
    b) Can Mrs. Grande rely on the *Merchants Consolidated v. Team Sports & Trophies* case discussed above?
    c) Does Mrs. Grande have any grounds for a defence? What are they and what is her likelihood of success?

16. Give the technical legal name for each of the following relating to a cheque:
    a) a person signing a cheque
    b) a person to whom a cheque is made payable
    c) the bank where bank account held
    d) a person to whom cheque signed over (negotiated) on reverse side

17. **Internet Research.** Visit the Bank of Canada website. Do a report on how a business can detect counterfeit money.

 *Websites*

www.cba.ca—Canadian Bankers Association. Information on banking issues, from the banks' point of view. Includes a special section on small business.

www.cdiaonline.org—Consumer Data Industry Association. Includes consumer information on credit checks.

strategis.ic.gc.ca/SSG/ca00669e.html—Site for Industry Canada providing a comparison of service charges at financial institutions.

Bank Guarantee Form

GUARANTEE
to the Bank of Credit and Commerce

IN CONSIDERATION OF THE BANK OF CREDIT AND COMMERCE (herein called the "Bank")
agreeing to deal with or to continue to deal with

Joseph Fine o/a Smythe & Fine

(herein called the "Customer"), the undersigned and each of them, if more than one, hereby jointly and severally guarantees payment to the Bank of all debts and liabilities, present or future, direct or indirect, absolute or contingent, matured or not, at any time owing by the Customer to the Bank or remaining unpaid by the Customer to the Bank, whether arising from dealings between the Bank and the Customer or from other dealings or proceedings by which the Bank may be or become in any manner whatever a creditor of the Customer, and wherever incurred, and whether incurred by the Customer alone or with another or others and whether as principal or surety, including all interest, commissions, legal and other costs, charges and expenses (such debts and liabilities being herein called the "guaranteed liabilities"), the liability of the undersigned hereunder being limited to the sum of

Forty-Eight Thousand

Insert Limit, if any. .... dollars

with interest from the date of demand for payment at the rate set out in paragraph 5 hereof.

AND THE UNDERSIGNED and each of them, if more than one, hereby jointly
and severally agrees with the Bank as follows:

1. In this guarantee the word "Guarantor" shall mean the undersigned and, if there is more than one guarantor, it shall mean each of them.

2. This guarantee shall be a continuing guarantee of all the guaranteed liabilities and shall apply to and secure any ultimate balance due or remaining unpaid to the Bank; and this guarantee shall not be considered as wholly or partially satisfied by the payment or liquidation at any time of any sum of money for the time being due or remaining unpaid to the Bank.

3. The Bank shall not be bound to exhaust its recourse against the Customer or others or any securities or other guarantees it may at any time hold before being entitled to payment from the Guarantor, and the Guarantor renounces all benefits of discussion and division.

4. The Guarantor's liability to make payment under this guarantee shall arise forthwith after demand for payment has been made in writing on the undersigned or any one of them, if more than one, and such demand shall be deemed to have been effectually made when an envelope containing such demand addressed to the undersigned or such one of them at the address of the undersigned or such one of them last known to the Bank is posted, postage prepaid, in the post office; and the Guarantor's liability shall bear interest from the date of such demand at the rate set out in paragraph 5 hereof.

5. The rate of interest payable by the Guarantor from the date of a demand for payment under this guarantee shall be the Bank's prime rate applicable at the time of demand, PLUS 2% per annum.

6. Upon default in payment of any sum owing by the Customer to the Bank at any time, the Bank may treat all guaranteed liabilities as due and payable and may forthwith collect from the Guarantor the total amount hereby guaranteed and may apply the sum so collected upon the guaranteed liabilities or may place it to the credit of a special account. A written statement of a Manager or Acting Manager of a branch of the Bank at which an account of the Customer is kept or of a General Manager of the Bank at which an account of the Customer is kept or of a General Manager of the Bank as to the amount remaining unpaid to the Bank at any time by the Customer shall, if agreed to by the Customer, be conclusive evidence and shall, in any event, be prima facie evidence against the Guarantor as to the amount remaining unpaid to the Bank at such time by the Customer.

7. This guarantee shall be in addition to and not in substitution for any other guarantees or other securities which the Bank may now or hereafter hold in respect of the guaranteed liabilities and the Bank shall be under no obligation to marshal in favour of the Guarantor any other guarantees or other securities or any moneys or other assets which the Bank may be entitled to receive or may have a claim upon; and no loss of or in respect of or unenforceability of any other guarantees or other securities which the Bank may now or hereafter hold in respect of the guaranteed liabilities, whether occasioned by the fault of the Bank or otherwise, shall in any way limit or lessen the Guarantor's liability.

8. Without prejudice to or in any way limiting or lessening the Guarantor's liability and without obtaining the consent of or giving notice to the Guarantor, the Bank may discontinue, reduce, increase or otherwise vary the credit of the Customer, may grant time, renewals, extensions, indulgences, releases and discharges to and accept compositions from or otherwise deal with the Customer and others, including the Guarantor and any other guarantor as the Bank may see fit, and the Bank may take, abstain from taking or perfecting, vary, exchange, renew, discharge, give up, realize on or otherwise deal with securities and guarantees in such manner as the Bank may see fit, and the Bank may apply all moneys received from the Customer or others or from securities or guarantees upon such parts of the guaranteed liabilities as the Bank may see fit and change any such application in whole or in part from time to time.

9. Until repayment in full of all the guaranteed liabilities, all dividends, compositions, proceeds of securities, securities valued or payments received by the Bank from the Customer or others or from estates in respect of the guaranteed liabilities shall be regarded for all purposes as payments in gross without any right on the part of the Guarantor to claim the benefit thereof in reduction of the liability under this guarantee, and the Guarantor shall not claim any set-off or counterclaim against the Customer in respect of any liability of the Customer to the Guarantor, claim or prove in the bankruptcy or insolvency of the Customer in competition with the Bank or have any right to be subrogated to the Bank.

10. This guarantee shall not be discharged or otherwise affected by the death or loss of capacity of the Customer, by any change in the name of the Customer, or in the membership of the Customer, if a partnership, or in the objects, capital structure or constitution of the Customer, if a corporation, or by the sale of the Customer's business or any part thereof or by the Customer being amalgamated with a corporation, but shall, notwithstanding any such event, continue to apply to all guaranteed liabilities whether theretofore or thereafter incurred; and in the case of a change in the membership of a Customer which is a partnership or in the case of the Customer being amalgamated with a corporation, this guarantee shall apply to the liabilities of the resulting partnership or corporation, and the term "Customer" shall include each such resulting partnership and corporation.

11. All advances, renewals and credits made or granted by the Bank purportedly to or for the Customer after the death, loss of capacity, bankruptcy or insolvency of the Customer, but before the Bank has received notice thereof shall be deemed to form part of the guaranteed liabilities; and all advances, renewals and credits obtained from the Bank purportedly by or on behalf of the Customer shall be deemed to form part of the guaranteed liabilities, notwithstanding any lack or limitation of power, incapacity or disability of the Customer or of the directors, partners or agents thereof, or that the Customer may not be a legal or suable entity, or any irregularity, defect or informality in the obtaining of such advances, renewals or credits, whether or not the Bank had knowledge thereof; and any such advance, renewal or credit which may not be recoverable from the undersigned as guarantor(s) shall be recoverable from the undersigned and each of them, if more than one, jointly and severally as principal debtor(s) in respect thereof and shall be paid to the Bank on demand with interest at the rate set out in paragraph 5 hereof.

12. All debts and liabilities, present and future, of the Customer to the Guarantor are hereby assigned to the Bank and postponed to the guaranteed liabilities, and all moneys received by the Guarantor in respect thereof shall be received in trust for the Bank and forthwith upon receipt shall be paid over to the Bank, the whole without in any way lessening or limiting the liability of the Guarantor under this guarantee; and this assignment and postponement is independent of the guarantee and shall remain in full force and effect until repayment in full to the Bank of all the guaranteed liabilities, notwithstanding that the liability of the undersigned or any of them under this guarantee may have been discharged or terminated.

13. The undersigned or any of them, if more than one, or his or their executors or administrators, by giving thirty days' notice in writing to the branch of the Bank at which the main account of the Customer is kept, may terminate his or their further liability under this guarantee in respect of liabilities of the Customer incurred or arising after the expiration of such thirty days, but not in respect of any guaranteed liabilities incurred or arising before the expiration of such thirty days even though not then matured; provided that notwithstanding receipt of any such notice the Bank may fulfil any requirements of the Customer based on agreements express or implied made prior to the expiration of such thirty days and any resulting liabilities shall be covered by this guarantee; and provided further that in the event of the termination of this guarantee as to one or more of the undersigned, if more than one, it shall remain a continuing guarantee as to the other or others of the undersigned.

14. This guarantee embodies all the agreements between the parties hereto relative to the guarantee, assignment and postponement and none of the parties shall be bound by any representation or promise made by any person relative thereto which is not embodied herein; and it is specifically agreed that the Bank shall not be bound by any representation or promises made by the Customer to the Guarantor. Possession of this instrument by the Bank shall be conclusive evidence against the Guarantor that the instrument was not delivered in escrow or pursuant to any agreement that it should not be effective until any condition precedent or subsequent has been complied with and this guarantee shall be operative and binding notwithstanding the non-execution thereof by any proposed signatory.

15. This guarantee shall be governed in all respects by the laws of the Province or jurisdiction in which the Customer's main account with the Bank is kept.

16. This guarantee shall not be discharged or affected by the death or any disability of the undersigned or any of them, if more than one, and shall enure to the benefit of and be binding upon the Bank, its successors and assigns, and the Guarantor, his heirs, executors, administrators, successors and assigns.

AS WITNESS the hand and seal of the Guarantor at _____ ,

this _____ day of _____ , 20 _____ .

SIGNED SEALED AND DELIVERED
  in the presence of

SIGNATURE AND SEAL

DATE RECEIVED
RECORDED
APPROVED
E.O. AUDITOR

_____

N.B.–Signature of this Guarantee involves personal liability.

Secured Transactions

Security Interests

When you borrow money from a bank, you will be asked to provide **collateral**—property of the debtor that can be seized and sold by a creditor if the debt is not paid, e.g., a car may be given as collateral for a bank loan. This collateral is called security, and because it is a type of property, it is subject to some of the laws surrounding property. Banks want collateral in order to minimize their risk of loss. The term *instrument* in this context means a formal written document.

collateral
property of the debtor that can be seized and sold by a creditor if the debt is not paid, e.g., a car may be given as collateral for a bank loan

Property Law

Property is divided into two classes in law—land, or real property, and all other property, called personal property (cars, televisions, boats, and so on).

Personal property is in turn divided into two types—tangible, or concrete, and intangible, or notional. For example, a computer is concrete property, but the right to collect money on a bill owed is notional. Notional property exists as a concept: it has no physical presence.

A business can possess all types of property, real and personal, both tangible and intangible. A small furniture manufacturing business, for example, might own the land on which the plant is built—real property—as well as tangible personal property such as machinery, tools, and inventory. It will also have **intangible property** (property that cannot be touched, such as accounts receivable) and, perhaps, a confidential formula for a special finish that makes the furniture unique.

intangible property
property that cannot be touched, such as accounts receivable

All property has two aspects that are important considerations for security purposes:

- ownership
- possession

Someone might have possession of a car but not actually own it. The vehicle could belong to a friend, or might be under lien to a bank. It is important to realize that possession of an item does not necessarily mean there is power to sell it with clear title.

Consider as an example the case of John Romanow, who purchased a clothing store from Leo Rodriguez. The store had a large inventory at the time the purchase was completed, and Romanow took possession. Shortly afterwards, the principal supplier removed most of the stock from the premises, as it had been placed on consignment and was not in fact owned by Rodriguez.

Giving Credit and Taking Security

The most important consideration in granting credit is not the asset the borrower might offer as security. The main concern is the borrower's ability to repay the sum involved in the transaction.

Security is a secondary concern. If the business cannot repay the loan, the assets that have been **pledged** (that is, taken possession of by a creditor as security and held until repayment) are seized and sold, and the proceeds applied against the amount owing. There is always a risk that the assets might not realize sufficient money to cover the loan. The value of any property can change over time. Even a house—which has a fairly stable market value—can drop dramatically in its worth because of a fall in land prices. Assets other than land are also very much subject to fluctuations in value.

The forced sale of personal property often brings only 20 percent of its retail value. People mistakenly compare personal property values with land values. With land, there is only one market, but with other assets, there are two markets—retail and wholesale. The forced sale of personal property often yields about half the wholesale price, or less.

The seizure and sale of assets involves other costs. The private bailiff who carries out the seizure must be paid; should the borrower resist, then obtaining a court order will involve further expense. In addition, resale of the items is normally handled by auctioneers or other liquidators—all of whom charge a significant fee for their services.

Why Take Security?

Security on a debt offers the lender a quick remedy if the borrower defaults, without having to go to court, for **repossession** of the property (the act of taking back possession of property that has been in the possession of another). The creditor can simply employ a bailiff to seize the assets, going to the courts only if some difficulty arises. For example, if a bank holds a chattel mortgage on a car and the borrower defaults, the bailiff can seize the vehicle from the borrower's property. The car can then be resold at a reasonable commercial value without the borrower's consent. However, if the car is in a locked garage, the bailiff can enter a locked structure only with the authority of a court order. Such an order relating to secured assets can usually be obtained fairly quickly.

Creditors who have security for their loans will be repaid before any other creditors, provided that security has been registered. Suppose, for example, that a bank holds a chattel mortgage on a car belonging to a business. One of the suppliers to the business has a judgment against it for $2,000. Because the bank loan is secured by the car, the bank can seize and sell the vehicle, and thereby have first claim on the proceeds.

Car selling price at auction	$6,000		
Bank loan outstanding	$5,000	Bank loan repaid	$5,000
Supplier's account	$2,000	Supplier paid	$1,000
Total debt	$7,000	Total paid	$6,000

The bank receives $5,000; the supplier—even though a court judgment has been obtained—receives only $1,000. The two creditors do not share equally in the proceeds of sale because the bank has specific security on the car.

Types of Security Instruments

There are several types of transactions in which the creditor obtains security. Some of these deal with real estate, and are discussed in Chapter 19. The documents involved in such agreements are called security instruments. *Instrument*, used in a legal context, refers to the written form of the transaction and is a synonym for *document*. Some of the most common methods of obtaining security on personal property are outlined below.

pledged

taken possession of by a creditor as security and held until repayment

repossession

the act of taking back possession of property that has been in the possession of another

Conditional Sales

Under this arrangement, the seller retains legal ownership—title—of the property until the final payment is made, but gives possession of it to the purchaser at the start of the agreement.

Used-car sales are sometimes made under a conditional sales contract, which is then sold, or assigned, by the car dealer to a finance company, which takes over collection of the payments.

Chattel Mortgages

Similar to a land mortgage, a chattel mortgage is a lien on personal property that is pledged as security for a loan. If you buy a car by borrowing money from a bank, the bank will put a chattel mortgage on the car until the loan is paid.

There are some limitations on the use of chattel mortgages. They are only possible for tangible property of some value, which can be identified—such as a car or a manufacturing machine. They are of little value over inventory such as shoes in a shoe store. While the shoes can be identified at the time the chattel mortgage is registered, they will be constantly sold and replaced, and a new inventory will not be covered by the chattel mortgage. It is obviously not realistic to register and discharge a chattel mortgage on each pair of shoes on delivery and sale.

Although chattel mortgages are still in use, they are gradually being replaced by the general security agreement (GSA) (see p. 398).

Chattel **Chattel** is the Norman French word for *cattle*. In medieval times, cattle were important personal property, and the term became associated in law with all moveable (personal) assets, as opposed to immovable assets, or real property.

Legalese

Assignment of Accounts Receivable/Book Debts

A business sells goods and services, for which customers pay. Frequently, that payment is not made at the time the items actually change hands or the service is provided, but is invoiced, with payment expected within a certain time. An accounting firm, for example, might have invoices totalling $50,000 awaiting payment by clients. This amount is known as accounts receivable, or book debts.

Most such accounts will probably be paid in the weeks or months following their issue. If collection of the amounts due does seem likely, a bank will lend money on the security of the accounts receivable. The accounting firm sends out bills, and some will be paid in any given time period, so that the actual accounts owing change continually. By using them as security for a loan, the business assigns the right to collect these debts to the bank. The bank can exercise these rights if the business defaults on its loan.

Banks have policies to evaluate the accounts receivable, and will seldom, for example, give any value to accounts outstanding more than 90 days.

General Security Agreements

Chattel mortgages and conditional sales relate to tangible property. The assignment of book debts relates to intangible property. None of these security instruments has the flexibility for dealing with all the types of personal property, tangible and intangible, that a business might have. A business is usually more valuable if it can be sold on an ongoing basis—chattel mortgages and conditional sales allow only pieces of the business to be seized.

Thus, a more general security instrument has been developed, taking into account the increasing amount and value of intangible property—such as information—in the modern business. The **general security agreement** is an agreement in which all the assets of a business are pledged as collateral. The GSA has wording that allows all the personal property of a business and the business operation itself to be seized, so that the business can be run as a going concern if there is any advantage to doing so. The GSA will include the right to information in computer systems, and to computer software, as well as any confidential formulas necessary for the success of the business.

Debentures

Debentures are simply another term for an instrument very similar to bonds. A **debenture** is a type of corporate bond, indicating a debt owed by a corporation. It combines security over personal and real property in one document. *Debenture* derives from the same word as *debt*, and can contain various terms. One of the most common of these is a **floating charge**—a form of mortgage on the assets of a corporation not affixed to any particular asset, but which does become affixed once a specified event takes place. A floating charge, for example, is often used with respect to inventory, which might be pledged as security for a loan—the firm can sell that inventory and replace it in the ordinary course of business. The purchaser can provide clear ownership without obtaining lien clearance. If, however, the corporation defaults on its loan payments, the security attaches to the property, and the corporation can no longer sell the inventory free and clear of the security interest. Once the security has attached, it is similar to a mortgage.

Debenture   The word **debenture** comes from the Latin *debeo*, meaning debt or to owe. So, like a bond, debenture simply means money that is borrowed on a loan basis, as distinct from an equity—purchase of shares—basis.

> **general security agreement**
>
> an agreement in which all the assets of a business are pledged as collateral

> **debenture**
>
> a type of corporate bond, indicating a debt owed by a corporation

> **floating charge**
>
> a form of mortgage on the assets of a corporation not affixed to any particular asset, but which does become affixed once a specified event takes place

> *Legalese*

■ *Business Law* Applied

❶ **Cristin Schmitz has** a small manufacturing business, and wants to sell three punch presses and replace them. She finds a purchaser who offers her $100,000 for the three machines. The purchase price is to be paid in instalments, with $10,000 down, and $10,000 a month for 9 months. The purchaser offers to give Schmitz postdated cheques for the payments.

   a) Do you think postdated cheques are sufficient, or is there anything else that Schmitz should do to ensure collection?

❷ **Phoenix Technologies Inc.** makes brake systems for automotive assembly plants. It wants to borrow $100,000 to buy new equipment for expansion, and has approached Venture Capital Inc. for a loan. Venture Capital has reviewed the business plan and the history of Phoenix, and has decided it is a good investment. You are an employee of Venture Capital, and your boss asks for any comments you might have about security that Venture could take from Phoenix for the loan.

   a) Discuss the possible assets that Phoenix might have and the types of security instruments that could be employed in the lending transaction.

Leases (Financing)

Leasing is the fastest-growing practice in the lending industry. Such a lease is often called a financing, or equipment, lease to distinguish it from a traditional lease in which ownership is never intended to be transferred to the **lessee** (the borrower, or the tenant or person who takes possession of the leased property). The lessee usually has the option to purchase at the end of a **financing lease**, which is a security arrangement in which a third person provides credit, purchases the property, and leases it to the borrower. While it is called a lease, and modelled on the rental form, it is a security instrument, and is used in place of conditional sales and chattel mortgages.

The borrower selects a piece of equipment, say a cash-register system, that it wishes to purchase for its business. It then approaches a small finance company for approval to borrow the amount necessary to purchase the equipment. Instead of having the business buy the equipment and placing a chattel mortgage on it, the finance company purchases the cash register and leases it to the business. That firm then has to pay rental—blended principal and interest payments—to repay the loan over the term of the lease. Often there is an option to buy out the equipment for a nominal value at the end of the lease.

Leasing was introduced in business financing but has recently become a consumer security technique, especially in the retail car business, where it is often advertised as "lease to own."

A lease of this nature is a loan with security. When the finance company has advanced the money, it has performed its obligations under the arrangement. There is always a term in the financing lease that expenses resulting from defects in the equipment cannot be set off against rental payments, so that the borrower's only recourse is action against the supplier. These clauses have been held by the courts to be enforceable.

One Percent Financing   Some car dealerships offer what appears to be extraordinarily low interest on leases. It's done by keeping a high sale price. If you start by telling the sales rep that you have cash or a bank loan, you can negotiate a much lower sale price. Try it! The difference in price will bring the supposedly low interest rate up to the market rate. There is no free lunch.

Defences

Leases and other security instruments are types of contracts, and so the normal contract defences apply. Some of those defences most relevant are discussed next in the context of leases. Contract defences such as these apply to all security agreements.

There is in most leases a clause stating that if the borrower defaults on any payment, the whole of the principal sum of the debt and of accrued interest immediately falls due. Such a clause is called an **acceleration clause.**

There may also be a clause that states interest at a higher rate is charged on overdue payments. The interest default rate is often as high as 36 percent per annum. In time this interest can far exceed the purchase value of the item under lease.

Fortunately the courts have given some relief against these onerous terms. If they are out of all proportion to the real damage suffered by the leasing company, there may be penalty clauses (see Chapter 6). Recall that the leasing company must mitigate its damage. That means it must try to find another customer to take over the lease. If it does so, then the value of the new lease must be deducted from the damages resulting from the breach of the first lease. The acceleration clause often does not take into account the duty to mitigate or give credit for any mitigation.

lessee

the tenant or person who takes possession of the leased property

financing lease

a security arrangement in which a third person provides credit, purchases the property, and leases it to the borrower

Business Alert!

acceleration clause

a clause stating that if the borrower defaults on any payment, the whole of the principal sum of the debt and of accrued interest immediately falls due

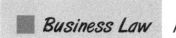

Business Law Applied

❸ **Bennett and Jones** Ltd. wants to lease a fax machine. It selects an MBI fax machine costing $5,000. The MBI sales representative tells Bennett and Jones Ltd. about Techlease, which specializes in financing business-equipment purchases. A lease is arranged by Bennett and Jones Ltd. with Techlease. The terms are: monthly installments of $100 for 60 months; and, if any payment is missed, the entire balance of the lease becomes due, and the leasing company can repossess the fax machine on default of payment.

Bennett and Jones Ltd. makes one year of payments, then defaults. Techlease repossesses the fax machine and releases it immediately to another company on the same terms. It sues Bennett and Jones Ltd. for $4,800, or 48 payments.

   a) Does the lease agreement permit Techlease to sue for the amount claimed?
   b) Does Bennett and Jones Ltd. have a defence?
   c) What damages can Techlease validly claim?

Defective Equipment

It seems that if the equipment that is leased is defective, the lessee should be able to set off the cost of repairing the defects against the lease payment. However, this is not the case. Recall that the real nature of a lease is a loan with security. When the finance company has advanced the money, it has performed its obligations under the arrangement. There is usually a term in the financing lease stating that expenses resulting from defects from the equipment cannot be set off against the rental payments, so that the borrower's only recourse is an action against the supplier. These clauses have been held to be enforceable by the courts.

Consumer Defences

Under consumer protection legislation in most provinces, if two-thirds of the loan is paid off, then the bank cannot seize the asset simply by using a bailiff. However, the bank can sue and obtain judgment, and then seize the item to satisfy that judgment. It may take a little longer, but the same result is achieved.

In British Columbia and Alberta, if the bank repossesses the car, it cannot sue for the balance should the sale of the vehicle fail to realize sufficient money to cover the outstanding amount of the loan.

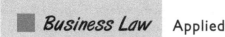

Business Law Applied

❹ **Linda Scott bought** a boat for recreational purposes, paid for in part by a bank loan of $44,000. As part of the security for the loan, the bank obtained a chattel mortgage on the vessel.

Scott made all the required payments on the loan, except the final one. The bank now wants to repossess the boat.

   a) Can the bank do so?
   b) Does it matter in which province this situation takes place?

Other Types of Securities

Consignment

Consignment is the placing of goods with a business for the purpose of sale. Goods are sometimes placed in a particular business by the manufacturer, to be sold by the business owner. The business does not buy these goods from the manufacturer, but simply stores them with instructions to sell. If the items are sold, the business keeps an agreed percentage of the selling price.

Whether goods on consignment are there as a security and have to be registered under the public registration system is a matter of intention between the owner and the person holding the goods for sale. (The **registration system** is a means of registering and tracking property deeds whereby the records are available to be examined.) The court will ask whether the consignment arrangement was intended to be a security arrangement, providing some security for the debtor's obligations towards the owner of the goods. Consignment can be of concern to a purchaser of the business. The business may appear to have a full inventory; however, if goods are on a true consignment basis—and therefore do not have to be registered—the purchaser may be misled as to the true size of the inventory.

consignment
the placing of goods with a business for the purpose of sale

registration system
a means of registering and tracking property deeds whereby the records are available to be examined

Purchase Money Security Interest

If a supplier sells and delivers a large quantity of inventory on credit one day, and the next day that business goes bankrupt, ownership of the goods has passed to the business. The trustee in bankruptcy of the business will sell that inventory and the supplier will only share with all other creditors. To protect suppliers of goods, a new security instrument called the purchase money security interest (PMSI) was devised, permitting a supplier of goods to register a lien under *Personal Property Security Act* legislation for goods supplied. If the business does not pay, or goes bankrupt, the supplier can repossess its own goods to the extent of the unpaid amount. An alternative remedy may be available under the *Bankruptcy and Insolvency Act*.

Business Law   Applied

❺ **On September 1,** Kipling Industries Inc. sells and delivers a quantity of sweatshirts on credit to Tough Sport Limited. The clothing is worth $10,000.

On September 2, Tough Sport arranges with a contractor for renovations to its premises and gives the contractor a chattel mortgage in the amount of $10,000 on the sweatshirt inventory.

On September 3, Tough Sport goes bankrupt.

a) Can the contractor seize the sweatshirt inventory, or can Kipling Industries take it back?
b) What could Kipling have done to protect its interests?

❻ **Slim Fitness Inc.,** a diet business, wishes to purchase a new type of computerized body-wrap machine that is reported to help in weight loss. It arranges with Sure Leasing Inc. to obtain the money to buy the equipment. Sure Leasing Inc. buys the equipment from EMS Systems Inc., and then gives it to Slim Fitness Inc. on a financing lease.

After using the equipment for a few months, the system breaks down almost completely.

a) Can Slim Fitness Inc. refuse to make payments on the financing lease?
b) If not, what remedy does it have?

Personal Property Security Act

financing statement

a document setting out details of a security interest that must be filed in order to protect that interest under personal property security acts

Until recently, each type of security instrument required different technical procedures for the time and place of its registration, form of agreement, and so on. To cut through some of the red tape involved, all provinces, except P.E.I. and Newfoundland, created one set of rules governing the registration of all security transactions involving personal property. Such registration is accomplished with a document called a financing statement, and should take place as soon as possible after the transaction has been completed. A **financing statement** is a document setting out details of a security interest that must be filed in order to protect that interest under personal property security acts (often referred to as the PPSA of the particular province). This means that the lender registers notice of all liens against personal property at one place, using one procedure. As well, a purchaser has only to search for lien notices at one location.

The registration concept puts the onus on the purchaser to search for liens before buying. The purchaser cannot plead ignorance as a defence—if a lien is publicly registered, it is enforceable even against innocent purchasers who were unaware of it.

■ Critical Concepts of Unexpected Liens

- Notice of liens can be registered in a government office, and the general public can search for evidence of a lien against any object.
- The registration of a notice of lien means it is enforceable against a stranger who purchased the object, whether the purchaser knew of the lien or not.
- Goods sold to consumers in ordinary retail sales are not subject to liens.
- Registration gives the first-registered lienholder priority over subsequently registered notices of liens.

Business Alert!

Liens Can Be Dangerous   Liens against personal property can cause businesses two serious problems.

Giving credit. When you give credit to a business, it is safest to assume that the bank and other financial institutions have liens on all of its assets. As a small business, you are concerned with the firm's ability to pay. If it should go out of business, there will very likely be little left over after the bank takes its first claim on security.

Buying. Before purchasing any item from a seller who is not selling in the ordinary course of its business, make certain that you search for liens. Because of the consumer/retail exemption for goods sold in the ordinary course of business, many people do not realize the real danger that a lien may exist on something bought outside the normal retail setting. Probably all purchases that you make as a business will be outside the retail/consumer context.

Lien Clearance Certificate

Recognizing that many consumers are not aware of the need to search and obtain lien clearance before buying an expensive object, the Ontario government has passed laws requiring the vendor of a motor vehicle to provide a lien-clearance certificate on the private sale of a car. Purchasers of cars sold by car dealers in the ordinary course of business are not subject to liens. To date, Ontario is the only province that has this legislation in place. It also applies only to cars, and to no other objects.

Business Law   Applied

❼ Franka Marques wanted two cars for her family. She bought a van for family use and a subcompact for driving to work. The van was purchased from a used-car lot; the subcompact she acquired by private sale from an ad in the local newspaper.

It turns out there were liens registered against both vehicles by banks, who now want to repossess the cars because the original borrowers have defaulted.

a) Is the lien registered against the van enforceable against Marques?

b) Is the lien registered against the subcompact enforceable against Marques?

❽ Chester Gryski saw a newspaper ad for the private sale of a car, and agreed to purchase the vehicle for $20,000 on August 1, from John Fairburn. Fairburn knew that he would soon be leaving the country, and borrowed $10,000 against the security of the car, giving the bank a chattel mortgage. Fairburn had no intention of repaying the loan.

At 9:30 a.m. on July 31, Fairburn obtained a lien certificate that the car was free and clear. At 10:00 a.m. the same day, the bank registered its security against the loan to Fairburn.

On August 1, Gryski met Fairburn at the Ministry of Transportation office, where Fairburn gave Gryski the lien clearance certificate and the ownership to the car in exchange for a certified cheque for $20,000.

Fairburn left the country. The bank seized the car and claimed the lien for $10,000.

a) Did Gryski know of the lien?

b) Does the bank have a valid lien for $10,000?

Receivers/Managers

When a business borrows money from a bank or other creditor, one of the terms may provide that on default the creditor can appoint a receiver. The **receiver** is a person appointed by a **secured creditor**—a creditor who has the right to seize and sell specific assets of a borrower to pay off a loan—to retrieve the assets to satisfy the debt. The receiver takes control of the business and/or its assets, according to the provisions of the agreement. The receiver replaces the current board of directors and has the powers of the board, which include firing all employees. In a typical case, the receiver and staff will arrive at the business premises and physically take control of the premises and all business records. If the owner resists, the receiver can make an application to the court. If the owner resists that court order, the owner may be in contempt of court.

Few business owners resist the receivership, so most proceed voluntarily and without the need of court intervention. In a receivership, the business is considered insolvent, that is, unable to pay its debts. However, a formal application in bankruptcy is not made. That expense is saved by the creditor. Receivers have to register with the Superintendent of Bankruptcy, so anyone can search at that office to see if a business is in receivership.

Frequently, the duties of receiver and manager are undertaken by one person or firm. However, the legal responsibilities of each position are distinct. A receiver/manager can be anyone. There are no requirements for specific qualifications. However, a receiver is usually a chartered accountant who is also a licensed trustee in bankruptcy. The bank has to guarantee the payment of the receiver's fees, but these are added on to the debt and eventually borne by the debtor if the debtor has sufficient assets.

receiver
a person appointed by a secured creditor to retrieve the assets to satisfy the debt

secured creditor
a creditor who has the right to seize and sell specific assets of a borrower to pay off a loan

A receiver:

- is an agent who takes over the assets that are subject to a general security agreement
- takes control of the assets with a view to disposing of them as quickly as possible, at a reasonable commercial value
- has no power to run the business

A manager:

- takes over the function of the board of directors, and has the power to run the company as an ongoing concern. Legally, the business is considered to have ceased operation at the time the receiver/manager is appointed, and afterwards is started afresh.
- has the power to fire all employees on one day's notice, with no compensation. This is a considerable advantage because many employees may be loyal to the business owner, and antagonistic to the manager who they feel has harmed their former employer. However, the ability of the manager to control their continuing employment helps to ensure their co-operation.
- is appointed when there is some hope of either making an agreement with the creditors to keep the business alive, or selling the business as an ongoing enterprise. Usually, a business has more value if it can be sold while it is in operation.

Types of Receivers

A receiver can be appointed by either:

- private arrangement under a general security agreement (GSA)/debenture type of security, or
- the court

A typical GSA provides for the appointment of a receiver on notice to the debtor. In this way, the bank or other creditor sends out a letter appointing a receiver, who goes directly to the business and takes over the assets. The courts do not want to become involved in this part of the debt-collection process if it can be avoided, and will appoint a receiver only if the self-help remedy is ineffective. Such a situation would be if the receiver goes to the business and the owner refuses to turn over the assets.

There are provisions for the appointment of a receiver whenever the court feels it is just and convenient—such as when another remedy is found to be ineffective, and the assets are in danger of disappearing.

A receivership is an expensive proposition, and receiver's fees are quite high. If the proceeds from the sale of the assets are not enough to cover the receiver's fee, the bank has to pay the difference.

In Summation

Security Instruments

- A financing institution's decision to lend money is based on the borrower's ability to repay the loan. This decision will include a request for property, real or personal, to be given as collateral or security for repayment of the loan.
- A security interest in real property is usually created through a mortgage.

- If personal property is involved, the financial transaction is secured by what is commonly referred to as a lien.

- There are several different types of security instruments for personal property, each with distinct advantages and limitations. The various types are: conditional sale contract; chattel mortgage; assignment of accounts receivable/book debts; general security agreement (GSA); debenture; lease; consignment; and purchase money security interest (PMSI).

Liens

- The lien against personal property created by the various types of security instruments may be registered under the *Personal Property Security Act* (PPSA) registry system in almost all provinces. It may then be enforced against subsequent purchasers of that property, even if the purchaser is unaware of the lien's existence.

- The lien created by the security instrument includes the lender's right to repossess the item. This gives the lender an advantage over other general, unsecured creditors of the debtor.

- Various consumer laws protect a purchaser in a consumer transaction from the financial institution's being able to exercise its lien in particular circumstances.

- The ability to appointment a receiver/manager is a further remedy that may be available to a financial institution in a lending transaction.

Closing Questions

1. What is the nature of each of the following types of property?
   a) the name associated with a doughnut/coffee-shop franchise
   b) a prize-winning show dog
   c) a mobile home
   d) a company's outstanding invoices to customers
   e) an office building
   f) a computer disk containing the original program for a highly successful word-processing program
   g) an acre of undeveloped land

2. Claudia Regona bought three videos that she found in a bin of previously viewed tapes at a video store. In talking to the owner, Regona mentioned that she had always wanted to operate her own video-rental outlet. The owner said that he wanted to get out of the business, and was trying to sell off his entire stock of tapes. He offered them to Regona at a price she could not refuse. To avoid tax, she arranged to pay cash for the entire inventory.

   Later that day, after renting a truck and visiting her bank to pick up the cash, Regona moved all the videos from the store to her basement. The next day, she was contacted by the Central Bank, which claimed it had a lien registered against all the videotapes owned by the video store.
   a) Is the lien enforceable against the three tapes that Regona bought from the bin of previously viewed videos?
   b) Is the lien enforceable against the sale by the owner of the entire inventory of the store?
   c) What steps should Regona have taken to protect her interests?

3. Rod Smith lived in Vancouver, British Columbia. He borrowed $10,000 from the Bank of Victoria to purchase a car, and the bank secured the loan by a chattel mortgage on the vehicle. Several months later, Smith found a contract job in Ontario for a period of one year. Two months after relocating to Ontario, Smith defaulted on his loan payments. The Bank of Victoria repossessed the car and sold it at auction. The bank received $6,000 from the sale of the car, and is now bringing a court action against Smith in Ontario for the balance of the $10,000 loan.
   a) Does Smith have a defence to the bank's court action for the balance of the outstanding loan?

4. Helen Symanski responded to a newspaper advertisement selling a 1992 Mustang. After negotiating with the owner, Symanski bought the car for an exceptionally good price, paying cash. Three days later, hearing a noise in her driveway, she looked out the window to see the car being towed away. She later discovered that a bank had a registered lien against the car.

Symanski claims she had no knowledge of the bank's lien, and was totally unaware that liens could be registered. The previous owner has already spent the money and she cannot get anything back from him. The bank claimed Symanski owed it $1,500 on the lien, as well as $250 in repossession charges—a total of $1,750.

a) Does Symanski have to pay the bank, or does her right to the car take priority over the bank's?

b) Can she successfully argue against having to pay the $250 in repossession charges?

c) If the car had been parked in Symanski's garage, what procedure would the bank have had to take in order to repossess the car?

d) Assume the same facts as above, except that the owner took out a bank loan on August 1, and signed a chattel mortgage on the Mustang for $5,000. Symanski does know that she must search for liens, and obtains a lien-clearance certificate. On August 2, she purchases the car from the owner, and transfers ownership that same day. The bank registers its chattel mortgage on August 3. Subsequently, the owner defaults on the loan. Can the bank claim a lien on the car for $5,000?

Bankruptcy

What Is Bankruptcy?

It has often been said that everybody loses when a business goes bankrupt. The owner loses the business and the investment, creditors lose money since they are not paid in full, employees lose jobs, suppliers lose a customer, and customers lose a source of supply.

A new *Bankruptcy and Insolvency Act* (BIA) was passed by the federal government in 1992 to reform bankruptcy law and shift the emphasis from merely distributing a bankrupt's assets among creditors to providing possibilities for saving the business. The main purposes of the act are:

- to ensure a fair distribution of the bankrupt's assets among creditors
- to save any ongoing business where possible
- to release an honest but unfortunate debtor from debts where the burden is too great to allow a fresh start

How Is Bankruptcy Declared?

There are three ways in which a bankruptcy can happen:

- voluntarily
- involuntarily
- by rejection of a commercial proposal

Voluntary

No one wants to file for bankruptcy. But when situations such as extraordinary health-care costs or business setbacks occur, it can become impossible to meet heavy financial obligations. In these circumstances, both individuals and corporations can apply to the court and make a voluntary assignment into bankruptcy.

The general test to justify voluntary bankruptcy is that is has become absolutely impossible to pay the debts owing. What a court considers impossible will vary with individual circumstances, and advice should be sought from a specialist. Many trustees in bankruptcy as well as bankruptcy lawyers offer a free initial half-hour consultation.

Involuntary

If a business's creditors have tried unsuccessfully to collect their debts by other means, they may decide to force the business into bankruptcy. This is done by way of a petition to the court. If the court agrees, it will make a **receiving order** (a court order for the transfer of debtor's assets to a trustee in bankruptcy), finding that the person is bankrupt. In order to initiate the process, a creditor must be owed a debt of more than $1,000, and the debtor must have committed an act of bankruptcy as set out in the act.

If the business is a corporation, the corporation is declared bankrupt. If the business is not incorporated (e.g., a partnership), individual partners are petitioned personally and declared bankrupt.

The Bankruptcy and Insolvency Act

Three of the most common acts of bankruptcy are listed in this excerpt from subsection 42(1) of the act:

> a debtor commits an act of bankruptcy in each of the following cases: . . .
>
> (f) If he admits to any meeting of his creditors in any statement of his assets and liabilities that show that he is insolvent, or presents or causes to be presented to any such meeting a written admission of his inability to pay his debts; or . . .
>
> (h) If he gives notice to any of his creditors that he has suspended, or is about to suspend payment of his debts; or . . .
>
> (j) If he ceases to meet his liabilities generally as they become due.

■ *Business Law* Applied

❶ **Joan Carlucci carries** on business as Aquarius Electronics Company. The firm's debts are too high, and it cannot continue in business. Carlucci wants to know if the company can declare bankruptcy.

　a) Can Aquarius Electronics Company file for bankruptcy?

Commercial Proposals

Before the BIA was passed in 1992, the greatest criticism of the Canadian bankruptcy system was the lack of inexpensive provisions to help a business get back on its feet. A creditor might act out of self-interest, or without sufficient thought, and destroy a business that could well have been saved. Under the new act, the majority of creditors now have a chance to vote on any proposal to keep the business alive, and overrule objections other creditors might have to doing so. The majority might force a dissident creditor to accept less than full payment on its claim. The guiding principle is that all creditors may eventually receive more from a proposal to carry on business than they would by putting the business into bankruptcy and having assets sold on a liquidation basis. By renegotiating—restructuring—its debts through a compromise with creditors, the business can continue, and everyone involved benefits.

The act allows persons who are insolvent, or their representative, to file a notice of an intention to make a proposal. When this notice is filed, the business obtains certain protections from creditors. The most important of these are:

- Creditors are prevented from taking steps to enforce rights to collect on their debts, either by way of self-help—seizing assets—or court order. The stay, or delay, in creditors' taking action does not apply to secured creditors who have already started to realize on the assets secured in their favour.
- No one can stop supplying essential services such as electricity, heat, water, or phone services. This applies to services, not to goods. However, an insolvent person can be made to pay **COD** (cash on delivery, a contractual term requiring the purchaser to pay the shipper cash on delivery of goods) for goods or services used or leased if those items are provided after the filing date. (An **insolvent person** is a person who is unable to meet, or has ceased to pay, his or her debts as they become due, but has not been declared bankrupt by court order.)
- No one can terminate or amend any agreement with the insolvent person.
- No one can terminate a lease or a licensing agreement.
- No one can accelerate contract or money-due provisions contained in an agreement.

The initial stay is 30 days, but the court can renew it for up to a total of six months to allow the insolvent business to attempt to make a deal with its creditors and continue in business. The renewals will be based on the fact that the business is making a valid attempt to reach a compromise, and that a deal is possible. If the business is using this process only as a delaying tactic, the renewal will be denied.

The proposal must be accepted according to a somewhat complicated formula that allows a majority of creditors to approve it, over the objection of others. If the proposal is rejected, the insolvent person is automatically declared bankrupt.

Insolvency   **Insolvency** describes a financial condition. If an individual cannot meet obligations as they generally become due, and has liabilities of at least $1,000, that person is insolvent, *but not necessarily bankrupt.*

Bankruptcy occurs when a receiving order is made against a person or corporation, or a voluntary assignment is made, or a commercial proposal is rejected.

COD

cash on delivery, a contractual term requiring the purchaser to pay the shipper cash on delivery of goods

insolvent person

a person who is unable to meet, or has ceased to pay, his or her debts as they become due, but has not been declared bankrupt by court order

Legalese

■ *Business Law*   Applied

❷ **Business has gone** badly for the Wellington Corporation, and it cannot continue to pay its creditors. Prescott Manufacturers, which supplied Wellington with an essential manufacturing machine, is threatening to repossess that machine. Wellington Corporation has a very good chance of securing a large contract that will help turn its fortunes around. However, Prescott refuses to wait for payment.

a) Can the Wellington Corporation take any steps to stop the supplier from taking its machine?
b) If so, for how long would the delay remain in effect?

❸ **Salvadore Holdings Limited** runs a plant that is heavily dependent on electricity, and has accumulated very large arrears on its account with the hydro company. The electricity supplier has threatened to cut off Salvadore unless the full amount owing is paid immediately. To make Salvadore's life even more difficult, a supplier of leather—vital to their production—has refused to provide any further product.

    a) Is there any remedy that Salvadore Holdings can take to prevent the hydro company from cutting off the supply of electricity?

    b) Will the hydro company have to supply electricity in the future? If so, on what basis?

    c) Can Salvadore Holdings obtain an order making the leather supplier continue to supply leather?

❹ **JMC Corporation gets** raw material from Bearskin Supplies. The invoice from Bearskin states "30 days is as good as cash" and, up till now, if JMC Corporation paid their account in full within 30 days, the company was not charged interest.

JMC has filed a notice of intention to make a proposal with the bankruptcy court, and now wants Bearskin to continue its supplies on the same basis. Bearskin refuses, saying it will supply, but on a COD basis.

    a) Can Bearskin insist on COD, or is it required by bankruptcy law to continue to supply on 30-days' credit?

    b) What is the downside risk in filing a commercial proposal for bankruptcy?

The Key Players

The Trustee

The **trustee in bankruptcy** is the person appointed to administer the property of a bankrupt for the benefit of creditors. This person is usually a chartered accountant, who must hold a licence from the Superintendent of Bankruptcy. The trustee is normally selected by the debtor. However if there is any disagreement, the creditors have the right to apply to the court to have a trustee of their choosing appointed.

The Superintendent of Bankruptcy

The federal government has established the Office of Superintendent of Bankruptcy and supervises this individual closely. The superintendent licenses and oversees the acts of trustees in bankruptcy, and also appoints a government official known as the official receiver.

Official Receiver

The **official receiver** is a government-appointed administrator responsible for the supervision of bankruptcy proceedings. It is the office of the official receiver that supervises individual bankruptcy cases. As part of the bankruptcy process, the bankrupt will be called to the official receiver's office and questioned by a member of that staff on the bankrupt's activities and assets.

What Happens When Bankruptcy Is Declared?

On bankruptcy, the assets of the insolvent person are transferred into the possession of the trustee in bankruptcy. Where the bankrupt is a business, the trustee will take over the business and decide whether to try to continue to run the operation for a time, or to liquidate it immediately.

    The trustee will examine the affairs of the bankrupt and report to creditors on the assets and liabilities. The trustee will also determine whether there have been any illegal transfers of assets. The official receiver may also interview the bankrupt to determine whether there have any fraudulent transactions.

Creditors will file a proof of claim and, in bankruptcy of businesses, are then entitled to attend a meeting of creditors to discuss the trustee's report and decide whether any action should be taken to recover assets.

Fraudulent Transactions in Bankruptcy

The main actions designated by the BIA as probably being undertaken in an attempt to defraud creditors are:

- gifts given to anyone by the bankrupt one year before the bankruptcy, if the trustee can prove that the now-bankrupt was insolvent at the time the gift was made. If the gift is to a relative the time extends to five years.
- payment for services or transfer of property to any related person one year before the bankruptcy. Such a transaction is a reviewable transaction.
- payment given to a creditor in preference over other creditors. A solvent business can pay creditors in any order that it wishes. However, if the business is insolvent, it must pay all creditors equally. The time limit for preferences is three months preceding the bankruptcy; however, if the payment is to a relative, the time limit is 12 months before the bankruptcy.
- payments to shareholders, either by way of dividend or repurchase of shares, made one year before the bankruptcy.
- taking any assets from the business and hiding them, or giving them to others to do so—this is a criminal offence.

The act also provides that these actions—named deceptive practices by the bankrupt during the course of the bankruptcy—are criminal offences.

Investigation of a Bankrupt's Actions

The bankrupt's improper actions are usually divided into two categories, known as fraudulent conveyance and **fraudulent preference** (an insolvent debtor's preferring (and paying) one creditor over another). An individual facing bankruptcy might take steps to place assets out of the reach of creditors. The *Bankruptcy and Insolvency Act* contains rules that target certain transactions, automatically declaring them ineffective, or presuming them to have been made with the intention of defrauding creditors. There are usually three factors involved in deciding whether this type of transaction has taken place:

fraudulent preference
an insolvent debtor's preferring (and paying) one creditor over another

- value given or received—either too much or too little is paid for the property or services
- timing—the event took place close to the date bankruptcy was declared, when the business was insolvent
- relationship—the transaction was done with a relative or close friend, or a related corporation

One of the key concepts is the non-arm's-length, or related-party, transaction. (A transaction is **arm's length** if it is between persons who are not related or associated in any way.) This is a transaction between the near-bankrupt and close friends or relatives who help the debtor to keep assets beyond the reach of creditors. Since corporations are often used today, they can be substituted for relatives. So, any corporation which is owned or controlled by a bankrupt is considered a related party.

arm's length
between persons who are not related or associated in any way

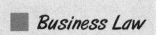 *Critical Concepts of* Bankruptcy

Certain transfers of assets by a bankrupt are considered deceptive practices:

- If it is to a creditor to whom the bankrupt does owe money, it may be a preference.
- If it is a person to whom the bankrupt does not owe money, it may be a settlement.
- If it is to a non–arm's length person, it may be a fraudulent conveyance.
- If it is for an inadequate consideration, it may be a reviewable transaction.

R. v. Spectrum Interiors (Guelph) Ltd., [1979] 29 C.B.R. 218 (Ont. S.C.)

Pressuring a business to pay may not benefit the creditor if the business goes bankrupt shortly after payment is made. The payment, or return of goods, may be considered a fraudulent preference if the transaction gives one creditor an advantage over another.

Spectrum Interiors was in a difficult situation, struggling to stay in business. Its principal supplier, which shipped a large quantity of flooring materials on credit, demanded return of the stock when it was not paid for. The supplier threatened that if Spectrum did not return the goods then in Spectrum's possession, it would be cut off from future shipments. If Spectrum did return the stock, the supplier would continue to ship on a COD-only basis.

Spectrum returned the flooring materials to the supplier, and shortly after doing so went bankrupt. The trustee in bankruptcy demanded the cash value of the returned goods from the supplier,

claiming the return was a fraudulent preference. The supplier refused, stating this was not a preference, and the main intention of the bankrupt was to stay in business, not to prefer the creditor.

The Court's Decision

The court found that Spectrum's hope of staying in business by returning the goods was unrealistic. In fact, returning 50 percent of its inventory made it impossible for Spectrum to carry on. The creditor did not agree to extend further credit; all it offered to do was to continue to ship, but on a COD basis. The only one to profit from the return of the merchandise was the supplier. That company was preferred three months before Spectrum's bankruptcy, and therefore the return of the goods was a fraudulent preference.

■ *Business Law* Applied

5 **Susan Suarez runs** her own business, a sole proprietorship called Suzy Suarez Designs. The business is doing badly and so, on August 1, she transfers ownership of her house to her husband. On September 1 of the same year, Suarez goes into bankruptcy. The trustee in bankruptcy wants to attack the transfer of the house to the husband.

a) Are there any special bankruptcy rules that will assist either the trustee or the business owner?

6 **John and Louise** Webber were the sole shareholders of Webber Feeds Ltd. As well as being in the feed business, the company owned a few acres of vacant land. One month before Webber Feeds Ltd. went bankrupt, that land was sold for fair market value to John Wilson, Mrs. Webber's brother. At the time of the land sale, Mr. and Mrs. Webber were given an option personally to repurchase the property at the same price. They paid nothing for the option, which was to expire in five years.

One year after the bankruptcy, the land significantly increased in value, and so the Webbers exercised their option and bought the property. The trustee in bankruptcy of Webber Feeds wants to have the Webbers hand over to the trustee the money they made by purchasing the property.

a) Are there any special bankruptcy rules that will assist the trustee?
b) Did the option to the Webbers have any value in itself?
c) If the corporation got fair market value at the time, was there any harm to the creditors because of the transaction?
d) What test will the court apply to decide whether the Webbers should pay their gain to the trustee?

7 **Verne Wilkinson was** the sole shareholder, officer, and director of Cleaningz Eazi Inc. when the firm declared bankruptcy. Wilkinson's aunt was a vice-president of Cleaningz Eazi, and proved a claim in the bankruptcy for unpaid wages in the amount of $5,000.

a) In which class of creditors is a wage claimant?
b) Are there any limits on the amount, or can the aunt claim the full $5,000?
c) Can the aunt claim as a preferred creditor?

8 **The Phoenix Corporation** operates a small manufacturing business. It was doing poorly and could not pay its creditors. The major creditor approached the owner and had him give a chattel mortgage on all of the Phoenix Corporation's machinery. The chattel mortgage was publicly registered.

One month after giving the chattel mortgage, the Phoenix Corporation went bankrupt. The trustee in bankruptcy wants to have the chattel mortgage set aside.

a) Are there any special bankruptcy rules that will assist the trustee?
b) Are all creditors being treated equally in this situation?

Types of Creditors

There are three categories of creditors in a bankruptcy:

- secured
- preferred
- unsecured

Secured

These are creditors who hold some form of security, such as a mortgage or general security agreement (GSA), on the assets of the bankrupt, and therefore have claim on the particular property named in that security. If the security is sold and does not cover the debt, then the secured creditor can claim before an unsecured creditor for the balance owing. If, for example, a building owned by a bankrupt business is sold for $400,000, and the bank has an outstanding mortgage of $500,000, the bank receives the $400,000, but must claim as an unsecured creditor for the additional $100,000. The bank's claim takes precedence over that of other unsecured creditors.

Preferred

The act specifically creates a class of preferred creditors who have priority over unsecured creditors. Preferred creditors include:

- funeral directors for funeral expenses relating to the bankrupt, if deceased
- trustee's and lawyer's fees incurred in carrying out the bankruptcy
- employees' wages for six months, to a limit of $2,000 per person
- landlord's rent arrears, subject to limitations
- amounts owed to government agencies for taxes and worker's compensation

Unsecured

unsecured creditors

creditors who have no security interest (such as a mortgage) in the bankrupt debtor's property

Unsecured creditors are creditors who have no security interest (such as a mortgage) in the bankrupt debtor's property. These are persons to whom the bankrupt owes money, but who fall outside the other two categories. The most common example is a supplier of goods on credit who has not been paid.

Payment of Creditors

This is a simplified version of what occurs in a bankruptcy distribution:

- The secured creditors take the assets subject to their security.
- If there is any money left over, the preferred creditors are paid in order of priority as they are listed in the act.
- If there is any money remaining, it is divided equally among the unsecured creditors. Since a bankruptcy happens only when the business does not have enough money to pay its creditors, that means it is very unlikely unsecured creditors will receive much. If, for example, there is $12,000 to be distributed among three creditors, each takes a pro rata share of $4,000. In fact, unsecured creditors often receive nothing in a bankruptcy.

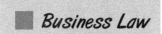 **Business Law**   Applied

⑨ **Padme Nanda is** the sole shareholder, director, and officer of Ganesh Imports Inc. The outstanding debts of the company total $200,000. Because it cannot meet its liabilities when they become due, Ganesh is declared bankrupt on August 1. At the time, the business has the following assets:

- a store valued at $100,000
- unpaid accounts from customers in the amount of $10,000
- inventory of small furniture and accessories valued at $10,000

Nanda also owns a house and a car, but he does not declare personal bankruptcy.

Scenario 1

a) Which of the above assets form part of the estate of the bankrupt company and can be sold so that the proceeds can be distributed to the creditors?

Scenario 2

One of the suppliers of Ganesh, who is owed $200,000, started a court action to reclaim that debt. Nanda also gave a personal guarantee of this debt, and has been sued in the same action. Neither Nanda nor the company has defended. On August 2, the supplier wants to obtain a default judgment against Ganesh and against Nanda personally.

b) Will the supplier succeed?

Scenario 3

The store has been sold for $100,000 and the other assets for $10,000. The following creditors prove their claims in the bankruptcy of Ganesh:

- the bank which holds a mortgage on the store: $90,000
- trustee in bankruptcy for fees: $10,000
- supplier of inventory: $20,000

c) Under which category of creditor does each of the above fall according to the *Bankruptcy and Insolvency Act*?

d) What amount will each receive on the distribution of the bankrupt corporation's estate?

Wage Claims   Under the *Bankruptcy and Insolvency Act*, the employee has a wage claim as a preferred creditor for up to six months' unpaid wages, to a limit of $2,000. This is against the corporation only. It is very unlikely that there will be sufficient assets to cover even preferred claimants' amounts.

Under the various corporations acts, the employee can make a claim against the directors personally if the business goes bankrupt. Also, many provincial governments have set up unpaid-wages funds for employees' claims, up to a limit of about $5,000 if both of the above remedies are valueless to employees.

Suppliers of Goods

A thorny problem in bankruptcy situations has been the position of a business that supplies a large quantity of **goods**—personal property consisting of tangible items that can be bought and sold—to the bankrupt and is not paid for the inventory. The trustee in bankruptcy will take this inventory, sell it, and distribute the proceeds among all the creditors. Usually the preferred creditors will take all, and the supplier will get nothing—even though it was the supplier's product that was sold.

As proved by the Spectrum case (see p. 412), the supplier cannot safely take the inventory back, even by threats, as the trustee could later recover it as a fraudulent preference. While the transaction in this case was undoubtedly a preference, the fairness of the result has often been questioned. The supplier, after all, was only getting back its own goods for which the retailer had not paid.

The BIA contains provisions that give an unpaid supplier the right to the return of goods delivered in the 30 days prior to the bankruptcy. However, for many reasons, this right is generally considered to be ineffective. The provision relates only to goods supplied up to 30 days before the date of the bankruptcy, a time period unlikely to include many of the goods supplied.

A far more effective remedy for suppliers of goods on credit is the purchase money security interest (PMSI) discussed in Chapter 12. A supplier can register a PMSI in provinces that have a *Personal Property Security Act*, thus ensuring the right to take back all goods supplied but not paid for.

goods
personal property consisting of tangible items that can be bought and sold

Consumer Proposals

Persons other than businesses can make a proposal under the *Bankruptcy and Insolvency Act*. The proposal works in the same way, and the consumer can offer creditors some lesser amount on their debts. To date, the consumer-proposal section of the act is not widely used—possibly because many consumers are not aware of its existence. Another deterrent is that credit-rating agencies give no recognition to the attempt to pay off debts under this method. They treat it the same as a bankruptcy, and so there is no incentive for a consumer to use this heading. After a bankruptcy, creditors will be reluctant to grant credit. While every creditor can have a different policy, most will not extend credit for five or seven years after a bankruptcy, and will do so only if the bankrupt has had a good track record since the bankruptcy.

Discharge from Bankruptcy

A **discharge** is a court order whereby a person who has been declared bankrupt ceases to have the status of a bankrupt person. The debtor is given a clean slate and is freed from the obligations to pay the debts. A discharge is given to a corporation only if it is able to pay off its creditors—a very unlikely event.

discharge
a court order whereby a person who has been declared bankrupt ceases to have the status of a bankrupt person

Discharges to natural persons are, however, almost automatic for first-time bankruptcies. This allows the person to begin afresh, free of past debts. In deciding whether to grant a discharge, the court will take into account the honesty of the bankrupt, particularly in revealing assets to the trustee. The court will also consider the circumstances contributing to the bankruptcy. If the court finds a bankrupt's conduct to be irresponsible, discharge will be refused. There are a few debts that are not discharged from bankruptcy. The more common ones are support payments for a spouse or children and necessities (rent, food, basic clothing) purchased prior to the bankruptcy.

Undischarged Bankrupt   Before a bankrupt is given his discharge that individual has a positive duty to advise anyone doing business with him of his status. Failure to do so means that the debt relating to that transaction is not discharged by the bankruptcy.

Business Alert!

R. v. Messier, [1981] 36 C.B.R. (N.S.) 118 (Alta. Q.B.)

Messier went bankrupt in April 1976, with assets of $40,500 and liabilities of $326,406.78. The federal and provincial governments were preferred creditors; unsecured creditors were lawyers, hotels, travel agents, florists, clothiers, restaurants, and a furrier. The trustee stated in his reports that carelessness was the cause of bankruptcy, compounded by gambling and domestic difficulties.

The trustee opposed the discharge. The reason was that Messier contracted liabilities when he knew that he was insolvent. For the three years preceding the bankruptcy, Messier claimed that he travelled with the boxer Muhammad Ali, and that he spent a great deal of money on high living, gambling, and prostitutes. The bankrupt was careful to make clear that the prostitutes were not for himself. Even during the period after his assignment into bankruptcy, Messier ran up another $100,000 in debts.

The Court's Decision

The bankruptcy was caused largely by the high living and irresponsible conduct of the bankrupt. Creditors received next to nothing on their claims. Messier continued his irresponsible behaviour even after **assignment in bankruptcy** (a voluntary declaration of bankruptcy). The court noted that a refusal of a discharge ought to be imposed only in cases where the conduct of the debtor has been particularly reprehensible, and that standard had been met in this case. The bankrupt had flagrantly disregarded the rights of his creditors. A discharge was refused, and the debt therefore remained.

assignment in bankruptcy

a voluntary declaration of bankruptcy

How Money Is Made by Going Bankrupt

People are often confused, if not annoyed to see a business person, whose business has declared bankruptcy, driving around town in an expensive car and living in a large house and very soon back in the same or very similar business to the one put into bankruptcy.

How is it done?   First recall how creditor proofing schemes are put in place to separate and protect personal assets such as cars, houses, cottages and such from creditors of the business.

Next understand the practical weaknesses of the sale of assets, or even the entire business, in a bankruptcy. Assets sold in a bankruptcy are usually at liquidation prices, which is often 10% of their value. Thus, if an owner has personal means, or can borrow funds, that owner of that bankrupt business (who knows the value of the assets) can outbid any other purchaser of the assets and, in effect, repurchase his business free and clear of all debts for little over 10% of the value of the assets.

In Summation

Bankruptcy

- Businesses or individuals are insolvent if there are debts greater than $1,000. However, until a receiving order is given or there is a voluntary assignment into bankruptcy, they are not bankrupt.

- Bankruptcy may occur voluntarily if it has become impossible for the debtor to pay outstanding debts. Involuntary bankruptcy happens when the creditor can show a debt greater than $1,000 and an act of bankruptcy, or if a debtor's proposal for carrying on business is rejected by the majority of creditors.

- Once an insolvent party files a notice of intention to make a proposal, several important factors come into effect for up to six months to provide some protection from creditors. Ultimately, the proposal must be approved by a majority of creditors in order to be put into effect.

When Bankruptcy Is Declared

- The trustee in bankruptcy, under direction of the Superintendent of Bankruptcy, assumes possession of the assets or business of the debtor. An examination of the bankrupt's affairs is done by the trustee and the official receiver to determine if any dishonest transactions, such as fraudulent preference or fraudulent conveyance, have occurred. The trustee then reports to the creditors who have filed a proof of claim.

- Suppliers of goods to a business that has since gone bankrupt are entitled to the return of any goods delivered within 30 days of the bankruptcy. The timing involved with this remedy may limit its usefulness. Suppliers may be better protected by relying on a purchase money security interest (PMSI), which can be registered under the *Personal Property Security Act* (PPSA), where available.

- Consumers may also make a proposal to creditors under the BIA.

Creditors

- Creditors are ranked in priority for the purposes of receiving assets or the return of the money owing.

- Secured creditors hold a security instrument registered against a particular asset, such as a mortgage on real property.

- The next creditors in priority are preferred creditors, who receive payment before the unsecured creditors, in an order detailed by the *Bankruptcy and Insolvency Act* (BIA). Examples are arrears for employees' wages and rent owed to a landlord. If any money remains after the first two levels of creditors are paid, it is divided among the unsecured creditors.

- There may be alternative remedies available to employees with a claim for outstanding wages, such as a provincial fund or liability on the part of a director.

Discharge from Bankruptcy

- Following a period of bankruptcy, the court will grant the bankrupt a discharge, and the debtor is cleared of past debts.

- Generally, a discharge is automatic for a natural person; however, a corporation will be discharged only if it is able to pay off its creditors.

Closing Questions

Bankruptcy

1. a) What is the general test to justify voluntary bankruptcy?
   b) Create a fact situation which you believe would clearly illustrate that test.

2. Which of the following is (are) entitled to review the bankrupt's activities to determine the nature of any transactions which have taken place?
   a) the Superintendent of Bankruptcy
   b) the official receiver
   c) the creditors
   d) the trustee in bankruptcy

3. Laffs Ltd. operated a standup comedy night club under the name Jocularity Jane's, having obtained exclusive rights for use of the name in Canada from the highly successful Los Angeles nightclub of the same name.

   Tamara Burton was the sole shareholder of Laffs Ltd. Unfortunately, the laughs were limited and Burton soon found herself in serious financial difficulties with her employees, landlord, trade creditors, and the Los Angeles company to whom she owed licensing fees. Burton owed her 10 employees wages for two months, totalling $32,000; she owed the landlord rent arrears for one month in the amount of $1,500; the general trade creditors were owed a total of $35,000; and the **licensee** (a visitor, other than an invitee, who enters premises with the consent of the occupier) of the name was owed $2,000. Much to her creditors' unhappiness, Burton voluntarily assigned Laffs Ltd. into bankruptcy.

   The only assets held by the corporation were the licence to operate under the name Jocularity Jane's and the balance of the five-year lease on the premises. The trustee in bankruptcy moved very quickly to sell the assets in order to recover some money for the creditors. Within a day, the trustee was approached by Biz R Corporation to purchase the licensed operating name and the balance of the lease on the premises. As no other interested party appeared to be forthcoming, a quick sale was arranged and the trade name and balance of the lease were sold for $40,000.

   Jocularity Jane's went on to become an enormous success and began to open other clubs across the country. It was not until several months later that it was discovered that the sole shareholder of Biz R Corporation was Tamara Burton. The creditors of Laffs Ltd. are outraged and have contacted the trustee in bankruptcy to see what, if anything, can be done about what they see as a gross injustice.
   a) In the bankruptcy, would the Los Angeles licenser of the name Jocularity Jane's be a secured, preferred, or unsecured creditor?
   b) Identify the classification of the various creditors, list the order in which they would be paid, and determine the total amount owed to the unsecured creditors, as well as the amount of money available to be divided among that class.
   c) Is there any legal recourse available to the creditors against Tamara Burton in these circumstances?

4. Audrey, Hank, Karin, and Mike carried on business as a partnership operating under the firm name Oceanic Importers. Time and again, their grand plans to import products for resale in Canada had stretched their budget to the breaking point, and time and again their trade creditors had agreed to a reorganization of their trade accounts in order to keep the firm afloat. When the firm's last plan to import petrified beetles to be marketed as novelty desk pets failed, the creditors had had enough.
   a) What procedures must the creditors follow in order to place the partnership in bankruptcy?

5. Terry Cavers was petitioned into bankruptcy, owing money to several creditors, including Francine Gardner, who held the first mortgage on his house. When Gardner had realized on the asset, she was still $20,000 short of the mortgage funds that had been advanced to Cavers. Gardner will rank as a preferred creditor in priority to Cavers's employees' claims for the balance of the money owed to her.
   a) With reasons, explain whether the last statement is true or false.

licensee

a visitor, other than an invitee, who enters premises with the consent of the occupier

6. Albert Bernard Cook owns all of the shares of ABC Limited. From the Company's cash flow Cook has the Company purchase half of his shares at fair market value.

   In the next month ABC Limited's main customer switches to another supplier. Because of the loss of this customer, six months later ABC Limited declares bankruptcy.

   Which of the following describes the above purchase of the shares by ABC Limited:
   a) fraudulent preference,
   b) deceptive consumer practice,
   c) an act of anticipatory bankruptcy,
   d) fraudulent settlement.

7. Joe Gladstone from Garden Tools Inc. delivered a large quantity of garden rakes to Happy Harold's Hardware Emporium. While making his delivery, Gladstone struck up a conversation with Happy Harold and learned that Happy Harold had been humbled and might have to make some drastic financial decisions in the future. Gladstone related this information to Carole Mathews, vice-president of finance at Garden Tools Inc.
   a) If Mathews is concerned about a potential bankruptcy or insolvency on the part of Happy Harold, what measures can she take to secure Garden Tools' interest in the goods supplied? What procedures must be followed to accomplish this end?
   b) Assuming Garden Tools was owed $30,000 for the delivery of the rakes, and had received and cashed a cheque for $5,000 from Happy Harold, would it be entitled to pick up the entire delivery made to Happy Harold's in the event of his bankruptcy? Explain the reasons for your answer.

8. Which category does each creditor in the following situations occupy? Why?
   a) Carmen Richter owes the city of Vancouver $7,085 in municipal taxes.
   b) Eduardo Maindroit owes Knit Kwik Ltd. $600 for knitting needles and a correspondence course.
   c) Gary Coonves has two mortgages on his property. The first, for $100,000, is with the Bank of Central Canada; the second, for $30,000, is with Lira Trust Company.
   d) Darlene Bairn's Flower Shop owes $4,000 to her two employees for outstanding wages, and $3,000 to her landlord for rent arrears.
   e) Backstab Corp. has a number of debts. It owes:
      - $2,000 in fees to its bankruptcy lawyer and the trustee in bankruptcy
      - $4,000 in outstanding payments to Workers' Compensation
      - $1,500 in rent arrears to the landlord
      - $25,000 to Avarice Financial Corp., for a metal press bought under a conditional sale agreement and registered under the PPSA by Avarice
      - $6,000 to Ferrous Ltd., for metal supplied over the past three months
      - $2,000 to Gertrude Elsinore, mother of the company's president, Wally, for a loan made to the company when it was started last year
      - $4,000 to Tracy, Wally Elsinore's sister, for a loan she made to Wally last year when he started the company

Websites

canadaonline.about.com/msub187.htm?once=true&—Canada Online, Personal Bankruptcy in Canada. General information on the bankruptcy process, via a variety of links.

www.duhaime.org/bankruptcy.shtml—Duhaime's Canadian Bankruptcy Law Centre. Links to articles on bankruptcy and debt collection.

Agency

Agents

What Is an Agent?

An **agent** is a person who is authorized to act on behalf of another, known as the **principal** (the person on whose behalf the agent acts). Agents' acts, when done within the scope of the authority they have been given, bind the principal as if that individual had committed those acts personally.

Agency is the relationship that exists when one party represents another party in the formation of legal relations. Often, as it is used in the law of agency, the term *agent* has a restricted meaning, and refers to a situation in which the agent has authority to bind the principal in contract. Sometimes agents with such authorization are higher-level employees of a company, but they may also include external agents. A company buyer, for example, has the power to place orders for supplies, and the company must pay for these items. However, the term is sometimes used for persons who do not have authority to bind their principals in contract, such as real estate agents.

agent
a person who is authorized to act on behalf of another

principal
the person on whose behalf the agent acts

agency
the relationship that exists when one party represents another party in the formation of legal relations

Agency Relationship

The relationship between principal and agent can happen in four ways.

■ By Express (Actual) Authority

The principal can expressly give the agent authority, either orally or in writing, to make contracts on the principal's behalf. This is called **actual authority**. A common form of written actual authority is a **power of attorney**. Today, powers of attorney are becoming widely used in personal affairs to deal with both property and issues related to health and medical treatment. In some provinces, this last type of document is referred to as a *living will*; in others it is known as a power of attorney. In either case, such authority is given by the principal to the agent. This arrangement allows the agent to make decisions in the principal's financial affairs, as well as in medical treatment should the principal become unable to do so personally.

■ By Appearance

apparent authority

a situation in which there is no actual authority but the conduct of the principal suggests to a third party that the agent does have authority to act

Apparent authority is a situation in which there is no actual authority but the conduct of the principal suggests to a third party that the agent does have authority to act. If a principal gives this impression, then that principal is bound to contracts made in its name.

For example, in a store, a buyer usually can place orders—make contracts—that bind the company. So, if an employee is given the title "buyer," that employee has apparent authority to act as the company's agent. If the store owner says to a particular employee, "You are appointed buyer, but I have to approve any order that you place," and does not tell suppliers this, the owner is bound for any orders placed by the buyer, who still has apparent authority. The owner is **estopped** (stopped or prevented) from denying the employee's authority.

estopped

stopped or prevented

■ By Approval

The agent may not have authority initially, but if the principal later learns of the contract, the principal can approve—ratify—it. Once the agreement is ratified, the principal is bound by it, and must pay the agent a reasonable fee for the services provided.

■ By Necessity

The common law, with a few exceptions, generally does not recognize agency by necessity. One exception—that of a wife not supported by her husband—meant that she could pledge her husband's credit out of necessity to support herself and her children. Changes in matrimonial law mean that this exception is rarely used today.

Legalese

Estoppel   The word **estoppel** comes from the same Latin root as *stop*, and has a similar meaning. It means that a person's own actions can prevent that individual from doing a certain thing. In an agency relationship, the principal is stopped from denying the agency by permitting a situation to exist that gives people the impression that the agent has authority.

Business Alert!

Estoppel   If you learn that other people wrongly believe someone is acting as your agent, you must take steps to put them on notice, by informing them that this is not true. The law states that if you allow others to believe that another can make contracts on your behalf, you will be stopped from denying the agent's apparent authority.

Agents' Liability to Third Parties in Contracts

One of the unique features of agency law is that the agreement made between the agent and a third party creates a contract between the principal and the third party. The agent has no liability on the contract as long as the third party knew that it was dealing with an agent.

Agency Triangle

Agency Triangle

Principal

Parties bound on the contract

Third party

Agent

Parties who signed the contract

In order to avoid personal liability, an agent should sign all contracts in the manner shown here. This caution applies especially to agents acting on behalf of their employer, when the agent must make it absolutely clear that the contract is with that employer and not with the agent personally. This is particularly important in small, incorporated companies, as the other party might not realize that it is dealing with a corporation. The accepted ways to sign as an agent are:

■ When signing on behalf of a person:

Mohammed Abdi

Per: ___Michael Silver___

Michael Silver

■ When signing on behalf of a corporation:

Prestige Enterprises Ltd.

Per: ___Linda Decahanas___

Linda Decahanas
Vice-President

There are two contracts involved—the first between the principal and the agent, and the second between the principal and the third party.

The Corporate Seal

Corporations have a corporate seal that, in the past, was used in place of a written signature on a contract, as proof of the authority to bind the corporation. This practice worked well when corporations were small, and had to sign only a few contracts. However, as corporations expanded and more officers and employees could sign contracts on their behalf, the corporate seal was not always available. In recent times, it is used infrequently, and the phrase "authorized to bind the corporation" can be written under the name of the employee-agent in place of the corporate seal.

Outside agents have never been required to have the corporate seal, and simply sign in any way that shows they are signing as agents. For example:

signed: ___Mark Deal___

As agent for the Compaq Corporation, Inc.

■ *Critical Concepts of* Agents

- ■ An agent's signature is final, and the principal cannot alter or reject the contract even if the principal does not agree.
- ■ The principal only is liable on the contract. The agent is not personally liable if the other party knows the contract is negotiated with an agent acting within the scope of the agency.
- ■ The agent need only reveal to the other party that the agency exists—the name of the principal does not have to be disclosed.
- ■ If the agency is not revealed to the other party, the third party can elect (choose) to hold either the principal or the agent liable on the contract.

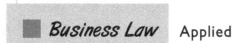

① Maurice Sosnovich asked his neighbour, Rod Carswell, owner of the Sun Seekers Travel Agency, to transfer $20,000 to a relative in Poland. Carswell said he would be glad to do so for a minimum fee of $100. Sosnovich handed over a cheque for $20,000, and Carswell gave him a receipt, signed:

> Sun Seekers Travel Agency Inc.
>
> Per: _Rod Carswell_
>
> Rod Carswell
> President

When the relative did not receive the money, Sosnovich asked Carswell what happened. Carswell replied that by mistake, his bookkeeper deposited the money in a general account, and used it to pay current creditors. Unfortunately, the travel agency has now gone bankrupt. Carswell owns a large home, free of any mortgage.

Sosnovich demanded the money from Carswell, who replied that he did not owe the money: the company—now bankrupt—did.

   a) Draw an agency triangle diagram and identify each party in this question on it.
   b) Is Sosnovich's contract with Carswell or with the corporation?
   c) Is Carswell personally liable?
   d) What could Sosnovich have done to ensure that Carswell would have been personally liable?

An Agent's Duties

Having someone act as your agent is not something to be allowed lightly. That person can attract legal liability to you by the stroke of a pen. You have to be able to trust your agent to do what you've asked, to the best of his or her ability. He or she is doing your business for you.

The law recognizes the seriousness of being an agent by imposing a set of duties or obligations on him or her. Failure to conform to these can result in the principal taking legal action against the agent.

Duty to Act in the Scope of Authority

Agents are often engaged to conduct a fairly specific set of business transactions. In the context of the business, they are less often given authority to conduct any business transaction whatsoever. So, for example, you may hire a lawyer to act for you in suing a supplier. Your lawyer is your agent—acting on your behalf—but only with respect to prosecuting or settling that particular lawsuit. Consequently, she could bind you to an agreement to settle that lawsuit (a contract). She would not have authority, however, to bind you on a contract with another supplier.

Therefore one of the primary duties of an agent is to act squarely within the scope of the authority given by the principal. If you are hired as an agent to sign up well-known sports personalities for speaking engagements, you must do exactly that. If you enter into a contract whereby you agree that a sports personality will endorse a certain sports competition, you have acted beyond the boundaries of your authority.

Duty to Act with Reasonable Care and Skill

An agent must be generally competent to carry out the task assigned to her. She has a duty to conduct the transaction or business to the level of any person claiming to be qualified to do that particular task. If she falls below that standard, and the principal suffers loss, she would be liable to compensate the principal for that loss.

You may be interested in buying small businesses. You hire an agent to scout these out for you, and buy them up. Your agent buys a roadside rest stop, with a restaurant, convenience store, playground and gas station—but also with leaking underground gas-storage tanks as part of the gas station. It could be argued that anyone buying a business including a gas station would check for leaking underground storage tanks_and thus the agent would be liable for the amount the principal lost in fixing the storage-tank problem.

Fiduciary Duty

The concept of fiduciary duty will be discussed in more detail in Chapter 4. Briefly, though, a fiduciary obligation is an ethical obligation. The agent must always be acting in good faith towards the principal, and put the principal's interest first. Fiduciary duty does not have to do with skill level or expertise.

An example of this "good faith" is not taking advantage of inside information received in the course of being an agent for the agent's own gain. You are trying to find a large tract of land to buy on behalf of your principal, for future development. In the process of doing this, you discover a great development opportunity, which you are sure will net a handsome profit in the future. There is plenty of undeveloped land in the tract, and you are tempted to buy a little for yourself. However, you are under an ethical duty not to "scoop" that land for yourself, but must put the interests of your principal first, obtaining it for him or her.

Limits on Fiduciary Relationships   Fiduciary duties apply only to a limited number of relationships. Many business relationships do not give rise to this duty.

For example, a customer may trust and like a salesperson. However, except in extreme circumstances, a salesperson does not have a fiduciary duty to a customer; in fact, the very opposite is true. A salesperson, subject to restrictions such as misrepresentation and the like, is entitled to try to get the best deal for his company and himself at the expense of the customer.

For example, a car salesperson's commission is usually linked to the sale price of a car being sold. Therefore, it is in the sales rep's personal financial interest to get the highest price possible. That representative does not owe a duty to assist the customer and is financially motivated to do the opposite.

Salespeople, to be successful, need to have the ability to be friendly and to inspire trust and confidence. However, the law says you must be on your guard and protect yourself against sales reps. They have no fiduciary obligation to assist you.

■ *Critical Concepts of* An Agent's Duty

- ■ The terms implied by law in any agency relationship are similar to those implied in a business advisor's relationship.
- ■ The agent must discharge the task with reasonable care and skill.
- ■ The agent owes a fiduciary duty to the principal.

Business Law   Applied

❷ **Mas Kikuta,** a sales representative with Hakimoto Electronics Inc., called on Geraldine Heider, vice-president of MacroSoft Computers Inc. Two weeks before the sales call, Hakimoto had warned all its representatives that they should not accept large orders for a particular microchip, as it was proving difficult to obtain component parts from other suppliers. As a result, supplies of the microchip were very low. Normally, Hakimoto's salespeople accepted sizeable orders for this chip from their clients every week, committing the company to supply the item quickly.

Heider ordered a large quantity of the microchips for MacroSoft, stating that delivery was needed by August 1, which was two weeks away. Kikuta wrote up the order, and faxed it to his head office.

One hour after receiving Kikuta's fax, Hakimoto sent a fax to Heider at MacroSoft, cancelling the order.

   a) In what legal position was Kikuta acting?
   b) Did Kikuta have actual authority to bind Hakimoto Electronics Inc., the principal? Is the contract that was signed by Kikuta and Heider binding?
   c) Is Hakimoto's restriction on the authority of its sales representatives effective?
   d) Can Hakimoto legally cancel the contract?

❸ **Mrs. McGregor owned** an 18-unit apartment building. She decided to winter in the Caribbean from November till May, and told the tenants that her son, Rob, would collect the rent cheques while she was away. Rob McGregor collected all the cheques for November, December, January, and February.

Tiring of her vacation, Mrs. McGregor returned in late February, and told her son not to collect the rents for March. During the morning of March 1, Rob McGregor went to the apartment building, where he collected all the rents for that month. He then went and paid a sizeable gambling debt, using the money he had collected.

Late in the afternoon of March 1, Mrs. McGregor visited the apartment block, intending to collect the rents for the month. All the tenants told her they had already paid. Mrs. McGregor demanded that they pay her again.

   a) By what type of authority did Rob McGregor collect the cheques on his mother's behalf for the first four months of her vacation? When he collected them on March 1, did he have any authority?
   b) Do the tenants have to pay a second time?

The Agent's Rights

Agents have duties to their principals; they also have rights against their principals. It may happen that there is no discussion between the agent and the principal about any fee for service or the amount. However, if an agent renders service of value to a principal, the principal must pay for that service and on a reasonable basis. What is reasonable is likely the going rate for similar services.

Owners sometimes put up land for sale privately and include a notation on the sign "Brokers Protected". This means that the owner will pay a commission at the going rate to any real estate agent who brings a purchaser.

Example: A real estate agent learns that an owner of a parcel of vacant land is intending to sell the land but has not yet listed the property for sale. The agent introduces a purchaser to the owner. The purchaser does buy the property. The owner must pay the agent a commission at the standard rate charged by real estate agents in similar situations if demanded by the agent.

■■ *Critical Concepts of* An Agent's Rights

- ▨ Once a principal/agent relationship is established, the principal must pay the agent a reasonable fee for service, even if there is no express agreement to do so.
- ▨ What is reasonable depends on what is paid to other agents in a similar situation.

■ *Business Law*   Applied

❹ Kamleh Nicola knew that Cadillac Enterprises Corp., Ltd. wanted to purchase a certain type of machine for its plant. Nicola learned of a used machine, available at an exceptional price; however, another firm was ready to buy it. Nicola signed an offer to purchase the machine as agent for Cadillac Enterprises Corp., Ltd. on the spot. She then took the agreement to Cadillac, which approved the deal.

Later, Cadillac decided it did not need the machine, and negotiated out of the contract. Nicola asked for the normal finder's fee payable in these situations—10 percent of the sale price. Cadillac refused to pay her, claiming the company had not asked her to do the work, which proved of no benefit to it anyway.

- a) What is the technical name for Cadillac's action in approving the agreement to purchase?
- b) What legal relationship did it create between Nicola and Cadillac?
- c) What legal relationship did it create between Cadillac and the owner of the machinery?
- d) Does Cadillac have to pay Nicola's commission?

In Summation

Agents

The Agency Relationship

- ▨ An agent acts on behalf of another party (the principal) and carries the authority to bind the principal in contract.

- ▨ The agency relationship may be created through express agreement, apparent authority, approval, or necessity.

- ▨ If done properly, the agent is not personally liable, and the principal alone is bound in contract for the obligations and benefits created by the agent on the principal's behalf.

- ▨ As agent, it is always important to ensure that the other party is aware of the agency relationship and signs documents in a fashion clearly indicating this.

Agent's Duties

- ▨ An agent owes a fiduciary duty (ethical duty) to the principal, and must exercise reasonable care and skill (competence) while acting on the principal's behalf. In addition, the agent must act within the scope of the authority given. In exchange, the agent is entitled to a reasonable fee for the services rendered.

Closing Questions

Agents

1. A third party entering into a contract made by an agent on behalf of an undisclosed principal may elect to sue the agent or principal. (An **undisclosed principal** is an agent who does not reveal either the identity of the principal or the fact that he or she is working for the principal.) What clarification would you need in order to be able to determine if this statement is true or false?

2. The agency relationship is said to be an exception to the doctrine of privity of contract. Why is this statement true?

3. You have been authorized to act as an agent on behalf of your employer in obtaining janitorial services for your small business, a retail antique shop. Are you breaching any of the duties of any agent if you do the following?
   a) Hire Breeze-Pro to come in twice a week to dust and vacuum and empty trash, and to clean windows and wash floors twice a month.
   b) Hire Breeze-Pro to do what is noted in a) above, for one year, in exchange for any two antiques of their choice.
   c) Hire Breeze-Pro to give the carpets an odour-free treatment.
   d) Hire Breeze-Pro to water the plants in your showroom.
   e) Hire Breeze-Pro to do a) above. You are the owner-operator of Breeze-Pro.
   f) Subscribe to a publication, *ACleaning News@*, which lists the latest in businesses offering janitorial services in your community.
   g) Hire Breeze-Pro to do what is noted in a) above. Breeze-Pro totally ruined all the carpets in your showroom in an attempt to clean them. It turns out Breeze-Pro was reported to consumer affairs six times in the last six months for shoddy work, and had its membership pulled from the Better Business Bureau.
   h) Hire Breeze-Pro to do what is noted in a) above. Your friend Louis runs Breeze-Pro, and has promised to do you a favour some time if you give him the contract. Breeze-Pro's quote was only slightly above that of two other bidders.
   i) Hire Breeze-Pro to do what is noted in a) above. Breeze-Pro has never cleaned an antique store before, and it damages several items in its first month on the job, causing a $5,000 loss.

4. Adam Chin met Tracy Geen, a real estate agent, while looking to purchase a house. Geen showed Chin a number of properties, and he found the home of his dreams, which, unfortunately, carried a high price. Chin had already organized a first mortgage with his bank, the Municipal Bank of Mellenville, but he would require a second mortgage to be able to purchase the house. While telling Geen of his need for a second mortgage, he also mentioned that he required fire insurance for the house once the purchase was completed. Geen, who also happened to be an *insurance agent* for Metro Life Insurance Company, offered to help Chin with his insurance needs and, for a fee, to assist him in placing a second mortgage.

   Unknown to Chin, the vendor of the house had indicated to Geen that she was prepared to take back a second mortgage on a three-year term at 15 percent if it would assist in helping to sell the house. Chin left it to Geen to negotiate the terms of the second mortgage saying, "The lower the interest rate, the higher the return—nudge, nudge, wink, wink."

   Geen negotiated the interest from the vendor down to 12 percent for a five-year term. The offer on the house was finalized. Geen and Chin met the day before the purchase of the house and completed the necessary insurance forms. Chin gave Geen a cheque for his first premium, and Geen put the forms and the cheque in an envelope, placed them in her briefcase and, patting it, told him he was in good hands. She would submit the insurance application to Metro Life later that day.

   Six weeks later, Chin's house was destroyed by fire and the Municipal Bank of Mellenville demanded payment under the mortgage, as did the vendor as second *mortgagee* (lender). Chin contacted Metro Life, which said it had no records of Chin's application, and refused to pay either the bank or the second mortgagee. Chin then contacted Geen, who vaguely recalled her meeting with

Chin. Checking her briefcase, she found the envelope containing his application forms and cheque stuck in the top corner of the lid. Geen phoned Chin, and told him the application had never been submitted. She felt just awful that all this had happened; however, he was not covered for insurance on his house.

a) Advise Chin as to the nature of his legal action, and whether it would be Metro Life or Geen that he would pursue for his remedy.

b) Has Geen met the terms of her agency relationship with Metro Life, and if not, explain what standard she has fallen short of and why?

c) Now that the parties are all talking directly to each other, the vendor/second mortgagee has found out about the second-mortgage financing arrangement between Chin and Geen. What advice would you provide her in the circumstances?

d) Other than finding a new profession, what advice would you offer Geen in order to help her arrange her future business dealings?

5. Portia Playfair had decided to take her money out of the bank and put it in the hands of a stockbroker in order to receive a better return on it. Clever Carl Corban, her stockbroker, strongly recommended that she place it in a mutual fund, and provided her with a prospectus from the fund. (A **prospectus** is a document issued to inform the public about a new issue of shares or bonds that a corporation is required to publish when inviting the public to buy its securities.) This document specifically emphasized that there were no fees payable by the investor, either at the time of making the investment or when the money was removed from the fund. Playfair decided to go with Clever Carl's suggestion, and placed $50,000 in the mutual fund based on the prospectus and his recommendation.

A year later, Playfair wished to remove half her money from the mutual fund in order to purchase a recreational vehicle to tour the Yukon. When she asked Corban to make the arrangements, he convinced her to leave the funds in and to arrange a bank loan to make the purchase. She followed his advice. Several months later, struggling to make her monthly loan payments, Playfair read an article in the financial section of the newspaper that indicated some mutual funds paid an annual fee of anywhere from 1 to 2 percent to the broker who placed the money in the fund, for as long as the money remained there. Curious, Portia looked through the prospectus for the mutual fund and found no reference to such a fee. She then telephoned the newspaper reporter and asked if his research indicated that her particular mutual fund followed this practice. When the reporter said that it did, she contacted Corban and asked him directly if he was receiving a fee from the mutual fund for the amount and length of time her money stayed in the fund. Corban said he would have to get back to her.

a) Has Corban breached a duty and, if so, what is the nature of that duty and the breach?

b) To whom did Corban owe this duty—Playfair or the mutual fund?

c) If the duty was owed to Playfair, what would be the result of a court action for breach of that duty?

prospectus

a document issued to inform the public about a new issue of shares or bonds that a corporation is required to publish when inviting the public to buy its securities

Insurance

The Concept of Insurance

Insurance is a contract that shifts a potential loss from the person who purchases the policy (the insured) to the company (the insurer) that gives the **insurance policy** (the written evidence of the terms of a contract of insurance). The insured pays a **premium** (the price paid by the insured to purchase insurance coverage) for the insurance policy. If you buy a car, you are legally required to carry insurance. If you accidentally knock down a pedestrian who breaks an arm, the pedestrian has a claim against you, which is paid for by the insurance company. The risk of paying for the accident has been shifted to the insurance company.

Because businesses face significant risks, failure to insure adequately for those risks could result in bankruptcy. Thus, insurance is an important part of business planning

How Does Insurance Work?

Insurance has been compared to a lottery. Many people buy tickets and only a few experience the specified occurrence, in this case winning. The ticket price is calculated by experts so that enough money is collected to cover the prizes, pay the costs of the lottery, and produce a profit.

Similarly, an insurance company giving, for example, fire insurance on buildings will set a premium based on the statistical data of the likelihood of a fire in a business building of the particular type in the area. When sold to a large number of customers, the premium will produce enough money to cover the occurrence, that is, fire in a business building, to be sufficient to pay its expenses, and to yield a profit. The risk is spread over a number of insureds by this method.

A key difference between a lottery and an insurance contract is the concept of **insurable interest**, which is an interest which gives a person a financial benefit from the continued existence of the property or life insured, or which would make the person suffer financial detriment from the loss or destruction of that property or life. An insured business owns its building and thus has a financial benefit from its continued existence, or it will suffer a financial loss if the building is destroyed. Of course, unlike winning a lottery, the occurrence is an unwanted event.

To continue the example, the insured is the owner of the building and so the risk of a real financial loss is transferred to the insurance company. Because of the insurable-interest rule, a person cannot insure another person's building for fire loss on the speculation that it might burn down. If this could be done, arson might be encouraged. Also, a person cannot insure another person's life without the express consent of that person. If a person could insure another person's life without consent, murder might be encouraged.

insurance policy
the written evidence of the terms of a contract of insurance

premium
the price paid by the insured to purchase insurance coverage

insurable interest
an interest which gives a person a financial benefit from the continued existence of the property or life insured, or which would make the person suffer financial detriment from the loss or destruction of that property or life

People other than the "owner" may have an insurable interest. The mortgagee of a property may be entitled by the terms of its mortgage to have the building insured and be a named beneficiary on the policy. Mortgage companies usually require a copy of the policy with such a clause before releasing the mortgage funds. A tenant may have an arrangement with a landlord for the provision of insurance on the building (a commercial tenant still has to pay rent to the end of the lease even if the building is destroyed). In this case, the tenant should check to see that its name is on the policy as a beneficiary.

Why Insurance Companies?

Imagine that a group of businesses, all of which own buildings, get together to provide fire insurance for the buildings of their group. There are 100 businesses and so each agrees in writing to pay one-hundredth of the loss of any other member of the group respecting buildings.

Consider the practical problems. What if a member's building burns? The replacement cost is $1 million. Will a member, whose building is worth $200,000, be willing to pay its full share? Will all the members pay willingly? How difficult will it be for the business claiming the loss to collect? Will all members agree that the damage was in fact the amount claimed? If not, how will the disputes be settled? The above example gives a few reasons why separate companies have been formed to provide insurance.

The Need for Advice Before Applying

There are a number of risks, various policies with different types of coverage, and different premiums available from a number of different insurance companies. A business person needs advice on all aspects of insurance before deciding on the final policy. It is important to know from whom you are getting advice in the insurance industry.

An agent usually acts for one insurance company and is in effect a sales representative for an individual company, hence owing a duty to the insurance company and not to the insured. An insurance broker, who is independent, acts for the insured. As such, the broker can advise on comparative coverage, rates, and such among the various insurance companies. Sometimes the terms *agent* and *broker* are used interchangeably. You will want to be clear on what type of advisor you are dealing with.

An insurance broker is a good source for information regarding a risk-management plan. Insurance coverage should be reviewed with the broker at least once a year. When you are speaking with the broker, he or she may do worksheets respecting coverage. It is a good practice to ask the broker for a copy of those worksheets so that if there is any dispute about coverage or amounts, you can refer to them.

insurance adjuster
a person who handles and investigates a claim of property losses

An **insurance adjuster** is a person who handles and investigates a claim of property losses. Adjusters often act for insurance companies. However, there are independent adjusters who will act for insureds in making a claim.

Types of Insurance

Personal

There are personal risks of loss of income because of untimely death, physical disability, old age, and unemployment.

If you are a sole proprietor of a business, you will want to plan for circumstances in which you cannot work for a period of time because of illness or accident. If you are a partner or a shareholder in a business, one of the group may become incapacitated. There may be a need to fund a temporary replacement. If a partner or shareholder dies, money may be needed to buy out the interest of that person's estate. Life insurance and sickness and accident (also called disability) insurance can provide for those needs.

There are a number of types of life insurance, which go by names such as indemnity, double indemnity, whole life, term, and such. Some of these contain a savings component as well as pure insurance. Personal insurance without any savings component is called **term insurance.** Term insurance premiums are usually the lowest because there is no savings component. Thus, it is often the preferred type of life insurance for business needs.

With key person insurance, the loss of very important executives is insured so that if they die, the insurance covers the cost of finding and training a replacement. For this reason a business has an insurable interest in the lives of its executives. The death benefit is paid to the business.

Many companies have requirements that their key executives cannot fly on the same plane, ride in the same car, or even ride in the same elevators to prevent a serious loss of leadership to the company.

term insurance

personal insurance without any savings component

Property

A large part of a business's wealth is often in the form of some kind of property: buildings, equipment, commercial vehicles, raw materials, inventory, field crops, and livestock, to name a few examples. Fire may destroy a building, thieves may steal inventory or equipment, and soil may give away and cause the side of a building to collapse.

The most common type of property insurance for a business today is called comprehensive general liability insurance. There are separate policies for perils such as fire, theft, flood, and such. But with business insurance the more general practice is to take out comprehensive general liability insurance rather than insuring for specific perils.

Vehicle insurance is mandatory in all provinces for public liability insurance. If a business's truck runs into a car, for example, the injuries suffered by the occupant and the car are covered by public liability insurance. Comprehensive insurance covers the cost of repair or damage to the business's truck.

The insurance of goods during transport is called marine insurance, as it was developed when shipping was the primary mode of transportation. Transportation insurance is important because when you order goods, you may be considered the owner at the time of the acceptance of the order and hence you have the obligation to insure the goods during transportation. Thus, you must read the terms of any purchase order or confirmation to determine which party has the obligation to insure goods during transportation. This is discussed in detail under the topic "Buying and Selling Business Products" in Chapter 9.

Computer Theft   According to the Insurance Bureau of Canada, the most common objects stolen are computers. Low buildings with an easy access from the ground are particularly vulnerable. Like lightning, thieves often strike in the same place. It frequently happens that stolen computers are replaced only to be stolen a second time. The thieves know that they are getting new computers this time.

Business Alert!

It is a good practice to review computer-theft prevention practices with your broker and the local police department. Most police departments have a computer-theft prevention program, which includes placing serial numbers in hidden places so that the ownership of the computer can be traced, and the police have the necessary elements to prove theft at trial.

Operation of a Business

Additionally, damage to physical property may have an effect on the operation of the business, and create a greater loss than the loss of the property. Assume your business manufactures parts for the car industry and your business's building is completely destroyed by fire. It takes one year to rebuild the plant and start production. There is no income during this time, but you still have to pay realty taxes, mortgage and loan payments, and such. It may take months to regain your customer base and your normal profit level. Business-interruption insurance can provide coverage for these risks.

Business-interruption insurance insures part of the loss of profit caused by specified peril such as accident fire and flood. It also covers expenses necessarily made to continue the business and expenses made to reduce loss, such as moving to a new premise. However, business-interruption loss is calculated according to a formula set out in the policy. It is not the same as loss of profit, as normally calculated on an income statement by accounting principles. Therefore, it is critical to have your agent or broker do a rough calculation to show you the difference between business-interruption coverage and loss of profit for your business.

fidelity bond

insurance against loss caused by fraud, theft, or embezzlement committed by employees of the insured

Fidelity insurance, or a **fidelity bond**, is insurance against loss caused by fraud, theft, or embezzlement committed by employees of the insured. The insurer is referred to as a bonding company. Recall that fidelity means faithfulness.

Credit insurance is available to protect against bad-debt losses from customers who do not pay. The premium depends on the insurance company's assessment of the collectibility of the debts (accounts receivable). Good credit-granting practices, such as those employed by banks and large companies, are essential to obtain the best premiums.

Employee benefits are frequently in the form of medical and dental plans covered by insurance. Plans of this type may have a premium shared by the employer and the employee. They usually cover members of the employee's family.

Business Alert!

Disaster Recovery The possibility of a complete disaster to a business either by data loss because of hackers or by acts of terrorism has become a prime concern for modern businesses. Thus, any plans for business-interruption insurance now often include a scenario for a situation where the business has to be rebuilt from scratch.

Public Liability

Businesses are exposed to many legal responsibilities or liabilities to the public, from slip and fall claims to claims for personal injury resulting from employee vehicle accidents. Recall that employers are responsible by the doctrine of vicarious liability for torts committed by employees.

Additionally, businesses are held to strict standards of product safety under the law of torts, and so they usually obtain product-liability insurance to cover claims by members of the public who are injured by their product.

errors and omissions insurance

insurance to protect professionals in the event that their own negligence causes injury to others

Professional liability insurance, also called **errors and omissions insurance** (E & O), is insurance to protect professionals in the event that their own negligence causes injury to others. For example, if an engineer makes a mistake on the design of the condominium structure so that it is unsafe and has to be repaired, a claim by the owner for a loss because of this mistake would be covered by an engineer's professional negligence policy. Directors of companies also may obtain coverage for claims against them for acts done in their role as directors by shareholders or creditors. Such coverage is recommended because it fully protects directors by providing insurance (including litigation costs), and makes them more willing to remain with a company in difficult times.

Applying for Insurance

utmost good faith

a duty owed when a special measure of trust is placed in one party by the other

When applying for insurance there is a common law duty on the applicant to act in **utmost good faith** (a duty owed when a special measure of trust is placed in one party by the other). That means that the applicant must reveal, whether specifically asked or not, any important matters that might affect the assessment of the risk. The clearest example is with life insurance. If the insured has a serious illness such as cancer, the insured must reveal that. Failure to reveal information that would materially affect the risk means that the insurance company can refuse to pay a claim made on the policy. Traditionally this duty has been strictly enforced and if there is a failure to disclose a material fact, the policy is ineffective for any claims. Where an insured failed to disclose a previous fire, a claim for stolen goods was denied.

That strict interpretation has been modified slightly in more recent times. In one case, a business said that it had a night watchman but it did not. A claim for theft that occurred in the afternoon was upheld by the court. The insurance company had to pay.[1]

Insurance companies refer to the causes of losses such as fire, flood, and tornado as perils. The situations which increase the likelihood of perils occurring are called hazards. If a building is situated by a river, it usually has a greater likelihood of flood. If that building is on a hill by the river, that hazard is less. Risk management can be seen as attempts to reduce hazards. Of course, a building worth $10,000 next to the river may be a lesser risk in total value to the insurance company than a building on a hill that is worth $1 million.

Critical Concepts of Insurance Policies

- An insurance policy is a contract and all rules of contract law apply to it.
- An applicant for insurance owes a duty of utmost good faith to reveal to the insurer any material facts that might affect the assessment of the risk, whether asked or not.
- Persons who advise on insurance coverage do not always owe a duty to the insured. An **insurance broker** is an independent business which arranges insurance coverage for its clients and deals with several insurance companies. It owes a duty to the insured, but an **insurance agent** (an agent or employee of the insurance company) does not.

insurance broker

an independent business which arranges insurance coverage for its clients and deals with several insurance companies

insurance agent

an agent or employee of the insurance company

Business Law Applied

① Slippery Sam is the president of Smooth Sales and Distributors Inc. About 10 years ago, one of the cans of grease, the contents of which are essential to Sam's method of operation, spilled and there was a small fire. Sam did not claim that fire on the current insurance policy because the damage was slight and he did not want the premiums to go up.

When applying for new all-risks coverage, Sam notices that the broker, who is filling out the application form, forgets to ask about previous fires. The broker also forgets to have Sam sign the application. Sam decides to say nothing about the fire.

Because of an unusually heavy rain, the storage area floods, damaging the Smooth Sales inventory. It makes a claim on its policy. During the investigation, the insurance company's adjuster notices signs of a fire, searches the record of the local fire department, and discovers a record about the undisclosed fire. On this basis the insurance company declines coverage.

Sam claims that he should be paid based on three factors:

- he was not asked about previous fires
- he did not sign the application form
- the non-disclosure was with respect to fire but the loss was caused by water damage

a) Discuss whether any of Sam's grounds will be successful in countering the insurance company's claim of non-disclosure.

---

1. *Case Existological Laboratories Ltd. v. Century Insurance Company* (1982), 133 D.L.R. (3d) 727.

Obtaining Adequate Coverage

To make certain that your policy contains adequate coverage for your needs, you need to review the coverage in detail with an independent broker. Where there are many risks, it is a good idea to have the broker attend at your business.

Each insurance company has standard clauses that are prepared in advance. A broker will assemble a number of these clauses into one document, which results in a policy. If some additional coverage above that company's standard clause is required, that coverage is done by a clause called a **rider** (an additional clause to a standard policy of insurance). If there is a later change in the coverage, this clause is called an **endorsement** (a clause which changes the terms of an insurance policy).

> **rider**
> an additional clause to a standard policy of insurance
>
> **endorsement**
> a clause which changes the terms of an insurance policy

The standard wording of insurance coverage clauses may not always meet a business's individual needs. For example, computer software companies cannot rely on standard product-liability insurance. This coverage insures for property damage or personal injury. If a pop bottle explodes in a consumer's car and damages the upholstery (property damage) and cuts the consumer's face (personal injury), this damage is covered under the standard product-liability clause.

However, the damage done by software will more likely be to data loss or loss of profits because of downtime. This type of risk is more similar to professional liability (also called errors and omissions) insurance. So, a software company will have to make certain that its new and unique risks are covered. It cannot rely on standard clauses.

As noted above, there are individual policies for specified risks such as fire, theft, and the like. There is also an all-risk policy, which is called comprehensive general liability insurance. The premiums may be higher, but the general coverage is usually recommended. However, the term *all-risk* is misleading, for there are exceptions to this coverage. One common exception is that machinery is covered for external damage such as fire, but not for design defects. Other common exclusions are normal wear and tear, war, or intentionally caused damage. (See Appendix to this chapter for an example of an All Risks Policy and exclusions.)

Standard coverage terms often provide that the insurance company has the choice of repairing or paying the value of the property. The value is normally based on the condition of the property before destruction and not the new or replacement value. Premiums for replacement value are much higher. Sometimes insurance companies will agree to buy a new machine if the insured agrees to pay for the difference between the value of the machine under the insurance policy at the date of destruction and the new machine. The increase is called a "betterment."

Business Alert!

Rider and Endorsement   **Rider** has a similar meaning as the term that is used to describe a person who sits on a horse. As the person is on top of the horse, so a rider clause is on top of the standard clause.

Endorsement derives from Latin word *dorsum*, which means back. A dorsal fin of a fish is the fin on the back of the fish. Endorsement originally meant adding something by writing on the back of a document. A judge's reasons, when written on the back of a court document, are called an endorsement.

Interpretation of Coverage Terms

Insurance policies are contracts; so the general rules of contract interpretation of standard form contracts apply. The courts first look at the language of the policy to determine the intention of the parties. If the provisions are ambiguous, the words will be given a meaning, which if reasonable, favours the insured. This is considered fair because the language used was chosen by the insurer.

Coverage issues are a frequent subject of litigation. Coverage provisions will be interpreted broadly and exclusions narrowly.

In the following *Goderich Elevator* case the insurance company could not meet the litigation burden of proof to prove that the cause of the defective grain was one of the exclusions. In the *Triple Five Corp.* case the court held that the insurance policy was not the equivalent of a warranty policy that a purchaser could obtain from a manufacturer.

Goderich Elevator v. Royal Insurance Co., [1999] 16 D.L.R. (4d) 763

Goderich Elevators stores grain in elevators (so called because the grain is lifted by a machine). It took out a policy for coverage of "all risk of direct physical loss or damage . . . except as excluded." The exclusion clause stated: "loss or damage caused directly or indirectly . . . by dryness of atmosphere, changes in temperature, heating, shrinkage, evaporation . . ."

Some of the loads of grain contained a large amount of poorquality grain called heated grain. Goderich sued for the loss to the heated grain. The insurance company claimed that the heated grain must have been caused by one of the excluded circumstances.

The Court's Decision

The experts called by the insurance company could not establish what the cause of the heated grain was. So, it did not establish on the balance of probability that the cause was one of the exclusions.

The court applied the principle of interpretation of insurance policies that coverage provision should be construed broadly and exclusion provisions narrowly. The insurance company was ordered to pay Goderich's claim.

Triple Five Corp. v. Simcoe & Erie Group, [1997] 5 W.W.R. 1 (Alta. C.A.) leave to appeal to S.C.C. denied [1997] S.C.C. no. 363

Triple Five corporation owned and operated the West Edmonton Mall, which featured an amusement park with a roller coaster. One car of the roller coaster overturned, killing two customers.

Triple Five had an all-risk policy which provided that certain name perils were excluded, including any occurrence caused by a "latent defect" (latent means hidden). The personal-injury claims were settled. Triple Five's claim for business interruption loss was denied by the insurer.

The accident was caused because the tracks at several points had been incorrectly spaced, a matter of fine tuning and not noticeable to the naked eye. This incorrect spacing created dangerous stress on the wheels of the cars, causing the accident. The importance for precise spacing was noted by a senior engineer employed by the manufacturer but this requirement was not put in the specification that went to the assemblers. This was held to be a design error. The question for the court was whether a design error was excluded by the term "latent defect."

The Court's Decision

The court held that, based on precedent, an all-risks policy insures against only perils external to the property, as opposed to perils that are somehow inside the property. The court considered several factors that made a design defect an internal or latent defect. First, this was not a policy warranting the fitness of the property. Also, this event was not purely accidental, but foreseeable by the manufacturer, which could have prevented the accident if it had used due care. Further, this design defect did not occur after the insurance policy was taken out: only the result of the defect occurred then. This defect could not have been discovered by a reasonable inspection by the insured or the insurer. Again, only the manufacturer could have discovered it.

The court concluded that this design defect was not external and hence not covered by the all-risks policy. Triple Five lost the case.

Business Law Applied

2. a) **Triple Five and** Goderich had similar all-risks policies. Why were there differences in results respecting their claims?
   b) Did Triple Five have a remedy against any other person? Did Goderich? Might the fact that Triple Five had the possibility of a claim against someone else have influenced the judges' decisions?
   c) The court in *Goderich* applied a principle of interpretation of insurance policies. Do you know of a similar principle of interpretation in general contract law? If so, what is it called?

Interpretation Examples

The typical car insurance policy covers injury caused by the "use or operation" of a vehicle. There have been a number of unusual claims under this wording:

- A car jack victim was covered for her injuries,
- A deer hunter who drove to this site and was wounded by a fellow hunter was not.

Example: Drive-by Shooting—A woman walking into a donut shop was hit by a wild bullet in a drive-by shooting which made her a paraplegic. She sued arguing that the shooter did not leave the car as in the deer hunter case. However, the court rejected her claim for coverage stating that the injury was not caused by the driving (use of the vehicle) but by the shooting. (*Russo v. John Doe,* 2009 ONCA 305 (CanLII)

Also the meaning of "Accident" has been interpreted. Risky activities are not an accident.

Example: Contraction of Herpes—An insured man under a group accident policy contracted herpes through unprotected sex. It caused a rare complication which paralyzed him from the waist down. He made a claim on the basis that his contraction of herpes was an accident.

The court found that this contraction of disease was a natural process and not an accident. Such a claim might have been covered under a health policy but not under an accident policy (*Co-Operators Life Insurance v. Gibbens,* 2009 SCC 59).

Business Alert!

Paper Trail   When discussing coverage with an insurance agent or broker, obtain and keep copies of all forms that you fill out. Especially ask for copies of the agent's or broker's worksheets, which will detail in handwriting the scope and the amount of coverage discussed.

If the insurance company denies a claim as being outside the coverage, the documentation will be essential in order for your lawyer to determine if there is a valid claim against the insurance company on the basis that the loss is indeed covered, or against the agent or broker for failing to advise you on adequate coverage.

The Bottom Line of Coverage

In placing an insurance policy for a business you will want to consider at least four elements of the policy to be able to determine what the final payout from the insurance company will be for various situations.

deductible

a fixed amount of loss that the insured is required to bear

- **Coverage.** The exact loss to be covered must be specifically noted. For example, fire insurance may cover replacement damage to a building but not loss for the businesses' downtime.
- **Exclusion.** Fire insurance on the building may not cover damage to the glass in the windows. There may be an express plate-glass exclusion item.
- **Deductible.** This is a fixed amount of loss that the insured is required to bear. To obtain a lower premium, the insured may agree to a deductible for any claim. This amount is deducted first from the loss.
- **Penalty.** Most policies contain an underinsurance penalty clause, explained below. The insurance company sets the amount, which it determines is adequate insurance. There is a penalty if you take out a lower amount.

Underinsurance Penalty

In most policies, the insurance company sets out what it determines is adequate insurance. There is a penalty if the insured takes a lower amount.

Take the example of business-interruption insurance: the policy will contain a formula that in effect requires coverage for a full year's loss. If a company purchases business-interruption insurance with a limit of $500,000 and its average annual gross profit is $1 million, the under-insurance clause will deem this to be 50% underinsurance. So, any claim for business interruption loss will be reduced by 50%. For example, that business may have a claim for $200,000. Its underinsurance penalty is 50%, and so the payout under the policy will be $100,000. Additionally, there may be other deductions under the policy.

Insurance companies defend this approach by saying that they set premiums on the assumption of complete loss, such as one year's profits. Critics respond that this reason is not logical. The insurance companies could set their premiums based on actual loss. Since the premiums would relate to actual loss, there would be no need for an underinsurance penalty.

Change in Risk

An insurance company issues a policy based on its assessment of the particular risk involved. Any changes to that risk must be reported so that the company can review the risk to see if it needs to increase the premium. For example, vacant properties are considered at high risk of vandalism and fire. The standard policy frequently states that if a building remains vacant for 30 days, the policy is cancelled. Sometimes the change in risk is not obvious to the insured, and so there is a need for continuing consultation with the insurance company or with a broker, as the case below demonstrates. Additionally, it is recommended that an insured meet with a broker once a year to review the insured's coverage and possible changes.

Review Annually   It is critical to review your business situation yearly with an insurance broker. There may be changes that affect coverage that are not obvious. If a business buys a new piece of equipment, that may not be covered by the insurance policy because only equipment specifically listed in the insurance policy is covered. An asset may have decreased in value and the coverage can be reduced. The business may have added a cafeteria for its staff. Any restaurant-like business is viewed as a special risk by insurance companies because of the increased likelihood of fire. Opening such a facility might even invalidate existing insurance.

Business Alert!

Making a Claim

Terms of an insurance policy usually require immediate notice of any possible claims, but in any event it will always include a very short time period for giving notice. Additionally, there is usually a limitation time for starting an action. The limitation for commencing an action on contract in law is six years; however, by the terms of the standard insurance policy that period is shortened to ranges as short as 60 days to one year. Thus, it is important to notify the company immediately by phone and to confirm this in writing so that there is evidence of the notification.

Insurance companies do receive fraudulent and exaggerated claims. They have staff trained in investigation techniques who visit the site of loss to determine both its extent and its validity. However, insurance companies cannot take an adversarial stance and deny a claim based on unfounded suspicions.

As the insured has a duty of good faith in disclosing all relevant matters to the insurance company in the application, the company has a duty of good faith in paying a valid claim. Breach of that duty may attract a serious amount of punitive damages.

The facts of the following case, *Whitten v. Pilot*, were extreme. Not every refusal to pay would result in a breach of a good-faith duty. Sometimes a company may have a valid reason for denying a claim even if ultimately that reason is proved wrong. The next few years will undoubtedly see cases which provide guidelines as to when an insurance company's conduct breaches the good-faith requirement.

Whitten v. Pilot Insurance Company, [2002] S.C.R. 1

Mrs. Whitten had insured her house for fire. She discovered a fire in the house just after midnight in January. She, her husband, and their two daughters fled from the house wearing only night-clothes into the –18 degree Celsius weather. Mr. Whitten gave his slippers to one of the daughters to go for help, and suffered severe frostbite to his feet. The fire totally destroyed their home and all contents.

The insurance company made a $5,000 expense payment and paid a few months rental, and then cut the Whittens off completely from any payments. The insurance company took the position that the Whittens set fire to their own house, even though the local fire chief and the company's own expert said that was unlikely. At trial a jury awarded $1 million in punitive damages against the insurance company for bad faith. The court of appeal reduced that to $100,000. Mrs. Whitten appealed to the Supreme Court of Canada and asked that the trial award be reinstated.

The Court's Decision

The insurance company's conduct was exceptionally reprehensible. It was intended to force the insured to make an unfair settlement. Insurance contracts are purchased for peace of mind. The more devastating the loss, the more the insured will be at the financial mercy of the insurer and the more difficult it will be for the insured to challenge a wrongful refusal to pay.

The obligation of good faith means that the insured's peace of mind should have been the company's objective and her vulnerability should not have been exploited by a negotiating strategy.

An award of punitive damages in contract cases are rare. Here, in addition to the contractual obligations to pay the claim, the insurance company was under a distinct and separate obligation to deal with its policyholders in good faith. This distinct obligation could support a claim for damages for bad faith.

The jury intended to send a powerful message criticizing the company's behaviour. While the amount was much higher than any previous award in this country, it was, in these circumstances, within rational limits. The trial judgment of $1 million was restored.

Business Alert!

Notice   It is a very good practice to give the insurance company notice of any potential claim. For example, a business has a public liability policy covering slip and a customer does slip, does not appear to be injured, and leaves without a comment. The insurance company should be notified because the next time the business hears from that customer may be a lawsuit served six months later. The insurance company may raise the lack of notice as a defence against the claim on the policy by the business.

Business Alert!

Claims Procedure   If you are making a claim on a matter of any complexity, you might consider the following suggestions:

- Ask the broker for instructions on what to do. Confirm the notice provision and the limitation time for commencing the action in the policy.
- Notify the insurance company by phone and in writing by fax, if possible, as the fax will have a record of the date and time. Copy the broker.
- Keep a detailed diary of all events, including a summary of what you were told by insurance company representatives. You can be assured that the insurance company representatives are recording in precise detail everything that you are telling them. Take frequent pictures of the damage and the repair process if possible.
- Cooperate fully with the insurance company representative in any investigation. Insurance companies do get fraudulent claims and nothing makes an insurance representative more suspicious than a failure of co-operation.
- If the claim is complicated, ask the insurance company to appoint and pay for an independent adjuster to assist you in making the claim. Even if the company refuses to pay, you might want to retain an independent adjuster to assist you with any complex claim.
- If there are any problems respecting the claim, contact a lawyer who specializes in claims against insurance companies (not all lawyers have experience with insurance claims). Keep in mind the time limits for when you can start a lawsuit under the policy.

In Summation

- Insurance can classified into three types according to risks:
  a) personal: untimely death, sickness, disability
  b) property: buildings, equipment, commercial vehicles, inventory, livestock
  c) liability to others: occupier's liability, vicarious liability for employees, negligence, product liability

- Insurance is a method of sharing the losses of the few individuals in a group who suffer the loss among the members of the group who do not.

- Insurance agents owe a duty to the insurance company for whom they work; insurance brokers owe a duty to the insured.

- When applying for insurance, whether specifically asked or not, there is a duty of good faith on the applicant to volunteer any fact that might influence the insurance company in setting the premium or determining whether to accept or reject the risk.

- Coverage clauses must be reviewed to see what is specifically included or excluded. "All risks" does not literally mean all risks.

- There is a rule of interpretation which assists the insured: coverage is to be construed widely and exclusions are to be construed narrowly.

- In determining whether the claim should be paid, and if so in what amount, an insurance company will look at:
  a) what is covered by the policy? (a building, a machine)
  b) what perils are covered? (fire, flood)
  c) are there extensions of coverage? (riders, endorsements)
  d) are there exclusions, deductibles, penalties?
  e) are there conditions? (notice of changing risk, timing of notice of loss)

- An insurance company has a duty of utmost good faith in paying a valid claim.

Closing Questions

1. a) How does insurance shift the risk of loss and then spread that risk?
   b) What is the difference between an insurance agent and an insurance broker? Which owes a duty to whom?
   c) What is an insurable interest?

2. Which of the following are valid insurance contracts according to the principle of insurable interest?
   a) a fan wants to insure the life of Céline Dion
   b) a mortgagee wants to insure a building on which it has a mortgage
   c) a partner wants to insure her business partner's life
   d) a business involved in a lengthy trial wants to insure the life of the judge

3. Match each term in Column A with its related term in Column B:

Column A	Column B
deductible	risk transfer
risk	consideration
liability	extent of protection
insurance	prevention
premium	risk retention
coverage	obligation
risk management	chance of loss

4. What is the difference between an insurance broker and an insurance agent? Why is the difference significant to a person seeking insurance?

5. a) What is meant by utmost good faith?
   b) How is it relevant to a person applying for an insurance policy?
   c) How is it relevant to an insurance company?

6. Match the following terms:

Column A	Column B
An insurance broker puts an ad in a paper indicating he has the best rates	offer
A customer sends an application to an insurance company	insurable interest
After an insurance company issues a policy, the insured pays the premiums	acceptance
The mortgagee's interest is shown on an insurance policy	invitation to treat

7. a) In the *Triple Five v. Simcoe & Erie* case, what factors did the court say made the event not an external defect and hence covered by the policy?
   b) The Alberta Court of Appeal reasoned that since the design error was hidden and unknown to Triple Five, the insurance did not cover the event. Did this latent or hidden factor make the overturning of the car more or less like an accident?
   c) What type of insurance would have covered this event?
   d) What should Triple Five have done to be successful in a lawsuit?

Comprehensive Condominium All Risks Policy

THIS SECTION INSURES FOR THE COVERAGE AND TO THE EXTENT SPECIFIED IN PART ii OF THE DECLARATIONS SUBJECT TO ALL PROVISIONS OF THIS SECTION APPLICABLE TO THE COVERAGES AND IS ALSO SUBJECT TO THE GENERAL CONDITONS SECTION OF THIS POLICY.

PROPERTY COVERED

On all property of every kind and description, including but not so as to limit the generality of the foregoing, the units and the common elements, all buildings and structures together with their additions extensions and attachments, and all equipment, furniture, fixtures, material and supplies and generally everything of an insurable nature whether specifically mentioned herein or not: the property of the insured or for which they are legally liable or for which they may be responsible and/or in which they have an insurable interest.

"COVERAGE AWAY FROM PREMISES"

This policy covers property as described herein normally kept at the premises insured, while temporarily removed from said premises but only within the territorial limits of Canada and the Continental United States (excluding Alaska). The insurers liability hereunder shall not exceed $150,000 any on occurrence.

PROPERTY EXCLUDED

This policy does not insure:

(a) Sewers, drains, watermains, gas and other utility lines located beyond the boundary of the premises:

(b) Electrical appliances or devices of any kind (including wiring) when loss or damage is due to electrical currents artificially generated, unless fire or explosion ensues.

(c) Street clocks, electrical signs, mechanical signs, vitrolite or terrazzo floor or wall tile or similar materials, unless loss or damage is caused directly by fire, windstorm, hail, lightning, explosion, riot, impact by aircraft or vehicle, smoke (meaning smoke due to sudden unusual and faulty operation of any stationary boiler or furnace or apparatus used solely or partly for heating the premises insured or for warming water), sprinkler leakage, malicious damage, vandalism or theft including attempt thereat:

(d) Pressure vessels over 24 inches in diameter and boilers (including all piping and apparatus attached thereto): if loss or damage is caused by or resulting from explosion, rupture, bursting, cracking, burning out or bulging of such boilers or pressure vessels or piping or apparatus attached thereto, while connected ready for use;

(e) Personal property belonging to the owners of individual Condominium Units;

(f) Animals, fish, birds, growing plants (except those which are used for decorative purposes within buildings), automobiles (unlicensed automobiles or tractors excepted) motor trucks, motor cycles, aircraft, watercraft or other conveyances, money, notes, securities, stamps, accounts, bills, deeds, evidences of debt, letters of credit, passports, documents, railroad or other tickets;

(g) Furs, jewels, jewellery, watches, pearls, precious and semi-precious stones, gold, silver, platinum, other precious metals and alloys.

(h) Improvements and betterments to individual Condominium Units made or acquired by the Owners of such Units.

PERILS INSURED

This Policy insures against ALL RISKS of direct physical loss or damage except as herein provided.

PERILS EXCLUDED

This Policy does not insure against:

(a) Loss or damage caused by or resulting from earthquake (unless such coverage is specifically endorsed hereon), except that the insurer shall be liable for damage caused by ensuing fire, explosion, smoke or sprinkler leakage not excluded elsewhere by this Policy;

(b) Loss or damage by flood, whether or not caused by water inundating or flooding land as the result of waves, tide or tidal wave, or the rising of or the breaking of boundaries of natural or man-made lakes, reservoirs, rivers, or other bodies of water, the accumulation on land of water immediately derived from natural sources: all whether driven by wind or not; or whether caused by or attributable to earthquake, except that the insurer shall be liable for ensuing fire, explosion, sprinkler leakage or smoke (meaning smoke due to a sudden unusual and faulty operation of any stationary boiler or furnace or its apparatus used solely or partly for heating the premises insured or for warming water) not excluded elsewhere by this Policy:

(c) Loss or damage caused by seepage, leakage or influx of water derived from natural sources through basement walls, foundations, basement floors, sidewalks or sidewalk lights, or the backing up of sewers and drains unless caused by or resulting from a peril not excluded elsewhere by the Policy;

(d) Loss or damage caused by settling, expansion, contraction, moving, shifting or cracking, unless caused by or resulting from a peril not excluded elsewhere by the Policy;

(e) Loss or damage caused by or resulting from explosion, rupture or bursting of pressure vessels over 24 inches in diameter, or boilers including all piping and apparatus attached to such pressure vessels or boilers, unless fire ensues and then only for the loss or damage caused by such ensuing fire;

(f) Loss or damaged caused by or resulting from dampness of atmosphere, dryness of atmosphere, changes of temperature, freezing, other than freezing of fire protection system or plumbing or air conditioning, heating, shrinkage, evaporation, loss of weight, leakage of contents, exposure to light, contamination, pollution, change in colour or texture or finish, rust or corrosion, marring, scratching or crushing, but this exclusion does not apply to loss or damage caused directly by fire, lightning, smoke, windstorm, hail, explosion, strike, riot, impact by vehicle or aircraft, leakage from fire protection equipment, rupture of pipes or breakage of apparatus not excluded under paragraph (a) hereof, vandalism or malicious acts, theft or attempt thereat. Damage to pipes caused by freezing is insured provided such pipes are not excluded in paragraph (a) hereof.

(g) Loss or damage caused by or resulting from rodents, vermin or insects;

(h) Loss or damage caused by or resulting from delay, loss of use or occupancy;

(i) Mechanical or electrical breakdown, latent defect or faulty material or workmanship, inherent vice, gradual deterioration, wear and tear;

(j) Loss or damage attributable to radiation of, or contamination by, any radioactive, lissionable or fusionable materials, whether or not consequent upon loss or damage otherwise insured hereunder;

(k) any mysterious disappearances; any loss or shortage disclosed on taking inventory;

(l) Loss or damaged resulting from misappropriation, secretion, conversion, infidelity or any dishonest act on the part of the insured or other party of interest, his or their employees or agents or any person or persons whom the property may be entrusted (bailees for hire excepted);

(m) Loss or damage to goods occasioned by or happening through their undergoing any process involving the application of heat;

(n) Loss or damage caused by war, invasion, act of foreign enemy, hostilities (whether declared or not), civil war, rebellion, revolution, insurrection or military power, and loss or damage caused by contamination by radioactive material directly or indirectly resulting from an insured peril under this Policy.

16

Employment Law

What Is Employment?

The law divides persons who provide services to employers into three categories:

- employees
- **independent contractors** (people who carry on an independent business and act for a number of other persons)
- dependent contractors

independent
contractors

people who carry on an
independent business and
act for a number of other
persons

These categories are determined by legal principles. It does not matter what the parties have called the relationship, for often the relevant contract will state that the person is an independent contractor so that the employer can avoid many obligations (such as those under employment standards legislation, paying employee benefit costs such as worker's compensation and employment insurance, and withholding taxes).

The courts have affirmed an intermediate category between employee and independent contractor in view of the number of relationships in which a person is economically dependent upon another business but would not meet the strict test of being an employee. This has been called a dependent contractor (*McKee v. Reid's Heritage Homes Ltd.*, 2009 OMCA 916 CanLii).

Example: An Independent Contractor:

A golf course hires a landscaping firm to cut its lawns. The landscaping firm provides this service to a number of other businesses.

Example: A person called an independent contractor who may be an employee:

A golf course hires an individual to cut its lawns and calls him an independent contractor. He bills them monthly. However, he uses its equipment and is subject to direct supervision by one of its staff.

Example: Dependent Contractor:

A person owns all his own equipment for lawn cutting but does about 80% of his business with the golf course which creates an economic dependency on the golf course. The balance of 20% of his business is done with various customers.

■■ *Critical Concepts of* Employee v. Independent Contractor

The courts generally use the following two tests to determine if a person is an employee:

■ Control—the individual is subject to control by the employer (when/where/how work is done).

■ Organization—the person is integrated into the business organization.

The courts generally use the following two tests to determine if an individual is an independent contractor:

■ Tools—the individual has ownership of that person's own tools and brings them to the workplace.

■ Risk—the individual has the potential for the loss or gain of profits from the arrangement.

Business Alert!

Tax Consideration   Many small businesses prefer to refer to personnel associated with the business as independent contractors when they are actually employees. This is done to avoid paying the many employee taxes and benefits and filling out a significant number of government forms. However, government agencies, such as Revenue Canada, often reclassify these relationships as employee relationships by applying the above tests. The employer then is assessed as owing all the applicable withholding taxes and similar employee deductions and must pay them.

It is the responsibility of the employer to pay these amounts and not the responsibility of the employee. Therefore, the risk of having a contract which is stated to be an independent-contractor contract being reassessed and found to be an employee contract is completely on the employer.

Hiring

Labour laws, as well as federal and provincial human rights legislation and the *Charter of Rights and Freedoms*, closely control the process of advertising for and interviewing new employees. Neither the advertisement nor the interview can include questions about an applicant's race, colour, nationality, age, sex, religion, marital status, past criminal convictions that are unrelated to employment, or mental and physical disability. Labour legislation also prohibits questions about trade union membership.

However, job applicants can be limited to those who meet the valid skill requirements—*bona fide* occupational requirements (BFORs)—for the job. These might include particular experience, or academic qualifications. For example, a company that provides security guards for residential apartments could refuse to hire someone who had been convicted of sexual assault. Equally, a school board would not hire a teacher who did not possess the appropriate professional qualifications.

The Canadian Human Rights Tribunal ruled in a 1994 decision that the Toronto Dominion Bank could enforce a policy of mandatory drug testing for new employees. The tribunal stated that the drug testing was intrusive but acceptable. New employees at the bank were to undergo a urine test within 48 hours of receiving a job offer. The bank justified the testing program by claiming that it was risky to put drug users near cash and bank records, and the test was therefore a *bona fide* occupational requirement. If an employee refused to take the test, or tested positive a third time, the employee could be fired. The Federal Court of Appeal, however, reversed the tribunal's ruling, finding that the policy discriminated against drug-dependent persons and was not shown to be sufficiently related to job performance.[1]

---

1. *Canada (Human Rights Commission) v. Toronto Dominion Bank*, [1998] 4 F.C. 205 (C.A.).

Some of the information an employer cannot seek is necessary for employment records, and can be obtained after the person is hired.

Ontario is the only jurisdiction that prohibits requiring employees and job applicants to take lie-detector tests.

■ *Critical Concepts of* Hiring

- Human rights legislation restricts the asking of questions on prohibited grounds of discrimination such as age, sex, or race.
- Labour legislation prohibits asking questions about trade union membership.
- Immigration law prohibits the hiring of persons who are not Canadian citizens or permanent residents of Canada, unless they have a valid immigration permit.
- Child labour laws set out minimum age requirements for young people working in certain industries. No person under the age of 16, for example, may work in construction. The minimum age in the shipping industry is 15; in mining, it is 18.

The Employment Contract

An employment agreement is a specific type of contract. It can be oral or written, or both—the hiring might be done orally, and the employee told that there is an employee manual setting out many of the terms of the employment, such as benefits. The manual is not considered part of the employment contract if the employee is not told about it at the time of hiring.

Many employment contracts are oral and for an indefinite term, automatically renewed from year to year with changes in position and salary. A contract may also be for a set term, such as one year. Such contracts have become more popular recently because of economic conditions. When the term ends, the obligations of the employer cease.

Terms of an Employment Contract

Many employers use a standard form contract that can be custom tailored for a few items, such as compensation, that are unique to individual employees. Such a contract usually includes:

- a job description
- a standard period of probation
- overtime and sick-pay policies
- details about vacations, leaves of absence, and holidays
- the remuneration to be paid, including benefits and bonuses
- the notice or severance that will be given in case of layoff or dismissal
- identification of the lines of responsibility
- protection of the company's ownership of inventions or improvements to products done as part of employment
- a non-competition clause
- a trade secrets confidentiality clause
- job evaluation methods
- certification by employees of their education and qualifications

One significant term from the above list is the limit on an employee's claim for damages upon being fired. As explained later an employee may be entitled to damages relating to reasonable notice for, say, one year, but a term in the employment contract may stipulate the employee can only claim three months' damages. These claims are often enforced.

Résumés   It is easy to falsify information on a résumé. Employers usually do not have the time to check all facts thoroughly; but false statements, and even forged documents, are common, particularly with the advances in cheap printing technology. In addition to thorough checks, businesses are advised to have a term in the contract requiring that employees verify that all statements in their résumés are true. Misrepresentation of a material fact in a résumé is a ground for immediate dismissal. Credit searches, with permission of the individual, are also a way to independently check on a potential employee's past. Employers are using social networking sites such as Facebook to investigate applicants.

■ *Business Law*   Applied

❶ **John Harris is** HIV-positive. He applies to be a file clerk in a business. At the interview, the business owner tells him that he must undergo drug testing on the first day of his employment. Harris does not want to take the test because it will reveal his HIV-positive status.

   a) Can the employer legitimately require Harris to take the test, or does Harris have any grounds for refusing without revealing his medical condition?

❷ **Saleh Mohamed was** hired by Promoters-Canada Limited. During the interview he was told of the employee manual, and on his first day on the job he was given a copy of it. The manual states that the employer can terminate an individual's employment with four weeks' notice. Five years later, because of a downturn in the economy, Mohamed is fired, and given the four weeks' notice.

He wants longer notice, but his employer points to the manual. Mohamed says that he did not read the document when he received it, and so it is not part of his employment contract.

   a) Is Mohamed correct?

Avoidance of Restrictive Covenants

You will recall in the chapter on contracts that employment that restricted an employee's ability to earn a living after leaving an employer are often not enforced by the courts on the grounds of public policy, i.e., the public have an interest in making certain that everyone has the ability to earn a living and then not be on welfare. One alternative to a restraint of trait clause, which may be enforced, is a repayment of training expenses if the employee leaves and works for a competitor.

   Example: An employee who had no experience in the real estate business was hired on a three-year contract and was to be trained by the employer. A term of the contract stated that he agreed to repay a specified amount relating to training expenses if he left before the three-year period, the amount to be determined according to a formula in the employment contract. The court found that the formula was a reasonable pre-estimate of damages the employer would suffer if the employee left before the three-year period and upheld the clause (*Renaud v. Graham,* 2007 CanLii 5680 (ONSC).

Government Regulations of Working Conditions

Both federal and provincial governments have legislation governing employee work conditions. In some provinces, there is an *Employment Standards Act*; in others, the provisions are included in a *Labour Act*. While the details vary from province to province, the legislation all deals with such areas as wages, rest periods, holidays and vacations, sick days, and maternity leaves. It is an ever-changing area of the law, and the Employment Standards Offices of the provinces will supply up-to-date information and answer any questions that you have. Here is a summary of the main issues:

Wages

- The minimum wage in most provinces is about $6 an hour for people 18 or older.
- Certain jobs, such as farm workers and waiters, are exempt from minimum-wage requirements.
- There is a minimum number of hours per day an employee should be asked to work.
- After eight hours a day, or 40 hours a week, overtime—in most provinces 1.5 times the regular rate of pay—must be paid.
- Male and female employees must receive equal pay for substantially similar work.

Rest Periods

- Employees are entitled to one 30-minute rest period, without pay, for every five hours worked.
- They are entitled to a minimum weekly rest of 24 continuous hours every seven days.
- In Ontario, an employee in a retail business establishment may refuse to work on Sunday.

Holidays and Vacations

- Employees are usually entitled to 11 paid statutory holidays a year (this varies by province). If an employee works on a statutory holiday, a premium rate must be paid, or time off given instead.
- Normally, a minimum of two weeks' vacation with pay is required, but some provinces guarantee three or four weeks after five or more years of service. Most employers simply continue to pay regular wages during employees' time off, as this usually amounts to the equivalent of vacation pay for two weeks. Vacation pay is calculated as 4 percent of the employee's usual annual earnings.

Sick Days and Maternity Leaves

- The laws governing sick days are unclear, but if most businesses in your line of work offer sick days, you must do the same.
- The minimum amount of unpaid maternity leave ranges from 17 to 18 weeks, depending on the province.
- Some provinces also guarantee additional unpaid parental leave for mothers or fathers, including adoptive parents.

Human Rights Issues

Discrimination

Human rights legislation is one of the developing areas of law (see Chapter 1). A business must take reasonable steps—short of causing the business undue hardship—to adapt any work rules that would discriminate against an employee. For example, a milk production plant, closed on weekends, was always extremely busy on Mondays as milk delivered on Saturday and Sunday was processed. The plant fired an employee who belonged to the Church of the Seventh-Day Adventists, and who refused to work on Easter Monday for religious reasons. The Supreme Court of Canada found that the employer could have accommodated the employee's request for Easter Monday off, as a supervisor or other employee could have taken his place. The business was found guilty of discrimination.

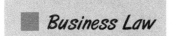

Business Law   Applied

❸ **John Goodman is** Jewish. He is an employee of a small business that has decided to stay open on Friday evenings. There are about 20 people on staff. Goodman protests, but the manager says that everyone has to work on Fridays.

  a) Does Goodman have any grounds for refusing to work?
  b) In what circumstances would the employer have to agree to let Goodman not work Friday evenings?

Sexual Harassment

Any unwelcome sexually oriented behaviour that makes an employee feel uncomfortable, or obstructs the ability to work, or interferes with employment opportunities, is sexual harassment. It may be obvious, such as crude jokes, but it may also be subtle, such as a request for dates by a superior that an employee feels compelled to accept.

Business Alert!

Sexual Harassment   The offender is personally liable for harassing conduct. However, the employer may also be responsible—even if unaware of the incident—unless the employer has been proactive in preventing sexual harassment. Employers are advised to:

- create a sexual harassment policy and post it in a conspicuous place
- encourage employees to speak up if harassed
- develop a clear complaint procedure
- discipline offenders by written warnings, suspension without pay and, if all else fails, dismissal

Non-Smoking Policy

There may be tension between policies to eliminate smoking in the workplace and the need to accommodate smokers who are addicted.

Governments are passing smoke-free legislation that requires businesses to create smoke-free environments in the workplace. On the other hand human rights tribunals may rule that addiction to smoking is a disability and require accommodation for that disability. Cominco Ltd. created a policy that its entire premises would be smoke free. However, the Ontario Human Rights Tribunal found that smoking was a disability and the policy had to be modified to accommodate this disability. (*Cominco Ltd. v. Steelworkers of America,* Local 9505 (2000), 59 C.L.A.S. 318).

Health and Safety

In some provinces, health and safety requirements are included in general labour laws; in others, they are dealt with specifically in occupational health and safety acts. The main purposes of these laws are:

- to provide safe working conditions, by identifying hazardous activities and substances, fencing dangerous areas, putting proper shielding around equipment, and similar measures
- to ensure safe employment practices and the use of protective equipment such as hard hats, goggles, and other protective clothing

- to establish programs that educate employers and employees on safety issues
- There are laws governing the amount of light and space per employee, as well as the type of lunchroom and washroom facilities that should be provided. An employee may also refuse to work with or operate a tool or machine that could create a danger to health. There are local industrial health and safety officers who conduct inspections, and will also answer any questions on behalf of employers or employees. Workers' compensation funds are also available to employees who are injured on the job.

Privacy in the Workplace

There are a few cases dealing with privacy in the workplace. In one of these cases, *Richardson v. Davis Wire Industries*, the B.C. Supreme Court allowed an employer to present evidence from a secret videotape that revealed a foreman was sleeping on the job (*Lawyers Weekly*, May 16, 1997, p. 20).

Firing

An employer does not have to keep an employee on the payroll for life. A worker can be dismissed because that individual breached the employment contract—this is known as firing for **just cause**, that is with a valid reason for dismissing an employee without notice. An employee can also be fired without cause, but then the employer is in breach of the contract and must pay damages.

Sometimes an employee is not fired outright, but the job is changed in an effort to force the employee to quit. Such acts by the employer are called **constructive dismissal**, employer conduct that amounts to a fundamental breach of the employment contract and justifies the employee quitting. For example, if an employee was hired to be a sales manager but was then demoted to be a sales representative, this would be constructive dismissal. If, however, the employee accepts the new position, the parties have agreed to change the employment contract, and the demotion is not actionable.

just cause

a valid reason for dismissing an employee without notice

constructive dismissal

employer conduct that amounts to a fundamental breach of the employment contract and justifies the employee quitting

"But enough of my little jokes. You're probably wondering why I asked you to come by my office!"

Shah v. Xerox Canada Ltd., [2000] 49 C.C.E.L. (2d) 166 (Ont. C.A.)

Viren Shah had been employed with Xerox for over 12 years when he was given a position as a Technical Support Analyst. Up until this transfer, Shah received positive performance appraisals, regular bonuses, and regular pay increases.

After Shah's transfer to the new position a personality conflict developed with his new manager. The manager gave Shah negative performance appraisals and two warning letters, criticizing his job performance in very strong language. Three days after the second warning letter, the supervisor advised Shah that he was on probation. Shah resigned from his employment and commenced a claim for wrongful dismissal on the basis of constructive dismissal.

The Court's Decision

The court held that a change in the fundamental term of an employment agreement amounts to constructive dismissal (technically, a fundamental breach) and justifies resignation. The factors must be objective and traditionally they included:

1. geographic relocation of employment
2. change in responsibilities
3. reduction in remuneration or benefits
4. technological changes

The court expanded the law to indicate that it was sufficient that the employee prove a poisoned work environment. The court said that the basic principles are:

- an employee is entitled to decent treatment from the employer; and
- an employer does not have the right to make the conditions of employment intolerable to the average individual.

Here the court found that the supervisor was not justified in his criticisms and was simply taking advantage of his position to indulge in a personality conflict. Shah was awarded damages for wrongful dismissal.

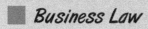

Business Law   Applied

④ Julie Stolzak is Vice-President, Public Relations, of Magnum Computer Corp. Limited. Her annual salary is $80,000. Because of difficult times, Magnum is restructuring, and has eliminated this particular position. Stolzak has been offered the position of General Sales Manager, at an annual salary of $70,000. She would then report to the Vice-President, Sales.

   a) Stolzak does not want to accept this position because she feels she would lose face in front of all the company employees. Does she have to accept the position?
   b) What are her alternatives if she does not accept the new job?

Privacy

Increased sensitivity to privacy rights has impacted on the law of constructive dismissal. An Ontario Judge ruled that an employer who secretly installed a hidden camera in an employee's office, without her knowledge and without a plausible explanation, had constructively dismissed the employee based on a privacy violation.

Colwell v. Cornerstone Properties Inc. [2008] CanLII 66139 (ON S.C.)

A commercial manager, Ms. Colwell, learned that a hidden camera was installed in her office by her immediate boss at Cornerstone Properties Inc., ("Cornerstone"). Ms. Colwell found out about the existence of the camera when she saw the image of her office on a monitor in the presence of her immediate boss and the vice-president of Cornerstone.

Ms. Colwell confronted her immediate boss, who indicated to her that the camera had been installed approximately nine months prior to her being aware of its existence. He also indicated to her that she was not considered to be involved in any alleged thefts—either as a victim or a suspect. The camera, she was told, was to assist in detecting theft by the maintenance staff. However, even though Ms. Colwell was the person directly responsible for the maintenance staff, she was never advised of any thefts or the camera set up to capture them. The camera in her office was the only hidden camera installed in Cornerstone's office area, yet there was no plausible explanation given as to why her office was thought to be most likely the subject of a theft.

The Court's Decision

The judge stated, "A secret camera installed in a trusted manager's office without her knowledge, although perhaps accept- able employer conduct in itself, coupled with a totally implausible explanation, renders the actions unacceptable." The judge found that Ms. Colwell's contract of employment contained an implied term of good faith and fair dealing, throughout the existence of the contract, which was breached by the actions of her employer. As such, the judge held that Ms. Colwell was constructively dismissed and was accordingly justified in leaving her position at Cornerstone. She was ultimately awarded seven months pay in lieu of notice (she had been employed by Cornerstone for in excess of seven years).

While there continues to be no privacy legislation that addresses an employee's privacy rights in the workplace, the *Colwell* case demonstrates that there is an implied right of privacy as a part of good faith and fair dealing in an employment contract.

Surveillance cameras which are set up without employees' knowledge and without plausible explanation may amount to constructive dismissal, especially if cameras are set up for a direct view into an employee's office.

Even if an employer has a plausible explanation (e.g., a need to investigate inappropriate activity), employers should consider all other less intrusive means of combating workplace issues before secretly invading employees' privacy.

Business Alert!

Just Cause

If an employer has a good reason to fire an employee, this is just cause in law and the individual can be dismissed immediately without notice, and without payment of damages. Not every transgression or fault of an employee amounts to just cause. Some of the most common situations involving just cause are:

- theft
- dishonesty
- frequent absenteeism, not because of illness
- intoxication affecting the employee's work
- insolence and insubordination
- frequent lateness
- incompetence
- conflict of interest
- illness that prevents the employee from doing the job for which the individual was hired

Just cause can also be discovered after the dismissal has taken place.

Incompetence

On the surface, it would seem that incompetence would be the easiest basis on which to have an employee dismissed—but it is not. It is therefore important to have a term of probation to make certain that new employees are capable of performing the job for which they were hired.

Before an employee can be found incompetent, the individual must be given written warnings. It is also important that the employer not be found to have approved the conduct. Sometimes, well-meaning employers are reluctant to correct an employee, who can then claim to have been doing the job for several years without being told of incompetence.

Misconduct

Misconduct as a basis for dismissal includes a wide range of activities such as dishonesty, cheating on expense accounts, disrespect, uncooperative attitudes, and failure to obey reasonable orders.

If employee behaviour can be improved—and misconduct is usually in this category—the individual must be given notice and the chance to alter the unacceptable behaviour. For example, where a manager is putting too much pressure on subordinates, that manager must be told of this. If the conduct continues, the manager can be dismissed. Traditionally, for other matters such as dishonesty—where a cashier steals from the cash register, for example—no notice need be given.

However, a recent Supreme Court of Canada case has said that dishonesty is not an automatic cause for dismissal. BC Tel dismissed an accountant, alleging he had been dishonest about a medical condition and the treatment available for it. The employee was successful in his wrongful-dismissal action. The judge told the jury that it could consider whether the dishonesty was completely incompatible with the employment relationship. The jury apparently found that it was not, for it awarded wrongful dismissal damages to the employee.

A relatively new grounds for dismissal for misconduct is the use of a company computer for downloading or distributing racist or pornographic materials. Where a company has a clear policy prohibiting employees from using company computers for such personal uses, the employee who does so can be dismissed without any need to give prior warnings to stop the misconduct (*Poliquine v. Devon Canada Corporation,* 2009 ABCA 216 CanLii).

There are limits on the type of conduct that can be used to justify dismissal without notice. In some cases changing values may influence the determination of what is relevant behaviour as the next case shows.

Disrespectful Blogging

Disrespectful comments in a blog about fellow employees may be grounds for dismissal. An employee wrote on her blog: "Does anyone else out there live in a world like mine with imbeciles and idiot savants (no offence to them) running the ship . . . and is anyone else's ship being sailed down the highway to hell?" An arbitration panel, upheld by the Alberta Court of Appeal held that the contempt expressed by the employee in her public blogs respecting her coworkers, management and administration of the department seriously and irreparably damaged the employment relationship justifying the termination (*Union of Provincial Employees v. Alberta* QB 2009 and ABQB 2008 [Nielsen J.]).

Dooley v. C.N. Weber Ltd., [1994] 3 C.C.E.L (2d) 95

John Dooley began working for C.N. Weber Ltd. in 1973 as a summer student. He rose to middle management and, in 1992, was appointed a member of the management operating committee. The Weber company had been in that family for over 100 years, and the current president was Jack Weber. The company was run as if all long-term employees were members of one family, and Dooley confirmed that he felt Jack treated him as a son.

While at the Kitchener location, Dooley had an affair with a subordinate woman employee. It was conducted outside working hours, and did not affect C.N. Weber's business. Dooley's wife was also a long-term employee of C.N. Weber, but the couple was in the process of separating at the time. They later divorced.

After this affair, Dooley was advised by a representative of the company that he would be laid off or suspended from his employment unless he sought counselling designed to prevent further sexual misconduct at work. Dooley refused this offer of counselling, since he did not feel he had a sexual problem as alleged.

Dooley was transferred to Toronto, and Jack Weber warned Dooley not to have any sexual relationships with female subordinates,

adding that if he did, it would be grounds for immediate dismissal. Dooley did have a second affair with another female employee in Toronto. It was also conducted after working hours. Dooley was fired for disobeying the order not to have affairs with female employees.

The Court's Decision

The court held that the question to be answered was whether the order given by Weber to Dooley that he not be involved sexually with female subordinates in Toronto was reasonable, and could be given within the scope of his employment contract with the company.

Earlier case law had accepted that an employer could order an employee not to have affairs with subordinate females. Disobedience was just cause for dismissal. However, the court noted that, since those earlier decisions, society's thinking had changed, and such an order was not reasonable in today's world, particularly when there was no evidence that the company suffered in any way, financially or otherwise. Accordingly, the court awarded Dooley damages based on 12 months' notice.

Conflict of Interest

Moonlighting—holding a second paid job—in the same area of work may be a conflict of interest, and the first employer must approve the extra work. An employee cannot compete with, or take business away from, the main employer.

Millard v. Seven Continents Enterprises Inc., [1992] 44 C.C.E.L. 119

Millard was a design artist for Seven Continents, a firm that prepared in-store and window displays for retailers. He did a little moonlighting, and prepared a Christmas display for a shopping mall, receiving $325 for 17 hours of work one weekend.

When Seven Continents heard about this, they fired Millard. He sued for wrongful dismissal, claiming that he had taken the project in the hopes of impressing the mall management, and gaining more business for his employer. Also, he said the project was so small, it would not have been of interest to Seven Continents.

The Court's Decision

The court found that Millard, as an employee, owed a duty not to take any business away from his employer. If he wanted to compete with Seven Continents in even the smallest way, he should have advised them of the opportunity and obtained their permission to go ahead. If it really was too small a job for Seven Continents' interest, it would have approved Millard's request.

The fact that the job was a very small one was not a defence. The employer was justified in terminating Millard's employment.

Sexual Harassment

If an employee engages in any act that violates human rights legislation, such as making discriminatory remarks or unwelcome sexual comments, that individual can be fired. The employer is responsible under human rights legislation for the acts of the employee, and could be fined.

Employers must conduct a proper investigation of any allegation of sexual harassment. There are several cases in which employers responded to claims of sexual harassment by firing the alleged offender immediately; it was held that the employers acted too quickly, and did not investigate the incident. The alleged sexual harassment allegations were found to be untrue. More recent cases have held that the employee must be given notice of the offensive conduct and an opportunity to change.

Personality Conflict

A conflict of personalities is not just cause for dismissing an employee.

Retaliation

Employers cannot fire an employee because that individual has filed a complaint with the government that the employer has violated employment laws.

Pollinger v. Bergman Graphics Limited, [1994] 18 O.R. (3d) 31

Pollinger, aged 50, was hired as a journeyman litho stripper on May 1, 1989, and dismissed 18 months later. He was given two weeks' pay in lieu of notice.

Pollinger was very sensitive to second-hand smoke, and advised the employer of this on hiring. He was assured the plant had a no-smoking policy. However, in October 1990, he was bothered by the smoking of a fellow worker, and complained to a

supervisor on several occasions. The supervisor told Pollinger that the other employee was working hard and needed a smoke.

Pollinger then told management that he had spoken to Ministry of Labour officials about the situation. He said further that he did not want to hurt the company, but "if that guy lights up again" he would file a complaint with the Ministry of Labour. The next day, Pollinger was given his walking papers.

The Court's Decision

Pollinger was not fired for cause. The company did not even claim it had cause to fire him, so the only question was what was reasonable notice in all the circumstances. The court took into account the type of employment, the length of service, the age of the employee, and the availability of similar work elsewhere. In light of this, and Pollinger's experience, training, and qualifications, he was awarded four months' pay as reasonable notice.

The court noted that the company's attempt to terminate the employee because of his threat to complain under a workplace statute was a serious matter. Such conduct deserved penalty by the court in the form of punitive damages. The court added one month's additional wages on this basis.

Human Rights Issues II

Human rights issues may also be relevant to ongoing management policies, not merely hiring.

Example: a provincial transit company instituted an attendance management program which would identify employees who are absent beyond the average of other employees. The Union grieved this policy claiming it discriminated against employees with disabilities contrary to the British Columbia Human Rights Code. However, the court held that the policy was a bona fide occupational requirement and upheld it (*Coast Mountain Bus v. CAW–Canada*, 2009 BCSC 396).

Firing without Just Cause

Reasonable Notice

reasonable notice

notice calculated on the basis of level of position and length of employment

An employee does not have lifelong job security. The employer has to give only **reasonable notice** (notice calculated on the basis of level of position and length of employment) or the equivalent in salary, the measure of damages at common law. Most companies prefer to give the equivalent in salary and have the employee leave at once. What is reasonable notice varies with individual circumstances. It is usually easier, for example, for a legal secretary to find alternative employment than it is for the president of a multinational corporation. Similarly, a 25-year-old worker will normally find a new job faster than one who is 50.

■ *Critical Concepts of* Notice at Common Law

- An employer can fire without just cause, but must give reasonable notice or pay the equivalent in salary.
- Reasonable notice depends on age, level of position, and length of time to obtain alternative equivalent employment.

Bardal v. The Globe & Mail Ltd., [1960] 24 D.L.R. (2d) 140

In 1942, Bardal was appointed advertising manager for the *Globe & Mail*. In 1959, the newspaper became dissatisfied with his efforts, and thought it could find an advertising manager who would produce better results. The position of advertising manager is one of the most important in the newspaper business, since it is the revenue generated by advertising that makes the newspaper profitable.

The president of the *Globe & Mail* informed Bardal that the newspaper wanted to get someone who could improve business in the advertising department, and asked for Bardal's resignation. When Bardal refused, he was given written notice of termination on April 24, 1959.

Bardal sought new employment immediately, and secured a position with an advertising firm on July 1, 1959, but at a lower salary. Bardal then brought an action against the *Globe & Mail* for his lost salary during the period of unemployment, and for the difference in salary between his old and new employment for the balance of the reasonable notice period.

The Court's Decision

The court stated that, although counsel for the *Globe & Mail* had cited many precedents where six months was the highest period given for reasonable notice, these did not establish that six months was, as a matter of law, the longest reasonable notice period. These cases were decided on particular facts, and different circumstances would suggest different notice periods.

The court held that what constitutes reasonable notice must be decided in each particular case, taking into consideration the type of employment, length of service of the employee, age of the employee, and the availability of similar employment given the employee's experience, training, and qualifications.

In applying this principle, the court found that Bardal had a lifetime of training and was qualified to manage the advertising department of a large metropolitan newspaper. He had been in the advertising departments of two large daily newspapers. There were few similar situations available in Canada, and so Bardal had taken employment with an advertising agency. However, that employment would be of a different character. Taking all these factors into account, the court decided that one year was reasonable notice in this case.

Bardal was entitled to the lost salary between his last day of employment and commencing new work. He was also entitled to the difference between his new and old employment for the balance of the reasonable notice period of one year.

Notice Periods

Each case is decided on its individual merits. A list of the average notice periods awarded by judges for all job classifications and ages is shown below.

Years of Service	Average Notice (in months)
1	5.33
2	6.00
3	6.19
4	8.73
5	7.38
6	7.46
7	8.71
8	8.37
9	8.41
10	11.66
11	10.50
12	11.47
13	12.67
14	11.33
15	7.88
16	13.67
17	13.25
18	12.27
19	14.56
20	15.14

Source: David Harris, *Wrongful Dismissal* (Toronto: Carswell, 1990), pp. 4–26.

Businesses often use the rule of thumb of one month for every year of service to determine notice awards. However useful this might be for settlement purposes, it is not what the courts apply, and is not supported by the above list, particularly in the earlier years.

Interpreting statistics, however, is always tricky. For example, the average notice awarded of 5.33 months for one year of service is probably affected by the fact that most employees who sue after one year of service are older, and have left positions where they held seniority. A 45-year-old who left a previous job after 10 years, and then was fired from a new position after one year, would likely receive several months' notice. A 25-year-old, with no previous experience, would probably only get a month's notice after one year's service. This factor is not accounted for in statistics.

Business Law Applied

⑤ Felipe Suarez was foreman of a meat-packing plant. One day several employees called in sick, and as a result his crew was short-staffed. Those employees who were present had to work hard to get the day's work done. At the end of the day, Suarez rewarded the workers by bringing in some beer.

The next day, the supervisor found empty beer bottles and now wants to fire Suarez for allowing employees to drink on the job.

a) Does the company have just cause for dismissing Suarez?

b) What do you think the company is legally required to do?

Statutory Notice Period

Some confusion exists in the area of notice because two separate, but overlapping, laws which govern it—common law and statutory law. The employment standards acts and labour acts set notice periods for dismissal without cause. These are minimum periods; the common law sets the maximum. In the past, notice for management-level positions has been decided according to common law, while more junior positions have been decided by statutory provisions. However, this may be changing, as there is a trend to apply common law notice periods to positions below the management level.

The various Employment Standards Acts provide for two types of pay on being fired: termination and severance. Termination pay applies to all employees, but entitlement to severance pay only applies to those employed by larger employers–usually with 50 employees or more. The examples in this text will assume only termination pay.

Example: Termination pay and pay in lieu of notice

An employee of 7 years is fired without just cause and entitled to pay in lieu of reasonable notice (at common law). Assuming the amounts in the table on the preceding page, the notice might be 8.73 months. However, the statutory notice period for termination pay might be 4 weeks. The employee does not get both but only the maximum.

Business Law Applied

⑥ Villma Mednic was a receptionist with Geller company for approximately one year. During that time, she had made personal long-distance calls during office hours, charging them to business files. The company's auditor discovered these calls—90 in all, for a total of about $500. On discovery, Mednic repaid the money and promised not to do it again. Geller Enterprises does not want an employee who is dishonest, and would like to fire her. Mednic claims the company suffered no harm, as the money was repaid.

a) Does the company have just cause to fire Mednic?

b) If the company fires Mednic and is wrong, what can Mednic claim in a court proceeding?

c) What are the relevant common law and statutory notice periods?

d) How long do you think it would take a receptionist to find another position?

e) If a company was found not to have just cause for her dismissal, could Mednic obtain an order that the company reinstate her?

▰■ *Critical Concepts of* Notice

- At common law, notice must be reasonable. This is a maximum period.
- Under provincial legislation, notice is set out on a sliding scale. It is normally two weeks after the first year of service, and one week per year of service after that, to a maximum of eight weeks. This is the minimum period.

Factors That Affect Damages

Factors that tend to increase the amount of damages the courts will award include:

- the employee was induced to move from one province to another to take the position from which the individual was subsequently fired
- the employee's health at the time of termination would make it difficult to find alternative employment
- the employee was laid off for three months before being recalled to work, then fired by the employer although the employer had intended the dismissal before the layoff
- the employee had a secure position and was enticed away from that position by the present employer
- the employee was terminated in a harsh or insensitive manner

Employees have often been given special consideration by the courts. One of the most recent indications that the employment contract will not be considered in the same way as normal arm's-length contracts is the principle that if any employer raises defences in a court action, which the court views as without merit or done for tactical reasons to force the employee to settle, the court will increase the damage award to the employee significantly.

The court recognizes that when an employee is terminated, it has a devastating financial effect on the employee. The employee will usually have ongoing obligations that demand most of that individual's salary and will suddenly be left without income. If an employer uses the court process to increase legal costs, the employee often cannot afford the expense of litigation. To discourage employers from raising sham defences to make it difficult for employees to sue, the courts will significantly increase the award to the employee in this circumstance.

Factors that have been found to reduce the amount of damages include:

- the employee had been looking for a position prior to dismissal
- the employee was employed in the construction industry, which is highly cyclical in nature
- the position itself was insecure, and before accepting employment the employee was aware of the fact that the employer was having financial difficulties
- the employer provided job-relocation counselling
- the employee rejected the employer's offer of free placement services

Near cause—that is, poor behaviour that is just short of justification for firing—cannot be used to reduce the award of damages.

Thus in determining the size of an offer of severance pay for an employee who has been fired without just cause, poor performance, which is less than cause for dismissal, does not reduce the amount of severance pay.

Business Law Applied

You are on your first day on the job assigned to assist the director of human relations for your employer. The employer has decided to fire one employee to cut costs but does not have just cause in law. However, in considering the amount of severance pay to be offered to the employee, the director has reviewed that employee's past performance appraisals and sees that he got very poor reviews. On the basis of these poor reviews the director decides to offer half the normal severance amounts. Is he correct in law?

Bad Faith Dismissal

One of the above factors that has invoked considerable litigation is employer conduct in the course of dismissing an employee. The dismissal must be done with due regard for the employee's dignity. Damages for breach of this obligation reached a high water mark in a case that lent its name to such claims: *Wallace v. United Grain Growers Ltd.*, 1997 CanLII 332 (S.C.C.). Wallace damages as an extension of the reasonable notice period became a frequent claim. Employers were held to a high standard of careful treat of terminated employees. Wallace damages were often awarded to compensate, for example, for humiliation, which did not require medical evidence in support. However, the Supreme Court of Canada restated the basis for awarding these damages in the following case requiring, in effect, medical evidence of psychological injury as a result of the conduct. The scope for Wallace damages, now sometimes pleaded as moral damages, may likely be severely restricted.

Honda Canada Inc. v. Keays, [2008] SCC 39 (CanLII)

Keays had worked 11 years for Honda, first on an assembly line and later in data entry, when, in 1997, he was diagnosed with chronic fatigue syndrome. He ceased work and received disability benefits until 1998, when Honda's insurer discontinued his benefits. Keays returned to work and was placed in a disability program that allows employees to take absences from work if they provide doctor's notes confirming that their absences are related to their disability.

Keays' employer became concerned about the frequency of his absences. Moreover, the notes Keays offered to explain his absences changed in tone, leaving the employer to believe that the doctor did not independently evaluate whether he missed work due to disability. As such, the employer asked Keays to meet Dr. Brennan, an occupational medical specialist, in order to determine how Keays' disability could be accommodated.

On the advice of his lawyer, Keays refused to meet Dr. Brennan without explanation of the purpose, methodology and parameters of the consultation. In March 28, 2000, the employer gave Keays a letter stating that it supported Keays' full return to work but that Keays' employment would be terminated if he refused to meet Dr. Brennan. When Keays remained unwilling to meet Dr. Brennan, the employer terminated Keays' employment.

Keays sued for wrongful dismissal. The trial judge found that Keays was entitled to a notice period of 15 months. He held that the employer had committed acts of discrimination, harassment and misconduct against Keays. He increased the notice period to 24 months to award additional aggravated damages (called informally: Wallace damages) because of the manner of dismissal. He also awarded punitive damages against the employer in the amount of $500,000, a costs premium, and costs on a substantial indemnity scale.

The Court of Appeal reduced the costs premium and, in a majority decision, reduced the punitive damages award to $100,000. The Court of Appeal otherwise upheld the trial judge's decision.

The Supreme Court of Canada's Decision

The Plaintiff was wrongfully dismissed and the award of damages reflecting the need for 15 months' notice should be maintained.

However, the court reversed the trial judge's finding first on facts as not supported by the evidence; Honda had not acted in bad faith in the manner of dismissing Keays.

Secondly, as a matter of law, while the court affirmed the availability of the remedy of damages that result from an employer's conduct in the course of dismissal which conduct is unfair or in bad faith by being, for example, untruthful, misleading or unduly insensitive (Wallace Damages), it stated that these damages should only be awarded on the same basis as other damages, i.e., proof of actual harm. Previously, courts had awarded damages on a more punitive like rationale, by extending the reasonable notice period, without proof of actual mental distress.

Similarly, punitive damages should not have been awarded. Punitive damages should be restricted to wrongful acts that are so malicious and outrageous that they are deserving of punishment on their own. The facts of this case demonstrated no such conduct. Courts should only resort to punitive damages in exceptional cases.

Firing: Employers   At the earliest sign of difficulties with an employee, you should seek legal advice.

Business Alert!

■ If the conduct can be remedied, you should give the employee notice in writing, and start a paper trail by keeping track of all incidents by writing and filing memos.

■ If you have to fire an employee, do so in a private office, and have a witness. Do not fire the individual in front of other employees, thus causing mental stress and humiliation.

■ Follow up the termination interview with a letter containing the amount and terms of any severance package offered if the firing is not for cause. A release for the employee to sign should be included, with a comment that legal advice should be sought. A release signed by an employee is probably not enforceable unless that individual has obtained independent legal advice.

■ If you are firing for cause, do not give a letter of reference without discussing the matter with your lawyer. It could be used by the employee to prevent you from establishing just cause.

Being Fired: Employees   If you are fired, do not sign anything or agree to anything; ask for time to consult a lawyer, and do so.

Business Alert!

Employee Notice

If an employee wants to resign, that employee is also obligated to give the employer some notice, although this notice is generally for much less a time from the notice an employer must give an employee. If the employee gives notice of two weeks, and the employer tells the employee to leave immediately, the employer must still pay the employee for the notice period of two weeks (provided there is no contractual term stating otherwise).

Employment Insurance

Employees who contribute to the unemployment insurance plan may be eligible to collect from it on being fired. Anyone who is fired without cause is automatically entitled to do so, after a delay period of a few weeks. This is a policy set by the Canada Employment Insurance Commission and may change from time to time.

If an employee is fired for cause, or leaves voluntarily, the individual is not entitled to receive payment from employment insurance. The commission recognizes, however, that not every employee who is fired is, in fact, fired for a just cause, and will make inquiries to decide whether the employer was correct in the dismissal. If it determines that the individual was fired without cause, employment insurance will be paid.

If employees receive a lump-sum settlement package from the employer, they must advise the commission of this. Employment insurance payments will commence when the severance amount is completed—for example, if an employer pays an employee the equivalent of six months' salary, that employee cannot collect employment insurance until six months have elapsed.

Business Law Applied

❼ The Vitale Group is facing large losses and, in order to survive, must fire the regional sales manager, Mary Meccelli, who is 45 years of age. Meccelli has been with the company for 16 years, and currently earns $60,000 a year. An employment agency says that it usually takes about one year for a person in Meccelli's situation to find another position.

    a) Is firing for economic necessity just cause?
    b) What will determine the length of notice that must be given to Meccelli?
    c) What notice do you think the court would award in this case?

Business Alert!

Employment Insurance and Severance   If an individual collects employment insurance for some time while negotiating a severance package with a former employer, that employer must deduct the amount that has been paid from the final agreed package. If the employer does not do so, and pays it to the employee, the employer is liable and may have to pay twice—once to the employee and once to the commission. When a settlement is reached, the employer, not the employee, must reimburse the commission for the payments made. If it pays the money to the employee, the commission will collect it again from the employer.

Agreeing to Lesser Notice

Some employment agreements have terms specifying the amount of notice required for dismissal for cause. These terms invariably set out substantially less time than the common law notice period. As a matter of freedom of contract, an employee is able to agree to terms that shorten the notice period, and several reported decisions have upheld such terms. The employee cannot, however, agree to a notice period that is less than the minimum outlined under statutory requirements.

Hodgson v. Sun Valley Co-op Ltd., [1991] 38 C.C.E.L. 34

In February 1988, Hodgson applied for the position, and was promoted to office manager/accountant on a probationary basis. She entered into an employment agreement dated February 29, 1988. This agreement included terms stating that she was on probation in this position for six months, and set a severance allowance equal to one week for each year of service upon dismissal without cause. There was also an employee information manual that outlined the same terms.

Hodgson, on being fired, had 12 years and four months of employment with the defendant, and claimed that reasonable notice should be in the range of nine to 12 months' salary. She also claimed reimbursement for moving expenses of $450, incurred when she relocated to Winnipeg in an effort to find employment.

Sun Valley took the position that the plaintiff was entitled to only one week's pay for each year of service, for a total of 12 weeks'

pay according to either the employee agreement or the employee information manual. The co-operative pointed out that the plaintiff had assisted in the preparation of this manual.

The Court's Decision

The court decided that the employment contract governed, and the term of that contract expressly set severance payment at one week per year of service when an employee was fired without just cause. The court felt it did not have to decide whether the employee information manual was part of the employee contract, but the same result would have been reached. As the employment contract did not provide for any damages for moving expenses, the plaintiff was not able to claim the moving expenses to Winnipeg.

Terms That Limit Notice   Although *Hodgson* and other cases have upheld terms limiting the notice period to less than reasonable notice, such clauses are likely to be attacked in future under two grounds in contract law:

- economic duress
- penalty/liquidated damages

Does an employee really have a choice when agreeing to such a term on being hired? Also, if that term is not a reasonable estimate of what a court would award—liquidated damages—it may be struck as a penalty (see p. 199).

If you are an employer and wish to use such a clause, it is essential to make certain that the notice is greater than the statutory minimum, and that the term is brought to the employee's attention at time of hiring. The notice should also be at least near the low end of the range for common law awards. Only a lawyer can advise you of the current ranges for various job levels and lengths of employment.

Mental Distress

Although courts have begun to allow damages for non-economic factors such as mental distress, they do not do so frequently. It is accepted that on being fired an employee will feel a sense of humiliation and loss of confidence, which will be stronger if the individual has been a long-time employee, expecting lifetime employment. Only in extreme cases will damages for mental suffering be awarded, and a psychiatric report will often be necessary to support such a claim.

In the case of *Bohemier v. Storwal*, the court awarded Mr. Bohemier $1,500 for mental distress because the employer sent a notice by taxicab, delivered to his house after he returned from work. His family testified that Mr. Bohemier was so distraught that he required medical attention on receiving the notice. The court was obviously giving a message to employers that they must treat their employees with respect, and sending notice by way of a taxicab was not acceptable.

Hence, the manner of giving notice is given great weight by the court in determining whether they will award damages for mental distress. If an employee is fired in front of other employees, for example, that would be considered an unnecessarily callous act, and would attract damages for mental suffering.

Pillato v. Hamilton Place Convention Centre Inc., [1984] 45 O.R. (2d) 662

John Pillato was the manager of the Hamilton Place Convention Centre. He had considerable experience in the hotel industry, and was hired because he was considered one of the top marketing men in that business. He was chief executive officer at the time of being fired.

When he was hired, there was an exchange of letters between Pillato and the board of directors. In one letter, the board told Pillato that it was a term of his employment that, if he were dismissed without cause, notice would be six months.

Pillato showed a pornographic video in his private office. The chairman and vice-chairman of the convention centre's board were both present. Later, the staff showed the video to other staff in a public meeting room at the centre, but no members of the public were present. Pillato heard of this, and told the staff not to do it again.

The board called Pillato to a meeting for his annual review. Some of the board members had heard about the showing of the film. Pillato was asked if any board members were present, and he answered untruthfully that they had not been. The board told Pillato that he showed bad judgment in the affair, and that he should not do it again. But, at the same meeting, the board told him that it expressed confidence in his performance generally, and gave him a raise in salary.

The media picked up the story about pornographic videos being shown at the convention centre. They also reported that Pillato had shown the film in Vancouver to promote convention-centre business. The mayor and city council of Hamilton heard about this. The mayor called Pillato in for a private meeting. At trial, the evidence of the mayor and Pillato differed as to what occurred at this meeting. But the court accepted Pillato's evidence that he denied the Vancouver showing, and that members of the public had never been shown any pornographic videos at the convention centre.

After the publicity, two board members called Pillato in for a private meeting. One of them said, "You'd better resign or we'll burn you."

Pillato went on holiday. The matter was still a very heated political topic. The city council directed the Hamilton Convention Centre to fire Pillato because of the videos, and the board did so while Pillato was on vacation—without advising him of its intention, or giving him an opportunity to explain. At the same time, the board issued a press release that was widely reported. Pillato found out about his dismissal by reading about it in the paper.

Pillato sued for damages for wrongful dismissal, mental suffering, and punitive damages. The convention centre defended, claiming they had three reasons in law that amounted to just cause:

- administrative incompetence
- improper claims for expenses
- the fact that Pillato lied to the board about the presence of two directors at the showing of the tapes

The Court's Decision

The court found that the allegations concerning the administrative incompetence and improper claim for expenses were not proven.

As for the grounds of lying, the court felt that the convention centre was using this as an excuse simply because earlier cases had accepted dishonesty as just cause for dismissal. However, the court indicated that not all lies are equal. The lie in this case was told to protect the reputation of members of the board who were also well known in the community. So, although it was a lie, it was of a minor type, and did not justify dismissal.

The court held that damages for mental suffering could be given for breach of contract, particularly in cases where an employee suffered because the employer failed to give proper notice, then carried out the dismissal in an inconsiderate manner. Pillato called a psychiatrist to testify at trial on his behalf. The psychiatrist filed a report that said:

"He has been experiencing several symptoms of stress, including sleep disturbance, obsessional thinking, fleeting suicidal thoughts, and social withdrawal. It was my impression that Mr. Pillato was suffering from a reactive depression, secondary to the intense stress of losing his position with the Hamilton Convention Centre. He had been struggling with intense feelings of anger, frustration, disappointment, embarrassment, and shame, and subsequent difficulties secondary to being unable to obtain employment... he did not suffer from any significant mental or emotional disturbances before this."

The court therefore held that Pillato was not given notice of termination of his employment, and was dealt with in a severe and unfair manner that had grave effects on his health.

The court then stated that punitive damages can also be awarded for a breach of contract in employment situations. The evidence of an outplacement specialist who said it was improbable that Pillato would be able to find appropriate employment in his field in Canada, because of what happened to him in Hamilton, was accepted. It was felt that Pillato had repeatedly been dealt with savagely and severely, to his lasting harm, and that the board had not only threatened to try to ruin Pillato if he did not resign, but it had made good its threat.

Because Pillato had agreed to six months' notice in his employment contract, his claim for notice was limited to that amount. However, mental suffering and punitive damages are separate issues. Therefore the court awarded Pillato:

a) for the loss of six months' salary—$32,500
b) for mental suffering—$25,000
c) for punitive damages—$25,000

Checklist for Termination Letter

It is best to consult a lawyer as early as possible when problems with an employee arise, and before actually dismissing that individual. The notice of dismissal should include:

- the reason for dismissal
- the termination date
- the proposed notice, or pay in lieu of notice
- details of any payout under employee benefit plans, or requirements to convert insurance coverage, such as group life insurance
- details of statutory amounts to be paid, such as severance pay, vacation pay, and wages to date, including overtime
- a request for the return of employer's property, such as computers, keys, company credit card, and confidential documents
- a time by which the employee's personal effects must be removed from the company's premises
- information about any relocation assistance, such as counselling, reference letters, or secretarial help, that the employer is willing to offer
- a release for the employee to sign

Re-employment   Employees are not required to reveal to employers that they have found re-employment after termination. Careful employers now insist on having employees swear an affidavit that they have not found re-employment when employers are negotiating settlements with the former employees.

Employers also often structure the settlement payments so that they are paid over a period of some months. The employee is required to report each month on whether that individual has found employment. Once the former employee has found re-employment, the payments either cease or are reduced significantly.

Mitigation

Under contract law, an employee who has been fired must mitigate, or reduce, damages, by making every effort to find new employment. It is advisable to keep a record of all attempts to find another job, especially copies of letters sent to prospective employers.

Is an employee required to accept a lesser position in order to mitigate the damages? The courts have stated that this depends on the circumstances involved. In a normal situation, if the alternative position offered is not particularly demeaning, or will not result in humiliation, the employee must accept it while looking for other work. Damages awarded in such a case would be the difference between the original salary and that of the lower position with the same employer for the extent of the reasonable notice period, or until alternative employment was found at an equal, or better, salary.

In most cases, it is likely that the circumstances would be such that the employee would not be required to accept the new position. However, in a case where an employee's job was being eliminated because of economic necessity and relations were amicable, the employee would likely be required to accept the alternative position on a temporary basis while seeking new employment. If an employee collects unemployment insurance, that amount is to be deducted from the damage award.

Business Law   Applied

⑧ **LeeRoy Devon was** a 20-year employee at Forzan Electric Limited. He began as a salesperson and signed an employment contract at that time, indicating that if he was dismissed for any reason, his severance package would be based on one month per year of service, to a maximum of four months. He worked his way up to his present position as vice-president of sales in the company. When Forzan was taken over by a competitor, most of the senior executives were fired.

Devon wants the equivalent of reasonable notice in a lump-sum payment. Forzan checked its files, found the employment contract, and said it would only pay four months. Devon replied that the contract was signed 20 years ago, and he had forgotten all about it.

a) What reasonable notice would be likely in these circumstances?
b) Is the contract term to limit reasonable notice to four months enforceable?
   The CEO has become a good friend of Devon over the 20 years, and is embarrassed. He feels that he cannot face firing him in person, and wants to send Devon a letter of termination by courier to his home address.
c) Is this a wise course of action?

⑨ **Dana Zubas was** vice-president of public relations for the Harris Group of companies for 10 years. Because of the need to restructure the company, this position has been eliminated. The

Harris Group offers her a position as a public relations officer, at the same salary. Zubas objects, saying that the head of public relations used to report to her.

 a) What is the technical name in law for the offering of the alternative position?
 b) Is Zubas required to accept it?

Post-Employment Obligations

The Duty Not to Compete with a Former Employer

By Contract You may recall in the section on contracts under illegal agreements, the topic of restrictive covenants. Employment contracts may contain two types of terms that govern employee's conduct after termination: non-competition and non-solicitation clauses.

These terms are considered against public policy and enforced only if they are reasonable in the circumstances. The trend of the law appears to be that non-competition clauses are viewed with disfavour as being too restrictive on an employee's ability to earn a living. However, non-solicitation clauses are more likely to be upheld. By such a clause, employees are prohibited from directly approaching customers of the former employer for a reasonable period, which varies according to the circumstances, but it appears that a period of six months will be upheld.

While an employee is prohibited from directly contacting a customer, the employee is permitted to make a general announcement such as an advertisement in a newspaper indicating his change of employment.

Implied by Law Employees are free to compete with their former employers generally. However, there are restrictions. If an employee has a high level position with considerable control and responsibility in the employer's operation, that employee may owe a fiduciary duty to the employer. A company's CFO (Chief Financial Officer) would be an example of a fiduciary.

This level of employee may be prohibited from competing against the former employer for a reasonable period after termination. The fiduciary employee may also be prohibited from directly soliciting the former employer's customers for a reasonable period. While the period may vary with the circumstances, it appears that a minimum of six months is a frequent finding.

However, there is no implied term on lower level employees not to compete with a former employer. The average (non-fiduciary) employee can compete freely with a former employer without the restrictions imposed on a fiduciary as the next case brief demonstrates.

All employees have a duty to give reasonable notice before quitting. Failure to do so is sometimes called: "wrongful resignation". The length of required employee notice is governed by the test of how long it would take an employer to find a replacement. This period is usually in the order of weeks and much shorter than employer notice on firing an employee, which is more likely calculated in months.

Recall also that all employees have a duty not to use a former employer's confidential information as discussed above.

■ *Critical Concepts of* Employees' Post-Termination Obligations

The law implies obligations on employees to their employers post-employment:

- fiduciary level employees owe a duty not to compete for a reasonable period
- all level employees owe a duty to give reasonable notice of quitting
- all level employees owe a duty not to use their former employer's confidential information

RBC Dominion Securities Inc. v. Merrill Lynch Canada Inc., [2008] SCC 54 (CanLII)

Don Delamont was the manager of the Cranbrook Branch of RBC Dominion Securities ("RBC"). Cranbrook is a small city in British Columbia. RBC is the stock broker arm of the Royal Bank of Canada. Delamont was a personal friend of the manager of a competitor, the defendant Merrill Lynch Inc.

In November, 2002 Delamont left RBC to join Merrill Lynch's Cranbrook branch and took with him almost the entire Cranbrook sales team. Prior to leaving Delamont copied all RBC confidential customer information and brought it to Merrill Lynch. The RBC branch was effectively hollowed out and all but collapsed. On discovering the confidential information, Merrill Lynch returned it immediately and RBC accepted that no damage had been done resulting from this breach.

RBC sued the former employees and Merrill Lynch successfully on the basis of several economic torts, which will not be discussed here, but also sued the departing employees alleging two implied terms in the employment contract of any employee at any level:

a) to give reasonable notice of termination
b) not to compete during the notice period.

The Supreme Court of Canada's Decision

This Court found that although contract of employment ends when either the employer or employee terminates the employment relationship, residual post-employment duties may remain. An employee terminating employment may be liable for failure to give reasonable notice in breach of these residual duties. Subject to these duties the employee is free to compete against the former employer.

The Court found that reasonable notice in this situation was 2.5 weeks. That is the time in which a replacement employee could be found. During this period of time the employee has a duty not to compete and is only liable for damages for failure to give reasonable notice. The damages relating to the failure to give reasonable notice were estimated at $40,000.00 for all employees.

The trial judge had awarded additional damages of $225,000.00 based on the loss of 7% of RBC's clients immediately after the employees left. The Supreme Court of Canada overturned this decision by saying there was no implied duty on the employees not to compete.

■ *Business Law*   Applied

⑫ Satinder Khalsa is the CFO of Think Prudent Mortgage Corp. Inc. ("Think Prudent"). Ami Raj is a bookkeeper in the same business. Both quit without notice.

Khalsa goes to a large bank and Raj goes to a credit union. Both of these businesses compete with Think Prudent in the mortgage lending market.

a) Does Khalsa have any obligation not to compete with Think Prudent for a reasonable period? Give reasons.
b) Does Raj have any obligation not to compete with Think Prudent for a reasonable period? Give reasons.
c) How could Think Prudent have prevented Raj from contacting its customers for a reasonable period?
d) Think Prudent has good reason to believe Raj took its customer list and has it hidden in his home. Is there any remedy available to Think Prudent to get the list back?

Alternative to Lawsuit

Provincial and federal ministries of labour have tribunals, run on similar lines as a court, but on an informal basis. A non-union employee can make a claim against an employer for wrongful dismissal. The employment tribunal's hearing officer will investigate, and make an award.

There are, in effect, two parallel systems—the judicial system, and the employment tribunal system. The employment tribunal system has been traditionally used by lower-level employees. The tribunal awards were also considered to be lower, and closer to the minimum standard set out in provincial legislation. However, in some provinces, there is an opinion that the tribunal awards are more sympathetic to employees, and are exceeding the notice periods that a court would award.

If a tribunal makes a decision, it is final. The parties cannot later apply to a court and ask for another hearing. This does not apply to grievance tribunals held under collective bargaining agreements.

Bankruptcy and Wages

If a company goes out of business or declares bankruptcy, most provinces have a fund administered through the provincial ministry of labour to pay for unpaid wages. This fund relates only to unpaid wages, not to a claim for wrongful dismissal or severance pay, which is for future wages. Bankruptcy is considered termination under employment standards legislation. Employees of bankrupt companies can claim severance pay in the company's bankruptcy.

There are also provisions in the corporations acts and the *Bankruptcy and Insolvency Act* that make directors personally liable for employees' unpaid wages for up to six months (see Chapter 13).

Trade Secrets and Other Confidential Information

The value of information and timing is well demonstrated by the historical example of how the Rothschild family gained control of a number of English banks. Before the Battle of Waterloo on June 18, 1815, Napoleon's reputation as a general was legendary. England was about to fight Napoleon, but its commander was a young, untried general named Wellington, who, it was feared, was no match for the experienced Napoleon. The battle was to take place at Waterloo (now part of Belgium). Anticipating a loss and subsequent invasion of their country, English merchants were trying to sell their assets in exchange for gold, which could be hidden or taken out of the country. The English bankers agreed with this strategy, and many banks were for sale at a fraction of their value.

The English Rothschild family devised a method of communication that used mirrors. They had a number of agents stationed at various points between London and Waterloo. When the outcome of the battle was certain, these agents flashed the information from one to the next, by this system of mirrors. In this way, the Rothschilds knew one full day before anyone else in England what the outcome of the battle was. They quickly bought up all the banks that were for sale, and thus gained control of the English banking system.

The above story is told and retold in business circles. As with all legends, it is impossible to know here what is myth and what is fact. There is great disagreement over the method the Rothschilds used to obtain their information. Some variations say it was carrier pigeons or a series of private couriers that brought the news from Waterloo to London.

What Is a Trade Secret?

Employees want to know what they can do if they go to work for someone else, or set up business on their own. Employers need to know how much of their business expertise and knowledge can be protected, so that employees cannot learn all there is to know, and then go into competition using that information.

It is sometimes difficult to draw a line between where an employer's confidential information ends and employees' general knowledge begins. Normally, the principle that separates confidential, protected information from general knowledge is that confidential information is objective—for example, formulas, processes, or market research such as consumer surveys or market analyses. However, knowledge or skill acquired by employees on the job—"know-how"—is subjective information, and is not the confidential property of the employer.

Confidential formulas and processes are obvious examples of protected information. Common disputes arise over information about customers. Employees, especially salespeople, may develop a personal relationship with a number of customers. Can the employee leave, go to work for a competitor, and call on the customers to get them to switch to the new company?

Employers argue that the customer relationship arose because of employer's expense. The employer may have spent a considerable amount of money on advertising and marketing to develop the relationship with the customer.

Under law, a former employee cannot directly contact customers from the previous employer for a reasonable time afterwards in an effort to try to get their business. What is a reasonable time will vary with each circumstance, but a rule of thumb would be about six months for most situations. Although direct solicitation is prohibited, former employees could place an advertisement in a newspaper announcing their new business. If a customer approached them as a result of the ad, the employees would be entitled to deal with the customer.

■ *Critical Concepts of* Trade Secrets/Confidential Information

There are three distinct areas of law that govern **confidential business information** (information that provides a business advantage as a result of the fact that it is kept secret):

- Breach of confidence—if information is given to a person in circumstances that make it clear the information is intended to remain confidential, that confidence can be enforced by court action.

- Breach of fiduciary duty—if there is a special relationship, such as employer/employee, and the employee learns of the information as a result of this relationship, then the employee is under a duty not to disclose it.

- Breach of contract—if the employee signs a term in an employee agreement (a non-competition clause), that clause is enforceable.

> **confidential business information**
>
> information that provides a business advantage as a result of the fact that it is kept secret

Remedies: Civil Search Warrant

The remedies are the same as for other breaches of intellectual-property areas (see Chapter 17), but there is one particular remedy more used in confidential information lawsuits than in others. This is the Anton Piller order, a secretly obtained civil search warrant. If an employer can provide sufficient evidence to satisfy the court that a former employee has taken confidential information, the court will make an order, without notice to the employee, permitting the employer to search named premises such as a house, garage, or new business, to try to locate the confidential documents. This order is carried out under the supervision of a court officer.

Example: Yong Lim was an engineer with Canadian Steel Consultants. He left on short notice and joined a competing engineering firm. Both firms were involved in the same type of construction projects. During the time Lim was with the firm, Canadian Steel Consultants had been working on a new procedure that could not be patented, but gave them a competitive edge against the other company.

After Lim left, it came to the president's attention that for the three days preceding Lim's departure he stayed late and was seen at the photocopy machine. Lim had worked for Canadian Steel Consultants for five years, and seldom worked after 5:00 p.m.

In this case the court would likely grant the employer the right to conduct a search of Lim's house.

■ *Business Law* Applied

⑩ Linda Castelino has been employed by The Car Doctor Auto Repair as a mechanic for over 10 years. She began as an apprentice and, during her employment with the firm, has become a Class A mechanic. Castelino quits and opens her own auto-repair shop across the street. There is no written employment agreement.

The owner of The Car Doctor Auto Repair is incensed, and wants to obtain a court order to stop Castelino, claiming, "I taught her everything she knows."

    a) Are the skills that Castelino acquired at The Car Doctor Auto Repair confidential information?

    b) How might the Car Doctor have protected himself from having Castelino open across the street?

⑪ Consuela Peres is an accountant at Canada Steel Bridge Corporation. The company has just developed a new steel product that it sells to a specialized market.

Watson Steel Manufacturing is a very small, local company that has discovered a process by which it can make the same steel product much cheaper—but as the market for selling the product is specialized, cannot find the potential customers.

Watson hires Peres from Canada Steel by offering her a significant increase in salary. The night before Peres leaves Canada Steel, she is seen in the sales office where she would normally not go, and where the specialized customer mailing list is kept.

    a) Does Canada Steel have any remedy to protect the customer mailing list?

    b) Does it have any remedy against Watson for hiring its accountant?

Trade Unions

collective bargaining
the negotiation between an employer and the union bargaining agent for its employees, in order to establish conditions of employment

At one time, the law prevented employees from forming groups to bargain with their employers. Now, many Canadian labour laws contain a preamble expressly stating that it is in the public interest to encourage the group bargaining process—**collective bargaining**, the negotiation between an employer and the union bargaining agent for its employees, in order to establish conditions of employment.

There are both federal and provincial statutes relating to unions and collective bargaining. It is estimated that about 90 percent of labour matters fall under provincial jurisdiction. While there are provincial variations, there are many common areas, and these are discussed in this section.

In collective bargaining, the union is called the bargaining agent, and the employee group is the bargaining unit. The unit includes all employees of that type of business, whether they are union members or not. The contract made as the result of collective bargaining is therefore called a group, or collective, agreement.

Government employees may also be members of unions. Some government-employee unions do not have the right to strike, but must use compulsory arbitration for bargaining disputes. There are also more preconditions to a strike than there are in the private sector. In spite of these restrictions, public-sector strikes account for an increasing proportion of Canadian strikes. In recent years, trade union growth in Canada has occurred mainly in the public sector, and more than half the trade union members in the country are public employees.

Certification

Employers can recognize unions voluntarily but, if they refuse to do so, a union can apply to the provincial labour board for certification. The labour board is similar to a court, but is more informal, and is called a tribunal. It is this body that settles most collective bargaining disputes. A person need not be represented by a lawyer to appear before a labour board.

In most jurisdictions, a vote of 50 percent of the employees is sufficient for the board to certify the union as the bargaining agent. Some provinces do not require a formal vote, but will certify the union if 50 percent of employees have signed union membership cards.

Unfair Labour Practices

Collective bargaining laws place restrictions on both the employer and the union. The labour boards keep a close eye on the employer while a union is organizing, so that no unlawful methods are used to resist its formation. Employer activity is scrutinized during this time, and any statements made to employees are interpreted very strictly. If those statements or the employer's conduct are tainted by anti-union sentiment, the employer may end up paying large damage awards, while the union is still certified as the bargaining agent.

Collective Agreements

Collective agreements are similar to standard form employment contracts, and are negotiated by the union on behalf of all employees. They apply to all bargaining union employees, and no individual worker can make a private employment contract. A collective agreement contains the usual terms of an employment contract, including clauses that:

- set out a procedure for laying off (temporary letting-go)
- give notice periods for termination (permanent firing)
- set salary, vacation time, and fringe benefits
- provide a method for settling grievances

Closed Shops

One of the terms in the collective agreement is usually that the union is entitled to a closed shop. There are several types of closed shops.

- Closed shop—an individual must be a member of the union before being hired
- Union shop—an individual must join the union on being employed
- Rand shop, or rand formula—an individual must pay union dues, but does not necessarily have to join the union as a condition of employment

In some provinces, the rand formula is mandatory, and the employer may be required to collect dues on the union's behalf.

Grievances

Labour laws require that all collective agreements contain a procedure for solving disputes over the interpretation of a collective agreement. Such disagreements are known as grievances. For example, an employee may have a dispute about the calculation of overtime pay, or a group of employees may object to hidden-camera surveillance, or mandatory drug testing.

The early stages of a grievance are usually dealt with by negotiation but, if this fails, the grievance goes to arbitration. The arbitrator is normally chosen by the employer and the union. In some provinces, if they cannot agree, either side can apply to the minister of labour to have an arbitrator appointed.

The Right to Strike

Legislation restricts when a union has the right to strike. A strike can be called only at the negotiation stage of a collective agreement; while the agreement is in force, there is no right to strike. There are certain procedures that must be followed before a strike; otherwise the strike is illegal.

- The parties must bargain for a specified period of time.
- The union must hold a strike vote, and give notice of a successful strike vote to the employer.
- Both sides must submit to a conciliation process, in which an outsider attempts bring the parties to agreement. The conciliator cannot force any terms on either side.
- If conciliation fails, there is a cooling-off period before the employer can lock out the employees, or the employees can strike.

Business Law Applied

⑬ **A truck driver** was required to drive his vehicle on a ramp beside an open pit at a mine. There was a slight rain, and the ramp was slippery. In addition, approximately 100 metres of the protective railing at the side of the ramp was missing.

The truck driver refused to drive on the ramp as it was unsafe, and the union called a strike.

a) Was striking the proper procedure? If not, what was?

Picketing

If the strike is legal, picketing is permitted. Picketing involves strikers' standing near the company's premises, or marching, as they display signs to dissuade people from doing business there. All such activity must be peaceful, and the information on the signs and banners the picketers carry must be accurate.

labour relations board
an administrative tribunal regulating labour relations

If picketing goes beyond simple communication and becomes intimidation, the **labour relations board** (an administrative tribunal regulating labour relations) may restrict the number of picketers permitted near the business at any one time. The individuals on the picket line are subject to other laws, such as tort and criminal law, and cannot commit defamation or any criminal offence.

Primary/Secondary Picketing

All provinces permit employees to picket the plant or factory where they work—this is called primary picketing. However, the employer may carry on business at other locations; if they, too, are picketed, this is called secondary picketing. In most provinces, secondary picketing is not allowed. Businesses that are unrelated to the main employer cannot be picketed.

Replacement Workers/Scabs

Everyone has the right to cross a picket line. Customers can continue to do business; suppliers can still deliver goods and services to the employer, which has the right to carry on normal business activities. If the employer can persuade other employees to cross the picket line, they must be permitted to do so.

Most controversy surrounds the crossing of picket lines by what are called replacement workers or scabs—depending on the point of view of the speaker. In most jurisdictions, employers are permitted to bring in substitute employees to help run the business during a strike. Under federal legislation, and in the provinces of B.C. and Quebec, there are statutes prohibiting the use of strike-breaking employees. Similar legislation was repealed in Ontario in 1995.

General Drywall Batteries of Canada Limited v. Brigenshaw et al., [1951] O.R. 522 (H.C.)

General Drywall Batteries made dry battery cells. Its factory employees were represented by Local 512 of the United Electrical Radio and Machine Workers of America, the certified bargaining agent.

The union employees went on strike and began to picket General Drywall Batteries' plant. The firm tried to carry on business using managerial staff.

Pickets blocked access to the plant, making it impossible for customers and managerial staff to pass. The next day, supervisory staff needed police assistance to cross the picket line. One staff member, Mrs. Zimmerman, had a needle driven into her shoulder. Two others were pelted with rotten eggs, and another was physically assaulted.

Railway officials were prevented from removing a box car containing 70,000 pounds of finished batteries that had been spe-

cially designed for several important customers, who needed them badly.

General Drywall Batteries applied to the court for an injunction stopping the union from picketing the plant.

The Court's Decision

A union is permitted peaceful picketing. Picketing that does not interfere with business, and is for the purpose of informing the public of the strike, will not be stopped by a court order.

However, behaviour that goes beyond peaceful picketing—such as preventing customers, managerial staff, and shippers of goods and services from crossing the picket line—is illegal, and will be stopped. Accordingly, the court ordered an injunction that stopped the picketers from interfering with General Drywall Batteries' carrying on business.

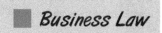

Business Law Applied

⑭ **Coal Codvill Inc.** was a distributor for the IGA food-store franchises. Its employees went on strike, and picketed the plant. One of the franchisees that Codvill supplied was Dussessoy's IGA, and Codvill's employees began to picket that location. All its signs said "Codvill—distributor to IGA—employees on strike." The picketing was peaceful, and customers were allowed freely past the picket line.

a) Did the Codvill employees have the right to picket this site to which Codvill delivers?
b) What could Dussessoy's IGA do about the picketing, if anything?

The *Charter of Rights and Freedoms*

While courts have been free in making new laws in many areas using the Charter, they have stayed away from collective bargaining situations, clearly meaning that any reform is in the hands of politicians.

This attitude of the courts of not interfering in labour laws was demonstrated in a case in which an instructor at Humber College objected to the Ontario Public Services Employee Union's using union dues to donate money to the New Democratic Party. The instructor claimed that using these dues for non-collective bargaining purposes, and for political activity, was inconsistent with the Charter's guarantees of freedom of association and freedom of expression. The court held that even if this was so, such position was justified as a reasonable limitation under section 1 of the Charter.

NAFTA

Changes in labour law in Canada have been viewed as generally pro-employee. However, Canada's participation in the North America Free Trade Agreement (NAFTA) may create economic and political pressures to change the labour laws further, so that Canada can compete more effectively with the United States and Mexico. How NAFTA will affect Canadian labour laws will only be known in the future.

In Summation

Hiring

▪ The process of advertising for and interviewing potential employees is closely controlled by human rights legislation and labour laws. *Bona fide* occupational requirements may be used in selecting applicants; however, questions related to certain matters, such as race, sex, and religion, may not be asked during the interview process. Some types of information maybe obtained from the employee for employment records after being hired.

Employment

▪ An employment agreement is often a standard form contract customized for the individual employee and the position being filled. Frequently, there is a reference to an employee manual stated in the employment contract. The manual details the terms of employment.

▪ An employer is advised to have the employee verify the truth of statements on his or her application and résumé. Misrepresentation by the employee on these documents is a ground for immediate dismissal.

▪ Employment legislation exists at both the federal and provincial levels. These statutes deal with such issues as wages, discrimination, sexual harassment, occupational health and safety, and maternity leave.

Firing

▪ An employer can dismiss an employee for just cause (actions inconsistent with the duties of employment). Such actions would include, among others, theft, conflict of interest, or incompetence.

▪ If the dismissal is not for just cause, it is a breach of the employment contract and will result in payment of damages based on a period of notice.

▪ Confusion exists as to what will constitute an appropriate notice period because both the common law and the statute law contain notice periods.

▪ Statutory notice, set through employment standards acts and labour acts, is the minimum notice period required.

▪ The common law requires reasonable notice to be given based on the circumstances of each case. It attempts to balance a number of factors, including age, length of employment, anticipated time to locate other employment, and level of position, when determining what would be reasonable notice.

▪ If the amount of notice required has been previously established and incorporated in the employment contract, it may be seen as enforceable.

▪ Damages for mental distress arising from termination may be available to the employee if the manner in which the termination has been handled has caused extreme mental suffering.

Mitigation

▪ An employee who has been terminated has a positive obligation in law to make an effort to find other employment. The employee's attempts to mitigate will be taken into consideration by the court in determining any award to be given as a result of the termination.

▪ If an employee's position has been so altered that the circumstances could be construed as constructive dismissal, that employee may have to accept the lesser position while looking for other employment.

▪ The severance package offered to a terminated employee may affect that individual's claims under such government programs as employment insurance.

- Government funds and tribunals have been established to deal with situations where the employer goes bankrupt, or the party arguing the issue of dismissal for cause wishes a solution without any further recourse to the courts.

Trade Secrets

- Confidential business information may be protected by the employer through a court action to stop the employee from using the material after employment has been terminated.

- The employer will not be successful in preventing an employee from using the skill or knowledge acquired on the job, either to benefit another employer or for the ex-employee's own purposes.

Trade Unions

- Both federal and provincial legislation exists dealing with unions and the collective bargaining process.

- Once certified in accordance with provincial requirements, the trade union becomes the bargaining agent on behalf of the employee group.

- The collective agreement details a number of terms and conditions on behalf of all employees. These would include salary, termination, grievance procedures, and whether the union is entitled to a closed shop.

- Matters such as the right to strike or picket, and the use of replacement labour during a strike, are dealt with through legislation and not through the collective bargaining process.

Closing Questions

Hiring

1. Biosyn Ltd. had recently purchased some new technology that claimed to be able to determine, through analysis of hair and fingernail samples, whether an individual would be prone to particular diseases. The vice-president, human resources, received a copy of the internal memo circulated concerning this new technology, and thought it might be used to Biosyn's advantage in dealing with its employees. If they could require new employees to undergo the testing, then they could determine whether they were susceptible to any diseases that might involve lengthy periods off work, or that could lead to less-than-optimum performance.

   Biosyn would be able to reduce absenteeism and increase production, or at least allocate the employee to an appropriate department where the impact of the potential illness could be lessened. A further benefit would be that it would be possible to monitor changes in the body chemistry of employees who worked in departments dealing with different bacterial life forms. In this way it would be possible to see if there were any change in their health status, so that the company could take active measures to assist that employee.

   a) The vice-president, human resources, has asked you to prepare a report, giving full reasons whether or not Biosyn can require the employees to provide hair and fingernail samples for testing. She also needs to know under what circumstances the testing would have to be done.

2. Melita Andersson had been employed by Computoch Inc. for three years in the sales department. When she was hired, she signed a standard form employment contract that included a job description, as well as terms relating to vacations and so on.

   Recently she was told by her vice-president that all employees in the sales department are required to sign a confidentiality agreement. This agreement includes a non-competition clause covering the possibility of the employee's leaving Computoch. When Andersson asked what would happen if she did not sign the contract, the vice-president merely laughed, pulled her finger across her throat, and pretended to throw something over her shoulder.

Before all this comes to a showdown, Andersson has decided to inform herself as to her rights, and has contacted you, knowing that you took a business law course.

a) Advise Andersson as to the nature of the issue that is being raised by Computoch's request and whether she is required to sign the agreement.

b) Would it make any difference if Computoch were requiring the same non-competition/confidentiality agreement to be signed by all its employees, and not just those in the sales department?

3. Morty Lake is a supervisor at a not-for-profit organization that advises people on occupational health matters. Lake's job is to review the case studies of the six field workers who do the interviewing and assist the clients. Because it is a not-for-profit organization, funds for leasing premises were limited, and so the organization is housed in what used to be a men-only club. Anna Lee recently joined the organization and, much to her surprise, on the first day found that, although 55 percent of the staff are women, there is only one women's washroom. This is housed in a very small trailer, attached to the far back of the building. The washroom is frequently crowded, and often it is an office joke that people need to take a number in the morning in order to ensure that they have an opportunity to use it in the course of the day.

This issue has been raised with Lake a number of times by his staff, and he has always promised to look into it. What he means by this, the staff are not sure, because the female staff have always been a little uncertain why he feels a need to close his office door whenever one of them is in discussing an issue with him. The director of the organization is usually absent from the premises, out looking for funding, and Lake is the next person in charge—consequently, the female employees have been reluctant to raise the issue of his interviewing techniques.

Today was the last straw for Anna Lee when, during an interview in Lake's office to discuss a client's file, he suggested he didn't need sugar in his coffee as there was "obviously enough sweetness present." Leaving the office as quickly as she could, she went through her employment package to see what procedures should be followed for complaining about this behaviour. The only help she found in it was a statement encouraging employees to speak up if harassed.

a) What grounds does Anna Lee have for registering a complaint, and which legislation deals with these issues?

b) With reasons, explain which of the following would be liable for the conduct complained of:
   i)   Morty Lake
   ii) the director
   iii) the not-for-profit organization

c) What steps would you suggest the employer immediately take to protect itself and ensure this type of situation does not arise again?

d) Does the not-for-profit organization have grounds for immediately terminating Lake's employment, or is there any other obligation which it must meet prior to taking that step?

4. If an employee works on a statutory holiday, can the employer require that individual to take another day off in compensation?

5. Alex Alexander was interviewed for a position with an advertising company. The interview was conducted by the vice-president, human relations, for the company, who had previously run as a candidate in a federal election. He asked Alexander if he had voted for the party currently in power (not the party with which the vice-president is affiliated). The fact that Alexander avoided answering the question was written down in the interview notes.

Later in the interview the vice-president, laughing, said to Alexander, "You seem to be an absolutely sterling, top-notch candidate: great recommendations, excellent academic background, almost too good to be true. Don't tell me you are a closet drinker." When Alexander responded with laughter as well, the vice-president wrote in his interview notes, "Did not deny potential drinking problem."

Alexander was not offered the job, and later found out from a friend who worked in the advertising firm that these notes had been made about his interview and, as a direct result, the job had gone to another candidate.

a) Which laws deal with the types of questions asked of Alexander in the interview process?

b) Is there any legal remedy available to Alexander as a result of this interview?

6. Waleed had been unemployed for three years. He found that most employers considered him overqualified for the positions for which he had applied. In desperation, Waleed rewrote his résumé, deleting the reference to his university degree, and describing his working experience in much more general terms. He was recently offered a position doing shift work in the bottling department of a brewery. On his first day on the job, he was asked to sign an employment contract which required him to certify the truth of his statements concerning his education and qualifications.

   Within the first week, Waleed had irritated his supervisor by making several suggestions as to how procedures could be streamlined to increase productivity, as well as pointing out a couple of occupational safety issues that needed to be dealt with. Waleed had implied that if corrective measures were not taken, he would register a complaint with the appropriate government department. His supervisor has spoken to some of Waleed's co-workers, and discovered that Waleed had let slip that he had a university degree and specialized training in time-management efficiency.
   a) Can the supervisor terminate Waleed's employment?
   b) If termination is possible, what would be the grounds, and what length of notice must be given Waleed?
   c) What defences are available to Waleed given the information you have from the fact situation above?
   d) If the company were to terminate Waleed's employment immediately, and to use him as an example to other employees by firing him in front of his co-workers, what damages would a court award in these circumstances?

7. Has an employer met his obligations related to industrial health and safety if he does so in the following manner? Explain.
   - Safety glasses are made available to employees working on drill presses.
   - To obtain the safety glasses, employees are required to ask for them at a specific office in another part of the building.
   - In an attempt to keep overhead costs low, employees are required to sign the glasses out and return them at the end of the day.

8. Anayat Daniels wishes to hire Asja Lublin as an accountant for his business but he wants to avoid a lot of government paper work so he has her sign an employment contract which states that she is an independent contractor. It is his belief that because of this term in the contract, if he fires her he does not have to pay her severance pay. Is he correct?

Firing

9. Harvey Keach was employed as a professor of advanced mathematics. He had an unusual style, and had won awards for excellence in teaching. Roger Slown approached Keach with the idea of making videotapes of his class lessons, and then selling them as review aids to mathematics students or, alternatively, selling them to the general public, who might wish to upgrade their mathematics skills. Keach's employer became aware of the videotapes and their sales, and has called Keach in for a discussion.
   a) On what basis could Keach's employer terminate his employment?
   b) Would such a firing be with or without cause?
   c) Would Keach have any legal rights regarding his termination?

10. Four days out of five each work week, Susan Douthwaite was 10 to 15 minutes late in arriving at her office in the building where she was employed. Her supervisor has told her that this lateness is unacceptable, and Douthwaite's response was that she was always in the company parking lot on the hour, but it took 10 minutes to walk to her office.
    a) Discuss whether the company has just cause for terminating Douthwaite's employment based on her lateness.

11. Brian Dooley had been employed as an instructor at a community college for 15 years. An internal study to meet budgetary restraints indicated that instructors could be hired on contract at half

the price of instructors on full-time employment. This would result in considerable savings to the college, allowing it to maintain its services to the student body.

Dooley, who is 50 years old, was approached about early retirement. The package offered was not particularly attractive, and he turned it down. The next week, Dooley received a termination notice.

a) Does Dooley's refusal to accept the early-retirement package allow his employer to terminate him with cause?

b) What other information would you require in order to be able to advise Dooley as to what would be a realistic settlement of this matter with his employer?

c) How would that information help you in arriving at your advice to Dooley?

12. Harold deSouza's employment with Arbour Inc. was terminated after 10 years. His dismissal was without cause, although there had been incidents of misconduct that could have justified terminating his employment. Arbour is currently negotiating with deSouza about the number of weeks of notice on which his severance package will be based. The company has suggested a minimum period given the background issue of misconduct, while deSouza is insisting on a much longer period of notice. DeSouza is currently looking for other employment and has requested a letter of reference.

a) What are the two sources of authority on which deSouza and Arbour are basing their negotiation for the necessary period of notice?

b) What potential problem could Arbour be creating if it were to provide the letter of reference?

c) What general principle of contract law is deSouza following in his attempt to locate other employment?

d) What are the qualifications on his obligation to accept an offer of employment elsewhere?

e) Arbour is considering referring the dispute to a tribunal for decision, and feels quite strongly about the issue of misconduct being a factor in any final resolution of the matter. What concerns should Arbour address before it makes its decision on whether to refer this matter to a tribunal?

13. Hector Berlioz was a student employed for the summer by Bob's Urban Reusable Products. When Berlioz received his first paycheque, he noticed that a sizeable amount had been deducted for union dues. He immediately called payroll to explain that an error had been made, suggesting that his paycheque had been confused with someone else's.

The payroll person replied that there was no mistake; union dues were deducted for everyone who was not management. When Berlioz persisted, complaining that he was not a union member, that no one had told him he must pay union dues (especially in this amount), that he was a summer student employee, and that this was unfair treatment, the voice from payroll said, "Quit whining, kid. Management doesn't like it either, and we have to collect the dues on behalf of the union. Take it up with them; they're your representatives."

a) What is the type of union shop operated at Bob's Urban Reusable Products?

b) In what document would Berlioz be able to find the details related to the union and its shop?

c) Does the union represent Berlioz in this situation?

d) Do you agree with the young man's assessment that this type of union shop is unfair in these circumstances?

e) Is there a *Charter of Rights* argument available to Berlioz in these circumstances? If not, should there be?

14. Match the following:

Column A	Column B
Constructive dismissal	Reduction of loss
Termination	Confidential information
Just cause	Demotion
Mitigation	Firing
Trade secret	Valid grounds for firing

Websites

canadaonline.about.com/msub22.htm?once=true&—Canada Online, Human Resources: Employees. General information on avoiding legal difficulty in the administration of human resources, via a variety of links.

www.duhaime.org/labour.htm—Duhaime's Labour & Employment Law Information Centre. Includes links to the Canada Labour Relations Board site and others in Alberta and British Columbia.

Intellectual Property

The Information Revolution

In the 1950s Canadian communications expert Marshall McLuhan stressed the importance of technology's effect on the speed of change in society. He identified Gutenberg's invention of moveable type as the single most important invention of past history. In the year 2000, Time Magazine echoed McLuhan's accolade and designated Gutenberg's invention as the most significant of the past 1,000 years.

Prior to Gutenberg's duplication by print was severely limited. Copies of books were done by hand or by whole pages carved on one wooden block. They were so expensive very few wealthy people could own more than a few. Gutenberg's idea of a single piece of type for each letter of the alphabet made book copying less expensive and available to everyone. This advance in technology also began to make copying and distribution of ideas easier and weakened the exclusive control over creative ideas. The law had to advance along with these changes to give protection to both the creator and the interest of the public.

The laws of intellectual property balance the rights of creators to have some control and financial reward to promote creativity, against the interests of the public. Because many advances in technology are based on prior innovations, the public benefits by making the breakthroughs known and used by later inventive minds. The debt to prior creative minds was perhaps expressed the best by Sir Isaac Newton (1855): "if I have seen further, it is only by standing on the shoulders of giants"—a concept traceable to ancient Greece but made famous by Newton.

The ease of copying and distribution was again accelerated with the invention of digital technology and the Internet. Now every household, and even children, can copy creative works and distribute them worldwide without paying royalties to the creators. One of the extreme examples is peer to peer sharing whereby an extremely large number of home computers can be linked, the owners can put files, for example music, that they have copied onto their computer hard drive into shared file folders which are then indexed on a central search engine. All who participate in the scheme can have access to copy music that is on any of the other participating computers throughout the world—for free.

Thus the ability to copy easily and distribute cheaply has impacted greatly both on business models and the laws of intellectual property.

The Age of Imagination

Business today depends more and more on the imaginations of those who work in it. Microsoft's principal factory asset is the human imagination. Disney calls its creative staff imagineers. *Fortune* magazine now lists Nike in its service category, rather than in the industrial section—because the company's value is created by design and marketing skills. Such businesses rely more and more on the intellectual component, and less on the material. Imagination is a major source of value in the economy. Virtually every business, no matter how small, owns some intellectual property asset.

Intellectual Property **Intellectual property** is non-tangible, created by mental effort, and cannot be held in your hand. Even though intellectual property cannot be seen, it is still protected by various rights, such as copyright, patents, and trademarks.

Legalese

Types of Intellectual Property

Most businesses today have some type of intellectual property of value. Business consultants indicate that it may often be overlooked. Intellectual property is often divided into three categories of assets. Each has a different set of laws respecting it which balance protection of the creator and the interest of the public.

Human Assets

These are the creative people. In some companies it is said the entire assets of some companies go up and down in the elevators at night. The protection of human assets is by fiduciary duties, enforcement of restrictive covenants in employment agreements, and economic torts such as inducing breach of contract that prevents stealing away of employees.

Internal Assets

These include: trade secrets, supplier and customer lists, marketing research and plans, similar confidential information. These are, if actually kept confidential, protected by the law of confidentiality.

External and Disclosed Assets

These include image, innovative and creative works that are disclosed. These are protected by the intellectual property laws that are discussed in this chapter.

Intellectual Property Rights

The main types of intellectual property rights are:

industrial design
a distinctive shape or design that is a pattern to be reproduced many times, such as the design on fine china

- Personality rights—protect against the unauthorized use of names and distinctive features associated with celebrities
- Copyright—protects creative works, such as a song or a book
- Trademarks—protect brand names, business names, logos, and symbols, such as the apple of Apple Computer, and the stylized M known as McDonald's "golden arches."
- **Industrial design**—protects a distinctive shape or design that is a pattern to be reproduced many times, such as the design on fine china
- Patents—protect inventions such as the Pentium computer chip or the electric light bulb
- Confidential information—protects trade secrets, such as the formula for Coca-Cola (which has never been patented)

Personality Rights

Celebrities, such as prominent political, sports, and entertainment figures, have rights relating to their personas—how they are seen by the public. When football star Elroy "Crazy Legs" Hirsch sued a women's shaving gel manufacturer in the mid 1970s and won, it proved that name and persona had value that would be recognized by the courts. Unauthorized use of these individuals' names, photographs, and other distinctive features associated with them may be prohibited.

At the time of writing this text, all provinces have this common law right, but British Columbia, Manitoba, Saskatchewan, and Newfoundland have also enacted specific legislation protecting personality rights.

John W. Carson v. Here's Johnny Portable Toilets Inc., [1983] 698 F. (2d) 831

Here's Johnny Portable Toilets Inc. marketed a portable toilet called Here's Johnny. They also had the slogan "The World's Most Famous Comodium" inscribed on each unit. Johnny Carson sued to prohibit the company from the unauthorized use of his name. He claimed there was commercial value in the use of his name, and that he did not want his name associated with toilets.

The corporation claimed there was no violation of Carson's rights because neither his image nor his name was used.

The Court's Decision

The court held that Johnny Carson had built up a persona, or personality image, that was famous throughout North America and other parts of the world. Even though neither Carson's name nor picture was used, there was no doubt that the toilets were referring to Carson, and making money by the use of his name. Carson had not registered his name as a trademark, and so there was no trademark infringement. There was no likelihood of confusion—the public would recognize that this was not a product put out by Johnny Carson. However, the only reason that the portable-toilet company was using this name was as a humorous comparison to the persona that Johnny Carson had made famous. Johnny Carson had the right to that persona and could prohibit its use.

The court therefore held that the portable-toilet company had to cease using the name Here's Johnny.

Copyright

What Is Copyright?

Copyright literally means "the right to copy," although it also includes other rights, such as the right to translate, and to change the work to another form—from book to film, for example. It is the right to prevent others from copying original works. Copyright is a protection for the originator of any literary, scientific, dramatic, or musical work, and means that that individual is the only person entitled to copy, publish, reproduce, or distribute the work. Computer software is protected by copyright.

Copyright is designed to encourage authors to produce these works by allowing them to keep the profits for themselves. As soon as the work is put in concrete form, it is protected by copyright—no registration is required in Canada.

It is the way in which an idea is expressed that is protected by copyright, not the idea itself. For example, the Canadian songwriter Leonard Cohen wrote a song entitled "Suzanne," about a short romantic encounter. This same topic is the subject of many songs, poems, and novels;

copyright
the right to prevent others from copying original works

it is Cohen's song—the individual expression of the idea, not the subject—that is copyright protected.

International Copyright Protection

Copyright protection occurs automatically in Canada. Often, however, a work created in Canada needs to be protected by copyright in other countries. There are two international copyright conventions, and most industrial countries belong to one or the other.

The Berne Convention

Canada is a signatory to the Berne Convention, under which it is not necessary to register copyright. Copyright works in the same way in all countries that have signed this agreement—a book that is copyright in Canada is automatically copyright in all these countries as well. Sixty countries have signed the convention, the United States being a notable exception.

The Universal Copyright Convention

Both Canada and the United States are signatories to the Universal Copyright Convention, which requires that a copyright notice appear at the beginning of the work, along with the owner's name and the date. For example:

© Muriel Fiona Napier, 1997

It is not necessary to include the copyright notice in order to protect a work in this country, but Canadian publishers normally do so to make sure their material is also protected in the United States.

Copyright Registration

Under the Berne Convention, an author does not have to register a work in order for it to be protected by copyright. However, if the work has been registered, it helps to establish the date of the copyright and the content of the material should disputes arise in the future. Registration of a copyright in Canada is very simple—a form must be completed and sent along with a small filing fee to the copyright office in Ottawa. Some authors do not register, but send a copy of their work to themselves by registered mail. The postal records and cancellation stamps are evidence of the date the work was created.

Ownership of Copyright   The ownership of copyright is set out in section 13 of the federal *Copyright Act*:

> 13 (1) Subject to this Act, the author of a work shall be the first owner of a copyright therein.
>
> 13 (2) Where, in the case of an engraving, photograph, or portrait, the plate or other original was ordered by some other person and was made for valuable consideration in pursuance of that order, then in the absence of any agreement to the contrary, the person by whom such plate or other original was ordered shall be the first owner of the copyright.
>
> 13 (3) Where the author was in the employment of some other person under a contract of service or apprenticeship and the work was made in the course of employment by that person, the person by whom the person was employed shall, in the absence of any agreement to the contrary, be the first owner of the copyright.

Corso v. NEBS Business Products Ltd. [2009] 176 A.C.W.S. (3d)

Mr. Corso worked for NEBS Business Products Ltd. which sold payroll services using cheques. On his own time, Corso developed software for a chequeless method of payroll called "eVault".

When NEBS learned of this they fired Corso and claimed ownership of the software.

Corso sued for wrongful dismissal and a declaration of ownership of the software claiming he developed it on his own time.

The Court's Decision

The court found that pursuant to Section 13(3) of the *Copyright Act* the eVault program was done while Corso was employed by NEBS. As an employee, Corso, had a good faith duty to give ideas for product improvement to his employer. His software was directly competitive to his employer's product.

As Corso breached his good faith obligation to his employer, his dismissal was justified.

Employment and Copyright

While intellectual property items done as part of employment belong to the employer by law (assuming there is no specific item dealing with the intellectual property in a contract) the property may not fit into one of the categories of intellectual property.

Example: George Lucas hired a designer to design and make the helmets for the storm troopers in the Star Wars films. The designer kept the molds and advertised and sold replicas through an internet site. Lucas sued in the U.K. claiming that the helmets were sculptures and subject to copyrights. However, the court rejected the claim and found that they were merely utilitarian and not sculptures and therefore not subject to copyright protection (*Lucasfilm Ltd. & Ors v. Ainsworth & Or* [2009] EWCA CIV 1326).

Business Law   Applied

❶ Ray Reynolds was a successful professional photographer whose work appeared in several coffee-table books. Because of Reynolds's reputation, Jim Head, a movie celebrity, asked him to take his portrait, for a specified fee. Reynolds did so, and the result was considered an excellent, creative photograph. Head did not like it, but paid for it anyway.

A few months later, Head heard from friends that Reynolds was exhibiting a copy of this picture at a local gallery as part of a collection of his works. Head demanded that Reynolds remove the photograph from his show.

   a) Who has the right to copy and display the picture?

❷ Jane Walker was walking down the main street in town when a camera crew from a local television station filmed her. The camera operator told Walker that the station was going to show a clip of her in a collage of snapshots of city life. Walker phoned the station owner and informed him that she did not want her picture shown on television.

   a) Who had the copyright in the film?
   b) Could Walker stop the television station from showing it by law?

❸ Digital Corp. Inc. employed Frank Rasta to train staff in the use of robotic assembly equipment. On his own initiative, Rasta prepared an instruction manual and, through using it with his trainees, made substantial revisions over a few years. He realized that there was a market for such a manual and wanted to publish it.

Digital Corp. Inc. claimed that it owned the copyright to the manual. Rasta claimed the copyright was his because he thought of the idea of using a manual in the training program, and wrote it entirely himself.

   a) Who owns the copyright in this manual?

Length of Copyright Protection

Copyright in Canada lasts until 50 years after the author's death. There are a few exceptions to this rule:

- photographs—50 years after the original negative is made
- records and tapes—50 years after the original recording is made
- government publications—50 years from the date of first publication
- joint authorship—50 years after the death of the last surviving author

Assignment or Licensing

The creators of works can assign or license others to copy their work. This is often necessary because authors cannot afford the cost of marketing a work. Books, for example, often contain a copyright in the name of the publisher, indicating that the author has assigned the copyright to that publisher.

Assignment involves a complete sale of the copyright, while a licence is permission to use it for a specified time. Most of us have purchased a license to use software whether we know it or not. When we buy a product such as Microsoft Office, in law we are buying a license to use that software according to the terms contained in the License Agreement. While we may also be buying a hard copy of a CD, that disc's value is very minimal. It is the content that is of value.

Example of License: The RCMP gave the Walt Disney Company (Canada) a five-year licence to market the Mountie image in making souvenirs, T-shirts, and so on, but retained the rights to that image. When the product licence expired at the end of 1999, it was not renewed; the Mounted Police Foundation now manages all product licensing.

Example of Assignment: One of the most famous assignments of copyright is that of the rights to the Beatles' songs. The Beatles' corporation owned the copyright of their songs but has sold—assigned—it to Michael Jackson. Every time a Beatles song is performed or played, a fee is paid to the copyright owner—Michael Jackson.

Copyleft

The copyleft logo shows a reverse "c" in the Circle.

Business Alert!

A play on copyright the term is the result of the free software movement, the goal of which, in the words of founder Richard Stallman, is to promote the development of "a sufficient body of free software ... to get along without any software that is not free."

This form of license permits any user to use the software without payment and permits changes (improvements) to be made provided only that the original creator is given credit for the first form of the software and the new product is also offered on the same basis, that is, free and with permission to make changes. It restricts only the use of the free software being used as a basis to develop software that is then sold for profit.

Internet Danger   If you have posted a piece of writing or other creative work on the Internet on a site to which the public has access, then you have published it and cannot assign "first rights." Sending to a few friends for comments is not publishing.

Many publishers will not pay for a work for which you can assign only "secondary rights," for example, a work which has already been posted on the Internet.

Moral Rights

moral rights

the rights of an author or creator to prevent a work from being distorted or misused

Even when an author assigns the rights of a work to someone else, the author retains the **moral rights** (the rights of an author or creator to prevent a work from being distorted or misused): these cannot be assigned. These rights mean that the work cannot be altered so that it no longer reflects the author's intentions when it was created. Moral rights, in other words, protect the author against someone destroying the integrity of a work.

Snow v. Eaton Centre Ltd., [1982] 70 C.P.R. (2nd) 105

The Eaton Centre commissioned Michael Snow to create a mobile, called "Flight Stop," of Canada geese. The completed sculpture was hung in the Eaton Centre in downtown Toronto. At the beginning of the Christmas shopping season, Eaton Centre management had the geese decorated, tying red ribbons around the birds' necks.

Snow took offence at this, and claimed the decorations were defacing the artistic value—destroying the integrity—of his work. Eaton Centre management refused to remove the ribbons, and so Snow sued for a mandatory injunction—a court order forcing them to do so. (A **mandatory injunction** is an order requiring a person to do a particular act.)

The Court's Decision

Although Snow had sold the copyright to the Eaton Centre, he retained the moral right over his work, since this right cannot be sold. Thus, the artist maintains a certain control over how any work is to be displayed. The purchaser cannot alter it, because it will injure the reputation of the artist and consequently that individual's ability to earn a living.

The court ordered the Eaton Centre to remove the ribbons.

Infringement

If anyone uses copyrighted material without the consent of the copyright owner, that copying is called an infringement. One copy is a copy and therefore possibly infringement. Any person who participates in the infringement may also be liable. For example, a video-store owner who sells pirate videos is liable, as well as the person who made the pirate edition. An individual who lends a book to someone to permit photocopying is technically guilty of an infringement, as is the printing store where the copying is done.

mandatory injunction

an order requiring a person to do a particular act

Video Piracy

The following notice appears on most commercially recorded videotapes.

> WARNING
>
> For private and domestic use only. Federal law provides severe civil and criminal penalties for the unauthorized reproduction, distribution, or exhibition of copyrighted motion pictures and video tapes.
>
> The international criminal police organization, Interpol, has expressed its concern about motion picture piracy and sound recording piracy to all of its member national police forces (resolution adopted at Interpol General Assembly, Stockholm, Sweden, September 8, 1977).

■ *Critical Concepts of* Legal Copying

There are some situations when it is legal to copy material without the consent of the copyright holder. These include the following:

- fair dealing with the work for the purpose of private study, research, criticism, review, or newspaper summary
- short passages photocopied for use in schools
- public readings of extracts from works
- performance of musical works for religious, educational, or charitable purposes by educational or religious bodies
- copying computer software onto the purchaser's hard drive, with a reasonable number of back-up copies made for the purchaser's own use

Fair Dealing

What constitutes fair use? When does copying reach the point that it is virtually reprinting the original, and therefore reducing the demand for it? Researchers may want to copy a few pages from a book in a library, rather than take notes. Teachers may wish to photocopy a page or two from a textbook to hand out to a class of students. These acts are considered fair dealing. In addition, a classroom is not considered to be a public place, and screening a video to students is also considered fair dealing. If a teacher photocopies a whole chapter, is this still fair? The question is not an easy one to answer, but as the purpose of copyright is to protect the artist's economic interest, the amount of copying permitted under the fair-dealing exception will be small.

Access to Copyrighted Materials

The Canadian Copyright Licensing Agency (Access Copyright) is a copyright collective for authors and publishers. It is a non-profit organization, representing thousands of authors and publishers across Canada. The purpose of Access Copyright is to collect royalties on behalf of its members when their material is photocopied or reproduced, and to make annual payments to them.

Access Copyright will take legal action to protect its members' rights. One of the initial targets was small copy firms near universities and colleges, which were copying parts or all of textbooks without permission and selling them to students at very reduced prices. In a much publicized raid on Copy Inc. near the University of Toronto campus, Access Copyright, acting under an Anton Piller order, seized a variety of material, including a price list for illegally copied college texts. Judgment was granted to Access Copyright against Copy Inc. in the amount of $132,000.

Socan

Creative people in the music world are represented by Socan, the society of composers, authors and music publishers of Canada. This body licenses the public performance of music in Canada so that all organizations using music publicly—from radio and television stations to banquet halls and bars—must pay a licence fee. The fees collected are then distributed to members.

The method of distributing the fees is based on a percentage of music sales. Thus, the most popular songs earn the highest proportion of fees for their creators.

■ *Critical Concepts of* Remedies for Copyright Infringement

The remedies for copyright infringement are the same as those for breach of contract, and apply to all intellectual property categories.

- Damages—a sum representing the financial loss to the copyright owner caused by the illegal use
- An accounting—a disclosure of profits made by the illegal use, and an order for payment of these profits to the owner
- An injunction—a court order to restrain violation of the copyright, possibly also including a requirement that any illegal copies be handed over to the rightful owner, or destroyed
- Penalties—criminal penalties in the *Copyright Act* provide for maximum fines of up to $1,000,000 and five years in jail

Business Law   Applied

④ LeeRoy Washington was an accountant who specialized in accounting and bookkeeping for small businesses. To advertise a new idea for on-time accounting, Washington designed a new brochure. He spent several days composing the wording and deciding on the format and illustrations. Washington did not mark it "© 1995 Washington," nor did he register it. The brochure was a success.

A few months later, Washington saw a brochure put out by a rival, Joe Cordeiro. It was obviously a copy of Washington's pamphlet but had "© 1995 Cordeiro" printed on it. When confronted by Washington, Cordeiro stated that he had registered this pamphlet with the copyright office in Ottawa, and had a Certificate of Copyright. As a result, Cordeiro claimed he was the owner of the copyright in the pamphlet.

   a) Who holds the copyright?

⑤ Edna Morrera bought the latest version of a much-improved word-processing software program. She copied the program onto several disks for back-up. She then lent the program to her brother, who copied it onto the hard drive of his own computer, and made more copies on floppy disks. These copies he sold for $25 each to friends at school.

   a) Did Morrera's brother infringe the copyright of the software manufacturer?
   b) Did the back-up copies made by Edna Morrera constitute copyright infringement?
   c) Did lending the disks to her brother so that he could copy the program onto his hard drive constitute copyright infringement?
   d) Is Edna Morrera liable in her brother's sale of copies to his friends?

⑥ Dalton Myers started a club at school called CD Swap. The idea of the club was that members would lend CDs to each other, and it was common knowledge that these CDs were frequently copied onto tape by their borrowers. Myers made no money, but simply acted as the organizer, making sure that the CDs were returned to the original owners.

   a) Did the members of the club have the right to make copies of the disks?
   b) Would the fact that Myers did not do the copying himself provide a defence to any claim of copyright infringement against him?

Trademarks

What Is a Trademark?

Distinctive marks and symbols are significant marketing tools. The early craft guilds of medieval times recognized the importance that purchasers placed on quality, and stamped a craft symbol or mark on their products as a sign of that quality. Competitors copied these marks and used them to sell inferior products disguised as the real thing. Laws were developed to prevent this passing off a copy as the genuine article. Passing off still exists as a tort, but the use of trademarks has become so essential to business that the protection of trademarks has been vastly expanded by the federal *Trademarks Act*.

A **trademark** is any visual characteristic of a product distinguishing it from a product made by competitors. A trademark can be a word, symbol, design, shape, picture, drawing, script, special colouring, or any combination of these which distinguishes a product or service from another.

trademark
any visual characteristic of a product distinguishing it from a product made by competitors

As well as having distinguishing visual characteristics, there are several other conditions that a trademark must satisfy. The most important of these are that it must not:

- be likely to be confused with an already registered trademark
- consist merely of words that are in general use, or are descriptive of the quality of the goods—instant, cold, or on time, for example—as they do not distinguish the goods and may apply equally to the competition
- be primarily the name or the surname of an individual who is living, or who has died within the preceding 30 years
- falsely suggest a connection with any living individual
- consist of the portrait or signature of any individual who is living, or who has died within the preceding 30 years
- resemble any government, charitable, or royal crest or symbol

---

Re: Application of Cross-Border Pharmacy.com [March, 2009] Decision, Trademark Opposition Board

The Applicant sought to register as a trademark the Domain name "CROSS-BORDER PHARMACY.COM" relating to the retail sale of pharmaceuticals to consumers primarily through the internet. A competitor opposed the registration on the grounds that the name contained only words that were in general use and merely descriptive but that did not distinguish the business from other businesses in the same area.

The Board's Decision

The hearing officer held that the name must be considered from the point of view of the average consumer. The officer concluded that the mark taken as a whole indicated the retail sale of pharmaceuticals to consumers over the internet and thus was merely descriptive and therefore not registerable.

Business Alert!

Trademark Search   Before deciding on any business or brand name or slogan, you can do an online trade mark search at the Canadian Intellectual Property office: cipo.ic.gc.ca.

Forms of Trademarks

Often a brand name or a short-form name by which a business is known is a trademark. For example, "The Bay" is a trademark of the Hudson Bay Company Limited. "Colgate," the brand name for a toothpaste, is a registered trademark of the Colgate-Palmolive Company Ltd. The practice of putting "®" or "™" or "® Registered Trademark" is not necessary to protect a trademark.

Slogans have become a powerful advertising tool, and are now frequently registered as trademarks. For example:

- "Just do it"
- "At Speedy, you're a somebody"
- "Everything you want in a drugstore"
- "Get cracking"

Trademarks can take other forms, including:

distinguishing guise

the distinctive shape of goods or their containers, or a distinctive way of wrapping or packaging, necessary to establish grounds for trademark

- A certification mark—a type of trademark indicating that the goods or services meet a special standard. For example, the "Good Housekeeping Seal of Approval" is a certification mark.
- A **distinguishing guise**—the distinctive shape of goods or their containers, or a distinctive way of wrapping or packaging, necessary to establish grounds for trademark. For example, the unique shape of the original Coca-Cola bottle is a trademark.

- A proposed trademark—not yet in use, but proposed. In most countries trademarks are only granted based on actual use. However, a few countries, including Canada and the United States, permit an application based on proposed use.

Registered trademark of
Shoppers Drug Mart, a Division
of Imasco Retail Inc: Courtesy of
Shoppers Drug Mart Limited

Registered trademark of Sears:
Courtesy of Sears Canada

Registered trademark of Shoppers Drug Mart, a division
of Imasco Retail Inc.: Courtesy of Shoppers Drug Mart
Limited

Registered trademark of Sears: Courtesy of Sears Canada

Surnames

Surnames cannot be registered as trademarks. The general rule is that no one should be able to claim a monopoly that is common to others. However, if you can show public recognition of your name as identifying you with particular goods or services, you have acquired a trademark in that name and can register it.

Some of the surnames that have acquired trademark status are:

- Dodge
- Eaton
- McDonald

Miranda Aluminium Inc. v. Miranda Windows and Doors Inc. [2009] F.C. 669

A father Antonio Miranda owned Miranda Aluminium Inc. and caused it to apply to have two trademarks registered by a company owned by his son expunged. The marks showed the names Miranda and an outline of a roof and chimney. The father claimed, among other grounds, that the trademark used a surname and could not be registered.

The Court's Decision:

The court held that a surname could be registered as a trademark only if it had acquired distinctiveness through use. On the evidence the court found that the son had established distinctiveness of use of that name by himself. While the father had used that name in the past there was a long hiatus of use by the father while he was incarcerated for cocaine trafficking. The son however had used the name continuously for at least several years before the father's application and so the name had acquired distinctiveness.

Trademarks as Domain Names

Domain names are the addresses of websites, such as *www.msn.com*. Trademark law is ineffective in dealing with domain names because trademarks are registered only in local jurisdictions, such as Canada or the United States. No one country has the jurisdiction over the Internet because it crosses international borders.

In order to establish some voluntary jurisdiction over the Internet, an organization called the Internet Corporation for Assigned Names and Numbers (ICANN) was established. It is based in California and is governed by 18 internationally elected directors. It has jurisdiction to decide disputes between parties claiming the rights to domain names. Often corporations, which already have a trademark in a name, try to register that name but the same domain name is held by someone who has registered that name simply to force the corporation to buy it (a cybersquatter). This is called a bad-faith registration.

The very first case to be heard was brought by the World Wrestling Federation. It went after someone who had registered *wwf.com* and the wrestlers won the match. In another early decision, Madonna won the right to *Madonna.com*.

In an arbitration decision rendered in August, 2000, an arbitrator deprived a Spanish couple of *www.barcelona.com*, a name that they had registered four years ago for their tourist site. The arbitrator awarded that name to the city of Barcelona.

According to the arbitrator, the couple was using the name in bad faith because part of the reason for the registration was to prevent the city of Barcelona from doing so. As well, the evidence indicated that the couple planned to demand a payment from the city in exchange for the name. The fact that they also validly used it for their business was not sufficient.

As part of the reasoning, the arbitrator ruled that the name was "confusingly similar" to trademarks owned by the Barcelona City Council and the city had better rights and more legitimate interest in the name than the registering couple. The ICANN decisions are posted on the Internet.

Business Law   Applied

❼ Readi-Mix Drinks Corporation has developed a new line of tropical fruit beverages and wants to register the following as trademarks:

■ a stylized line drawing of a trader with the words "Trader John's."

■ the words "Thirst Buster"
■ these names for the different flavours:
■ Shaka's Revenge
■ King Tut's Curse
■ The Grape Gretzky

a) Which of the above could be registered as trademarks?

❽ You are an employee in the Trademarks Registry Office and receive the following applications. Which do you think can be registered?

a) a new brand of bandages called Red Cross Bandages
b) a brand of records showing a portrait of Elvis Presley, bearing the slogan "The King's Choice"
c) the logo of a small mortgage broker which displays the Canadian coat of arms
d) a computer software shareware organization that uses the name in the following style: d'LOAD.

■ *Critical Concepts of* Trademark Registration

- Applications are made to the Registrar of Trademarks. The registrar will review the application to determine whether it complies with the law, and to ensure that the trademark will not be confused with others.

- If the registrar believes the trademark can be registered, the application will be published in the *Trademark Journal*, a government magazine. This gives notice of the trademark application.

- Anyone can object to the registration by filing a notice of objection with the registrar within 30 days of publication in the *Trademark Journal*. A hearing, similar to a trial, will take place if necessary, to determine whether the trademark should be registered.

- Once registration is approved, the owner of the trademark has the exclusive right to use it throughout Canada, and in countries party to the international trademark agreement, even if the use has been confined to only one province at the time of application. The registration period is for 15 years, although it is renewable indefinitely.

- Once the trademark is registered, no unauthorized person may then sell, distribute, or advertise any goods or services using a trademark that could be confused with it, or decrease the value of the goodwill attached to the mark. There is still, however, an opportunity to attack the trademark registration. Someone who has used the same trademark before the successfully registered trademark can apply to have the trademark cancelled.

- Trademark registration is also of assistance because it can be used as a basis for making application for foreign trademark recognition.

- Failure to use a trademark may result in the loss of that trademark through abandonment.

Who Can Apply?

Registration of a trademark is on a "first come, first served" basis. The owner of a trademark can apply for registration on any of the following grounds:

- actual use in Canada—the trademark is already known in Canada (usually a foreign trademark that has appeared in Canadian media advertising)
- proposed use in Canada—the trademark must actually be used within the following six months
- registration in a country outside Canada

Facebook Cybersquatting   Facebook Registration. Although not a government regulated registration system and not enforceable through the courts, Facebook permits a business to register its trademark with Facebook so that its users will not be allowed to adopt the trademark as a user name. This procedure may be more effective and much less costly than any legal remedy.

Business Alert!

Losing Protection

If a registered trademark is no longer descriptive or distinguishing, and has become the name by which the goods are generally known no matter who makes them, the trademark loses its status as a mark even though it is registered. *Linoleum* was once a trademark, but has become the name for a certain type of floor covering and has lost its trademark standing. Similarly, *Aspirin* was once the trademark of one manufacturer of analgesic pills. *Scotch tape* was once the trademark of the 3M Company, but has become the name for transparent adhesive tape. *Escalator* was also a trademark at one time.

■ *Critical Concepts of* Infringement of Trademarks

- Any use of a trademark without permission of the owner is infringement.
- The owner of a registered trademark need only prove that the infringing mark is so similar that it will likely confuse the public as to the source of the goods.

Montres Rolex S.A. v. Balshin et al., 31 C.P.R. (3d) 180

Technology has made copying infinitely easier. Knock-offs, or imitations, are easily found today for many products. Montres Rolex S.A., the Swiss watchmaker, marketed expensive watches through the Rolex Watch Company of Canada. Palmer imported and sold similar watches that included the crown design, and the name Rollex (itself a registered trademark) in small letters on each watch.

The imitation watches sold for $40, while the Rolex watches range from $2,500 to $10,000 and more. Palmer provided a card that included a disclaimer indicating that the Rollex was not a Swiss Rolex. This card clearly stated that it was an imitation.

Palmer argued that the buyers were not fooled—they knew they were not getting a genuine Rolex for $40. He further claimed that there was a thriving industry generally known as imitation art—even famous oil paintings are copied and sold as imitations.

The Court's Decision

The court stated that the relevant question was whether the imitation watches were so similar to the Swiss watches that they would confuse the public as to the source of the goods. A unique point of this problem was that the buyer was not fooled. The buyer bought the imitation watches because of the goodwill of the Swiss Rolex watches. The buyer wanted to give the public the impression of owning the expensive luxury watch; thus, the public was deceived by the buyer, not by the imitator/seller.

Part of the appeal of the Rolex watches was that they were known to be a high-quality timepiece. If it became widely known that very similar watches were selling for $40, the market for Swiss Rolex watches would be badly affected.

The court held that Palmer was infringing the trademark of the Rolex Watch Company of Canada and ordered him to cease marketing these watches.

Trademarks and Passing Offence

Trademark infringement and passing off are very similar. Trademark infringement is a right of action given under the federal *Trademarks Act*. Passing off is a tort that was developed by common law. Both passing off and trademark infringement require use of a competitor's project in a way that deceives the public.

The differences are slight. One is that trademark registration gives protection across Canada, while passing off gives protection only in the area of actual use.

The test for determining whether the purchasers would be confused is not that of a careful and deliberate purchaser, nor on the other hand is it the moron in a hurry; it is a middle type, a consumer who is the ordinary hurried purchaser.

In an action for trademark infringement fought between two competitors who supplied products in the nuclear reactor industry over two trademarks of a similarly stylized "A", the judge commented in rejecting the moron test, that Homer Simpson may have been confused in looking at the 2 trademarks, but that was not sufficient to find confusion for the purpose of trademark violation infringement (*AECL v. Areva NP Canada Ltd.* [2009] F.C. 980). The court found that the purchasers, a very sophisticated and small target market, would not be confused. The Homer Simpson test was rejected.

Registration While trademark registration may not be absolutely necessary because the mark may be protected by passing off, there are advantages to registration in proving length of use and ownership.

Business Alert!

McDonald's Corporation et al. v. Yoggi Yogurt Ltd. et al., [1982] 66 C.P.R. (2d) 101

Yoggi Yogurt Ltd. ran a restaurant business with two outlets in Toronto. It applied to register the trademark McYogurt for milkshakes.

The Registrar of Trademarks circulated notice of the application in the *Trademarks Journal*. McDonald's Corporation filed a notice of objection, and a hearing of the Trademarks Opposition Board was held to determine if the trademark should be registered.

The board cleared the trademark for registration, and McDonald's Corporation appealed to the federal court.

McDonald's Corporation is the registered owner of a number of trademarks with the prefixes *Mc* and *Mac*. There are 21 registrations in connection with a particular food, including Big Mac, Egg McMuffin, MacSundae, McCheese, and McFeast.

Although not registered, McDonald's has used the term *McShake* in advertising. McDonald's markets a milkshake which it calls McDonald's Shamrock Milkshake.

Since coming to Canada in 1960, McDonald's has embarked on a very aggressive advertising campaign directed at overwhelming both potential customers and competitors. It has also been zealous in defending its trademarks. Weston Foods sought an application to register trademarks such as McCandy and others. McDonald's opposed this, and Weston withdrew its application.

Vast sums have been expended in all types of advertising. Between 1974 and 1977, $21 million was spent advertising McDonald's trademarks in Canada. In the years 1974 and 1975, McDonald's sold more than 45 million milkshakes.

Yoggi Yogurt claimed that McDonald's did not have a monopoly on trademarks that use the prefix *Mc*. For example, McCain's was a registered trademark of the McCain Food Corporation, associated with frozen foods.

Yoggi Yogurt also asserted that *McYogurt* could not be confused with any of the McDonald trademarks. *McYogurt* and *McMuffin* were clearly distinguishable.

The Court's Decision

The court held that McDonald's had established a family of trademarks, and had appropriated the use of *Mc* and *Mac* in association with food products. Other registrations with the *Mc* prefix were well-known surnames, and not the *Mc* or *Mac* prefix with a food product name. When *McYogurt* was compared with the whole family of McDonald's trademarks, it might lead consumers to assume that *McYogurt* was associated with McDonald's. The ruling of the Trademark Opposition Board was overturned, and the application by Yoggi Yogurt to register its trademark *McYogurt* was refused.

■ *Business Law*   Applied

⑨ **BoneChill Company,** a large U.S.-based multinational marketing firm, wants to register the following trademarks in Canada, and has asked your advice on which will be permitted. What will you tell them?

a) A brand name registered and used in the United States as a trademark, but only in the southern states. It has not been heard of outside those states. It is to be used in Canada in about two years' time.

b) A brand name registered and used extensively in the United States as a trademark. The advertising appears in U.S. magazines that have a high circulation all over North America.

c) A new name for a brand to be introduced into Canada in three months' time.

⑩ **New Tech Company** Limited has been operating since 1980 in Fredericton, New Brunswick, marketing alarm clocks under the brand name SureWake. On a trip to Regina, the president of New Tech sees that the Ultra Clock Company has an identical brand, using the same name and configuration. Ultra Clock operates only in Saskatchewan, and had registered the trademark one year prior to the discovery by New Tech Company. New Tech wants to attack the trademark registration.

a) Does New Tech Company have a remedy, or is the trademark registration final?

b) What is the basis for any claim that New Tech Company may have? Is it likely to be successful?

Industrial Designs

What Is Industrial Design?

Industrial designs are essentially unique patterns, shapes, or ornaments that appeal to and are judged solely by the eye. For example, icons, which are used universally in computer software, can be registered as industrial designs. There is much room for dispute over whether a design should be subject to registration as an industrial design, or as patent, trademark, or copyright work, since designs can often be classified as any one of these. This is another example of a term having a specific technical legal meaning that is different from the way the word is used generally.

Companion with Other Intellectual Property

There are several criteria to consider when deciding if a particular item is an industrial design.

- An industrial design is judged solely by the eye, and is primarily ornamental—a pattern of china, or Web page design.
- A patent must be useful, and not just ornamental.
- An industrial design can also be registered as a trademark, as a distinguishing guise.
- Designs may also be copyrighted as distinguishing shapes. However, if they are used for patterns to produce articles in quantities of more than 50, the design cannot be copyrighted but must be registered under the *Industrial Design Act*.
- No principle of manufacturing or construction can be registered as an industrial design.

Reproduced with the kind permission of the copyright owner,
Royal Doulton

■ *Critical Concepts of* Registering an Industrial Design

- Registration must be made and completed within one year of the design's becoming known to the public.
- Protection is granted for ten years.
- The word *Registered* or *Rd* and the year of registration must be placed on an article conforming to the design (e.g., Rd, 2001), or protection is lost.
- Two or more variations can be registered, thereby effectively providing protection for a class of designs.

Thurston Hayes Developments Ltd. et al. v. Horn Abbot et al., [1985] 6 C.I.P.R. 75 (Fed. C.A.)

Thurston Hayes Developments Ltd. developed a board game called Trivial Pursuit. They registered the name and script as a trademark, and the board design as an industrial design.

Horn Abbot Ltd. marketed a game called Sexual Pursuits. The name was in the identical script to that used by Trivial Pursuit. The design and shape of the box and board were very similar.

Thurston sued Horn Abbot for infringement of Thurston's trademark and industrial design, and applied to the court for an order before trial—an interlocutory injunction—that Horn Abbot stop marketing the Sexual Pursuits game immediately.

The Court's Decision

The court found that Horn Abbot designed its Sexual Pursuits game to be as similar as possible to Trivial Pursuit, with only minor differences in an effort to escape a finding of infringement. The court ordered that Horn Abbot cease to market Sexual Pursuits until the trial of the action.

■ Business Law Applied

⑪ **Tookta Van Kunek**, an architect, devised a new construction system for building large residential subdivisions. The prefabricated components of the house were built in a factory on site. The factory itself was designed so that on completion of the houses, the factory could easily be converted to a shopping centre. Van Kunek wants to have this system registered as an industrial design.

    a) Is this system the proper subject matter for registration as an industrial design?

⑫ **Helena Theodoseos designed** a new pattern for wallpaper, to be sold throughout Canada.

    a) Is this wallpaper design the proper subject matter for registration as an industrial design?
    b) What is the length of time that Theodoseos has to complete registration of the design?
    c) How long will the protection last?
    d) Could Theodoseos also obtain copyright on this design?

Patents

The Nature of a Patent

The patent system applies to inventions, and is designed to encourage further inventions. To obtain a patent, the inventor must reveal the invention process in exchange for an exclusive right to use it for 20 years. Although the patent cannot be copied outright, it can suggest ideas for new inventions that build on the original idea. Perhaps one of the most famous patents ever granted was to two Canadians, Dr. Frederick Banting and Dr. Charles Best, in 1923 for the insulin used to treat diabetes. Other examples of patented inventions are the fax machine, which was originally patented in the late 1800s, and the telephone.

A patent:

- is a government-granted monopoly to use an invention
- protects the idea itself in a working model, not the expression of the idea
- comes into existence only when registered
- gives protection for 20 years, but requires disclosure of the invention

After 20 years anyone can use the item patented, and the monopoly ceases. Some inventors do not wish to reveal the invention process and do not apply for patent protection. They simply keep the process a secret. The formula for blending Coca-Cola, which was invented in 1891, was never patented, and has been maintained by secrecy.

Patent   Once a patent has been granted, the invention process is made public. The grant of a patent from the government is given in a form called **letters patent**. *Letter* is used here in an older meaning of written communication. The word **patent** is derived from a Latin word meaning *open*, *disclosed*, or *revealed*—hence, to make public.

What Can Be Patented?

Only inventions can be patented. The *Patent Act* defines an invention as: "Any new and useful art, process, machine, manufacture or composition of matter."

Farcus
© 1992 Farcus Cartoons/dist. by Universal Press Syndicate   WAISGLASS/COULTHART

"Okay, so what else does it do?"

Any new and useful improvement on a previously patented invention is also patentable, but a new patent must be sought.

In order to be patented, an invention must have three qualities:

- ingenuity—it must be more than just an obvious step that a person with reasonable skill would have taken
- utility—it must be of practical use. It must cause a change or condition in the character or condition of the physical object.
- novelty—it must not already be known to the public (in the public domain), although the Patent Act permits disclosure 1 year before the application for a patent.

What Cannot Be Patented?

Not all inventions can be patented. An invention that is to be patented must contain a novelty value; therefore, certain already-known inventions are not patentable. Other inventions that cannot be patented are:

- methods of medical treatment
- business systems or method
- industrial designs, copyrighted items, and trademarks
- devices that simply change the shape of existing devices
- mathematical formulas or abstract theorems

There is much debate as to whether computer programs should be a matter of patent or copyright. Computer programs are considered similar to mathematical formulas, and currently cannot be patented. However, they are subject to copyright. Computer programs that are an integral part of a new machine (computer apparatus) may be patentable. There is considerable pressure from the electronics industry to make programs patentable, and the law in this area may change. However at present software standing alone is not patentable.

Example: One Click Method-Amazon.com Inc. filed a patent application for the software for its 1-click online purchasing method. The Patent Appeal Board rejected this patent application finding, among other reasons, that this was a business method and as such could not be patentable (Patent Appeal Board Decision No. 1290, March 5, 2009).

With the development of bioengineering, a new issue has arisen as to whether life forms should be patentable. In the first case in Canada to consider this matter, Harvard University applied for a patent for a genetically engineered mouse called the Harvard Mouse. The patent was rejected because the mouse was not reliably reproducible. The issue of whether higher life forms can be patented was left open.

Business Law   Applied

⑬ **On a visit** to some Pacific Rim countries, Marlene McIvor discovered a surprisingly effective traditional herbal remedy for the common cold. Its advantage was that it came in a small sugar-coated tablet about the size of an aspirin, and would be easily saleable in the North American market, where it was hitherto unknown.

   a) Could McIvor obtain a patent for this item in Canada?

⑭ **After several years** of experimentation, Vivian Prus developed a system for home water filtration. She lived in Edmonton, Alberta, but hoped to market the system throughout North America. On a trip to New Brunswick she found a local manufacturer had been selling a similar system for about five years, but only locally.

   a) Is this water filtration system a subject for a patent?
   b) If so, who can obtain the patent—Prus or the New Brunswick manufacturer?

⑮ **Robert Roth invented** a machine that made frames for aluminum doors and windows much more cheaply than any similar machine on the market. He started his own small company, and supplied window frames locally for about five years. A friend advised him that he could sell his machine nationally to other manufacturing companies. First, however, Roth decided to apply for a patent on his machine.

   a) Would he be successful in obtaining a patent?

Innovations

The law governing intellectual properties is rapidly changing because of international trade agreements such as NAFTA. Rapid improvements in technology are also having their effect. The international trade agreements are influencing all signatory countries to have the same intellectual property laws. Some of the new technologies that require special treatment are biotechnology—the production of new life forms—and cable and satellite retransmission facilities. Some of the recent intellectual property legislation has been:

- *Intellectual Property Law Improvement Act*, 1993
- *Integrated Circuit Topography Act*, 1993
- *Plant Breeders' Rights Act*, 1990
- *Patent Act Amendment Act*, 1992

Impeachment

If anyone believes that a patent does not meet the criteria for registration, that person can ask the patent office to re-examine the patent grant, or can bring a court action for impeachment to have the patent revoked. **Impeachment** is, in effect, an action challenging the validity of a patent, claiming that the letters patent should not have been granted in the first place. (**Letters patent** is a document incorporating a corporation, issued by the appropriate authority, and constituting the charter of the corporation.)

Applying for a Patent

Copyright exists as soon as you create an original work; patents, however, must be applied for. It is possible to apply for a patent yourself, and there are many self-help books and inventors groups that can explain the process.

Most inventors use a **patent agent**—a registered agent (often an engineer) who pursues applications for patents on behalf of individual inventors. An examiner at the government patent office will then check the patent application and, if it conforms with the law, the patent will be granted. A grant of patent gives the holder monopoly rights to the invention for 20 years.

Canada now uses a first-to-file registration system. If two individuals quite independently create the same invention, the first to file will be granted the sole patent rights. As with copyright, if the invention is found by the patent office examiner to have been made under the terms of an employment contract, the patent rights will belong to the employer. An inventor, therefore, must be very careful in outlining what is, and is not, the employer's in any employment contract.

Non-Disclosure Agreement

Because obtaining a patent can be expensive, sometimes an inventor does not have the money to do so and must approach a large business to obtain funding. In order to protect the invention rights, the inventor should have the business sign a non-disclosure agreement, in which the business acknowledges that it does not already know of the invention, and agrees that it will not use the invention or disclose it to anyone else. This is some protection for the inventor in the event that the negotiations for funding fall through with this business.

Identifying Patents

If a patent is granted, anything produced under that patent must state that it is patented and the date the letters patent were granted (e.g., Patented, 2001). It is an offence under the *Patent Act* not to display this patent identification. It is also an offence under the act to use this identification if the item is not in fact produced under that patent. You will often see the words "Patent Pending" on goods. They are of no legal effect.

International Patent Protection

There is no international convention that gives foreign protection, and so inventors must register in every country in which they seek protection. Many inventors register in both Canada and the United States. The Patent Co-operation Treaty permits inventors to file in Canada for patent protection in 43 countries, with a single international application.

Patent Applications   The Canadian Patent Office publishes a manual of its practice and procedure, which can be obtained by contacting that office. There are branches in major cities in all provinces, and they are listed in the government section of the telephone directory. Most libraries carry self-help books on how to make your own patent application. There are also inventors groups that can assist. These are often listed in classified sections of newspapers and special interest magazines dealing with topics such as electronics.

Patent Protection vs. Copyright, Trade Secrets

Patents give the strongest form of intellectual property protection. Copyright and trade secrets only protect against copying. Independent creation is a defence against claims to copyright or trade secrets.

Example: Two independent creators of same product: John, in Ontario, designs a software program that speeds up on-time delivery for business products. He successfully registers a copyright for this software.

Mary, in British Columbia, develops, completely on her own and without any knowledge of John's product, the identical program. John cannot stop the sale of Mary's product for she did not "copy" John's work.

However, if the product had been patentable, the first to register would hold the patent rights and be able to prevent the other from using the invention.

Confidential Information in Business Deals

Trade secrets and confidential information were examined in Chapter 16, with specific application to the area of employment law. In that chapter, the difference between confidential, protected information and knowledge or skills acquired on the job was outlined as being the distinction between objective and subjective information. A formula is an example of objective, protected information, while the learning of a skill by an employee is subjective information.

A trade secret will be protected as long as it is kept secret. It is information of any type or form that has an economic value because it is not generally known in the trade. To succeed in a court action based on the unauthorized disclosure or use of confidential information or a trade secret, it is necessary to show that reasonable efforts have been made to maintain the secrecy of the trade secret; that the information was given out in a relationship of confidentiality; and that there has been unauthorized use of the information which has caused an injury to the person who first communicated the trade secret.

What will constitute reasonable efforts to maintain secrecy will depend on the circumstances in each case. Restricting access to the information to only a few people, holding closed-door meetings with no record of the discussions, and not permitting copies to be made of the information, are all examples of the types of actions that would support a claim that efforts were made to keep the information secret.

When the trade secret is disclosed to another party, it does not require a formal act or some special handshake to maintain its confidential nature. If the information is given out in circumstances where the other party has notice of its confidential nature, either because there is a contract with an express or implied obligation of confidence or because they are requested to keep it confidential, then a duty to maintain the secrecy of the information is created.

There are three distinct areas of law that govern confidential business information. One of them, the breach of a contract with an express confidentiality clause, was examined in Chapter 16.

A second area involves a breach of confidence, and occurs when confidential information is provided on a business-like basis with some common objective in the minds of the parties. This might be between individuals who may be discussing a potential business operation or partnership, and one party uses that information to its own advantage, against the interests of the party who revealed the information.

The third area of law involves a fiduciary duty. An employee, agent, officer, or director of a corporation has a duty to act in good faith and in the best interests of the principal at all times. A key element of the duty created by this special relationship is the obligation to keep information given by the principal confidential. Disclosure or personal use of the information is a breach of the fiduciary duty, and is viewed very seriously by the courts because of the nature of the trust and dependency that exists in this type of relationship.

LAC Minerals Ltd. v. International Corona Resources Ltd., [1989] 61 D.L.R. (4th) 14 (S.C.C.)

Corona was in the business of exploring potential gold-mining properties in northwestern Ontario. The company decided to purchase the property next to the land on which it already held a claim. Corona entered into negotiations to purchase this adjacent property, which was referred to as the Williams property. LAC Minerals Ltd. heard about Corona's exploration plans and began discussions with the company for the purpose of forming a joint venture or partnership to develop a gold mine on the Williams property. Through information provided during the negotiations, LAC found out Corona did not yet own the Williams property. When discussions between LAC and Corona broke down, LAC purchased the Williams property itself and developed the gold mine, which yielded huge profits.

Corona brought a court action against LAC for breach of confidentiality and breach of fiduciary duty.

The Court's Decision

At the trial and Ontario Court of Appeal levels, LAC was found liable for breach of confidence and breach of fiduciary duty because the information about the Williams property was confidential. It had been revealed in confidence in the course of well-developed joint venture discussions.

The Supreme Court of Canada confirmed that a breach of confidence had clearly occurred. However, three of the five judges found the element of dependence by one party on the other required to establish a fiduciary duty was not sufficiently proven on the part of Corona.

Breach of confidence was enough to enable the Supreme Court to confirm the lower courts' decisions requiring LAC to turn the gold mine over to Corona after Corona paid LAC's development costs.

Remedies

Remedies for disclosure of confidential information are the same as those for infringement of other intellectual property rights.

In Summation

Intellectual Property

- Your creativity, expressed through such media as drawings, a new process, a new machine, a multi-coloured logo, a design, or a formula, is known as intellectual property. It is a type of non-tangible property that carries with it enforceable rights. These rights allow you to protect the ownership, use, reproduction, copying, and goodwill value of the intellectual property.

Personality Rights

- Celebrities have the right to control the use of those elements of their personality which have become attached to their celebrity status, such as some aspect of their physical image, or their name.

Copyright

- This area of intellectual property is governed by the federal *Copyright Act*. Copyright protects the author's creative expression but not the idea expressed. No other person may use the author's intellectual property for a period that extends to 50 years after the author's death. There are some limited exceptions to this period of time for protection.

- Protection in Canada is automatic without any requirement to register, although registration may assist in providing evidence as to when the work was created. Protection in other countries is available through international copyright conventions.

- The author of the work is the owner of copyright except in particular circumstances, such as when a work is created in the course of employment.

- While ownership of copyright can be assigned or a licence can be given, the moral rights, aimed at protecting the integrity of the created expression, cannot be assigned.

- Infringement of copyright occurs when someone uses, or assists in using, copyrighted material without the owner's consent. Special situations exist permitting copies to be made without consent. Copies made of short passages for use in schools or for research are examples of these exceptions. Remedies for infringement include damages, an accounting for profits made from the illegal use, an injunction, and criminal penalties under the *Copyright Act*.

Trademarks

- A trademark is a distinctive mark or symbol that distinguishes and identifies the product or service of one party from those of another.

- Trademarks can take many forms, from a name to a shape, and include slogans, certification marks, and distinguishing guises based on a distinctive shape.

- Several factors are involved for protection of a trademark to be granted. Use or proposed use, along with such elements as being confused with an existing trademark, are looked for when registration is sought.

- The registration process follows a particular procedure and, if granted, protects the trademark for 15 years, renewable indefinitely.

- Infringement is proven by showing that the other mark is likely to cause confusion in the mind of the public as to the source of the goods.

Industrial Design

- An industrial design is aimed at protecting the shape or design pattern of an object from being reproduced. Visual appeal in a useful object such as a bottle shape is a key element in applying for protection for this type of intellectual property.

- Once granted, protection for reproduction of the item is given for up to 10 years. The word *registered*, or an abbreviation, along with the year of registration, must appear on the article reproduced from the protected design.

Patents

- A patent protects an idea for 20 years and gives its inventor a governmental monopoly on the use of the invention that embodies the idea.

- To make it through the rigours of the patent application process, an idea must first be seen as an invention. This is defined by the federal *Patent Act* as any new and useful art, process, machine, manufacture, or composition of matter. The invention must then be seen as possessing the qualities of ingenuity, utility, and novelty. A thorough examination process follows, leading, possibly, to a grant of letters patent.

- A patent application requires full disclosure of the invention and consequently ends any protection available under the area of trade secret or confidential information.

- Anything produced under the patent must bear a statement that it is patented along with the date the patent was granted, although protection begins from the date of application.

- Applying for a patent in every country in which use is anticipated is necessary as there are no international conventions for patent protection.

- The owner of a patent may be required to give a licence for the use of the invention if the patent rights are being abused through, for example, improper use.

- The ending of the compulsory licensing of medicines in 1992 created considerable controversy and possibly hefty profits for large international drug companies.

- The area of intellectual property law is changing rapidly because of new and unanticipated technologies, improvements in existing technology, and international trade concerns. Recent legislation in this area has attempted to respond to the business sector's need to protect valuable assets.

Trade Secrets

- Certain types of information may be considered confidential and capable of being protected from disclosure.

Closing Questions

The Protection of Creativity

1. Could Einstein have patented the theory of relativity?

2. Dudley Cooke enjoyed making homemade wine. In September 1994, in the course of his experimentation, he discovered a new process by which berries from a particular plant could be distilled and a rather exotic flavour obtained. He kept this process a secret, and enjoyed the curious looks and questions that were raised whenever he introduced anyone to his particular wine, which he labelled Dudley Do It Right.

   Unknown to Cooke, Jennifer Paik, another inventor, was hard at work attempting to create a new fragrance. By accident, Paik discovered the same process used by Cooke, and which could be applied to any fruit or berry to create an enhanced flavoured wine. Excited, she packed up her notes and headed off to talk to an intellectual-property lawyer, who applied for a patent on the process on her behalf. Paik's patent for the new process was granted on July 16, 1996. Two years later, when she discovered that Cooke was now marketing his wine-making process locally, she brought an application to stop him.
   a) Would Paik be able to enforce her patent against Cooke and stop him from being able to use the process that he discovered on his own and has been using since then?
   b) To what date will Paik have a monopoly over the process that she has patented?

3. Previous or proposed use is required for which of the following?
   a) patent protection
   b) copyright
   c) trademark
   d) industrial design

4. Winston Basset was an aspiring composer, and had been writing music for a couple of years. He entered a radio station's contest, submitting a tape of his music along with the entry form which stated that all entries became the property of the radio station and would not be returned. Basset was not one of the winning entries.

   Several months later, while listening to the radio, he heard his music being played as background for an advertisement for the radio station. When Basset telephoned the station manager to complain about the use of his music without his permission, the station manager replied, "You're a big boy; you knew the rules. We can do what we want with it."

a) What would be the legal remedy that Basset would pursue, and in what area of law does that remedy lie?

b) With reasons, explain the issues concerning the ownership of the music being used in the radio station's advertisement, and give a decision as to who would be successful if this matter went to court.

5. Tokay is an artist who often painted her own designs on T-shirts and sweatshirts that she wore. She had done a few T-shirts for friends on which she drew exotic birds with bright-coloured feathers. The body of the bird was on the front of the T-shirt, and the tail feathers extended around the body to cover a good percentage of the shirt's back. Her friends enjoyed the designs so much that she decided to begin marketing them. Tokay arranged to buy T-shirts and have the designs reproduced on them. She decided to market the shirts under the name Too-Right-Designs.

a) What measures should Tokay take to protect her designs and business name?

b) One day, while wandering through a mall looking for potential customers for her designer T-shirts, Tokay saw sweatshirts that had designs of exotic birds on them, almost exactly like hers. The only differences were that other colours had been used and, rather than having the tails of the birds finishing on the back, the entire bird was produced on the front of the sweatshirt. Tokay is extremely upset because she has not yet signed up any store outlets to sell her T-shirts, and with the sweatshirt already on the market she may be out of luck. Explain with reasons whether Tokay has the legal right to stop the sweatshirt company from selling its product, and in which area of law she would base her court action.

6. Walt Whitmore liked to carve figures out of wood. He worked in construction and one day, while on coffee break, he picked up some of the foam sponge insulation that was used in the new houses that were being built. He took out his pocket knife and carved a small football out of the sponge, which he and his co-workers then used to play tag ball during their breaks.

Suddenly struck with brilliant inspiration, Whitmore realized that he had a new product on his hands, so to speak. Calling it a Squange ball, he ordered several sheets of the foam sponge insulation and began to experiment with various shapes that could be used for different types of games. He began to market these items under the name Squange and became independently wealthy in a short period of time. His old tool belt now hangs on the wall as a symbol of his retirement from the construction trade.

a) Will Whitmore be successful in applying for a patent for his Squange ball?

b) If he were unsuccessful in patenting the ball, what areas of intellectual property would offer Whitmore protection from competitors, and what elements of his new business should he be looking to protect?

7. Aurora and Sonia co-wrote a manual on golfing techniques. The manual was completed on April 1, 1996. Aurora was in a car accident, and died from her injuries on June 1, 1997. Sonia continued to enjoy the royalties paid on the sale of their manual until her death on January 30, 2015.

a) If Aurora and Sonia did not register the copyright in the manual would they have protection under the *Copyright Act*?

b) What advice would you give them if Aurora and Sonia intended to sell the manual outside Canada, particularly if they were thinking of selling it in the United States?

c) Assuming that copyright in the golfing manual was registered on May 30, 1996, on which of the following dates does that copyright expire?

i) April 1, 2016

ii) May 30, 2046

iii) June 1, 2047

iv) January 30, 2065

8. Would the *Industrial Design Act* provide the best protection from competitors for your product if the shape in which it is designed distinguishes it from other goods in the same field?

9. Carmen was commissioned to create a mural for the lobby of an office building. The mural that she designed had a picture of a farmer's field, with three-dimensional trees emerging in the foreground from the wall. One day, while walking past the building, Carmen was surprised to see what appeared to be blinking lights hanging from the trees in her mural. When she asked the building superintendent who had hung the lights, he told her that they changed the tree decorations according to the seasons, and since this was Christmas they thought flashing coloured lights would be a great idea. He added that she wouldn't believe what they have planned for the Canada Day celebrations.

   a) Does Carmen have any right to have the lights removed from the trees and, if so, on what would she base her legal action?

10. Angela Wong had an elderly grandfather who required a walker in order to be able to move about. Noticing that he would tire quickly and require a place to sit down, Wong designed a walker that could be easily collapsed and restructured into a chair with the use of two levers. She has named her prototype stroller/chair the Supportive Stroller.

   Which of the following areas of intellectual property would protect Wong's creation, and for what period of time?

   a) industrial design
   b) trademark
   c) patent
   d) copyright
   e) trade secret

11. Medikant Ltd., a European drug manufacturer, had obtained patents in several countries, including Canada, for a new drug that was effective in slowing the symptoms experienced by AIDS patients. The drug cost Medikant $0.50 a tablet to manufacture, and it was sold to the patients at $5 a tablet. Redbow Inc. approached Medikant for a licence to manufacture the drug in Canada and was refused.

   a) Explain whether Redbow would be able to force Medikant to grant it a licence.
   b) Given your answer to question a), do you support the current arrangement in this area? Why or why not?
   c) If Marlene is an AIDS patient with a low income and cannot afford the tablets manufactured by Medikant, is there anything she can do about the company's pricing policy?

Websites

patents1.ic.gc.ca/intro-e.html—Canadian Patent Database. Includes links to the trademark database.

www.siia.net—Website for the software and information industry. Site compiles techlaw, trends, and insights on industry activities.

Computer Law: Civil and Criminal

Information Technology and the Law

Information technology law does not exist. What was once known as computer law consists in fact of several areas of the law that deal with rapidly advancing technology and the new value that has been attached to information.

Your purchase of a video CD player by credit card in Singapore on March 1 is sent by telecommunication networks to various locations around the world, one of which compiles a data bank on individuals who purchase this type of equipment. In turn, that consumer data service company sells the information to video CD retailers. By the time you return home one week or less later, a complete listing of recently released CDs available via the Internet is waiting in your e-mail.

Information about you, your business, and your spending habits is worth money to someone, somewhere. Technology that gathers, collates, manipulates, and distributes this information worldwide in minutes—if not seconds—is evolving constantly. Being first in the market with new technology that is faster, more accurate, or less expensive than the competition may make or break a company financially.

Advancing technology has made it possible to put a company's entire financial history on a hard drive or floppy disk. It has also made it very easy to steal that information by copying it onto a disk that is no bigger than a credit card and can easily slip into a pocket as you leave the office for your new job with a competitor.

The various areas of law involved in information technology try to encourage the development of technology and recognize the increasing importance attached to information. At the same time, they discourage piracy, theft, and fraud. But technology changes and develops rapidly. Thus, the protection offered by the current laws is stretched to the limit, and certain elements may well remain unprotected.

Protection for information technology comes primarily from four main areas of the law.

Civil Law

Intellectual Property Law

- Patents protect the inventions themselves—computer hardware such as the laptop computer

- Integrated circuit topographies, found in computer chips, microprocessors, and integrated circuits used in data processing are protected under a federal statute called the *Integrated Circuit Topography Act*.
- Industrial design protects anything that has a distinctive shape or visual design.
- Copyright law protects the creative expression found, for example, in the computer program or the manuals associated with it.
- The law covering trade secrets and confidential information protects sensitive information not known to the general public.
- Trademarks protect the business name or logo—the apple used by Apple Computer, for example.

Contract Law

- Particular terms and conditions in a contract can help to define who owns the property or has rights to it. Specific conditions might outline the terms under which the property can be licensed.

Criminal Law

- Criminal prosecution or the threat of prosecution can be used to protect the technology and data from theft, unauthorized use, and mischief by hackers or unhappy employees.

Tort Law

- This area of law provides an opportunity for compensation if someone has injured you or your business through negligence or by an intentional tort. In March 1994, an Australian court awarded an internationally known professor of anthropology the equivalent of US$28,000 for defamation published on the Internet.

Patents

The patent system is designed to encourage and reward inventiveness. It grants a monopoly to the inventor to use the invention for 20 years, in exchange for full disclosure of the invention and its processes. In order to qualify for protection under the *Patent Act*, the invention has to meet the criteria set out in the act. It must be ingenious, useful, and new (see Chapter 17). Most patents related to information technology are concerned with hardware such as monitors, laptop computers, modems, or a new type of cable material.

The *Patent Act* specifically excludes mathematical formulas or abstract theorems. Currently, computer programs are considered to be similar to mathematical formulas and cannot be patented in Canada. There is considerable pressure from various interest groups in the information technology sector for change in this area of the law.

Business Alert!   Software Patents in the United States   In the United States it is possible to protect a computer program by a software patent. Because there is no international convention for patent protection, you need to obtain patents in those countries in which you want protection. If you are planning to carry on business in or export to the United States or any other country you should check with a lawyer on the possibility of obtaining patent protection in that location.

Programs and Processes

If a computer program is part of a new machine or process which meets the tests for patentability, the program may be protected as part of that item. A new invention for testing the quality of water in rivers or lakes, for example, consists of a waterproof box with a series of chambers and lasers that are opened and activated by a computer program—the machine performs several types of analysis of a water sample. Such a computer program would be protected by virtue of being an integral part of the invention for which the patent is granted.

Patent Applications

Changes and developments in information technology occur rapidly. The processing of a patent application may take a few years and be quite expensive, involving patent agents and highly technical diagrams and descriptions of the invention. Disclosure in the application also means the invention process is made public and the common law protection for trade secrets is lost. After that, the invention may not meet the tests for ingenuity, utility, and novelty required for a grant of letters patent.

The decision whether to pursue the protection available under the *Patent Act* or some other source of intellectual property law, such as trade-secret law, requires serious consideration and the balancing of many practical business issues.

▓ *Business Law* Applied

❶ Jorge Jose wrote a software program that causes various carbon-based compounds to be measured and integrated into a new material that is used for manufacturing extremely lightweight and durable items such as canoes and violins for public-school music students.

a) Explain whether Jose will be successful in obtaining a patent to protect his invention.

❷ Franklin More is a geologist with a special interest. He is fascinated by earthquakes and the prediction of the location and intensity of the aftershocks. More developed a small device that could be attached in a previously unheard-of manner to a seismograph that measures and records the vibrations of earthquakes. Because it is attached directly to the seismograph, More's invention could pick up the most sensitive of the data recorded by the seismograph. Then, through use of a built-in computer program, information from previous earthquakes not normally used could be accessed and combined with the current earthquake's information to give a printout estimating the location and intensity of the aftershocks.

a) Would More be able to obtain patent protection for his invention?
b) If the computer program were removed, would the attachment qualify for patent protection?

Computer Chips

Robotics, artificial intelligence, and More's seismograph attachment described above might incorporate a computer chip for data processing. It was the development of the computer chip that led to the meteoric advances in personal computers and the current state of information technology.

Chips, microchips, or integrated circuits are used in data processing and a wide range of commercial activities and products. They are miniaturized electronic circuits on a single piece of semiconductor material, usually silicon. The design of the electronic circuit is what causes the chip to do what it is supposed to do. The electronic elements are built up in layers, creating an overall three-dimensional pattern that is then deposited on a wafer of silicon for use in the end product—for example, a computer's memory. The three-dimensional pattern is known as the topography of the chip.

Research and development of a new chip is expensive. However, a chip is easily duplicated through such means as reverse engineering—a procedure in which you start with a known product and then take it apart, working backward to figure out the process by which it was developed so that it can be recreated.

Rights Granted under the Act

The federal government's *Integrated Circuit Topography Act, S.C. 1990, c. 37*, is aimed at protecting the original design of a topography. The act does not give a monopoly on the idea, but does give a limited monopoly to the owner of the registered topography, providing the right to reproduce, manufacture, and import or commercially exploit the registered topography or any product that incorporates it. This limited monopoly does not give any exclusive rights to the idea or process embodied in the topography or an integrated circuit product. Anyone can independently create a similar topography without infringing the rights of the owner of a registered topography.

■ *Critical Concepts of* Topography

Only the owner of a topography may apply for its registration, and the topography must meet the following criteria:

- It must be original.
- The application for registration must be filed before the topography is used commercially, or within two years after it is.
- The owner must be Canadian or, among other possible qualifications, have a manufacturing site for integrated circuit products or topographies located in Canada.

Business Alert!

Topography Protection   A topography registered under the act is protected for up to 10 years. Protection begins either the year in which it was first commercially exploited or the filing date of the application, whichever is earlier. Commercial exploitation is defined in the act as occurring whenever the topography or an integrated circuit incorporating the topography is sold, leased, or exhibited for sale or lease for the first time any place in the world by or with the consent of the owner of the topography.

Exceptions to Protection

There are several exceptions to the rights granted under the act. These exceptions generally allow the reproduction and manufacture of a protected integrated circuit topography for the purposes of analysis, education, evaluation, or research.

The rights granted under the act may be transferred by the owner in whole or in part, as well as licensed. If the topography is created by an individual in the course of employment, ownership of the topography will belong to the employer or the person for whom that topography was created.

■ *Business Law* Applied

❸ **Elena Raco works** in a laboratory in which foreign viruses are analyzed. Her job is to manipulate a robotic arm that opens the tubes containing the viruses, and to squeeze the gel in which the viruses are suspended onto a specimen (Petri) dish.

While on a leave of absence from her job, Raco developed a microchip that can be installed in the robotic arm to increase its sensitivity to the pressure required to squeeze the gel out of the tubes, and reduce the risk of damaging the specimen or squirting it onto the floor.

   a) Can Raco patent the automatic robotic arm?
   b) Is there alternative protection available for the chip other than through an application for a patent for the automated arm? If so, what would it be?
   c) Who should apply under the *Integrated Circuit Topography Act* for registration of the chip, Raco or her employer?

Industrial Design

Protection under the *Industrial Design Act, R.S.C. 1985, c. 1-9* is available for any new shape, configuration, or design element that is incorporated into some useful object in which the eye sees the design as being part of the finished product.

The act gives the holder of a registered industrial design the exclusive right to stop anyone else from manufacturing or selling in Canada any item that incorporates the protected design. This protection is available for up to 10 years. For example, the shape or configuration of the package used for the display and sale of a joystick for a computer/video game might possess such visual elements that it would qualify for industrial design protection. The main criterion to remember in industrial design is that the visual design element must be part of a useful object.

■ *Critical Concepts of* Industrial Design

- The design must be new, original, and unknown in Canada longer than one year before the application for registration.
- *Registered* or *Rd* and the year of registration must be placed on the article incorporating the design, or protection is lost.

■ *Business Law*   Applied

④ **Helga Birnbaum spends** hours a day sitting on a commuter train, travelling to her job in Winnipeg. Frustrated at not being able to use her laptop effectively while travelling, she created an attachment that uses a gel to absorb the vibrations of the train. Between the layers of gel is an air chamber that can be inflated, raising the laptop to the right height for working. The gel and air chambers are encased in a one-piece, durable, non-slip rubber sheath that slips around the edges of the laptop to hold it securely in place. The whole thing has a unique appearance and seems to be one unit.

Just after completing her prototype, Birnbaum was sent overseas for a 14-month contract placement where she used the attachment daily. She has now returned to Canada and is planning to market her invention with an aim to early retirement and trips overseas for vacation only in the future.

- a) Is the laptop attachment the proper subject matter for registration as an industrial design?
- b) Is Birnbaum too late to apply for registration?
- c) Is 10 years of protection automatically granted on successful registration of the industrial design?

Copyright and Trade Secrets

In the past, ideas and information were committed to paper or canvas that could be held in your hand and read. Musical notes were written on sheet music with the lyrics below. An instruction manual was typed up and printed. Most, if not all, techniques, plans, directions, and procedures were paper based. If you wanted protection, you kept the original document containing the sensitive information in a restricted area or locked cabinet. If someone tried to remove the document or copy it, that individual would probably be noticed photocopying the pages or physically carrying the item.

Today, the computers in many companies are networked, giving access to the records and data of various departments. This information can be downloaded in seconds and transferred outside the company within minutes. There is no bulky document to remove and no extra time in which to learn of the problem and try to stop it. In addition, information itself has become a commodity carrying a dollar value, often a very high one.

Two systems of law deal with this situation: criminal law and **civil law** (the law in common law system which applies to private rights, such as contracts). Civil remedies may be based on the law of copyright and the law of trade secrets/confidentiality.

But the major principles underlying these areas of law were formulated at a time when milk was delivered in horse-drawn wagons. The laws could not have anticipated the type of technological growth nor the value that would be attached to information. Now the issue is how existing laws can be adapted by business to help in protecting its interests in the face of the unforeseen problems created by new technology.

Copyright

A computer program such as Microsoft Word or Lotus 1-2-3 takes considerable time and money to create. Unauthorized and unpaid-for copies might be obtained in various ways. It is the sale of such pirated copies of a program that drains the life blood from a business.

Since June 1988, computer programs have been specifically included in the *Copyright Act* under the definition of literary work. Section 2 of the act defines a computer program as "a set of instructions or statements, expressed, fixed, embodied or stored in any manner, that is to be used directly or indirectly in a computer in order to bring about a specific result." The author of computer software can stop anyone else from copying it—including by way of the Internet, though how this can be accomplished is a moot point.

Business Alert!

Copyright Act   The act states that in the absence of an agreement in writing stating otherwise, the author of the work is the first owner of the copyright unless that individual was employed by someone else or under a contract, and the work was done in the course of employment. In that situation, the employer would own the copyright.

Protection of Interface Elements (I Like Your Trash Can!)

The "look and feel" of the program—the way in which a user interfaces with it—is also protected. Images; moving figures; the ability to point an arrow, click a button, and remove an item from the screen—these are part of the look-and-feel element of a computer program. The images themselves (the hourglass seen frequently in MS Windows, for example) might be viewed as artistic and literary works and thus be protected by copyright.

Exceptions to Infringement

The *Copyright Act* recognizes that a business might need to adapt, modify, or convert a computer program, or possibly translate it into another language, in order to make a back-up copy or ensure compatibility with the particular system used by the business. This type of copying is exempt from being considered infringement under the act, provided such copying is authorized by the author of the program.

Making Back-ups

It is best to make sure that the contract for the sale or licensing of software includes appropriate terms and conditions that clearly state under what circumstances back-up copies or translation will be permitted.

SOFTWARE LICENCE AGREEMENT

1) Coreware Inc. grants you the right to use the Software in the quantity and on the platform(s) indicated on the proof of purchase form you received in the Software package.

2) You may make copies of the written documentation, which accompanies the Software, in support of your authorized use of the Software product. You may also make an archival copy of the Software for each Licence obtained under this agreement.

3) You may not rent or lease the Software without the written permission of Coreware. You may not decompile, disassemble, reverse engineer, copy, create a derivative work or otherwise use the Software except as stated in this agreement. Irrespective of the number of sets of media included with the Software, you are granted the right to use the Software only in the quantity indicated on the enclosed proof of purchase form. Certain qualifications may apply to the purchase of this Software; when present, they are printed on the Software package and form part of this agreement.

4) You are authorized to use a copy of the Software on a home or portable computer, as long as the extra copy is never loaded at the same time the Software is loaded on the primary computer on which you use the Software.

If other people come up with an idea for software similar to yours on their own, that is perfectly acceptable. Copyright protects only the expression of the idea, not the idea itself. A good example of this is all the different word processing programs that are now on the market—WordPerfect, Word, AmiPro, etc.—which all basically do the same things.

Business Law   Applied

⑤ **Tamara Tikal wrote** an accounting software program for small businesses that she sold, along with a manual, to some local merchants, including Duggy's Hardware. Several weeks later, Tamara was called by some hardware merchants she did not know; they had questions about how to use the program. They also wanted page 25 of the manual—it was missing from their copies. Investigation revealed that Duggy had provided copies of the program to a hardware merchants' association of which he is a member.

a) Does Tikal have a legal right to stop the association from providing either copies of her program or the manual, or both, to its members?
b) Can Tikal get the pirated copies back from those who have them?
c) If Tikal had licensed the program to Duggy, what action(s) could she take as a result of his behaviour?

Trade Secrets/Confidentiality

Before writing a new computer program, any company would have analysed the market's needs and wants, collecting lists of potential customers and much other information. Maintaining the secrecy or confidentiality of this information could be critical to the success or failure of the software program when it is finally released for sale.

New companies are always being formed in the technology industry as executives, technicians, sales personnel, and scientists establish other companies in competition with their previous employers. Often, they want to use their previous employer's marketing plans or trade secrets and confidential information, such as software programs and design elements, in their new positions.

The competition in this field is very strong. Businesses in the information technology sector regularly monitor their competitors' improvements and products. They often try to buy those items for study and analysis. If they cannot obtain the product they might try to get hold of internal documents and information by retaining someone to hack into the other company's computer system.

Trade Secrets and Employees

A firm's employees are another possible source of information. Some workers might simply be unhappy in their jobs and glad of a chance to "get at" the business; others might need the money they get from passing on confidential information. Studies show that 90 percent of the time, any security breach involving the loss of a trade secret or confidential information is due to an employee with a problem of some kind—financial difficulties, long-term illness, substance abuse, or family difficulties.

Employees have a broad knowledge base obtained from their experience with previous employers in the information technology industry. An employee cannot be prevented from using that information in a new position if it is general knowledge or a skill that has been developed as a result of employment. However, if a prior employer has given that employee information the individual knows is to be kept confidential, then legal remedies are available to stop the ex-employee from using the knowledge.

Protection of Trade Secrets

There is no statute law to protect the confidential information or trade secrets of a business. Protection is based on the legal principles available at common law and equity. It reflects the court's willingness to assist businesses in protecting themselves from being taken advantage of by those to whom they have entrusted confidential information. So, even though patent or industrial design protection might not be available, protection of confidentiality through common law and equity often will be, sometimes along with other areas of law such as copyright.

Trade secret law protects only information that is not generally known. There is no time limit to that protection, as long as the information has not become public knowledge. The idea behind trade secret law is the enforcement of the policy that confidences or secrets must be respected.

Normally, the only person that a business can sue for breach of trade secret is the person who received the information in confidence. If that individual passes it along and it becomes generally known, there is nothing that can be done about those other people who received the information from the person to whom it was originally given if they were unaware of its confidential nature. In that event, the only remedy is to try to financially recover some of what was lost from the person who betrayed your confidence. The responsibility of businesses and management for the wrongful actions of employees was discussed in Chapter 4. That responsibility also extends to a business knowingly using confidential information brought to it by a new employee.

Consultancy Contracts

It is possible to create a requirement of confidentiality by including a specific term to that effect in a contract, or by establishing a relationship that involves a fiduciary duty—for example, that owed by a director to a corporation.

A carefully worded consultancy contract would include, among other things, statements that outline:

- the confidential nature of the information
- the basis on which the information is being disclosed
- the obligations for maintaining the confidential nature of the trade secrets
- the manner in which the information is to be handled
- to whom it may be disclosed
- what use can be made of it

At the very least, a non-disclosure agreement with the consultant should be signed before revealing any information relating to your business and the purposes of the proposed consultancy arrangement.

Non-disclosure Agreements   Depending on the circumstances, a non-disclosure agreement may be enough to protect confidential information. It is usually a simple one-page document, specific to the situation, and not as lengthy or complex as an employment contract. One aim of a non-disclosure agreement is to have the person signing acknowledge that he or she did not know the information before it was disclosed and to agree not to disclose it to anyone else.

Business Alert!

Creating Confidentiality

Even if there is no written contract or relationship involving a fiduciary duty, it may still be possible to claim that the information was given in circumstances that communicated a duty of confidentiality. Confidentiality is an aspect of law currently evolving, and incorporates elements from contract, equity, and property law. It is being used to enforce the policy that, whether it be oral or written, if information is related in confidence, it must be respected and kept confidential. (See *LAC Minerals Ltd. v. International Corona Resources Ltd.*, p. 502.)

■ *Critical Concepts of* Confidential Information

Secret decoder rings or complicated handshake rituals are not necessary to obtain the protection of trade secret law. What must be established to protect sensitive information is:

■ The information is obviously of the type you want kept secret.

■ The other party should have known from the circumstances in which it received the information that it was told in confidence.

■ Without your permission, the other party used the secret information itself or told it to someone else.

Steps to Creating Confidentiality   Writing the words backwards so that the other person has to read them in a mirror might be helpful in proving that some of these elements are present, but is not necessary. What is required is the implementation of reasonable security measures to protect your trade secrets and confidential information. What is reasonable will be based on common sense in the circumstances. There are a number of practical measures which can be taken:

Business Alert!

■ Mark all hardcopy or tangible items that are truly confidential in nature with notices that they are confidential and not to be copied. The indiscriminate marking of all items as confidential may actually work to your disadvantage.

■ Put controls on who has access to the confidential data—use computer passwords that are changed on a regular basis or deleted when an employee leaves.

■ Keep the confidential information in one location that can be locked up, so that the material has to be signed out.

■ Use entry-control badges or other forms of identification.

■ Limit access to the information on a need-to-know basis.

■ Create and distribute a policy on confidentiality, advising employees on how they are to handle any confidential information or trade secret to which they may have access in the course of their employment.

■ **Encrypt** (make data on the Internet unreadable without the key for privacy and security) any high-value material by placing a code on the software requiring a password or descrambler to access the data.

encrypt
make data on the Internet unreadable without the key for privacy and security

■ Restrict the number of copies which can be made of sensitive information and, if it is to be used by outside parties, require all copies to be returned upon completion of the project along with a written certificate stating all copies have been returned or destroyed.

The bottom line is to put in place whatever measures are necessary to protect the confidential information of the business from being pirated or accessed. At the same time these measures will demonstrate the information has been consistently treated in a confidential, protected manner to ensure that it is not available to anyone other than those who have been authorized to use it.

Restrictive Covenants

The issue of whether information has been consistently treated in a confidential manner may also arise in the enforcement of non-competition or confidentiality clauses against previous employees. The purpose of such clauses is to make sure the employee does not use your confidential information for some other employer or for personal benefit when he or she is no longer in your employ. It must be reasonable in the circumstances. It must also relate to trade secrets that have a commercial value and that have been treated consistently in a confidential manner.

Protecting Information from Employee Abuse

Other practical methods may also help protect confidential information or trade secrets from misuse by employees. Putting employee support programs in place to help deal with drugs, alcohol, or family problems could help avoid such situations entirely. Some businesses offer cash incentives for ideas submitted by employees for new products that they might want to pursue, as well as bonuses paid for ideas that result in a successful industrial design or patent application. The philosophy behind this approach is to stop the theft before it ever happens.

Another active step is to hold a termination interview when an employee leaves to remind that individual of the obligations about confidentiality that were taken on when the employment contract was signed. Some businesses have also adopted a policy of making employees aware of the personal financial consequences of information theft. Infringement of intellectual property rights could result in stiff fines or other penalties. It is also possible that an employer could launch a civil action against the individual—resulting in serious financial consequences for the employee.

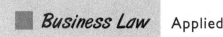

Business Law Applied

⑥ **Jean interviewed Salim** and Alex for a position with her new business to develop highly confidential software for drug companies. For a particular project she required the skills of both applicants. Jean decided to hire Salim as an employee of the company and Alex only for the particular project.

    a) What steps should Jean take in her employment arrangements with Salim?
    b) In what capacity is Alex being hired?
    c) What concerns might Jean have in her arrangement with Alex and what measures can she take directly with Alex to resolve those concerns?
    d) What internal company policies could you suggest to Jean to protect the confidentiality of the information?

Criminal Law

Misuse of confidential information through either the elimination of or interference with data carries the possibility of a criminal prosecution and a criminal record. The criminal offences most likely to arise where there has been an unauthorized or illegal taking of confidential information or a trade secret by an employee are theft, fraud, unauthorized computer use, and mischief in relation to data *(Criminal Code, R.S.C. 1985, c. C-46, s. 322, 342.1, 380,* and *430 (1.1)* respectively).

The liability extends further than just the individual who has committed the criminal act. An ex-employee's new employer may also be held liable if the knowledge or information that the new employee brings is used for the benefit of the new employer. If the new employee has a disk containing confidential marketing information, or a copy of a software program, or has knowledge that would be considered a trade secret or confidential information and that will be used for the benefit of the new employer's business—then the ex-employee may be facing possible imprisonment, and the new employer's business or corporation, as well as the officers and directors, could be fined and required to hand over any monetary gains resulting from the ex-employee's criminal act.

Theft

Theft (section 322 of the Criminal Code) is the intentional and unauthorized taking of another person's property dishonestly and with knowledge that there was no right to do so. It can take any form—from an ex-employee's removing documents, design printouts, or computer disks with information stored on them, to a stranger's entering the premises and taking a prototype. It could also involve the theft of an idea that has been written on a piece of paper—stealing an idea is not a criminal offence, but taking the paper (tangible property) is.

Theft—Canadian Criminal Code, R.S.C. 1985, c. C-46

---

s. 322. (1) Every one commits theft who fraudulently and without colour of right takes, or fraudulently and without colour of right converts to his use or to use of another person, anything whether animate or inanimate, with intent,

   (a) to deprive, temporarily or absolutely, the owner of it, or a person who has a special property or interest in it, of the thing or of his property or interest in it;
   (b) to pledge it or deposit it as security;
   (c) to part with it under a condition with respect to its return that the person who parts with it may be unable to perform; or
   (d) to deal with it in such a manner that it cannot be restored in the condition in which it was at the time it was taken or converted.

s. 334. Except where otherwise provided by law, every one who commits theft

   (a) is guilty of an indictable offence and liable to imprisonment for a term not exceeding ten years, . . . where the value of what is stolen exceeds five thousand dollars,
   (b) is guilty
      (i) of an indictable offence and is liable to imprisonment for a term not exceeding two years, or
      (ii) of an offence punishable on summary conviction, where the value of what is stolen does not exceed five thousand dollars.

R. v. Stewart, [1988] 1 S.C.R. 963 (S.C.C.)a

The accused, Stewart, was asked by a representative of a union seeking to form a bargaining unit in a large hotel complex employing approximately 600 people to obtain the names, addresses, and telephone numbers of the employees. The information, which was confidential, could be obtained only through the personnel files or a payroll computer printout.

Stewart contacted a security worker at the hotel and offered to pay for the information. He suggested the information be secretly copied from the confidential records without removing or otherwise affecting the records themselves. Stewart was charged with counselling a hotel employee to commit the offence of theft by stealing information which was the property of the hotel and its employees.

The Supreme Court's Decision

The court held that confidential information is not considered property under the Criminal Code and that if information of a commercial value is to be given protection through the Criminal Code, it should be left to Parliament to enact laws that did so. Confidential information is not tangible property. The accused's conviction for theft at the appeal court level was reversed.

The court went on to consider whether the confidentiality of the information could be the subject of theft. It decided that since the confidential nature of the information cannot be taken or converted in a way that would deprive the owner of the use or possession of the information, confidentiality itself cannot be the subject of theft.

Fraud

If the actual document or disk containing the information is not taken, but an unauthorized copy of it is made with the intention of using the material in a way that would or could cause a financial loss to the original owner of the property, the offence of fraud has been committed.

The criminal offence of fraud (section 380(1) of the Criminal Code) occurs when someone is defrauded of any property, money, or valuable security, by deceit, falsehood, or other fraudulent means. In essence, this means any act that would be considered dishonest by a reasonable person and that is done with the intention of causing an economic loss to the victim. That economic loss might occur through either an actual loss or merely by putting the victim's economic interests at risk.

R. v. Ram, [1987] 47 Can. Computer L.R. 109

Mr. Ram had operated a business through which, for several months in 1985, he copied without permission and sold computer software (Display Write 2) and a manual owned and copyrighted by IBM Corporation. During that same period, Ram had also copied and sold without permission computer software and a manual entitled Advanced Productivity Systems, owned and copyrighted by Arrix Logic Systems Incorporated.

The Court's Decision

The court held that the unauthorized reproduction of the software and the manuals caused a risk of economic loss to the software manufacturers. Ram was convicted on three counts of fraud involving the unauthorized reproduction of software and computer manuals. He was given a jail sentence and also put on probation for three years, during which time he was required not to take part in any business that made copies of computer software for renting or resale.

Unauthorized Use of a Computer

The unauthorized use of a computer (section 342.1 of the Criminal Code) is aimed at protecting the privacy of your computer system from people who might try to intercept your data, either directly at the source or from a remote location. The actions of hackers who enter your system and retrieve computer programs or data from your files would fall within this section of the Criminal Code.

An example of this type of activity involved a hacker who broke into a telemarketing firm's database, getting names, credit card numbers, and expiry dates. He used the credit card numbers to make purchases and generously shared some of the numbers with friends. To avoid detection, he reformatted his hard drive and reinstalled all his programs. Unfortunately, the RCMP's High Tech Crime Section recovered enough file fragments to allow the telemarketing firm to confirm that the information had been copied from its database. The hacker was outsmarted and convicted.

For the purposes of section 342.1, "computer service" includes data processing and the storage and retrieval of data, while "computer system" is defined to include a computer program. Unauthorized computer use occurs when, without authorization, a computer service is intentionally obtained, or data is intentionally retrieved. It also occurs when a function of a computer system (for example, data processing) is intentionally intercepted by a computer system being used for that purpose. Consequently, if an employee dishonestly and without authority were to use a new employer's computer system with the intention of accessing a previous employer's computer service or intercepting communications within the previous employer's computer system, then likely the offence of unauthorized use has occurred.

Mischief Related to Data

The aim of section 430 (1.1) is to control, for example, the actions of people who might access a computer system and encrypt a software program so that the owner is unable to get into the data. As another example, the records of an intensive care unit in a Los Angeles hospital were tapped into by a hacker who, with a warped sense of humour, altered the data in the computer system by doubling the dosage of medication for all the patients.

Section 430 (1.1) of the Criminal Code states:

Every one commits mischief who willfully

(a) destroys or alters data;
(b) renders data meaningless, useless or ineffective;
(c) obstructs, interrupts or interferes with the lawful use of data; or
(d) obstructs, interrupts or interferes with any person in the lawful use of data or denies access to data to any person who is entitled to access thereto.

The offence of mischief in relation to data includes both data as it is usually understood as well as computer programs. Computer programs are defined to mean data that represent instructions and statements that, when executed in a computer system, cause the computer system to perform a function.

The combination of sections 342.1 (unauthorized use) and 430 (1.1) (mischief related to data) will certainly help deal with problems unique to the area of information technology, such as computer viruses, mail bombs, and time bombs. Should an unhappy employee, when creating a piece of software, deliberately implant a time bomb or virus to destroy the program after a certain period of use or if some future event occurs, such as the employee's termination, the act of implanting the virus or time bomb would fall within the offence of unauthorized use of a computer (section 342.1). If, when the time bomb goes off or the virus surfaces, data is destroyed, that act would be seen as mischief in relation to data and an offence under section 430(1.1).

■ *Critical Concepts of* Criminal Liability

Criminal responsibility for wrongful actions related to information and technology will likely fall within the following four sections of the Criminal Code, depending on the nature of the action and the item affected:

■ Section 322 (theft) will assist if a disk or some tangible property is removed without authority. It is of no assistance at this point in protecting such intangible elements as confidentiality or information itself.

■ Section 80 (fraud) may be available for actions that do not constitute theft but are dishonest acts done with the intention of using the commercially valuable information or technology to cause or threaten to cause the victim an economic loss.

■ Section 342.1 (unauthorized use of a computer) may be available for retrieving data (a "computer service") or downloading a computer program (a "computer system") intentionally and without authorization, whether at source or remotely, which may be seen as the criminal offence of unauthorized, punishable in certain circumstances by a prison term of up to 10 years.

■ Section 430 (1.1) (mischief related to data) may apply for willful destruction, interference with, or interruption of data or computer programs or access to them, which constitute the crime of mischief related to data. An action which attracts the criminal liability of section 342.1 will often entail liability under section 430 (1.1) as well.

■ *Business Law* Applied

❼ Using his own disks, Jody Canard made copies of a software program used by his employer for calculating the odds for bets placed on horse races. Each night before leaving work, he would print out 10 hardcopies of the five-page manual for the program on coloured paper he had bought for that purpose. Jody would then sell the manual along with copies of the program at the racetrack.

Jody was fired when his employer learned of his activities. However, before being escorted from the building, Jody had an opportunity to access the software and change some of the data so that the odds would be miscalculated in a subtle but effective way.

a) Explain whether Jody has committed one or more of the offences of: theft; fraud; unauthorized use of a computer; mischief related to data.

Business Practices

The protection afforded information technology by the various areas of law does not always come from the enforcement of legal rights once a problem has surfaced. The various areas of law can also be used to create a legal framework in which the parties have a clear understanding of their rights and duties from the start. This goes a long way toward avoiding the expense of having the courts enforce your rights.

The legal principles discussed in this text provide the tools to ensure effective business operations. The procedures, policies, and decisions made by a business put them to work. As an example, to help in establishing the confidential nature of your information to obtain protection under trade secrecy law, consider implementing procedures such as those suggested in this chapter.

Business Alert!

Negotiating Contracts   When entering into contract negotiations, keep in mind that there are particular issues related to information technology that are most effectively handled through a structured contract format. For example, transfer of ownership of copyright in software must be put in writing whether you are hiring someone to develop software for you or purchasing your software from another. The purchase of new hardware or software should involve some element of acceptance testing before delivery and payment in full occurs. If the new technology must be integrated into an existing system, a definition of integration, an allocation of responsibility, and the tests or dates for its accomplishment will assist both vendor and purchaser in creating a smooth, effective business relationship because legal obligations have been clearly set out.

Limiting Liability through Contract

Compliance with statutes such as the provincial *Sale of Goods Act* may also need to be addressed through the contract or the business procedures of the company.

Warranties, conditions, and limitation of liability are key issues to include in any contract. The following are typical examples of some clauses found in a licensing agreement for software.

LIMITED WARRANTY/LIMITATION OF LIABILITY

This Software is licensed AS IS. IF FOR ANY REASON YOU ARE DISSATIS-FIED WITH IT, RETURN THE SOFTWARE, INCLUDING ALL MATERI-ALS, WITH PROOF OF PURCHASE TO (NAME OF COMPANY) WITHIN 90 DAYS OF THE DATE OF PURCHASE FOR A FULL REFUND. If any materials or media in this package are defective, return them within 90 days of the date of purchase, and they will be replaced at no charge.

THESE WARRANTIES ARE IN LIEU OF ANY OTHER WARRANTIES, EXPRESS OR IMPLIED, INCLUDING THE IMPLIED WARRANTIES OF MERCHANTABILITY AND FITNESS FOR A PARTICULAR PURPOSE. IN NO EVENT WILL (NAME OF COMPANY) BE LIABLE TO YOU FOR DAMAGES, INCLUDING ANY LOSS OF PROFITS, LOST SAVINGS, OR OTHER INCIDENTAL OR CONSEQUENTIAL DAMAGES ARISING OUT OF YOUR USE OF OR INABILITY TO USE THE SOFTWARE, EVEN IF (NAME OF COMPANY) OR AN AUTHORIZED (NAME OF COMPANY) REPRESENTATIVE HAS BEEN ADVISED OF THE POSSIBILITY OF SUCH DAMAGES.

Some jurisdictions do not allow excluding or limiting implied warranties, or limiting liability for incidental or consequential damages, and some jurisdictions have special statutory consumer protection provisions which may supersede this limitation. As a result, this limitation of liability may not apply to you if it is prohibited by the laws of your jurisdiction.

Consumers' Association of Canada v. Hamilton-Avnet International (Canada) Ltd. et al., [1984] 23 A.C.W.S. (2d) 59

Consumers' Association of Canada purchased computer components from Hamilton-Avnet, which were to be linked together to create an operating system. Because of a limited budget, the purchase of a system already set up was not possible, but both Hamilton-Avnet and the association believed a volunteer worker for the plaintiff had the necessary expertise to link the components together. The volunteer was not able to make the components link up and the association sued for the return of the purchase price.

The Court's Decision

The court held that the Consumers' Association of Canada did not rely on Hamilton-Avnet's expertise. The association's dealings with Hamilton-Avnet were dominated by issues of price. The *Sale of Goods Act* did not apply. The association had purchased separate components which were both merchantable and fit for the general purpose sold. The association was bound to the contract, including the limitation clause, and the action was dismissed.

■■■ *Critical Concepts of* Creating Effective Contracts

To create an effective and efficient contract:

■ identify what issues are essential to successful completion of the contract

■ ensure that there are terms and conditions present to deal with these items.

Should problems arise, these are the legal issues which will be addressed by the court in determining the parties' rights.

e-commerce

doing business on the Internet

E-Commerce

New forums for doing business have been created along with, and as a result of, the advances in information technology—the Internet, the World Wide Web, and e-mail (electronic mail), to name a few. The rules and regulations applying to doing business in a traditional form also apply in these new arenas. Vendor permits and licences must be obtained when required, and income tax will have to be paid. If an action is illegal or against public policy, its nature does not change just because of the use of an electronic medium. The distribution of child pornography is a criminal offence and remains so on the Internet. Although it may often be very difficult and time consuming for the authorities to trace the offender, it can be done.

R. v. Pecciarich, [1995] 22 O.R. (3d) 748

The accused was charged with distributing child pornography. Using the code name "Recent Zephyr," he had uploaded to a computer bulletin board (BBS) files consisting of images and text that were found to be obscene or pornographic. That BBS was accessible through the Internet, and the files could be downloaded by anybody.

The Court's Decision

Evidence established that the accused was Recent Zephyr, and it was admitted that the images and text were obscene and pornographic. The court held that, as a matter of law, uploading files onto a computer BBS where the public has access to them was distribution of pornography, and a conviction was entered.

Deleted, Not Erased

Other unanticipated problems may arise from the benefits created by advanced technology. E-mail is used by millions of people in the workplace as well as at home via the Internet. Depending on the type of hardware and software used, e-mail messages may remain hidden in a computer storage system long after they have vanished from the screen. This ability to recall a message may prove to be a double-edged sword. While an employer may be able to call back an accidentally deleted e-mail message containing a suggestion for a marketing plan, it is also possible for an unfriendly individual to do the same.

This technology has enabled electronic private-eye firms to make a profitable living from simply reconstructing deleted e-mail to obtain incriminating evidence. In the United States there have been several cases in which e-mail was used as evidence, often promoting a settlement rather than a court trial. For example, DuPont waged a battle against hundreds of lawsuits for crop damage alleged to have been caused by a defective fungicide. However, many of these actions—including one for US$4.5 million—were settled after a DuPont scientist, in an e-mail message, appeared to admit a "labelling mistake" by DuPont on the fungicide's instructions for use.

Deleting Data   When data is deleted, the computer usually simply changes the first letter of the file name to an asterisk so that the data cannot be called up. However, the data may physically still remain on the hard drive. Many systems now feature an "undelete" function to permit the information to be retrieved. Only if other data is written to the disk on top of the old does the earlier file become irretrievable.

Experts say never sell a hard drive—always destroy it. If a company is considering selling its used equipment, the components containing memory should be thoroughly checked to ensure any data has been truly deleted. Valuable information has been obtained through the purchase of used equipment and an undelete function key, much to a competitor's delight.

Privacy

The privacy of your electronic correspondence and business information as well as of electronic communications is, obviously, a concern.

It is now possible to obtain a loan from some financial institutions over the Internet. What level of comfort should a business require when providing the necessary financial, marketing, and income records over the Internet, and what can it realistically expect from the level of the technology available? Although the Criminal Code and other areas of law provide remedies, you must first be able to detect that someone has intercepted the information or data and then trace it back.

The financial institution considering the Internet loan application will provide a response within minutes. While the customer waits, the lending institution is checking with a credit reference company to determine the risks of making a loan to the business. An individual or business's credit record contains information ranging from the type of material read or ordered, to the purchases made on the last trip overseas, business or personal. Every survey completed, every transaction paid for by a credit card, and countless other sources, provide information relating to a business's operations. This is collated, sorted, categorized, and stored as data in a memory bank.

Concerns must arise as to the accuracy of the data. What if there is an error in inputting the information? What if the data suggests an inaccurate pattern of business behaviour or spending? This information might be interpreted as a problem by a financial institution considering a loan application, a potential employer, or a crucial supplier considering the payment terms on which it will supply inventory.

Business Advantage

The trademark a business uses becomes a valuable asset and plays a vital role in developing goodwill within the information technology sector. The choice of a distinctive mark, symbol, word, or slogan is an important marketing tool requiring protection. The trademark adopted will distinguish the products or services of one business from those that are being provided by someone else.

Because technology is changing so fast, businesses should be aware of new opportunities in which to use a trademark as well as new areas from which it may need protection. It is uncertain, for example, whether a trademark registration using the word *Internet* can be claimed by any company as a property right, although several companies have registered names incorporating that word for various services.

A business considering the Internet for the purposes of marketing or sales should ensure its use of the trademark by registering it as an Internet address. Registration is available only as a business service and not a government protection of that mark. Individuals or businesses on the Internet are given an address that is based on a name (for example, *isolde@found.net*). Generally, there is no central monitoring agency, and anyone can register an address for the purposes of

Business Alert!

marketing products, services, or information on the Internet. The Net has become a major marketing tool in a very short period of time. If some other business or individual used an address that incorporated your trademark, that trademark's value to you would be much reduced. Many of these same concerns arise around the creation of websites and pages.

Remedies

In order to ensure the enforcement of a right within the area of information technology, it must, as in all other areas of business, fall within the protection offered by existing legal principles. And these principles, because of unforeseen technological advancements and applications, are often stretched to the limit to offer protection, and in some instances may leave certain elements unprotected.

A legal action must be based on some principle of law for the courts to have jurisdiction over the matter. In the realm of information technology the primary areas are likely to be the law of contract, property, intellectual property, tort, or equity (breach of confidence).

The remedy requested from the court will depend on the injury the business has suffered. Speedy remedies such as an interim injunction might be required to stop another business's advertising campaign if you believe that it is based on information that has been obtained through theft. This type of remedy allows the infringing action to be halted until the trial of the issue, in this example, breach of confidence or the tort of conversion, has taken place.

Another possible interim remedy is an Anton Piller order, which is the civil action's equivalent to the criminal law order permitting search and seizure. This remedy would be available, for example, in the event that pirated copies of a business's software are being distributed and there are either verifiable suspicions or strong reasons to believe that evidence is being held in a particular location and, unless it is obtained now, it will probably be destroyed prior to the trial of the legal issue.

The permanent remedies available under contract law, such as damages or specific performance, would be used in the event the other party fails to honour contractual obligations such as are found in a licensing agreement or employment contract. These remedies, along with permanent injunctions, accounting for profits, delivery up of all the infringing material by the defendant to the plaintiff, damages, and passing off are discussed in the various chapters detailing the legal principles giving rise to the right or duty which is being protected.

In Summation

Information technology law is the application of a number of rights from various areas of law which consider new problems created by advances in technology and the increasing value of information. The main areas of law relevant to information technology are:

Intellectual Property Law

- patents
- *Integrated Circuit Topography Act*
- industrial design
- copyright
- confidential information/trade secrets
- trademarks

Contract Law

- licensing agreements
- exemption (limitation of liability) clause
- confidentiality clause
- non-competition clause
- co-employee enticement clause

Criminal Law

- theft
- fraud
- unauthorized use of a computer
- mischief relating to data

Tort Law

- defamation
- conversion

Patents

Computer hardware innovation can be patented. Computer software cannot be patented in Canada but it can be in the U.S. A computer program which is a necessary component of a new machine or process can be protected as part of the patent for the new machine.

Copyright

Software is subject to copyright protection.

Topography Act

Computer chips do not fall into the category of intellectual property, and so a new *Integrated Circuit Topography Act* was passed to protect them. The protection is the exclusive right to manufacture or sell that specific integrated circuit topography for 10 years.

Industrial Design

This applies to the visual aspect of design in a functional product.

Protection of Business Secrets

Advances in technology have made theft of business secrets by insiders and outsiders easy. The most effective legal protections are found in the areas of trade secrets/confidentiality, copyright, and criminal law.

Trade Secrets/Confidentiality

The legal protection for business secrets has expanded as the importance of information has increased. There are three main areas of civil law for the protection of business secrets.

- contract—by specific terms
- fiduciary duty—created by an employment relationship
- confidentiality—created by obviously confidential information being given to a person clearly in confidence

Criminal Law

While theft was surprisingly interpreted by the court not to cover information because it was not property in law, the traditional crime of fraud may apply to technology information theft. There are two new Criminal Code provisions directly relating to computer crime.

- unauthorized use of a computer
- mischief relating to data

Purchasing Technology

The usual contractual concerns apply to purchasing technology. Make certain you understand what is warranted and what is not, and for how long. Test it out at your location and have contractual terms to allow you to verify that the technology works in your business situation with your equipment.

Remedies

The remedy under criminal law is to go to the police. The civil rights all give rise to civil remedies. The most relevant of these are:

- damage for:
  - breach of contract
  - infringement of copyright
  - trademark, patent, industrial design
- injunction
- civil search warrant

Closing Questions

Information Technology Law

1. Is it true that an Anton Piller order will not be granted unless an extremely strong case is made out by the defendant?

2. The research and development department for Loxana Industries, a microchip company, announces that it is launching the first android operating with a neural network very similar to a human brain. This development has been made possible by a chip which uses a topography identical to the human brain for certain neural pathways.
   a) Discuss some of the difficulties Loxana Industries would encounter if it attempted to patent the prototype of its chip in Canada.
   b) Explain what types of protection, if any, are available for this chip in Canada.

3. HiMem Corp. is considering automating its accounting and inventory systems, which are still manual operations. It will require hardware and a custom-written software program. Kimber, vice-president of finance, was asked to write a memo to the board of directors discussing four areas which he sees will lead to problems later on if they are not dealt with during the procurement/contract negotiation process. Kimber hasn't a clue.
   "What do they expect? I'm not a lawyer," he complained to you at a party last night. Handing him your business card as president of Ghostwriters Inc., you suggested he call as you had taken an excellent law course. A desperate Kimber has e-mailed you with the request that you prepare the memo in his name for the board. In the hope of getting a raise, he has also asked you to include suggestions as to how these problems can be avoided or planned for.
   a) Draft a memo on behalf of Kimber dealing with the issues he has indicated.

4. Based on the *R. v. Stewart* case (p. 518), is it true that legal protection for trade secrets is based on statute law? Explain your decision.

5. Explain whether an inventor may still claim the protection of confidentiality for information disclosed in a patent application filed with the government.

6. You have registered your copyright in a very successful video game. You discover that Harry Flash, who has been sued for this sort of thing before, has launched a marketing campaign for an exact copy of your program under his own name. You first realized that there was something wrong when your sales orders suddenly dropped. You are not going to make anything like your expected profits. Through various sources you have very strong and reliable evidence that a large number of disks with your program and Harry's name on them are being stored in a warehouse belonging to Harry. Discuss in detail and evaluate:
   a) the benefits of the various remedies available to you to stop Harry Flash
   b) on what basis you could sue Harry and what you might expect from the court if you are successful in your action

7. Arnie, a stockbroker, worked from a home office with his computer and modem and a link-up to Index High, the brokerage house where he was employed. He decided to upgrade his system and placed an advertisement selling off his old components.

   Maxine, a competitor, saw Arnie's ad in the paper and decided to purchase the central processing unit from the old system. At home, Maxine connected the purchased unit to her system and when she turned it on, Arnie's client files began to appear on her screen. Gleefully, Maxine printed out the information and began to call Arnie's clients with reasons why they should switch to her employer, not least of which was lack of security at Index High's office.

   When clients began to phone to complain about their files being given to a rival broker, the president of Index High called Arnie for an explanation. "Oops," was the response. Arnie is now giving stock advice to patrons at the Burger Barn and Rib Emporium between taking orders.
   a) What remedies are available to Index High and against whom for the loss of clients resulting from Arnie's actions?
   b) Explain the basis for any court action Index High might take.
   c) What remedies are available to Index High's clients for the actions that have taken place? Against whom would those remedies be made?

8. Compare and contrast the different kinds of protection for intellectual property in relation to computer products and services. What do you think about the reasons that are generally given as to why we protect such kinds of property when they are applied to information technology?

9. You have been operating a computer consulting business in Toronto for six years under the name Computers for You. In the past six months your business has fallen to half its normal amount. Recently, you saw a van with the name Computers 4 U printed on its side, parked outside a building where one of your clients is located. You telephoned the number printed on the side of the van to complain about the name they are operating under and were told, "Tough terminals, buddy."
   a) Explain (with reasons) what remedies, if any, are available to stop your competitor from using the name Computers 4 U.

10. A friend of yours who developed a unique software package has just telephoned for advice. Apparently, an unhappy employee who had been terminated on Friday, accessed the computer system over the weekend and uploaded the software onto the Internet. Calls are coming in from all over the world from people who have downloaded the program and want to obtain the next version of the software when it comes available.
   a) Advise your friend if there is anything she can do about the actions of Rex, her ex-employee.
   b) Identify and explain to her the intellectual-property law issues which have arisen now that the software is on the Internet. How does this situation affect copyright? How does it affect confidentiality?
   c) Do the implied warranties and conditions of the relevant *Sale of Goods* legislation help the people who have downloaded the software but are experiencing problems with it?
   d) Assuming clever Rex used his own phone to do the deed and it can be traced back to him, explain what criminal charges, if any, he might face.

Websites

www.cybercrime.gov—U.S. Department of Justice site devoted exclusively to cyber crimes.

www.mcconnellinternational.com—Reports of private organizations on cyber crimes.

Real Estate

General Concepts

Karl Marx believed that whoever controlled the land controlled a country's economy. The American humorist Will Rogers is famous for rephrasing Marx's principle as "Buy land; they're not making it anymore." The importance of land in the economic development of a country has long been recognized, and land law was one of the first branches of the law to develop. As a result, most of the legal terms and rules used in land laws today were first heard in medieval times.

Land has always been recognized as unique. One area of land is not interchangeable with another. A hectare of land at the busiest intersection of the main street of a large city is worth far more than a hectare of land a few blocks away. Land on a hill overlooking the ocean has a view that cannot be valued in money. In medieval times, a court action claiming compensation other than money was called a real action. An action respecting land had to be brought procedurally by way of a real action. Land, then, took on the name *real estate*.

What Is Land?

Land includes the surface of the land, all that is under the surface (including the minerals and oil), and everything above the surface permanently fixed, such as buildings. It includes all that is attached to it—trees, fences, buildings, and so on. A deed to land might therefore describe that land in measurement terms only, making no mention of anything that is on it. However, because of the legal concept of land, all **fixtures** (objects that are permanently attached or fixed to land or to a building) automatically go with the land. So, if you lease a house and build a garage beside it, the garage is considered part of the land. The landowner automatically owns the garage.

In earlier times, it was said that land rights extended down to the core of the earth and upwards to heaven. Since the time of that rather idealistic image, the practical realities of modern living have severely restricted the use of air space. The right of aircraft to fly over land without having to pay anything to the property's owners is one example. Similarly, ownership of land does not always mean possession of mineral rights to the area. In mining areas, it is not unusual to find that the deed of land does not convey the right to mine the minerals. That right has been sold by a previous owner to a mining and exploration company. Grants of land from the Crown typically contain a clause that the mineral rights are kept by the Crown.

land
the surface of the land, all that is under the surface (including the minerals and oil), and everything above the surface permanently fixed, such as buildings

fixtures
objects that are permanently attached or fixed to land or to a building

Types of Ownership

In feudal times, it was established in England that the Crown owned all of the land, and that the nobles merely held that land for the Crown. They, in turn, were able to grant a portion of their estates to their vassals. Ownership of land then became known as an estate in land. That concept is maintained in law today. While we say that a person owns a house, in law, the Crown owns the house and that person holds the fee simple estate.

The monarch of Britain is still nominally the head of state in Canada, and so the federal government is referred to as the Crown. Thus, government-owned land is called Crown land.

■ Critical Concepts of States in Land

The only relevant estates today are:

- estate in fee simple
- life estate
- leasehold
- condominiums

Legalese

Tenant   The current meaning of **tenant** is someone who rents a building, apartment, or house from a landlord. The original meaning of tenant is derived from the Latin *tenure*, to hold. The tenant is one who holds land.

Fee Simple

fee simple

the highest form of ownership of land in law, allowing a person to dispose of the land during life or after death

Fee simple is the technical term for what is commonly called ownership of land. It is the highest form of ownership of land in law, allowing a person to dispose of the land during life or after death.

Life Estate

life estate

an estate in land that lasts only while the person is alive

A **life estate** is an estate in land that lasts only while the person is alive. It is created when the owner of a property in fee simple divides the ownership and use of that property. Usually used within a family arrangement, the owner in fee simple gives the fee simple interest to one person or retains it himself while giving a lifetime right to use the land to another. The person who holds the fee simple interest subject to the life estate is said to have the remainder, or reversion, interest. The existence of a life estate usually makes it impossible to sell the land, as the purchaser would be subject to the life estate as well.

Leasehold Estate

leasehold

an interest in land for a period of time created by a lease

A **leasehold** estate is commonly called a lease. It is an interest in land for a period of time created by a lease. The landlord gives the tenant a right to exclusive possession of the property for a limited time—a term. At the end of the term, the tenant's right to occupy reverts to the landlord.

The rights concerning the property are split. The tenant has the right to occupy, while the landlord has the right to enforce the terms of the lease (primarily, collect the rent) and the right to repossess the property at the end of the lease. The landlord has no right to occupy the property if it is leased out, unless specifically given that right in the terms of the lease.

Business Law Applied

① **Angela Bennett buys** a hectare of land from the Crown and builds a house on it. She rents the house to Carol Dodd for two years. About three months into the lease, Bennett is driving by and sees that Dodd is out and has left every light on in the house.

Muttering about the waste of electricity, Bennett uses her key, goes in, and turns off all the lights. Dodd learns of this, is furious, and wants Bennett charged with trespassing. Bennett says that is nonsense; she has every right to enter the house since she is the owner.

a) What is the legal name for Angela Bennett's ownership of the land she purchases from the Crown?
b) What is the legal name for Angela Bennett's and Carol Dodd's interest in the renting of the house?
c) Does Bennett have the right to enter the house as she did?

Condominiums

Land law has not changed significantly in its basic theories since medieval times. However, one particular new concept of ownership, or estate in land, has developed in the last 40 or so years—the condominium. Shortage of land created the need for a combination of individual and shared ownership, and this is the basis of condominium properties. Condominium projects take many forms: some are apartment buildings; others are row houses; others are detached dwellings. Some office buildings, too, have become condominiums in recent years. A **condominium corporation** is a corporation allowing a way of holding property co-operatively, in which the members are the unit owners.

In condominium ownership, an individual owns one unit in a larger development, such as an apartment building, townhouse complex, or office block. As well as owning the actual unit, that person also owns a share of all of the other features necessary for the running of the project as a tenant in common. These are known as the **common elements**, the structures and areas external to a unit in a condominium, including hallways, elevators, swimming pools, and such.

condominium corporation
a corporation allowing a way of holding property co-operatively, in which the members are the unit owners

common elements
the structures and areas external to a unit in a condominium, including hallways, elevators, swimming pools, and such

Condominiums

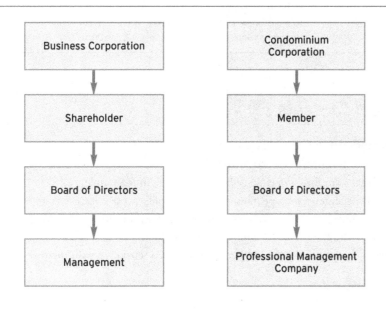

The individual owner has the right to exclusive possession of the unit owned, and a membership in the condominium corporation which has control over all of the common elements. The condominium corporation functions like a normal corporation; however, the homeowners are called *members* rather than *shareholders*. The day-to-day running of the corporation is usually looked after by a professional management company.

Tenancy in Common

Tenancy in common

co-ownership of land whereby each owner can deal separately with his or her interest, may have unequal interest, and can sell his or her interest or dispose of it by will

When two or more people own property together, they are called either tenants in common or joint tenants. **Tenancy in common** is co-ownership of land whereby each owner can deal separately with his or her interest, may have unequal interest, and can sell his or her interest or dispose of it by will. This is one type of estate in fee simple.

Joint Tenancy

joint tenancy

shared ownership with right of survivorship

Joint tenants are equal owners with a unique type of relationship, known as the right of survivorship. **Joint tenancy** is shared ownership with right of survivorship. If one of the joint tenants dies, the surviving tenant automatically becomes the sole owner. The deceased's interest is considered to have died with the owner. A joint tenant cannot will an interest in the property to a third party, because at death that interest has ceased to exist. Most husbands and wives hold the matrimonial home in joint tenancy.

Joint tenants can break a joint tenancy by severing, so that it is then changed to a tenancy in common. The normal way of doing this is to transfer the interest to another person. Of course, a person cannot benefit from a wrongful act—AB could not kill CD and thereby become sole owner.

While the term *co-owners* is used, it is not a legal term. Co-owners are either joint tenants or tenants in common.

Property

Property is divided into three classes:

Real Property	Personal Property	Intellectual Property
Land—subsisting soil plus fixtures.	*Tangible property* (hard assets)—car, inventory. *Intangible property* (conceptual assets)—right to collect on a bill sent to a customer, right to withdraw money on deposit in a bank.	*Ideas*—creative works, as embodied in books, music, visual art, etc. and/or protected through patents and copyright.

■ *Critical Concepts of* Real Estate

- Land includes all things affixed to it.
- All land is technically owned by the Crown.
- The legal term for ownership of land is an estate in fee simple.
- Sole ownership is one type of estate in fee simple.
- Joint tenancy has the right of survivorship, which means that the deceased's right ceases and the surviving joint tenant becomes the sole owner.
- Tenants in common are co-owners who can deal separately with their interest.

Business Law   Applied

② **Adam Barnes sells** his house to Cliff Dares. Before the date of closing, Barnes removes the garage from the house and sets it up at his farm. Barnes claims he did not sell it to Dares, as it is not specified in the agreement of purchase and sale.

   a) Is Barnes correct?

③ **Brothers Don and** Jon Davis own an apartment building in joint tenancy. The brothers are on bad terms. Don Davis dies and, in his will, leaves his interest in the apartment building to his son.

   a) Does his son own the interest in the building?
   b) If Don Davis had transferred his interest to his son before he died, would that transfer be effective?
   c) What type of ownership would the son have with his uncle?

④ **Amy Bondi and** Calvin Donald are business associates and hold a piece of vacant land in joint tenancy. The land goes up in value. Donald experiences severe financial difficulties and murders Bondi.

   a) Does Calvin Donald becomes the sole owner of the property?

⑤ **Ron Starr and** Cynthia Brookes are married, and they own two vacant lots. Lot A is owned in joint tenancy, and Lot B is held as tenants in common. In his will, Starr leaves his interest in Lot A to his son, and his interest in Lot B to his daughter.

   a) Does the son become owner of the interest in Lot A?
   b) Does the daughter become owner of the interest in Lot B?

Other Rights over Land

Other rights over land are termed interests lesser than estates. Such interests give the right to use the land for a limited purpose, but do not give exclusive possession. The most common are:

- easements
- licences

Easements

An **easement** is a right enjoyed by one landowner over the land of another for a particular purpose, such as access to water, but not for occupation of the land. The most common easement is a **right of way** (an easement that gives the holder a right to pass back and forth over the land of another in order to get to and from his or her own land). Mutual driveways are examples of easements. Each owner owns the half of the driveway on that individual's side of the property, and has an easement for the use of the other half.

There are also statutory easements for public utility and telephone companies, giving such firms the right to lay cables and enter properties for maintenance and repair.

easement

a right enjoyed by one landowner over the land of another for a particular purpose, such as access to water, but not for occupation of the land

right of way

an easement that gives the holder a right to pass back and forth over the land of another in order to get to and from his or her own land

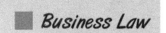

Business Law Applied

❻ **Two neighbours,** Anthony Bello and Doug Coombes, share a mutual driveway. Over some time, they start to quarrel. Out of spite, Bello leaves a garbage can on his side of the property, blocking use of the driveway. When asked to remove it, Bello tells Coombes that the garbage can is on Bello's own land and he has a right to put it there. In retaliation, and claiming he has an easement, Coombes leaves his car parked in the driveway for long periods of time.

  a) Does Bello have the right to leave the garbage can on his own side of the driveway? Does Coombes have any rights over this part of Bello's property?
  b) Can Coombes park in the driveway?

Licences

Licences can apply to all property, not merely land, and are technically a matter of contract law. In the context of land law, a licence gives permission for the use of land. One of the most common is the implied licence to enter that a retailer gives the public for the purposes of shopping. That licence can be withdrawn by the retailer.

Business Law Applied

❼ **Bo's Bootery,** a retail shoe store, gives Angie Carr, a neighbourhood kid, the right to set up a table in front of the store to sell jewelery she has made. Some time later, arguments develop because the store owner believes customers are not frequenting his store because of the number and type of clients Carr is attracting. He asks her to leave, but she refuses.

  a) What is the name of the right by which Carr was allowed to set up on the business property?
  b) Can the store owner revoke that right?

Oil and Gas Leases

The potential value of mineral rights makes their ownership crucial. The owner of land can sell the right to minerals under that land, in an agreement which is called a lease. Technically, though, this document is not a lease as that term is traditionally used in law. Rather, it is a combination of several interests in land. Oil and gas leases are becoming a complex area, and all that can be done in this text is to point out that mineral rights can be separated from surface rights.

In Alberta, most owners of land do not own the mineral rights below the surface.

If oil, for example, is discovered on someone's land, the government will negotiate the deal for removal of that mineral with the oil company. The government collects royalties from the company, based on the amount of production. The owner of the land will receive some periodic payment similar to a royalty payment.

adverse possession

the exclusive possession of land by someone who openly uses it for a long period like an owner, but without the permission of the owner

Adverse Possession/Squatter's Rights

A principle that developed early in the concept of land ownership was that of adverse possession—popularly known as squatter's rights. **Adverse possession** is the exclusive possession of land by someone who openly uses it for a long period like an owner, but without the permission of the owner. Land went to those who used it, was the principle underlining this rule. It is still used today to settle neighbourhood boundary disputes where land is registered in the registry system. There are two land registry systems in Canada:

- registry system
- land titles system

All new subdivisions, condominiums, and so on, are registered under the land titles system.

For example—the Smiths buy a house and, after a new survey is prepared, discover that the fence put up by the Joneses next door is one foot on their property. The Smiths cannot force the Joneses to remove the fence if it has been there for a reasonable length of time. The length of time varies from province to province, and can range from 10 to 20 years.

The principle of adverse possession can be also be expressed as "What you see is what you get." The Smiths saw the backyard of their new house, and bought according to what they saw. Only when the survey was completed did they realize they were entitled to more land. The concept of adverse possession settles the dispute in favour of the long-term user of the land—the Joneses become for all purposes the owner of that strip of land, and can sell it with their house.

There is no adverse possession against the Crown, which may own large tracts of vacant land in remote areas. It would be impossible for the government to supervise these properties and make certain that no one was using them without permission. Land owned by municipalities is Crown land.

Easement by Prescription

Similar to adverse possession, in some provinces an easement over land owned by another person may arise from visible, uninterrupted use of a right of way over that other person's land for a long period of time. This is known as a prescriptive right of easement. The continuous use of the right of way must be in disregard of the land's ownership by someone else and be done with the owner's knowledge, or in circumstances where the owner would normally be aware of the use.

Restrictive Covenants

The ownership of land may be subject to a restrictive covenant. This is a clause registered on title that places an obligation on the current owner of land not to use the property in a particular way. An example would be a restriction not to erect a satellite dish, or a multiple-family dwelling, on the property. This type of restriction, which usually benefits the owners of adjacent properties, will run with the land, in the sense that it will be binding on each successive purchaser of the property and can be enforced, provided it is reasonable.

Public Registration

Transfers of land in feudal times were done by the owner handing a piece of dirt from the land to the new owner. Later, transfers were recorded by documents written on sheepskin. The deed was written twice on the same sheet of sheepskin, which was then cut in a very uneven, indented form. A **deed** is any document (not only a deed to land) under seal, which today is usually a small red paper wafer. If anyone claimed to possess a duplicate of the deed, it was matched to the indentations of the original to see if there was a fit. This helped to reduce forgery. You will see some legal documents even today beginning with the phrase "This indenture made the. . . . " The word *indenture* goes back to the old practice of uneven cutting of the two sides.

deed

any document (not only a deed to land) under seal, which today is usually a small red paper wafer

In the early days of the use of documents, people kept them at home in a tin box. They were liable to be lost, stolen, or destroyed by fire, and so a system of public registration was devised. Owners could file the original of the deed to their land with the public registration office, and receive a stamped, certified duplicate copy of the original. The system of public registration provides two services:

- protecting the document
- giving of public notice

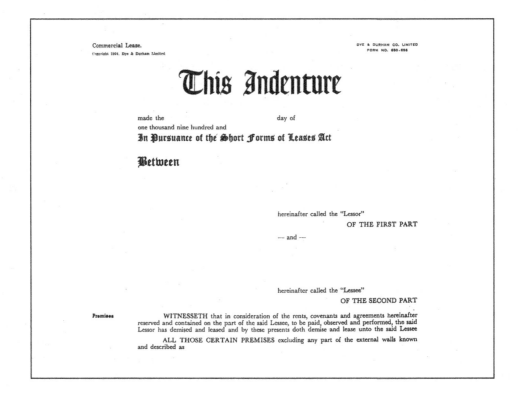

Buyers need a lawyer to act on their behalf in purchasing real estate. They understand that the lawyer has to search the publicly registered documents to be certain that the seller does in fact have title. What buyers often do not realize is that they also need a lawyer at the contract stage, before they sign the agreement of purchase and sale.

Public Notice

The giving of public notice by registering a deed is important because it is deemed notice—a buyer is judged in law to have notice of a publicly registered document whether the individual actually had notice or not. The buyer then must search the public registration system for registrations affecting any land purchased.

The scheme behind the public registry system is a "first come, first served" concept. The documents that are registered first have priority over other documents. The date a house was sold is irrelevant; what matters is the date the deed representing that sale was publicly registered. Consider the following example:

July 1—XY sells to CD, who delays in registering the deed
July 2—XY mortgages the same house to AB, and AB registers the mortgage
July 3—CD registers his deed to the property

AB's mortgage has priority over CD's deed. That means CD owns the house, but must pay off the mortgage amount to AB. What governs is not the time of the deal, but the time of public registration.

Registry Acts

All provinces have a registry act specifically stating that unregistered deeds are considered completely ineffective against those that have been registered. The following extract is from the *Registry Act of New Brunswick*.

R.S.N.B. (1973), s. 19

All instruments may be registered in the registry office in a county where the lands lie, and if not so registered, shall . . . be deemed fraudulent and void against subsequent purchasers for valuable consideration whose conveyances are previously registered.

Under the registry system, the buyer's lawyer must search the property's title, to make certain that the seller is the legal owner. This means more than searching the last deed to see that the owner's name is on the registry book. The search must make sure that the owner bought from someone who legally owned the property, and that individual also bought from a legal owner and so on, thus establishing a chain of ownership that goes back for a long period, usually 40 years.

There may be some mistakes or inaccuracies in the document. If they occur in a deed more than 40 years from the date of the current sale, then they are made ineffective. The buyer's lawyer has to check all of the documents in the chain of title to the last deed beyond the 40 years to make certain that every owner in between had good title, and that all mortgages are discharged.

The Land Titles System

Searching title back 40 years and beyond can be treacherous. A small error in a document can go undetected by a series of lawyers for many years, only to be discovered by the lawyer for a later purchaser. Given the number of documents that can be registered against a piece of land over a 40-year period, and the need for technical precision, mistakes are inevitable. To solve this problem, a system called the land titles system was devised.

The **land titles system** has been in use in western Canada for some time and is also sometimes known as the Torrens system of land registration. It is a system of land registration in which the land titles office certifies registered interests as being correct. The rules concerning the system are set out in the land titles acts of the various provinces. Generally, the system requires that the provincial government maintain a registry which records the following on a document called the Certificate of Title:

land titles system
a system of land registration in which the land titles office certifies registered interests as being correct

- the legal description of the land
- the "highest" type of interest held (for example, an estate in fee simple)
- the owner(s) of that interest
- other parties who have a lesser interest in the land, and what type of interest they claim

The key feature of the land titles system is a guarantee—what you see on the title to a piece of property is what you get (with a few notable exceptions listed below). You do not have to search back in time to figure out who owns a piece of property and who else claims an interest in it. The *Land Titles Act* guarantees that what is on the Certificate of Title is right—and if it is not, you can make a claim for compensation against a government-maintained fund (called an assurance fund).

Some other important features of the land titles system:

- If there is no registration, then there is no claim against subsequent owners. The idea is that registration of your interest at the land titles office lets everyone know you are out there. Persons acquiring an interest in the land are supposed to check the registry to see what interest others may have.
- The order of registration determines the order of priority. The rule is simple—interests which are registered first have first priority. So if the Bank of Money registered its mortgage ahead of yours, it gets first chance at the proceeds of the property to cover the amount of its loan.
- The land titles acts set out some important exceptions to the "what you see is what you get" rule. For example, section 65 of the Alberta *Land Titles Act, R.S.A. 1980 c. L-5*, states that the following interests can be claimed in land, against subsequent owners, even if they are not registered: unpaid taxes; any public highway; any subsisting lease for a period of not more than three years, if there is actual occupation of the land. Some of these exceptions could be quite important to a land transaction, and so inquiries should be made at the appropriate government agencies.
- There is an exception to the Land Titles guarantee, if fraud is involved. In other words, if you acquire your interest by some fraudulent means, you cannot necessarily be assured that whatever interest appears on the Certificate of Title is what you will get.
- Rights by prescription or based on adverse possession are not allowed under the land titles acts.

fraudulent transfer

a transfer of property by a debtor, usually to a related person, so that creditors cannot seize it

Paramount Life Insurance Company v. Hill et al., [1986] 34 D.L.R. (4th) 150 (Alta. C.A.)

Audrey Hill owned a house. Her husband was in a business partnership with a Mr. Laidlaw, and the partnership needed a loan. The partnership approached Paramount Life Insurance, who demanded security. Mrs. Hill refused to put up her house.

The husband forged his wife's name on a deed to Laidlaw, who then gave a mortgage to Paramount. The life insurance company advanced the loan on the basis of this mortgage as security. Not long after, Mr. Hill died. The mortgage went into default, and Paramount sought to have the house sold.

Mrs. Hill resisted, saying that the transfer was a forgery and therefore of no effect. Laidlaw could not give a mortgage on the basis of this **fraudulent transfer** (a transfer of property by a debtor, usually to a related person, so that creditors cannot seize

it). As her husband had not owned the house, the transfer existed on paper only.

Paramount relied on a Certificate of Title given by the Alberta land titles registry office, saying that the transfer and the mortgage were valid.

The Court's Decision

The transfer and mortgage were registered under the land titles system. The *Land Titles Act* gives the mortgagee a good title on registration, except in the case of fraud. However, the fraud must be the fraud of the mortgagee. In this case, Paramount was not involved in the fraud, and so the mortgage to Paramount was valid under the *Land Titles Act*.

Business Law   Applied

⑧ On June 1, 1995, Delroy Robinson agreed to purchase a small manufacturing plant from Iveta Holdings Limited. Robinson's lawyers did a **title search** (an investigation of the registered ownership of land) and found that the property was registered under the registry system. There was a deed to Iveta Holdings from Anne Hodgkin in 1953. However, there was also a deed in 1952 from Anne Hodgkin to Accurate Investments Inc.

Delroy Robinson's lawyer concludes that Robinson should not purchase the property because of the deed to Accurate Investments.

a) Is the purchaser's lawyer correct?

⑨ Lambert Fisk was a farmer in southern Saskatchewan. He wished to purchase an additional quarter section of land for his operation, but had to borrow money to so do. His uncle, Filbert Fisk, agreed to lend him the money, but wanted a mortgage against the new farmland to protect himself in case Lambert could not pay him back. Lambert and Filbert signed the mortgage and Lambert because the proud owner of a new quarter section of land. Filbert did not register his mortgage at the land titles office.

Soon after purchasing the property, Lambert found that he could not make the payments and made a quick sale of the newly acquired land to his neighbour, Elmer Filkowski. Uncle Filbert is very unhappy and feels he should be able to get the farmland for himself, since he has a mortgage on it.

a) Can Uncle Filbert enforce his mortgage against Elmer (that is, foreclose on the land to try and recover his loss)?

b) What should Uncle Filbert have done to protect his claim against the land?

c) What should Elmer (or his lawyer) have done prior to going through with the land sale, to find out who else had a potential claim against the property?

title search

an investigation of the registered ownership of land

Commercial Leases

Commercial leasing is a complex area in which there can be many different leasing situations. This section focuses on the small retail business in the shopping centre or plaza—a relatively common situation that contains concerns beyond those of renting an isolated unit. A shopping centre tenant, for example, must consider not just the aspects of the store rented, but also those of the whole shopping centre. A tenant might rent a store on a five-year lease to start an upscale jewelry shop. What happens if the mall then rents a kiosk that sells hotdogs right in front of the door? Or what can be done if the landlord rents another jewelry store nearby? The tenant is stuck for five years unless the lease contains protective clauses.

A new trend in leasing law is adding to its complexity. Leasing law was developed in accordance with very strict and technical land law principles, and contract principles were developed quite distinctly. However, the old and very technical principles of leasing law are now being replaced with contract principles that are more in accord with the modern business environment. Also, most conflicts between a landlord and tenant are governed by the terms of the lease—the contract—and not by the principles of leasing law. So it is often more important to understand the terms of the lease than it is to have an in-depth knowledge of general leasing law principles.

Note that residential tenancies (like the type that would cover an apartment you rented) are covered by special legislation, and the rules which apply to commercial leasing may well not apply to the residential situation. Generally, the rules concerning residential tenancies afford special protection for the tenants.

Negotiating a Lease

From a business point of view, the important considerations in any lease are rent and location. There are different concerns from a legal point of view, and these seldom seem significant until something goes wrong.

Some of the questions that should be answered when negotiating a lease are:

- What use is permitted?
- Who is responsible for repairing and maintaining the unit leased?
- Who is responsible for repairing and maintaining those things outside of the leased premises which are needed for its successful operation?
- Will the person responsible be able to pay for the repair or maintenance, especially in the case of some catastrophe such as fire or storm damage?
- Will other tenants be allowed to carry on a competing business?

Agreements to Lease

When the negotiations have been concluded and the major terms agreed, it is common for a landlord to produce a document entitled "Offer to Lease," "Letter of Agreement," "Memorandum of Agreement," or something similar. This document will set out a number of terms that are to be included in the lease.

It is important not to sign this agreement until all of the terms that a tenant wants have been expressed as part of the agreement at this stage. The clause at the bottom of the first page of the sample memorandum of agreement notes: "Tenant to execute a lease upon the landlord's standard form." The tenant cannot insist on any significant changes to that standard form agreement.

The Terms of the Lease

Permitted Use

The landlord will insist that the premises be used only for the stated purposes. Other uses might cause more wear and tear, interfere with other tenants, or even result in the cancellation of the landlord's insurance. If a store is leased as a clothing store but the owner converts it to a restaurant, for example, the landlord's fire insurance policy would likely be cancelled.

Tenants will also be concerned that the landlord obtain similar clauses from other tenants, so that a competing business cannot be set up in the same mall. An exclusive-use clause states that the tenant shall be the only business of the type in the shopping centre.

Spike v. Rocca Group Ltd., [1979] 23 Nfld. & P.E.I.R. 493 (S.C.)

A new concept in leasing law is developing as a result of the modern multi-tenant situation found in shopping centres, malls, and plazas. The courts realize that what one tenant does may greatly affect another. This is called a community interest and, in some circumstances, permits tenant A to sue tenant B, based on the terms of the lease between tenant B and the landlord.

Louise Spike operated a women's hairdressing salon under the name of Plaza Beauty Parlour. She signed a lease with the Rocca Group for space in its University Plaza. That lease contained a clause that said Spike would restrict her business to the cutting of women's hair.

> 7.26 The tenant will not use or occupy the leased premises or any part thereof for any purpose other than the operation of the business of women's hairstyling under the name of Plaza Beauty Parlour.

The lease also contained an exclusive-use clause.

9.19 The landlord agrees that during the term of this lease or any renewal thereof, it will not lease any other premises in the shopping centre or in any addition built to the present shopping centre to a tenant doing women's hairstyling and/or operating a unisex beauty salon.

John Muise, who operated a men's barber shop called Big John's Place, signed a similar lease with the Rocca Group. That lease contained a clause limiting the use of the unit to men's hair cutting. Another clause guaranteed him the exclusive right to carry on the business of cutting men's hair similar to the Spike clause.

Big John's Place began to cut women's hair. Spike complained to the Rocca Group but it refused to do anything about the situation. Spike brought an action against Big John's, requesting an injunction to stop the firm from cutting women's hair. Big John's defended, claiming Spike was not a party to the lease containing the permitted use clause and therefore had no legal basis to sue.

The Court's Decision

The court held that the growing number of shopping malls across the country is creating a new body of law particular to it. Spike thus had the right to an injunction against Big John's to stop it from violating its permitted-use clause. Even though there was no privity of contract, each business had agreed not to use the premises except for specific uses. Each business received the benefit of this covenant. This is the essence of a shopping mall lease.

The mutual advantage created a community of interest between tenants of similar businesses, giving each a direct interest in the carrying out of the terms of the lease by the other. Therefore Big John's was prohibited from the business of cutting women's hair.

■ **Business Law** Applied

⑩ **Andrew Reich ran** a news stand and variety store at a major intersection for a number of years. A developer wanted to buy it and the surrounding properties to convert them into a shopping mall. Reich agreed to sell and took a lease for a kiosk at the entrance of the new shopping mall. He agreed as a term of the lease to limit his business to that of a news stand.

Business went well for about a year, and then it dropped off. Reich learned that a pharmacy had opened in the mall and was selling newspapers and magazines. A clause in the pharmacy's lease stated that it would only carry on the business of a pharmacy.

Reich wants to know if there is anything that can be done to stop the pharmacy from selling newspapers and magazines.

   a) What additional clause could Reich have negotiated in his lease?
   b) Does the landlord have any right to stop the pharmacy from selling newspapers? What is the technical name for that remedy?
   c) Will the wording of the permitted-use clause in the pharmacy's lease give it a possible defence?

Exclusivity Clauses   Being a tenant in a multi-tenant situation such as a shopping centre or plaza creates new problems. Tenants need to negotiate for an exclusivity clause, but landlords resist because it restricts their ability to rent to others.

There is also a difficulty in the wording of these clauses. Many businesses, such as drugstores, discount stores, and small department stores, carry on a wide range of activities that can overlap with other businesses. It is wise to have an experienced leasing lawyer examine any lease before you sign it.

Business Alert!

MSM Construction Limited et al. v. Deiuliis, [1985] 49 O.R. (2d) 633 (H.C.)

Can a landlord permit a new tenant to start or carry on a business that completely interferes with an existing tenant's activities, making it impossible for the first tenant to carry on business? In such a situation, the courts have applied contract law principles rather than strict leasing laws, and implied terms in a lease that the landlord will not permit a nuisance in the area of any tenant. A **nuisance** is an activity that substantially interferes with the enjoyment of the land of others in the vicinity. It is an intentional tort—an interference with the occupier's use and enjoyment of the land.

Jean Deiuliis operated a women's hairdressing salon in leased premises in a plaza owned by MSM Construction Limited. Towards the end of the lease, the landlord rented the next unit to a fish market. Deiuliis complained, but the landlord refused to do anything about it. Deiuliis saw his business drop off and one staff member quit because of the smell emanating from next door.

Deiuliis vacated the leased premises before the end of the lease, and the landlord sued for the balance of the rent due. Deiuliis counterclaimed for damages for loss of business due to

the landlord having committed a nuisance—renting to the fish store.

The Court's Decision

There is no right that allows a tenant to withhold rent because of a breach of a term by the landlord, and so the landlord obtained judgment for the amount of the rent owing.

However, although there was no written term in the lease that the landlord would not permit letting space in the plaza in a way that would constitute a nuisance, there must be one implied in law. Such a term was necessary to bring about the desired business result of the lease arrangement. It would be contrary to the very purpose of the lease if a landlord could rent a space and then do something that reduced the ability of the tenant to carry on business.

The tenant therefore had a claim for loss of business against the landlord. The court found this was exactly the same amount as the rent owing.

---

nuisance

an activity that substantially interferes with the enjoyment of the land of others in the vicinity

Rent

In a modern retail store lease, especially one in a shopping centre, there may be many items other than rent included in the tenant's monthly payment obligation. The most common of these include:

- percentage rent (a percentage of annual sales, and is applicable only in a retail situation)
- utility charges (water, heating, air conditioning, ventilation, and so on)
- a proportionate share of common-area costs, such as escalators, elevators, or hallways, and the cost of the housekeeping, maintenance, and repair to them
- merchants' associations dues and other advertising costs
- a proportionate share in business and realty taxes and insurance

The landlord will want all of these items to be called rent, so that it can take advantage of special leasing remedies for enforcement if a tenant fails to pay. The tenant, on the other hand, will want such costs to be called tenant's expenses.

Radius Clauses

When a tenant agrees to pay percentage rent, the landlord will insist that a radius clause be included in the lease.

Radius is used in its ordinary geometrical meaning of a distance from a point measured in a circular motion. So, a tenant may agree not to open another branch within, for example, a radius of five kilometres of the shopping centre. Landlords insist on such a clause in case a tenant is able to lease other space in the neighbourhood, where a percentage rent is not demanded.

These radius clauses are covenants in restraint of trade and, like non-competition clauses, must be a reasonable restraint regarding subject matter, time, and distance.

Gross/Net Lease

Often landlords will want all expenses to be paid by the tenant. The landlord will assume certain specific financial obligations, and the tenant will pay insurance, realty taxes, and utilities. This is called a net lease.

> Section 201 Net Lease
>
> The tenant acknowledges and agrees that it is intended that this lease is a completed care free net lease to the landlord. Except as expressly herein set out, the landlord is not responsible during the term for any costs, charges, expenses, and outlays of any nature whatsoever arising from or relating to the leased premises, or the use and occupancy thereof, or the contents thereof or the business carried on therein, and the tenant shall pay all charges, impositions, costs, and expenses of every nature and kind relating to the leased premises except as expressly herein set out.

In a gross lease, the tenant pays only regular rent, and the landlord is responsible for the other expenses. The landlord and tenant may agree to any combination of the two leases.

Repairs

Common law puts the responsibility for repairs on the tenant, except when the premises become so unusable that it amounts to eviction. Repair obligations are expressly set out in the lease, and they should be reviewed with care. The normal clause reads that the landlord will be responsible for structural repairs, and the tenant for repairs to the internal part of the premises.

The tenant will normally insist that the landlord be responsible for internal repairs caused by problems with construction, or by a catastrophe such as fire or hurricane, for which the landlord can carry insurance. Also, the tenant is exempted from having to repair deterioration caused by reasonable wear and tear.

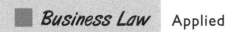

Business Law   Applied

11 Insect Communications Inc. has leased a retail unit in a plaza. The standard form lease contains a term: "The landlord will be responsible for structural repairs and the tenant for repairs to the interior portion of the premises."

A pipe for the air conditioning system travels from a central unit at the back of the premises through the wall to the exterior. It cracks along the whole length.

a) Who must repair the pipe?
b) How could the landlord and tenant have avoided the problem of deciding responsibility?

Repair Clauses   The drafting of repair clauses requires the advice of an experienced leasing lawyer. Do not rely on standard form agreements purchased from a stationery store. For example, are the piping and wiring that are located within the walls and floors part of the interior or the exterior of the premises? Countless court actions have been commenced on the wording of repair clauses. A careful draftsperson will refer specifically to completed, as-built, drawings of the property to remove some of the ambiguity.

Business Alert!

A tenant should also insist on a clause stating that the landlord has insurance to cover agreed repair costs. An agreement by the landlord to repair will be of no value if the landlord cannot raise the money to do so. Discuss the repair situation with an insurance agent, to establish your position on such matters as business interruption loss or loss of profits if the repairs prevent the carrying on of business.

Breaches of the Lease—Landlord's Remedies

The emphasis in this section is on the landlord's remedies—not because the tenant's remedies are less important, but simply because they are less complicated. Also, a tenant must understand that, although traditional leasing law gives landlords special and very effective remedies, the courts restrict the landlord's use of these by demanding absolute technical compliance. The tenant must know these technicalities if it wishes to take advantage of them in defending against a landlord's actions.

Eviction

The events that permit the landlord to evict the tenant are divided into two categories:

- failure to pay rent
- breach of a condition of the lease, unrelated to rent

When a landlord evicts a tenant, this is a termination of the lease, and is called the forfeiture of the lease. Locking the tenant out by changing the locks is a common method of terminating the lease. The landlord can also apply to the court for an order ending the lease and evicting the tenant.

Failure to Pay Rent

Specific rules relate to a tenant's failure to pay rent. Under them, the landlord is given far more effective remedies than would be available in contract law. A landlord can retake possession of the premises and evict the tenant without need of a court order. For this reason, a landlord will attempt to have as many tenant expenses as possible included as rent in a lease.

By statute and the common law, the landlord can take possession of the premises, without notice to the tenant, for failure to pay rent after 15 days. (The period can be varied by the lease.) The tenant has until midnight on the day the rent is due to pay the sum owing.

■ *Critical Concepts of* Eviction for Not Paying Rent

- The landlord can evict the tenant 15 days after the rent was due.
- The tenant has until midnight on the day the rent is due to pay.
- The landlord need give no notice to the tenant before taking possession—that is, evicting the tenant.

Business Alert!

Franchises and Rent In franchises, the parent company often attempts to become the landlord by renting the premises and then subletting to the franchisee. The franchisee's royalty payments and other fees are described as rent in the sublease, so that the parent company can take advantage of the special lease rent-default remedies.

■ *Business Law*   Applied

⑫ **The rent is** due on the lease on the fifteenth of the month, and when it is not paid by close of business at 5:00 p.m. on that day, the landlord has the bailiff change the locks and post a notice to the tenant that it is evicted. The tenant comes in the next morning and is shocked. It has an automated computer system and by some mistake, the rent cheque was not sent to the landlord when it should have been.

   a) The tenant claims that it received no notice of the overdue rent, and so the landlord's taking possession is improper. Is that correct?

   b) Does the tenant have any defences?

Eviction for Breach of Other Terms

Terminating the lease and evicting the tenant for breaches other than those involving rent must follow strict procedures. Notice of the breach must be given to the tenant, detailing the problem and giving the tenant time to deal with the situation. The slightest mistake in following this process will be fatal to the landlord, as the courts are very ready to protect the tenant's rights. One notice of breach given by a landlord mistakenly described the lease as being dated January 11 instead of January 8. The judge declared the **re-entry**—the landlord's remedy of evicting the tenant for failure to pay rent or for breach of another major covenant—by the landlord invalid and said, "A little inaccuracy is as fatal as the greatest."

re-entry
the landlord's remedy of evicting the tenant for failure to pay rent or for breach of another major covenant

■ *Critical Concepts of*   Notice

- Notice of the breach must be given to the tenant.
- The notice must be accurate in every detail.
- The notice must clearly advise the tenant of the nature of the breach, e.g., that the roof is leaking and it is the tenant's responsibility to repair this.
- The tenant must be permitted a reasonable time to remedy the breach.
- If the landlord accepts rent after it first becomes aware of the breach, it cannot terminate the lease.
- Even though the landlord loses the right to terminate or evict the tenant for breach of a condition of the lease by accepting rent after notice, the landlord can apply to the court for an order remedying the situation.

■ *Business Law*   Applied

⑬ **A tenant signed** a lease that contained a clause permitting it to operate a variety store that will not sell dairy products. Because a competing variety store a short distance away began to sell dairy products, the tenant began to sell them also.

The landlord served the following notice on the tenant:

> Take notice that you are in breach of the terms of your lease and unless you remedy the breach immediately, the lease will be terminated.

The tenant ignored the notice and continued to sell dairy products. Three days later, the tenant came to the store to find it padlocked, and a notice on the door saying that the premises had been seized on behalf of the landlord.

a) Does the tenant have any grounds to attack the termination of the lease?

⑭ A tenant agreed by terms of the lease to repair the plumbing in the premises. A pipe began to leak; the landlord noticed this, and gave the tenant written notice on November 30 to repair the leak. The next day, December 1, the landlord came again to collect the rent which was due on the first day of every month. While taking the cheque, the landlord noticed that the leak had increased, and became worried that, as the pipe went across the ceiling, the entire ceiling could collapse unless it was repaired immediately. The tenant said that it didn't have money to do the repair, and so the next day the landlord had the tenant locked out. The landlord terminated the lease and began to do the repairs.

a) Was the landlord's re-entry proper?

Seizure of Tenant's Goods

distress

the right of the landlord to distrain (seize) a tenant's assets found on the premises and sell them to apply to arrears of rent

If the tenant has the ability to pay and the landlord wants to keep the lease alive, the landlord has the remedy of **distress**, the right of the landlord to distrain (seize) a tenant's assets found on the premises and sell them to apply to arrears of rent. Distress must be done strictly according to the proper procedure, or the landlord will be liable in damages for the improper seizure of goods.

The process is normally carried out by a licensed bailiff. If the value of the goods seized is far in excess of the rent owing, the landlord will be liable for the value of the goods seized, and for any consequent business loss. While the landlord has this very unusual remedy, the courts make certain that the landlord does not abuse its privilege. In one case, the landlord's lawyer was ordered to pay the tenant's damages after the lawyer failed to instruct the landlord's bailiff on distress procedures, and the distress was irregular.

The landlord should not need to use force because the landlord should have a key to the premises. If the tenant has changed the locks, the landlord can change the locks back, but must give the tenant a key.

The remedies of suing for rent arrears and taking goods are alternatives. If the landlord seizes the goods, it cannot sue until the goods are sold and the proceeds applied to the amount owed, and any arrears remaining become evident.

■ *Critical Concepts of* Distress

- Seizure of a tenant's goods can be done only during daylight hours, and never on Sunday.
- The landlord cannot use force to enter the premises.
- The landlord must hold the goods for five days before selling, and have them valued by two appraisers.
- The goods must be sold for the best price.
- The quantity of the goods seized must not be excessive.

Business Law   Applied

⑮ The Thompson Corp. is a tenant, and is in arrears for two months' rent—$2,000. It has inventory of furniture which could be sold at an auction for $2,000 if seized by the landlord. Thompson Corp. has changed the locks, and the landlord can't get in. The landlord has a locksmith change them again and puts a notice on the door to the tenant that the goods are seized. The furniture would retail for $5,000 if sold by the tenant in the normal course of business.

a) Can the landlord seize the tenant's inventory without a court order? If so, what is the process called?
b) Is the seizure by the landlord proper?
c) If the seizure is not proper, what damages could the tenant claim?
d) How could the landlord have made a proper seizure?

Distress   A common mistake landlords make is to evict a tenant for non-payment of rent by changing the locks and also seizing the tenant's goods. If the landlord evicts the tenant, the lease is terminated, and the landlord cannot seize the tenant's goods.

Business Alert!

Breaches of the Lease—Tenant's Remedies

Apart from defects in the strict procedure that may make actions by the landlord invalid, the tenant's main remedy is relief from forfeiture. The courts are very ready to order the lease reinstated upon payment of rent arrears or performance of the breach—such as repairing damage or paying the landlord's costs of doing so.

BP Canada Limited v. Bamsa, [1976] 14 O.R. (2d) 508

Gary Vanneck leased a service station from BP Canada Limited (now part of Petro-Canada). It was a term of the lease that Vanneck would observe all laws and regulations. Vanneck had a friend, David Taylor, who was a bookie. Taylor sometimes worked a shift for Vanneck without pay. While there, Taylor used the phone for his bookmaking business. Taylor was caught, and convicted for bookmaking and keeping a common betting house arising out of the use of the telephone at Vanneck's.

The landlord served a notice on Vanneck that he had breached the lease and then had a bailiff take possession.

Vanneck claimed that he was not given the chance by the landlord to remedy the breach, and therefore the notice was invalid, and so he (Vanneck) should be given relief from forfeiture. Vanneck also claimed that he didn't know that Taylor was using the phone for bookmaking and that Vanneck had now taken steps to prevent this from happening in the future. Vanneck claimed that Taylor was banned from the premises. Vanneck promised to monitor future use of the telephone closely.

The Court's Decision

The court stated that, although there was precedent to say that generally an illegal activity was a breach not capable of remedy, the court still had discretion to give relief from forfeiture if the illegal activity was a minor one.

In all of the legal precedents, the tenant was directly involved in matters such as keeping a common bawdy house or a gaming house. In this case, the tenant himself was not directly involved. The tenant depended on operating a service station as his way of life. Apart from the bookmaking problem, Vanneck had been a good tenant. The court held that, although the fact of the conviction had to be considered, the property suffered no great harm. The court therefore allowed Vanneck relief from forfeiture, but required that he pay the landlord's legal fees and the costs of the court application.

Withholding Rent

The tenant's agreement to pay rent is considered a term separate from any of the landlord's agreements in the lease. So, if the landlord breaches the agreement by, for example, not repairing damage to the structure, the tenant cannot withhold rent. Instead, the tenant must bring a court action for an order compelling the landlord to perform, or for damages for the cost of doing the repair by the tenant, including, for example, loss of business if that happened because of the lack of repair.

Critical Concepts of Tenant's Remedies

- If a tenant is locked out, the tenant can apply to the court to have the lease reinstated by a remedy called relief of forfeiture.
- The court will usually order the tenant to make good any loss to the landlord before reinstating the lease.
- The court is usually very ready to grant tenants relief from forfeiture.
- A tenant cannot withhold rent if the landlord fails to perform one of its agreements in the lease.

Canadian Silk Manufacturing Co. Limited v. Badalato, [1950] O.W.N. 186

If the landlord enters the tenant's premises improperly, the landlord may be liable for damages in trespass.

Canadian Silk Manufacturing Co., supplier of cleaning cloths to industrial businesses, leased space in a large warehouse complex from Badalato. The soiled cloths were temporarily stored in the warehouse and then shipped to another location for cleaning. The landlord knew nothing of the day-to-day details of this business. The lease contained the term that the tenant would not conduct any business that would amount to a nuisance.

Six months into the lease, Badalato was notified by the fire marshal after a routine inspection that the storage of these cloths was a fire hazard, as they contained grease and oil. The landlord had to notify his insurance company, which said that it would cancel the insurance on the entire warehouse complex if the hazardous activity was not stopped.

On May 26, Badalato sent a notice to the tenant that it had another location available, and requested the tenant to move to that location. If the tenant did not agree, Badalato would bring a court action to have the lease declared forfeited. The tenant would not agree to the move.

On June 24, Badalato sent a telegram to Canadian Silk stating that, because of the fire hazard, the lease was terminated that day. The landlord took possession of the premises, and the tenant's goods were removed.

The Court's Decision

The court held that the question was whether the landlord's procedure for taking possession was proper. It felt that there was not the urgency that the landlord implied. The deputy fire marshal, although he did say that the premises were a fire hazard, did not issue a fire marshal's order or treat the matter as urgently as the defendants had done. The insurance company also had not taken steps to cancel the policies. The landlord, however, on the evening of the same day that the telegram was sent, had a truck come to the premises and remove all of the material owned by the tenant.

The notice was defective because the first letter did not require the tenant to remedy a breach, but requested the tenant to find other premises. The court held that what was required from the landlord was not that he give notice of intention to cancel the lease, but that he draw the tenant's attention to what was wrong. The tenant also had to be given reasonable time to remedy the breach.

The court found that the Badalato's notice to Canadian Silk was defective, and therefore the landlord had illegally evicted the tenant. The tenant was awarded damages for trespass to goods.

Termination of Lease by the Tenant

If a statute or a lease provides that a tenant must give notice to end a lease, that notice must be given in clear days. For example, if a tenant could terminate a lease on two months' notice and rent was to be paid on the first of the month, the notice must be given on the 31st of the preceding month and not on the first. There must be a full—clear—month's notice. If notice is given on the first, there is not a complete month.

■ *Business Law*   Applied

⑯ **A tenant rented** a building and saw a crack in the plaster ceiling. The landlord promised to repair it, but was slow getting around to it. After the tenant began business, a piece of plaster fell and hit a customer. The customer successfully sued the tenant for $6,000 in Ontario small claims court, and the landlord refused to reimburse the tenant for this amount.

When the next rental amount of $1,000 was due, the tenant refused to pay, saying that this amount would be offset against the $6,000 the landlord owed. The rent was due on the first of the month. On the 20th of the month, the tenant came to work to find the locks changed by a bailiff, and a notice that the landlord had seized the property and terminated the lease.

a) Is the termination of the lease by the landlord proper?
b) Can the tenant deduct the $6,000 from the rent?
c) Does the tenant have any remedy? If the tenant succeeds in getting the lease reinstated, what amounts will the tenant likely have to pay the landlord in addition to the rent?

Mortgages

Early Mortgages

Mortgage, foreclosure, and *equity* are words that appear often in the language surrounding the purchase of a house and the raising of money for a business. These words have their origins in lending practices that go back to feudal England. The church in the Middle Ages condemned lending money in exchange for interest as the sin of usury, so that lenders had to take actual possession of land that was pledged in support of a loan if they wanted to avoid punishment by the church. The land was returned to the borrower when the debt was repaid. Since this was an actual transfer of the land, it was called a *live pledge*.

This situation was not satisfactory to many lenders, since taking possession of the land involved assuming the responsibility attached to it—such as growing crops. The borrowers were not happy about giving up land that they could use to earn income. So, a more sophisticated method was developed, in which the borrower simply transferred title to the land, but kept possession. This was called a passive or dead (**mort**) pledge (**gage**)—hence the word *mortgage*. **Mortgage** is the title of property that is held by the lender as security. Under this arrangement, the lender had the right to take over the land if payments were not made, but the borrower kept possession as long as the mortgage loan was paid.

The law of mortgages developed through the common law courts. The principles developed were binding and became quite inflexible. The borrower transferred title of the property to the lender. On default, the borrower lost the right to get the title back and lost the property. Technically, under common law, the lender becomes the owner—that is, the holder in fee simple—of the mortgaged property.

mort
passive or dead

gage
a pledge

mortgage
the title of property that is held by the lender as security

To soften the harsh consequences of the common law, the court of equity developed principles of fairness, including the concept of the equity of redemption. From this term, we derive the term *equity*, referring to the cash value that an owner has in the house. The **equity of redemption** is the right of the mortgagor to redeem the title to the mortgaged land on payment of the debt in full.

The Mortgage Transaction

A mortgage is a two-step transaction. First, money is borrowed; second, land is pledged as security for that loan. In ordinary terms, these two transactions are referred to as one—giving a mortgage if the land is under the registry system, and a charge if it is under the land titles system.

To understand the legal concepts involved, the two parts of the transaction must be kept distinct. In fact, under the registry system, giving the mortgage legally is the transfer of the land as security. Under the land titles system, ownership of the land is not transferred, but rather the land is charged with the repayment of the debt. The **transfer** is the equivalent (under the land titles system) of a deed transferring ownership, not made under seal. For example, in a typical residential mortgage/charge, a person wants to buy a house for $200,000. That individual has $30,000 as a down payment, but must borrow the rest and give a mortgage/charge on the house to secure payment of the loan. If the borrower defaults, the lender has the right to sue for recovery of the loan, and also to sell the mortgaged/charged property and apply the proceeds of the sale to the outstanding loan amount.

In everyday terms, the $30,000 down payment is considered the owner's equity. If the owner pays $10,000 off the mortgage loan, that equity will increase to $40,000. If the market value of the house increases from $200,000 to $300,000, then the owner's equity is increased by the difference, rising to $130,000. Most lenders demand about 25 to 30 percent equity before they will advance money on the security of a mortgage. This is mainly because:

- There may be a fluctuation in the market value that would reduce the amount the lender could recover on sale of the property.
- Appraisals will be off by between 10 and 15 percent. This can translate into a significant amount of money—an error of 10 percent on a house worth $200,000 would be $20,000, and would effectively wipe out the cushion of owner's equity.
- With a large equity, the owner will fight to keep the house. If the owner has very little equity there is no incentive to make payments, and the individual might simply walk away at the first occasion of difficulty.

Mortgagee   The lender is the **mortgagee** (a lender who takes a mortgage as security for a loan); the borrower is the **mortgagor** (a borrower who gives an interest in land as security for a debt). To simplify matters, we refer to the mortgagee as the lender throughout this text. The borrower is also referred to as the owner of the property, since this is common usage for the holder of the equity of redemption. The courts have so restricted the rights of the lender (holder of title in fee simple) that the popular concept is more accurate than the technically legal concept.

Series of Mortgages

It is very common to hear of second, third, and more, mortgages. Technically, under the registry system, since the owner has conveyed title in fee simple to the first lender, the owner now has the equity of redemption. So, all subsequent mortgages are transfers by the owner of the equity of redemption. This is not the case under the Land Titles System, where the land is charged with the repayment of the debt and the transfer of ownership does not occur.

Remember that the registry system governs the priority of interest in the land. Therefore, for all practical purposes, mortgages take their priority by the timing of the registration—not when the mortgage document is signed. First in priority means that the first lender takes the full amount of the outstanding loan relating to that mortgage. All other lenders take the full amount of their loan in priority according to the date of registration of the mortgage.

For example, a house has been sold for $200,000 after default of the registered mortgages:

First mortgage	$150,000
Second mortgage	$100,000
Third mortgage	$ 25,000
Total mortgages	$275,000

The distribution of the proceeds of sale would be as follows:

First lender receives	$150,000
Second lender receives	$ 50,000
Third lender receives	Nil

In order to protect their interests, holders of other mortgages may have to pay the first mortgage and keep it in good standing until the property has sold. They might also have to take over the sale of the property, because if the first lender conducts the sale, it will be done so as to cover the first mortgage amount. Although the first lender is obliged to obtain a fair market value for the property, it is difficult to prove any fault if the house is sold for between 10 to 20 percent less than that amount. In addition, forced sales almost always bring a lower price. Thus, in order to obtain the best price, the second lender will probably be forced to take over the expenses and time involved in conducting the sale.

Types of Mortgages

A number of different names have been devised for different mortgages and related lending transactions. Some of the more common are as follows.

Conventional Mortgage

The term *conventional* is used because it is a standard model for lending agreements. This document is a standard form agreement and is roughly the same for all mortgages of the same type. If there are special terms negotiated, it is then called an unconventional mortgage. Conventional mortgages are easily available from banks and trust companies. They will provide a loan of up to only 75 percent of the property value.

Insured Mortgage/High Ratio

Beginning in the 1950s, the government recognized that some people could not afford the 25 percent down payment demanded by lending institutions. This type of mortgage was called a low-ratio mortgage because the ratio of the mortgage to the full value of the property was low. In order to encourage lending institutions to lend high-ratio mortgages, based on 90 or even 95 percent of the value of the property, the concept of an insured mortgage was developed. If the borrower defaults on the loan, the insurance company will pay.

This type of mortgage insurance may be obtained either privately or publicly. The public, or government-initiated, insurance company is the Canada Mortgage and Housing Corporation (CMHC). The CMHC provides the insurance; however, the banks still administer the mortgage. There is also private insurance available. The largest private mortgage insurer in Canada is the Mortgage Insurance Company of Canada (MICC).

The mortgage loan contains an additional amount which goes to pay for the insurance. The premiums form a pool of funds to cover defaults. The premium normally adds anywhere between 1 and 3 percent to the loan amount.

Vendor Take Back Mortgage

A purchaser may not be able to raise all of the money required to buy the house. The seller might then take a mortgage back on the property for the additional amount. While it is not a legal category, it is commonly called a vendor take back. If the vendor is willing to do this, it will be noted on the listing agreement as VTB.

Collateral Mortgage

In a business lending transaction, various types of security are often given. When obtaining a business loan, the business person may be required to sign a promissory note as well as a general security agreement on the business assets. An additional mortgage on a personal residence might also be required. This is known as a collateral mortgage, because it is not the prime security, but additional security. The term *collateral* refers to the property pledged. If a bank manager asks a business person what collateral is available, the answer may be a car, a house, a boat, or any other property.

Variable Interest Mortgage

In recent years, interest rates have fluctuated dramatically, and mortgage lending practices have been adapted to account for this. Previously, an interest rate was usually fixed at the beginning of the mortgage term. The variable interest rate mortgage allows interest to vary according to an agreement between lender and borrower. The interest rate is normally set based on the Bank of Canada, and the rate varies as the Bank of Canada changes the prime rate.

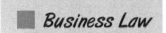 **Business Law**   Applied

⑰ **Mauricio Martinez wants** to buy a house for $200,000 and has $20,000 as a down payment. He hopes to get a bank loan, secured by a mortgage against the house.

   a) Assuming his credit is otherwise good, will the bank likely give him a mortgage loan? If so, what type of mortgage loan?
   b) Will the monthly payments be increased because of the low down payment?
   c) What is the common name for Martinez's financial interest?
   d) If Martinez does purchase the house as planned, and the following month the fair market value increases to $300,000, how much equity does Martinez have in the house?

Sources of Mortgages

The mortgage market is competitive, and different arrangements are offered by different sources—a borrower should shop around before deciding. It is not only interest rates that should be considered. Some of the optional terms, especially those relating to repayment, can make a significant difference to the borrower. Many newspapers publish comparative rates for the various sources in their financial sections. Some of the usual sources for the borrower for mortgage loans are:

- banks and trust companies
- insurance companies, credit unions, and pension funds
- private mortgage companies

The Terms of a Mortgage

Borrowers have come to realize that it is not only interest rates that are negotiable, but also the other terms in a mortgage. Open and prepayment terms allow payment of the mortgage in full at any time, or the right to make advance payments during the course of the mortgage. This type of term is most important because of the way interest is calculated on a mortgage. The difference between the term of the mortgage and the amortization period is a critical concept to remember.

Term is the date when the mortgage comes due. For example, a $200,000 mortgage may end in three years. At that time, the borrower must pay it off. Practically, that cannot be done, and so the mortgage is renewed, or a new loan is obtained elsewhere.

The amortization period is the time it will take to pay off the entire mortgage loan, usually 25 years. The amortization is normally based on the blended payment of principal and interest. So, for example, if the mortgage payment is $800 per month, a certain amount of that is repayment of principal, and the balance is interest. The interest on a mortgage has to be paid first. This is the key concept in understanding how important prepayment privileges are.

Amortization and Interest

Examine the amortization schedule provided by your instructor. The relevant data from that schedule are:

Monthly Payment $894.49

	Interest	Principal
First payment	$816.48	$ 78.01
End of three years (36th payment)	$790.80	$103.69
Last Payment (after 25 years)	$ 7.21	$887.28

By the end of the third year, the borrower has paid total monthly payments of $32,201.64 but only $3,250 of that has gone to reduce the loan amount.

Solutions to Front-End Loading of Mortgage Interest

Borrowers are increasingly aware of the fact that for many years over the life of their mortgage they are simply repaying interest and very little of the monthly payment is applied to the principal. There are a number of ways to lessen the burden, including:

- Prepayment privileges—allowing additional payment of smaller amounts, such as multiples of $100 at certain periods. These payments are to go against principal only.
- Weekly payments—allowing weekly payments significantly reduces the amount of interest over the amortization period.
- **Open mortgages**—mortgages permitting repayment of the debt at any time without notice or bonus.

open mortgages

mortgages permitting repayment of the debt at any time without notice or bonus

Saving Mortgage Interest

Payment Option	# Payments per year	Payment Amount	Amortization (years)	Potential Savings
Monthly	12	$662.38	25	—
Semi-monthly	24	$330.58	25	$360
Bi-weekly	26	$304.50	25	$785
Accelerated bi-weekly	26	$331.19	19.3	$32,127
Weekly	52	$152.12	25	$946
Accelerated weekly	52	$165.59	19.3	$32,497

The chart is based on a mortgage of $80,000, at 9 percent per annum, compounded annually, with no prepayments.

Taxes and fire insurance premiums are often added to the monthly mortgage payments and paid by the lender.

■ *Critical Concepts of* Obligations Under a Mortgage

Apart from paying the monthly installments as they become due, there are several other requirements under a mortgage.

- The owner must comply with all laws affecting the mortgaged property. For example, if the building is zoned for office use only, the owner cannot open a restaurant, as this would be a violation of the building by-law and a default under the mortgage.
- Fire insurance must be maintained with the mortgagee named as first loss payee. This is important to the lender because if the property is destroyed by fire, the lender is entitled to the insurance proceeds.
- All realty taxes must be paid. If the property taxes are not paid, the property may be sold by the city government for payment of the outstanding taxes.
- The property must be kept in good condition—the owner must prevent waste. The borrower must not allow any damage or destruction to the property that would affect its value.
- The property may not be sold without the consent of the lender. If the borrower does sell without consent, the mortgage becomes due.

Lender's Remedies

The mortgage loan is a contract and involves obligations on all sides. The lender advances the money at the beginning of the contract. The borrower must conform to the agreement as well. The main default is, of course, failure to make the monthly payments.

The lender has several remedies if the borrower defaults:

- Sue on the promise to pay for the outstanding amount. There is usually an acceleration clause in the mortgage document, stating that on any default the full amount of the mortgage becomes due.
- Sue the previous owner on the covenant. If a house is sold and the mortgage is taken over by the new owner, the previous owner is still obligated on the loan covenant.

To protect against this, the seller may require the purchaser to arrange a new mortgage and discharge the current one. This law varies among the provinces—in some, the lender is not permitted to sue the previous owner.

- Sell the property under court supervision (judicial sale). If the sale realizes more than the amount owed, the difference must be paid to the owner.
- Foreclose. This is a court proceeding. The lender will ask the court for an order foreclosing the interest in the property (equity of redemption) so that the lender becomes the owner of it. The lender can sell it and apply the sale proceeds against the loan. Even if the property exceeds the value of the loan, the lender can keep the excess amount.
- Sell privately (often called power of sale). A standard form mortgage agreement usually contains terms allowing the lender to sell privately. The private sale is regulated by legislation. There is a notice requirement, usually one month or a little longer. On the sale, the lender must attempt to obtain fair market value, and any amount over the loan amount must be paid to the owner.
- Take possession. The lender can obtain possession of the property by court order and have the owner evicted.

Power of Sale

Power of sale is a right of the mortgagee to sell mortgaged land by the terms of the mortgage or by statute upon default. If the lender opts to use the private power of sale, there are no grounds for any extensions. The borrower must be given notice—usually 30 days or a little longer. If the borrower refuses to vacate the property, the lender must obtain a court order for possession. This can add a short time on to the borrower's ability to stay on the property, but from the time of service of the notice of intent to exercise the power of sale, it will be a matter of only a few months before the lender can have the borrower evicted.

Foreclosure   In everyday language, remedies to do with mortgages are often referred to as **foreclosure**. Technically, *foreclosure* refers to closing out the legal interest of the owner. This means that the lender has the common law title (fee simple) and therefore can sell the property as sole owner. The judicial and private sale remedies are often called foreclosure, but this is technically inaccurate.

power of sale

a right of the mortgagee to sell mortgaged land by the terms of the mortgage or by statute upon default

Legalese

Critical Concepts of Lender's Remedies

On default, the lender can take the following actions to enforce the mortgage loan transaction:

- suing for the loan amount
- foreclosing, to extinguish the owner's rights and become sole owner of the property
- judicial sale—sale of the property under court supervision
- power of sale—private sale by the lender
- possession—evict the owner by court order, and take possession of the property

Provincial Differences

Three provinces, Alberta, British Columbia, and Saskatchewan, provide rules that prevent the lender from taking the property and suing for any balance still owing on the personal covenant. This is done by restricting the lender's right to **foreclosure**—an order by a court ending the mortgagor's right to redeem within a fixed time—but also requiring a judicially supervised sale. In Saskatchewan and Alberta this applies only to residential mortgages.

foreclosure

an order by a court ending the mortgagor's right to redeem within a fixed time

In all other provinces, the lender can seize the property and sue on the covenant by choosing to exercise the right to a private sale (power of sale). In Nova Scotia, the technical action is called foreclosure, but a personal action for debt on the covenant is permitted. The restriction on the right to take the property and not sue for debt on the covenant is a fair rule. However, in practice, it is of little effect, for if a mortgage is in default the borrower usually has no other assets anyway. The sale of the property usually does not exceed the mortgage debt—if it did, the borrower would be able to sell it and pay off the loan, or even refinance the mortgage loan transaction.

Borrower's Remedies

The borrower has a defence if the money has been paid and the lender has not given proper credit. But, when a real default occurs, the lender has the remedy of taking the property and having it sold. If the lender chooses foreclosure, the borrower can:

- Ask for a redemption period. This is normally about three to six months, but will be extended if the borrower can show that there is a possibility of paying the debt in the near future.
- Require a judicial sale. This means the foreclosure action is converted to a sale action. In some jurisdictions, this is done automatically.

Practical Solutions for Borrowers

There is often some room to negotiate when problems arise, since the lenders realize that they are facing a loss in a collection situation. Practical solutions include the following.

Rescheduling the Debt

The borrower may be able to convince the lender that the default is only the result of a temporary difficulty. The lender may agree to waive immediate collection of the amount in default, and add it on to the principal of the loan. The lender may also be willing to forgive a small amount of the debt because that much would be lost in the collection process. There is also a possibility of the lender's agreeing to lower payments if it can be shown that the mortgage can be paid off over a longer period of time. A variation of this can be a lowering of payments for two years, and then an increase in later years.

Transfer of the Mortgaged Property to the Lender for a Full Release

This saves collection fees, and also helps the borrower avoid a bad credit rating. If a court proceeding has started, that fact will go on the borrower's credit record. Collection agencies monitor court registers.

Buying and Selling Real Estate

The buying and selling of real estate has evolved into a fairly complex transaction, often involving many parties besides the vendor and purchaser.

Banks/financial institutions: They provide part of the money for the purchaser to be able to buy the property. Usually, they take a mortgage against the property purchased to protect their interest. In the event of non-payment, the mortgage gives the institution the right to the property to recover its money. As well, these lenders want to ensure that municipal property taxes are paid (to prevent the prospect of the municipality selling the land to cover these), and they also want to ensure that they are entitled to insurance proceeds in the event that the property burns down (and their security "goes up in smoke").

Lawyers: They generally protect the interests of the three main parties involved: the vendor, the purchaser, and the financial institution which provided the money to the purchaser (often the same lawyer acts for these last two parties). Ideally, the lawyers examine the offer to purchase prior to the parties' committing themselves to the transaction. Prior to closing, they prepare documents and check out the title, correcting any defects that are not assumed by the new purchaser prior to closing. As well, the status of property taxes, zoning, and utility payments are also checked.

Land titles offices/registry offices: These are the places where the documents of and the mortgage are registered. Registration fees apply. These are also the offices to check for others who claim an interest in the property being sold.

Surveyors: They determine that the vendor is selling the property that he says he is, and also identify if there is any part of neighbouring property encroaching on the sale property, or vice versa (for example, if your fence is over the property line onto the adjoining land).

Municipal offices: They confirm that the property taxes and local improvement levies have been paid (through the issuance of a tax certificate) and that zoning by-laws have been complied with (through the issuance of a compliance certificate).

Appraisers: They are generally required by financial institutions to confirm the value of the property, and to ensure that the security (that is, the property) is of sufficient value to cover the amount of the loan.

Title insurers: They are private companies which provide protection as to a property's compliance with zoning and the status of encroachments. If the property does not comply as stated, and loss occurs, a claim may be made against the policy.

Tenants: Particularly in the commercial transaction, tenants of an existing property may be asked to verify that there are no outstanding claims against the previous owner/landlord that the new owner may be responsible for. Terms of the lease are also verified.

In general, the flow of the typical real estate transaction goes as follows.

The Real Estate Transaction

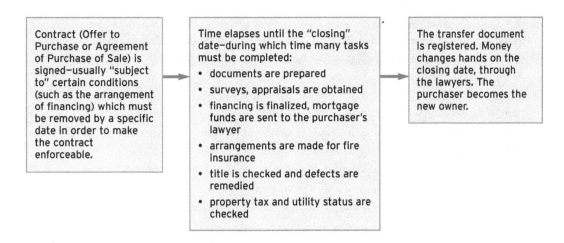

Contract (Offer to Purchase or Agreement of Purchase and Sale) is signed—usually "subject to" certain conditions (such as the arrangement of financing) which must be removed by a specific date in order to make the contract enforceable.

Time elapses until the "closing" date—during which time many tasks must be completed:

■ documents are prepared
■ surveys and appraisals are obtained
■ financing is finalized and mortgage funds are sent to the purchaser's lawyer

> - arrangements are made for fire insurance
> - title is checked and defects are remedied
> - property tax and utility status are checked

closing date
the date for completing a
sale of property

The transfer document is registered. Money changes hands on the **closing date** (the date for completing a sale of property), through the lawyers. The purchaser becomes the new owner.

In Summation

Land

- Real property includes the land and all items attached to it.

Interests in Land

- There are various types of estates in land. A fee simple estate is the broadest form of ownership; a life estate allows one party lifetime use of the land; a leasehold estate gives the tenant the right to possession for a fixed period of time; and condominium is a combination of private ownership along with a share of a corporation that allows access to areas used in common with other individual owners.

Title/Ownership

- Ownership of land by an individual is held in fee simple. If more than one person is holding title to the land, it is held in fee simple either as tenants in common or as joint tenants.
- Joint tenancy carries the right to survivorship, and is often used between spouses.

Other Rights over Land

- An easement allows one property owner the right to use the land of another for a particular purpose. Access to a beach by crossing the land of another is an example of an easement.
- The exercise of an easement over another's land without consent for a period of time may give rise to a prescriptive easement.
- Ownership of land by occupation under specific conditions for a period of time without permission of the owner may give rise to a claim of ownership based on adverse possession.
- Adverse possession and prescriptive easements are not possible against the Crown, or under the land titles system.
- Restrictive covenants may be present to limit the use of the land by current and future owners.

Licences

- A licence applied to land relates to its use by the licensee.

Public Registration

- Registration of documents indicating an interest in the land is done under either the registry system or the land titles system.
- Registration of the document provides public notice of the interest in the land, as well as establishing priorities among interest holders. It also allows a search to be done to establish outstanding interests in, and ownership of, land before it is purchased.

Commercial Leases

- Commercial leases are a complex area in which contract principles are playing a greater role.

- Negotiations usually conclude with the parties signing an offer to lease that sets out a number of terms and conditions to be incorporated into the lease itself. These terms will be included along with a number of other basic terms relating to the use of the premises.

- The lease terms to be negotiated by the parties will cover whatever issues are of importance to them for the operation of the business. Some terms of particular concern are: permitted use, exclusivity, disturbing uses, and radius clauses.

- The rental payment may include a number of other charges to be paid by the tenant, such as insurance or water, and should be made clear by the parties in the lease.

Breach of the Lease—Landlord

- In the event the lease is breached, the landlord must comply exactly with the technicalities required to exercise the remedies available, or the remedy will not be upheld by the court.

- Eviction is possible for failure to pay rent, and for breach of some other conditions of the lease.

- The form, content, and notice period required by statute and common law in order for a landlord to exercise its rights must be followed to the last detail.

- The right to seize the tenant's goods (distress) and sell them for rent arrears must be done under set circumstances and according to the proper procedures, or the landlord may become liable for damages.

- Distress and lease termination are alternative remedies.

Breach of the Lease—Tenant

- The tenant can ensure that the landlord follows the terms and conditions of the lease by using such remedies as an action for trespass or a court order to compel performance. The tenant may not withhold rent.

- The tenant's main remedy is relief from having the lease terminated, and the courts are often ready to have the lease reinstated upon the tenant bringing the outstanding issue, whether it be arrears of rent or performance of some condition under the lease, into good standing.

- Termination of the lease by the tenant must be done in strict accordance with the lease or the governing statute.

Mortgages

- A mortgage, or charge of land, acts as security for the loan of money by a lender to the owner of the property. It must be registered against the property to be effective in protecting the interest of the lender. There will often be more than one loan secured against the value of the property. These mortgages or charges will rank in priority according to their date of registration.

- There are a number of types of mortgage available to correspond with the nature of the loan made. Each type of mortgage offers different rights, benefits, terms, and conditions. Examples are insured mortgages, collateral mortgages, variable rate mortgages, and open mortgages.

- The term and the amortization period of a mortgage are two separate elements that are used in determining the amount of money to be paid on a regular basis in repaying the mortgage.

Default of a Mortgage

- In the event the borrower defaults in making regular payments or breaches some other condition of the loan, the lender has several remedies available. The lender may sue on the loan, may exercise rights under the mortgage to take over ownership of the land (foreclosure), or may decide to sell the property to recover the debt owed (power of sale).

■ The borrower has the opportunity to ask for a redemption period in which to pay off the debt, or for a judicial sale if foreclosure has been exercised. There are usually practical solutions available as well that can be used prior to the lender exercising rights under the mortgage.

The Real Estate Transaction

■ The typical real estate transaction involves many parties, and can therefore be quite complex. Lawyers are generally involved to protect the interests of the three main players: the vendor, the purchaser, and the financial institution lending the purchaser funds to buy the property.

Closing Questions

General Concepts

1. Would a central air conditioning unit attached to the side of a house be considered real property or personal property? Explain the reasons for your answer.

2. Samson Mephisto's house was for sale. He was an avid gardener and had collected unique plants from a number of different sources which he had planted in his garden. Delia Jones submitted an offer to purchase the house.

   The transaction was completed, and Jones took possession, anticipating the joy of giving her first garden party. She was horrified when she walked out into the garden to discover that all that remained was a couple of small trees. The rest of the garden was a series of deep holes where all the shrubs and plants had been dug out.
   a) What are Delia Jones's rights in this case of the missing plants?

3. Which of the following is correct? The purpose of registering documents of ownership for property is:
   a) giving public notice
   b) generating money for the government
   c) protecting the document from theft or fire
   d) saving on sheepskin

4. According to section 19 of the *Registry Act* from the revised statutes of New Brunswick, what element other than previous registration is required of a subsequent purchaser in order for that purchaser to take precedence over an earlier, unregistered deed?

5. Charles and Beatrice Clarke purchased a vacation property on a lake. The first summer in possession they were very upset to find that a number of people used their property for access to the lake for swimming and boating. When Charles Clarke attempted to stop people from crossing the land he was told that this access to the lake had been used for years.

   The Clarkes quickly huddled over their deed of land and found no wording indicating that such a right existed. They decided to erect a fence to stop people from crossing their property. Several days later, they were disturbed by the sound of Gavin Sellars using a chainsaw to artfully sculpt an entrance way through the wood fence. When confronted by Mr. Clarke, Sellars cheerfully waved the chainsaw and an affidavit (statement) from a local resident who had lived in the area for 30 years. This document stated that the walkway had been used for access to the lake for at least 25 years.
   a) What is the nature of the interest in land which the affidavit would support?
   b) Would someone wishing to use this access as a boat launch be successful in claiming a right to do so based on the fact situation described?

6. Laina Ballantyne had a survey done of her property and found that for the past 30 years her back fence had actually been located half a metre into the laneway owned by the municipality.
   a) What right does Ballantyne have to claim ownership of that strip of land which has been fenced?

7. Nora Mogambo had a beautiful piece of lakefront property in Slime Lake, Alberta. She wished to sell it and use the proceeds to travel. Not too long after putting the property up for sale, Nora agreed to sell to Alex Fontana for $150,000. Alex did a search on the property at the Land Titles office and found nothing registered as an interest against the title.

A few days before closing, Corey Kazima called up Alex and said, "You realize, of course, that I have a lease on this property for the next seven years." Sure enough, when Alex went out to a remote corner of the property, he found that Corey was living in a cabin.
a) Is Alex stuck with Corey as a tenant? Why or why not?
b) Would it make any difference to your answer above if Corey's lease were for 12 months?

8. Refer to the certificate of title provided by your instructor. Explain what you learn from this document.

Commercial Leases

9. Linda Chierne operated a pet shop under the name Urban Pets, in the Runnymede Shopping Centre. She specialized in the sale of cats and small dogs, such as toy poodles, cairn terriers, Scotties, and chihuahuas. Her lease contained a clause restricting her business to the carrying on of a pet shop, and the sale of small dogs and cats.

Several months after opening her shop, another pet shop opened in the same shopping centre under the name Exotic Pets and Fish. It was run by Gregory Pushkin, known as Push to his friends. Push specialized in the sale of such exotic pets as iguanas, snakes, and saltwater marine fish. He had a clause in his lease restricting his business to the carrying on of a pet shop, and the sale of exotic pets and fish.

After a few months, Push decided to begin selling Shar-Pei dogs (Chinese wrinkle dogs), and basenjis (barkless dogs). When Chierne complained to Covert Ltd., the firm that managed the shopping centre, it wanted nothing to do with the problem. She next approached Push, and he responded, "People want real dogs, not those rats with hair you sell. What'cha gonna do about it? Want to borrow a cup of real kibble?" She left in a furious temper, determined to bite back.
a) Who can Chierne bring action against in these circumstances?
b) What remedy would she be asking for?
c) What measures could Chierne have taken to avoid this situation?
d) What is a Shar-Pei, and is it exotic?

10. You are interested in leasing a main floor location in a shopping plaza for the purposes of operating a book and art shop, where customers can buy coffee to drink while browsing.
a) What particular terms and conditions would you want to include in your negotiations with the landlord?
b) As a landlord, you think this operation might be very successful and you would like a percentage of the gross income. What clause would you want included in the lease?

11. Which of the following best describes distress?
a) a remedy for the tenant
b) another expression for being upset
c) a remedy enabling the landlord to end the lease
d) a remedy enabling the landlord to get money for rent arrears
e) something educators practice on their students

Mortgages

12. Helmut and Luzinda Schwartz bought a 10-hectare piece of undeveloped real estate for $130,000. They took out a first mortgage of $100,000 when it was bought, and later decided to build a house on the land. Once their plans for the house were drawn up, a real estate appraiser gave them an estimate that the property, when all was completed according to the plan, would be valued at $350,000.

With their plans and appraisal in hand, the Schwarztes approached a wealthy friend of theirs, Aaron Ritche, about financing for the house construction. Ritche, who made his money in the stock market, was not very knowledgeable about real estate financing. Nevertheless, he agreed to lend the Schwartzes $150,000, secured by a promissory note from both of them, with a collateral mortgage registered on the property. Ritche figured the promissory note would allow him to get his money back faster if he needed it.

The Schwartzes began work on construction of their house but it was not long before things went terribly wrong. The contractor they hired to build the foundation was inexperienced. Originally the foundation was to be finished in September, but it was not completed until December that year. The carpenters and bricklayers who had been scheduled to begin work in September were required to look for other contracts as a result, and then were not available in December when the foundations were finished. Because of poor workmanship and exposure to winter conditions, the basement walls cracked and collapsed over January and February, so that the entire foundation had to be rebuilt in the spring. Helmut and Luzinda Schwartz ended up in a long court battle with the contractor over the bill for the foundation work, as well as with the carpenters and bricklayers who had lost money because of the delays.

By this time, the Schwartzes were short of money again and the house was only three-quarters finished. The real estate market in the area had gone flat, and a recent appraisal put the value of the land and house at $240,000. However, the appraisal noted that it was anticipated land values in the area would rise again in one year once a new car-manufacturing plant was completed and operating in the area. The estimated value in those circumstances would be $280,000.

The Schwartzes lost their court case with the builder, and are unable to pay the money the court awarded him. They are considering personal bankruptcy proceedings.

Aaron Ritche has been told all this by Helmut and Luzinda, who are no longer close personal friends, and has come to you for advice on where he stands in all this financial mess, and what his options are to protect his interests.

a) Advise Ritche with full reasons as to what actions he might take under the promissory note and the collateral mortgage. Include in your discussion the effect, if any, a bankruptcy would have on your advice. Complete your advice by suggesting a course of action for Ritche to take, and why you recommend it.

13. Mario Montell entered into a mortgage for $100,000 with the Canadian Commercial Bank. He then took out another mortgage with Cross Town Credit Union for $55,000. Unknown to the other two lenders, Montell also had taken out a third mortgage with Kiva Sivananda for $30,000. All three lenders registered their mortgages at various times in the following order—Cross Town Credit Union, Canadian Commercial Bank, and Kiva Sivananda.

Montell has defaulted on his payments on the mortgages, and all three lenders have recently become aware of one another. Cross Town Credit Union has indicated that it intends to proceed by power of sale, and hopes to do a quick sale for approximately $150,000. Canadian Commercial Bank had recently done an appraisal on the property, and estimated that even under power of sale it should go for $175,000.

a) List the lenders in order of priority.

b) What is the nature of the interest that Montell transferred to the Canadian Commercial Bank, Cross Town Credit Union, and Kiva Sivananda?

c) If Cross Town Credit Union proceeds under power of sale, what would be the financial results for Canadian Commercial Bank and Kiva Sivananda?

d) If you were advising the Canadian Commercial Bank, what actions would you suggest it take once it receives notice from Cross Town Credit Union of the intention to proceed by power of sale?

e) What remedies, if any, does Kiva Sivananda have if Cross Town Credit Union proceeds by power of sale?

f) Would your answer to e) be different if this situation took place in Alberta?

14. a) What is the amortization period for the schedule (provided by your instructor)?

b) Assuming this mortgage had a five-year term, what would be the principal due and payable on the maturity of the mortgage?

c) What is the amount of interest you are paying each day after having made your mortgage payments for one year?

15. Your lottery numbers came up and you won $50,000. When you returned from your round-the-world cruise on February 26, carrying all your duty-free gifts, you found you had spent $4,818.41 of your prize money. Coming to your senses and having taken a business law course, you decide to use the remaining prize money against the principal outstanding on your mortgage when you make your next monthly payment on the first day of March.
    a) You quickly flip through the pages of your mortgage document looking for what particular term or condition?
    b) Assuming you have found, to your great relief, that the term you require is present in your mortgage document, what would be the amount of your next monthly payment and the amount of interest you are now paying per day?

16. Ashley Marchbanks and Joe Magee were partners and decided to purchase an office building at a busy downtown intersection. In order to complete the purchase the partnership took out a first mortgage against the property in the amount of $250,000. Several months later, Magee left the partnership because he was tired of dealing with the problems associated with being a landlord.

    Two years later, Magee received a letter from the bank that held the mortgage. In it, the bank indicated that the mortgage was in default, and the bank would be looking to Magee for any funds owing if the sale of the property was not sufficient to meet the balance due on the mortgage.
    a) With reasons, advise Magee whether he is liable for the balance due under the mortgage with the bank.
    b) What steps, if any, should Magee have taken in these circumstances?

17. On Saturday night Maxwell Grant just happened to be driving by the house on which he held the first mortgage. He noticed that a rather large and noisy party was taking place on the premises. Several windows appeared to be broken, the lawn was full of tall weeds, and the eavestroughs were hanging off the house. On Sunday, he returned to talk with the neighbours about the party, and discovered that over the past few months the neighbours had became more and more upset because the owners have been letting the house fall apart. The neighbours are also concerned that the property values in the area will drop if the house is allowed to get any worse.
    a) As lender on the mortgage, what action should Grant be taking at this time to protect his investment?

18. Which of the following covenants would you not expect to find in a mortgage document?
    a) payment of property taxes
    b) maintaining the property in good condition
    c) obtaining the consent of the mortgagee prior to the sale of the property
    d) maintaining fire insurance
    e) obtaining the consent of the mortgagee to negotiate a new mortgage on the property

19. Refer to the amortization schedule.
    a) When do the payments finally "break even"—that is, you pay as much in interest as you do in principal?
    b) What do you think can be done to avoid a situation where you are paying so much in interest for such a long period of time?

Website

www.duhaime.org—Property law, including some case summaries.

Glossary

absolute privilege complete immunity from liability for defamation, whereby the defamatory statement cannot be the grounds for a lawsuit

acceleration clause a clause stating that if the borrower defaults on any payment, the whole of the principal sum of the debt and of accrued interest immediately falls due

acceptance an unqualified and unconditional agreement to the terms of the offer

accounts receivable (book debts) amounts owed to a person which can be sold, usually at a discount, or pledged as security for a loan

act of God the violence of nature

ADR (alternative dispute resolution) private procedures, such as mediation or arbitration, to resolve disputes, replacing or supplementing the traditional court process

adverse possession the exclusive possession of land by someone who openly uses for a long period like an owner, but without the permission of the owner

age of majority the age at which a person is recognized as an adult according to the law of his or her province

agency the relationship that exists when one party represents another party in the formation of legal relations

agent a person who is authorized to act on behalf of another

aggravated damages compensation for injuries such as distress and humiliation caused by the defendant's reprehensible conduct

allegations statements made that have not yet been proved

annual general meeting (AGM) the general meeting of shareholders of a corporation that is required by law to be held each year to transact certain specified business, including election of directors

Anton Piller order an order that the defendant must permit its premises to be searched without informing the defendant, made without notice to the defendant if giving notice would defeat the plaintiff's ability to obtain the remedy

apparent authority a situation in which there is no actual authority but the conduct of the principal suggests to a third party that the agent does have authority to act

appeal a request that a higher court review a decision made by a lower court

arbitration a form of alternative dispute resolution in which the parties agree to refer the dispute to an arbitrator, who decides the matter

arm's length between persons who are not related or associated in any way

articles of incorporation the basic document creating a corporation in most Canadian jurisdictions

assault the threat to do harm to a person

assignee the third party to whom rights under a contract have been assigned

assignment a transfer by a party of its contract rights to a third party

assignment in bankruptcy a voluntary declaration of bankruptcy

assignor the party that assigns its rights under a contract to a third party

attorney a lawyer in the United States

auditors outside accountants ("watchdogs" over accountants) who review financial statements for a company

according to accepted auditing principles to determine whether the statements are properly done

authorized share capital the maximum number (or value) of shares that a corporation is permitted by its charter to issue

bailment transfer of possession of personal property without transfer of ownership

bait and switch advertising advertising a product at a bargain price but not having a supply in reasonable quantities

bankrupt declared insolvent by the court, incapable of paying debts

barrister lawyers who represent clients in court; compare with solicitor

battery physical contact with a person without consent

beneficiary the person who enforces the contract against the insurance company and receives the benefits

bid-rigging agreeing in advance what bids will be submitted

bill of exchange a written order by A to B (usually a bank) to pay a specified sum of money to a named party or to the bearer of the document

bill of lading a receipt signed by a carrier or transportation company acknowledging that certain goods have been given to it for shipment

board of directors the governing body of a corporation, responsible for the management of its business and affairs

bona fide **occupational requirement (BFOR)** a genuine requirement for a job, such as the need to wear a hard hat when working on a construction site; a BFOR is a defence that excuses discrimination on a prohibited ground when it is done in good faith and for a legitimate business reason

bond a certificate of a debt owed by a corporation

breach failure to live up to the terms of a contract

brief a summary of a case (for use at trial) including evidence and law, or a summary of a court decision such as those used in this text

broadly held corporations corporations whose shares are publicly traded on the stock market

burden of proof the requirement that a party who claims a fact to be true must lead evidence to establish it in a court proceeding

capacity the legal capability of entering into an agreement; some individuals, such as minors, and mentally incompetent or intoxicated persons, are not seen in law as having the capacity to enter into a contract

causation one of the elements of negligence, relating to whether the action produced the damage or injury

caveat emptor let the buyer beware

certified cheque a cheque on which a bank has indicated that it will be cashed when presented for payment

chattel mortgage a mortgage of personal (chattel) property

cheque a bill of exchange drawn against a bank and payable on demand

C.I.F. cost, insurance, and freight, a designation for goods, making the seller responsible for arranging the insurance (in the buyer's name) and the shipping charges, with the goods remaining at the seller's risk until delivery to the purchaser

civil law the law in a common law system which applies to private rights, such as contracts

claim a written statement or basic summary of a plaintiff's allegations against a defendant in a lawsuit

class action an action in which one individual represents a group and the judgment decides the matter for all members of the class at once

click-wrap rule contract terms which are accepted when the user clicks an appropriate icon on a website document

closely held corporations corporations which do not sell shares to the public

closing date the date for completing a sale of property

COD cash on delivery, a contractual term requiring the purchaser to pay the shipper cash on delivery of goods

collateral agreement a separate, side agreement between the parties made at the same time as, but not included in, the written contract

collateral property of the debtor that can be sold by a creditor if the debt is not paid, e.g., a car may be given as collateral for a bank loan

collective bargaining negotiation between an employer and the union bargaining agent for its employees, in order to establish conditions of employment

common elements the structures and areas external to a unit in a condominium, including hallways, elevators, and swimming pools

common law rules that are pronounced in judgments

common shares shares carrying no preferential right to distribution of assets on breakup, but usually carrying voting rights

compulsory licensing granting a licence to a person to use a patent without the consent of the owner of the patent

conditions major, essential terms which, if breached, give the innocent party the right to terminate the contract and claim damages

condominium corporation a corporation allowing a way of holding property co-operatively, in which the members are the unit owners

confidential business information information that provides a business advantage as a result of the fact that it is kept secret

confidentiality the obligation not to disclose any information without consent

consideration the price paid for a promise, something of value promised or paid that is taken to indicate that the person has considered the agreement and consents to be bound by it

consignment the placing of goods with a business for the purpose of sale

constructive dismissal employer conduct that amounts to a fundamental breach of the employment contract and justifies the employee quitting

consumer notes promissory notes arising in a consumer credit sale

contract an agreement that is enforceable in a court of law

contributory negligence negligence by an injured party that helps to cause or increase (contribute) to his or her own loss or injury

conversion unauthorized use of the goods of another

cooling-off period a specified time after a contract is made during which a buyer may terminate the contract by giving written notice to the seller

copyright the right to prevent others from copying original works

corporation a business organization that is a separate legal entity (person) from the owners

costs legal expenses that a judge orders the loser to pay the winner

counsel a lawyer, usually a barrister

counterclaim a claim by the defendant against the plaintiff arising from the same facts as the original action by the plaintiff, and to be tried at the same time as that action

counter-offer the rejection of one offer and the proposal of a new one

covenants terms of agreement

crumbling skull plaintiff rule the principle that a defendant may be responsible for increasing a pre-existing weakness

cybersquatting the registration of a domain name containing a business name of another person, with the intention of selling the domain name to that business

damages monetary compensation in a lawsuit for the loss suffered by the aggrieved party

debenture a type of a corporate bond, indicating a debt owed by a corporation

deceit fraud, deliberately misleading another and causing injury

deductible a fixed amount of loss that the insured is required to bear

deed any document (not only a deed to land) under seal, which today is usually a small red paper wafer

defamation making an untrue statement that causes injury to the reputation of an individual or business, including both libel and slander

defendant the party being sued

deposit a sum of money paid by the buyer to the seller, to be forfeited if the buyer does not perform its part of the contract

discharge a court order whereby a person who has been declared bankrupt ceases to have the status of a bankrupt person

discharge of contract occurs when all the parties have done exactly what they were required to do under the terms of the agreement: the promises have been completed and the parties have no further obligations to each other

discovery of documents making each side's relevant documents in a litigation available to the other side

discrimination the act of treating someone differently on grounds that are prohibited by human rights legislation

distinguishing guise the distinctive shape of goods or their containers, or a distinctive way of wrapping or packaging, necessary to establish grounds for trademark

distress the right of the landlord to distrain (seize) a tenant's assets found on the premises and sell them to apply to arrears of rent

dividends sums declared by the board of directors as payable to shareholders

domain name the address of a website

dominant position the offence of taking unfair advantage of a monopoly or dominant position in the marketplace

double ticketing the offence of failing to sell at the lowest of the two or more prices appearing on a product

down payment a sum of money paid by the buyer as an initial part of the purchase price, and not completely forfeited if the contract is breached

drawee the party required to make payment on the bill of exchange

drawer the party who draws up or signs a bill of exchange

due diligence a defence to certain charges, by doing everything reasonable to prevent the problem leading to legal liability

duress actual, or threatened, violence, or unreasonable coercion used to force agreement

duty of care an obligation (in torts) to take care not to injure another

easement a right enjoyed by one landowner over the land of another for a particular purpose, such as access to water, but not for occupation of the land

e-commerce doing business on the Internet

encrypt make data on the Internet unreadable without the key for privacy and security

endorsed signed with one's name on a negotiable instrument, e.g., on the back of a cheque

endorsement a clause which changes the terms of an insurance policy

entire agreement clause a term in a contract in which the parties agree that their contract is complete as written

equitable assignment an assignment, other than a statutory assignment, which does not require that the assignment be absolute, unconditional, in writing, or that notice, written or oral, be given by the assignor

equity rules of law developed by the courts of equity to relieve the harshness of the common law

equity of redemption the right of the mortgagor to redeem the title to the mortgaged land on payment of the debt in full

errors and omissions insurance insurance to protect professionals in the event that their own negligence causes injury to others

estopped stopped or prevented

examination for discovery processes allowing each party to examine the other party orally on all issues in the lawsuit, and to have the testimony recorded by a reporter

exclusive dealing the supplier requiring that the retailer use only, or primarily, its particular products in the retail outlet

executed contract a contract in which both parties have performed their obligations

executors the personal representatives of a deceased person named in his or her will

executory contract a contract in which an agreement has been made but there has been no performance

exemption clauses (disclaimers) clauses in a contract that limit or completely eliminate the damages or other relief that the court would normally award against a party who has breached a contract

expectation damages an amount awarded for breach of contract based on the expected results if the contract had been properly performed

express terms actual stated terms, written or oral

factor the business of buying accounts receivable, usually at a discount, and then collecting directly from the customer

fair comment a defence to an action for defamation in which the harmful statements were made about public figures

false arrest causing a person to be arrested without reasonable cause

false imprisonment unlawfully restraining or confining another person

fee simple the highest form of ownership of land in law, allowing a person to dispose of the land during life or after death

fidelity bond insurance against loss caused by fraud, theft, or embezzlement committed by employees of the insured

fiduciary duty a duty of good faith imposed on a person who stands in a relation of trust to another

financial statements annual accounting statements that normally consist of a balance sheet and income statements

financing lease a security arrangement in which a third person provides credit, purchases the property, and leases it to the borrower

financing statement a document setting out details of a security interest that must be filed in order to protect that interest under personal property security acts

fixtures objects that are permanently attached or fixed to land or to a building

floating charge a form of mortgage on the assets of a corporation not affixed to any particular asset, but which does become affixed once a specified event takes place

F.O.B. free on board, a designation for goods when the seller must arrange and pay for transportation to the shipper, and the goods remain at the seller's risk until delivery

foreclosure an order by a court ending the mortgagor's right to redeem within a fixed time

forfeiture loss of money, such as a deposit, or of a right because of a breach of contract

franchise agreement an agreement under which a franchisor (the founding company) grants to the franchisee (the small-business outlet) the right to market the franchisor's products

fraudulent misrepresentation an incorrect statement made knowingly with the intention of causing injury to another

fraudulent preference an insolvent debtor's preferring (and paying) one creditor over another

fraudulent transfer a transfer of property by a debtor, usually to a related person, so that creditors cannot seize it

frustration an outside event that makes the performance of the contract impossible, and excuses a party from performance

fundamental breach a breach of the whole contract or of an essential term that is so serious that it means that the contract is not fulfilled in a fundamental manner, and the defaulting party cannot rely on an escape clause to avoid liability

gage a pledge

general meeting of shareholders a formal meeting of shareholders at which they are able to vote on matters concerning the corporation

general partner a partner in a limited partnership whose liability is not limited, and who usually runs the business

general security agreement an agreement in which all the assets of a business are pledged as collateral

goods personal property consisting of tangible items that can be bought and sold

goodwill the value of the good name, reputation, and connection of a business

gratuitous promise a promise for which no consideration is given

guarantee a collateral promise by one person to pay the debt if the primary debtor defaults

guarantor a co-signor, a person who signs a guarantee

hearsay evidence by a witness who simply repeats a statement by another person who will not testify at the trial

holder in due course an innocent third party entitled to collect on a negotiable instrument in spite of any defences of the original parties

illegal contracts contracts which cannot be enforced because they are contrary to legislation or public policy

immediate parties the parties who have had direct dealings with each other

implied terms terms which are added to a contact by statutes, by custom and usage of a particular business, or by the courts, based on what they think is necessary to meet the fair and reasonable expectations of the parties (the "officious bystander" test)

implied term of fitness a term implied into the contract that the goods are of a type that is suitable for any special purpose for which they are bought

Incoterms a set of standard contractual terms commonly used in purchase orders, and adopted by the International Chamber of Commerce

indemnity an agreement in which the third party undertakes to be equally liable for the loan owed by the main debtor

independent contractors people who carry on an independent business and act for a number of other persons

indoor management rule the principle that a person dealing with a corporation is entitled to assume that its internal rules have been complied with unless it is apparent that such is not the case

inducing breach of contract intentionally causing one person to breach his contract with another, e.g., persuading a key employee of a competitor to leave that company to join yours

industrial design a distinctive shape or design that is a pattern to be reproduced many times, such as the design on fine china

injunction an order instructing one party to halt a particular process or action

injurious falsehood a false statement about goods or services that is harmful to the reputation of those goods or services

innkeeper a person who maintains a business offering lodging to the public

innuendo a statement that implies something derogatory about another individual without directly saying it

insider trading the use of a corporation's confidential information to buy or sell its securities

insolvency the inability of a business to pay debts as they come due

insolvent person a person who is unable to meet, or has ceased to pay, his or her debts as they become due, but has not been declared bankrupt by court order

inspector a person appointed by the court to investigate the affairs of a corporation

insurable interest an interest which gives a person a financial benefit from the continued existence of the property or life insured, or which would make the person suffer financial detriment from the loss or destruction of that property or life

insurance adjuster a person who handles and investigates a claim of property losses

insurance agent an agent or employee of the insurance company

insurance broker an independent business which arranges insurance coverage for its clients and deals with several insurance companies

insurance policy the written evidence of the terms of a contract of insurance

insured the one who buys insurance coverage

intangible property that cannot be touched, such as accounts receivable

intellectual property personal property in the form of ideas and creative work, created by the intellect

intentional torts harmful acts that are committed on purpose and for which the law provides a remedy

interlocutory injunction a temporary injunction which lasts only until trial

invitation to treat the technical legal term for the invitation to engage in the bargaining process

impeachment an action challenging the validity of a patent

joint liability a liability shared by a number of persons, each of whom is personally liable for the full amount of a debt

joint tenancy shared ownership with right of survivorship

joint venture an agreement between two or more independent businesses to cooperate on a particular project only

judgment debtor a party who has been ordered by the court to pay a sum of money

jurisdiction the province, state, or country whose laws apply to a particular matter

just cause a valid reason for dismissing an employee without notice

labour relations board an administrative tribunal regulating labour relations

land the surface of the land, all that is under the surface (including the minerals and oil), and everything above the surface permanently fixed, such as buildings

land titles system a system of land registration in which the land titles office certifies registered interests as being correct

lease a contractual arrangement where the owner of property (the landlord) allows another person (the tenant) to have possession and use of the property for a certain period in return for the payment of rent

leasehold an interest in land for a period of time created by a lease

legal person an entity (a corporation or a human being) recognized at law as having its own legal personality

lessee the tenant or person who takes possession of the leased property

letter of credit a written promise by one person's bank to pay another person when specified conditions are met

letters patent a document incorporating a corporation, issued by the appropriate authority, and constituting the charter of the corporation

libel defamation in which the harmful statement is written or broadcast

licensee a visitor, other than an invitee, who enters premises with the consent of the occupier

lien a claim against property

life estate an estate in land that lasts only while the person is alive

limitation periods rules requiring that a lawsuit be started within a specified time after the offending conduct takes place

limited liability the principle that a corporation can shield owners, directors, and managers from liability for many obligations of the corporation

limited liability partnership a partnership in which partners who are not negligent are not personally liable for losses caused by the negligence of another partner or of an employee directly supervised by another partner

limited partner a partner in a limited partnership whose liability is limited to the amount of his or her capital contribution

limited partnership a partnership in which some of the partners limit their liability to the amount of their capital contributions and are not active in conducting the business

liquidated damages the amount of damages (in cash, or liquid, form) to be paid should the agreement be breached

litigation a court action when one person sues another

maker the party who signs and delivers a promissory note

malicious prosecution causing a person to be prosecuted for a crime without an honest belief that the crime had been committed

mandatory injunction an order requiring a person to do a particular act

mediation a form of alternative dispute resolution in which a neutral third party assists the parties to reach a settlement

memorandum of association a document setting out the essential terms of an agreement to form a corporation

mens rea a guilty mind

minor (infant) a person who has not attained the age of majority according to the law of his or her province, and therefore is not legally an adult

mitigation acts by the plaintiff to reduce loss caused by the defendant

moral rights the rights of an author or creator to prevent a work from being distorted or misused

mort passive or dead

mortgage the title of property that is held by the lender as security

mortgagee a lender who takes a mortgage as security for a loan

mortgagor a borrower who gives an interest in land as security for a debt

necessities (necessaries) the basic goods and services required to function in society

negligence an act or omission that carelessly causes injury to the person or property of another

negligent misrepresentation an incorrect statement made without due care for its accuracy

negotiation direct communication between the parties to agree on a contract, or efforts to resolve disputes without third-party intervention

non est factum ("it is not my doing"), a plea that a person didn't know what he or she was signing

notary public a person (usually but not necessarily a lawyer) authorized to take sworn testimony such as an affidavit

novation the process of substituting a new contract for an old one

nuisance an activity that substantially interferes with the enjoyment of the land of others in the vicinity

occupier any person with a legal right to occupy premises

offer a promise made by one party that contains all necessary terms so that the other party need only say "I accept" and a contract is formed

offeree the person who receives the offer

offeror the person who makes an offer

official receiver a government-appointed administrator responsible for the supervision of bankruptcy proceedings

open mortgages mortgages permitting repayment of the debt at any time without notice or bonus

oppression remedy a statutory procedure allowing individual shareholders to seek a personal remedy if they have been unfairly treated

option a new and separate contract to keep an offer open for a specified time in return for a sum of money

parol evidence rule the rule that a court will not ask the parties to a contract for their testimony as to the meaning of any term

partnership the relationship between two or more persons carrying on a business with a view to profit

partnership agreement an agreement between persons which creates a partnership and sets out its terms

passing off misrepresenting goods, services, or a business in order to deceive the public into believing that they are another's goods, services, or business

past consideration the consideration has already been given

patent agent a registered agent (often an engineer) who pursues applications for patents on behalf of individual inventors

payee the party named to receive payment on the bill of exchange

penalty clause terms specifying an exorbitant amount for breach of contract, intended to force a party to perform

pleadings the documents used in a court action, including the statement of claim, the statement of defence, and any counterclaim

pledged taken possession of by a creditor as security and held until repayment

postdated dated later than the time when it is given to the payee

power of attorney a type of agency agreement authorizing the agent to sign documents on behalf of the principal

power of sale a right of the mortgagee to sell mortgaged land by the terms of the mortgage or by statute upon default

precedent the principle in the common law system which requires judges to follow a decision made in a higher court in the same jurisdiction

premium the price paid by the insured to purchase insurance coverage

principal the person on whose behalf the agent acts

priority right to be repaid out of the debtor's property ahead of other claimants

privity of contract the principle in law that since a contract is created by two or more people exchanging promises, it is generally only those individuals who are direct parties to the agreement who are subject to its obligations and entitled to its benefits

promissory estoppel a remedy against a person who made a promise without giving any consideration for it, often used when a creditor waives strict compliance with payment dates and then notifies the debtor in default for not making timely payments

promissory note a written promise to pay the amount stated on the instrument

prospectus a document issued to inform the public about a new issue of shares or bonds that a corporation is required to publish when inviting the public to buy its securities

punitive damages (exemplary damages) compensation for damages beyond the plaintiff's actual losses, awarded to punish the wrongdoer

qualified privilege immunity from liability for defamation when the statement is made in good faith to a person or body which has authority over the person defamed

quantum meruit "as much as is merited," the amount a person deserves to be paid for goods or services provided to another person requesting them, even if some of the elements of a contract are missing

real property land, buildings, and fixtures; land and anything attached to it

reasonable foreseeability the test of what a person could have anticipated would be the consequences of his or her action

reasonable notice notice calculated on the basis of level of position and length of employment

reasonable person test a test or standard based on what a reasonable person would have done in similar circumstances

rebutted proven to be false

receiver a person appointed by a secured creditor to retrieve the assets to satisfy the debt

receiving order a court order for the transfer of debtor's assets to a trustee in bankruptcy

rectification a court order which corrects a written document to reflect accurately the contract made by the parties

re-entry the landlord's remedy of evicting the tenant for failure to pay rent or for breach of another major covenant

registration system a means of registering and tracking property deeds whereby the records are available to be examined

rejection the refusal to accept the offer

release a written or oral statement freeing another party from an existing duty

remoteness of damages the principle of whether the damages are too far removed from the original negligent act

repossession the act of taking back possession of property that has been in the possession of another

repudiation an indication by a party that he or she will not go through with the agreement as promised

retail price maintenance the attempt by a supplier of goods to control their resale price

res ipsa loquitur the facts speak for themselves

rescission the cancelling of the contract, with both parties put back into their original positions

respondent the party who defends on an appeal

revocation withdrawal of an offer before acceptance, and communicating the withdrawal to the offeree

restrictive endorsement an endorsement with a limitation

rider an additional clause to a standard policy of insurance

right of way an easement that gives the holder a right to pass back and forth over the land of another in order to get to and from his or her own land

risk the possibility of loss

rule of law established legal principles that treat all persons equally and that government itself obeys

secured creditor a creditor who has the right to seize and sell specific assets of a borrower to pay off a loan

self-defence a response to an assault or battery with as much force as is reasonable in the circumstances

share the holder's proportionate interest in the assets of a corporation

shareholder agreement an agreement between two or more shareholders, similar to a partnership agreement

shrink-wrap rule contract terms relating to a shrink-wrapped product, often including a limitation-of-liability clause which limits or excludes the manufacturer's liability for damages that may occur from the use of the product

slander defamation in which the harmful statement is spoken

sole proprietorships one-person businesses

solicitor lawyers who deal with commercial and other legal matters that do not involve going to court; compare with barrister

special damages damages to compensate for expenses and quantifiable losses, e.g., hospital bills

special meeting any meeting of shareholders other than the annual general meeting

specific performance an order requiring the defendant to undertake a specified task, usually to complete a transaction

standard form contract an offer presented in a printed document, the terms of which are the same for all customers, and which becomes a contract when signed (accepted) by the customer

stare decisis the principle by which judges are required to follow the decision made in a similar case by an equal or higher court

statement of claim the document which often starts a lawsuit, setting out briefly the nature of the complaint and the facts alleged as the basis of the action

statement of defence the response to a statement of claim by the defendant

statutes summarized or codified short-code formats of common law, comprising acts or legislation passed by Parliament

statutory assignment an assignment that complies with statutory provisions enabling the assignee to sue the debtor without joining the assignor to the action

stop payment an instruction from the drawer of a cheque to the bank not to pay the cheque

stoppage in transit reclaiming possession from the carrier of the goods while in transit, in order to stop delivery to the buyer, if the seller discovers that the buyer is insolvent

strict liability offences offences in which responsibility is imposed even when there was no intention to do the act, unless the defendant can show that he or she took reasonable care (due diligence)

subrogation the right of an insurer who has paid a claim to "step into the shoes" of the insured and sue the person responsible for the loss

subsidiary corporation a separate corporation owned or controlled by a parent corporation

systemic discrimination discrimination that is the consequence of a policy, whether the effect of discrimination was intended or not; for example, a policy that a police officer be 6 feet tall would discriminate on gender and race

telemarketing the use of the telephone to sell products

tenancy in common co-ownership of land whereby each owner can deal separately with his or her interest, may have unequal interest, and can sell his or her interest or dispose of it by will

term insurance personal insurance without any savings component

thin skull plaintiff rule the principle that a defendant is liable for the full extent of a plaintiff's loss even where a prior weakness makes the harm more serious than it otherwise might be

third party a stranger to the agreement, a person who is not one of the parties to a contract

title a legal concept roughly equivalent to ownership

title search an investigation of the registered ownership of land

tort a wrongful act done intentionally or unintentionally to the person or property of another for which the law gives a remedy

trade name a name used by a business, often in addition to the registered or incorporated name

trademark any visual characteristic of a product distinguishing it from a product made by competitors

transfer the equivalent (under the land titles system) of a deed transferring ownership, not made under seal

trespass the entry onto the property of another without the owner's permission, or some lawful right, to do so

trespasser one who enters without consent or lawful right on the lands of another, or who, having entered lawfully, refuses to leave when ordered to do so by the owner

trustee in bankruptcy the person appointed to administer the property of a bankrupt for the benefit of creditors

ultra vires beyond the powers of

unascertained goods goods that have not been set aside (identified and separated from a group) and agreed upon as the subject of a sale

undisclosed principal an agent who does not reveal either the identity of the principal or the fact that he or she is working for the principal

undue influence the misuse of influence and the domination of one party over the mind of another to such a degree as to deprive the latter of the will to make an independent decision

unsecured creditors creditors who have no security interest (such as a mortgage) in the bankrupt debtor's property

utmost good faith a duty owed when a special measure of trust is placed in one party by the other

vicarious liability the responsibility of an employer to compensate for harm caused by employees in the normal course of their employment

void never formed in law

waiver an agreement not to proceed with the performance of a contract or some term of it

warranties minor terms which, if breached, permit only a claim for damages but not the refusal to complete the contract

winding up dissolving, ending a corporation

workers' compensation a scheme in which employers contribute to a fund used to compensate workers injured in on-the-job accidents, in place of their right to sue in torts

Index